SECOND FRONT

Anglo-American Rivalry and the Hidden
Story of the Normandy Campaign

MARC MILNER

YALE UNIVERSITY PRESS
NEW HAVEN AND LONDON

For information about this and other Yale University Press publications, please contact:
U.S. Office: sales.press@yale.edu   yalebooks.com
Europe Office: sales@yaleup.co.uk   yalebooks.co.uk

Set in Adobe Garamond Pro by IDSUK (DataConnection) Ltd
Printed and Bound in the UK using 100% Renewable Electricity at CPI Group (UK) Ltd

Library of Congress Control Number: 2025930625
A catalogue record for this book is available from the British Library.
Authorized Representative in the EU: Easy Access System Europe, Mustamäe tee 50, 10621 Tallinn, Estonia, gpsr.requests@easproject.com

ISBN 978-0-300-27887-3

10 9 8 7 6 5 4 3 2 1

Dedicated to
Norman H. Gibbs, PhD
Chichele Professor of the History of War, 1953–77
Oxford University
and
Martin Blumenson, MA
Historical Officer, Third US Army, 1944–5
Historian, Center for Military History

CONTENTS

CONTENTS

ILLUSTRATIONS

MAPS

ABBREVIATIONS

ABSIE	American Broadcasting Service in Europe
AEF	American Expeditionary Force
AFHQ	Allied Forces HQ, Algiers
AG	Army Group
AHEC	US Army Heritage and Education Center, Carlisle, PA
AHQ	Army Headquarters
ASF	US Army Service Force
ASW	Anti-Submarine Warfare
BAD	British Armoured Division
BBC	British Broadcasting Corporation
BEF	British Expeditionary Force
BID	British Infantry Division
BIHR	Borthwick Institute for Historical Research, University of York
BIS	British Information Services
BLINY	British Library of Information, New York
BSC	British Security Coordination, New York
CAD	Canadian Armoured Division
CBC	Canadian Broadcasting Corporation
CBS	Columbia Broadcasting System
CCS	Combined Chiefs of Staff
CID	Canadian Infantry Division

CMH	US Army Center for Military History, Washington, DC
COI	Coordinator of Information
COSSAC	Chief of Staff, Supreme Allied Commander
CPRG	Canadian Press Relations Group
DD	Duplex Drive (tank)
DHH	Directorate of History and Heritage, National Defence Headquarters, Ottawa
ETOUSA	European Theater of Operations, US Army
FAD	French Armoured Division
FOO	Forward Observation Officer
FUSAG	First US Army Group
JCS	Joint Chiefs of Staff, US
LAC	Library and Archives of Canada
LCA	Landing Craft Assault
LCI(L)	Landing Craft Infantry (Large)
LCS	London Controlling Section
LCT	Landing Craft Tank
LHC	Liddell Hart Centre for Military Archives, King's College London
LST	Landing Ship Tank
MOI	Ministry of Information
NARA	National Archives and Records Administration, USA
NBC	National Broadcasting Company
OFF	Office of Facts and Figures
OKW	Oberkommando der Wehrmacht
OWI	Office of War Information
PAD	Polish Armoured Division
PGR	Panzer Grenadier Regiment
PGW	Panzer Group West
PWB	Psychological Warfare Branch
PWE	Psychological Warfare Executive
RAF	Royal Air Force
RCAF	Royal Canadian Air Force
RCN	Royal Canadian Navy
RCT	Regimental Combat Team
RN	Royal Navy

TAF	Tactical Air Force
TNA	The National Archives, Kew
USAAF	US Army Air Force
USAD	US Armored Division
USID	US Infantry Division
USN	United States Navy
USNI	United States Naval Institute
SCAEF	Supreme Command, Allied Expeditionary Force
SHAEF	Supreme Headquarters, Allied Expeditionary Force
SSF	Canadian-American 1st Special Service Force

ACKNOWLEDGEMENTS

I was introduced to problems with the Normandy narrative at the tender age of eight. My father had landed in the assault wave on D-Day, and in great anticipation he took a gaggle of neighbourhood boys to see *The Longest Day*. We were mesmerised by the film: my father was crestfallen. While we nattered like magpies outside the theatre, I vividly remember him looking bewildered, muttering, 'We were there, why didn't they show us?' His reaction to the film was typical in Canada. My father never stopped reading about Normandy and questioning. 'If closing the Falaise Gap was so friggin' important,' he asked to his dying day, 'then how come the only people down there trying to close it were us and the Poles?' Good question.

At the University of New Brunswick I bumped into a very fine history department, and a military history programme run by Professor Dominick Stewart 'Toby' Graham, DSO, MC. A gunner, like my father, Toby started his war in Norway in 1940, fought in the Western Desert including first siege of Tobruk, spent a year as a POW in Italy and then arrived in Normandy with Guards Armoured in the summer of 1944. The Germans finally got a piece of hot metal into him in the Netherlands in February 1945 in an action that earned him a Military Cross.

Toby was a force of nature. He was fascinated by ideas and doctrine, by the way in which habits of thought, contemporary ideas and pressures, and the great sine curves of western philosophy shaped how armies were organised and fought – and how historians wrote. Every book – and every historian – was fodder for his fertile mind. Toby used his grant money from the Department of Defence to bring a steady stream of distinguished historians to UNB to 'explain themselves' and have their work dissected in seminar. Jay Winter, Robin Higham, Richard Kohn, Carlo D'Este, John Terraine, Bill McAndrew, Forrest Pogue, Ian Beckett, Terry Copp, Alec Douglas, Keith Jeffery and Martin Blumenson immediately spring to mind. There were many more. Distinguished people appeared in our classes, too, including General William Westmoreland, Conor Cruise O'Brien and Dean Rusk. Nothing was sacred. We 'seminared' drafts of Toby's books with equal vigour: he could not only dish it out, he could take it. The process never stopped. Long glorious winter afternoons skiing the woodland trails of central New Brunswick with Toby were spent working out 'problems'. The objective was never perfection. It was to push the boundaries of knowledge – and surrender an untenable position when a better case came along. For Toby, history was an iterative process, not a zero-sum game.

Toby was also a great believer in experiential learning and he used the Canadian Army's Combat Training Centre – just a few miles down the road – as part of his teaching programme. Students got to see it 'done', they got to drive tanks, and fire everything from a pistol to 155mm howitzer. Knowing how stuff worked was important. 'Do you know how hard it is to hit a moving tank with the field gun?' he barked at one unfortunate seminar guest who had the temerity to criticise British problems killing tanks in the Western Desert. 'Well, I can tell you! It's bloody hard!' He had done it at Tobruk with a battery of French 75mms: 'Get it right!' As a budding naval historian, I was not excused this experiential education: Toby arranged to send me to sea for five weeks with the Canadian Navy. I retained that close connection with experiential learning when I took over his programme in 1986. When I was struggling to explain a barrage to my Great War class, one of my grad students, who was an 'Instructor in Gunnery' at the artillery school, arranged a visit to a battery in the field. The class watched shells land from the safety of the observation bunker, then fused, loaded and fired its own five-round barrage! Those were the days.

While I wrote naval history, most of my time at UNB was spent teaching and supervising graduate theses on 'army stuff'. Visits to battlefields reinforced that bias. Toby squired me through my first in 1985 to the Gothic Line in northern Italy, and then in 1993 we went to northwest Europe with my father. From the outset I was struck by the fact that no amount of pre-travel research and study ever survived contact with the ground. When Terry Copp asked me in 1997 to help lead tours for what is now the Canadian Battlefields Foundation, I leapt at the chance. I have been at them ever since for various Canadian and American organisations. As my personal interest in the Normandy campaign morphed into a professional one, the CBF kindly allowed me to explore well beyond Canada's battlefields.

The result of all this is a book on the Normandy campaign that has been a lifetime in the making.

In addition to support from the CBF, the Social Science and Humanities Research Council of Canada and the Security and Defence Forum of the Department of National Defence funded the research. Their generous support allowed me to visit over two dozen archives in Canada, Britain and the USA. I am enormously grateful to the archivists and staff of those institutions for their help and support. The staff at UNB's Harriet Irving Library were unstinting in their help. Thanks to the thoughtfulness of my university's great twentieth-century patron, Lord Beaverbrook – who bought whole libraries from faltering English country estates in the 1950s and shipped them to UNB – they oversee a remarkable collection of rare and obscure books which were enormously helpful to this project.

The scores of graduate students, many of them serving army officers, who wrote seminar papers and graduate theses on this stuff over more than three decades contributed more than they could ever imagine. Some will find their work cited in the references. Several of my graduate students tracked newspapers for me, including Chris Heenan who compiled an enormous clippings file from Canadian papers, and Jamie Horncastle who tracked coverage in American, Australian and South African newspapers. Chris Kretschmer helped with German sources. A very kind grad student in Eau Claire – whose name, sadly, I have lost – copied the Dupuy papers at the University of Wisconsin–Madison for me. Friends and colleagues provided continuous support and encouragement. These include Mike Bechtholdt, Steve Bourque, David Charters, Peter Clark, Tim Cook, Terry Copp, Doug Delaney, Jonathan Fennel, Jack Granatstein, Steve Harris, Nick Hewitt, Norman Hillmer, Sean Kennedy, Peter Kent, John Klug, Doug Knight, Clive Law, Brian J. McKercher, John McManus, Keith Neilson, Alan Sears, Roger Sarty, Dennis Showalter, Bruce Vandervort, Rob von Maier, Gerhard Weinberg and Steven Zaloga. Bonnie Huskins and Glenn Leonard very kindly copied documents at The National Archives in Kew. Special thanks to Steve Harris and David Charters for reading the whole manuscript and recommending improvements. Mike Bechtold, Jon Klug, Steve Prince, John McManus, Nick Hewitt and Steve Bourque helped with the photos.

Thanks to Andrew Lambert for the introduction to Julian Loose, the Yale UP (London) Editorial Director, and to Julian for having faith in the project – even when the manuscript was still monstrously large. Frazer Martin, Julian's assistant, did a great job managing the project and helping track down images. Rachael Lonsdale, the Managing Editor and Design Manager, suffered through the copy editing – and the randomness of my referencing 'system'. I am eternally grateful for her patience and diligence. Meg Pettit, the Production Editor, handled the maps and final work on the text superbly. Thanks to David Watkins for his excellent copy editing, and to Robert Davies for his proofreading. Thanks also to the manuscript's referees for their support and encouragement. I am grateful to Mark Kunkel for keeping my old Mac running during the long writing process, and to the administrative staff in my department, Carole Hines, Elizabeth Arnold and Misty Chisholm, for all their help over many years. To those whom I have missed in this accounting I can only offer my apologies and heartfelt thanks.

I have taken the liberty of dedicating this book to two official historians of the Second World War to whom I owe a special debt. Canadian military historians of my generation were typically students of Canadian official historians: Charles Stacey, G.W.G. Nicholson, Dan Goodspeed and their colleagues. Their focus was very much on Canadian history for Canadians. UNB was focused on Canadian military history in an international context, as the steady stream of foreign visitors (and this book) attests. In 1975–6 the recently retired Chichele Professor of War History at Oxford, Norman Gibbs, replaced Toby at UNB for a year. Gibbs had just completed volume one of the British *Grand Strategy* series of official histories. To us undergraduates he was a charming elderly English gentleman in a sweater vest. He taught to a typically mixed group: 'You are not all *reading* in history, are you?' he said in bewilderment to the Second World War class after marking the first midterm test. He also taught a general European military history survey course which I took. I managed to do well enough to be invited to his home for a reception at the end of the year. When the subject of the Dieppe raid came up, Mrs Gibbs explained quietly that the Canadians were being such a nuisance that they had to do something. Professor Gibbs and I exchanged letters after I too became an official historian. Many decades later, as an older gentleman in a sweater vest, I gave my final lecture in the military history survey course that Gibbs had taught and in the same classroom.

Martin Blumenson, the author of the *Breakout and Pursuit* volume of the US Army's official history, editor of *The Patton Papers*, and writer of many other books as well, was a regular visitor to UNB in the late 1970s and early 1980s. I got to know him well. He and Toby were an odd couple: a tall, rather gruff Englishman in a tweed jacket, corduroy pants and suede shoes, and a diminutive, soft-spoken New Yorker with the delicate hands of a gifted pianist, always dressed in finely tailored suits and highly polished shoes. But they shared a passion for the history of the Second World War. Martin was visiting in January 1983 when I learned of my appointment as an official historian. One of my first tasks when I got to Ottawa was to shred the draft copy of his *Breakout and Pursuit* which had been sent to Charles Stacey for comment. As I peeled the pages off into the shredder I noted that there were virtually no comments in the margins, so I did not feel so bad when I later told Martin of my crime. During research for this book, I found a lengthy critique of his draft in Stacey's papers and when I checked it against the published version my esteem for Blumenson as an historian only increased.

Finally, I have to thank my friend and companion for the last fifty years, Barbara Jean (aka Bobbi). She is long familiar with the distraction and grumpiness associated with producing books – and this one has been a bruiser. She eased that burden by sharing in the research, working alongside me in the British Library trolling through newspapers, and completed a very close reading of the *New York Times* for 1942–4 that proved invaluable. Thanks Bud.

Without question I have omitted someone in this long list and for that I ask forgiveness. This has been the work of many hands over several decades, but ultimately the errors and omissions that remain are mine alone.

INTRODUCTION

Operation Overlord remains a subject of endless fascination and debate. The international media buzz surrounding the eightieth anniversary of the landings in 2024 is proof of that. When and how the 'Second Front' was launched, how the campaign ashore unfolded and who 'won' it mattered a great deal then, and they still do. Failure in Normandy in the summer of 1944 would have changed not just the course of the war but world history, too. The success of Overlord not only ensured the defeat of Nazi Germany, but it also prevented the Russians from driving deep into western Europe, and the Allies from using atomic weapons in Europe. In the process Overlord marked the arrival of America as the global hegemon and the concurrent demise of Great Britain and her empire in that role. Small wonder, then, why participants and historians have been arguing over the course and conduct of the campaign since 6 June 1944.

Second Front began as an effort to explain how our understanding of Operation Overlord and the Normandy campaign was shaped by contemporary factors. The initial assumption was that the existing Normandy narrative was the result of a clash between expectations and the hard reality of events as they unfolded, and the reconciliation of these into the story we have accepted for eighty years. In short, a dialectic: thesis, antithesis, synthesis. This proved to be largely true. However, the search for expectations about Operation Overlord drew me back further into the story of Anglo-American relations than 1944

1

or even the Second World War. Indeed, as will be clear, I might well have gone back to the American Declaration of Independence. But the immediate roots of the context for our current understanding of Operation Overlord were found in the complex and interwoven legacy of the Great War, in the decline of the British empire and the emergence of its Dominions as independent states, in the Anglo-American economic and political rivalry, in the media revolution of the interwar era, in the battle over strategy after 1941, and ultimately in America's pathological anti-British sentiment and the effort to undermine the British empire.

The decisive battles that ended the Great War in 1918 profoundly shaped contemporary expectations in the summer of 1944. Indeed, many senior politicians and military officers were veterans of that earlier campaign. By 1918 America had amassed an army of a million men in France, enough to launch one of several major Allied offensives that led to German capitulation in November. For many Americans the simple logic of the sequence of events that year was irrefutable: the Great War was stalemated until they attacked en masse in the Meuse–Argonne in September, then the war ended. *Ipso facto*, America won the war. On top of that, Woodrow Wilson's Fourteen Points – liberating oppressed nations and guaranteeing their right to self-determination – formed the basis of the peace process that followed at Versailles.

For the British, the notion that America's fumbling expeditionary force had somehow won the war in 1918 was absurd. The heavy lifting in the final push had been done by the British Expeditionary Force (BEF). For their part, Canadians believed that their celebrated Canadian Corps carried much of that burden. Worse than America's claims of victory, Wilson's misguided idealism and meddling in the peace process had laid the groundwork for economic and political instability in Europe, and ultimately another great war.

In the interwar years these views hardened. For many Americans the British remained what they had been in 1776: a ruthless, class-ridden society bent on oppressing and exploiting the people of the world. The fact that Britain had evolved into a modern democracy, and that its settler Dominions – like Canada – had developed peacefully into modern liberal democracies as well, did not fit the paradigm. The British were the shysters who ran the world, suckered America into the Great War with crafty propaganda, and accumulated a great debt to America in pursuit of their imperial ambitions. Then, when the world spiralled into economic crisis in the 1930s, British mismanagement of the crisis threw America into depression. The British solution was imperial preference in trade, excluding America from the sterling bloc and reneging on their debt. For many Americans in 1939, Britain was an enemy: more present, more pressing and certainly more impactful than Germany.

Many in Britain believed, naively, that America was motivated by the same liberal democratic values that shaped their own society, and for which they had fought the Great War and, in 1939, stood up to Hitler and the Nazis. Roosevelt had articulated them in his famous four freedoms: freedom from fear, freedom from want, freedom of religion, and the political freedom of a liberal democratic society. Even so, the British remained discreet enough – or too dependent on the good will of southern Democrats – not to highlight the Jim Crow laws across the south and the hypocrisy in America's claims for moral leadership.

There was, nonetheless, some expectation in the summer of 1939 that America's money and industry would again be needed to beat the Germans, but with luck not the American military and the benighted influence that might engender. Even after the fall of France in June 1940, when Britain and her empire and Commonwealth stood alone, Churchill felt that it would be best if this new war could be won before America once again claimed victory and wrecked the peace. So for the next three years the British gnawed at the edges of the Third Reich, striving to bomb and blockade the Nazi regime into capitulation while trying to foment rebellion among the subject peoples – 'setting Europe ablaze'. This strategy is usually attributed to British weakness and fear of another bloody war of attrition on the Western Front. There is truth in that. The Great War had been a searing experience, one not to be repeated.

But in the summer of 1940 Britain remained the global hegemon, and the British sought to control the war in Europe in order to shape its outcome. Churchill's hopes that he could do that were buoyed by the Lend-Lease arrangement with America in March 1941 – securing the tools to finish the job. Lend-Lease ensured Britain's ultimate survival, but only at the cost of transferring control over its economy to the US Treasury Department. Churchill's hopes got a boost from the German attack on Russia in June 1941. The Soviets were hardly ideal allies, but the vastness of Russia and sheer weight of their forces soon trapped Germany in a brutal war of attrition. Europe might yet rise in rebellion and Britain would be there to shape the peace.

As the war dragged on, and as British military and economic power waned, growing American power made it harder for Britain to control strategy and exclude Franklin Roosevelt from shaping the postwar world. Evidence of this shifting balance was confirmed at Tehran in November 1943, when Roosevelt threw Europe to the tender mercies of Joseph Stalin, whom he credulously believed he could control. In the process, Roosevelt undermined the solidarity of the Anglo-American alliance and made it clear to Stalin that America would not support British efforts to restore Europe and contain Russian power. Instead, America and Russia would rule the postwar world, imposing an international 'New Deal' on the recalcitrant nations and empires – including the British. This would all be managed through a new international body called the 'United Nations'. In the process, all the world's empires, except those of America and Russia, would be dissolved.

On the eve of Operation Overlord the Allied war in western Europe was still overwhelmingly British, and in the summer of 1944 the British empire and Commonwealth had more troops engaged in direct combat with the Japanese Imperial Army than the Americans. Allied seapower in the western hemisphere was predominantly Anglo-Canadian, and the strategic bombing campaign against Germany was still a balanced effort between the United States Army Air Force (USAAF) and the British Royal Air Force (RAF). The scope and scale of Britain's war effort remained unknown to Americans. The British Ministry of Information (MOI) never developed an effective PR campaign in America. In part this was because of a fear of repeating the overt propaganda of the Great War which so alienated Americans. The British also discovered that being heard in the cacophonous American media landscape was problematic at best. American newspapers and radio were part of an infotainment industry that catered to the public nature of American politics and government. The President relied on the media not simply as a form of communication with the people but with other branches of government. American politics was – and remains – a full-contact public sport. Lord Lothian, the British ambassador until his tragic death in December 1940, understood this. Lord Halifax, who replaced him, did not – at least, not for several years.

In any event, once America was 'in' and the war supplies were flowing, the MOI was not really interested in wooing the Americans. Under Brendan Bracken's leadership, the thrust of the MOI's overseas PR effort was towards uniting the empire and Commonwealth to ensure that Britain was able to sustain its Great Power status. Nonetheless, America mattered enormously to Britain. At a minimum the outcome of the war itself depended on American goodwill, industrial production, and ultimately money and – after 1941 – American armed forces. Given the fraught nature of American politics and, as we shall see, the very strong anti-British sentiment in much of America, the British played their hand very carefully when dealing with the Americans – perhaps too carefully.

Much of the historical writing on the effort to keep the empire united has focused on India, the Jewel in the Crown and home to one-fifth of the world's population. Britain could not be a Great Power without it. But keeping the self-governing Dominions in the fold was no less important. The Statute of Westminster, passed into law in 1931, offered the Dominions status as fully independent nation states. By 1939 Ireland was already gone, and the Union of South Africa had charted its own route to unilateral independence. Only Canada signed on completely to Westminster, leaving Australia, New Zealand and Newfoundland still as de facto colonies. Many in Britain, not least Winston Churchill, preferred to see all the Dominions that way: still colonies. The unity of the empire and Commonwealth was crucial to the maintenance of Britain's position as a Great Power. As will become clear, their war efforts would all be subsumed under the 'British' umbrella.

Only Canada pushed back consistently against the smothering embrace of the mother country. The commander of First Canadian Army, the irascible and always difficult Andrew McNaughton, acted like the national contingent commander he was. He missed few chances to chastise the Chief of the Imperial General Staff, Alan Brooke, for moving Canadian formations and units around without authorisation from him. McNaughton even had the temerity to *summon* Montgomery to explain his plan for the invasion of Sicily, before giving the go-ahead to use the 1st Canadian Infantry Division (CID). Montgomery never forgot and never forgave him.

None of this would have mattered much had Canada not guarded its new independence jealously, and had its war effort been insignificant: it was not. In 1939 Canada was the world's fifth-largest trading nation and by late 1941 its economy eclipsed that of Italy. By 1943 it was delivering more war supplies to Britain than the United States. As McNaughton observed after the war, the British victory at El Alamein was 'trucked and gunned' by Canada. Its navy was second only to Britain's in the Battle of the Atlantic, and its air force grew to over fifty operational squadrons, while upwards of a quarter of all aircrew in RAF squadrons were Canadians. And by 1943 First Canadian Army was the lead British Commonwealth formation in the Overlord plan. It was a remarkable accomplishment for a nation of only 11 million people. 'British' power by 1944 depended in no small way on Canada. McNaughton told his biographer many years later that in 1943 Churchill felt it was time to 'put Canada in its place'.

Churchill certainly hoped that that place was the bosom of a united empire and Commonwealth under one foreign and defence policy. His ultimate attempt to demonstrate that solidarity came in the May 1944 conference of Prime Ministers in London, the only one of its kind during the war. The literature, including Churchill's own account, ignores the conference completely. Perhaps that is because Churchill's hopes for united 'British' power were scuppered by Canada. As the American journal *Business Week* concluded at the time, the real winner from the Prime Ministers conference was the United States.

In keeping with the idea of imperial solidarity, in the spring of 1944 the British deliberately wrote the Canadians out of the Overlord media coverage, subsuming their effort under the 'British' label. Press releases and the communiqués of the Supreme Headquarters, Allied Expeditionary Force (SHAEF), would talk of 'Anglo-American' forces only. The documentary film slated for release the week of the landings, *Eve of Battle*, never mentioned Canada's role – even describing the troops coming from North America to liberate Europe as all 'American'. The bias was so blatant that even the Americans demanded that *Eve of Battle* be re-edited to build in the Canadian story. That never happened.

Canadians reached a compromise with SHAEF to use the generic term 'Allied' rather than 'Anglo-American' to cover non-specific references to forces in Normandy. The American media happily adapted that to read 'American and Allied', leaving Britain's enormous effort obscured among the 'also-rans' of the Overlord campaign. This subtle, but critical, change in the terminology played to the existing American belief in early 1944 that the Second Front was primarily an American operation.

A key theme of *Second Front* is therefore the central role played by Canada in the planning, launching and conduct of Operation Overlord, and the unfolding of the campaign in Normandy. Making this case is not special pleading. As will become evident, First Canadian Army lay at the heart of all plans for a Second Front from 1941 onwards, nurtured by the legacy of the Canadian Army's role as 'shock troops' in the Great War. For reasons that will become clear, Canadian official historians could not or would not talk about the role of First Canadian Army in the planning and conduct of Operation Overlord, and Anglo-American historians were uninterested or unaware. In the event, the Canadian Army – a small force by any standard – played a decisive role at critical points in the Normandy campaign that has simply gone unnoticed by everyone except the Germans.

The complex power struggle going on within the British empire and Commonwealth and between Britain and America profoundly shaped the way in which Operation Overlord was reported, and therefore how the received narrative of the campaign developed. That story, which unfolded at the very moment that global hegemony shifted from Great Britain to the United States, forms the ultimate focus of this book. As will be evident, the context for the development of the prevalent Normandy narrative is deeply embedded in the two decades that preceded the campaign. Ultimately, Americans believed – then as now – that Normandy was largely an American battle, that Montgomery was too cautious, that the British Army sat idle while Americans fought, and that the break-out at the end of July and the subsequent sweep across France was, as Robert McCormick described it at the time, an 'all American' victory. There would be no repeat of the contested victories of 1918: America won the decisive battle and its massive army swept onto the continent and won the war in 1945.

The notion of an Anglo-American battle for power and influence – indeed, for global hegemony – during the Second World War is not new. Decades ago Christopher Thorne explored the problematic nature of the Anglo-American relationship in the context of the Pacific war in *Allies of a Kind* (1978). Randall Bennett Woods traced the contours and the details of the power shift between 1941 and 1946 in *A Changing of the Guard* (1990), and B.J.C. McKercher filled in the earlier period from 1930 to 1945 in *Transition of Power* (1999). John Charmley exploded the myth of a special relationship between Britain and America, and Churchill and Roosevelt, in 1995 with his then controversial *Churchill's Grand Alliance*. None of these important works integrated the military story in Europe with the political, diplomatic and economic contexts as well as Peter Clarke's *The Last Thousand Days of the British Empire* (2007). But Clarke only tracks the story from the high summer of 1944 to the loss of India in 1947. His book is the inspiration for this one, which is in many ways an effort to present the backstory to Clarke's work. Anyone who wants to know more about all this during the last eight months of the Second World War should read Clarke.

Second Front is therefore a fresh look at the troubled Anglo-American and British Commonwealth relationships from 1918 to 1945 and the origins and development of our understanding of Operation Overlord. Much of this might well have emerged sooner had the Canadian role been more comprehensively illuminated. As it turned out, that could never have happened. Canadian official historians were denied access to Overlord planning documents and deception operation files, and knew little of what is revealed here. In any event, the sacking of the commander of First Canadian Army in the autumn of 1943 was a subject too sensitive to touch in the postwar period. For their part, the British were content to bury the Canadian effort under the wider rubric of 'British'. The Americans, too, developed their own narrative and myths about Operation Overlord and the Normandy campaign. For all these reasons – and more – this story has lain hidden in the files for eighty years.

Book I

RIVALS

CHAPTER 1

HALF-FORGOTTEN THINGS

'The bloody Bosche has got the knock;

'And soon they'll crumple up and chuck their games.

'We've got the beggars on the run at last!'

Siegfried Sassoon, 'The rank stench

of those bodies haunts me still'[1]

In March 1918 the German Army launched a massive assault on the British Expeditionary Force on the Western Front. Over the next four months the Germans made increasingly desperate attempts to rupture the Allied line and win the war. Then, starting in July, the new Allied Supreme Commander, Field Marshal Ferdinand Foch, orchestrated a relentless counter-offensive, a series of 'hammer blows' all along the Western Front. As Germany's Allies slipped away, and as the socialists took power in Berlin – sending the Kaiser into exile – the German Army began to disintegrate. By November the war was over: the Allies had won. That much they could agree on.

In early 1918 the BEF was still recovering from the butchery of 1917. With Russia in rebellion, the French Army mutinous and the American Army still an unfulfilled promise, the British had carried the burden of the war. They fought their grimmest battle yet, the Third Battle of Ypres (Passchendaele). From late July until mid-November, clawing forward yard by yard in drowning mud, they added 300,000 casualties to a list that now approached 2 million.[2] If, as its generals claimed, 1917 had been a year of victories, Britain could not afford many more like it. The BEF Commander in Chief, Field Marshal Sir Douglas Haig, was forced to reorganise his entire army to keep units up to strength, and to extend the line held by the Fifth Army by 25km southward to free French troops for service elsewhere. When the weight of Operation Michael fell on the Fifth Army on 21 March 1918 it disintegrated into what John Terraine called 'forty-two miles of continuous catastrophe'.[3] The rupture soon threatened the critical connection between the British and French armies at Amiens. The British now feared that the French would fold their line south, to the Seine – or perhaps even the Loire. The French worried that the British would bolt for the coast. Casualties on both sides were staggering. By the time Operation Michael faltered outside Amiens on 9 April the Germans had lost 250,000 men, the British 178,000, and the French some 77,000. And 1918 was just getting started.[4]

* * *

The second great German offensive of 1918, Operation Georgette, struck the BEF in the Ypres sector, along the Lys River, in early April. All the painful British gains of the previous three years were swept away in hours. Britain now sent out boy soldiers to help stem the tide. While Haig pleaded for French support, he also looked longingly at the rising strength of the American Expeditionary Force (AEF). By the spring of 1918 there were 400,000 American troops in France, and they were arriving at the rate of 100,000 per month thanks largely to British shipping. These men were not yet an army. The US Army had little combat experience beyond counter-insurgency operations in the Philippines and Mexico, and few trained staff officers. Equipment, too, was in very short supply. Most of their artillery and machine guns were French, while their Enfield rifle was a British design manufactured in the US. Like the British before them, Americans would have to build a massive army under the strain of war.

Woodrow Wilson, the American President, brought his country into the war to fix the problem of conflicting European empires, and planned to use an American victory to dictate the peace. The commander of the AEF, General John 'Black Jack' Pershing, had his own ideas of how all this was going to happen. Pershing flatly rejected the Anglo-French experience on the Western Front as evidence of the effete Europeans' failure to understand how to fight effectively. 'Pershing came late into the war,' David Zabecki and Doug Mastriano wrote, 'with an unshakable belief in American exceptionalism and a steadfast faith in "self-reliant infantry", based on superior American marksmanship and the power of the bayonet.'[5] When the French Prime Minister George Clemenceau was told of this he observed laconically, 'If the Americans do not allow the French to teach them, the Germans will do so.'[6]

During the crisis in March and April, Pershing was pressed hard to simply put his newly arrived battalions and regiments into British and French formations. The War Department recommended that he attach novice divisions to Allied corps and armies, but that was as far as Pershing would go. 'The only hope of really winning the war', Colonel Fox Connor, the American Expeditionary Force's G3 (Plans), wrote just before the second German offensive stuck the British at Ypres, 'lies in an American army'. Moreover, Connor warned, only an American army could deliver 'a peace satisfactory' to America.[7] When amalgamation was put to Pershing at the Supreme War Council meeting in Abbeville on 1–2 May he rejected it. 'I have thought this problem over very deliberately,' Pershing told his French and British counterparts, 'and will not be coerced.'[8]

Nonetheless, all five US divisions engaged in front-line service in the spring of 1918 were seconded to British and French armies. Two served primarily alongside the Australians, who were now chronically short of men. These two divisions eventually became II US Corps and remained with the BEF until the Armistice. And by late May three American divisions were serving with the French Sixth Army north-east of Paris along the Chemin des Dames. The French believed that this would be a quiet sector and good place to ease the Americans into the fighting. The third great German attack of 1918 fell on them starting on 27 May.[9]

The line along the Chemin des Dames recoiled as the Germans drove towards the Marne River crossing at Château-Thierry. The motorised machine-gun battalion of the 3rd US Division arrived just in time on 31 May to hold the bridgehead over the Marne, while the rest of the division filled in along the river. The Germans were now only 60km from Paris. A few days later the 2nd US Division took position along the western side of the salient – earning the nickname 'Rock of the Marne'. Over the next few days the Germans launched furious attacks, all to no avail: the American line held. Within days of the Armistice in November a pamphlet was published in Boston claiming that the actions of American divisions at the Marne constituted the turning point of the Great War.[10]

Meanwhile, the 1st US Division was ordered to pinch out a small salient in the German line near the town of Cantigny. What followed was the first division-level deliberate attack by the AEF. One of the staff planners for the 1st Division was Major George C. Marshall. Among other notables at Cantigny was the ambitious and energetic Robert R. McCormick, the scion of a well-to-do Chicago family which ran the *Chicago Tribune*, who commanded the 1st Battalion, 5th US Field Artillery. McCormick had reason to be proud of the American effort at Cantigny. The supporting artillery fire, heavily reinforced by French guns, worked superbly. Tank–infantry cooperation was also excellent, impressing French liaison officers with 'spirited and intelligent' cooperation.[11]

The final German offensive came north-east of Paris in July. Franco-American counterattacks threw it back. The Germans were a spent force. Their front line was a third longer than it had been in March at a cost of 800,000 dead, wounded or missing; and the Allies were still in the fight. In fact, by July – thanks to British shipping – 250,000 Americans were arriving in France each month. 'The threat of an American Army gathers like a thunder-cloud in the rear of our other enemies,' German officer Rudolph Binding wrote in his diary that summer.[12]

Another menace lurked as well, on the slopes of Vimy Ridge north of Arras, the only sector of the Western Front between Rheims and the sea that the Germans did not attack in 1918. There sat the Canadian Corps, arguably the most cohesive Allied formation on the Western Front. Victories at Vimy, Hill 70 and Passchendaele in 1917 set the Canadian Corps apart as the elite troops of the BEF.[13] Its commander, General Sir Arthur Currie, a portly pre-war real estate agent, declined to adopt the new British organisation for divisions and brigades in early 1918. Had he done so, he would have commanded six divisions, enough to establish a 'First Canadian Army'. But the change offered no appreciable increase in combat power, and Currie could only get the staff needed by relying on British officers – something he was reluctant to do now that most of the key staff positions in the corps were held by Canadians. So Currie reorganised the Canadian Corps his own way. He drew the men and materiel of the 5th Division to France to strengthen each infantry battalion over war-establishment, created combat engineer battalions to free infantry from labour duties, absorbed the 5th Division's artillery to increase the corps' firepower, expanded logistic support, and increased the number of heavy machine guns. According to Shane Scheiber, each Canadian division now became 'the combat equivalent of a small British *corps*'.[14] The organisation, command and control of the Canadian Corps artillery was also unique: it was the only corps in the BEF to command its own heavy and siege artillery. By the summer of 1918 the Canadian Corps was an army in all but name.[15]

The Canadian Corps' uniqueness and ability was fostered by its patron, Lord Beaverbrook, the owner of London newspapers the *Daily Express* and the *Globe*, and one of the great press barons of his age. Raised in New Brunswick, Max Aitken was a millionaire by age thirty, when he moved to Britain in 1910 following a business scandal. His penchant for scheming and powerful friends earned him a seat in the British Parliament by the end of the year and a knighthood in 1911. When war broke out Aitken was unofficially appointed by the Canadian government 'to assert Canadian independence' within the empire's war effort, and champion the deeds of Canadian troops.

He succeeded admirably in both. As early as the Second Battle of Ypres in the spring of 1915, when the 1st Canadian Division made a valiant stand in the face of the first major gas attack in the history of war, even Americans were getting the impression that all the serious fighting in Europe was being done by Canadians. It helped that Aitken's commission as a Lieutenant-Colonel in the Canadian Army gave him unfettered access to the front: more than British press barons enjoyed. In 1915 Aitken was appointed Canadian records officer, and in early 1916 created the Canadian War Records Office in London. He went at all this with unbridled enthusiasm. He hired photographers and film-makers, and eventually established the Canadian War Art programme – sponsoring and supporting both the famous and the promising to paint great monuments to Canada's war effort.

Aitken was also engaged deeply in British politics. He was a key player in the movement to unseat Prime Minister Herbert Asquith and replace him with the fiery Welsh Minister of Munitions, David Lloyd George, in December 1916. His reward was a peerage, becoming Lord Beaverbrook, and appointment as Minister of Information. No Allied formation had a better-connected and more devoted publicist than the Canadian Corps.[16] The British would come to resent his over-selling of the Canadian role on the Western Front.

With strong political and public relations backing, and unqualified success in action, the Canadian Corps enjoyed quasi-independent status. Currie was a de facto national contingent commander, and he acted like one. When senior British officers threatened to move his Corps HQ into reserve in April 1918 and parcel out his divisions and guns to other British formations, Currie threatened political intervention to stop it. The British were not amused with Currie's 'swollen head'.[17] A myth soon emerged that the Canadians did nothing in the spring of 1918 while the Allies nearly lost the war.

By the end of July 1918 many believed that the war had reached a new stalemate. Pershing told Robert McCormick in early August that 'The war is over for the summer. We may have a little scrap here and there, but we don't expect any more fighting until next spring.' McCormick later recalled that 'While I was on the ocean the Germans broke. They had been fighting like hell until that time. Something went wrong with them.'[18]

* * *

The BEF was probably that 'something'. On 30 July the Canadian Corps began to slip away from Vimy Ridge and, under the cover of a complex deception scheme, concentrated south-west of Amiens. Since March the Germans had consolidated that sector. General Erik Ludendorff, Quartermaster-General of the German Army and its effective Commander in Chief, recalled that 'the divisional fronts were narrow, artillery was plentiful and the trench system was organized in depth'. Only German morale was questionable.[19]

The Australians held the Amiens front and they screened the Canadian deployment. Everyone knew that the Canadians were the great uncommitted reserve of the BEF. A German situation report from the summer observed that 'The Canadian Corps, magnificently equipped and highly trained in storm tactics, may be expected to appear shortly in offensive operations.'[20] Everyone thought the Canadians would attack across the Douai Plain from their base on Vimy Ridge. In early August an Australian patrol 'returned round-eyed with wonder' from a reconnaissance south of the Amiens–Saint-Quentin road: 'the woods are right full of Canadians. Canadians? We thought they were at Arras.'[21]

Also cleverly hidden from prying German eyes (and ears) were 450 tanks, over 1,200 guns and a massive Allied air force. The tanks included new types, like the fast 'Whippets' designed to support cavalry, logistics tanks carrying ammunition and equipment, and the Mk IV* designed to carry an infantry section across the battlefield. To this increasingly mechanised battlefield the Canadians brought two Motor Machine Gun brigades of armoured cars fitted with Vickers heavy machine guns suitable for roads and limited cross-country mobility. The artillery fireplan, too, was highly sophisticated in both its initial phase, with extensive neutralisation, wire cutting and counter-battery work – the 450 heavies on the Amiens front effectively silenced their German counterparts on the day[22] – and the supporting barrages. Innovative schemes were developed to leap-frog field and medium batteries, as well as trench mortars and heavy machine guns, forward to provide continuous support as the attack moved.

The plan worked superbly. On 8 August the Australians and Canadians (supported by French and British divisions) sliced through the enemy defences. By evening the Australians and Canadians were 13km from their start line. Ludendorff called it 'The Black Day of the German Army'. On 10 August the offensive 'culminated' in modern army jargon at a depth of 23km. The British later identified the Battle of Amiens as the start of the 'Hundred Days Campaign', an allusion to the final campaign against Napoleon in 1815 that ended with the defeat of France.

The French Tenth Army, under the redoubtable General Charles Mangin, was the next to attack and pushed the Germans back with comparative ease towards the Hindenburg line. Sensing German weakness, and with Germany's allies anxiously looking for a way out of the war, Foch now called for a series of attacks pounding at Germany's army until it broke. Things were now happening fast. When Winston Churchill, the Minister of Munitions, visited the front on 21 August, he was stunned to hear Haig declare that victory was imminent. The next day Haig informed his army commanders that the push to victory was on.

Quite apart from the desire to end the war, there was ample reason for the European Allies to push for victory in 1918: neither Britain or France wanted an American victory in 1919 or the American peace that would follow. The British situation was even more complicated than that. In August they began curtailing the movement of American troops to France. Britain had committed to supporting a 100 division American force on the Western Front, and shifted a significant portion of their carrying capacity to make that happen. By 1918 virtually all of the 1 million American troops in France had arrived on British ships. In the meantime, President Wilson began a quiet war against British maritime and economic power. His 1916 Naval Act, designed to build a 'navy second to none', was directly targeted at the Royal Navy (RN). But the act also provided for a massive, state-controlled expansion of the US merchant fleet.

As the US merchant fleet grew in late 1917 the Allies expected to see more of it in European waters, but by the end of the year barely 7 per cent of shipping using British and French ports was American.[23] Not surprisingly American shipping losses to German U-boats were tiny. In contrast, British losses to U-boats in the last two years of the war outstripped new construction, resulting in a steady decline in the size of the British merchant fleet. This suited Wilson fine, and he was content to limit American tonnage in service in the North Atlantic in order to allow the overall size of the fleet to grow. Appeals to the American government as late as May 1918 to abide by their agreement to share information with the Allies 'to form the basis on which the general allocation of tonnage of each nation will be . . . made to the services most essential to the prosecution of the war' fell on deaf ears.[24]

In fact, Wilson's new merchant fleet was never intended to help the Allies win the war. He wanted priority on merchant ships 'not', in Edward Parsons's words, 'to sustain the Allied war effort', but, as the

Secretary of the Navy Josephus Daniels recorded in his diary, because 'merchant ships would get the trade and that was the chief need'. So while the British suffered heavy losses at sea and carried the AEF to France, the US merchant fleet launched a direct assault on British carrying trade. As Parsons notes, the resulting deficiency in carrying capacity 'forced the British to virtually abandon their Latin American and Asian markets in order to divert ships to the carriage of military necessities. The British had stated that this meant that they could not win back markets thus lost to the Americans while the war lasted.'[25] Even appeals to help move food for troops and civilians in Europe were rejected by Wilson's government because of the importance of the new commercial ties to South America and Asia.

The British decision to 'limit' Pershing's army to eighty divisions rather than 100 therefore had as much to do with the nascent economic and naval struggle with America as it did with concern over who would shape the European peace. Parsons concludes emphatically, 'the evidence suggests that the British reduced the flow of American troops to France in order to advance their own economic interests and to constrict Wilson's power to forge the armistice and peace terms.'[26] His choice of words is revealing. A British historian might have observed that the British acted to 'preserve' their economic interests.

As the French Tenth Army's assault petered out in mid-August, the British began a series of attacks. On 21 August, the Third and Fourth British armies south of Arras began the Battle of Albert, and on the 26th, the British First Army attacked east of Arras in the Battle of the Scarpe. Terraine later described the success of both of these attacks as 'breathtaking'. The opening of the Battle of the Scarpe began when two Canadian divisions arrived in Arras by train from Amiens and went straight into the attack. They quickly captured the critical high ground overlooking the Drocourt–Queant Line. Meanwhile, the Australians pressed across the Somme in the Battle of Albert, capturing Mont Saint-Quentin and Peronne. 'So August ended with a flourish for Haig's army.'[27] More was to come.

By the time the Australians reached Peronne, the British First Army was ready to renew the attack east of Arras, along the road to Cambrai. On this sector the Hindenburg Line fanned out like the main branches of an elm tree across a broad rolling 40km plain. There were three main positions: the Drocourt–Queant (DQ) Line closest to Arras, the Vise-en-Artois switch line about halfway down the road, and then the main position along the Canal du Nord. The flat plain west of the critical rail hub of Cambrai was also laced with defensive lines, well supported by gun positions tucked away in the valley of the Scarpe River. Haig selected Currie's pocket-army because only it possessed the resources and the staying power to fight its way to Cambrai. Foch agreed. The Canadians, Foch said, will be 'the ram with which we will break up the last line of resistance of the German Army'.[28]

It is significant that Haig bypassed the First Army commander, General Henry S. Horne, and issued his instructions directly to Currie. Horne knew only too well that the Canadian Corps was a semi-autonomous formation. Currie had already defied Horne's order to capture Lens in August 1917 and captured Hill 70 instead. Currie's Counter-Battery Staff Officer, the brilliant if somewhat brittle electrical engineer Lieutenant-Colonel Andrew L. McNaughton, declared Horne's original scheme a 'bloody fool operation'.[29] It made little sense to take Lens, which lay in a saddle between two hills held by the Germans: better to capture the low whale-back of Hill 70 north of Lens and let the Germans die trying to get it back. Canadian artillery squired the two attacking divisions onto their objectives within an hour. The Germans launched twenty-one counterattacks over the next three days. Fighting was intense, often hand to hand, but the Canadians mauled five German divisions in the process.

Currie had had his own way again in the fall of 1917 at Passchendaele, again in the spring of 1918 when the Canadian Corps reorganised itself uniquely, and of course at Amiens. Now on the eve of the great push to crush the hinge of the Hindenburg Line, Haig once again gave Currie free rein. That meant that Currie's de facto artillery commander, McNaughton, was at liberty to organise his own plans without interference by Horne's new Chief of Staff, Lieutenant-Colonel Alan Brooke.

Brooke and McNaughton were already uneasy colleagues. Brooke joined the Canadian Corps just prior to Vimy to command its heavy batteries, and stayed with it for the rest of 1917. David Fraser, Brooke's biographer, comments that 'his initial and greatest reputation as a gunner staff officer [was made] in the 1st Canadian Corps in the artillery plans he drew up for and executed in the capture of the Vimy Ridge'.[30] In fact, Brooke developed the fire plans for Canada's three great victories of 1917: Vimy, Hill 70 and Passchendaele. But Brooke had an unruly subordinate in McNaughton, his counter-battery (CB) officer. Prior to Vimy, McNaughton arranged to remove his CB organisation from Brooke's command and established it as a separate entity. This was an unprecedented arrangement that offended Brooke. It did not help that McNaughton took the liberty of relocating some of Brooke's guns at Vimy when he deemed them to be improperly sited. That said, the two worked out their differences. Among the other skilled gunners in the Canadian Corps at Vimy was Captain Freddie Morgan, who left for the 42nd Division in the summer.

By any standard, McNaughton was an impressive gunner. In May 1918 he was offered the job as Chief of Staff of the First Army.

1. Troubled legacy: gunnery staff of the Canadian Corps, 1917. Major General E.W.B. Morrison (centre) is flanked on the left by a scowling Major Andrew McNaughton and on the right by a dreamy-eyed Major Alan Brooke.

McNaughton declined. 'I am a Canadian,' he told Currie, 'not a professional soldier.' And he was not enamoured of Horne's artillery concepts and organisation. So Brooke, fresh from staff college in the UK, got the job at the First Army. He learned later that he was the second choice, after a 'colonial soldier'.[31] Haig gave the First Army – and Brooke – a largely supporting role in the Canadian attack down the Arras–Cambrai highway. To help, Currie was given command of several British divisions. McNaughton ran the heavy guns. The CB task, which he brought back under his command, he passed to a promising young gunnery officer named Harry Crerar. McNaughton and Currie orchestrated the advance to Cambrai.

The fighting down the Arras–Cambrai highway was a successful combination of superb artillery tactics and determined infantry assaults. In preparation between 27 August and 2 September the Canadian Corps fired 847,000 shells into the DQ Line, including roughly 75 per cent of the gas shells used by the entire BEF in this phase of the war. The attack began at 0500 hours on 2 September and by the evening the Germans were in full retreat to the Canal du Nord: Currie shut the battle down the next day. It was superbly done. Gary Sheffield described the Canadian methods at the DQ line as 'strikingly modern' in concept and conduct, limited only by the technology of 1918.[32] Ludendorff responded by pulling no less than six armies (Second, Fourth, Sixth, Ninth, Seventeenth and Eighteenth) into the Cambrai sector.[33]

With British armies on the move it was now time to get the burgeoning AEF into the fight. By August there were nearly 1 million Doughboys in France, all in various states of training, with newly minted staff officers struggling to understand the basics of handling formations. Pershing preferred to start modestly by pinching out the Saint-Mihiel salient, a triangular indentation in the French line east of Verdun. This was to be the AEF's first major set-piece battle, and, according to Mark Grotelueschen, 'the start of the decisive American offensive that would win the war'.[34] Some 550,000 troops from sixteen US divisions, supported by six French divisions, were to attack the base of the salient from two sides simultaneously. Lieutenant Colonel George Marshall, now on the staff of the US First Army, was the driving force behind the plan, which included 1,500 aircraft, 3,000 guns and 400 French tanks.

When the offer of 150 heavy British tanks needed to crush the wire was suddenly withdrawn Marshall scrambled to develop a prolonged wire-cutting program for his guns. This was too much for Pershing, who ordered planners to attack without any preliminary bombardment at all. Marshall took the extraordinary step of writing a special unsolicited letter to the army commander 'appealing to him not to undertake the attack without artillery preparation'.[35] Marshall wanted eighteen hours of preliminary fire: Pershing allowed him four. Pershing expected his American riflemen to go fast and deep from the opening whistle.

Historians have often commented that the attack at Saint-Mihiel was like pushing on an open door because the Germans were in the process of withdrawing anyway. Mark Grotelueschen effectively debunked that myth,[36] but as one artillery unit reported, 'what we had expected to be a battle proved to be little more than a foot race to Nonsard'. Anticipating the American attack, the Germans pulled back. The battle ended on 13 September with the salient secured, 450 artillery pieces captured and some 16,000 German soldiers killed, wounded or missing. AEF planners had expected a hefty butcher's bill, perhaps 50,000 casualties: in the event the US First Army lost 7,000 men at Saint-Mihiel.

Success at Saint-Mihiel obscured the doctrinal problems of the AEF, especially Pershing's belief that his men could achieve deep penetrations with modest artillery support and minimal planning. As a result, planning for the much larger Franco-American assault in the area of the Meuse River and the Argonne forest slated for late September 'established such ambitious – indeed essentially unlimited – objectives that they were completely unattainable by the forces employed'.[37] This new offensive would nonetheless be monumental in scale: nearly 1 million men under American command targeted at the critical rail junction of Sedan.

The Franco-American attack in the Meuse–Argonne was one part of the wave of attacks ordered by Foch. The offensive would begin in the Meuse–Argonne on the 26th. The next day the Canadian Corps would resume its attack towards Cambrai, and on 28 September a combined Franco-British-Belgian offensive would start north of Ypres. French attacks towards Laon and from the Chemin des Dames area would follow on the 29th and 30th. By the end of September the whole Allied front from Verdun to the sea would be on the move.[38]

Pershing and his staff moved 600,000 men to make the Meuse–Argonne attack happen. Most of the fifteen US divisions in the initial assault were new to combat because the veteran formations were still on the move or just arriving from Saint-Mihiel. American staff work was barely up to the task, but the French moved heaven and earth to get the US First Army into place. 'Despite all the difficulties the job was done,' Forrest Pogue wrote, 'thanks in large part to Marshall's energy, drive, skill and perhaps above all his ability to improvise coolly when something went wrong.'[39] Critically, the artillery brigades of three divisions in the first echelon of the attack 'were still strung out along the line of march' on 25 September.[40] 'It was thought reasonable,' Pershing explained in his memoirs, 'to count on the vigor and the aggressive spirit of our troops to make up in a measure for their inexperience.'[41]

The Meuse–Argonne offensive was launched over some of the most difficult ground on the Western Front and against exceptionally formidable defences. The axis of the attack was astride the deep and unfordable Meuse River through rolling and occasionally heavily forested areas, and along the spine of the Argonne forest. To American soldiers the Argonne resembled 'a tropical jungle'.[42] The Germans augmented all the natural advantages of terrain and observation through three years of intense preparation. Defences extended some 20km in depth. Behind them lay Sedan, the great rail hub of this sector of the front. It was assumed that if Sedan fell a general German retreat across the Western Front would follow.

The French considered the defences in the Meuse–Argonne impenetrable. Pershing agreed that they were – to everyone but Americans. Pershing expected his army could do it in four phases. The first, and most important, was a sudden and massive surge 16km deep into the German positions, culminating in breeching the Kriemhilde Line. Phase two was another 16km charge to Le Chesne-Stenay, which would loosen the whole French line along the Aisne. The high ground east of the Meuse would fall in phase three, followed by a dash to the Sedan–Mézières railway line in the final lap.[43] Pershing's plan was wildly ambitious. The French expected the Americans to stall early in phase one.[44]

American planning for the Meuse–Argonne contrasts sharply with Canadian plans to reach Cambrai. Currie and his staff were not happy with the way battles became bogged down once the infantry reached the limits of their supporting artillery. Pushing beyond that point simply increased casualties without corresponding gain. The solution was to use operational pauses to move guns up and lay on new fire-plans. The Canadians also developed 'galloping batteries' of field artillery, motorised machine gun and mortar brigades, and medium guns pulled by four-wheel-drive trucks, to keep the guns right behind the advance. The Canadian Corps' enormous combat engineer component facilitated rapid movement of supporting units. All of this required extraordinarily efficient staff work, something the Canadians were now very good at.

The final Canadian lap to Cambrai entailed crossing the Canal du Nord, breeching the main Canal du Nord Line just east of it, and then pressing on through a series of defensive lines across a flat plain. The area was overlooked by the great bump of solid rock at Bourlon that provided unimpeded vision over the whole corps battle space. German heavy guns in dead ground along the Scarpe River to the north and east would need to be silenced.

The immediate task for the Canadians was getting across the Canal du Nord. Where it intersected the Arras–Cambrai highway it was full of water and surrounded by extensive flooded areas and marshland. But a 2,600-yard-long unfinished section – about the frontage of a single division – remained dry near Inchy. Currie built his plans around that dry gap. Using a very complex fireplan Currie proposed to send two divisions – one after the other – through the gap. Two more Canadian and two British divisions would then spill out onto the plain, and head towards Bourlon. The supporting barrage would unfold on the other side of the canal like a blossoming flower, from 2,600 yards wide at the canal to 15,000 yards once all the divisions were across.[45] The staff work for this was nothing short of spectacular.

When General Horne learned of Currie's scheme he declared it too complex and too dangerous. If anything went amiss every German gun for miles around would target that tiny gap in the canal and slaughter the Canadians. Currie would not budge. Horne appealed to Field Marshal Haig to intervene. Haig refused. Horne eventually persuaded the commander of the British Third Army, General Sir Julian Byng,

Currie's old friend and mentor, to talk sense to the portly Canadian. After reviewing the plan Byng said to Currie, 'Do you realize that you are attempting one of the most difficult operations of the war?' Byng expressed his faith in the ability of the Canadian Corps to pull it off, but warned Currie that, 'if you fail, it means home for you'.[46]

The contrast between Currie's plan for the Canal du Nord and Pershing's for the Meuse–Argonne is striking. Whereas the Canadians made elaborate plans to crush German artillery fire, provided sustained and massive artillery support for their attack, and phased it to ensure that the guns could come forward for each tactical stage, Pershing hoped to break the back of the German defences in a single bound. Pershing expected the US First Army to outrun its artillery support long before it reached the main German positions on the Kriemhilde Line. This would leave the Doughboys to take the Kriemhilde Line with 'their own skills and weaponry'.[47]

* * *

Marshal Foch's final great offensive began at 1130 hours on 25 September in the Meuse–Argonne. Once again the fury of the initial bombardment fell on a lightly defended front. It was impressive, nonetheless. 'To the new, inexperienced U.S. Divisions, and even to some older ones,' Donald Smythe wrote, 'the opening artillery barrage on September 25 seemed incredible. Four thousand guns rained incessant fire' on the Germans. According to the American fighter ace Eddie Rickenbacker, aloft before sunrise, the horizon was 'one mass of jagged flashes'.[48]

The opening advance surpassed all expectations – until noon, and then everything began to go wrong. For the inexperienced troops and their staffs a morning fog coupled with the fog of war quickly left them, in George Marshall's words, 'disorganized and confused to a remarkable degree'.[49] Coordination of infantry movement with artillery timetables fell apart, guns were slow to move up, and traffic jams quickly clogged the few available roads. In the centre, General George H. Cameron's V Corps reached Montfaucon quickly and then stalled. The delay stopped III Corps on their right, too, allowing Germans to re-occupy key positions that were vacant just hours before. Hard fighting by III and V Corps on 27 September took these objectives, but by then their momentum was lost. Things went no better with General Hunter

Ligget's I Corps fighting along the edge of the Argonne forest. Among the wounded that day was Colonel George Patton, commander of the 1st US Tank Brigade, shot in the buttocks while leading a small band of infantry. In those hours, Carlo D'Este writes, 'the legend of George S. Patton the warrior was born'.[50]

There was no shortage of heroic deeds on the Meuse–Argonne battlefield but no amount of flesh and will could overcome the German defences. Artillery fire from beyond the Argonne forest and on the heights above the Meuse was, in Smythe's words, 'simply devastating'. As one Doughboy later said, 'Every goddam German there who didn't have a machine gun had a cannon.' The muddle arising from green troops and their staffs engaged in their first major battle did much of the rest. General Max von Gallwitz, in command of that sector of the German line, claimed that 'we had no worries'.[51]

Robert Doughty concludes that the British 'made the most important advances in the first phase of the offensive'.[52] About the time III US Corps was teeing up its attack on Montfaucon, the Canadian Corps launched phase two of Foch's great offensive. At 0530 hours on 27 September the leading edge of the Canadian Corps surged across the gap in the Canal du Nord and began the move on Cambrai. By noon all the first day's objectives were captured except Bourlon Wood.[53] The third blow of Foch's great offensive fell the next day when the Northern Army Group, notionally commanded by King Leopold of Belgium but led by General Harold Plumer's British Second Army, burst out of the Ypres salient. The German Fourth Army in front of them crumbled. As Nick Lloyd concluded, 'there seemed little in the way to prevent the Allies from liberating all of Belgium'.[54]

South of Cambrai, the British Fourth Army had been pounding away at the Hindenburg Line along the Saint-Quentin canal since 26 September. In this sector the canal was 50 feet deep and filled with enough water and mud to drown a man. Behind it lay 3 miles of dense defences: the whole Hindenburg system compressed into a narrow band. The Australians considered this the critical section of the Western Front. 'If this position could be broken', Prior and Wilson wrote, 'the entire line to the north would be turned.'[55] Since there was no opportunity for surprise, the British spent four days systematically destroying the German front. Among the three-quarters of a million shells fired were 30,000 rounds of mustard gas, which seeped into deep dugouts, and penetrated clothing. As Lloyd wrote, 'those who had hoped the Hindenburg Line with its miles of bunkers and acres of concrete would be a refuge' now realised that 'this last line of defence was fast becoming an anvil upon which the remaining German armies would be broken'.[56]

The attack on the Saint-Quentin canal began at dawn on 29 September, and it proved a grim fight. Both the Australian Corps and II US Corps fighting alongside them failed to breach the line in the initial push. When it looked like the Germans would hold, the British IX Corps crossed the canal at Bellenglise in a bold and desperate action. The 46th (North Midland) Division determined to cross the canal even if the men had to swim. A truckload of life jackets from channel ferries were brought forward to do the job. While some swam the foetid canal in life jackets, a crucial bridge fell to the Midlanders just as it was about to be blown: the 46th Division was across. They were aided by an enormous supporting barrage: every 500-yard segment of the German front between the 46th Division's start line and their final objective was struck by some 50,000 shells.[57] Despite all this effort, the Germans in front of the Fourth British Army did not break and run: they fought hard and continued to do so. As Lloyd concludes, 'At the time it did not feel like victory.'[58] Even so, all up and down the BEF front ordinary British divisions – well supported by superb artillery – did extraordinary things.[59]

By the end of September the whole British front was on the move. The Americans, too, pushed hard until the end of September. Pershing's army had little choice other than to hurl flesh against steel. Waves of Americans, attacking in dense formations, made little impression on the Germans – other than amazement. The poor road system in the Meuse–Argonne was aggravated by a logistical muddle. 'First Army was wallowing in an unbelievable logistical tangle,' David Trask wrote. 'It was as if someone had taken the army's intestines out and dumped them all over the table.'[60] The whole affair reminded British liaison officers of their own army in 1915 or worst, 1 July 1916. A formal British report in late October observed that the AEF 'has suffered severely through ignorance of modern war and it must take at least a year before it becomes a serious fighting force'. The French agreed.[61] By 29 September, Pershing's offensive had stalled, having lost 117,000 men.

Thomas Johnson, a reporter with the *New York Sun*, wrote later that the British and French press took little interest in the American Expeditionary Force: two British newspaper men covered the Meuse–Argonne, no French correspondents did. Most relied on official US Army communiqués which, in Johnson's words, claimed that the AEF was 'always perfectly equipped and supplied, advancing gloriously, even blandly, from victory to victory'. When it was clear that the British and French were ignoring the AEF's accomplishment, 'We started a campaign to sell the Meuse–Argonne to the world.' According to Johnson, the AEF itself was responsible for the exaggerated praise that newspapers subsequently printed.[62] The American experience in the Meuse–Argonne left a lasting impression on the British and would influence their expectations of American combat power in the next war.

Foch had not expected much more from the Americans, but the sheer scale and relentlessness of their efforts – at enormous cost, as Johnson noted – drew German reinforcements south which helped the British to break through. Meanwhile, Foch was genuinely frustrated by the tentative efforts of his own French armies. Robert Doughty wrote that Foch was 'incensed at the lack of French progress' in every sector where they attacked.[63] As early as 30 September the British complained that the French were 'hanging back', 'leaning on the enemy' rather than attacking. Moreover, as the Allies advanced and the front shortened, French armies began to withdraw from the front. In July, Pétain deployed ten armies; by mid-October three of those were gone.[64]

In fact, the only great French success in September came in the Balkans, where General Franchet D'Espèrey's Franco-Serbian-British Army burst out of its Greek 'internment camp' at Salonika and quickly drove north. By 28 September, Bulgaria quit as British and Greek troops poured across the border. Turkey was now isolated from the rest of the Central Powers, while French cavalry reached Skopje, Serbia (now Macedonia), by the 30th. Meanwhile, Austria-Hungary teetered on the brink of collapse. Once the Allies broke out of Salonika, Austro-Hungarian garrisons began to withdraw from the Balkans. As early as 16 September, Emperor Karl appealed to Woodrow Wilson for peace based on the

American President's 'Fourteen Points'. With Germany now facing ruin along the whole Western Front, Hindenburg and Ludendorff recommended to their government on 1 October that it ask for 'peace at once'.[65]

* * *

Finding a way out of the looming catastrophe was not easy. The alternatives – defeat and invasion or revolution – were inconceivable. So the thin reed which the Germans now grasped was Wilson's Fourteen Points. Obviously, the Americans – with less 'sunk costs' in the war, guided by their ideals and their natural mistrust of Britain and France – offered the best hope of salvaging something from the debacle now unfolding. A request to President Wilson for negotiations to end the war was sent on 3 October.

Wilson's reply on the 14th came, in Holger Herwig's description, as a 'bombshell' and caused panic. Wilson condemned Germany for its 'wanton destruction' in France and Flanders, and for its 'illegal and inhuman' submarine war. Germany would have to accept 'the present military supremacy of the armies of the United States and of the Allies in the field'.[66] It was also now patently clear that the 'right to self-determination' meant that vast tracts of eastern Europe – modern Poland, the Baltic states and much of Ukraine and Belorussia – secured by Germany under the Treaty of Brest-Litovsk would be forfeit, and so, too, Germany's colonies.

Negotiations between Wilson's representatives and the German government began in The Hague on 17 October. Wilson's true intent was revealed in his third diplomatic note of 23 October. It was a complete rejection of 'Prussian militarism' and the autocratic government of the Kaiser. While the new German Chancellor, Prince Max von Baden, scrambled to find a solution, Hindenburg and Ludendorff flatly rejected Wilson's 'boundless will of conquest and annihilation'. That day they ordered Germany's armies to stand fast.

Few German soldiers on the Western Front were prepared to do that. By October the army reported that perhaps 1.5 million soldiers had already 'deserted', slipped away, shirked their duty, many simply starting the long walk home. The Canadian Corps captured the critical northern rail junction of Cambrai on 9 October, and the whole northern flank of the German position in the west folded back. Ludendorff now escaped to Sweden to pen his vitriolic memoir blaming the Jews and the Communists for 'stabbing the army in the back'. The navy, ordered to sea on a Wagnerian death-ride, rebelled. The virus of Bolshevism was creeping into the body politic of Germany – to join the Spanish-flu epidemic which was already devastating both the army and home front. No one knew how far the rebellion would go, but the ruling elites feared Germany would slip into Communism as Russia had a year before.

Meanwhile, the Italians, avenging their humiliation a year earlier at Caporetto, launched a crushing offensive against the Austrians in late October.[67] By 30 October Hungary, Bohemia, Croatia, Slovenia, Dalmatia, Moravia and Silesia had all declared some form of independence. Late on 2 November, Emperor Karl accepted an armistice: now Germany was alone.

Amid relentless pressure on all fronts and the total collapse of its Allies, the Germans hastened to placate Wilson. At the end of October a new executive, led by Socialists, was installed, and its powers were now made answerable to the people through the Reichstag. The Germans now looked to Wilson for salvation. All that now remained to do was get rid of the Kaiser, although many thought that the people and the army would fight to keep him. They were wrong. General Wilhelm Groener, Ludendorff's replacement as First Quartermaster General of the Army, reported on 9 November that the army would not fight to save the Kaiser – but it would fight to defeat Communism at home. The Kaiser had to go, and the army was needed in Germany. The war had to end. The Kaiser slipped into exile in the Netherlands the next day, twenty-four hours after the Social Democratic Party declared Germany a Republic. The new government sent delegates to Compiègne, north of Paris, to work out armistice terms.

While the diplomats and politicians talked, the fighting continued. Foch was intent on defeating Germany's army in the field. Pershing was frustrated by the failure of his army to achieve a quick and decisive victory in the Meuse–Argonne. The First US Army gnawed away at the Kriemhilde Line before finally breeching it on 11 October. The achievement prompted Pershing to send a sharp rebuke to Foch for his criticisms of American performance. Foch, as it turns out, was under pressure from the French Prime Minister, Georges Clemenceau, to 'fix' the American problem.

Many others within the AEF were trying to fix it, too. By mid-October the AEF had enough units in the field to establish the Second US Army. When this happened Pershing became the AEF commander, giving command of the First US Army to General Hunter Liggett, who immediately ordered a halt to all major operations. Over the next two weeks Liggett fundamentally altered the AEF's doctrine. 'For the upcoming attack,' Grotelueschen writes, 'Liggett chose objectives that, although relatively deep, were all within range of supporting artillery.' The planning fell to General Charles P. Summerall, an accomplished artilleryman, commander of V Corps and the architect of the final breaking of the Kriemhilde Line. His orders for the next assault were a marked departure from Pershing's belief that flesh and aimed rifle fire would conquer: 'fire superiority, rather than sheer manpower, [would] be the driving force of the attack'.[68] On 1 November, Liggett's First US Army launched 'the most powerful and comprehensive American attack plan of the war'.[69] It finally broke the stalemate in the Meuse–Argonne and the Germans began to withdraw.

Despite Liggett's achievement, Pershing remained 'upset by his failure to gain a brilliant victory' and, in David Trask's words, he 'railed at what he considered the premature end of the war'.[70] In the very last days of the war, he sought to crown the AEF's achievement by finally capturing Sedan, and presenting it to France as a prize to redeem the humiliation of Napoleon III's surrender there to the Prussians in 1870. The problem was that Sedan lay in the French sector. On 5 November, when the First US Army was well ahead of the French forces on their left flank, Pershing secured French permission to enter Sedan. The order to the First US Army contained a final unfortunate sentence: 'Boundaries will not be considered binding.' Pershing had meant the boundary between the French and American armies: American division commanders had a different understanding.[71]

Given this apparent licence, General Summerall ordered the 1st US Division to make a dash for Sedan that cut across the rear of three other divisions. 'The resulting chaos,' Zabecki and Mastriano write, 'brought the three American divisions and the French 40th Division to a dead halt, with their troops hopeless entangled.'[72] Liggett went ballistic. Meanwhile the French, 'who had overcome their difficulties and came storming up, panting to take Sedan, were as mad as hell'.[73] No one got to Sedan before the war ended, but nearly 600 Doughboys were killed, wounded or missing in the attempt.[74] As Smythe concluded, the whole affair 'was an action unworthy of any army'; Liggett labelled it a 'tactical atrocity'.[75]

The armistice came into effect at 11.00 a.m. on the morning of 11 November. John Terraine described the BEF's offensives in late 1918 as 'the greatest succession of victories in the British Army's whole history – victories won against the main body of the main enemy in a continental war, for the *only* time in British history'.[76] Field Marshal Haig claimed that it was the unrelenting British advance that finally defeated the Germans. And it did so at enormous cost: some 411,636 men killed, wounded and missing in the Hundred Days Campaign. The French lost over half a million men – 531,000 – and the Americans 127,000.

For Currie and his Canadians the capture of Mons on 11 November was a fitting metaphor: what the BEF had started four years earlier, the Canadian Corps had finished. Since 8 August the Canadians had come 100km, at a cost of 45,835 killed, wounded and missing: a casualty rate of nearly 46 per cent. Their effort was sustained by a steady stream of conscripts, raised at the cost of sectarian violence and near civil war in Canada. In the process the Canadian Corps met and defeated some forty-seven German divisions, about a quarter of their strength on the Western Front. As General Horne observed laconically, 'the Canadian Corps is perhaps rather apt to take all the credit it can for everything and to consider that the BEF consists of the Canadian Corps and some other troops'.[77]

By November 1918 expectations, myths and ghosts of the Great War were already haunting the corridors of power in the western world. Now the peace had to be settled – and the debate over what they had achieved, who owed what to who, and who had 'won' the war could begin in earnest.

CHAPTER 2

THE SHADOW OF 1918

Great Britain is faced in the United States with a phenomenon for
which there is no parallel in our modern history.

Robert Craigie, UK Foreign Office, 1928[1]

'Wilson drove America to the forefront of world politics in 1916,'
Adam Tooze concluded, 'to ensure not that the "right" side won
in World War I, but that no side did.'[2] Allied indebtedness and a victorious US Army on the field in Europe by 1919 would allow Wilson to
dictate the peace and reshape the world in ways amenable to American
trade, culture and finance. Franklin Delano Roosevelt's aims two decades later were identical.

Wilson's Fourteen Points captured the imagination as the pathway
to a more peaceful future. Self-determination would free Europe's
people from imperial oppression and eliminate the primary cause of
Europe's wars. To cap it all, Wilson proposed a 'League of Nations' with
enough power to regulate the peace. There would be no more secret
treaties, no retribution, no unjust claims, no indemnities. The will of
people everywhere expressed through free association in liberal democracies and defended by the might of the League would, perhaps, free the
whole world of war, too. This was the straw that the new German
republic grasped in November 1918.

When the Allies convened in Paris early 1919 to settle the terms of
Germany's surrender, Wilson controlled the agenda.[3] At the top was the

League of Nations. The French were not interested. They wanted back their lost provinces of Alsace and Lorraine, and they wanted the Germans to pay for four years of destruction wrought on their country. France had paid Prussia following its defeat in 1871; it was only fair that the Germans pay this time. The British focused on balance-of-power politics. France required compensation, and a powerful Germany was needed as a bulwark against Bolshevism. But the French also wanted an Anglo-American security agreement to guard it against renewed German aggression, while the Americans wanted to secure the freedom of the seas against unfettered British seapower. The British were not ill-disposed to Wilson's plans for the League and were prepared to ensure peace through international cooperation.[4]

That winter Wilson returned to the US to push his plan for the league. When he spoke in Boston in late February he had the draft of the League covenant – which the Senate had not yet seen – placed on every seat. By the time he got to Washington, Republican senators were irate, but Wilson refused to see them. The vast majority of the American people, he claimed, supported his scheme. The problem, which he refused to address, was that the Senate, not the American people, would decide.

The final Versailles Treaty was put before the German delegation in June 1919. It was largely a victory for the French. Germany was stripped of her colonies, territory was ceded both east and west – to France and a new Polish state – and new states were established across eastern Europe. Self-determination was, nonetheless, denied to the Germans living along the German border in Alsace-Lorraine, the Sudetenlands of the new Czechoslovak state and in Poland, and Austria was forbidden to unite with Germany. German armed forces were limited to 100,000, with no heavy artillery and no air force; the navy was forbidden to own or operate submarines. Germany was to pay an indemnity to cover the costs of the war and reconstruction. The ultimate humiliation was Article 231, which declared that Germany was solely responsible for causing the war.

The Versailles Treaty came as a total shock to the Germans. They believed that the new democratic republic, which took Germany out of the war and exiled the Kaiser, would get a lenient peace. This, they believed, is what Wilson's Fourteen Points had promised. The reality brought a deep sense of betrayal. As Margaret MacMillan said, Wilson went from a prophet of hope to 'a wicked hypocrite'.[5]

Worse followed. Many Americans supported the League of Nations but rejected the notion that any foreign body could command American forces. Wilson rode the rails for weeks drumming up support and rejecting compromises. Then his health collapsed. Appeals for the inclusion of reservations to the Treaty and the League Covenant continued to arrive, but Wilson rejected them all. By November, both he and his vision for the world were done. Wilson was awarded the Nobel Peace Prize in late 1919, but the Senate rejected the Treaty and the League in March 1920. Wilson's health never recovered, and he died in 1923 aged 67.

America's rejection of the League haunted every major European Cabinet room for the next two decades. America was the world's richest nation by a long mark, its national wealth estimated to be $245 billion – more than that of Britain, France and Germany combined. It also owned a fair portion of Europe's $120 billion debt.[6] The great fear among Europeans was that the management of that debt would become tangled in American domestic politics and the hands of the rough parvenus of American capitalism. They faced, according to Tooze, 'the incongruous spectacle of Chicago meatpackers, provincial senators and manufacturers of condensed milk lecturing a Prime Minister of France, a British Foreign Secretary or an Italian dictator about the virtues of disarmament and world peace. These were the uncouth heralds of America's drive towards "world hegemony".'[7] Tooze was only too right: after 1919 everything was affected by American domestic politics.

At the heart of the debt issue lay conflicting views of what the war had been about, who had carried the burden, who had won it, and who's vision would shape the postwar world. Many educated and well-travelled Americans shared Wilson's view that American exceptionalism, not just money, justified its emerging leadership. In this they clashed directly with the British, who, of course, saw themselves as the progenitors of the liberal and democratic values that Americans arrogated to themselves as leaders of the 'free world'. After all, British parliamentary democracy, the model for the whole world to emulate, had evolved in a fairly peaceful manner over many centuries. The values of peace, the rule of law and liberalism were why the British empire stood against Prussian militarism for years before America entered the war. American money may have assured Allied victory, but comparatively little American blood had been spilt fighting for these fundamental values.

This was not, of course, how the majority of Americans saw things. For the meatpackers, the provincial senators, and much of middle America, the British were no better than the rest of Europe's decaying empires. In fact, they were worse, for two reasons. The first and most obvious was that they commanded a global empire and the world's largest navy. They exercised command of the sea with a quiet ruthlessness that offended American sensibility, and virtually everywhere Americans went in the world they found the British, or British investment or British ownership, or British coal, or British newspapers. Worse still, the British oppressed hundreds of millions of subject peoples, especially in India, a nation that resonated with the founding myths of America itself. For most Americans in 1918 – and in 1939, too – the British empire itself was inherently evil, as it had been in the eighteenth century when America threw it off. The notion that Britain was animated by the same liberal political and economic philosophers that America claimed as its own – from Thomas Paine to Adam Smith, Richard Cobden and John Bright – was anathema. As Tooze observed, 'precisely because Britain was the nation from which America's own political culture had historically derived, it was essential for Wilson that Britain itself remain fixed in the past'. The very thought that British democracy 'might be advancing along the path of democratic progress, alongside rather than behind America, was deeply unsettling'.[8]

Tooze might have pushed his argument even further by exploring Canada's evolution into a peaceful, stable, liberal democratic state under the British empire. The great problem for Americans was that Canada was the very antimatter of America's founding myths. As recently as 2000 Robert Cowley could write that had the revolution failed, Americans would have ended up like Canadians, 'tame, humble colonials in the triumphant British empire, without an iota of the independent spirit that has been the heart of the nation's identity'.[9] No

British politician, official or military officer who had to deal with Canadians in the early twentieth century ever found them tame, humble or lacking in independence. Canada was proof that there had been another way in 1776. But as Wilson observed in 1916, and as Franklin Roosevelt assumed, the British were part of the problem.

* * *

Defeat of the Kaiser's Germany had been achieved at a ferocious cost: 12 million soldiers and perhaps as many civilians dead. The wounded, crippled and disfigured haunted the streets of every European village and town.[10] In France and Belgium the fighting left a wrecked, barren, shell-torn strip of landscape that snaked in a lazy 'S' from Switzerland to the North Sea.[11] The German occupation had also been ruthless. As one recent history has commented, 'French civilians endured a war ancient in its cruelty and very modern in the ways it regulated and extorted from the subject people.'[12] If anything, the exploitation of Belgium, including the enslavement of its people, was more harsh than anything the Nazis imposed a generation later.[13] One American Army engineer estimated that it would take two years of hard work simply to estimate of the costs of repairing the damage.[14]

By the summer of 1920 the only thing about Europe that Americans cared about was the debt. The bright young British economist John Maynard Keynes argued that to stabilise the world and get economies moving, both Britain and the US needed to forgive debt: wipe the slate clean. The American delegation at Versailles rejected the idea, and threatened to cut off further loans to smaller European nations if the idea was pushed.[15] The British government proposed the liquidation of all war debts again in the summer of 1920. If, as Chancellor of the Exchequer Austen Chamberlain warned the British Cabinet at the end of 1919, 'Europe cannot buy for want of credit',[16] then it was impossible to restore the world's economy. But the Americans wanted their money back, and in a presidential election year, no candidate was going to deny them that. The issue of debt and protectionism overshadowed Anglo-American relations for the next twenty-seven years.

Britain remained a Great Power after 1918 – in land area the largest it would ever be – but the war hollowed out the heart of that power. Trade suffered from the conversion of industry to war use, which in turn eroded the commercial and financial activity that made London the financial capital of the world. 'To restart the flow of trade,' John Darwin writes, 'required a massive injection of loans and credits.'[17] This money proved all but impossible to find. Prior to the war the British relied heavily on exporting textiles and coal. Control over the world's steaming coal – and other key industrial varieties like Yorkshire 'smalls' for Scandinavian industry – had allowed a declining British shipping industry to prosper before 1914: British tramps always had a secure outbound cargo. But as demand for coal slipped after 1919, the viability of the British shipping industry slipped as well.[18] Overseas trade, already hurt by the war, fell dramatically. This was especially so in Latin America, which American interests penetrated extensively in 1917–18 while the British carried the AEF to France. British shipbuilding and shipping industries – prime sources of foreign capital before 1914 – were soon in sharp decline.[19]

And then there was the war debt. Between 1914 and 1917 Britain funded the war, acting as the entente's banker. To find that cash Britain sold off nearly $1 billion in US assets, over $825 million in gold, and borrowed $1.4 billion from New York banks. The latter debt was entirely paid off by 1919. Britain also guaranteed $3.3 billion in loans from New York banks – which preferred the reliability of the British economy as collateral – to Russia, Italy and France. When America declared war on Germany, the US government, through the Liberty Loan Act, took charge of all loans, and the British had hopes that America would assume the role of entente banker. America's most important contribution to the war effort would be its money. 'If not one penny of it is returned,' Senator Reid from Utah remarked during debate on the Liberty Loan Act, 'I wish to say that every penny of it will be expended for the defence of principles . . . which we entered the war to uphold.'[20] Similar remarks by the Secretary of the Treasury in December 1917 indicated that funding the Europeans enabled them 'to do the fighting that otherwise the American Army would have to do at much expense, not only in terms of men but of money, money that could not be returned to us and lives that could not be restored'.[21]

The debt at the heart of the Anglo-American impasse was incurred after April 1917: money that, at the time, seemed like an exchange of cash for blood. From then until the end of the war Britain borrowed roughly $4 billion from the US. That debt was roughly equivalent to what Britain's Allies owed her by 1918.[22] Had the British been able to secure payment from their own debtors, resolution of the Anglo-American impasse would have been little more than a cashflow issue. But Bolshevik Russia repudiated its debt and France was in no position to pay the $3 billion it owed the UK (on top of its own $3.9 billion to the US).[23] The situation was further complicated by the shifting dynamics of the economy, and the nature of the goods acquired with the loans. The $4 billion Britain borrowed from the US after April 1917 was spent entirely in the USA, on American goods and services at inflated late-war prices. Now the money was to be repaid when currencies were devalued. Moreover, these loans had no commercial value. As Robert Self explained, 'they were neither productive nor self-liquidating in that they could never generate the means by which the borrower could repay the loan . . . like the shells on which they were largely spent, these loans were blown to pieces'.[24]

'The political trap', Benjamin D. Rhodes wrote, 'was that if Britain did not pay, the American tax payer was left with the bill', and no American politician could fight that battle and win.[25] It did not help that many Americans assumed that the British had used American money to pad their own civil economy. The US Secretary of the Treasury, Andrew Mellon, said that emphatically in 1927. 'American loans to England were not so much to provide war supplies,' one American journal concluded in 1927, 'as to furnish sterling for home and foreign needs and to save England borrowing from her own people.'[26] Given the statutory requirements of the Liberty Loan Act, Mellon was also emphatically wrong, but it seemed to matter little. 'American politicians and their voters', Self concludes, 'regarded the Europeans as untrustworthy "welchers"', and the war debt issue 'effectively poisoned great power relations with endless bickering, mistrust and resentment for two decades'.[27]

Americans would soon come to blame the British for most of their economic woes.

* * *

While the British empire was under stress economically, forces thrown up by the war threatened to rip it apart from within. Keeping the empire 'British', and keeping British power united, grew increasingly problematic after 1918.

In the early 1920s Ireland was finally granted Home Rule, minus the six northern counties of Ulster. The compromise was bound to offend, and civil war soon followed. Bloody unrest flared in India as well. Mahatma Gandhi's relentless mantra, 'We want the same rights as an Englishman enjoys', ran hard against the repressive Rowlatt Act, introduced in 1919, that extended the powers of preventative detention and detention without trial and without recourse to judicial review. 'Whatever its justification,' Darwin wrote of the Rowlatt Act, 'this was to be a staggering political blunder.' In March 1919 Mahatma Gandhi, the emerging focal point of India's anti-colonial movement, launched a campaign of civil disobedience that soon erupted into rioting and violence. His subsequent arrest fuelled the protest, and then, in April, 400 protesters were shot dead by the Indian Army at Amritsar. India's large Muslim population – the main source of manpower for the Indian Army – also joined in the wave of protest. Gandhi exploited their discontent. 'The "new politics" [of India] had arrived with a vengeance', Darwin concludes of the events in 1919–20.[28] The Indian 'problem' became the yardstick by which many Americans judged British rhetoric about liberal democratic values.

Britain's great Dominions – Australia, Canada, New Zealand and South Africa – also drifted away from the mother country after 1918. Together they had fielded a million men, and all of them signed the Treaty of Versailles in their own right. The Dominions were also granted seats in the new League of Nations. 'As the largest and oldest of the Dominions', Darwin writes, 'Canada's attitude was of key importance' to the British empire. Sir Robert Borden, Canada's wartime Prime Minister, had championed a common British foreign policy and, like many other British-Canadians, expected Canada to 'exert a significant influence' over that policy. In 1921 William Lyon Mackenzie King's new Liberal government flatly rejected Borden's policy of imperial integration. From Mackenzie King's perspective, the greatest 'potential threat to Canadian autonomy . . . came from London'.[29] Not surprisingly, when Britain sought help from its Dominions in 1922 to stop Turkish forces threatening the Anglo-French neutrality zone along the

Dardanelles – the Chanak Crisis – Canada simply refused to help. The League provided Canada with an international stage for its new independence, and Mackenzie King's government embraced it. Canada was to be a 'British' nation, but it would make its own foreign policy and sign its own treaties.[30]

The 1926 Imperial Conference was convened in part to resolve the issue of Dominion status. The case for independence was made by the Prime Minister of South Africa, General J.B.M. Hertzog. South Africa was willing to remain within the family of British nations 'only if she can be made to feel implicit faith in her full and free nationhood upon the basis of equality with every other member of the Commonwealth'. As Charles Stacey concluded, 'The clear implication was that if South Africa did not obtain satisfactory clarification of her status she would secede.'[31] The Irish, for their part, pushed the agenda even further by arguing that the mother Parliament in Westminster should no longer have the right of veto over legislation passed by the Dominions. When that discussion arose in committee it was decided to consider other issues, such as the power to sign treaties and have formal diplomatic relations with other countries. Mackenzie King supported this initiative, but softened Hertzog's direct appeal for 'independence' – it smacked too much, he said, 'of 1776' and the United States.[32] He persuaded the conference to accept Hertzog's other language: 'autonomous Communities within the British empire, equal in status, in no way subordinate to one another in any aspect of their domestic or external affairs, though united by a common allegiance to the Crown and freely associated as members of the British Commonwealth of Nations'.[33] With that, the path to independence was set.

By 1926 both Canada and Ireland had already opened legations in Washington.[34] The British ambassador to Washington, Sir Esme Howard, supported these initiatives. 'Our policy if we want to hold the Empire together is, I think,' he warned London, 'to encourage the national feeling in the Dominions in every way we can. To do this we have ourselves to recast our old ideas about Empire.'[35] Mackenzie King would have agreed wholeheartedly. When Canada ran for a chair on the Council of the League of Nations in 1927 the British were taken aback. They nonetheless supported Canada's bid, although a noticeable scowl was observed on the face of the British Foreign Secretary, Austen Chamberlain, when it was announced that Canada won the seat.[36] Canada's embrace of an international body as a counterpoint to close ties with Great Powers would be echoed again in 1945 with the founding of the United Nations.

Senior British military officers got a taste of what the future of the empire might be like in 1927 when Brigadier Andrew McNaughton attended the new Imperial Defence College (discussed in chapter 3). The IDC was part of the effort, largely successful, to integrate the armed forces of the empire into a single coherent force – a development somewhat at odds with the constitutional evolution of the British world. When called upon to give a 'lecture presenting the results of my past studies and experiences', McNaughton expressed the view that 'the time had gone by when any of the principal Dominions would accept a dictum from the central government of the United Kingdom'. In future, Dominion governments would retain 'responsibility in some measure for the overall direction of their [troops'] employment'. Through it all, McNaughton felt the 'opposition of [Alan] Brooke to the general idea'.

> I recall discussions in the syndicates and so on in which he took quite a different view. The concept I put forward was 'not on'. The idea that anybody except the central authority should have any power of discussion before decision was anathema to him. He was just against it. That, of course, was the way he thought afterwards. That was his attitude.[37]

The clash between McNaughton and Brooke would reach its climax in the Second World War, with important consequences for Operation Overlord.

A report prepared by A.J. Balfour, a former Prime Minister and by the late 1920s a senior member of Stanley Baldwin's Cabinet, emerged from the 1926 conference and set the stage for the new relationship between Britain and her senior colonies. The Statute of Westminster of 1931 offered full legal independence to Canada, the Irish Free State and the Union of South Africa. Mackenzie King arranged a quiet formal adoption ceremony.[38] The application of the Statute to Australia and New Zealand required ratification by their Parliaments, which did not happen before the Second World War. This left them legally still British colonies. The complex legal status of Britain's great Dominions created problems during the Second World War. As will be evident, the meaning of the Statute of Westminster escaped the understanding of many senior British officials and military leaders. It was also a source of utter bewilderment to the Americans – who seemed confused by the idea that independence could be achieved gradually and peacefully. However, for Canada the new situation was clear: as of 1931 Britain and Canada were separate countries with a shared head of state.

Andy McNaughton had foreseen the impact that this changed legal status would have on command and control of armed forces of the British empire and Commonwealth. And so he initiated the drafting of a 'Visiting Forces Act' as a corollary to the Statue of Westminster. This specified two types of cooperation for Canadian troops serving alongside those of Great Britain (or any other Commonwealth nation): 'serving together' or 'acting in combination'. The former maintained independence of command and control under national staffs, while the latter allowed for subordination of national contingents or formations under (presumably) British command and control. The Visiting Forces Act was passed into law in 1933 and adopted by Canada.[39]

* * *

Interwoven into the fabric of these political and economic developments of the 1920s was the process of memorialisation of the Great War. The differences between what the war meant to the British and their empire, and to the Americans were profound. Those differences would echo in the Anglo-American discourse during the Second World War, and in the ways in which the development of strategy was understood.

The most obvious and powerful memorialisation of the dead was the proliferation and formalisation of cemeteries and monuments. In the age of liberalism and nationalism it was necessary to honour the sacrifice of individuals for the common good. Lawrence Binyon's exhortation in his September 1914 poem 'For the Fallen', 'We will remember them', became a commitment by the whole of the British world. The British decided early that their dead – eventually totalling a million from Great Britain and the empire – should lie where they fell. By 1927 the Imperial War Graves Commission had built over five hundred cemeteries, most of these in France and Belgium. They became carefully manicured versions of English country gardens. The Belgians were deeply impressed by the solemnity and quiet dignity of British commemoration.[40] Edmund Blunden later lamented, 'No one can say they are not buried well / At least as much of them as could be found.'[41]

Between Paris and Zeebrugge the Imperial War Graves Commission also built twenty-seven major war memorials. Some are massive, constructed to honour the legions of the missing. The Menin Gate in Ypres bears the names of some 54,000 troops from Britain and the empire who disappeared in the suffocating mud of the salient. A few miles to the east a curved wall behind the Tyne Cot cemetery lists another 35,000 more who vanished elsewhere in Belgium. The names of the missing on the Thiepval Monument on the Somme add another 73,000 names of men with no known grave. All told, over 300,000 British soldiers remain missing in action. Among them are over 18,000 Canadians, nearly a third of Canada's 60,000 war dead.[42]

The spiritual reverence for the war dead carried over into postwar 'pilgrimages' to the Western Front and its cemeteries. The first tourist guidebooks appeared in 1919,[43] and major British travel agencies booked tourists in tens of thousands. It helped that the sites of the greatest British battles and their cemeteries were within easy reach by boat and rail, and within the budget of almost every British family.[44] For many Britons the notion that the war had been a tragic loss of life combined – uneasily – with the idea that it was also just, and that victory was due in no small part to British arms. Many veterans of the BEF comforted themselves in the 1920s with the belief that their cause had been just and the BEF's final push had tipped the Germans over.

American memory of the Great War was starkly different. Most importantly, it was only dimly shaped by the experience of combat and loss. The most important, and lasting, influence of the Great War in America was the radicalisation of its politics. The American 'establishment' embraced the war with unbridled enthusiasm and used it as an opportunity to crush everything 'un-American', including the socialist party, labour unions, African Americans and immigrants. The Espionage

45

Act of 1917 and the Sedition Act of 1918 were used to suspend civil liberties and jail thousands. When Robert Goldstein released his film, *The Spirit of '76*, in 1917 he was arrested, charged under the Espionage Act, fined $5,000 and sentenced to ten years in jail. His sin was portraying America's new ally, Great Britain, as brutal and repressive.[45] Even questioning the merits of the war could land someone in jail – or worse. Gangs of armed thugs, legitimised by local and federal authorities, helped the police track and arrest dissenters. The war at home fired anti-Black racism; fear of Communism fuelled xenophobia and the assault on the American socialist party and labour unions.[46] This rise of nativism would, by 1939, align much of the American right more with Nazi Germany than with Great Britain.[47]

In contrast to the troubled impact of the war on America's domestic front, combat and loss on the Western Front left little in the way of scars on the American collective psyche. America's memory of the war, Steven Trout argues, was shaped largely by the simple experience of army life for the millions of men who never left the lower forty-eight states.[48] The dominant memory of the Great War was the 'chicken shit' of army life. The result was what Trout calls a 'failed memory', and the 'absence of a stable "Myth about the War"'.[49] If there was a 'lost Generation' of Americans resulting from the war, Malcolm Cowley argued in his 1934 collection of essays, *Exile's Return*, it was both the American literati and the millions who were called into military service and never engaged in combat or even got close to the front. Like Ernest Hemingway, Cowley served in that most literate of frontline duties: ambulance drivers. 'School and college had uprooted us in spirit,' Cowley wrote, and 'now we were physically uprooted, hundreds of us, millions, plucked from our own soil as if by a clamshell bucket and dumped, scattered among strange people.' He goes on,

> We were fed, lodged, clothed by strangers, commanded by strangers, infected with the poison of irresponsibility – the poison of travel, too, for we had learned that problems could be left behind us merely by moving elsewhere – and the poison of danger, excitement, that made our old life seem intolerable. Then, as suddenly as it began for us, the war ended.[50]

It says a great deal about the legacy of the war in the United States that much of its important Great War literature was written by non-combat veterans. Ernest Hemingway, F. Scott Fitzgerald and John Dos Passos were all rejected for military service – the 'emasculating embarrassment' of not being able to fight like 'real men'. 'Instead of speaking uniformly for a Lost Generation,' Trout observes, American 'interwar literature, through its contradictions and divisions, documents a lost consensus over the meaning of America's first overseas crusade.'[51] This contrasts sharply with the British literature of the late 1920s and early 1930s, written largely by combat veterans, where a clear consensus on the absolute futility of the war emerged.

It may be that this muddled cultural, literary and folk memory of the war encouraged Americans to rally around the one certainty from their Great War experience: that they had won it. It was, however, not entirely clear how this had been done. As Trout writes, 'was it the vast reservoir of manpower in the United States, most of it still untapped by the time of the armistice, that . . . crushed the Germans' will to fight?' Or was it a combat victory on the Meuse–Argonne? Some, who knew better, questioned Pershing tactics and the claims of signal American victory on the battlefield in 1918.[52]

That dissenting voice was articulated most clearly in Thomas M. Johnson's 1928 book, *Without Censor*. Johnson had reported on the AEF for the *New York Sun* and was intimately familiar with the events and the players. He justified Pershing's brutal tactics and American casualties as proof of America's commitment to winning the war in 1918. The 'American's job was to keep up that attack and die in the thousands on the Kriemhilde Heights if need be to save another year of war that would take tens of thousands'.[53] So while the 'French and especially the British were winning great and glittering success. Ours was great, not glittering.'[54] As Johnson points out, the success of the final push to victory was based on concentric attacks. The great merit of the Meuse–Argonne campaign was that the AEF continued to push and draw in German forces, opening other parts of the front for rapid movement.

The idea that the Meuse–Argonne was the decisive blow that defeated Germany was nonetheless widely accepted and became the defining feature of American battlefield commemoration from the

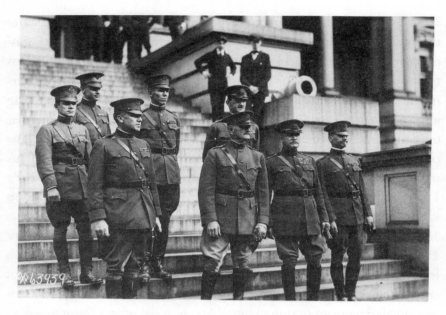

2. The men who won the Great War? General John Pershing
and staff, Washington, DC, 1919. Colonel George Marshall,
Pershing's G3 (Operations), is behind him in the centre.

outset. This was abundantly evident in 1923 with the establishment of
the American Battle Monuments Commission (ABMC), with General
John Pershing himself as its first chairman. The ABMC arose in part, as
Lisa Budreau concluded, 'In the midst of fears that America's contribution to the war effort was being overlooked by its allies'.[55] This was not
going to happen under Pershing's watch. '[T]he ABMC's memorials in
the Aisne-Marne, Saint-Mihiel and Meuse–Argonne are,' Trout writes,
'in part, Pershing's personal rebuke to Allied generals who had belittled
America's military contribution . . . These colossal monuments, visible
from miles away and dominating the surrounding landscape, leave little
question, at least for Americans visitors, that the AEF won the war.'[56] It
was also Secretary of War Newton D. Baker's idea that these great
monuments should 'mark the advance of freedom' and 'the further
advance yet of the American ideal'.[57]

Baker was not alone in his views. According to Budreau, what distinguished the American process of memorialisation from others was the

'degree to which the U.S. military and political elites were expected to respond to mass opinion expressed through newspapers and organized groups'.[58] In particular, American popular media championed the idea that the AEF had won the war. After all, they had done just such a thing in the war against Spain. The Cubans and the Filipinos had not been able to defeat the Spanish after long years of insurrection. Victory came only through American intervention, and then America settled the peace and imposed its writ on the newly 'liberated' islanders.[59] It only made sense that the Great War followed a similar pattern.

No other Allied combatant nation experienced American claims of victory more than Canada, where 'American pulp war magazines such as *Battle Stories* and *War Stories* . . . flooded across the border in the 1920s . . . Soldiers from other nations had no role in the Allied triumph,' Jonathan Vance observes of this American populist view. Veterans of the Canadian Corps were so incensed that some called for an outright ban on all American fiction about the war.[60] Canadians knew that they had played a key role in the Allied victory on the Western Front in 1918. J.F.B. Livesay's monumental *Canada and the Hundred Days*, published in late 1919 based on detailed reports from the British First Army and General Currie himself, demonstrated that. After presenting essentially Currie's account of the Canadian role between 8 August and 11 November, Livesay concludes emphatically that these Canadian attacks 'broke the back of enemy defense on the West Front'.[61]

Canadians got a taste of the official British view of their role when the first draft of the second volume of the British official history of the war landed at army headquarters in Ottawa. The volume, prepared by Sir James Edmonds, covered the Second Battle of Ypres in April–May 1915. For three days the 1st Canadian Division had borne the brunt of the first mass use of gas as a weapon. The Canadians had buckled, but they did not break – even when the French Colonial Division on their left fled. In a little more than seventy-two hours the Canadians suffered over 6,000 casualties, including 2,000 dead: virtually the entire rifle strength of the division.[62]

Edmonds's draft shocked senior Canadian Corps officers. T.V. Anderson summed up the general feeling when he wrote to Fortescue Duguid, the Canadian official historian, in May 1926, 'It is obvious that the actual writer, whoever he may be, starts his work prejudiced against the Canadians and takes every opportunity of belittling them and the work they did.' General Sir Arthur Currie was more direct, not least because Edmonds questioned his integrity as a brigade commander during an unexplained absence from the front at a critical moment. 'His statements, particularly his insinuations,' Currie wrote, 'are ungenerous, unjustifiable and untrue, if not contemptibly base . . . his mind must, to some extent, have been poisoned.'[63] Tim Cook concludes that Edmonds deliberately 'downplayed the role of the Canadians'. In Edmonds's view the Canadians had panicked and fought a confused battle until a British commander arrived to sort them out. In any event, the Canadians were British and Second Ypres was a British battle.

Duguid buried Edmonds in a barrage of material refuting his allegations. The retort landed with a scolding admonition to 'appreciate the importance to Canada of having the account in the British official history, of this battle in particular, meticulously accurate'. Duguid was backed by a letter from the Canadian Chief of Staff, General J.H. MacBrien, to the Chief of the Imperial General Staff, and the threat of an intervention by Lord Byng (formerly General Sir Julian Byng, who commanded the Canadians at Vimy), now serving as Canada's Governor General, directly to the King if the Canadians did not get the corrections they wanted.

What came to be known in Ottawa as the 'Third Battle of Ypres' went on for years. It was widely known in military circles, as was Edmonds's seven greater and more public spat with the Australians over how he treated them. Duguid eventually travelled to London to reconcile his differences with Edmonds, and believed they had worked it out. Edmonds was not so sure, especially after Duguid's entry in the latest *Encyclopaedia Britannica* on Second Ypres lauded the Canadians and neglected the British role. The odour of a cover-up for Currie lingered, and so too did Edmonds's bias against the Canadians.[64] Cook concludes that Edmonds was 'bludgeoned' into changing his account in favour of the Canadians, but he was not happy. Summoned to explain himself before the CIGS, General Sir George Milne, in April 1926, Edmonds warned, 'As the history proceeds, many and very serious difficulties with the Canadians will crop up.' As Cook observes, 'Edmonds believed that the Canadians were still fighting Beaverbrook-like publicity battles.' Edmonds was more candid with the CIGS about the grasping Canadians: 'There was no limit to their lying as the war went on. It is important to make a stand now.'[65] Events in the Second World War suggest that at least some in the British establishment heeded Edmonds's advice.

Rather typically, while the Canadians fought Edmonds over their treatment by the British, they defended the British empire from the Americans. The North American battle over who won the war reached something of a zenith in 1927 when Brigadier Henry Riley began serialising his forthcoming book *America's Part* in *Liberty* magazine. Riley was a graduate of West Point who worked for Robert McCormick's *Chicago Tribune* before the war. Between 1914 and 1917 he served as an ambulance driver and correspondent on the Western Front. When America entered the war Riley joined up and he advanced quickly, commanding the 42nd Rainbow Division by 1918. His articles in *Liberty* were probably published to coincide with the great American pilgrimage to the battlefields of France in 1927 (about which more below).

Riley's January 1927 article 'Who Won the War?' was a full-scale assault on the British contention that their victories in 1918 were decisive. Not only did Americans win the Great War, Riley charged, but in the process they 'had saved the British Empire, whose forces had floundered incompetently for three years'. Echoing popular American sentiment that would resonate for generations to come, Riley charged that the 'Allies did not win the war sooner because the British empire retained an unnecessarily large force in England proper', and squandered its resources fighting for a greater empire in the Middle East. More generally, the British failed to mobilise the manpower of the empire effectively through conscription. The cost of all this British bungling, faulty strategy, incompetence and imperialism was paid in American blood on the Western Front in 1918.[66]

Riley's claims ignited a firestorm in Canada. George Drew, a wounded Great War veteran and successful lawyer, provided what Jonathan Vance describes as a 'meticulous demolition' of Riley's main points in *Maclean's Magazine* on 1 July 1928.[67] In 'The Truth About the War', Drew attacked the 'slanderous statement, often reiterated in the United States publications of a certain type . . . that the British Empire did not bear her full share of the brunt of battle'.[68] Given that Canadians did not yet have a good history covering their own contributions to the war, and that the Canadian media lacked the clout to hold American opinions at bay, there was some urgency in Drew's words. He took exception to Riley's claim that American's soldiers' sense of 'altruism' and 'justice' paved the way for Allied victory. Where were these traits in 1914, Drew asked rhetorically, when other countries rose to stop Germany from imposing 'its brutal will upon the world and civilization'? 'Drew's article touched the wellspring of anti-Americanism that lies in the Canadian psyche,' according to Vance. The edition of *Maclean's Magazine* carrying Drew's article sold out so quickly that an additional 100,000 were printed for veterans' organisations and schools.

If Canadians needed reminding of the power of American popular media they experienced it first hand during their 1928 pilgrimage to the Western Front. At Vimy Ridge, site of their iconic 1917 victory, the French had erected a triumphal arch for the veterans to pass through. It was a kind gesture, meant to be welcoming, but the soldiers depicted on the arch were identifiably US Doughboys.[69]

The idea that the US Army won the war was affirmed by the American Battle Monuments Commission (ABMC) in 1927, when it published *A Guide to the American Battle Fields in Europe*. Production of the volume was overseen by Major Dwight David Eisenhower, an armoured officer who had not made it overseas during the war. The guide definitely reflected Pershing's views.

> Between September 26 and 1 November the French, British and Belgians in the west and north gradually increased the vigor and strength of their attacks and made enormous inroads into hostile positions.
>
> Damaging as were these drives to the German cause, and valuable as they were to the Allied plan for victory, such was the importance to the enemy of retaining intact his defences south of Sedan, in order to protect his lateral railroads, that he brought reserves from almost every sector of the Western Front to throw into the path of the American advance.
>
> When the American Army, in spite of increasing reinforcement and against a well-nigh impregnable defensive system, had driven

forward to a position dominating the German communications near Sedan, the termination of the war in 1918 was assured.[70]

It was a very carefully crafted conclusion. None of it is demonstrably wrong, but the overall impression implies a great deal beyond what America's allies would accept as truth.

The ABMC guide was ready for the 1927 American Pilgrimage to France, dubbed the 'Second AEF'. The return was an enormous success, but it was not without sniping from Europeans. The French were already weary over American plans for grand memorials stretching across the Western Front wherever the US Army fought. At one stage the ABMC proposed a major highway linking all the American battle-fields, with appropriate monuments along the way. The plan was looked upon with horror by the French. The ABMC also tended to run a bit roughshod over French sovereignty. And while the US government demanded that France pay its war debt, the ABMC demanded that France waive the import duties on stone shipped from Italy to build America's monuments. By the late 1920s French opposition to American persistence about war debts and their insistence that they won the war was visceral. 'Three mortal years we waited to hear America say, "France is the frontier of freedom",' Georges Clemenceau opined in 1926. 'Three years of blood as well as money flowing out of our pores. Come see the endless list of dead in our villages . . . Is the life force of lost youth not a bank note?'[71]

It did not help that what the French media saw of the Second AEF was primarily in Paris, where Americans took full advantage of France's abundant wine and spirits. Some Frenchmen were apparently shocked by 'the lack of excessive dignity'. Those who travelled to the Meuse–Argonne region for the more sombre ceremonies came away with a different impression of their American liberators. But both British and French journalists 'generally agreed that "America should be shown that they were not the only ones who won the war!" '[72]

By then Winston Churchill had already challenged the American claims in the final volume of his massive work, *The World Crisis*, published in 1927.[73] Churchill was already an enormously successful politician and accomplished historian. His florid work was serialised and published virtually simultaneously in both Britain and the United States. *The World Crisis* made it clear that the British won the Great War – not alone, by any means, but the final push by the BEF was the killing blow. Britain's contribution to the war by late 1918 consisted of a vast army of 4.5 million engaged on all fronts, the lion's share of Allied naval power, 20,000 merchant ships supplying the Allies and carrying the American Army to Europe, and war production, including a whole programme of medium artillery for the rapidly expanding US Army.[74] He might have added banker for the entente. Less than twenty years later Americans would be making the same claims for their effort in another, greater war. Churchill went on to explain how the BEF broke the back of the German Army in the Hundred Days Campaign. The Americans he lauds for their spirit and sacrifice, but ultimately damns with faint praise. The victory of 1918 belonged to Haig.

Not all British historians agreed with Churchill's assessment, not least because of their dislike of Haig, but their views did nothing to endorse the American claim. The most prolific of contemporary military historians, Basil H. Liddell Hart, supported Pershing's case for the decisive importance of Sedan in his 1928 book *Reputations: Ten Years After*. The rail line between the American front and the Ardennes, Liddell Hart wrote, 'was obviously Germany's most sensitive point'.[75] But the 30 miles to Sedan was beyond the AEF's capabilities, and in any event the British had already broken through the Hindenburg line at Cambrai–Saint-Quentin before the Americans drew German reserves to their front. As for the ABMC guide's claim that the renewed attack on 1 November was what pushed the Germans over the edge, Liddell Hart rejected that emphatically. The 'last offensive, beginning on November 1st', he writes, 'had only supplementary influence . . . the enemy was already suing for peace before Liggett struck'.[76] *The Real War*, which Liddell Hart published two years later, was equally dismissive of Pershing's claims for the decisiveness of the Meuse–Argonne campaign.[77]

Not surprisingly, Liddell Hart's review of Pershing's *Memoirs* in the *New York Times* in April 1931 drew fire from Americans. The most telling letter came from Wendell Westover, late an infantry Captain in the AEF. Westover's main contention was that the BEF was simply not capable of the combat power necessary to achieve what the British claimed for the Hundred Days Campaign. 'With the British Army at lower strength than in previous years,' Westover contends, 'its ranks filled with war-worn veterans and last-resort infants, it is portrayed as suddenly inspired to great offensive deeds, to the accomplishment of objectives sought for three years. Here is rank deception.' More importantly for the debate over the British effort in the Second World War, Westover noted that the British had done most of their fighting with Colonial troops: 'years of giving the Scotch [sic], the Australians, the New Zealanders, or the Canadians the "honor" of all important attacks – and the losses that went with them'.[78] Westover's response well illustrates the enduring belief among many Americans that the British were prepared to fight to the last colonial soldier – or perhaps the last American.

The British were sensitive to the view then and later, that troops from the empire did all the heavy lifting. The pernicious influence of Beaverbrook's press overselling the Canadians unquestionably contributed to this view. Brigadier Maurice Pope recalled that in 1918 the London press praised 'the fighting qualities of Australians, Canadians, Newfoundlanders, New Zealanders, the Scots, indeed everyone except the English. Then an occasional editor allowed himself gently to enquire if it was not a fact that the English, too, were carrying their fair share of the burden.' British officers noticed. When Pope attended the staff course at Camberley, the Commandant, Edmund Ironside, who had been Chief of Staff of 4th Canadian Division in 1917–18, took some 'swipes at Canadians which made the back of my neck glow a bit warm'.[79] The notion that imperial troops had done most of the fighting resonated with the editors of major American newspapers in the Second World War, when the 'pattern' seemed to be emerging again. In this climate, every claim by Canadians to have accomplished great and decisive things simply reinforced American belief that the British themselves were not sharing the burden equitably.

* * *

As the 1920s drew to a close the battlelines in the war of words over how the Great War had been won were well drawn. British writers, especially popular ones like John Buchan but also veterans of the war like Haig's former intelligence officer Sir John Charteris, and analysts like Churchill and Liddell Hart, were content with the view that Britain and her empire had won the war. Canadians differed only in their belief that it was the Canadian Corps, the undefeated shock troops of the empire, which struck the critical blows. For their part, the Americans saw the British, Canadians, Europeans – the whole lot – as bungling incompetents unable to achieve a decisive battlefield victory until the AEF arrived. Pershing and his troops had not needed the years of dawdling and attrition that the French and the British had endured. Once the AEF was big enough, the Americans launched themselves against the enemy and, in the careful language of the 1927 guide, 'the termination of the war in 1918 was assured'.

Wrangling over who won the war, who owed what to whom, and how the blood sacrifice was to be measured against money provided the context for a sharp decline Anglo-American relations by the late 1920s. Europe's economic recovery was precarious, and tension in the international financial community resulting from the war-debt issue remained high. The British and Americans were at loggerheads over naval disarmament and the enduring issue of belligerent rights at sea – what Wilson described as British 'militarism' – versus the American preference for freedom of the seas. This issue had festered since the War of 1812, and most recently in the Great War when the British restricted American trade with Europe again.[80]

The struggle between contending British and American views about how the world ought to be run also continued unabated. If Robert Self is to be believed, the state of Anglo-American relations by the late 1920s 'created the gravest alarm within British foreign policy circles'. Indeed, the challenge from America, as Foreign Office official Robert Craigie put it in 1928, was immense.

> Great Britain is faced in the United States of America with a phenomenon for which there is no parallel in our modern history – a State twenty-five times as large, five times as wealthy, three times as populous, twice as ambitious, almost invulnerable, and at least our equal in prosperity, vital energy, technical equipment and industrial science. This State has risen to its present state of development at a time when Great Britain is still staggering from

the effects of the superhuman effort made during the war, is loaded with a great burden of debt and is crippled by the evil of unemployment.[81]

There was a good reason that John Darwin titled the part of *The Empire Project* covering the 1919 to 1951 era as 'The great liner is sinking'. But, to extend that *Titanic* metaphor, it was not until 1944 – the year of Normandy – that the great ship suddenly settled by the bow, rose vertically, and began her final plunge.

Until then, the band played on.

CHAPTER 3

THE DISSOLUTION OF HOPE

[A]s the halls emptied and the doors closed, the spectre of international anarchy walked, and post-war became pre-war.

Paul Jankowski, *All Against All*[1]

It is customary to start the tumble into the Great Depression, which laid the foundation for the calamitous war which followed, with the Black Friday collapse of the New York stock exchange on 29 October 1929. Modern historians are less sure. The precipitous drop of share prices in late 1929 has recently been seen as a correction in the markets.[2] But with America holding much of the world's gold and a fair portion of its foreign debt, how America responded to the downturn tipped the balance. In the wake of Black Friday the US Congress opted for protectionism. In June 1930 it passed the Hawley–Smoot Tariff bill, raising import duties to their highest levels in US history. The signal sent to the world was unambiguous. One thousand economists petitioned Hoover not to sign the bill into law. 'I almost went down on my knees to beg Herbert Hoover to veto the asinine Hawley–Smoot Tariff,' one senior partner of J.P. Morgan wrote. 'That Act intensified nationalism all over the world.'[3]

The American action sent a ripple through the global economy. When negotiations on Germany's debt and reparations convened again in early 1930 to – in Adam Tooze's words – 'normalize Germany's debts', the new American tariff changed everything. Under the scheme proposed in 1929 by Owen Young, an American industrialist and diplomat, Germany would manage its own debt and make payments through a new 'Bank of International Settlements'. Under the Young Plan, more of the money Germany paid to France and Britain as reparations would simply slide through to the USA.[4] The carrot in all this for Germany was the withdrawal of French troops from the Rhineland. The Young Plan passed through the Reichstag with a resounding majority.

The Germans had hoped for salvation by working with the Americans on economic stability. But with American tariffs now at record levels, Germany turned east, engaging in a series of bilateral trade agreements, including a huge export credit to the Soviet Union and a customs union with Austria. This was 'kept secret until the spring of 1931', Tooze writes; 'it was to be this German initiative that unleashed the first true landslide of the Great Depression'.[5] The revelation of the customs union led to wild speculation in the Austrian stock market, which spilled over into Germany and put enormous downward pressure on the German currency. Gold and foreign currency were soon draining out of Germany.[6] Hoover tried to stop the tumble in 1931 by announcing a freeze on all reparations and war debts, but France vetoed the idea of a freeze on reparations. The whole affair reflected sharply different views between the Anglo-Americans and the French over how the peace of Europe might be maintained. The British and Americans sought that end through financial and fiscal means: the French wanted commitments from the Anglo-Saxons for a continental economic and political system that would bind Europeans together. The continuous tinkering with war debts and reparations, and the constant rejection of France's schemes for some form of international-security arrangement, as well as its claims that Germany was well able to pay what it owed, lay behind the French rejection of Hoover's freeze. The results were soon evident: the German economy collapsed, and the British sterling plunged, which led to a run on British gold as American bankers converted their extensive holdings.[7] The global economy began to tumble like a line of dominoes.

Faced with a surging deficit, and despite assistance from both New York and Paris, the British abandoned the gold standard on

18 September 1931. The impact was catastrophic. The resulting crisis effectively destroyed the last vestiges of parliamentary democracy in Japan, ensuring the ascendancy of the nationalists and military. The results in Germany took a little longer to manifest themselves but were similar. In the United States '522 American banks with deposits of $705 million failed'.[8] Instead of pouring money into the system, as later economic theory dictated, the US Federal Reserve, in the face of appeals by Hoover to the contrary, pulled money back and opted for deflation. The end of sterling convertibility drove the US economy from recession into depression and focused American animus on Perfidious Albion as the progenitor of all their suffering.

Over the next two and a half years, as the depression deepened, the British further aggravated their relationship with the US. To deal with the crisis Ramsay MacDonald, then Prime Minister in a minority Labour government, established an all-party coalition and went to the country in a general election in October 1931 asking for a mandate to tackle Britain's economic woes.[9] The new National Government sought to mitigate the impact of devaluation, and 'guard what remained of their agriculture against impending disaster' by forming a 'sterling bloc' within the empire to control the movement of British currency. These issues were hammered out in Ottawa in February 1932. The Ottawa Agreements created a global trade zone with over 500 million citizens, the largest number of captive consumers of any economic system in the world.[10]

Americans watched the Ottawa Conference with no little concern. They had always seen Canada as a bulwark of the British empire, and a direct challenge to American ambitions for continental domination. But Canada was also a major site of American investment: by 1931 about the same as their investment in all of Europe.[11] The return to the US on Canadian investment in 1931 was larger than all war-debt payments remitted from Europe, and larger than the return from any other single country. But imperial preference now excluded Americans from trading on favourable terms in a large portion of the world outside of Europe. In 1934 the Americans established an ad hoc 'British Empire Committee' in the state department 'to determine the best means of undermining the imperial preference system'.[12]

* * *

In a little more than one twelve-month period, mid-1932 to late 1933, what remained of Wilson's dream for Europe and the world – democracy, disarmament, free trade, international cooperation and a League of Nations with enough will and power to stop aggression – came crashing down. Paul Jankowski encapsulated this momentous shift in his aptly titled book *All Against All*. 'In 1933,' he writes, 'as the delegates left Geneva without a disarmament convention and London without a concerted approach to economic recovery, as the United States and its former allies bickered, as Germany and the Soviet Union rearmed, Japan consolidated one conquest and Italy contemplated another – as the halls emptied and the doors closed, the spectre of international anarchy walked, and post-war became pre-war.'[13]

For the British it was American intransigence over the war debt that was the engine driving the crisis. 'It is largely because of them,' a pamphlet published in 1932 by the *New Statesman and Nation* claimed, 'that the world is threatened in 1932 with a widespread financial collapse which may lead to wholesale repudiation and possibly to war and revolution in Europe.'[14] Some Americans agreed. Frank H. Simonds published his own take on the crisis in 1933, *America Must Cancel*, trying to explain that the war debts were a charade. The American people 'saw the making of the war loans as the conveyance of their own money through some colossal transatlantic pipeline to foreign shores'. In fact, the bulk of that money was 'promptly turned . . . back to the American farmer, factory-worker and miner . . . almost all of it stayed home.' Moreover, the food and material sent to the Europeans were 'not employed to create new wealth, but to win the war, and when the war was won little or nothing was left of them'.[15] What they got in exchange was Allied victory.

The year 1932 had opened with promise, when sixty-one nations gathered at Geneva for a conference on the Reduction and Limitation of Armaments. Herbert Hoover sought to buttress his domestic position in a presidential election year by demonstrating America's 'moral leadership' at Geneva.[16] In June he proposed that the major powers adopt a sharp reduction in armaments across the board. The British were not prepared to go that far and scuppered that idea. However, the part of Hoover's international scheme which the British did support was to mollify the Germans – who were pressing for rearmament – by eliminating their reparations to European countries under the Versailles Treaty. The carrot Hoover offered to the British, French, Belgians and Italians was that their debts to the US would then also be revised or perhaps liquidated. In the grand scheme of things the amounts were not large, roughly 2 per cent of annual Anglo-French budgets and the same for the US.[17] A tentative agreement to eliminate German reparations was reached at Lausanne in July.

For the French, however, the American demand to eliminate German reparations was the last straw in a long and difficult year. France had agreed to German rearmament and, under strong pressure from the United States and Britain, the elimination of the German debt to France.[18] But since reparations had been used, for the most part, to pay off the American debt, many in France expected, on the strength of Hoover's rhetoric, that their war debts would be liquidated, too. But nothing could be done about that in an American election year. Then Hoover lost the presidency in November, and all work in Washington stalled until the new President was sworn in on 4 March 1933. In the meantime, the Geneva Disarmament Conference ended in rancour over war debts and a hasty American retreat into renewed isolationism. When the usual year-end American request for debt payment went out to Europe's capitals it occasioned furious debate in the French Chamber of Deputies and street protests. The Premier, M. Herriot, wanted to pay to keep America on side in the fight for 'liberty against dictatorship'.[19] But he lost the vote, France refused to pay and Herriot's government fell.

The British were no more enamoured of the American demand, although they were able to bend to the Americans without breaking. There was some faint hope that President-elect Franklin Delano Roosevelt would extend Hoover's moratorium on payments, but Roosevelt steadfastly refused to discuss anything until his inauguration. As the *Manchester Guardian* lamented, the debt issue was stuck in America's 'quadrennial frenzy'. Nor was it probable that FDR would do much to adjust – let alone retire – the debts. American populists were, in Jankowski's words, 'fastened like a predator onto the war debts'.[20] The final result was that at the end of 1933, the British and French, 'once pillars of the global financial system and eager members of a democratic alliance with the United States, had suspended payment on billions of dollars of debt they owed to the people of the US'.[21]

The Germans simply stopped paying, too, in 1933. That was no surprise. The National Socialist Workers Party (NSDAP, the Nazi party), led by the beguiling and messianic Adolf Hitler, became the largest party in the Reichstag in the fall elections of 1932. German power brokers installed Hitler as Chancellor in January 1933 amid promises of a new election. It was a miscalculation of cataclysmic proportions. What followed was essentially a coup d'état from within. When President Paul von Hindenburg died in 1934 Hitler appointed himself to the post. Hitler withdrew Germany from the League of Nations and set off on a path of rearmament and genocide.

If all that were not bad enough, events in the Far East revealed the weakness of the League of Nations. On 18 September 1931 a small explosion by a railway in northern China precipitated an invasion of Manchuria by Japan and the establishment of the puppet state of Manchukuo. The League of Nations sent Lord Lytton to investigate. He blamed Japan for a 'false flag' incident, unwarranted aggression and the seizure of territory from another member state. His report was praised for its objectivity. The League voted to censure Japan in February 1933. Japan walked out of the League the next month and continued its war against China. As Jankowski concludes, domestic politics in the west trumped the League's principles every time.[22]

* * *

The economic crisis of the early 1930s radicalised politics across the western world, and America was no exception. At the heart of Roosevelt's revolution lay what he dubbed the 'New Deal', an unprecedented intervention of the federal government into the social and economic life of Americans.[23] The radical nature of the New Deal was matched only by the speed and determination of Roosevelt's action. At his inauguration, FDR reminded Americans, 'The only thing we have to fear is fear itself.' His first act on 5 March 1933, in response to the latest round of bank failures and an eight-day banking holiday announced by Michigan, was to announce a four-day national 'banking holiday'. A week later, in his first 'Fireside Chat' using the new medium of radio, Roosevelt's calming voice explained to the average American how banks worked and why they needed to develop a little faith.[24] The banking crisis ended. Over his first 'Hundred Days' Roosevelt totally redefined the role of the federal government in the affairs of the nation. David Kennedy sums up the change:

> The New Deal had decisively halted the banking panic. It invented wholly new institutions to restructure vast tracks of the nation's economy, from banking to agriculture to industry to labor relations. It authorized the biggest public works program in American history. It had earmarked billions of dollars for federal relief to the unemployed. It had designated the great Tennessee watershed as the site of an unprecedented experiment in comprehensive, planned regional development. No less important, the spirit of the country, so discouraged by four years of economic devastation, had been infused with Roosevelt's own contagious optimism and hope.[25]

Dealing with the implications of Roosevelt's revolution dominated American domestic politics for the next decade. As seemingly benign as the New Deal was and remains to many outside America, Roosevelt's critics saw it as a usurpation of power no less egregious than that of Hitler or Stalin. During his presidency Roosevelt would be vilified in the Republican press as dictator, fascist, Communist, tyrant and much more besides. His four terms as President, which culminated in 1944, changed American politics forever.

During FDR's first two terms America turned inward to resolve its social, economic and political problems. Evidence of that came early. In April 1933, in the face of a run on American gold and pressure for the US to abandon the gold standard – as the British had done – Roosevelt committed the US to participation in a World Economic Conference in London to 'stabilize currencies'. The next month he made an impassioned plea to fifty-four heads of state to participate. When the conference met in July, Roosevelt killed it. On 3 July he sent a telegram saying that the US preferred to seek national solutions to its own currency problems. The best that Kennedy can come up with to explain Roosevelt's sudden change of heart is that he needed inflation, not stability, for the New Deal to work. The Europeans, not least the British with whom Roosevelt had worked to organise the conference, were stunned. Only two men seem to have drawn comfort from the collapse of the World Economic Conference in July 1933: John Maynard Keynes, who believed that Roosevelt's economic policy under the New Deal was right, and Adolf Hitler, 'who drew the lesson that the United States intended to play no consequential international role'.[26] Indeed, as Adam Tooze has argued, America's decision to effectively withdraw from the international community was one of the key causes of the accension to power of Hitler and the Nazis.[27]

To keep his agenda Roosevelt had to focus on domestic politics, play to America's isolationism, and in particular to abandon his Wilsonian urges. In 1934, as mid-term elections loomed, Roosevelt mollified the liberal wing of the Republican Party by signing off on an act proposed by Republican Hiram Johnson 'prohibiting loans to governments that were in default on their existing obligations to the U.S. Treasury'. The target of the Johnson Act was obvious: Britain and France had repudiated their outstanding debts to the US just months before. As Kennedy observed, the Johnson Act 'would in time threaten to stifle Roosevelt's efforts to get American aid into the hands of Hitler's foes'.[28] But its adoption in 1934 helped ease the acceptance of Roosevelt's domestic agenda.

Canada, too, was unable to escape the pressures of political radicalism during the Great Depression, but its response highlights the fundamental differences between the two North American nations. Farmers, labour and the small Progressive Party in the west coalesced around a new social democratic political party, the Co-operative Commonwealth Federation. Democratic socialism was alien to Americans – indeed, what there was of it was effectively destroyed by the radicalism engendered by the Great War – but many in Canada, Britain and Europe embraced it. Alberta, settled primarily by Americans, opted instead for a form of state corporatism advocated by radio evangelist William 'Bible Bill' Aberhart. His 'Social Credit' movement proposed that the government manage the economy by putting money into everyone's hands for basic needs. Social Credit also found favour in Quebec, where it mixed with latent Quebecois nationalism and a powerful devotion to Catholicism and the church to create its own unique right-of-centre movement. Canadian politics never assumed the extremes of Europe or the cooperative character of Great Britain's National Coalition. However, the pressure was strong to create a kinder and gentler country, and for interventionist federal programmes. Throughout the 1930s the role of the Canadian federal government changed, too, especially after Mackenzie King was re-elected as Prime Minister in 1935. In this, as in many other things, 1944 would be a decisive year.

* * *

'Where is the world we fought to establish?' Canon F.G. Scott lamented at the Canadian Corps reunion in Toronto in 1934. 'Where are the workings in civil life of those high principles which drew us, a mighty host, into the furnace of a war to end war? We stand aghast,' Scott concluded, 'at the dissolution of our hopes.'[29] For many in the British empire and Commonwealth, disillusionment morphed into resolve to settle the 'German problem' once and for all. In this, and in their general worldview, the British and Americans were worlds apart in the 1930s.

The British shared, with other Europeans, something of German philosopher Oswald Spengler's belief put forth in *Decline of the West* (published in its definitive edition in 1923) that a 'crisis in civilization' loomed. Richard Overy captured the mood well in the British title of his book on Britain between the wars, *The Morbid Age*.[30] Like Karl Marx, Spengler assumed that societies evolved inexorably through a series of stages from primitive to advanced. But unlike Marx, who foresaw a workers' paradise, Spengler offered nothing but cataclysm. Like many of his day, especially in the defeated countries, Spengler took exception to the triumph of the Anglo-Saxons, their media-dominated democracy and their faith in liberalism. Men 'hope for salvation from somewhere or other,' Spengler wrote, 'for some real thing of honour and chivalry, of inward nobility, of unselfishness and duty.' As Philip Blom concluded, Spengler believed that the 'great system' which had achieved victory in 1918 'was doomed to fail because it would undermine itself'.[31] By 1930 the crisis affecting Europe's stability and its civilisation had become the subject of intense intellectual debate.[32] Aldous Huxley's classic dystopian novel *Brave New World*, published in 1932, emerged from this firmament.[33]

America was largely unaffected by European intellectual movements. Belief in the 'unseen hand' of capitalism, minimalist government, and personal freedom united an otherwise fractious people around the idea of America itself: something akin to a secular religion. The sanctity of America as 'The City on the Hill' kept it free from the evils of European violence and decadence.[34] Events in Europe were reported by the American media, and there was genuine fear that European radicalism would infect the American body politic. Orson Welles's radio play *The War of the Worlds* in October 1938 – which sent many Americans into a panic – well captured the notion that threats to America came from outside. The contrast with contemporary British ideas of threats is telling. H.G. Wells's science-fiction novel about a dystopian future, *The Shape of Things to Come* (released as a feature film, *Things to Come*, in 1936) described the collapse of civilisation into a pointless war that lasts thirty years. The war ends when the 'Aviators' arrive to create a soulless, modern high-tech society, which the people ultimately reject. In Wells's view, it was people themselves who were the authors of the coming apocalypse. America's Martians might well have been Europeans.[35] These radically differing mentalities had a profound impact on Anglo-American discourse over the meaning and purpose of the war that broke out in Europe in 1939.

Few legacies of that great liberal system erected at Versailles epitomised hope for a peaceful world more than the League of Nations, and none proved more disappointing. The weakness of the League was laid bare during a series of crises in the 1930s – Manchuria, Ethiopia, Spain primarily. Only Britain, in control of the sea approaches to the war zones, might have intervened, but no one else in the League was willing to do so. By 1936 Roosevelt was already positioning himself for re-election and neither Congress nor the country would abide siding with the League of Nations.[36] Roosevelt's isolationism reflected the national mood. In 1935 Congress passed no less than five neutrality acts 'that aimed to insulate the United States from the war-storms then brewing across the globe'.[37]

The pace of international chaos quickened in 1936. The Spanish Civil War soon took on the character of a proxy war between contending belief systems. General Franco's Nationalist forces drew strength, and eventually military contingents, from Nazi Germany and fascist Italy, and they overlaid their campaign against the 'Godless Communists' in Madrid with Catholic religious fervour. Communists, leftists, labour activists and anti-fascists supported the Republic. Aircraft and tanks from the Soviet Union, and legions of foreign volunteers, arrived to defend the Spanish Republic. The great disappointment for liberals and socialists in Britain, especially those like George Orwell and thes great pacifist Norman Angell, was that none of the liberal democracies moved to openly support Spain's democratically elected government. At best most participated in the useless international blockade. And while European statesmen dithered and fussed, Roosevelt acceded to Congress's wishes and in 1937 signed a Neutrality Act which re-affirmed in perpetuity the Neutrality Acts of 1935. 'With stout legal thread,' Kennedy writes, 'Congress had spun a straitjacket that rendered the United States effectively powerless in the face of the global conflagration that was about to explode.'[38]

Roosevelt responded to the increasing tensions in the world with his 'Good Neighbour Policy', targeted primarily at Latin America, where America ran its own quasi-empire. Roosevelt's policy seemed, in the words of Kennedy, to represent 'a systematic retreat from the world'. That suited Hitler just fine. He viewed Americans as a 'mongrel race . . . doomed to the trash heap of history', and on the eve of the Second World War he was simply not worried about American military power. As Kennedy concludes, 'that conclusion was for the time being not without foundation in fact'.[39]

With Europe descending into chaos the British could not be so cavalier. The Ethiopian crisis highlighted the direct challenge which fascist Italy presented to critical British communications through Suez and the Red Sea. Not only did Italy sit astride the Mediterranean route to India, but Italy's possessions on the Horn of Africa – especially in Eritrea – were a direct threat to the Red Sea and the Bab-al-Mandab Strait. Unrest in Egypt, notionally independent as of 1936, also threatened the route to India and Britain's eastern empire.

Historians generally focus on Britain's weakness in the face of these enormous threats and set the out stark options for British statesmen by the late 1930s: appeasement or rearmament. In the event, Britain chose both, but not from a position of abject weakness. By 1939 Great Britain was still the single most powerful and most industrialised country on the earth, and the second wealthiest behind the USA.[40] British politicians and military staffs felt that, with France as an ally, the British empire possessed unique strengths that made her position virtually unassailable – a view apparently shared by Hitler.[41] That said, few British politicians were prepared to squander Britain's strength by acting unilaterally.

As war clouds gathered, positions hardened, and British rearmament accelerated, but there were limits to how far Britain could go. Foreign trade and exports were crucial to keeping the country – and the empire – solvent. Shifting from automobiles and radio sets to Spitfires and tanks was not a simple choice. Gold reserves to sustain a long war were critically low: Britain's pockets in 1939 were not as deep as they had been in 1914. For its part, France, too, was unprepared for war in 1938: appeasement seemed the best option.

Nevertheless, Britain expected more from the Commonwealth than it got. It helped Mackenzie King's struggle for independence from London that Roosevelt had provided Canada with reassurance about its security. How tightly the Canadians would accept the American embrace remained to be seen. Certainly they were reticent to get involved in America's own fledgling empire, the Organization of American States.[42] The fear that the British Dominions would be swept up in an emerging American global empire lay behind much British anxiety by 1942, not least because it was openly discussed in the American press. In the meantime, Roosevelt accepted that Canada was part of the British empire. And as he told Canadians during a speech at Queen's University in Kingston, Ontario, in August 1938, 'I give you assurance that the people of the United States will not stand idly by if domination of Canadian soil is threatened by any other empire.'[43]

* * *

Although informal ties between Roosevelt's administration and the British warmed during the late 1930s, the popular American perception of the British as untrustworthy manipulators hardened. By the 1930s 'America knew,' according to Nicholas Cull, 'that, throughout the [First World] war, the British had shamelessly manipulated war news, had peddled pictures of bloated Prussian beasts, had invented tales of "Huns" atrocities, and had faked evidence to fit.'[44] This idea had, in fact, been a continuous thread in American literature about the war. In 1928 historian Sydney Fay finally published all his ideas on the origins of the war in a two-volume work, *The Origins of the World War*. It was a commercial and a critical success, was translated into French, German and Russian, and earned Fay faculty positions at both Yale and Harvard. It was Fay, perhaps more than any other major historian, who convinced Americans that the Great War was a general European calamity, that Germany was no more responsible for starting it than any other country, and that it was never a war between good and evil as British propagandists had claimed.

By then Harry Elmer Barnes, taking a lead from Fay's earlier work, had put his finger on the nub of the problem with his 1926 book, *The Genesis of the War*: the subtle shaping of American public opinion about Germany by British press services. American newspapers relied heavily on copy from Britain's Northcliffe chain. The First Baron Northcliffe, Alfred Harmsworth, was the father of British popular journalism, the owner of the *Daily Mail* and the *Daily Mirror*. Beaverbrook, whose career closely resembled Northcliffe's, described him in 1928 as 'the greatest figure who ever strode Fleet Street'.[45] He was also stridently anti-German, and took on the role of Britain's chief propagandist in 1917–18.[46] As Barnes explained, 'most American news concerning Germany came through the notoriously anti-German English papers controlled by Harmsworth [Northcliffe]'.[47]

The idea of British manipulation of American support for the Great War gained credibility throughout the 1930s. C. Harley Grattan's book *Why We Fought*, published in 1929, was largely dismissed as a polemical attack on the Allied role – primarily British – in luring America into the war. But Grattan identified two critical claims about the role of the British in luring America into the war. The first was that British propaganda was very good, and it appealed in particular to the American 'elite' who shared many of the same values. The second was that no matter how good British propaganda was, it got no purchase at all in the mid-west.[48]

Grattan also strengthened Barnes's point about British manipulation of the American media. In fact, one of Britain's first steps when the war began was to sever all of Germany's overseas cables, preventing any alternate views of the war emerging. 'Control of the cables,' Grattan wrote, 'is now recognized to be the most important cause of the astounding success the British had in manipulating the American mind, quite apart from the favourable disposition of the American people.'[49] And if all that was not enough, American papers frequently employed British journalists to write copy on the war and serve as correspondents. Grattan cited the example of the *New York Times*, which, despite its claim to impartiality, relied almost entirely on material from the Northcliffe chain. Even the *Chicago Tribune*, run by Robert McCormick, drew on material from Northcliffe's correspondents.[50]

Although Grattan's work was a commercial and critical failure, his ideas and those of the propaganda critics of the 1920s were captured for the popular American readership in Walter Millis's 1934 book, *Road to War: America 1914–1917*. Millis was an editorial writer for the *New York Herald Tribune* with a gifted pen. Writing about Millis's influence on American attitudes towards British propaganda in the Second World War, Robert Calder described *Road to War* – which became a Book of the Month Club selection – as having 'considerable influence on public opinion'.[51]

Works which questioned the legitimacy and morality of America's Great War, and the nation's vulnerability to foreign manipulation, contributed to 'a surge of Anglophobia and paranoia' that fed American isolationist sentiment in the mid-1930s.[52] So, too, did scholarly confirmation of the worst American fears. If anyone doubted the critical and pernicious role of British propagandists in drawing America into war in 1917, Professor James Duane Squires's *British Propaganda at Home and in the United States from 1914 to 1917* laid that to rest. Publication with Harvard University Press in 1935 gave the book enormous credibility. It was Squires, taking the lead from Grattan, who demonstrated the depth of British penetration of American newspapers before and during the Great War. Squires damned the British effort with evidence from Sir Gilbert Parker, the Canadian who ran the British propaganda machine in the United States. Writing about the success of British efforts, Parker had observed, 'Among other things we supplied three hundred and sixty newspapers in smaller states of the United States with an English newspaper which gives weekly reviews and comments on the affairs of the war. We established connections with the man on the street through cinema pictures of army and navy, and by letters in reply to individual American critics, which were printed in the chief newspaper in the State in which they lived, and were copied in newspapers in other and neighbouring states.'[53] Britain ended the Great War, Squires concludes, 'with the best developed and probably the most effective organization dedicated to propaganda of any of the belligerent nations'.[54]

Two books in 1938–9 solidified the American view of the British as gifted and dangerous manipulators. H.C. Peterson's *Propaganda for War: The Campaign Against American Neutrality 1914–1917*, published in 1939, came to a much sharper conclusion than Squires. The British had crafted a 'blind hatred of everything German' in the minds of Americans. 'After this hatred had distorted American neutrality,' Peterson wrote, 'it created a willingness to sacrifice American youth in an attempt to punish the hated nation.'[55]

The other major book which solidly confirmed British perfidy – and warned that they would try again to manipulate American public opinion – was British. In 1938, as part of Liddell Hart's monograph series *The Next War*, Sidney Rogerson published *Propaganda and the Next War*. Rogerson stated emphatically that the main target of propaganda in a future war would be the United States. At a minimum Britain needed to keep the US 'benevolently neutral'. At best, the British needed to 'define a threat to America, a threat, moreover, which will have to be brought home by propaganda to every citizen, before the republic will again take arms in an external struggle'.[56] Setting the British plan so directly into words gave both American isolationists and the Nazi propagandists a coup of exceptional value.

'The cumulative effect of Squires, Peterson, Rogerson and others,' Calder concludes, 'was to instil in many Americans a supersensitivity to British propaganda which verged on paranoia.'[57] One writer in the *American Mercury* warned in 1937 that it was possible to gauge the tenor of British fortunes by looking at the passenger lists of ships arriving in New York. Events soon proved him right. Within a month of the outbreak of war in 1939 Duff Cooper, a Conservative critic of

Appeasement who had reassigned his position as First Lord of the Admiralty over the Munich Crisis of 1938 (see below) and by 1939 one of Britain's staunchest anti-German politicians, and a gaggle of writers and literary critics arrived for a speaking tour.[58] The next day a New York paper ran the headline, 'The British Are Here to Get Us In'.[59] The headline was right, but the battle had only just begun and the British had no option but to try.

America's lingering mistrust of the British, fostered in its founding myths and propagated in schools across the land, had been confirmed by recent experience. Britain was the most powerful country on earth, controlling vast swaths of the globe, and possessed of enormous wealth. And yet it had, through its own self-interest, apparently turned the financial crisis of 1930 into the catastrophic Great Depression and then walked away from its debts to Americans. If that were not enough, the British had deliberately lied to and manipulated the American people to draw them into the Great War, and then had the audacity to trivialise America's decisive victory in the fall of 1918 and claim that victory for themselves.

For many Americans this lingering and very deep anti-British sentiment took precedence over any fear of fascism. In 1917 Americans had embraced war with Germany with unbridled enthusiasm, and staunchly defended Britain as an ally in a worthwhile cause. In the decades since the Armistice much had changed. The radicalisation of American nativism engendered by the Great War continued to be fuelled by an almost pathological xenophobia, racism, anti-Semitism and fear of Communism. For many on the American right – enough to impact domestic politics – the feeling that they had been duped by the British into fighting the Great War paired naturally with strong sympathy for what the Nazis and other fascists were doing to 'cleanse' their societies and root out the Communists – and the Jews. Fascist movements in America, supported by Nazi Germany, were so pervasive by the late 1930s that a special 'House Committee on Un-American Activities', chaired by Congressman Martin Dies, was struck to investigate foreign influence in American politics. Dies found plenty of fascist activity, but no one was really interested in that. His committee was soon consumed with rooting out Communists and their Jewish fellow travellers.[60]

Strong support for what Hitler and the Nazis were trying to do in Europe meant that much of Britain's rhetoric about the fundamental evilness of Nazi Germany, and the righteousness of the war, simply failed to resonate in America. As will be explained, even on the eve of Operation Overlord the majority of Americans were unclear about the purpose of the war in Europe.

For many Americans, bred on anti-British sentiment and America's founding myths, British claims to stand for the liberal democratic values shared by the two great Anglo-American powers were a chimera. Only America could lay legitimate claim to speaking for the oppressed and downtrodden of the world. Its history, after all, was evidence of America's ability to throw off the burden of imperialism and to prosper as a result. Canada, as an alternative model for evolution towards independence within the British imperial system, never entered the calculus.

After March 1939, when Hitler occupied what remained of Czechoslovakia, the British understood their fate: Germany would have to be fought again. Their resolve arose not out of fear or resignation, but recognition of what the Third Reich was. 'A great deal of the public understood long before the final crisis of 1939 what the new German leader stood for,' Richard Overy concludes, 'and did not approve it.' Wyndham Lewis, in his 1939 book, *The Hitler Cult*, described being neutral in the face of Nazism as 'anti-British'.[61] So while America wrapped itself up in splendid isolation, the British prepared to fight. Their hope for success lay in the depth and staying power of their empire, and in the manifest strength of France's army.

CHAPTER 4

DIFFERENT TRAJECTORIES

He expected his country to go to war in a panic, in pitiful weakness. But now, splendidly, everything had become clear. The enemy at last was in plain view, huge and hateful, all disguise cast off. It was the Modern Age in arms.

Evelyn Waugh, *Men at Arms*[1]

When Americans thought of their country prior to the Second World War they thought of the 'Lower Forty-Eight'. Continental America was effectively an island, shielded from the world by vast oceans and weak neighbours. For most Americans what lay beyond was foreign. This was partly because of a conscious and successful effort to disguise the empire with words: America did not have colonies, it had 'territories' – where 19 million people, overwhelmingly Asians, lived under the American flag by 1939.[2] As a wartime report later observed, 'Americans are sometimes amazed to hear that we, too, have an "empire." '[3]

America's empire played an important role in shaping Roosevelt's defence policy in the 1930s. Like Britain's, America's empire was oceanic. At its greatest extent it stretched 7,000 miles across the vastness of the Pacific to the Philippines. Colonial possessions dotted the way across: Hawaii, Wake, Guam. The Alaska territory, too, could only be reached – and defended – by sea. A formal and informal empire existed in the Caribbean: Cuba, Puerto Rico, Guantanamo Bay, the Panama Canal zone, and many countries of central and Latin America.

And so Roosevelt focused his defence spending on the US Navy. Initially that was part of his economic recovery plan. America had never built up to its treaty limits, while a major naval expansion promised lots of jobs in desperate times. Working with Democrat Congressmen Carl Vinson and Park Trammell in March 1934, Roosevelt announced the construction of six new battleships, with 85 per cent of the work going to civilian yards.[4] It was not enough to guarantee the security of America's empire, but as George Baer observed that was not the objective. In 1934 Roosevelt wanted to avoid war, not prepare for one.

That changed when Japan walked out of the London Naval Conference in 1936 and began open warfare in China in 1937. Japan held a League of Nations mandate over the Marshall and Caroline Islands, two vast archipelagos that straddled the US route to the Philippines. Defence of the empire now meant that the US would have to fight. This much was clear to Roosevelt, but in his famous 'Quarantine Speech' delivered in Chicago he urged Americans to think about the global threat. The speech failed to move the isolationists, but the Second Vinson–Trammell Act of 1938 funded expansion of the US Navy (USN) beyond treaty limits, including the construction of three Iowa-class battleships, a number of 40,000-ton aircraft carriers, a score of cruisers and many smaller craft.[5] The concurrent establishment of the US Maritime Commission and a scheme to build modern, high-speed tankers and freighters, ostensibly for civilian use, provided the USN with auxiliary vessels when needed.[6] It was all good business and policy. Even more was to follow in 1940.

In the meantime, the US Army languished as little more than a colonial police force.[7] Ed Coffman's seminal book *The Regulars* captures that notion wonderfully. The army had an authorised strength of nearly 300,000 throughout most of the interwar period, but it usually numbered half that. Understrength units were scattered across a vast country in legacy nineteenth-century garrisons and coastal defences, and in garrisons throughout the empire. During the 1930s, the US Army lived a penurious existence at a languid pace. The upside, according to Coffman, was that the army got to spend time in places that 'were virtually inaccessible to most Americans: thus the military people . . . enjoyed a rare and exotic experience'.[8]

In the circumstances it was impossible to create a modern army. The US Army was unable to concentrate enough to work out the problems of modern war, let alone to field a major expeditionary force. The lessons of the Great War were distilled well enough in the *Field Service Regulations* of 1923: these affirmed the primacy of infantry supported by artillery. This concept dominated interwar thinking. In 1937 the Chief of the Army Staff, Malin Craig, finally concluded that tanks were also needed to support the infantry. But the Cavalry Corps fought a successful rearguard action against mechanisation. Mechanisation might work in Europe, the cavalry claimed, where there were lots of roads, but horses remained critical in more rugged terrain. By 1939 most of America's cavalry was still horsed.[9]

The artillery fared little better. By the late 1930s the primary field piece was still the French 75mm from the Great War mounted on wooden wheels. The shift to 105mm as the primary howitzer in infantry divisions, and later the 155mm gun, was agonisingly slow, and nowhere near complete by 1939. As a consequence, most of the army's artillery remained horse-drawn because wooden wheels were not suitable for high-speed travel. In any event, the Chief of Field Artillery liked horses, too. He told the Army War College in 1939 that 'the horse still remains superior as the prime mover off roads, through mud, the darkness and the rain . . . To discard him during peace in favor of the motor, 100 percent, is simply putting all our eggs in one basket and is, in my judgement, an unsound policy.'[10]

A half-hearted attempt was made to update the army's doctrine with *FSR 1939*, but according to William Odom the result was 'an archaic concept of combined arms' prepared by one staff officer. Douglas MacArthur, as Chief of the General Staff from 1930 to 1935, had elected to maintain the larger skeletal structure of the army's establishment – with all its corps, formations and units – rather than cutting his coat to suit his cloth. The result, Odom concludes, was that 'without money, men, or materiel, the army was hard pressed to conduct any maneuvers, let alone dedicate a portion of its thinly spread forces to experimentation'.

What saved the US Army during these dismal years, according to General J. Lawton Collins, Jr., who served with distinction in the

Second World War, was its schools: infantry at Fort Benning, artillery at Fort Sill, cavalry at Fort Knox, and the Army Command and General Staff School at Fort Leavenworth.[11] It was there that the hard thinking and planning for modern war was done, not least the problems of integrating tanks, scientific gunnery and airpower into the modern battlefield. But American refusal to countenance any return to a major continental war in Europe undermined efforts to put new ideas into practice. Modernisation of the army was primarily an intellectual problem for officers, not an issue for Congress or the President.

It did not help that the army was itself sundered by civil war, with Army Ground Forces pitted against the brash ideologues of the Army Air Corps (USAAC). Inspired by its firebrand prophet, Billy Mitchell, the USAAC was wedded to the idea of strategic bombing. Long-range four-engine bombers were sold to Congress as a form of coastal defence, but the real intent was to create a force that could act independently of armies and achieve a decisive victory through airpower alone.[12] In the circumstances, providing support for the army was never a priority. The development of heavy artillery in 1920s in particular was checked by the air-force claim that it could do the work of interdiction behind the enemy frontlines better than long-range guns.[13] Heavy reliance on airpower in lieu of artillery would eventually affect the conduct of operations in the Second World War, including the Normandy campaign.

The fundamentals of Roosevelt's defence and foreign policies remained largely unaltered throughout the 1930s. The American people, the Senate, the House and many of the key senior members of the administration in Washington were isolationist at best, or anti-British at worst. 'In 1940,' the well-known American broadcaster Raymond Swing wrote, 'Americans were still so isolated as to think tolerantly or even approvingly of National Socialism in Germany and fascism in Italy.'[14] A few bumps and bruises on malcontents, Communists and Jews seemed unavoidable. In any event, for many Americans the New Deal was a much greater threat to the American way of life than Europe's fascists. Harold Ickes claimed that the State Department was 'shot through with fascism'.[15] The Trade Department was, and would remain, pathologically anti-British. For the Trade Department, the Second World War would be fought primarily against the British empire.

Even Roosevelt's senior army staff was anti-British. 'In the Army, there was a tendency among officers of both ground and air forces to admire Germany for her achievements in building up these arms,' Robert Sherwood wrote. 'This led in some extreme cases to the hope that Germany would conquer England . . . thereby providing historic demonstration of the superiority of land- and airpower over seapower.'[16] This was certainly true of the US Army's planning and intelligence staff, which had strong ties with the German Army. Among them was General Stanley Embrick, former Deputy Chief of the Army Staff, and a close friend of George Marshall. When Marshall became Chief of Staff on 1 September 1939, he made Embrick his 'Senior Military Advisor'. It was a decision, Lynne Olson concludes, 'that would have profound consequences for American military policy, especially with regard to Britain, throughout the war'.[17] Marshall's senior advisor on Germany, Colonel Truman Smith, was perhaps an even greater problem. An active isolationist, Smith was a personal friend of the German Army Attaché, General Frederick von Boetticher, and had been since Smith's first posting to Germany in the 1920s. Smith's 'bitter opposition to Roosevelt and his friendship and admiration for Germany', Boetticher confessed after the war, 'were well known'. This friendship allowed Boetticher to wander unimpeded into the US Army's intelligence offices. When Roosevelt tried to court-marshal Smith, Marshall refused to cooperate, suggesting that doing so would simply make him a martyr. Smith was ordered to disappear for a few weeks, lodging with Albert Wedemeyer, who had just returned from the German Army staff college and shared Smith's views.[18]

By the late 1930s only the USN had a clear idea of its role in American strategic planning, and the money to support it. The Royal Navy remained its only global challenger, but the recent experience of serving alongside the British in European waters in the Great War had generally been positive. The Canadian-born commander of American naval forces in European waters, Admiral William R. Sims, may have played a role in this rapprochement.[19] In any event, the Anglo-Americans had reconciled many of their naval differences through a series of disarmament conferences, and shared strategic concerns over the threat of fascist and Japanese seapower.

Worrying about the US Army was well down Roosevelt's list by the late 1930s as he fought to impose his New Deal on America. That task seemed to become easier after his landslide win in the 1936 presidential election, when he won the highest percentage of popular votes and the highest number of electoral college votes since 1820. In any other country this would have been a writ to do whatever he wanted at home or abroad. But the US Supreme Court had overruled several of his key New Deal programs and promised to further obstruct his legislative agenda. In early 1937 Roosevelt proposed a ham-fisted plan to appoint new justices to replace everyone on the court over seventy years old – six would be needed. That scheme blew up in his face, and tarred him for many as a ruthless politician who would abuse America's sacred institutions for his own political purposes. Then he had the 'Roosevelt Recession' of 1938–9 to tackle.

Roosevelt's distraction by domestic issues forestalled any American effort to restrain Hitler. When the British pressed for help in 1939, FDR told his emissary in Brussels to tell the British 'that there is such a thing as public opinion in the United States'. In the midst of the recession he could not afford 'to be made, in popular opinion at home, the tail of the British kite'.[20] This proved to be true for the whole course of the Second World War.

* * *

The public nature of American political discourse confounded many senior British officials in 1939, and throughout the war. The President was the head of the state and the head of government. It was, and remains, a post to which the powerful and successful can aspire, including well-known generals. The President appoints whomever he wants as his 'Secretaries' (Cabinet ministers). They report to him, but also to Congress and the Senate through committees which meet sometimes in private, often in public session. The relentless electoral cycle makes virtually every issue political. Then as now, American elections run on two-year cycles in even-numbered years: the whole Congress and one-third of the Senate every two years, and the President every four years. The result is an endless election campaign.

The British parliamentary system was perhaps just as perplexing to Americans. The Mackenzie King, of course, was the head of state, but his powers were nominal. Parliament, where the people were represented, served at the Mackenzie King's 'pleasure', but following the 1911 Parliament Act, Parliament sat for a maximum of five years before a general election was required. The political party with the majority of seats in Parliament formed 'the government'. Elected Members of Parliament held ministerial posts under the *Prime* Minister. The upper house, the House of Lords, represented the landed gentry, hereditary nobility and the church, as well as appointed distinguished citizens – especially the new monied class. It serves to keep a check on the Commons. All the important work – including legislation, budgets and policy – was done by the Cabinet, which is answerable to Parliament.

Historians of the Second World War seldom reflect on what these political systems – especially the American one – meant to the conduct of the war. Churchill's 'right' to govern derived from the continued support of Parliament, to whom he was obliged to explain his government's actions. The National Government coalition established by Ramsay MacDonald to tackle the Depression in 1931 was replaced by a Conservative-led coalition following the 1935 general election, which wrestled with the rapidly developing crisis in Europe. When the crisis finally broke in 1939 the coalition agreed to continue, and so Britain did not have another general election until 1945. This quirk of the parliamentary system was used by American critics during the Second World War as evidence of the inherently undemocratic nature of the British empire.

In the American system, continuous engagement with the electorate through the press meant that the media was a critical part of the electoral process. A free press and cheap postage – as well as literacy – were the handmaidens of American democracy.[21] The American masses, Paul Starr asserts, therefore had a practical and cultural predisposition for 'information' from the outset. Until the advent of AM and shortwave radio in the 1920s, newspapers provided that information. By the end of the nineteenth century major newspapers coalesced into conglomerates controlled by powerful owners – like William Randolph Hearst and Robert McCormick and his cousins – with powerful partisan agendas. Most of what newspapers carried was domestic news, and infotainment – sports, articles on celebrities, local gossip, fashion,

3. Government, Roosevelt style: FDR addresses the nation by radio from Hyde Park on the eve of the 1938 mid-term elections.

comics – sprinkled with strong editorials and syndicated columnists. Only the *New York Times*, with a large staff assigned to cover the world, claimed to be a 'national' newspaper – although its circulation was limited to the north-east.[22]

Roosevelt was not the first President to actively engage the media as part of his governance, but he was, according to one correspondent, 'The best newspaperman who has ever been President of the United States'.[23] In the process, 'he became this century's prime manipulator of the new and increasingly powerful modern media'. From the outset Roosevelt promised reporters two news conferences a week. According to David Halberstam, 'he held to that', conducting almost 1,000 news conferences in his first three terms. Roosevelt changed the way America's news was reported. Before FDR, Halberstam claims, 'Washington was filled with journalists who covered regional stories for their regional papers'. After Roosevelt it was filled with 'highly trained specialists who wrote of national implications for the entire country'. It was not simply the frequency of the news conferences that mattered: Roosevelt orchestrated them, manipulated his small coterie of selected newsmen, took them into his confidence and told them how to shape the news. He became casually familiar with the small group that travelled with him, dining, drinking and playing poker. 'Roosevelt's hold on his press corps was very powerful,' Halberstam claims: a misstep could leave a reporter on the outside. Roosevelt knew that they all worked to deadlines, so he fed them just enough to make headlines the next day but not enough time to do the background work to provide deeper context – or criticism. When he thought the reporters were getting the story wrong he told them so, suggesting how they might shape the headlines the next day.

Roosevelt was also the first President to use the radio extensively – and very effectively. Herbert Hoover and his ilk had looked on radio 'with contempt . . . beneath their dignity', Halberstam claims, and his rare radio broadcasts were, 'awkward, stilted, pedantic, words written and spoken in governmentese'. Roosevelt fully embraced the new medium. He worked on his radio speeches until they were polished, casual and memorised, and he understood intuitively the importance of timing and cadence. Then, in his soothing New England Brahmin accent, he entered the kitchens and parlours of America and spoke to the people with a voice that was 'strong, confident and totally at ease . . . a consummately professional performance'. Many, indeed perhaps most, of the editorial opinion in America's papers was often against him, but FDR never lost track of his base. The power of his message was clearly manifest in his landslide victory in the 1936 presidential election. The advent of the American Institute for Public Opinion, established by George Gallup in 1935, and the publication of bi-weekly public-opinion surveys – the Gallup Polls – lent powerful weight to Roosevelt's predilection to play to the crowd.

Radio also profoundly changed the way America heard about the wider world. Throughout the nineteenth and early twentieth centuries foreign news crept into America through the new technology of wire services. The global system of submarine cables laid before the Great War was 80 per cent British owned, and all connections between Europe and the rest of the world – including America – went through the

British Isles. The British built the system largely to control their empire, but it also allowed them to control news.[24] It was this monopoly which British propagandists exploited so effectively in the Great War. The advent of wireless, especially the explosion of global shortwave radio after 1919, broke the British monopoly on international news and fundamentally altered the information landscape in which the Second World War was fought.

The British and Americans also had starkly different approaches to the new medium of AM radio. The British (and indeed European) approach was close regulation, and the establishment of what Starr calls a 'unified private broadcasting organization', the British Broadcasting Corporation (BBC) in 1922. This mirrored the previous European approach to print media.[25] The purpose of British radio was to inform and educate. In contrast, American radio was unregulated: stations and abuse of frequencies abounded. What Americans received on the AM band was mostly local news and music. The British found it, in Starr's words, 'chaotic and vulgar'. The Radio Act of 1927 empowered the Federal Radio Commission to control frequencies and broadcast strengths, but the US remained wedded to commercial radio.

The economics of radio and the need to sell advertising led to the development of radio networks on a national scale. Networks, Starr writes, soon had 'an unbreakable hold on broadcasting'.[26] The National Broadcasting Corporation (NBC) was the first in 1925, a conglomeration of radio equipment producers and the telegraph giant AT&T. The rival Columbia Broadcasting System (CBS) was established two years later. The upstart CBS proved to be more entrepreneurial and soon gained a hefty market share of American stations, advertising and broadcasting. By the late 1930s American had several highly successful national radio networks, but CBS remained the largest and most influential throughout the Second World War.

The power and reach of the new medium of radio transcended international boundaries and opened countries to unregulated influence through the ether. Foreign governments could now talk directly to people around the world. Weimar Germany began shortwave broadcasts to the US in 1929. Not surprisingly, one of Hitler's first acts in early 1933 was to commence regular shortwave service to America precisely because America's entry into the Great War was seen to have been decisive.[27] Within a year the shortwave service at Zeesen, outside Berlin, was broadcasting nineteen hours of English-language programming a day to the United States. It was a judicious blend of German music and propaganda, including Hitler's major speeches, nicely balanced to entice those drawn to the music to stay tuned for the message. In 1937 – two years ahead of the BBC – the Germans began multilingual programming globally. The news delivered was just accurate enough to be technically right, but always contained a strong critique of anything British. 'German Study Circles' and group listening were fostered, and individual requests for music, birthday wishes and the like were encouraged – which allowed local security officials to develop lists of known Nazi sympathisers.[28]

The long-established wire services and newspapers fought back, attempting to starve radio of news,[29] but improvements in broadcasting allowed radio to generate its own news, especially international news through direct reporting on shortwave. This was well demonstrated by the Moose River mine disaster in Nova Scotia in 1936. A collapse in a gold mine trapped three miners on 12 April. The rescue attempt was still going on when a radio engineer from the Canadian Broadcasting Corporation (CBC), J. Frank Willis, arrived with a transmitter. For the next two and a half days Willis broadcast two-minute updates every hour on the progress of the rescue. His reports reached over 100 million people worldwide, through the CBC, the BBC and 650 stations across the United States. The Moose River mine disaster began the modern practice of live, on-the-spot minute-by-minute coverage of events.[30] Global news radio was born. By the late 1930s when Americans wanted the latest news they turned on the radio.[31]

It is difficult to overstate the importance of developments in communications technology between 1919 and 1939 to media coverage of the Second World War, and the Normandy campaign in particular. As early as 1922, in his seminal work *Public Opinion*, Walter Lippmann astutely prophesised that 'A revolution is taking place'. The impact of state intervention in news during the Great War, Lippmann claimed, was 'infinitely more significant than any shifting of economic power . . . None of us begins to understand the consequences, but it is no daring prophesy to say that the knowledge of how to create it [public opinion] will alter every political calculation and modify every political premise.'[32] In modern society, Lippmann warned prophetically, it will be possible to 'manufacture consent'.

The expansion of public radio during the interwar years accelerated and enhanced the trends Lippmann identified. But the power to manufacture consent increased enormously with the advent of the Gallup Poll. Gallop confidently predicted, against the general consensus and other 'polls', that Roosevelt would win a second term as President. American politics would never be the same. The British Institute of Public Opinion (BIPO) was established two years later. Typically, the British tended to focus on polling for social-engineering purposes. But by the start of the Second World War no American politician could afford to neglect the results of the Gallup Poll, as Roosevelt warned the British during the Munich Crisis of 1938. The manufacturers of consent now had a way to measure their success. They did so during the Second World War, and – as outlined below – they established agencies to shape not only the news in support of the war effort but also ways of thinking about events as they unfolded.

And so as the British struggled to influence American politics and public sentiment at the start of the Second World War, they confronted a revolution in telecommunications, a target audience they poorly understood and one that was already hostile to British 'information'. In retrospect, it was naive in the extreme to imagine that British agencies could shift American public opinion in 1939–41 to support participation in the war in Europe. Even more fantastic was the notion after 1941 that Americans could be persuaded that the British empire was a good thing and that it was worth supporting.

* * *

By the late 1930s, as America wrestled with its ongoing economic woes and confirmed through its Neutrality Acts its intent to remain isolated from the growing global unrest, Britain faced the chilling prospect of another continental war. Until the mid-1930s, any thought of sending a British expeditionary force to the continent was little more than an intellectual exercise. Britain's Ten-Year Rule, in force until 1932, mandated that there would be no continental commitment for the next decade: a 'rule' that renewed itself every day. In this climate the Royal

Navy and the Royal Air Force, the most technical and – given that Britain is an island – the most critical of the services, took precedence. Much of Britain's army was in overseas garrisons throughout the empire. By the late 1920s it was estimated that the UK could raise one cavalry and four infantry divisions in a pinch, but they would be undermanned and poorly supported.[33]

The British Army was sharply criticised at the time for failing to 'think' about the problems of continental war, and subsequent historians have echoed the charge.[34] But the British were not without ideas. The BEF had fought well in 1918. It had beaten the German Army through superior artillery and constant adaptation of its fire and movement tactics. Tanks had helped, but in the final Hundred Days Campaign the lumbering rhomboids of the Royal Tank Corps had been too slow, too few in number and too prone to breakdown to have much impact.[35] Tank enthusiasts like Major-General J.F.C. Fuller nonetheless argued for a mass of tanks turned loose on the battlefield. By late 1918 this was conceivable: the British had some 4,500 Mk VIII tanks on order for delivery in 1919. Fuller wanted them to attack the enemy in depth and sow paralysis. His scheme, dubbed 'Plan 1919', he described as a 'psycho-tactical plan' – a 'shot to the brain'.[36]

Plan 1919 never came off, but the British were aware of the need to increase the tempo of battle and to find the means of turning a tactical breach into an operational or – better yet – strategic result. In February 1926 the British Army established the 'Experimental Mechanized Force' (soon renamed the Armoured Force) to conduct trials in the use of tanks. The exercises that followed in the summers of 1927 and 1928 were suggestive. Budget restraints in the autumn of 1928 led to the disbanding of the armoured force.[37] A review of the lessons of the Great War under Lieutenant-General W.M. St G. Kirke, which reported at the end of 1932, concluded tanks were clearly essential. But for the moment, cavalry was all the army had available to turn a tactical victory into an operational one, and the cavalry refused to mechanise. The Kirke Committee report was quietly shelved. Instead, as David French concludes, 'In the late 1920s and in the 1930s the British developed a doctrine not of ruthless exploitation, but of rapid consolidation.'[38] The Great Depression acted as a brake on innovation and mechanisation.

The British were committed, nonetheless, David Edgerton asserts, to a future 'war of machines', of tanks, aircraft and ships, not the war of flesh and bone fought a generation earlier.[39] Fortunately, Britain possessed the world-class industry and research-and-development expertise to put a war of machines into effect.

The recognition that war on the continent was increasingly possible gave focus to British Army reforms by the mid-1930s. The recommendation to Cabinet in 1936 was that Britain prepare seventeen divisions for an expeditionary force. Cabinet approved just the five regular divisions. The new Prime Minister, Neville Chamberlain (who assumed the office in 1937), preferred to deter Germany by other means. Shielded by the enormous French Army, now safely ensconced in its impregnable Maginot Line, Chamberlain wanted to protect Britain from a knock-out blow from the air, and, by keeping the British economy in good trim, threaten Germany with another long war. As Brian Bond argued many years ago (and Dan Todman recently),[40] 'Chamberlain did not invent appeasement'. He pursued it because both the British public and, crucially the Dominion governments as expressed at the 1937 Imperial Conference (discussed below), did not want a war. As for the Americans, they were unlikely to help and if they did – in Bond's words – 'the price might compromise Britain's economic independence'.[41]

British Army modernisation was renewed under General Sir Cyril Deverell, as CIGS in 1936. 'The official line', Bidwell and Graham concluded, was that the 'basic formation of the Army would continue to be the marching infantry division, its transport and artillery mechanised'. It would be supported by the Royal Tank Corps, equipped with 'small, slow and heavily armoured tanks'. The newly established Royal Armoured Corps, composed of recently mechanised cavalry units, would coalesce around a 'Mobile Division' designed for screening and reconnaissance. The Mobile Division was soon converted into an 'armoured division' of fast tanks to exploit a breach in the enemy line.[42] This organisation into separate infantry and armoured divisions seemed to answer the 'break-in, break-out' problem the British had been wrestling with since 1918. As a result, the British conceived of two basic types of tanks: heavy for close infantry support, and 'cruisers' for exploitation. The armoured division would be essentially 'pure in race' – primarily cruiser tanks.[43]

By 1939 the British had identified and addressed the lessons of the Great War, albeit within the confines of their own peculiar national culture, organisations and limits. Within a matter of years British war industry would be out-producing any other country in the world. On the eve of war the British Army was already the only fully mechanised force in the world. That said, a new BEF was not going to change the outcome of a major continental war: the mass conscript armies of France and Belgium would have to do that.

While much has been written about British military thinking between the wars, a much-neglected critical part of British thinking was about strategic issues. In this, the new 'Imperial Defence College' (IDC) established in 1926 played a crucial role. Churchill had first articulated the idea in 1912 when he proposed a college to create a 'common brain' to oversee the conduct of Britain's wars. The IDC went a long way towards doing that. Claude Auchinleck, a member of the first class, recalled that the IDC allowed senior officers from all three services to develop a habit of 'thinking big'.[44] Brigadier Andrew McNaughton, his friend John Dill and his uneasy colleague Alan Brooke were also among the first class.

The intellectual father of the IDC was the British maritime historian and theorist Sir Julian Corbett. Often misidentified as a 'navalist', Corbett subscribed to Karl von Clausewitz's idea that war was the continuation of politics by other means. Corbett had argued before the Great War that Britain needed a *national* strategy to counteract the tendency of the Royal Navy and the British Army to think in stove-pipes, and the Government to abrogate its responsibility to oversee the strategic direction of war. The Great War proved the truth of his assessment. The first Commandant of the IDC was one of Corbett's disciples, Rear Admiral Sir Herbert Richmond. It was organised into syndicates to explore a wide range of strategic problems, from imperial defence generally, to defence of India, to some future alliance with France and Belgium against Germany, to Russia's role in the international strategic scene, to Palestine, the defence of Hong Kong and Singapore, etc. It was a broad, comprehensive and innovative program of study, and it had a profound impact on the ability of Britain, her empire and Commonwealth to coordinate strategy and military operations in the

Second World War. Many scenarios that arose after 1939 had already been 'gamed' at the IDC.

The IDC also challenged senior officers to think about what kind of war Britain ought to fight. Among those who championed the idea of a 'British way of war' was Captain B.H. Liddell Hart, who accepted Corbett's theory that Britain's natural strength lay on the sea and from economic power skilfully applied. The great continental armies could be left to fight the battles on land – subsidised by British wealth as needs be. And when continental allies were scarce, a peripheral strategy, gnawing at the edges of the enemy's position and plans, was perfectly acceptable. As a sea power, Britain could afford to wait. The belief that there was a natural 'British way of war' was imparted by the IDC.[45]

The comprehensive and sophisticated nature of British strategic thinking and staff planning was often attributed by the Americans to centuries of exercising global power. But the recent advent of the IDC was critical to the integration of military and national strategy under effective political control. As the Second World War revealed, there was nothing in the American system, either organisationally or conceptually, that compared. Because of Corbett's ideas and the education imparted by the IDC, the British were comfortable – if not content – with a peripheral strategy after 1940.

* * *

Chamberlain's reluctance to commit an expeditionary force to the continent stemmed in part from his knowledge that the Dominions, which together with India put 2.5 million men in the field during the Great War, wanted nothing to do with another major European war. In the case of Canada, the senior Dominion and by 1939 the fifth-largest trading nation in the world, this was never in doubt. For Mackenzie King this meant keeping the army small – and home. His first government (1921–6) slashed defence spending to the bone, and he was able to keep the regular army, officers and men tiny: roughly 4,000 between 1921 and 1939.[46] But Canada's tradition of militia service, which permeated even the smallest towns and villages of the country, was powerfully reinforced by the experience of the Great War. Mackenzie King worked relentlessly to tamp that volunteer enthusiasm down. Andrew McNaughton, who became Chief of the General Staff on 1 January

1929, developed plans for a three- to seven-division expeditionary force.[47] The Great Depression crushed those plans. When Mackenzie King returned as Prime Minister in 1935, he kept a close watch on the army's ambitions.

In November 1936, as tension mounted in Europe, Africa and Asia, the Minister of National Defence, Ian Mackenzie, laid a plan before the Cabinet to fix Canada's ageing coast defences and equip two 'mobile divisions', a euphemism for an expeditionary force. The timing of this request was probably not accidental. The army was riding a wave of popular sentiment arising from the dedication of Canada's Vimy monument. In July 1936 over 7,500 Canadians descended on Vimy in a pilgrimage. The French and Belgians gave them a rousing welcome that left a lasting impression on the visitors. The unveiling ceremony atop Hill 145 – towering over the plains of Douai and ceded in perpetuity by France – took on an imperial flavour when Mackenzie King Edward VIII agreed to preside. The Canadians were greeted in Britain like conquering heroes. The Royal British Legion described this 'Second Canadian Expeditionary Force' as a critical display of imperial unity, especially as war with Germany seemed more and more likely.[48] Mackenzie King was well aware of these popular enthusiasms, but he was also acutely aware that French Canada would never be reconciled to the experience of the Great War. If Canada had been 'born on the slopes of Vimy Ridge', as the English-Canadian mantra had it, the cost had been too high. Mackenzie King needed Quebec electors to hold power, and so had to balance the radically different views of English and French Canadians on Canada's role in both the empire and the world.[49]

Taking a lead from Stanley Baldwin's advice in 1936 that Britain was focusing on airpower, Mackenzie King's government emphasised an increase in the Royal Canadian Air Force (RCAF). A modest programme of aircraft purchases, and the letting of contracts in Canada for building Stranrear floatplanes, Bristol Blenheims, Handley Page Hampden two-engine bombers, and Hurricane fighters, followed. It was not much, but it laid the foundation of a substantial wartime aircraft industry. By 1939 the RCAF consumed approximately 49 per cent of the Canadian defence budget.[50] A dramatic expansion of Royal Canadian Navy (RCN) was also proposed in January 1939, as sabres began to rattle in the Czech crisis. That scheme would have made the navy the largest of Canada's three services.[51] Both the air force and the navy would help defend Canada, and could be sent off to help the empire without fear of the massive casualties which an army on the Western Front promised.[52]

As for direct military aid to Britain, Mackenzie King remained – as Charles Stacey described him – 'a prickly, difficult, unpleasant character'. This was evident at the 1937 Imperial Conference, convened by the British to draw the empire and Commonwealth into a common defence and foreign policy. Position papers were circulated by the British government beforehand, outlining what might be done – including sending a Canadian expeditionary force to Europe. These sent the notoriously anti-British, Irish-born Canadian Under-Secretary of State for External Affairs, O.D. Skelton, into a rage.[53] Mackenzie King was nonplussed. Canada was simply not going to commit to any unified defence or foreign policy under British direction. The Irish, headed for neutrality, did not attend, and Newfoundland had reverted to colonial status. South Africa under President Hertzog, himself pro-German and an admirer of Hitler, wanted to be neutral, too. Only the Australians and New Zealanders, fearful of Japan, clamoured for Commonwealth and imperial unity.[54] They would do so again in 1944 – in response to the American threat.

In 1937 Mackenzie King refused to make any commitments: he even forbade the senior Canadian military staff travelling with the delegation from talking formally with senior British officers. In tones that must have infuriated the British, Mackenzie King lectured the delegates about Canada's ethnic diversity and the role of its Parliament in deciding defence and foreign policy commitments. Canada – the only full signatory to the Statute of Westminster – would commit to nothing. Mackenzie King spent a week reworking the final communiqué of the conference producing, in Stacey's words, an 'anodyne paragraph . . . eliminating every phrase that might suggest a commitment'.[55] Correlli Barnett later concluded that Mackenzie King had completely derailed the British agenda in London in 1937: 'Not one of the English [sic] objectives in promoting a co-ordinated imperial alliance – in strategy, military and naval organization, industrial development or diplomatic effort – had been achieved.'[56] He would do the same again in May 1944, just days before the D-Day landings.

Mackenzie King nonetheless knew where his loyalties lay, and where the passions of English Canada would take the country in times of crisis. Privately he made it clear to both Neville Chamberlain, who replaced Baldwin as Prime Minister in the midst of the conference, and the Foreign Secretary, Anthony Eden, that if war came Canada would be at Britain's side. Chamberlain accepted that pressing the issue of military aid now would lead to rejection: when the guns began to fire things would be different. It was reported to the British Cabinet that Mackenzie King had told Herr Hitler that, if Germany ever threatened the United Kingdom, 'all the Dominions would come to her aid and that there would be a great numbers of Canadians anxious to swim the Atlantic!'[57] It is doubtful if the threat of war with Canada ever entered Hitler's calculus, but Mackenzie King was right about the willingness of Canadians to fight Germany again.

The 1937 Imperial Conference also failed to find a mutually beneficial way of mobilising war industry in Canada. Typically, the Canadians wanted the British to underwrite the costs of building new plants by purchasing weapons and equipment, leaving the Canadian Army with an affordable domestic supply. The British declined because Canadian costs were too high.[58] Apart from a small contract for Bren guns and the building of a few obsolescent aircraft, the largest pre-war armaments initiative came from Quebec. In 1938 Edouard Simard, owner of Marine Industries, convinced the huge French armaments firm Schneider-Creusot to build a plant in Canada to produce field guns. It was a radical idea. Canada did not even produce the steel necessary for gun barrels and breechblocks. Simard's bold scheme was to build a huge plant at Sorel, Quebec, which would receive scrap iron at one end and send guns out the other. The Canadian government got interested in early 1939 and by August of that year – even before the plant was built – the first orders were obtained from the British. In time, the Sorel plant became a critical source of supply for the Commonwealth.[59]

However, when the British approached Mackenzie King in 1937 about developing air-training facilities in Canada, as the RAF had done in the Great War, the request was rejected. The British sent a mission of exploration nonetheless in 1938, to check out the possibilities of using Canada as an air-training base. When Mackenzie King found out, the mission was withdrawn. The RCAF liaison officer in London later confirmed that the British were trying to build a conduit for Canadian manpower. The best that Mackenzie King would permit prior to 1939 was the continued training of Canadian volunteers in the UK and the building of a modest programme of flight schools in Canada, run by the RAF, to train British pilots.[60] It was a bizarre compromise that suited Mackenzie King's political situation and bewildered the British.

By the late 1930s English Canadians had their own reasons for getting involved in the looming world crisis. For many, especially those who fought on the Western Front and later marched through despoiled Belgium in the wake of the retreating Germans, the job had not been completed in 1918. But Canadians also had a sense of global citizenship derived from being in the British Commonwealth and empire. In this they differed profoundly from their American cousins, for whom the world outside was foreign. Canadians were part of the world's first global community. The map of the British empire that hung in every Canadian school, on the walls of church, service club and Legion halls, in Scout and Girl Guide camps, and a myriad other places, reminded Canadians that they were part of something much bigger. Radio and newspaper coverage of events in distant lands was often as not accounts of their own British community of nations. By the 1930s the shortwave broadcasts of the BBC beamed to Canada brought that news into their homes. The Canadian worldview in 1939 was far more cosmopolitan than that of their American cousins. When Great Britain went to war, most Canadians felt that they too had a stake in the outcome.

* * *

By all accounts Chamberlain was not disheartened by the failure of the 1937 Imperial Conference. The British world was not prepared to go to war, and neither was Britain herself. Chamberlain remained convinced that Hitler's ambition could be contained. Having joined Austria to the German Reich in March 1938, however, Hitler began a quasi-war against Czechoslovakia in September in an effort to bring the Sudetenland Germans – who lived in western Czechoslovakia – into the German state. This, he claimed, was the fulfilment of his ambition. Poland and Hungary threatened to take pieces of Czechoslovakia as well. The Czechs mobilised a million troops and were prepared to fight:

only the Russians offered to help. Britain and France convinced the Czechs to trade their country for a general European peace. The Munich Agreement of September 1938 seemed proof that Hitler's ambitions had been fulfilled. Chamberlain landed at Heston Airfield west of London on 30 September waving the agreement to surrender the Sudetenland to Germany, declaring 'Peace for our time!' Seldom have more tragically misplaced hopes been expressed.

Hitler betrayed Chamberlain's trust in March 1939, when he discarded the Munich Agreement and dismembered what was left of Czechoslovakia. Having squandered thirty Czechoslovak divisions, the British General Staff now advised that it was better to fight Germany with Poland as an ally. The Polish Army possessed roughly fifty-four divisions, enough to engage about sixty German divisions. And even if Poland succumbed eventually, that would leave Germany with a long common border with Russia which she would have to guard.[61] All things considered, it made sense to draw the line.

On 31 March 1939 Chamberlain announced the Anglo-French guarantee of Polish independence. The British would do their part. 'In late March,' David French writes, 'the Territorial Army was doubled as a public gesture to Britain's new resolve and in April conscription was introduced [for the first time ever in British history during peacetime] to encourage the French.'[62] The Anglo-French plan in the spring of 1939 was sensible. They had to withstand the initial German onslaught, mobilise their global empires, and, when the time came, launch a counterattack.

* * *

The initial response to British mobilisation plans from the Commonwealth and empire was disappointing, although not unexpected. Mackenzie King eased Canada's entry into the war. In March, as Hitler unmasked his intent, Mackenzie King's Quebec Lieutenant, Ernest LaPointe, explained to his fellow Quebecers that Canada could not be neutral: but there would be no obligation to send troops. As Darwin claims, French Canadians were comforted by the idea that sending troops to fight in a major European war was 'out of date'.[63] That meant no conscription – the ghost that haunted every interwar Canadian Cabinet meeting. In any event, Canada's entry into the war would be decided by the Canadian Parliament.

The situation for Australia and New Zealand was rather different: they remained technically colonies. But they reserved the right to determine what their war effort would look like. South Africa, which had declared itself independent, took its lead from Canada, and for much the same reason. Afrikaners and British settlers had not yet 'fused' into a distinct White South African identity. South Africans would fight in Africa. Ireland, recently established as a republic, declared neutrality.

India, the Jewel in the Crown and home to one-fifth of the world's population, was not in a position to declare anything. Its latent power was critical to the British, but it could not be mobilised by fiat. The ethnic diversity of India's population and its complex politics precluded easy mobilisation. The majority, about 68 per cent, were Hindus and a quarter were Muslim. About 6 million Christians, 6 million Sikhs and a welter of other faiths made up the rest. Some two hundred languages were spoken. Two-fifths of India's territory and a third of its population were encompassed by 562 nominally independent Indian states (sometimes referred to as the princely states). Their people were not British subjects and had become completely self-governing in 1937. By the mid-1930s Home Rule for India had been successful in putting elected Congress Party governments in provinces ruled directly by the British Crown. But in the absence of a promise in writing setting a date for Indian independence, Gandhi and his Congress Party refused to cooperate. The Congress Party was always small: by the Second World War it was estimated to have a membership of just 1.5 million. For the British at least, the Congress Party was unrepresentative of the complex issues facing Indian independence.[64] But Gandhi and the Congress Party were enormously successful at mobilising support, especially in America where the push for Indian independence was followed closely.

The situation was further complicated because the Hindu-dominated Congress Party had a troubled relationship with Mohammad Ali Jinnah and his Muslim League. Jinnah was prepared to work with the Hindus, but he wanted recognition of the League as the Muslims' sole representative. The rejection of Jinnah's demand by the Congress Party had little immediate impact on India's role in the war. Muslims and other so-called martial races, like the Sikhs, already made up the bulk of the Indian Army. The predominantly Muslim Punjab and Bengal, India's most heavily industrialised regions, offered (in Darwin's words) 'unconditional backing to the imperial war'.[65] That meant that Indian industry could be mobilised, and the Indian Army confidently deployed throughout the Middle East.

The Canadian pattern of mobilisation in 1939 reflects the quickly declining strategic situation in Europe. In February 1939 the army simply went ahead without government approval with planning for an expeditionary force. As Europe sped towards war, the Canadian general staff grew increasingly anxious that Mackenzie King's government would announce its own mobilisation plans without consulting the army. In the event, the army got approval to mobilise for home defence on 24 August 1939, but only if and when war broke out in Europe. Canada's small navy, six destroyers and some auxiliary vessels shifted to a war footing on 28 August, in line with the Royal Navy's initiation of Naval Control of Shipping.

By then the very nature of the coming war had changed profoundly. The Soviet–German Non-Aggression Pact, signed on 22 August, shocked the world, and made nonsense of Anglo-French war plans. An economic blockade of Germany had been a decisive element of Allied war strategy during the Great War, and there was hope that it be so again. With the stroke of a pen the whole Eurasian landmass was open to German industry. Just as alarming, Poland was now caught in a vice. The Soviet Union, defeated and driven east in its war with Poland two decades before, had its own scores to settle.

Despite this profoundly altered strategic situation, and the uncertainty of support from the empire and Commonwealth, Chamberlain was forced to act. When the Germans crossed the Polish border on 1 September 1939, the British and French governments issued an ultimatum to cease hostilities and withdraw, or face a war. Weariness and resignation came across in Chamberlain's voice when he spoke to the British people on 3 September. The Germans had been asked to stop but 'no such undertaking has been received . . . consequently, this country is at war with Germany'.

CHAPTER 5

IN GOD'S GOOD TIME

Heaven knows, I don't want the Americans to fight for us – we should have to pay too dearly for that.

Neville Chamberlain, September 1939[1]

The speed and audacity of the German attack on Poland stunned the world.[2] Polish defences were 'unhinged within four days'. Then on 17 September the 'axis of evil' was unmasked when Poland was attacked from the east by the Soviet Union. By 6 October 1939 the war in the east was over. Germany, backed by the enormous power of the Soviet Union, was free to direct all its might against the western Allies. Nowhere in the Anglo-French vision of a war with Germany was this nightmare scenario imagined.

Everyone suspected that the attack in the west would come through Belgium, as it had in 1914. Fear of just such an eventuality led the Belgians to declare their neutrality in 1938. That made it impossible for the French General Staff to develop a coordinated plan. Nonetheless, the French field army – backed by the BEF – would surge north to help the Belgians as soon as the Germans crossed the border. By the end of 1939 a BEF of five divisions was deployed north of Lille, on the French–Belgian border.[3] The novel threat of air attack meant that the new BEF's logistics tail did not begin at the Pas-de-Calais, but stretched south to Normandy and Brittany. Over the winter of 1939–40, 160,000 British troops built and sustained supply routes from Cherbourg, Brest and smaller ports in between to the combat forces in Picardy. The ultimate British plan in early 1940 was to mobilise a total of fifty-five divisions, about the size of the BEF in 1918. Territorial divisions began to arrive in France in January 1940. If all went well, by June, the BEF would be organised into four corps of two armies and well on the way to a force large enough to make a difference.[4] The effort in France and Belgium would be the focus of the British Army: what it could mobilise and equip. Virtually everything was in the shop window.

The Dominions and India also expanded their military efforts over the winter of 1939–40, working towards what the British hoped would be a force of fourteen divisions from abroad. Australia began mobilising a four-division corps in late 1939 and, along with New Zealand, began sending troops to Europe and Egypt in early 1940. Australia had not fully adopted the Statute of Westminster but an agreement was reached in March, whereby their divisions would constitute a separate force under an Australian commander, with deployment agreed by mutual consent of the two governments. 'The force would however', the British official history notes, 'come under the operational control of the Commander-in-Chief of the theatre in which it was serving'.[5] The Royal Australian Navy, with six cruisers and a dozen smaller vessels, was by far the most capable of the Dominion navies. It immediately came under British operational control, and by early 1940 had forces in the eastern Mediterranean.

In 1939 the Indian Army was composed of roughly 160,000 Indian and 40,000 British troops, organised into four infantry divisions. The 4th and 5th divisions were soon on their way to Egypt. As the crisis unfolded in the spring of 1940 the Indian government was asked to mobilise a further five infantry divisions and one armoured division. The bulk of these were earmarked for duty in Iraq and Iran, to shield British oil fields from Germany's allies – including the Russians. By the spring of 1940 South Africa, too, was being drawn into the war, with plans to field a division. The primary focus of the military effort east of Suez was defence of the Middle East, with its critical oil supplies and imperial communications. This would be done primarily by Indian, Australian, New Zealand and South African troops.

Canada's efforts would be focused on the European front. On the day Britain declared war, 3 September, Mackenzie King sent a personal telegram to Chamberlain explaining Canada's efforts to defend itself, and offered to help with the defence of Newfoundland and the West Indies. Most of Canada's tiny navy was soon in the Caribbean hunting German raiders. Then he asked, tepidly, where the British expected to fight and under what arrangements. The Dominion Secretary responded three days later saying there was, 'no urgency', but a 'token force' would be very much appreciated. This was just the kind of answer Mackenzie King wanted. While the army sorted out its plans, Parliament debated a declaration of war which was finally passed on 10 September.[6]

Two days after the Soviet troops attacked Poland, Canada made a formal offer of a division for the Western Front. The offer was quickly accepted. As Colonel G.P. Loggie at the Canadian High Commission reported, 'the reputation Canadians earned in the last war has not been forgotten'.[7] Andrew McNaughton was the logical choice to command the expeditionary force. As he explained to the Canadian Cabinet, his vision was a war of machines, with an army structured to spend materiel and equipment, not lives. 'This humane approach,' John Swettenham wrote, 'so close to his own, struck the Prime Minister very forcibly.'[8] Although Swettenham does not mention it, it is likely that McNaughton's strident nationalism had a great deal to do with his appointment, too.

The arrival of the 1st Canadian Division in the UK just before Christmas 1939 occasioned much fanfare. Anthony Eden, Secretary of State for Dominion Affairs, and other dignitaries steamed out aboard HMS *Warspite* and HMS *Hood* to greet the Canadian convoy. 'It was when the tune of "O Canada!" came drifting across from the transports,' *The Bulletin and Scots Pictorial* reported, 'that it was realized what these soldiers were who were landing on Britain's shore and a tremendous cheer went up.'[9] The British expected the Canadians to join the BEF in France in June.[10]

In December, Canada also committed to building and operating the 'British Commonwealth Air Training Plan' (BCATP) to train aircrew from across the empire and Commonwealth and funnel them into the RAF. The BCATP would – it seemed – consume much of the Royal Canadian Air Force's effort at home – which suited Mackenzie King perfectly. So, too, did the agreement that the British would pay for the whole thing – and buy more Canadian wheat. It was nonetheless a major coup for the RAF. Aircrew from around the globe (including Europeans in exile) would now have a safe place to train and then pour into the RAF, making it the largest international air force in the world – all ostensibly 'British'. The Dominions received assurances that their personnel would remain members of their distinctive air forces, and that the Dominions would field their own squadrons and higher formations.[11] According to J.R.M. Butler, 'The Air Training Plan was the most spectacular contribution from overseas countries of the British Commonwealth to the Allied cause in the early part of the war.'[12] The butcher's bill for the bomber offensive was still a long way off.

Mackenzie King had similar ambitions for the RCN: a meaningful contribution, with major industrial impact at home, without heavy casualties. Leonard Murray, in 1939–40 in charge of the Plans Division in Ottawa, recalled that the only restriction on the RCN's budget that first winter was that it could not ask for more money than it could spend. The navy's ambition (lingering from the failed January 1939 plan) was a fleet of Tribal Class destroyers: sleek, fast, powerful vessels designed to take the war to the enemy. Canada could not build them, so a scheme was hatched to swap Canadian-built auxiliary vessels for British-built Tribals. The new 'Flower Class' corvettes could be constructed at yards on the Canadian coasts and even along the shores of the Great Lakes. By the spring of 1940 sixty-four corvettes and eighteen Bangor-class minesweepers were on order in Canada, and plans were underway to build merchant ships.[13]

One of McNaughton's first tasks in Britain was to clarify the lines of command and control over Canadian forces. This was sorted out in a series of conferences held in early 1940. As will be recalled, the Visiting Forces Act specified that Dominion forces were either 'serving together' or 'in combination'. The niceties of this legal arrangement were foremost in McNaughton's mind, but few senior British officers were either aware of them or willing to abide by them. It did not help that only Canada had fully adopted the Statute of Westminster, and therefore the Visiting Forces Act – for the moment – only applied to Canadian troops. It would come to nettle McNaughton's relationship with the British.

McNaughton's position was enhanced in mid-February when the Canadian government announced plans to send a second division

overseas and form a new Canadian Corps. The decision was a calculated move on Mackenzie King's part to keep the army's role from
becoming a political issue in the forthcoming general election in
March.[14] It worked. Mackenzie King's majority in parliament increased.
But he was never free of the challenge of balancing Canada's domestic
politics against the burden of fighting the war. In the depths of the war
the pressure of Canadian domestic politics would come to have an
impact on events scarcely imagined by Anglo-American historians.

* * *

In the early hours of 10 May 1940 Lieutenant-General Alan Brooke,
General Officer Commanding of II British Corps, was awaken by 'an
infernal bombardment of AA guns'. German planes were overhead, as
they had been before. This time, however, there was other news. Word
soon arrived that the Germans had attacked Belgium and the
Netherlands. 'It was hard to believe on a most glorious spring day with
all nature looking quite its best,' Brooke – the birdwatcher – wrote, 'that
we were taking the first step towards what must become one of the
greatest battles of history!'[15] What followed was even more unbelievable.

In response to the German assault, General Maurice Gamelin's best
formations, fifteen French divisions and ten divisions of the BEF, moved
north through Belgium to link up with the Dutch at Breda. As they did
so, German Army Group A pushed westward through the Ardennes
forest in Belgium. The result was like a giant turnstile. By 14 May,
Panzers had crossed the Meuse at Sedan and were racing for the sea.
When news of the breakthrough was confirmed, General Alphonse
Georges, commander of the French northern armies, collapsed into
tears.[16] The speed of the German advance induced paralysis in the French
high command. Expecting a controlled form of linear warfare, French
orders were largely carried by motorcycle despatch riders. Their travels
across France and Belgium were impeded by clogged roads, Luftwaffe
attacks and the need to move at night at high speed. 'Scores of these
motorcyclists,' Lloyd Clark observes, 'were killed or seriously wounded
in accidents.' It took days for 'time-sensitive' orders to be delivered. In
contrast, German formations required little intervention by high
command. Everyone knew that their task was to push forward relentlessly, and that everyone else was hustling up from behind.

Well before the collapse of the Allied position in the west, the German attack on Norway in April – and its implications – had provoked a crisis in the British government. The British and French had hoped to forestall a German occupation of Norway by launching their own. It turned into a disaster. Chamberlain, already tainted by the failure of appeasement, had to go. Churchill was selected as a compromise candidate for Prime Minister on 10 May. He was by no means a popular figure, but Churchill shouldered the burden of trying to salvage something from what was rapidly becoming an unmitigated disaster.

On 14 May, Churchill flew to Paris and arrived to find the French frantically burning state papers. William Manchester observed that Churchill 'dominated the proceedings from the moment he entered the room'. In butchered but comprehensible French he reminded Prime Minister Reynaud and his officials that they – the British and French – had been here before, in the spring of 1918. They had weathered that storm and would do so again. Then the metaphorical bomb burst in the room. 'Où est la masse de manoeuvre?' Churchill asked. Where are the reserves? 'Gamelin shook his head,' answering with one word, 'Aucune.' There were none.[17] The Germans were pouring through and there was no way to stop them.

The discussion that followed became acrimonious, with the French demanding that Britain send its air force to stop the Panzers and the British demanding that the French counterattack. British and French intentions were sharply divided from then onwards. The French expected the British to commit everything to the continent and, if necessary, go down fighting with them. The British were already starting to think about retreating to their island. For the moment Churchill relented and agreed to send several squadrons of Hurricanes.[18] The next day the Netherlands capitulated. Premier Reynaud phoned Churchill to tell him, 'We are beaten, we have lost the battle.' The retreat from Belgium had begun.[19]

By 20 May the leading elements of General Heinz Guderian's XIX Panzer Corps reached Abbeville, where the Somme runs into the sea. The impossible had happened: Britain's army was trapped, cut off from the bulk of the French army and from its logistical base in Normandy and Brittany. All that the BEF could do was fight for time and space. A slashing attack by seventy-four heavy tanks, two battalions of infantry, some artillery and a motorcycle battalion south of Arras on 21 May momentarily stunned the Germans. General Erwin Rommel reported an attack by five divisions. It stalled when it ran into German 88mm anti-aircraft guns deployed in a direct-fire role – the only German guns which could penetrate the heavy British tanks.[20]

The 'counterattack' at Arras bought time, but on 21 May it was not yet clear what should be done with it. The British had only two divisions in the UK to commit to the battle, the 52nd Lowland Division and the 1st Canadian Division. Among the many decisions facing General Edmond Ironside, the Chief of the General Staff, was if, when and how to deploy them, and how the fighting strength of the BEF might yet be preserved. It speaks to the stature of General Andrew McNaughton that on 23 May Ironside ordered him to assess the situation in France and, if necessary – and plausible – take charge of the BEF's rear area in the Pas-de-Calais. Elements of the Canadian division would be sent to assist.

McNaughton arrived at Calais just before midnight and conferred with the British and French garrison commander and the local French Admiral. Calais was already under threat and rumours abounded of German forces along the coast to the north. McNaughton determined that the men on the ground would fight, and if the Canadians arrived Calais would hold. He sent Ironside a report recommending that the Canadians be sent,[21] and then set off for Dunkirk. The situation there was better, with two French divisions securing the perimeter. A further report was sent, and then McNaughton returned to Dover, where he was ordered to London to brief the War Cabinet. After hearing from McNaughton, Cabinet decided to abandon Calais and send the Canadians back to their barracks. An appeal from Lord Gort, the BEF commander, for the Canadian force on 25 May briefly revived the planned reinforcement.

In late May and early June, while the remnants of Gort's army and thousands of French were lifted miraculously off the beaches of Dunkirk, plans were afoot for a Second BEF. The idea was to establish a bastion in the Brittany peninsula, where the remnants of the Anglo-French armies could hold on. There were still some 150,000 British soldiers in France south of the Somme.[22] The French had been thinking along these lines and were encouraged by the news that the British would send 'every fit division' they had. When they discovered that this meant just two the French understood immediately that the Second BEF was a political gesture not a military one. They wanted the RAF.

The man tasked with leading this forlorn hope in Brittany was Brooke, late commander of II British Corps. Brooke received his orders on 10 June, the day Italy declared war on Britain and France. As Brooke left for Brittany, 'There were officers at the War Office who never expected to see him again.'[23] The same was true of the Canadians. As they prepared to board the transports, the new Chief of the Imperial General Staff, General Sir John Dill, fired off a telegram wishing 'my Dear Andy and all the splendid men under your command good fortune and every success in all that lies ahead'.[24] McNaughton was not naive about what his Canadians could achieve. For just this reason he had modified the terms of the Visiting Forces Act, making himself de facto national contingent commander and in personal control of any deployments of Canadian troops.

Brooke's orders were very general, little more than to cooperate with the French, but the plan was to secure the Brittany peninsula between Saint-Nazaire and Pontorson – about 70 miles – with two divisions and bits and pieces of two more. They and British troops in the area, mostly service corps, engineers and transport, along with the French, would create a redoubt into which the French government could retreat to carry on the war.

When Brooke met with the staff of 1st Canadian Division on 11 June to explain all this it was understood clearly that the Canadians would concentrate just outside Brest as a full division before moving east.[25] What neither Brooke nor McNaughton knew was that British Army 'Movement Control' in France still operated on orders to pushed combat troops forward to concentration areas at Laval and Le Mans, 70 miles east of the redoubt's baseline. When the 1st Canadian Infantry Brigade and its supporting artillery arrived on 12 and 13 June, they were immediately sent inland. The leading elements of the 52nd Lowland Division fared no better. By the time Brooke arrived on 13 June to establish his HQ at Le Mans, his force was strung out along road and rail lines between Le Mans and Brest or Cherbourg.

The situation at the French Army headquarters near Orleans early the next morning was worse than Brooke could have imagined. The French Army had disintegrated, and Paris had been abandoned. The French admitted, as Brooke recorded in his diary, 'that the Brittany Defence Scheme was quite impossible owing to lack of troops'. Brooke wired his conclusions to the War Office and then motored back to Le Mans, 'through masses of refugees'.[26] Meanwhile the French government appealed directly to the United States to intervene. 'Reynaud continued to hang onto a slim hope,' Lloyd Cark writes, 'that a positive message from Washington and a hard line by the British would be enough to ensure that France would continue to fight.'[27] The Americans responded the next day declining to get involved: no help was coming from them.

By the time Brooke got back to Le Mans the decision to abandon the Second BEF was made. It was now just a matter of getting as many troops out as possible. The first to go were the Canadians. They were forced to abandon their transport but refused to leave their artillery.[28] All the Canadians, except one unfortunate infantryman who spent the rest of the war as a POW, were gone by 17 June. In the meantime, the 52nd Division was held in France 'for political reasons'.[29]

Over the next few days the British acted quickly to save what was left. 'It is a desperate job,' Brooke wrote in his diary on 15 June, 'being faced with over 150,000 men and masses of materiel, ammunition, petrol, supplies etc. to try and evacuate or dispose of with nothing to cover this operation except the crumbling French army'. Two days later a new French government was formed and initial contact was made with the Germans for an armistice. With that the 52nd Division was ordered to evacuate as well. They and most of the line of communications troops got away.

McNaughton watched all this from Britain frustrated that two Canadian brigades waited on the wharf to go, and angry when 1st Brigade returned having lost everything but their guns. Dill tried to console him, explaining that 'Even the Canadian Division could not have saved the situation'.[30] The whole affair had been a shambles. McNaughton seethed. Some indication of this frustration made its way into McNaughton's letter to Dill at the end of June.[31] Two decades later he was still angry.[32]

McNaughton and Brooke were not the best of colleagues, and the fiasco of the second BEF did nothing to fix that. In August, Brooke, now the Commander in Chief of Home Forces and McNaughton's commanding officer, visited the Canadians, and at the end of the day the two ended up alone together in a staff car. It did not go well. McNaughton recalled that it was Brooke who broached the subject. 'Andy,' he said, 'I hear you are very disconcerted and you've been very critical of the way I've handled the division in France.' 'Brooky, I certainly am,' McNaughton replied. 'I'm not going to hide it. I was very upset. We had an arrangement.' The 1st Canadian Division was to be concentrated before deploying and instead 'we were thrown into chaos'. As McNaughton recalled, the discussion deteriorated quickly after that. 'I want you to know,' Brooke said, 'that you're under my orders now and I'll fight the division as I see fit.' Brooke then apparently confided that he had always intended to do that anyway, regardless of what McNaughton thought. 'What can you do with a man like that?' McNaughton opined to his interviewer in 1965. 'I let him know that I didn't approve of that sort of thing and that I wouldn't have it.' After that, McNaughton filtered every operational order received by Canadians through the Visiting Forces Act, to ensure that 'they could be in combination only so long and until I otherwise directed'.[33] With the victorious Germans now just across the Channel and threatening invasion, the last thing that Brooke needed was a constitutional spat with his old nemesis over the handling of one division. Things did not improve between them as the war went on, and as the Canadian Army grew in size and importance.

* * *

By the end of June 1940 British hopes and plans of a year before lay in ruins, and Britain's field army was shattered. The European states had fallen like dominoes, until the greatest asset in a prolonged war against Nazism – France – simply collapsed. Alistair Horne claims that it was news that Americans would not come to their aid that tipped the French into capitulation.[34] Nazi Germany could not have timed her attack any better: 1940 was an American presidential election year. In June, as the Nazis marched through the Arc de Triomphe, the first of the semi-annual notes from the US Treasury Department arrived in Paris demanding a payment on France's Great War debt.

As the tragedy unfolded, Churchill remained defiant. On 4 June 1940 he told Parliament that Britain would never succumb to Nazi tyranny: 'We shall fight on the beaches, we shall fight on the landing grounds, we shall fight in the fields and in the streets, we shall fight in the hills.' Britons, he asserted without bombast or ostentation, would 'never surrender'. They 'would carry on the struggle, until, in God's good time, the New World, with all its power and might, steps forth to the rescue and the liberation of the old'. No one ever doubted what Churchill meant by the 'New World' coming to rescue the old. Even before the final collapse of France the Chiefs of Staff warned Churchill that, as David Reynolds writes, 'without the 'full economic and financial support' of the United States '*we do not think we could continue the war with any chance of success*'.[35] Emphasis in the original text obscures the fact that the British Chiefs of Staff focused on American economic and financial aid, not military. Over the next eighteen months, securing America, backing for Britain's war proved far more difficult than anyone – especially Churchill – could imagine. Indeed, it seemed that God was taking her own sweet time.

The logic of the two great 'Anglo-Saxon' powers teaming up to save the world – as they eventually did – seemed inescapable to postwar historians. But the wartime rhetoric about the 'special relationship' between Britain and America was a chimera. Their respective populations remained blithely ignorant of each other, their notions based on myths developed over a century and a half of separation, war and mutual mistrust. For Britons, America remained a land of wealth and opportunity, but one governed at best by oligarchs and the 'hidden hand' of capitalism, and at worst by mob rule. Polls conducted in early 1942 revealed an alarming lack of both knowledge and, perhaps more importantly, interest among Britons about the USA. At best, their view was locked in a pre-1939 vision of a country where 'Trade Unionists are ignored or attacked, corruption is common, social legislation is primitive and commercialism rampant'.[36]

If anything, Britain's politicians and senior civil servants harboured much stronger feelings. This bitter anti-Americanism, in Robert Self's words, was 'typical of an entire generation within a British policy elite which displayed an astonishing degree of continuity throughout the interwar period'.[37] 'You will get nothing from America but words,' Stanley Baldwin warned in 1932. Baldwin's opinions were unchanged in 1935 when he was briefly Prime Minister again. Robert Vansittart, the Permanent Under-Secretary of State for Foreign Affairs, had all but given up on the Americans by the mid-1930s. 'It is still necessary, and I desire as much as ever,' he wrote in 1934, 'that we should get on with this untrustworthy race. But we shall never get very far: they will always let us down.'[38]

The mood in Britain was well known to American diplomats. When Neville Chamberlain became Prime Minister in 1937 the American ambassador to Britain, the pathologically anti-British Joseph Kennedy, sent off a note to Roosevelt warning him of Chamberlain's anti-Americanism. According to Self, Chamberlain knew he would come to depend on America to win any new war with Germany, but he deeply resented that fact and hoped to win without them – as Britain had done in 1918. 'Heaven knows,' Chamberlain said shortly after the war began in 1939, 'I don't want the Americans to fight for us – we should have to pay too dearly for that.' The Permanent Under-Secretary of State at the Foreign Office, Sir Alexander Cadogan, was even more stridently anti-American. After watching what Self describes as 'pious American declarations of goodwill' without any practical support for a policy of containment against Japan in 1934, Cadogan quipped prophetically that the 'U.S.A. will give us no undertaking to resist by force any action by Japan short of an attack on Hawaii or Honolulu'.[39]

The general American view of Britain was just as stubbornly ossified, locked in images of brutal British Redcoats and their Tory toadies imposing the will of mad King George. In 1919 it had been essential to Woodrow Wilson's foreign policy to see Britain as unchanged from the empire that Americans had thrown off in the eighteenth century. Nothing that happened between 1919 and 1939 changed those views. Robert McCormick's *Chicago Tribune* well reflected the depth of that intransigent hostility. The *Tribune* hammered away relentlessly on the fundamental evilness of the British empire throughout the Phoney War and on into that dreadful summer of 1940.

Between May 1940 and December 1941 Britons saw themselves as the last bastion of decency and democracy in Europe, the guardians of all that both British and American society stood for. Britain had not gone to war to save its empire, as many Americans believed. Sir Harold Nicolson, one of Britain's great diplomats and statesmen, made it clear in his little book *Why Britain Is at War* in the fall of 1939 that the issue was the evilness of Hitler's regime and the threat it posed to the world. Nicolson was one of the few MPs who refused to cheer Chamberlain's efforts to appease Hitler in September 1938. Writing of the plans as outlined in *Mein Kampf* Nicolson wrote, 'Here speaks the fanatic, the nihilist, the revolutionary, the anarchist; here speaks the maniac who is prepared to bring the whole world to ruin in order to satisfy the only lust he possesses: the lust of power.'[40]

This moral righteousness underlay all of Britain's appeals to – and expectations of – the United States throughout the war. It lay at the heart of Churchill's unrelenting optimism that America would declare war soon, or in a matter of days, or right after the 1940 election. It was here that the starkly different worldviews of Britons and Americans – the clash of ideals in a battle for civilisation versus splendid isolation – made effective dialogue and discourse problematic. Churchill's expectation that Americans saw the issues in the same way as Britons proved to be utterly unfounded.[41] 'Churchill was tone-deaf when it came to American culture,' Todman writes, 'and he consistently overestimated the extent of American fellow feeling with the U.K.'[42] Many Americans – not least the isolationists and much of the mid-west – saw Britain's situation by the summer of 1940 as something of its own making.[43] Robert Bruce Lockhart, the perceptive Scot who eventually became the head of Britain's Political Warfare Executive, made this discovery during his 1939 speaking tour. Lockhart summed up his impression of the average American attitude: 'We pulled you out of a hole [in the Great War] and we received grudging thanks . . . Now, largely through your own fault, you are in trouble again and you want our help. Well, we've learned our lesson.'[44] The manipulative and perfidious British were reaping what their power and wealth had sown.

In any event, before Pearl Harbor most Americas believed that they did not need the world to be 'nice'. As Orson Welles had suggested with his Martians, all the trouble came from outside. By 1940 the American economy was doing fine, thanks largely to British and French war orders.[45] Americans would trade and live with whomever dominated Europe. If they had a peculiar anxiety it was over Central and Southern America, where American investments and foreign policy had carved out an informal empire. Even isolationists seemed to agree that the Nazis must not be allowed to infiltrate 'their' part of the western hemisphere.

* * *

The problem the British faced in the summer of 1940 is that they had no clear idea of how to persuade America to come to their aid. The undertaking was monumental. As one *New York Times* writer pointed out on 10 June – even before the fate of France was sealed – the British government could not decide whether to pitch their appeal optimistically, pessimistically, or just to present the facts. In any case, they had no idea of the mood of America, little idea of how American politics worked, and no clear plan to try to shape public opinion – assuming that was what they wanted to do. 'There was,' as Alan Dudley, for some time the Director of the 'British Library of Information in New York' (BLINY), opined in 1942, 'no policy.'[46]

That was not for want of trying.

On 26 June 1940 – four days after the French capitulation – Churchill sent a brief note to his Minister of Information, Duff Cooper, asking him to 'submit a memorandum to the Cabinet of your views on propaganda in the United States, together with definite proposals'. Cooper responded a week later. 'It has hitherto been the policy of His Majesty's Government to do no propaganda in the United States,' Cooper replied, 'and no machinery for the purpose therefore exists'.[47]

This was not strictly true. Since the 1920s the British government had maintained the British Library of Information. Its task was to dispel the odium of propaganda that clung to every British utterance in America since the Great War. It was not successful. But the BLINY pushed out information and served as a resource for – as Cull describes it – 'all things British'.[48] It also started a routine survey of the American press, which was forwarded to London. According to Cull, this survey became the 'British Government's principal barometer of American public opinion'.[49] The press survey expanded during the Second World War.

The British had also been broadcasting into the northern American states since 1932, when the BBC began its 'Empire Service' to Canada.

The BBC soon received more mail from Americans than from Canadians. Three years later, at Roosevelt's urging, a regular transatlantic exchange of radio programmes explaining Britain and America to each other began between the BBC and CBS. The opening of New York offices of the BBC that year, and the quest for material, launched the career of Alistair Cooke, who for generations worked to explain America to Britons.[50]

As tension mounted in Europe during the late 1930s the urgency of shaping American sentiment towards Britain grew apace. The British Foreign Office tracked American print and radio correspondents in Europe, monitoring their attitudes towards Britain, and encouraged film actors and directors (like Alfred Hitchcock) to use their opportunities in Hollywood to put a positive spin on things British. When a shadow 'Ministry of Information' was established in 1937 to begin handling the media and the message, an American Division was created. As we shall see, it remained a small cell of clerks tasked with pushing information out to British agencies in the US. Cull sets the origins of this effort solely within the Anglo-American discourse arising out of the Great War experience and attempt to undo the damage already done. But by the late 1930s the British were also reacting to the aggressive and highly sophisticated efforts of Dr Joseph Goebbels and his Reichsministerium für Volksaufklärung und Propaganda.[51] The German propaganda task in the US was simple: confirm the correctness of isolationism, nurture the radical extremism of the American right, and foster Americans' anti-British sentiments.[52] Throughout the Second World War a steady stream of protests was sent home from Washington by British and Canadian diplomats about the effectiveness of German propaganda efforts in America.

The job of running the American Division of the MOI was initially given to Sir Frederick Whyte, a veteran of the propaganda machine of the Great War. Whyte was the director general of the 'English Speaking Union' and a key player in British efforts to bring Anglo-American scholars and intellectuals together under the rubric of 'English Atlanticism'.[53] It was Whyte, acting on a recommendation from Alex Fletcher of BLINY, who settled on the idea that the best way to get the British story into America was to enlist Americans to do it. The group of correspondents the British set out to woo on the eve of war was anti-Nazi but many were not evidently pro-British. 'Drew Middleton of AP', Cull writes,

> confessed himself 'sceptical' upon first arriving in Britain: Eric Sevareid of CBS found the nation's 'little England' mentality quite a match for isolationism in his native Midwest; and Edward R. Murrow [appointed European director for CBS in 1937] initially thought of Britain as a 'pleasant' but relatively unimportant 'museum piece'. Complaints about British complacency, classism and cooking abounded.[54]

Only a few, like Dorothy Thompson and Walter Durant, who had British connections, were sympathetic from the outset. The key to turning these sceptics around was opening the British war effort to full and frank reporting. Not everyone, least of all the military and security people, agreed with this approach. But using American reporters to put a positive spin on Britain was the preferred course for senior MOI officers, who hoped to avoid anything that smacked of propaganda.

There was, nonetheless, a clandestine counterpart to this British effort: 'British Security Coordination' (BSC), also based in New York. It was, as Nigel West explained, an umbrella organisation eventually consisting of MI5, the Secret Intelligence Service, Special Operations Executive and the Political Warfare Executive. BSC was tasked with tracking and countering German propaganda in the US, as well as fighting Britain's secret war in the Caribbean, and Central and South America.[55] Its founder, and guiding light, was the 'quiet Canadian' and inveterate self-promoter William Stephenson.

An exceptionally talented and fearless fighter pilot in the Great War, Stephenson had a passion for radio which, coupled with his 'inventive and commercial genius', made him a multi-millionaire by 1939.[56] Among his early triumphs was inventing a machine to send photographs over telegraph wires. By the mid-1930s Stephenson's work obliged him to spend considerable time in Germany, where he witnessed the Nazi transformation of Germany industry to war production. In 1936 he began to report his observations to Churchill, and eventually Britain's new

Secret Intelligence Service (SIS), the Industrial Intelligence Centre, the Ministry of Economic Warfare and the Committee of Imperial Defence.[57]

In spring 1940 Stephenson was sent off on a secret visit to the US to sound out the possibility of cooperation between SIS and America's Federal Bureau of Investigation (FBI) to root out German espionage and saboteurs. The head of the FBI, J. Edgar Hoover, proved enthusiastic and Roosevelt gave his approval for the 'closest possible marriage between the FBI and British Intelligence'.[58] When Stephenson reported all this his reward was to be sent back to New York to 'do all that was not being done and could not be done by overt means to assure sufficient aid for Britain and eventually to bring America into the war'.[59]

So by the time Churchill asked Duff Cooper what the propaganda plan was for the USA, there were at least three British campaigns underway: the general push of information through the MOI and BLINY; the project to coopt American overseas correspondents; and Stephenson's covert organisation. Officially there was no British propaganda campaign. In early July a fourth was recommended to the British Cabinet by Mr Emery Reves, a publisher, Hungarian ex-pat and Churchill's literary agent. The Germans, Reves asserted, were winning the propaganda war in America, and with control of the huge French news agency Havas now in their hands, things could only get worse. He recommended that the British government buy or establish its own news agency (perhaps the financially strapped and very pro-German Hearst newspaper chain) and commit some 10 million in sterling to engage in a proper propaganda war in the USA – which he would run.[60]

Reves's proposal formed the basis of much discussion over selling the British case in America. By early August some in the MOI, the Foreign Office, the BBC and a few other senior officials had pulled together a scheme for one large PR organisation for the USA. That plan was scuttled by senior MOI civil servants, who felt that 'turning' American correspondents and pushing out information was enough. This proved to be the first of several occasions when the MOI grossly mismanaged Britain's PR campaign in America. As for Mr Reves, his plan was dismissed as being too German, and he for being not quite British.[61]

Reves was sent to the USA to coordinate what he could, while the MOI carried on with its 'plan'.

The best propaganda agent Britain had in the US in 1940 was its ambassador, Philip Kerr, Lord Lothian. Kerr, who inherited the title Marquess of Lothian in 1930, had wide experience as a diplomat during and after the Great War. His credibility was soiled slightly by association with the 'Cliveden Set' named after the estate of Lady Mary Astor, whose home was 'the headquarters of a reactionary group sympathetic to dictators and exercising a baneful influence on British politics'.[62] By 1938 Lothian was anti-Nazi, but his qualities for service as ambassador to America were more than just a title and notoriety. Lothian was secretary of the Rhodes Scholarship committee and by 1939 had completed fourteen trips to the USA, visiting over forty-four states in the previous twelve years. 'Unlike most British officials', Lynne Olson claims, Lothian was familiar with 'how Americans look at the world and what [they think] in the Middle West, South, and on the Pacific Coast as well as in New York and Washington'.[63] Lothian's casual informality and his genuine love of America endeared him to Americans. He both understood and was sympathetic to the way the American political system worked. This made him virtually unique among senior British officials.

* * *

America gave grudgingly of its wealth and armaments in the first eighteen months of the war. Americans were strongly in favour of the Allies in September 1939 – 84 per cent according to Gallup's surveys[64] – but also strongly against intervention.[65] Attempts by Roosevelt in June to have the Neutrality Act revoked were soundly defeated in both the House and the Senate. By mid-1939, Kennedy concludes, the US was making 'a piddling contribution to munitioning the democracies'.[66]

America itself was utterly unprepared for war. Roosevelt had tried since January 1939 to nudge America towards some level of preparedness without much success. When he petitioned Congress for $300 million to purchase 15,000 aircraft, the Chief of the Army General Staff professed himself unsure of what he would do with so many planes.[67] To the extent that Roosevelt had a military policy it consisted of sheltering behind a powerful navy and keeping hostile powers at arm's length. When Congress invoked the Neutrality Act on 3 September

1939 Roosevelt's hands were tied: nothing could be sold or delivered to any belligerent. When the Neutrality Act was reviewed less than three weeks later in a special session, most conservatives in Congress aligned with the isolationists. The core of Roosevelt's support for softening the Act came from Southern Democrats, who voted 110 to 8 in favour.[68] This was the first of many times that the fate of American support for Britain's war effort depended on politicians from the segregated and racially troubled deep south. Clearly the memory of British support during the US Civil War remained strong. But this also meant that the charges in the anti-British press of the inherent racism and oppression of the British empire could not be countered by pointing out America's own racism and repression of its citizens of colour. As we shall see, in early 1942 the new British ambassador, Lord Halifax, wanted to do that but his hand was stayed for just that reason.

The revised Neutrality Act, passed into law on 4 November 1939, allowed trading with belligerents on a strict cash-and-carry basis, and prohibited American-flagged shipping from operating in a war zone. The legislation also prohibited flying military aircraft directly to belligerent countries. These restrictions could only favour the Allies. The pressing Anglo-French need in the winter of 1939–40 was modern combat aircraft. The American aircraft industry was soon in the throes of expansion, funded by enormous French and British investment. By the spring of 1940 5,000 aircraft and 10,000 aero engines were on order for the Allies.[69] Money and gold poured in not just to pay for the aircraft, but to expand and build the plant necessary to produce them. The investment would pay enormous dividends later when America began to mobilise.

In the meantime, every spare military aircraft in America was snapped up. Many went overseas via Canada through a loophole in the Neutrality Act. Aircraft could not be flown directly to a belligerent country, but they could fly to some farmer's field in Montana and South Dakota where they were towed across the border (often by horses) and flown away. A few came across the border between Maine and New Brunswick. Some 600 aircraft arrived in Canada in this way over the next five months. Once the invasion of France began, the US government eased these restrictions and allowed aircraft to fly direct to Canada. This made Montreal the hub of regular transatlantic flights.

Meanwhile the hard core of isolationism coalesced around the 'America First Movement'. Among its prominent members were Charles Lindberg, the famous flyer who was totally smitten by Herman Göring and his Luftwaffe; Senator Gerald Nye, whose report on big business and the Great War confirmed most Americans' suspicions of British perfidy; and Robert McCormick, the owner and editor of the *Chicago Tribune*. Kennedy describes McCormick as 'militantly anti-New Deal and obstreperously isolationist . . . a bully . . . towering colossus of provincialism'. His newspaper had a circulation of over 1 million in 1939 and was 'enormously influential'; only the *New York Times* competed with the *Tribune* for status.[70] The power and reach of the isolationist movement, supported effectively – if for many Americans unknowingly – by Axis money and propaganda, acted as a powerful break on Roosevelt's efforts to help the Allies. This was true even as western Europe succumbed to Nazi aggression: 1940 was a presidential election year, and Roosevelt had to move carefully.

The pace and intensity of Roosevelt's own plans for military preparedness nonetheless changed when the Phoney War ended. On 15 May, just five days after the attack on France began, Roosevelt asked Congress for an additional $1.3 billion for defence – essentially doubling the budget. His intent now was to complete the plan for a massive 'two ocean navy', and build 50,000 aircraft, most of the latter to be sent overseas.[71] The 1940 Naval Act was the largest in American history, ultimately costing some $4 billion, and called for a 70 per cent increase in the size of the fleet. It would be years before the fruits of what is usually called the Third Vinson Act were ready, and a long time before enormous American aircraft production influenced the war. A start at army mobilisation (discussed in the next chapter) would follow later in the summer.

In the meantime, Britain needed help, and that could only come from the Commonwealth and empire. All of Britain's frontline divisions were effectively destroyed by the end of June, along with virtually all of Britain's modern military equipment, including 2,500 artillery pieces, 64,000 vehicles and 20,000 motorcycles.[72] For a time in the summer of 1940, the only full-strength, fully equipped division in the UK was the 1st Canadian Infantry. With the Italian declaration of war and the defection of France, Britain faced calamity. The Mediterranean, the Suez Canal, the overland route through Palestine to Iraq and Iran, their oil fields and the pipeline between Iraq and the Mediterranean were all in peril. Some, like Lord Halifax, the Foreign Secretary, recommended accommodation with Hitler. Churchill urged the British Cabinet to refuse any offers of peace on Hitler's terms, and convinced them to stay in the fight. It was a bold and perhaps foolhardy decision. It seemed that the Germans would soon invade, and Britain had only the tattered remnants of an army and little equipment to stop them.

The Commonwealth and empire responded to the challenge. As early as 17 May Mackenzie King told the Canadian War Cabinet that 'The Empire is in extremis'.[73] Orders for the 2nd Canadian Division to leave for England were cut, and mobilisation of the 3rd Canadian Division and elements of a fourth begun. Five days later Canada's seven modern destroyers began sailing for Europe. And Canada's only fighter squadron, No. 1 with its Canadian-built Hurricanes, was despatched in June: it arrived in time to fight in the Battle of Britain.[74]

While Canada's direct military contribution in 1940 was modest, the disaster of June 1940 kicked war production into high gear. Over the summer forty more warships were ordered from Canadian yards. By late 1940 Canada had some 129 ocean-going warships under construction. The production of weapons and vehicles was also increased. In 1940 Canada produced 100,000 rifles and 42,600 Bren guns, as well as small-arms ammunition and some artillery shells.[75] The Canadian automotive industry, well developed by 1939, soon became the main source of motor transport for the Commonwealth and empire. The first orders from the War Office for 20,900 trucks arrived in July 1940. 'Following this initial order,' Clive Law has written, 'the flood-gates opened.'[76] Thousands of 15-cwt and 30-cwt 'Canadian Military Pattern' (CMP) trucks would go overseas in 1941, many to the Middle East, where Canadian vehicles became ubiquitous – even General Erwin Rommel briefly used a Canadian Chevrolet staff car. The Canadians developed a pre-packed vehicle kit – a truck in a crate – that was easy to ship, and easy to assemble at the final destination. The Canadian Army in Britain was soon assembling Canadian trucks, and the British established some thirty depots to put them together.[77]

Canadian production of the British 25-pounder field guns in the new plant at Sorel, Quebec, was slower off the mark. By June 1940 nothing had come of the British contract signed in August 1939 for 100 guns and 200 carriages.[78] When France fell, the French engineers from Schneider-Creusot went home, and Sorel brought in new management unfamiliar with gun production. Major investment by the British and Canadian governments followed, and at British request plans were adopted to triple the production rate. All that occasioned delays. The first guns were not delivered until July 1941: by the end of that year 122 had been shipped. These were Mk II guns, fitted with a muzzle brake to fire more powerful charges. By mid-1942 virtually every 25-pounder field gun in North Africa came from Sorel.[79] So, too, did most of the 6-pounder anti-tank guns in the Middle East, pouring from the Dominion Engineering Works in Montreal at the rate of over 600 per month (and the same number of spare barrels) by early 1942. They were accompanied by thousands of 2-pounder guns, 3.7" anti-aircraft gun barrels, 20- and 40mm Bofors guns and barrels, and carriages for 4.5" and 5.5" artillery.[80] The expansion of Canadian industry, and its contribution to the war effort, starting in the summer of 1940 was prodigious. It has been overlooked by histories of the war. Within a year Canada's economy was as large as Italy's and growing quickly.[81]

India's industrial capacity did not expand as much during the war, but its guns, ammunition, armoured vehicles, food and miscellaneous goods accounted for nearly 20 per cent of British military supplies in the Middle East by late 1942. By then the Indians, Australians, New Zealanders and South Africans had arrived in some strength to help British formations secure the Middle East. They would do much of the actual fighting until late 1942, while the British Army reconstituted itself in Britain and secured the home country from invasion.

Churchill had expressed hope that Britain could hold on until, in 'God's good time', the New World – by which he meant America – would come to save the old. But in the meantime, the Commonwealth and empire stepped up and sustained Britain in her hour of greatest need. As the David Low cartoon of June 1940 put it, the British were indeed alone, all 500 million of them.

CHAPTER 6

VERY WELL THEN, ALONE!

In the war of attrition which raged ceaselessly against the human
spirit, anti-climax was a heavy weapon.

Evelyn Waugh, *Officers and Gentlemen*[1]

Between the fall of France and the German attack on Russia, Britain,
her Commonwealth and empire fought alone. The enormous power
and wealth of the British world, and hope of imminent American involvement, lay at the heart of British optimism in those dreadful months. That
optimism was also predicated on the belief that blockade, aerial bombing,
rebellion and a peripheral strategy would lead to collapse of the Nazi empire. The secretive 'Special Operations Executive' (SOE), set up by
Churchill in the summer of 1940, would set Europe ablaze. American
money and industry were absolutely vital, and their naval and airpower
would help weaken the Nazis. But when the time came to invade the
continent, a comparatively small, highly mobile British expeditionary
force would make the final push.[2] By 1942 they expected to have twenty
or thirty divisions ready, enough to topple a crumbling Nazi empire.[3]

In the meantime, it was necessary to convince America that Britain
had the resolution to fight on. This was an open question in July 1940.
Joseph Kennedy, Roosevelt's ambassador in London, reinforced those
fears with endless prognostications of doom. The bold and ruthless
British attack on the French fleet at Mers-el-Kébir in Algeria, which
refused a British demand to join them or be sunk at anchor, impressed

Roosevelt: three of the four battleships in the harbour were sunk or severely damaged. So, too, did the decision in August to despatch 100 tanks to Egypt at a time when Britain was facing invasion. But as David Edgerton points out, Britain had lots of tanks: sending a few to Egypt was 'not heroic folly, but calculation'.[4]

The Americans did what they could in 1940, sending 500,000 rifles, 8,000 machine guns, 130 million rounds of ammunition, 900 75mm guns and 1 million artillery shells to the UK.[5] The weapons were sorely needed, and gave the British hope that they could defend their island. But it was not the stuff of a modern field army. One 75mm gun issued to the Canadians in October had '1878' stamped on the barrel.[6]

* * *

In 1940 the USA had little to offer except moral support. In mid-May, Churchill suggested to Roosevelt that 'the loan of forty or fifty of your older destroyers' would help. Throughout July, as the German Army consolidated along the coast of France and Belgium, Lord Lothian let it be known that Britain desperately needed the ships now to fend off invasion. Roosevelt, worried about the prospects for a third term, allowed the Century Group – a collection of well-connected Americans devoted to full aid to Britain – to work the public and the backchannels of Washington. Lothian fed the Century Group information about the sharp decline in British destroyer numbers, while a formal appeal from Churchill on 31 July threw the debate wide open.[7]

The very public discourse over the destroyers proposal lasted three and a half months: the British simply could not fathom the delay.[8] Wendell Willkie, the Republican candidate for President, broke the logjam when he agreed to craft the destroyer deal as an act in defence of America. Americans had long been frustrated by the proximity of British possessions in the western Atlantic looming over America's east coast. The USN had secured permission to use Trinidad, St Lucia and Bermuda to support their neutrality zone patrols.[9] Now, in August 1940, Roosevelt proposed to exchange obsolete destroyers for base rights in the Bahamas, Trinidad, St Lucia, Jamaica, Antigua and Guiana. As a token of good faith, the British also offered bases in Newfoundland and Bermuda. FDR signed the deal on 30 August.[10] The Americans got the best of it. It was not until late January 1941 that all fifty destroyers

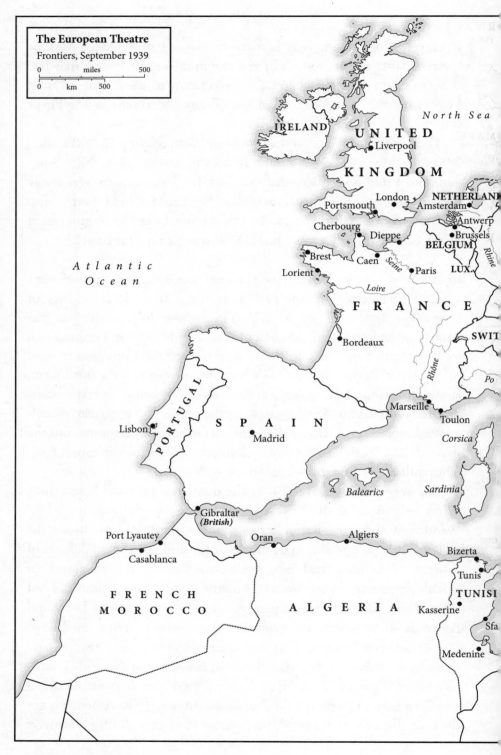

1. The European theatre.

were transferred.[11] Some went to sea immediately and did yeoman service. Many simply added to the burden on Britain's already over-stretched dockyards.[12]

In 1940 America's pressing concern was the narrow seas between west Africa and Brazil. Since the early 1930s the Germans had invested heavily in Brazilian coffee and cotton. This, in Adam Tooze's words, occasioned 'American concern about growing German influence in Brazil'.[13] With Vichy France now sympathetic to the Nazis, the shortest route for the fascists to the western hemisphere lay via French West Africa. Robert Sherwood wrote later of the almost insensible anxiety Americans felt about the fascist threat in the summer of 1940.[14] Bases in the Caribbean helped secure that vulnerability.

In fact, the destroyers-for-bases deal was part of Roosevelt's hemi-spheric defence plan. On 16 August he announced that talks were underway with Canada about North American defence. This was news to Mackenzie King, who received a phone call from Roosevelt later that day asking him to meet in Ogdensburg, New York, for a little chat. On 18 August the two leaders revealed the establishment of a 'Permanent Joint Board on Defense' of North America. It was both Canada's and America's first formal alliance.[15] The US media loved it. Robert McCormick saw the PJBD as the start of drawing British Dominions into an expanded United States.[16] This prospect alarmed the British Secretary of State for the Dominions, Lord Cranborne, who warned Churchill that the Ogdensburg Agreement had been signed 'without any reference to or consultation with us' and that it might 'drive a wedge between us and Canada'.[17]

With new bases and an alliance with Canada secured, in September Roosevelt introduced a scheme to conscript 1 million men for one year. This was unprecedented in American history, and Roosevelt had to 'work the system' to make it happen. Once again, Wilkie saved the day. 'I would rather not win the election', Wilkie told reporters, than oppose the act.[18] The Selective Service Act passed on 16 September, the day after the decisive defeat of German bombers in the skies over southern England, and the very day the massive Italian attack from Libya into Egypt stopped and started to dig in.

As America began to rearm, it began to renege on its contractual obligations to Britain. Between June and December 1940 the British invested as much in the American armaments industry as they had in their own in all of 1938.[19] But starting in September America began renegotiating contracts, and reducing shipments of machine tools. The British official history of *North American Supply* concludes that only 12 per cent of Britain's war needs (by monetary value) came from the USA in 1940: these were paid for in cash.[20] 'We have not had anything from the United States we have not paid for,' Churchill opined on 20 December, 'and what we have had has not played an essential part in our resistance.'[21] In fact, by the end of 1940 British capital investment had provided an enormous boost to American industry. By one estimate the British investment gave the United States as much as a year and a half head-start on their own rearmament. Without the kick-start provided by the British, Henry Stimson – Roosevelt's Secretary of War – admitted in early 1941, 'we would be in a very grave situation'.[22] The British hoped and expected to get something in return for all that investment.

The Americans not only got British investment, they also got access to the latest developments in British science and technology when Sir Henry Tizard arrived in September. Tizard was a brilliant scientist, and since 1933 had led British development of radar which culminated in the invention of the 'cavity magnetron'. In essence, the cavity magnetron produced powerful centimetric wavelengths, allowing high-definition radar to be miniaturised. Tizard brought the cavity magnetron and latest in British atomic research with him to America. James Phinney Baxter, author of the US official history of wartime scientific developments, described the cavity magnetron as 'the most valuable cargo ever brought to our shores'. His mission laid the groundwork for the highly successful Allied scientific research that lay behind victory in 1945.[23]

Not surprisingly then, Churchill had high expectations of the Americans. Roosevelt won the presidency in early November by a comfortable margin, and the Democrats also won control of both the Senate and the House. Churchill sent him an enthusiastic telegram of congratulations: 'I prayed for your success, and . . . am truly thankful for it.' Like many other Britons, Churchill anxiously awaited Roosevelt's announcement that the US was entering the war. 'Curiously,' Churchill wrote years later, 'I never received any answer to this telegram.'[24]

However, as Reynolds observed, the 1940 election did not really alter the strategic calculus of American domestic politics. And so Roosevelt continued to prevaricate.[25]

If anything, Britain's disappointment with the Americans in 1939–40 solidified Churchill's resolve to win the war without them.[26] On 8 December 1940 he announced his famous appeal to Roosevelt to 'Give us the tools and we will finish the job'. This was not hyperbole. So long as the war was confined to Europe and the Middle East, the British empire and Commonwealth expected to finish the job in 1942 without much direct American military help. God, it seemed, would help those who helped themselves.

* * *

As Churchill brooded over Roosevelt's inaction, the might of Nazi Germany was unleashed on the British people. On the night of 14–15 November waves of Heinkels blasted the city of Coventry. The initial incendiary strikes started a firestorm that provided a beacon for what Juliette Gardiner called 'the endless waves of bombers that kept coming all through the night'. They reduced Coventry and its 600-year-old cathedral to a smouldering ruin: 568 people died.[27] A few nights later the Germans hit Birmingham, starting nearly 600 fires. The destruction of civilian infrastructure left 20,000 people homeless.[28] By the end of 1940 cities from Aberdeen to Plymouth had been bombed: London 126 times, and the great western port of Liverpool nearly half as often. Some 18,000 people died in the first four months of the Blitz.

The bombing of British cities was routine fare in the American media in the autumn and winter of 1940–1. In part this was the result of the MOI's successful nurturing of a small coterie of American correspondents. Eric Sevareid of the CBS arrived in England after the fall of France with a decided dislike of the British, and doubted that they would stand up to Hitler. Life in London under the threat of invasion and German bombs changed that view entirely. When he was invalided home in October 1940, Sevareid spread the message about the importance of helping Britain. He was not alone. Edward R. Murrow, also of the CBS and perhaps the most famous American radio journalist of the war, broadcast regularly from bomb-scarred London and no American could mistake his sympathies. 'In their advocacy of the British cause,' Olson concludes, 'there was no question that Murrow and other American reporters in London were blurring the line between journalism and propaganda . . . Objectivity and neutrality had been mantras for CBS News from the beginning of the war . . . Murrow made mincemeat of that policy from the start.'[29]

By the autumn of 1940 Murrow and other Americans were openly working with the BBC on propaganda films, perhaps the most important of which was the ten-minute short *London Can Take It*, narrated by Quentin Reynolds, correspondent for *Collier's* magazine.[30] The film was released in Britain on 21 October and was an immediate hit. Warner Brothers in the US acquired it, and Reynolds used it during a speaking tour – without British titles or credits, just his name as narrator. An Oscar nomination followed the American release in December.[31]

Churchill worried about civilian morale, but he also knew that the suffering, the little victories and the careful crafting of myths were all essential parts of the greater propaganda war. Even the Blitz itself was mythologised for public-relations purposes.[32] In a globalised media market it was important that everyone, but especially Europeans under occupation and the dithering Americans, knew that *Britain* could take it.

In late 1940 Churchill's gravest concern was the impact of the German naval blockade: Britons needed to eat, but they also needed the sinews of war to continue the fight. The southern and eastern coast, especially the great ports of London and Southampton, were effectively closed by the Luftwaffe. It took nearly a year to reorient cargo handling, rail lines and manpower to the west, away from the immediate threat of air attack.[33] In the process, imports declined. There was a general tendency to attribute these declines directly to enemy action at sea rather than disruption at home, but there was no denying in late 1940 that the German noose was tightening. The U-boat attacks were part of a comprehensive German assault on Britain's lifeline. At the end of 1940 Britain really needed America's navy.[34]

* * *

The architect of the plan that 'saved' Britain and made Allied victory possible was Lord Lothian, who persuaded Churchill to lay bare Britain's situation and seek salvation from the Americans. And it was Lothian, upon his return to Washington in early December 1940, who 'sparked off a major press and political debate which obliged him [FDR] to act'. Reynolds concludes that it was Lothian's innate understanding of how the American political system worked – and the critical role of the press and media in the formulation of policy – that 'brought the issue to the attention of the opinion leaders and key policy-making groups whose support would be essential'.[35]

Roosevelt was already well aware that Britain was running out of US dollars and gold. But Roosevelt and others, not least Henry Morgenthau, the Treasury Secretary, believed that the British still controlled enormous wealth: perhaps as much as $18 billion in disposable assets. Had British sterling remained convertible the cash crunch would not have been serious. But the Americans wanted US dollars or gold. Roosevelt was also well aware of Britain's shipping situation. An internal British document, secured through the British Embassy in early December, confirmed what Americans suspected: losses to merchant shipping now outstripped Britain's ability to replace them, by a wide margin.[36]

Churchill's appeal to Roosevelt for help on 8 December 1940 runs to just 5,000 words. Eighty per cent of it is devoted to the U-boat peril, shipping losses and declining imports, and the prospect of the main German fleet – especially the new super-battleships *Bismarck* and *Tirpitz* – loose in the North Atlantic in early 1941. What Churchill really wanted was merchant ships and a decisive intervention in the North Atlantic by the US Navy to secure 'freedom of the seas'. 'Shipping, not men, is the limiting' factor in British strategy, Churchill observed. But ships were not what the American press at the time – and subsequent historians – latched onto. When Lothian returned to the USA in early December he is alleged to have told reporters, 'It's your money we're after.' If so, John Wheeler-Bennett was surely right: 'Never was indiscretion more calculated.'[37] This revelation spread across the American media like a prairie fire and forced Roosevelt's hand.

As Churchill explained, he wanted to attack Germany where 'the use of seapower and airpower' will allow its immense armies to be defeated in detail by smaller forces. 'For these reasons,' Churchill said, 'we are forming as fast as possible, as you are already aware, between fifty and sixty divisions.' In view of the lingering threat of invasion, Churchill pointed out that most of these divisions would be kept at home. Nonetheless, 'Even if the United States was our ally,' Churchill asserted, 'we should not ask for a large American expeditionary army.'[38] What Churchill wanted – immediately – was help with the Battle of the Atlantic.

Churchill could not control the agenda, not least because Lord Lothian suddenly died. Having drafted a speech slated for Baltimore and given a final polish to Churchill's letter to FDR, Lothian became drowsy and weak on Sunday, 8 December. His Christian Science beliefs forbade him from taking the simple treatments for uremic poisoning that would have saved his life. By Wednesday he was dead.[39] It is impossible to underestimate the impact of Lothian's death on Anglo-American relations, and on the fate of the British empire. Americans of all socio-economic groups felt some fondness for him. In Britain the news stunned those who knew the value of the man to Britain's war effort. Only the death of Churchill himself, one commentator observed, would be graver.[40] Walter Lippmann observed in 1942 that Lothian's death left 'an almost complete intellectual vacuum' in Anglo-American relations.[41] Lothian was given a state funeral at the Washington National Cathedral, and buried in Arlington National Cemetery.

Churchill eventually settled on Lord Halifax, the Foreign Secretary, as Lothian's replacement.[42] The awkward nobleman epitomised everything that Americans thought was wrong with Britain, and he took months (perhaps years) to find his feet. However, Halifax was perceptive enough to know that Britain was losing the public relations war in the USA and within weeks of his arrival in Washington was petitioning for change.[43]

Meanwhile, Roosevelt was furious with Lothian for stealing a march on him and forcing his hand. Like many senior American officials, Roosevelt believed that Britain was hoarding its wealth.[44] Churchill's abject appeal offered Roosevelt and Treasury Department Secretary Henry Morgenthau an opportunity to achieve two long-desired goals: recover the debt from the Great War and, in Darwin's words, 'blast the sterling empire open'.[45] Dan Todman is more blunt: Roosevelt wanted to 'defeat Fascism *and* imperialism, and to replace British with American power – which was exactly what he was doing as he manoeuvred to implement Lend-Lease'.[46]

Britain's position in the American public eye might have been improved in December 1940 had a concerted effort been made to trumpet the success of General Archibald Wavell's offensive against the Italians in Egypt. This was one of the great victories of the war, in which a small force of Australian and Indian infantry supported by British armour captured virtually all of Italy's African Army. But Wavell's victory failed to make a splash. The MOI declined to launch a PR offensive in support of Churchill's appeal. Rather, they urged 'delicate handling' and planned to confine 'our propaganda . . . to general statements and not attempt to specify the nature or extent of our requirements'. 'Is it not a scandal,' Emery Reves opined in a letter to Churchill on 20 December, 'that today the 11th day of our magnificent offensive in Africa, not one picture has been published in *The New York Times* about our victories?' The dearth of gripping British stories and photos left the front pages of American newspapers to the Germans.[47]

Prodded into action by Lothian's Baltimore speech (delivered by Neville Butler) and Churchill's appeal, Roosevelt now acted with uncharacteristic quickness. On 17 December he spoke to the Washington press corps that his plan was to 'eliminate the dollar sign', and used that now familiar phrase of lending a neighbour a garden hose when his house was on fire.[48] What Roosevelt promised Britain was unrestricted materiel support. In return, Morgenthau wanted an equally unrestricted commitment on the part of Britain to liquidate all of its assets in America – securities, investments and business ownership. Preliminary negotiations led to the seizure of British gold reserves and to orders to start selling off securities. When Roosevelt suggested that the British surrender their gold bullion sequestered in South Africa it was, William Manchester observed, 'an offer akin to a noncombatant lifting the boots and pocket watch from a dying trooper'.[49] When Churchill protested, Roosevelt told him that a USN cruiser was already on the way to get it. Attempts to seize Canada's gold, and that of France stored in Ottawa, were resisted.

To buttress the case for aid to Britain Roosevelt broadcast his second 'Fireside Chat' at the end of December. Reminding his listeners of the consequences of a British defeat, America, he said, needed to become '*the* arsenal of democracy'.[50] His choice of words prompted a quick response from British public-relations officials. They had in mind a publicity campaign emphasising that Britain, too, was an arsenal of democracy, and that through 'Reverse Lend-Lease' American forces would enjoy the benefits of British production and bases. Roosevelt's administration recommended against any mention of Britain's industrial effort – or the possibility that America might benefit from it – according to Wheeler-Bennett, in order 'to get the Lend-Lease Bill through'. The long-term effect was 'That America's pride in her industrial strength and mass production made them unwilling to hear of the industrial prowess of other countries'.[51] Americans would soon hear how they were doing it all, and all by themselves.

To further deflect criticism of the legislation, Morgenthau's office pushed Lend-Lease forward as a 'Bill Further to Promote the Defense of the United States'. It was introduced to Congress on 10 January 1941 with the number 'HR 1776'.[52] This was just a portent of the snubs to follow. Harold Ickes despaired of the attitude evident among many Americans, including some in Roosevelt's Cabinet. As he confided to his diary in late January, 'they are so ungenerous that they wanted to be perfectly sure that England was fighting naked, with bare hands, before they would be willing to go to her aid.'[53]

While the Lend-Lease debate went on, Roosevelt launched a series of intelligence-gathering expeditions to the UK. The first to depart was Harry Hopkins, Roosevelt's personal friend and long-time associate. Hopkins spent five weeks in the UK in January and February 1941, getting to know Churchill and the country, and was deeply impressed by both. Roosevelt instructed Hopkins to 'get an understanding of . . . the men he sees after mid-night'.[54] There were really only two: Brendan Bracken, soon to become Minister of Information, and Lord Beaverbrook, then Minster of Aircraft Production. Hopkins spent a good deal of time with Beaverbrook and may well have carried home with him the Canadian's jaundiced view of how the whole British system worked – or failed to – and how 'easy' it would be to return an army to France.

The path to Lend-Lease proved to be fraught for the British. The debate in Congress, in the American media and ultimately in the Senate lasted until mid-March. Clearly buoyed by victory in North Africa, on 8 February 1941 Churchill spoke in a broadcast directed primarily at

Americans, saying plainly, 'Give us the tools and we will finish the job.' American troops were not needed. 'In the last war,' Churchill said, 'the United States sent 2 million men across the Atlantic. But this is not a war of vast armies, firing immense masses of shells at one another. We do not need gallant armies which are forming throughout the American Union. We do not need them this year, nor next year; nor any year that I can foresee.'[55]

In the end, the debate in America over Lend-Lease had everything to do with domestic politics. While the Germans bombed British cities and sank their shipping, Republicans used the debate to attack Roosevelt. The Lend-Lease Bill, it was claimed, confirmed the dictatorial nature of his Presidency. As the *New York Times* reported on 16 February, the issue was 'primarily, not of aid to Britain, but the powers of the President'. The *Chicago Tribune* echoed the charge against Lend-Lease, opposing FDR's new grab for a 'dictatorship'. Senator Burton Wheeler from Montana famously protested that Lend-Lease would 'plow under every fourth American boy'.[56] Letters to McCormick from his readers in the mid-west made similar claims.[57]

The hyperbole of the American debate was softened somewhat by the knowledge that the British would pay this time – no reneging on this debt. For Morgenthau this meant getting the British to sell everything in the USA and strip their imperial assets bare to cover their costs.[58] Postwar accounting estimated that between the start of the war and the passing of Lend-Lease in March 1941, the British spent some $6 billion in the USA: building, buying and investing. The transfer of ownership of American munitions plants recently constructed with British money was fairly straightforward: the US government simply took them over for $46 million,[59] about one-tenth of their value.[60] Securities were sold for US dollars and their British owners compensated by their own government in sterling.

But Morgenthau also demanded that the British sell off their American companies, subsidiaries and branch plants. Britain was America's largest foreign investor, and British investment and ownership were deeply embedded in the fabric of the American economy. The firms cut across all industries. British-Dutch Shell was the largest foreign-owned corporation in the USA, and a critical part of America's fuel (including the new 100-octane aviation fuel), synthetic rubber and explosives industry. American Viscose, a wholly owned subsidiary of the British firm Courtaulds, was America's largest producer of rayon, other synthetic fabrics and parachute silk. It operated seven plants in the US and employed 18,000 people. Dunlop Tire and Rubber, and Lever Brothers (of soap and cosmetics fame), were British, as was Brown and Williamson Tobacco, and Decca Records. And the list went on. Disentangling these from their parent corporations risked losing much of their viability and their worth.

Morgenthau forced this part of his agenda when he announced to the Senate Foreign Relations Committee on 29 January that the British agreed to sell 'every dollar of property, real property or securities that any English [*sic*] citizen owns in the United States'. The public pronouncement of this intent came as a shock to the British. They responded by sending out Sir Edward Peacock, the Canadian Director of the Bank of England, to try to forestall the worst of the fire-sale.

Peacock protested that ripping the American part out of British multinational firms was much harder to do than Morgenthau thought, and in any event if Britain was to survive as a viable economic entity it would need its American investments. Morgenthau remained unmoved: America had no other rival than the British empire. On 9 March, two days before the Senate vote on Lend-Lease, Morgenthau gave Peacock an ultimatum. 'The British must stop procrastinating,' Mira Wilkins wrote, about the sale of their real property.[61] Peacock relented and negotiations began to find a buyer for the largest British owned firm in the US, American Viscose.

Roosevelt signed the Lend-Lease Bill into law on 11 March, but it was understood by senior officials in Washington 'that meaningful aid under that program was a year or more away'.[62] They were right. Even so, the British would always have to pay according to their means. British gold and dollar reserves were closely monitored by the Treasury Department, and when they exceeded $1 billion the British had to pay. How much could be squeezed from British assets in America was not resolved until May. As Kennedy concludes, 'the public spectacle of forced British sales in the early months of 1941 helped see the Lend-Lease bill through Congressional passage'.[63]

The sale of American Viscose was announced by Peacock on 16 March. It was estimated to be worth $100 million: it sold for $54 million. No other major British firm was seized in this fashion. Rather, an arrangement was formalised in June through the Reconstruction Finance Committee of the US government to essentially float the British a loan with their US companies as collateral. Some $900 million in British investment in America – not the $2.5 billion that Roosevelt and Morgenthau estimated for British investments in the US at the start of the Lend-Lease process[64] – was secured and so, too, was Britain's long-term supply of essential war materials.[65]

The cost was high. By May 1941 the Pax Britannica, in Darwin's words, 'was dead'.[66] Hitler's propaganda machine crowed about the British humiliation. Outwardly Churchill was grateful; inwardly he seethed, 'we are not only to be skinned, but flayed to the bone'. As one of Churchill's Tory colleagues put it, 'They are a quaint lot,' the Americans; 'if we lose the war they will be next on Hitler's list . . . and yet they seem quite content to leave the actual fighting to us: they will do anything except fight.' Benn Steil is emphatic in his conclusions about Lend-Lease. Morgenthau, Henry Dexter White (Morgenthau's Assistant Secretary) and Cordell Hull, the Secretary of State, 'would for years use Lend-Lease to press the British relentlessly for financial and trade concessions that would eliminate Britain as an economic and political rival in the postwar landscape'.[67]

* * *

Victory in the Western Desert in February 1941 was a much-needed tonic to the people of Britain, the Commonwealth and empire. Lester Pearson, on the staff of the Canadian High Commission in London, reported that the African victories 'cheered people up because it shows that not only can they "take it"; they can "dish it out" too. It also shows that we can wage the new warfare.'[68] But these North African victories, and the ones that followed in Sudan and Ethiopia against the Italians, captured little attention in the USA. As Sherwood observed, 'it was impossible to be greatly impressed by victories over Mussolini's reluctant legions, who were being subjected to a severe and humiliating mauling by the surprising Greek Army'.[69]

Moreover, what Americans saw in their newspapers' accounts was the empire at war, not Great Britain. Indian, Australian, New Zealand,

South African and African divisions played a prominent role. As Churchill had informed Roosevelt in his 9 December 1940 letter, Britain was husbanding its own troops at home to guard against invasion and to build divisions for expeditionary forces. This was not as self-serving as it sounds. The threat of a German invasion remained real in the spring of 1941. By early February senior American officials estimated that Germany would launch a 'desperate assault' on the UK within sixty to ninety days.[70] Nonetheless, for Americans the war news simply confirmed their belief that the British were once again fighting the war on the backs of their colonies. City editors of American dailies were only too keen to highlight the combat exploits of colonial and Dominion troops.

The Canadians were guarding Britain, too, and by early 1941 they were not happy about it. 'The troops are, of course, restless,' Pearson wrote to Grant Dexter, editor of the *Winnipeg Free Press*, on 10 January. 'It is difficult to maintain morale now that they are fully trained and equipped and nothing to do but train some more. Denied an opportunity of assaulting the Siegfried Line, I suppose it is not surprising that they occasionally assault the village pub or a local girl.' McNaughton was not happy either. In January 1941 during Exercise Victor, the guiding principle that Canadian formations could not be broken up and used piecemeal was, in John Swettenham's words, 'flagrantly disregarded'. McNaughton could not let this 'second' incident slip, not least because Brooke was only too well aware of Canada's policy following the Brittany affair in June. So on 31 January McNaughton visited Brooke to sort things out again. McNaughton's constitutional position was unassailable. According to McNaughton's recollection, Brooke got the point. The incident was recorded in Brooke's diary for 31 January as resolved amicably. But in fact, Brooke had no intention of surrendering authority over any Commonwealth or imperial troops. 'I quote this as an example of McNaughton's warped attitude to this Charter,' Brooke commented after the war.[71] The war effort of the Commonwealth and empire was to be 'British' and British alone.

That point was made abundantly clear to John Menzies, the Australian Prime Minister, during his visit to the UK in 1941. By late 1940 the Australian government knew little about what its divisions

4. Churchill's wartime Cabinet. Back row, from left to right: Sinclair, Alexander, Cranborne, Morrison, Moyne, Margesson, Bracken. Front row, from left to right: Bevin, Beaverbrook, Eden, Attlee, Churchill, Anderson, Greenwood, Wood.

were doing in the Middle East, or British plans for their use. 'According to Menzies', David Day wrote, 'the 'general feeling of [his] Cabinet' resented the British tendency to 'treat Australia as a Colony and to make insufficient allowance for the fact that it is for the Government of Australia to determine where and when Australian Forces shall go out of Australia'.[72]

What Menzies needed most by the winter of 1941 was clarity on Britain's commitment to Singapore and some Australian involvement in the higher direction of the war. His route to London took him through the Middle East, where he met with General Thomas A. Blamey, the Australian Imperial Force commander. Like McNaughton, Blamey was a distinguished Great War veteran, animated by the same desire to keep his forces grouped as a national contingent, as agreed with the British in March 1940. By the time Menzies arrived in Egypt

Blamey's troops were scattered all over the Middle East. 'If you give these English generals an inch,' Blamey warned, 'they'll take an ell.'[73] When Menzies met with Wavell he was told that the Australians and New Zealanders were now tagged for an expedition to Greece, and that this was done in consultation with Blamey. Jeff Grey concluded bluntly that 'Menzies was lied to'. Blamey had not been 'consulted in the manner suggested at all'. Under pressure for a quick decision and assuming that Blamey had already reviewed the plan, Menzies agreed to send Australians to Greece.[74]

Menzies then flew on to London 'in blissful ignorance of the crisis beginning to well up around him'.[75] Everyone knew that the expedition to Greece was a forlorn hope. As Sir Alexander Cadogan, the Permanent Undersecretary for Foreign Affairs, observed in his diary on 24 February, 'On all moral and sentimental (and consequently American) grounds, one is driven to the grim conclusion' that Britain had to fight alongside Greece. The reference to America was not idle. The Americans made it clear that they would back-fill for the British in the North Atlantic, to allow them to pursue their Mediterranean strategy. The knock-on effect was an expectation of help for the Greeks.[76] 'But it *must*,' Cadogan insisted, 'in the end, be a failure.'[77]

And so it was. One Australian and one New Zealand division, one British armoured brigade and a few RAF squadrons were never going to be enough. Meanwhile, the British position in Libya, now held by the newly arrived 2nd British Armoured and 9th Australian divisions, and one Indian brigade, was attacked by Rommel's recently arrived Afrika Corps on 24 March. Soon the Western Desert Force was in full retreat across Cyrenaica. A week later Iraq erupted in rebellion. Then on 6 April the German Second and Twelfth AGs, supported by the First Panzer Group and Hungarian and Italians forces, attacked Greece. Only in Ethiopia, where the Indian, South African and African divisions were fighting, did things go well for the British.

The unfolding tragedy in Greece and the relentless pursuit of the Western Desert Force by Rommel into Egypt, focused Australian attention on the failure of Menzies's mission to London. The British flatly refused to establish anything like the Imperial War Cabinet, which ran the final phase of the Great War, nor would they accept someone like

Menzies in the existing War Cabinet as a representative of Dominion interests. It did not help Menzies's cause that Canada had no interest in an Imperial War Cabinet. The Australian War Cabinet, David Day writes, was also bitter about the fact that Australians seemed to be carrying the burden of the fighting. 'The Australians looked enviously at their Canadian cousins, ensconced in the relative safety of Britain, and urged Menzies to press for their despatch to the Middle East.'[78]

By the middle of April the situation in the Mediterranean was dire. In the Western Desert the 2nd British Armoured Division (BAD) was a shattered ruin, and the 9th Australian Division was besieged in the port city of Tobruk. In Greece the 6th Australian and New Zealand divisions began evacuating on 23 April: 50,000 men were saved, leaving behind another 'mountain of wrecked equipment'.[79] Many of the troops, especially the New Zealanders, were taken to Crete, where they struggled to prepare the island against attack. All of this meant heavy losses to the Royal Navy at a time when no less than six British capital ships were undergoing repairs in US dockyards – generous support at a time when America was still technically neutral. Meanwhile, British forces in Iraq were under siege at Habbaniya airfield as a detachment of the Luftwaffe, staged through French Syria, arrived to help the rebels.

Fed up with British intransigence and their refusal to allow the Dominions a voice in the conduct of the war, and appalled by the Middle Eastern disasters, Menzies demanded that the British evacuate the Australians from Tobruk. Churchill urged them to stay and make a stand reminiscent of the Greeks at Thermopylae – an analogy not likely to endear him to Australians. Menzies persisted, and over the summer – at some cost to the British in lives and warships – the Australians were removed.[80]

At the heart of Menzies' dispute with Churchill in early 1941 was that there were simply too few British troops actually fighting. Even Britons themselves noticed. Jock Colville, Churchill's Assistant Private Secretary, recorded in his diary on 28 April that there was little in British newspapers about British troops in ground combat. '[T]oo much emphasis has been laid on the part played by Anzacs and New Zealanders. From the papers,' Colville noted, 'one would hardly suppose British troops had been fighting in Greece or Africa.'[81] Public perception was about right. Of the approximately fifteen divisions engaged in the Western Desert, Greece, Crete, Syria and East Africa in the spring of 1941, only three were actually British. For the moment, the British General Staff simply refused 'to let troops out of the country' for fear of invasion.[82] When Churchill complained to the Chief of the Imperial General Staff, Sir John Dill, about hoarding British troops at home, Dill set him straight. 'A successful invasion alone spells our final defeat,' Dill reminded the Prime Minister on 6 May. 'It is the United Kingdom therefore and not Egypt that is vital.' Churchill took exception to Dill's caution, but the British plan in the spring of 1941 was still to commit only three to four metropolitan British divisions for the Middle East and prepare eight to ten for expeditions elsewhere.[83]

All of this provided the Germans with a propaganda coup in America. Lord Halifax cabled on 24 April to advise the MOI and British Cabinet that the Germans were inflicting major public-relations defeats on the British day after day. After a three-week study of the American press and 'its effect on public opinion, so far as this can be estimated', the results were 'chiefly noteworthy for the conspicuous success which Dr Goebbels has obtained on the propaganda front'. Halifax warned 'that there has been an almost complete absence of concerted British countermeasures, and in consequence Germany has had for some days past a virtual free rein in this vital sector of the war front'. Not only was the German story presented in a more engaging and entertaining fashion, they had an effective 'monopoly' on published photographs. Much of Halifax's conviction of British press failure derived from the recent Associated Press Convention in New York, where an embassy representative talked to 'nearly one hundred proprietors and editors from all over the United States. Friends and enemies alike spoke to him about our failure to get the right material across in sufficient quantity at a moment when we should be doing our utmost to present our case in its most favourable aspect.'[84] Rather typically, the MOI responded that it was hard to sell defeats and, in any event, the problem was not their fault.

* * *

While America was not yet in the war, American military planners were deeply engaged in planning for it. Concurrent with the opening of negotiations over Lend-Lease in December 1940, a delegation of senior British staff officers arrived in Washington to hammer out the basics of a joint Anglo-American war plan.[85] The agreement they reached, 'American-British Conversations-1' (ABC-1), became the foundational document of the military alliance between Britain and the USA.

The genesis of ABC-1 lay in a series of scenarios developed in the fall of 1940 by Admiral Harold Stark, the professional head of the USN. Stark believed that the British were over-optimistic that they could beat Germany without a major land campaign, and only America could do that. As Mark Stoler points out, the introduction of a draft in September 1940, and the subsequent federalisation and mobilisation of National Guard divisions (of which more in the next chapter) laid the ground-work for a powerful US Army. 'Stark had accepted the close link between British victory and U.S. security,' Stoler observes. However, 'In this conflict, the United States would determine its own strategy for its own interests.'[86] American negotiators were issued a 'sharp warning' not to entrust 'our national future to British direction'.[87]

The ABC-1 agreement confirmed a 'Germany first' strategy. Everyone accepted that the Japanese could be easily contained until the war in Europe was finished. British attempts to draw the US into the defence of Singapore went nowhere, and Churchill ordered his team to drop the plea entirely. However, the US would retain the bulk of its fleet in the Pacific as a major deterrent to the Japanese. In pursuit of the Germany-first strategy, the US would begin to deploy its army in the North Atlantic area and prepare the USN to start convoying ship-ping. It was generally agreed that the USN would eventually assume primary responsibility for North Atlantic trade convoys.[88] As Matloff and Snell write, American representatives 'made it clear that, in their opinion, the security of the North Atlantic and of the British Isles was the common basis of American-British strategy, and that it was up to the British to do the best they could to take care of their interests else-where.' For the moment, however, there was 'no plan for employment of land forces in a major offensive against Germany'.[89]

Under the ABC-1 agreement the United States was to assume stra-tegic control over the western hemisphere from the mid-Atlantic west-ward across the Pacific. The British retained strategic control over the eastern Atlantic, Europe, the Middle East and up to an undetermined point on the far side of the world.[90] The Canadian government declined to accept the provisions of ABC-1 placing Canada under American strategic direction. A formal protest was made to the British reminding them that they could not make international agreements affecting Canada without Canadian participation and assent. Senior Americans officers understood this.[91] But they preferred to keep their relations with the 'British' – writ large – bilateral.[92] An annexe II to the ABC-1 agreement was added excluding Canadian territories and waters. A separate bilateral arrangement, ABC-22, was negotiated between the two North American countries.

* * *

The Lend-Lease Bill specifically rejected Churchill's appeal for help in the North Atlantic, one of the compromises Roosevelt made to get the bill passed.[93] For his part, Stimson was well aware that far from helping the British import crisis, Americans were actually contributing to it. By March 1941 labour unrest had increased the turnaround time for British ships in American ports from an average of five days to nearly twenty-five days. As he told his Cabinet colleagues on 8 March, that amounted to an annual loss of 1.8 million Gross Registered Tons (GRT) in British carrying capacity.[94] Had he known, Stimson might have added that that figure was nearly the equivalent of all Allied shipping losses to Germany's U-boats in 1941.[95]

Having been 'skinned and flayed to the bone', the British could have used the help at sea. The very week that the Lend-Lease became law, the German battlecruisers *Scharnhorst* and *Gneisenau*, along with the heavy cruiser *Admiral Hipper*, were trolling for convoys north of the Cape Verde Islands. They were supported by very long-range aircraft and U-boats from French bases. The new battleship *Bismarck* would soon join them. By March 1941 Churchill's worst fears were about to be realised, and Congress had seemingly tied Roosevelt's hands. On 29 March, Frank Knox, Secretary of the Navy, told FDR that the USN was ready to start escorting convoys from North America to Britain.[96] A few days later, on 4 April, Roosevelt ordered the transfer of three battleships, one fleet carrier, four cruisers and two destroyer squadrons from Pearl Harbor to the Atlantic.[97] They were due to arrive in late May. Then Roosevelt got cold feet. As he told Mackenzie King at Hyde Park on 20 April, 'convoying would be an act of war'.[98]

A similar paralysis affected Lend-Lease. In the days following the signing of the bill Roosevelt had promised swift action. 'Every plane, every instrument of war that we can spare now, we will send overseas,' FDR pledged on 15 March. 'But then,' Olson writes, 'nothing happened.' There was no executive power to force American industrialists to produce war materials. While Britain fought for its existence, American automobile sales were up by 35 per cent, refrigerators by 42 per cent and new stoves by over 51 per cent. As one unsolicited report on the failure of British propaganda efforts in the USA observed, 'The materials and skills workers used in producing these articles are precisely those required in the defence industries . . . In June of this year the defence industry in their entirety only accounted for 15% of the total U.S.A. production.'[99] Vilified in the mid-west press for 'the New Dictatorship' he was forging, an exhausted and ill Roosevelt was, in Harry Hopkins's words, still forced to be a 'consolidator of public opinion'.[100] Kennedy's assessment is less kind: FDR 'flipflopped, dodged, waffled and dissembled' his way through the spring and summer of 1941, to everyone's dismay.[101]

The agonising indecision of April carried forward into May, spurred by illness that virtually sequestered the President. Doris Goodwin wrote that 'Roosevelt was like a man staring into a fog'.[102] Pressed by Ickes, Stimson and Knox at a Cabinet meeting on 23 May to do something to help the British in the Atlantic, Roosevelt declined to act. The recent neutrality pact between Japan and the Soviet Union cemented the President's view that the Pacific could not be weakened: the transfer of major warships from the Pacific was cancelled. As for the Germans, Roosevelt 'was not prepared to fire the first shot'.[103] That day *Bismarck* and the heavy cruiser *Prinz Eugen* slipped through the Denmark Strait and out into the Atlantic.

The ageing battlecruiser *Hood* – nearly *Bismarck*'s weight and her rival in speed – and the newly commissioned battleship *Prince of Wales*, with dockyard workers still on board, caught up to *Bismarck* on 24 May. A lucky shot from *Bismarck* detonated *Hood*'s aft magazine, and the pride of the RN disappeared in a shattering blast. *Prince of Wales* sheered off, and *Bismarck* and *Prinz Eugen* continued their course into the Atlantic. For four days the world waited for the drama at sea to unfold. Then, on 27 May, Robert Post, the *New York Times* reporter who broke the news about *Hood*, filed an account of how the British hunted down and sank *Bismarck*. The victory over *Bismarck*, Post reported, 'is not a tale only of gallantry and courage at sea but also of excellent staff work and quick, effective action into which the British threw all the might of their sea and air power'.[104]

Roosevelt seized the moment. The day the *Bismarck* was sunk, he declared an 'Unlimited National Emergency'. A new Office of Civil Defense was being established, and measures taken to ensure the delivery of Lend-Lease goods to the UK. Among the latter was an extension and more rigorous enforcement of America's self-declared 'Security Zone'. The new zone shifted eastwards, from 60 degrees west to 23 degrees west, with a major extension to the north-east to encompass Iceland. American troops would soon garrison Iceland, while air and sea patrols – especially from the new bases in Newfoundland – vigorously watched the western Atlantic.[105] It was not quite what the British had in mind, but it was FDR's most emphatic statement of support yet. Robert Dallek described it as 'all but a declaration of war'.[106]

But there was no commitment to escort convoys. It was now that the Canadians came to Britain's rescue.

* * *

New British bases in Iceland in the spring of 1941 extended the range of anti-submarine escort of convoys to 35 degrees west. That left a gap in the transatlantic anti-submarine escort of convoys between 35 degrees west and the Grand Banks of Newfoundland. U-boat packs found that gap by mid-May. On the 20th the Admiralty asked the Canadians to fill it.[107] By May the RCN had roughly fifty ocean-going escorts available, most of them Flower Class corvettes built in Canadian shipyards. At British request, the 'Newfoundland Escort Force' (NEF) was quickly established at St John's. A steady flow of newly commissioned escorts followed for the rest of the year.[108] As the Commander in Chief of Western Approaches Command, Admiral Sir Percy Noble, put it, 'The Canadian Navy solved the problem of the Atlantic convoys.'[109] The New World had indeed come to the rescue of the Old.

Ottawa was also the North American regional centre of Britain's global naval control of shipping (NCS) and naval intelligence network, and ran a shadow network of 'Consular Shipping Agents' in American ports. Allied merchant-ship movements in the western hemisphere north of the equator were controlled from Ottawa. Information on arrivals, cargoes, departures, safe routes and Axis shipping, as well as Confidential Books and Secret Publications, flowed routinely throughout North America from Ottawa.[110] The first contacts between the USN and the RCN in the summer of 1940 dealt with naval intelligence and NCS, and the RCN helped the USN establish a 'trade section' in Washington. In the aftermath of the ABC-1 talks, naval liaison expanded, including the appointment of a Canadian Trade Liaison Officer to the US Navy Department.[111] In June a USN observation officer specialising in NCS was appointed to Halifax, and work was underway to integrate the USN into the British global NCS system.[112]

* * *

The quiet success of Britain and her Commonwealth and empire in waging war across half the globe apparently left the MOI with little to crow about in early 1941. Defeats in the Mediterranean, fighting the French in Syria, putting down a nationalist revolt in Iraq, or beating the Italians in the Western Desert and Ethiopia were not going to win the hearts of Americans. Nor indeed was trumpeting the small victories and great sacrifices of Dominion and colonial troops, such as the Australians holding out in Tobruk, much less the arrival of the Canadian Navy in sufficient numbers to complete the transatlantic escort of convoys.

By the spring of 1941 the British people were tired of the steady diet of stoicism coming from the MOI, and the lack of news of British victories – and victories by British metropolitan troops. After lunching with two senior civil servants on 4 June, Colville recorded in his diary that 'No 10 [Downing Street] was partly to blame for the inadequacy of our news and propaganda to the U.S.: the spokesmen of service departments are terrified of saying anything that might incur the Prime Minister's displeasure and so took refuge in silence.'[113] It was widely accepted that the MOI had failed miserably, both at home and abroad. Its message to stay calm and carry on was tiresome, and its overseas work uninspired. Lord Halifax was but one in a chorus of complainers. As Colville lamented in late May, the MOI was trying to woo German soldiers by broadcasting classical music, when what young Germans craved was jazz – a form of western music prohibited by the Nazis.[114] It was not until late 1943, with the establishment of the 'Black Ops' radio station 'Soldatensender Calais' that the British got around to this method of subversion.[115] By the spring of 1941 it was clear that the MOI was in need of a wholesale change. The so-called 'Battle of Bloomsbury', of which more in the next chapter, occurred that summer.

Meanwhile, the most successful penetration of American mass media at this stage was by the brilliant Scottish documentary filmmaker John Grierson, of the National Film Board (NFB) of Canada. Grierson believed that 'the international circulation of newsreels was one of the most powerful and important means by which a country makes itself known across its borders'.[116] To avoid being labelled a British propagandist, Grierson buried the British news in his popular series *Canada Carries On*, and more importantly in his *World in Action* series.[117] The latter was an enormous success, distributed to 7,000 theatres across the USA, part of a total of 15,000 American theatres that routinely showed NFB documentaries and newsreels. The *World at War* series film *Churchill's Island* won the Oscar for the best documentary of 1941.[118] As Cull concludes, Grierson 'plugged a gap in British film propaganda' and 'showed London how it should be done'.[119]

All that said, there was some reason to think that a massive new offensive by the Western Desert Force in June would redeem Britain's sagging fortunes. Churchill pinned great hopes on it. Wavell as Commander in Chief Middle East hoped to capture the escarpment west of Sollum: beyond that nothing was certain.[120] Operation Battleaxe was over in forty-eight hours when Britain's armoured force, operating largely without infantry or artillery support, was shot to pieces. It was clear that the British Army still had a great deal to learn.[121] The disappointment of Battleaxe, coming on the heels of Greece and Crete, piled injury onto a litany of woes: it had been a dreadful spring. There were renewed calls for a confidence vote in Parliament, and Churchill was muttering to his old confidant Lord Beaverbrook about resignation.

And then redemption came in the form of a tap on his door. Churchill was recovering from a long boozy evening with the new American ambassador John Gilbert Winant, the Foreign Secretary Anthony Eden and others. Much of the discussion was on the massive German build-up along the border with Russia; the press was full of it and had been for weeks. There was general agreement that America and Britain would come to Russia's aid. The next morning Colville stuck his nose into Churchill's room to tell him that Germany had invaded Russia. Churchill broke into a broad grin: 'Tell the B.B.C. I will broadcast at 9 to-night.' And then Churchill sent his valet to Eden's bedroom 'with a large cigar on a silver platter and a message' telling him of the good news.[122] In a heartbeat, everything had changed – again.

CHAPTER 7

THANK THE JAPANESE

'The Ministry of Information,' said Sprat defiantly, 'have shown great interest. They are only waiting for a successful operation to release the whole story to the press. Civil morale,' he faltered, '. . . American opinion.'

Evelyn Waugh, *Officers and Gentlemen*[1]

On 22 June, Churchill assembled a coterie of decision-makers at Chequers to help him shape the new policy towards the Soviet Union. Eden was already there, and so was the New Zealand Prime Minister, Peter Fraser – he had arrived to protest against the British use of his Dominion's troops in Greece and Crete. Sir Stafford Cripps, the British ambassador to Moscow home on leave, arrived before lunch, as did Viscount Cranborne, the Dominions Secretary, and Lord Beaverbrook, then 'Minister of State' – essentially a Cabinet minister without portfolio. Eden dashed away just after lunch to meet with the Soviet ambassador Maisky, but came back for dinner.

Beaverbrook, who historians – including Churchill – have written out of the story, was Churchill's confidant, and a force of nature with powerful influence on British domestic and foreign policy. Historians still cannot agree on whether his tenure as Minister of Aircraft Production was a success, but they all agree that he struck the government establishment like a thunderbolt. His work habits and tireless energy bewildered the staid British civil administration. He could interview several people at a time, take calls, correct memos and track it all in his head. By some measures, he tripled aircraft production in six months in 1940 and probably helped win the Battle of Britain – notions roundly dismissed as myths. There is widespread agreement, however, that Beaverbrook bruised egos and left a trail of resentment in his wake. Harold Macmillan, who served under Beaverbrook in the Ministry of Supply, concluded that he was 'half mad and half genius'.[2]

It may be, as Chisholm and Davie conclude, that Churchill wanted him in the government rather than scheming outside. In 1916 Beaverbrook had helped unseat Asquith and install Lloyd George as Prime Minister, and he had engineered Bonar Law's elevation to Prime Minister in 1922. Beaverbrook was an old friend, who had used his wealth and influence to foster Churchill's political career. But he was not to be trifled with. In 1941 Beaverbrook was 'undisputed lord of the press'. His *Daily Express* was the largest-circulation daily in the world, with 2.5 million copies sold. His *Evening Express* captured much of the evening readership, and the *Star*, featuring the cartoons of David Low, was popular with the working class.[3] Beaverbrook was a fierce critic of what he believed was the casual British approach to the war, and he was a trenchant critic of Churchill's peripheral strategy. For the Beaver the only way to victory was through France.

By the spring of 1941 Beaverbrook was ensconced at No. 12 Downing Street, with direct access to No. 10. 'Beaverbrook was one of the few people he [Churchill] sought out,' Chisholm and Davie conclude, 'and was always prepared to listen to, and by whom was invigorated.' Clement Attlee claimed that Churchill took Beaverbrook 'as a kind of stimulant, or drug'. He was the only one who could match Churchill's drinking and late nights, and who would argue endlessly with Churchill without recrimination or betrayal of confidence. Brendan Bracken, Churchill's other late-night drinking partner and confidant, commented to Colville that Beaverbrook took up 'more of the P.M.'s time than Hitler'.[4] All three were staunch Tory imperialists, with an unshakable faith in the enduring power of the empire. Whatever contemporaries and historians might say about Beaverbrook, there is no doubting his importance to Churchill and to the unfolding Anglo-American debate over strategy.

In the darkest scenario, and one not limited to the British, the German attack on Russia offered the prospect of another Nazi victory, and if that happened it made invasion in the spring of 1942 almost a certainty.[5] Beaverbrook's role in this gloomy drama was to provide optimism. He was, in David Farrer's words, 'ebullient, impatient of difficulties of delay, refusing to see obstacles, rejecting counsels of caution ... the breaker time and again of the pessimist front'.[6] Russia would endure, Beaverbrook insisted, and British help would matter. British salvation now demanded that all aid possible be shipped to Russia. Stafford Cripps's biographer Peter Clarke admitted that in the combination of Eden, Beaverbrook and Cripps the Prime Minister had collected 'probably the three most prominent pro-Russian figures in British politics'.[7] Churchill's broadcast that evening on the BBC reflected Beaverbrook's optimism and offered the Soviet Union a de facto alliance: 'The Russian danger is therefore our danger, and the danger of the United States.'[8]

* * *

The widening of the war brought little change in America's mood. Indeed, for many on the right the German attack on the homeland of Communism was good news. In any event, the civilian economy was booming, and industrialists had no interest in building tanks and military aircraft. In June 1941 there was still no clear plan (apart from naval construction) for American mobilisation, no idea of what to build, and for what purpose. The only thing that seemed certain to most Americans was that, at some point, a huge US Army would probably go to Europe to finish the job. As Kennedy says, FDR 'breathed no syllable about it to the public'.[9] But to mobilise America he needed a plan. And so, on 9 July 1941, he finally instructed the War Department to create one war. As Sherwood lamented, FDR 'believed in the policy of making haste slowly'.[10]

On 1 July 1941 the strength of the US Army stood at 1,326,577 officers and men. This was impressive, but the figure was an illusion. One million of those men were Selective Service Act conscripts from 1940 enlisted for only one year. There was genuine concern that if they were not released in October mass desertions would follow. However, if the army released them, expansion would have to start all over again.[11] The authorised strength under the state of emergency declared in June

1940 was just 375,000 personnel, in theory just enough to field sixteen divisions. The federalisation of the National Guard, which began in the autumn of 1940, allowed for a total of twenty-seven infantry, and four armoured and two cavalry divisions. Progress towards even this goal was much slower than Marshall wanted because Roosevelt kept giving away equipment, and American industry largely ignored political pressure to mobilise war production.[12]

Marshall's army faced other vexing issues. The lack of trained and experienced officers affected everything. As General Leslie McNair, appointed by Marshall to sort this all out, opined, 'Inadequately trained officers cannot train troops effectively.'[13] 'Officer Candidate Schools' began to appear in July 1941 to produce junior officers – the 'sixty-day wonders' who carried the burden of command at the lower level by 1943–4. But the problem did not end there. Division-, corps- and army-level staffs needed trained officers, so they in turn could train and mentor their subordinates.[14]

Part of the problem was that the American Army was still wrestling with fundamental doctrinal issues. The US Army prided itself as a force equipped and trained for attack, and what it saw in the recent campaigns in Europe reinforced the predilection for relentless movement. The 'Armored Force', established in response in July 1940, took control of all tanks, tank formations and supporting troops. As Greenfield and Palmer observe, from the outset the Armored Force was 'a strong autonomous organization', with its own board and schools under the firm direction of Brigadier General Adna R. Chaffee – an enthusiastic proponent of mechanisation described by the President of the Army War College in 1929 as 'visionary and crazy'.[15] For Chaffee, speed and hitting power exemplified the essence of America's offensive doctrine. 'With the blueprint of modern war provided by German operations', William Odom concluded, 'the army raced to revise its doctrine'.[16]

The Armored Force claimed responsibility for defeating enemy armour. The infantry divisions that made up the bulk of the army therefore lacked anti-tank guns, and, in any event, guns belonged to the artillery who seemed uninterested in the anti-tank role. The German defence against tank attack, as it turned out, was well-sited anti-tank guns. The slaughter of British armour during Operation Battleaxe confirmed McNair's belief in the need for a strong anti-tank capability.[17] His solution was the 'Tank Destroyer Force' built on self-propelled anti-tank guns. In the end, this proved to be very costly and for some analysts a misdirection of effort. The US Army never warmed to its towed anti-tank guns and so 'the tank remained the prime U.S. anti-tank system'.[18]

What is missing almost entirely from the literature on the expansion of the US Army after 1940 is its artillery. This reflects an interwar belief that artillery was primarily a defensive weapon, and over-reliance on it in the Great War was one of the key reasons for the stalemate. The 'new' war was all about manoeuvre and speed. Even the British, who had developed highly sophisticated artillery methods by 1918, had forgotten how important artillery was.[19] They were in the process of re-learning that lesson in a series of 'live fire exercises' against the Germans and Italians in the Western Desert. The weakness of the US Army's artillery would dog it throughout the war.

The doctrinal debate in the US Army in 1941 was dwarfed by the ambitions of planners. In July, Roosevelt instructed the War Department to plan for full mobilisation. The resulting 'Victory Program', signed off by Marshall in September, called for, in Mark Stoler's words, 'the creation of an army of 8.7 million men, organized into 215 ground divisions and a huge air force, to be used for a massive invasion of Europe no later than mid-1943'.[20] Clearly, once America got its hands on the war, there would be no dithering peripheral strategy.

The lethargic pace of American industrial mobilisation and the expansion of US armed forces meant that little military aid was sent to Britain in 1941. When Hopkins arrived in London on 12 July to coordinate a joint response to the wider war he found the British suspicious that the 'long-restrained hope of armed aid from America was a delusion'.[21] Of the $7 billion in Lend-Lease promised in March 1941, virtually nothing had arrived by mid-summer. 'We are deceiving people on both sides of the Atlantic', William Whitney, the American administrator for Lend-Lease in Britain wrote in his letter of resignation in July, 'by allowing them to think that there is today a stream of lease-lend war materials crossing the Atlantic, when in fact there is little or nothing'.[22] Most of what America had sent since March was powdered eggs and beans. Fortunately, American-built aircraft kept arriving, and so did critical alloys and chemicals for British war industry. The largest equipment shipment was 170 M3 light tanks, 'Stuarts' in British service, to Egypt. But for the moment, the arsenal of democracy was struggling to find its feet.

In contrast, Canada's war industry – already well developed – got a boost from Lend-Lease through an agreement worked out between Mackenzie King and Roosevelt at Hyde Park, New York, on 20 April 1941. Roosevelt agreed to purchase war supplies from Canada to offset Canada's cashflow problem, and to allow American goods, equipment and parts needed by Canada for its British contracts to be supplied under Lend-Lease.[23] The Hyde Park Declaration cost America virtually nothing, but it allowed Canadian industry to soar. In 1941 alone Canada financed and delivered to Britain $1 billion worth of military equipment and supplies: more than Britain received from the US in the first six months of Lend-Lease (and in proportion nearly twice what the Americans promised).[24] Canada produced over 120,000 military trucks and Bren carriers in 1941, making it 'the main source of mechanised transport for the British Empire'.[25] The Canadian Ford FG-T Field Artillery Tractor became 'the most widely used 4x4 tractor of the Second World War'.[26] By the end of the year Canada had produced nearly 500 million rounds of artillery and small-arms ammunition, over 1,300 field guns, and 17,860 machine guns – and production had only just begun; these figures would be dwarfed by the end of 1942.[27]

The key, for the moment, was keeping Russia in the fight. Hopkins told the British that America was prepared to extend Lend-Lease to the Soviets. The British agreed to tranship some of their own Lend-Lease aid to Russia and add to it from British production. All but thirty of 1,420 Canadian-built Valentine tanks, powered by reliable North American diesel engines, were soon on their way to Russia, where they proved to be a tough, versatile 'light' tank used until the end of the war.[28] To deliver these and other aid the British would now have to start running convoys to northern Russia, to Murmansk and Archangel, and open a route through Iran.[29] Roosevelt was ready to help make the Arctic convoys happen and build infrastructure in Iran. The USN was now to enter the fight in the Atlantic. In a broadcast to the British people before he departed for Moscow, Hopkins created, in Dallek's words, 'the impression, helped by British propaganda, that an inevitable clash of American arms with German naval forces in the Atlantic would bring the United States into the War'.[30] Churchill thought so, too.

* * *

Arrangements for America's entry into the shooting war were worked out at the new USN base in Argentia, Newfoundland, in August. Roosevelt and his Chiefs of Staff arrived aboard the cruiser *Augusta*; Churchill and the British Chiefs of Staff, joined by Hopkins, steamed in aboard HMS *Prince of Wales*. Beaverbrook, now the Minister of Supply, and Sir Arthur Purvis, the Scots-Canadian who ran the British Supply Council in New York, would arrive later by air. The Anglo-American meeting in Argentia was highly symbolic, and the irony was probably not lost on the attendees. The political and military brain-trust of the British empire had been summoned by the Americans to an American base in British territory. By the time *Prince of Wales* cast her anchor into Placentia Bay, the transition of power was well underway.

Churchill came with a list of objectives, which amounted to American participation in the war. The Canadians had resolved the problem of the North Atlantic convoys in May, but Churchill now wanted the USN engaged in these convoy operations to free British ships to run convoys to Russia. He wanted British and Canadian troops in Iceland replaced by Americans, and an American ultimatum to Japan to restrain its ambition in South East Asia. Roosevelt promised it all. American troops would garrison Iceland. The US Maritime Commission had established a pool of American merchant ships in Halifax to ensure that at least one was available to join every transatlantic convoy.[31] The USN would commit fifty destroyers to escort these 'American' convoys between the Grand Banks and Iceland. The first British convoy to Russia, Operation Dervish, had already sailed from Liverpool on 12 August, but with the British escorts released from the North Atlantic a regular series to Murmansk and Archangel could begin in September.[32]

For his part FDR had one major objective at Argentia: a statement of joint war aims that would serve him and America well. The 'Atlantic Charter', as Roosevelt's statement came to be called, championed 'the right of people to choose the form of government under which they will live' and restore 'sovereign rights and self-government to those who have been forcibly deprived of them'.[33] Churchill understood these words to mean the people living under Nazi oppression, and that they were largely 'symbolic and nothing more than a gesture by the two leaders, a non-binding piece of paper, ratified neither by Congress nor Parliament'. It only slowly dawned on him that the implications for the British empire were enormous. As Manchester and Reid conclude, 'That is exactly how Roosevelt, from the start, intended it to be construed.' The Atlantic Charter, 'an eight-barbed hook on which Roosevelt could reel in empires, evil or benign', was made public on 14 August 1941.[34]

As for drawing America into the fight, Lieutenant-Colonel Ian Jacob, Military Assistant Secretary to the British War Cabinet, noted that 'not a single American officer had shown the slightest keenness to be in the war on our side'.[35] They listened to the British explain why the Middle East mattered, and to their plans for defeating Germany. 'We do not foresee vast armies of infantry as in 1914–18,' Admiral Sir Dudley Pound the First Sea Lord made clear. 'The forces we employ will be armoured divisions with the most modern equipment.' Moreover, these forces would only be employed once conditions for a general uprising against the Nazi occupation had been achieved. Aerial bombing, a raiding strategy, and now the war against Russia would all contribute to a landing when, as Churchill informed FDR in July, 'the opportunity is ripe'.[36] At that point, 'Small forces, chiefly armoured, with their power of hard hitting, would be able quickly to win a decisive victory.'[37] The Americans were not officially opposed to British strategy: they just thought it would not work. Sooner or later, as one planning document concluded, 'we must come to grips with and defeat her [Germany's] ground forces and definitely breaking her will to combat.'[38]

Beaverbrook arrived in Argentia in the middle of the proceedings, and he might have returned immediately to Britain had Purvis not died when his plane crashed on take-off. To coordinate the delivery of war materials to the Russians, Beaverbrook carried on to Washington after the conference.[39] Churchill risked a great deal in sending the Beaver unsupervised. Beaverbrook was not only sharply critical of Britain's war effort and Churchill's peripheral strategy, he was an advocate for a

Second Front in France at the earliest possible time – perhaps even in the autumn. While in Washington Beaverbrook told FDR, an old friend with whom he shared New Brunswick connections, 'to start building landing craft on a large scale . . . Here already,' A.J.P. Taylor observes, 'was his first attempt to translate the Second Front into practical action.'[40] We can only imagine what else he said that might have confirmed American prejudices about Britain's war effort.

* * *

Beaverbrook's role was not the only thing that Churchill and Anglo-American historians left out of their accounts of the war. The agreement at Argentia to transfer convoy escort operations in the north-west Atlantic to the USN had profound implications for Churchill's vision of a united empire and Commonwealth. Canada already had major naval and air operations in the north-west Atlantic. Without any consultation, Churchill threw this all over to American control.

The liberty the British took at Argentia was more than Mackenzie King could abide.[41] This was 'how the British lose friends,' the Canadian Prime Minister confided to his diary.[42] Churchill arrived home from Argentia to find the Canadian PM on his doorstep. Mackenzie King did not come to the UK to start a constitutional battle, but that was the thrust of his visit. Canada's position was made clear to both Churchill and the British War Cabinet, especially at the meeting on 28 August: the day that Menzies was forced to resign as Australian Prime Minister. Mackenzie King was acutely aware of Menzies' efforts, since he had passed through Ottawa on the way home. Churchill's solution to this problem was to establish a council of ministers in London to act as a conduit between the British and the Dominions. Mackenzie King wanted none of it. Only the elected heads of the Dominions could speak for them. 'I added that the less it appeared that all matters were being settled by Cabinet sitting at Downing Street, the better it would be for the war effort of the several Dominions', Mackenzie King wrote in his diary: 'our people took their stand on the Statute of Westminster'. Mackenzie King was not so churlish as to demand a change to the command arrangements made at Argentia, but not for the last time he made it clear that Churchill's ambitions about the 'empire' were not shared by Canada.

Mackenzie King also brought a sobering message to the British War Cabinet. The Americans, he warned, were prepared to let the Japanese strike the British empire in the Far East, and they would not come into the European war anytime soon. Roosevelt had played both sides of the street: supporting Britain while telling the American people that he would keep them out of the war. As Mackenzie King warned Churchill's Cabinet, 'I did not think the British should bank on Americans coming in too quickly.'[43]

* * *

By mid-1941 every effort the British had made to convince Americans that they needed to join the war against fascism was a failure. Everyone in the information business seems to have known that. John Grierson said as much to the Canadian Club of Montreal as early as 17 February. The English, he observed, took for granted that others would accept the truth and honesty of what they said, but their passive information campaign was not working. In contrast, the Germans carefully crafted their message to the United States, presenting 'a calculated, impressive and positive picture' of Hitler and Nazism.[44]

The British response to the power of the German propaganda in the United States was finally to launch their own campaign. Beaverbrook, Eden and the Director of the Ministry of Information, Duff Cooper, were tasked in May to recommend how this might be done.[45] At that point, none of Britain's existing information organisations reached further west than Chicago, and none had a presence in Washington. Sir Gerald Campbell, the former British High Commissioner to Canada with extensive experience in America, was parachuted into New York in May to take charge. Campbell brought the British Press Service and the British Library of Information under a new umbrella organisation, the British Information Services (BIS).[46] He intended to open a BIS office in Washington and branch offices across the USA. Rather typically, the British Embassy objected to such overt public relations and forbade Campbell from opening the Washington office in a conspicuous place. So the BIS Washington office was opened quietly in July, so as not to alarm the Americans. As Wheeler-Bennett lamented, 'the task of launching a publicity bureau without publicity was not an easy one'.[47]

After a month taking stock, Campbell and Wheeler-Bennett set off for the UK in early July to make the case for a huge expansion of the BIS across the US. They arrived in the midst of the 'Battle of Bloomsbury' over the purpose and fate of the Ministry of Information. The MOI was ensconced in the new, and coldly austere, art-deco high rise, Senate House, at the University of London in the heart of the Bloomsbury district. Orwell used that building as the model for his 'Ministry of Truth' in *Nineteen Eighty-Four*. In the Second World War Britain's information war coalesced around Senate House. Beaverbrook had recommended to Churchill that the MOI either be vastly expanded and given real authority over the distribution of information, or that it be eliminated: 'piss or get off the pot'. By general consensus the MOI was a shambles. Sir Kenneth Clark, Controller of Home Publicity, described it in 1941 as 'a perfectly useless body'. Even the MOI Director, Duff Cooper, thought his organisation was 'a misbegotten freak'.[48] Significantly, Cooper got little cooperation from the military services. They refused to either let the MOI collect material from them, or allow the MOI to attach reporters to operational forces.[49] Cooper also got little cooperation from the Ministry of Economic Warfare, which was responsible for propaganda to enemy and occupied territories (through its Psychological Warfare Executive, PWE) or from the European Service of the BBC – both ostensibly under MOI direction.[50] And Cooper had precious little help from Churchill and the War Cabinet, neither of which backed him in the battle with the service chiefs over access to news. Even the public viewed the MOI as a failure.[51]

At Beaverbrook's urging Churchill replaced Cooper with Brendan Bracken, his Parliamentary Private Secretary. Bracken accepted, provided that Churchill backed him up. He did, up to a point, although the MOI never did resolve its lingering problems with the armed services which would haunt British press coverage of Operation Overlord three years later. The consensus among historians is that Bracken was a good choice to run the MOI. He went through the organisation 'like a dose of salts'. 'His tours of inspection were abruptly dramatic,' Andrew Boyle writes. 'From one office to another he went, introducing himself and saying, "Ah yes, you're Mr so-and-so. Well, you're out. The letter terminating your appointment is on its way." '[52] Bracken also began regular meetings with Eden (Foreign Office), Dalton (Economic Warfare) and Robert Bruce Lockhart, the PWE representative. Ian McLaine contends that Bracken made the MOI work.[53] That may be so. But Bracken, like his mentor Churchill and their drinking partner Beaverbrook, was a Tory imperialist. As we shall see, Bracken was more interested in unifying the empire and Commonwealth than pandering to the Americans.

Nonetheless, Campbell returned to America with £1 million and a writ to remodel British propaganda in the US.[54] Over the summer he reorganised and expanded the BIS. Five sub-sections and a number of 'Special Assistants' were established, and a new office opened in Chicago in August – the first of several planned across the US. The British would no longer shirk from propaganda. The previous mantra of 'Give us the tools and we will finish the job' shifted to a more direct 'We want the USN to help us finish the job'.[55] The gloves were off.

The second part of the British information counter-offensive in the US in 1941 was the launching of a covert attack on the German media and propaganda system in the US, and on American anti-war organisations which drew on German material and funds. This task fell to William Stephenson and his shadowy British Security Coordination, which in April began to identify and secretly support pro-British organisations, to root out and expose the Nazi supporters of America's anti-war movements, and expose treasonous activity by Americans. The BSC conducted its own espionage and counter-propaganda campaigns against America First leaders, speakers and meetings. Links to German money and agents were exposed in planted news stories. A scandalous level of fifth column activity was exposed, and in June Roosevelt closed all German consulates and agencies across the country. Perhaps the greatest coup of the BSC campaign was the revelation that members of Congress were using their postal privileges – free postage available to senators and Congressmen, known as 'franking', from the French *affranchir* ('free') – to distribute materials funded by German agents. Among the senior American Firsters tarred by the franking scandal was Senator Barton Wheeler, whose fiery rhetoric had accused Roosevelt's Lend-Lease scheme of 'burying every fourth American boy'. But Wheeler was not alone. The establishment of a Federal Grand Jury to investigate the franking scandal and the role of German agents in America kept the links between anti-war organisations and the Nazis in the news for years.[56]

Stephenson's secret war in the USA and the British shift to an overt propaganda campaign did not go unnoticed. Adolph Berle, the Assistant Secretary of State, and J. Edgar Hoover, head of the FBI, had Stephenson and the BSC in their sights by mid-1941. US authorities had been tracking Communist influence for years and were well aware from the Dies Commission of the scope and scale of Nazi influence. And as early as September the *Washington Star* was editorialising that propaganda from friendly nations was resented, too.[57] For the moment Stephenson had friends in high places. America possessed nothing comparable to the BSC: even the FBI paled in comparison to Stephenson's reach and ability in the US. William Donovan, a Great War combat veteran, former US Attorney and one of Roosevelt's secret emissaries to Europe, was particularly interested in the 'cloak and dagger' work of Stephenson's office. Between them they persuaded FDR to establish a comparable American organisation with Donovan at its head. The Office of the Coordinator of Information (COI) was set up in July in 1941 with the mandate to conduct foreign and domestic influence operations.[58] Hoover was furious over the establishment of a rival organisation to the FBI, while Berle took his concerns about foreign influence to the Justice Department, which began an investigation. A battle over control of all foreign information agencies and agents, including those of Great Britain, was soon underway.

The unsettling implications of the COI were further exacerbated in October when the Office of Facts and Figures (OFF) joined the fray. OFF's job was to sample public opinion and give 'Americans an accurate and coherent account of government policy'.[59] Roosevelt clearly wanted a slick spin on the work of the OFF. To run it he appointed Archibald MacLeish, the Librarian of Congress and one of the great American intellectuals of the age. America was an enormously diverse country, MacLeish observed, and an early OFF policy directive warned that 'It is not enough to make the full story available in Washington' or, one might add, New York or Chicago. 'The American people drew their ideas from a remarkably diverse array of what OFF officials called 'information channels', Justin Hart writes. 'The complexity of these channels reflected the vast range of interest groups and identity politics in the United States. As OFF analysts recognised, "in this country we do not have a homogeneous society. We have a nation of groups".[60] This view was shared by Wheeler-Bennett, who observed that prior to Pearl Harbor America 'was a playground for spreading discord'.[61]

'MacLeish's staff – one of the most erudite groups in Washington', according to Sydney Weinberg – 'was hand-picked and noted for intelligence, integrity and ability'. It was their job to explain to Americans why they would 'have to fight the coming war'.[62] Like the BIS, the OFF operated on the premise that only by telling the truth could the message be accepted to its best advantage.[63] The reach of the new American propaganda machine became global in the fall of 1941 when Donovan recruited a Hungarian, John Houseman, to start broadcasting shortwave on what became 'The Voice of America'.

For his part, Donovan was primarily interested in the 'Foreign Information Service' of COI, run by Robert Sherwood. Like MacLeish, Sherwood was an intellectual, author of several Pulitzer Prize-winning stage plays, speech writer for FDR and, like many who now joined the COI, committed to the social-justice ideals of the New Deal. Sherwood was also a combat veteran of the Great War, who was wounded while serving in the Canadian Corps. Like MacLeish, Sherwood believed that – in Justin Hart's words – 'the prevalence of "Nazi lies" had created a vacuum, even a hunger, through many parts of the world for any sort of credible information'.[64] This set Sherwood immediately at odds with Donovan, who wanted to use 'black' propaganda – contrived lies – to subvert and reshape foreign public opinion. The major intellectual and political differences between Donovan's conservative black-ops side and Sherwood's New Dealers in the OFF created tension from the outset.

Lost in all the discourse over the various players and organisations emerging in America's information war in 1941 is the coalescing of a direct challenge to British global dominance of the moral high ground. 'Between June 1941 and June 1942,' Hart writes, 'the Coordinator's Office played a major role in the creation of a worldwide propaganda program.'[65] America and Britain were now to clash in a battle over the hearts and minds of those they were fighting to free.

* * *

The USN entered the shooting war on 17 September 1941, when five USN destroyers took over convoy HX 150 south-east of Argentia. With that America assumed operational and strategic control of the north-west Atlantic. The U-boats were there, too, concentrated well inside America's neutrality zone. A few days earlier they had intercepted the slow convoy SC 42, sixty-five ships escorted by a Canadian force south of Greenland. Poorly trained and badly equipped, the escort was over-whelmed. 'The battle lasted for days,' Patrick Abbazia wrote, 'a moving red glow against sea and sky: sixteen merchant vessels were sunk.'[66] Canadian and British reinforcements arrived and sank two U-boats: American destroyers arrived too late to help.

The Admiralty and Naval Service Headquarters in Ottawa under-stood that defence of trade rested primarily on avoidance of the enemy using good intelligence and evasive routing. Essential wartime rhetoric lauded the close escort as the first line of defence, but it fought only if everything else failed. It was the system that mattered. By 1941 the flood of Canadian corvettes allowed the whole transatlantic system to operate, but the results were not often pretty. Commissioned and trained in haste, Canadian corvettes lacked rudimentary skills and basic equipment. The tiny cork-like corvettes seemed to spend so much time immersed in the sea that American sailors joked that the Canadians ought to get submariner's pay. The agreement reached in Argentia assigned the fast convoys to the USN's destroyers, leaving the plodding and vulnerable slow convoys to the Canadians. Canadian shortcomings drew the ire of seasoned British officers and did little to impress the Americans with 'British' efficiency. Indeed, all the British rhetoric about the fundamental importance of escorted convoys seemed to pale in the face of what Americans witnessed in the north-west Atlantic in the autumn of 1941. The experience would profoundly influence the USN's response to the U-boat assault along their coasts in 1942, and the fate of Britain's own merchant fleet.

At the heart of Britain's war strategy was the belief that the German will to resist could be broken, just as it had been in late 1918. By 1941 part of that strategy was attacking civilian morale from the air. This, as it turned out, was the great German fear about war in the west: an inability to withstand an enormous aerial onslaught by the

Anglo-Americans.[67] So far British raids on German cities were small and achieved little. By mid-1941 the RAF wanted a fleet of 4,000 heavy bombers to strike German cities every night: no rest. If that happened, the Germans – unlike the stoical British – would break. The RAF could win the war in 1943.[68] Churchill was not so sure. But he was content to give the RAF its head on this, and the 4,000 heavy-bomber programme was approved.[69]

While all this was being discussed in the late summer, the German offensive in Russia slowed noticeably. Some speculated that they had reached their limits. It was during this relatively quiet period that a major US–UK mission travelled to Moscow for talks with Stalin. Beaverbrook and Roosevelt's special envoy for Lend-Lease, Averell Harriman, agreed before leaving that they were going there to give Russia what it needed to survive. And so they did. 'Time and again,' Taylor wrote, 'Beaverbrook gave up Britain's share of American supplies so that it could be allotted to Russia.'[70] Harriman supported Beaverbrook's generosity by signing a deal for $1 billion in Lend-Lease aid, which exceeded his brief. Beaverbrook and Harriman promised 400 aircraft and 500 tanks per month before the summer of 1942, as well as machine tools, equipment and raw materials. Todman concludes that Beaverbrook's insistence that 'British deliveries were kept up, was the one thing during the whole war that Beaverbrook got right'.[71]

Not surprisingly, Beaverbrook and Stalin also discussed the possibility of a Second Front. Stalin's demand for a landing in France had been a persistent theme of Soviet propaganda since July.[72] British trade unions – now free to support the Communists openly – clamoured for immediate action. So, too, did Beaverbrook's papers: the *Daily Express*, the *Sunday Express* and the *Evening Standard*. Beaverbrook had submitted a paper to Churchill in early September, supported by Eden, urging immediate action. By Stalin's estimate, the British now had thirty divisions ready for combat. Somewhere along the 2,000 miles of enemy coastline they could force a landing – and stay there. As the Canadian diplomat Charles Ritchie lamented in his diary on 18 September, 'There is only one question of any real importance at this moment. Everyone is asking "Why can't we make a landing in France or Italy or Greece?" '[73]

Beaverbrook came back from Moscow fired by the need to open a Second Front. The urgency in doing so became clearer in October as the Germans renewed their advance. Beaverbrook pressed hard for a Second Front – now – and for further increases in military supplies for Russia. The latter put him in direct conflict with Ernest Bevin, the trade-union boss who was also Minister of Labour. Beaverbrook believed that Bevin was part of the problem. He would not force the unions to work harder, and was reluctant to bring more women into the workforce: still one million women short of where it had been in 1918. To push his agenda Beaverbrook urged Churchill to give control of labour and production to one minister, himself or Bevin. He knew that Churchill could never choose Bevin. Once again rumours swirled of threats by Beaverbrook to resign because the British were dawdling instead of taking the war seriously. The contretemps was sufficient to elicit a protest from Lord Halifax in Washington that Beaverbrook's latest shenanigans were 'being used to make mischief here'. In the meantime, Beaverbrook pressed relentlessly for a Second Front. 'Right or Wrong, I follow you,' Beaverbrook told Churchill in late October. 'But I am a victim of the Furies.'[74]

At a minimum something needed to be done to convince the Germans that a landing in the west was a possibility. British radio propaganda was busy creating that expectation,[75] while Churchill pressed the Chiefs of Staff to land as soon as possible in Norway. Plans for a landing at Trondheim were shot down by the Chiefs of Staff on 12 October. Unless the British could control the air, everything would fall apart – as it had in 1940, and in 1941 Greece and Crete. From the perspectives of the COS (and subsequent historians), the Trondheim operation died there. But Churchill was not yet done.

A week or so after the Chiefs of Staff dismissed the Trondheim scheme, a 'limp looking McNaughton walked into [Brooke's] room and literally poured himself into my armchair!' McNaughton had spent the weekend at Chequers with the Prime Minister. Two late nights and heavy drinking had left McNaughton exhausted and 'dumbfounded'. Churchill wanted McNaughton to send the Canadians into Trondheim. Mackenzie King had given McNaughton wide discretion in August to accept tasks for the Canadian Army, but McNaughton threw this back to his Prime Minister. Churchill immediately appealed to Mackenzie King.

5. Behind Brooke's back: General Andrew McNaughton and Winston Churchill scheming at First Canadian Army headquarters, March 1941.

By the fall of 1941 McNaughton commanded a force large enough to make a Canadian operation against Trondheim plausible. The 1st and 2nd Canadian Infantry divisions were 'hard, thoroughly trained and burning for action', and they had performed well in the recent Exercise Bumper.[76] The 3rd Canadian Division, the 5th Canadian Armoured Division (CAD) and the 1st Canadian Armoured Brigade (CAB) were also now in the UK. These were the parts of the 'First Canadian Army' which McNaughton was building. The Canadians constituted a major part of the combat-ready forces in the UK, and they were – in a legal sense – independent of the British COS committee. Not for the last time, Churchill tried to use the Canadians to do an end-run around his own chiefs. Brooke noticed. In 1941 it was Trondheim, in 1942 there would be more 'mad plans'.

McNaughton was able to allay Brooke's concerns about Trondheim: the Canadians would not go. In fact, McNaughton remained focused on France. When Brooke pressured McNaughton to have the Canadians relieve a British corps in the anti-invasion role in Sussex, McNaughton agreed on one condition: 'that in assuming the role of a static corps, the claims of the Canadian Forces to form the spearhead of any offensive [in France] would not be forgotten'. Brooke agreed.[77] McNaughton's small, but highly mechanised and modern army was just what the British envisaged dealing the final blow to a Germany tottering on the brink of collapse. By the autumn of 1941 McNaughton could tell reporters – and the world – that 'The Canadian Army is a dagger pointed at the heart of Berlin.'

For their part, the British service chiefs were appalled in late 1941 by what Beaverbrook gave away in Russia and were in no mood to entertain notions of a landing in France – or anywhere else. In addition to rebuilding an army for home defence and expeditions, the British spent the summer rebuilding their army in the Western Desert (now designated the Eighth Army) in preparation for a major offensive in November, and were obliged to build yet another army (the Tenth) to defend Iraq and Iran – and British oil – should the Russians collapse. There was a limit to what could be done.

Throughout autumn Churchill pushed General Claude Auchinleck, Commander in Chief of the Middle East, to start his long-anticipated Egyptian offensive, and relieve the siege of Tobruk. Auchinleck refused to be pushed. It was critical to get it right this time, not least because the MOI needed a victory to trumpet. Moreover, success in North Africa might be followed by a landing in Sicily, which could be sold as a Second Front.[78] In the meantime, Britain had to secure herself against the possibility of a 'supreme onslaught' of fifty or sixty battle-hardened German divisions in the spring of 1942. Unlike the Russians, Britain could not trade space for time.

Auchinleck's Operation Crusader, launched on 18 November, proved to be the most fiercely contested battle of the desert war so far. The newly constituted Eighth Army remained an 'imperial' force, its infantry predominantly South African, New Zealand and Indian, and its armour British. Of the 450 tanks employed, 165 were the new American M3 Stuart light tanks. The heart of Operation Crusader was the three armoured brigades of the 7th Armoured Division. The openness of the

Western Desert still encouraged a predilection for speed, and tanks operating 'independently'.[79] As Correlli Barnett put it succinctly, the plan 'was based on seeking and winning a decisive tank battle'.[80] It also reflected the current vision of how the final thrust against a defeated Germany was expected to transpire on the continent: a campaign of modern, fast-moving armoured forces.

The auguries for British success were good. Attacks on Axis supply convoys to Africa, interdiction by the RAF and Rommel's inability to open Tobruk as a forward port limited Axis fuel and ammunition supplies. There was reason to hope that the Axis could be driven back to Tripoli. Certainly, the American Army liaison team, which helped the British adapt to the M3, felt optimistic. Major Bonner Fellers noted that despite problems of training, supply and cooperation with the RAF, 'the unquestioned courage' of the British plus their 'air superiority and tank strength will win a decisive much needed victory'.[81]

Other Americans shared Fellers's optimistic view of the British in the autumn of 1941. Eugene Meyer, editor of the *Washington Post*, was hosted in the UK for two weeks in October. Typically for a high-profile American visitor, he was shown around and dined with the powerbrokers. His talk to the *Post* staff after his return to Washington provides unique insights into the view of the British by some informed Americans on the eve of the Japanese attack on Pearl Harbor. The English, Meyer explained, are sharply critical of themselves and everyone else, 'as you know . . . there are a lot of things that come over as news to us in the nature of self-criticism that really I think are exaggerated'. It was a warning that contemporaries – and subsequent historians – needed to hear. As for Churchill, his popularity was 'unassailable'; the only dissenters were the Communists, who wanted a Second Front. On that Churchill refused to move. Meyer paraphrased Churchill saying, 'a few men over [to France] would be ridiculous, and to send a lot would be disastrous'. Very little American news got through to the average Briton, Meyer informed his staff, but in any event, the British were not dwelling on 'our entry into the war'. Churchill had his scenario mapped out: Germany would be worn down as she had been in 1917–18 and then – as in November 1918 – she would collapse in ruin.[82]

* * *

In late 1941 Churchill's scenario for the unfolding of the war considered everything except the Japanese. Like Nelson at Copenhagen, he put his telescope to his blind eye and carried on. British reluctance – in fact inability – to commit anything substantial to deterring Japan had, of course, been the reason for Prime Minister Menzies' demand that Australian troops be relieved in Tobruk and sent home. The occupation of French Indochina by the Japanese in July spoke to their willingness to feed on shattered European empires. Anxiety to stop that lay at the root of Churchill's plea to Roosevelt at Argentia in August for the Americans to warn the Japanese not to attack British possessions. Roosevelt declined to do that. But America imposed economic sanctions on the Japanese, including an oil embargo. It was not clear how far the Japanese could be pushed. The Secretary of State, Cordell Hull, wanted carrots as well as sticks.[83] The German assault on the Soviet Union raised the anxiety level over Japanese opportunism, although revelations from the Japanese diplomatic cypher (intelligence codenamed Magic) suggested that they were focused south, towards the oil fields of Borneo.

One way to temper Japanese ambition was to keep General Chiang Kai-shek's Kuomintang army in the fight. It was supplied by the west through two routes. The high-profile Burma Road, a sinuous mountain track to Yunnan carved out of the wilderness by 200,000 Chinese labourers, was delivering roughly 3,000 tons a month by 1941 to the Kuomintang. A similar volume of supplies also reached Chiang's army in its main operational area of Hunan via a much shorter and easier route through the British colony of Hong Kong. Churchill had been adamantly opposed to reinforcing the Hong Kong garrison. The German attack on Russia changed that: it was critical to keep the Japanese fighting in China and off Stalin's back.

When the former commander of British troops in China, Major-General A.E. Grasett, a Canadian in British service, passed through Canada on his way back to Britain in the late summer of 1941 he pitched the idea of Canadian troops reinforcing Hong Kong. It turns out that Lieutenant-General Harry Crerar, Grasett's classmate from the Royal Military College of Canada and now Chief of Staff of the army, had done a major study of the defence of Hong Kong at the IDC in 1934,[84] and he needed little convincing. The formal British request was made on 19 September, and the Canadians quickly offered two battalions.[85]

Roosevelt, too, was interested in reinforcing Hong Kong.[86] In the early autumn his economic advisor, Canadian-born Laughlin Currie, came to Canada looking for ammunition and more besides for Chiang's army. Currie had leverage. Some 25–30 per cent of the steel used in Canada's burgeoning war industry came from the US, which already had a steel shortage. Currie got the Canadian ammunition, plus 15,000 Bren light machine guns for the Kuomintang.[87] As Dave Macri concludes, the Canadian government's China policy was made in Washington by Roosevelt. In November, the Canadian reinforcement plan was expanded to include another battalion, a brigade headquarters, field artillery and engineers.[88]

The British government also agreed in October, after intense pressure from Australia, to send capital ships to Singapore. The choice was agonising. Britain only had fifteen battleships and battle cruisers: five were in refit, and six were too old, too slow or too vulnerable to send. It was not much to work with. On 20 October it was agreed that the *Prince of Wales* would go, joined later by the battlecruiser *Repulse*.[89]

Meanwhile, negotiations between the Americans and Japanese dragged on without resolution. Throughout all of this Roosevelt kept Churchill largely in the dark. The British were unaware that the Americans were reading the Japanese diplomatic code, and, according to Reynolds, 'failed to grasp the hardening of US policy in late 1941 and the way this provoked rather than deterred Japan'.[90] It did not help that American bluster was not matched by a show of force. American possessions in the western Pacific were virtually defenceless. Plans were hatched to send out more US troops and modern equipment, and retrain the Philippine Army. A squadron of B-17 heavy bombers was sent to provide the garrison with a long-range strike force. Stimson put great faith in the deterrent value of America's heavy bombers.[91]

* * *

By the time that the first two Canadian battalions settled into Kowloon in late November it seemed that Sir Alexander Cadogan's prophecy from 1934 was coming true: the Americans were fickle and unreliable allies, who 'can never deliver the goods'. Certainly, Beaverbrook – still the Minster of Supply – felt that way. US production was 'falling into confusion', Taylor writes in the Beaver's biography. 'Deliveries to Russia were in arrears. The Americans were keeping for themselves supplies that they had promised to Canada and Great Britain.'[92]

As for Churchill's fervent hope that actually fighting the Germans in the North Atlantic would push FDR to declare war, that never happened. When the USS *Greer* was attacked by a U-boat east of Newfoundland on 4 September, Roosevelt went on the radio to inform the American people of the incident and issue a stern warning to the Axis that Americans would fight back. Their ships did, but that did not mean America was at war. Not even the torpedoing of the destroyer *Kearney* or the sinking of the USS *Reuben James* – in which 115 sailors died – in October prompted Roosevelt to declare war.

Lord Halifax conveyed Roosevelt's dilemma to Churchill in mid-October: FDR could not secure a declaration of war against Germany. Although the Democrats enjoyed a solid majority in the House and Senate, the Southern Democratic caucus, which held the whip hand, was notoriously unpredictable. As evidence of Roosevelt's problem, it proved almost impossible to keep the 1 million men drafted in 1940 under the Selective Service Act in the army. To have cut them loose would have seriously impaired the Victory Program. The bill to extend their service had been approved on 7 August by a single vote, thanks largely to the Southern Democrats.[93] Confrontation with U-boats in the North Atlantic did not change that. For the moment, Roosevelt was content to secure the 'northern' and 'southern' approaches to the western hemisphere against any Axis threat. With Iceland now occupied by American troops and the USN deployed in force in the North Atlantic, FDR instructed the US Army to prepare plans for a landing in French west Africa.[94]

In the meantime, America was in no mood for war, and many had already had enough of foreign propaganda, including that now emanating from the Britain. It would seem that the MOI plan in 1940 to use Americans reporters to sell the British story in America was a success. When Henry Hoke, a well-known advertiser and author, complained in late 1940 about rampant German propaganda one of his detractors told him, 'You have the nerve to complain about German propaganda, when half our radio commentators spew out volumes in praise of the British.'[95] According to Cull, by the late summer of 1941 'The interventionist culture reigned all but unchallenged: the British publicists and their American allies had won the day'.[96]

However, the intrigues of Stephenson's BSC, including the distribution of false documents designed to manipulate American opinion, had caught the attention of Adolf Berle in the State Department. Berle resolved to end all foreign propaganda, but especially British. Berle used a young State Department employee to ferret out the details of the British information network, and then designed legislation specifically targeting it. By November legislation was in the US Senate to amend the Foreign Agents Registration Act (FARA) of 1938 which would shut down every British information and public relations agency except the embassy in Washington. This 'unfriendly act', as Wheeler-Bennett politely described it, confirmed for many what they already suspected: 'that British prestige had suffered monstrously during the interwar years as a result of much political and academic propaganda in the United States'.[97] Buoyed by their friends in high places and the expectation that Roosevelt would veto the legislation, the British carried on. However, the battle over the revision of the FARA was not over until March 1942. In the meantime, the British propaganda campaign in America was on notice.

It was in this climate of mounting uncertainty that Japanese carrier-based aircraft attacked the USN fleet at Pearl Harbor in the early hours of 7 December. Within hours attacks spread across the Pacific, including the Philippines and Hong Kong. On hearing the news, Lord Halifax quietly ordered a bottle of champagne. He really ought to have informed Churchill, since no one else did. Churchill was late switching on the 9.00 p.m. BBC news and just caught the tail end of the announcement. It was left to his butler to confirm the Japanese attack. Churchill immediately telephoned Roosevelt. 'We are all in the same boat now,' the President exclaimed.[98] Churchill later said that he slept soundly that night for the first time in the war. 'So we had won after all.'

This was not quite true. Roosevelt's position on the European war remained unchanged: armed neutrality and an undeclared shooting war in the Atlantic. 'This,' Kennedy writes, 'was precisely Churchill's worry, and it was not easily laid to rest.'[99] Days clicked by without a declaration of war on Germany. Finally, on 11 December Hitler declared war on the United States. America was in. Britain and the United States were once again allies in a great war against the German empire – although for years to come many Americans could not imagine why.

Book II

PARTNERS

Book II

CHAPTER 8

GYMNAST TO RUTTER

[I]t is considered that the principal target for our first major offensive should be Germany, to be attacked through Western Europe . . . WPD further believes that, unless the plan is adopted as the eventual aim of all our efforts, we must turn our *backs* upon the Eastern Atlantic and go, full out, as quickly as possible, against Japan.

US War Plans Division Memorandum, 25 March 1942[1]

The western Allies expected to contain the Japanese in South East Asia. Nothing prepared them for what followed. When *Prince of Wales* and *Repulse* followed the American battle fleet to the bottom of the sea on 10 December, there was not an Allied battleship afloat between San Francisco and Africa. Then, on 18 December, Italian frogmen sank *Queen Elizabeth* and *Valiant* with limpet mines in Alexandria harbour. In just three weeks most of the American battleline and fully one-third of Britain's battlefleet was lost. The early success of Operation Crusader in the Western Desert was the only good news during that gloomy December. That, too, soon faded. By 20 December, Brooke admitted that 'hopes of carrying on with the conquest and reclamation of North Africa are beginning to look more and more impossible every day'.[2] The British march on Tripoli stalled once again at El Agheila.

There is a tendency to see Britain's steady rejection throughout 1942 of American desires to land somewhere on the coast of France as evidence of weakness. There is some truth in that. But students of the Second World War are wont to forget that in the months after December 1941 there was only one Great Power actually waging a global war: Great Britain. British forces were fighting on land, sea and in the air from the Arctic Ocean to the jungles of Malaya. The fact that Great Britain and her empire were able to do all of this suggests strength rather than weakness.

* * *

While the Japanese ran rampant across the western Pacific and South East Asia, Churchill was on his way to Washington. An eight-day brutal winter passage aboard the *Duke of York* allowed Churchill and his staff to solidify their strategy and prepare polished briefs for the first meeting with their new ally. Among the entourage was Field Marshal Sir John Dill, recently replaced as CIGS by Alan Brooke. Brooke had forced Churchill to appoint Dill, who Churchill found 'unimaginative and obstructionist',[3] to Washington as the key British permanent staff representative. Dill's charm, integrity and professionalism wooed his American counterparts. Brooke later claimed Dill's appointment to Washington as 'one of my most important accomplishments during the war'.[4] Churchill also brought along Beaverbrook, who was, Churchill wrote later, 'as usual in times of troubles optimistic'. The Beaver also knew, better than anyone else, the industrial potential of both Britain and the US, and he would employ his usual guile and directness to push the Americans to do more.

The British had five objectives at the Arcadia conference: confirm the Germany-first strategy; deflect American enthusiasm for an immediate descent on France; draw the Americans into the defence of the Middle East; entice the Americans to help defend Singapore; and push the Americans into producing more of everything. All but one of these objectives were accomplished.

The British found America utterly unprepared for war – materially or psychologically. America had not yet mobilised, and Lend-Lease had faltered to the point where Canada's rapidly expanding industry threatened to out-produce American production. Only aircraft production and shipbuilding, much of it initiated and funded by the British, were starting to boom.[5] Wheeler-Bennett commented that Americans were stunned by being thrust into a war which they fervently hoped to avoid. More alarmingly, isolationists and Anglophobes believed that the British had once again engineered American entry into another British imperial war (more on this below).[6]

No one knew better than senior US naval and army officers that America was unprepared. The Joint Board Estimates of 11 September 1941, which outlined the initial production targets for US industry and an army of 10.5 million men,[7] clearly revealed American strategic intent. There was no chance of revolution in Germany, the estimate concluded, 'until Germany is upon the point of military defeat'. That required a 'sustained and successful land offensive against the center of German power'. George Marshall's massive army would provide that force. In the meantime, the British strategy of blockade, bombardment and attrition would have to do.[8]

Meanwhile, America's effort was focused on securing the lower forty-eight states and its own empire, including the Philippines, Hawaii, Alaska and the Panama Canal. By January 1942, 600,000 American troops were committed to the defence of the western hemisphere.[9] Four divisions, the 32nd, 34th, 37th Infantry and 1st Armored, were earmarked for garrison duty in Iceland and Ireland: most of these were at 30–50 per cent of establishment. American ability to move troops globally was severely restricted. In January 1942 the US had the capacity to transport 25,000 troops at a time. By the summer that figure might rise to 60,000 – three divisions – hardly sufficient to take on the Wehrmacht.[10] For the moment, British troopships were heavily employed reinforcing the Far East. But soldiers needed equipment to train and fight: in 1942 there was little of that to be had.

The Arcadia Conference lasted from 22 December until 14 January 1942. The basics of western Allied strategy were affirmed, and the infra-structure for the command and control of the western Allies' war effort was established. Agreement was reached quickly on some basic issues. 'Germany first' remained the priority: only Germany's defeat would bring the others down. Getting the USAAF into the air over western Europe was one way America could help quickly. American staff officers needed little persuasion that holding the Middle East was key to ensuring ultimate Allied victory. As Ashley Jackson demonstrates, the oil fields of

Iraq and Iran fuelled the British war effort, especially in South East Asia. German advances in Russia put these at risk. It was also necessary to secure Iran as a conduit for Lend-Lease supplies to Russia. Throughout 1942 the British scrambled to assemble combat formations in Iraq and Iran to defend them.[11] American help came in the form of engineers and labour in Iran, while US Army combat formations assigned to Iceland and Northern Ireland released British divisions for deployment to operational theatres.

The toughest issue faced at Arcadia was what to do in Europe in 1942. 'Ten million American soldiers', Trumbull Higgins wrote, 'would necessarily mean a real cross-Channel invasion' on a scale which Britain could never hope to match.[12] Churchill had anticipated this and tackled it in one of his major position papers. Echoing his words of 1941, Churchill wrote that 'It need not be assumed that great numbers of men are required' for the final invasion of Europe. An elite, highly mechanised force of 600,000 Anglo-Americans, backed by 1 million support troops, supported by a general uprising of Europeans, would suffice to finally defeat Germany. Churchill proposed to launch this operation in 1943.

Marshall and his staff were deeply suspicious of Churchill's intent. US Army strategic doctrine derived from a long educational dependence on Baron Antoine Jomini's classic Napoleonic interpretation *The Art of War*. For Jomini, war was a function of military operations guided by scientific principles, primarily the concentration of mass against weaker enemy forces at some decisive point.[13] If landing in France with a huge continental army was the only the way to actually defeat Germany, then like the Meuse–Argonne campaign of 1918, the Americans were prepared to attack as soon as they could get everyone into line. Dwight D. Eisenhower, still a staff officer in Washington, opined in the aftermath of Arcadia, 'We've got to go to Europe and fight – and we've got to quit wasting resources all over the world – and worse still – wasting time.'[14]

At Arcadia the coat had to be cut to fit the cloth, and both Churchill and Roosevelt had to consider the wider politics of the war – something that Jomini's concept of war ignored. So if they 'had' to do something in 1942, they agreed that it should be North Africa. There were good military reasons for doing that, although most senior US Army officers could not think of any. Many, like Marshall's Anglophobic personal advisor General Stanley Embick, were opposed to anything that smacked of support for British interests.[15] Embick advised Marshall to have the British abandon Libya entirely and concentrate on stopping the Japanese. And, in Mark Stoller's words, he warned Marshall that London's entire Mediterranean approach was motivated 'more largely by political than by sound strategic purposes'.[16]

In fact, Roosevelt had entertained thoughts of occupying French North Africa for some time. Caribbean bases were secured from Britain in 1940 to guard against the impact of a Nazi seizure of French North Africa. The combination of German airpower and the remnants of the French Navy posed a significant threat from the French base at Dakar. But nothing had come of Roosevelt's instruction in October to the War Department to plan a landing in French North Africa. Stimson and Marshall, Lord Halifax reported, 'thought that he [FDR] was going off the deep end'.[17] Roosevelt revived the idea of occupying both the Azores and Dakar during his pre-conference discussions with US senior military staff on 21 December. When Roosevelt broached the idea to Churchill during their informal meeting on the 22nd the die was cast. Churchill's first memorandum for the Arcadia Conference argued for the occupation of North Africa. On Christmas Day FDR ordered the War Department – again – to start planning.

In light of the US Army's subsequent enthusiasm for an assault on France in 1942 it is interesting that Marshall's planners found the prospect of landing along the undefended coast of French North Africa in 1942 too risky. This was especially so given the lack of aircraft carriers to provide full air coverage. If the US Army was going to go, Marshall wanted nearly 400 aircraft landed as soon as possible to provide coverage: he did not want 'an American version of Greece'.[18]

Nor did Churchill. But Churchill wanted the Axis eliminated from North Africa altogether. The British already had a plan codenamed 'Gymnast' to land perhaps as far east as Tunisia, and crush Rommel and the Italians between two forces. As British fortunes in the Western Desert and in the Middle East faltered, the urgency to do something in North Africa mounted. American staff planners remained unmoved.

North Africa was just a distraction. But Roosevelt was adamant about a landing in North Africa and the British could only agree.[19] 'Super Gymnast' (soon redubbed just Gymnast), with an American landing in Morocco and the British inside the Mediterranean, would go ahead sometime in March 1942.[20]

At Arcadia it was also clear that the Allies needed more – much more – of everything. Beaverbrook urged Roosevelt not to follow the 'casual' British approach to expanding war industry.[21] As he told Roosevelt, 'Anything I can do [in the UK], you can do better.'[22] Beaverbrook's biographers credit him with encouraging America to become the massive producer of war materials that it was by 1944. But here the British were pushing on an open door. Roosevelt's own industrial planners had reported that the current guesstimations of war supplies were – in Jim Lacey's words – 'just sufficient to start waging major offensive operations in 1943'. To actually win the war, and especially to 'reenter the continent of Europe in 1944', the Victory Program would have to nearly double.[23] Roosevelt had the expanded figures at his fingertips. When he presented the Victory Program to Congress on 7 January 1942 he stunned politicians and planners alike by announcing increases in the previous industrial targets by an average of 50 per cent, and that these would double again for 1943.[24]

The prod that Beaverbrook gave to American war production was nonetheless one of his most important contributions to winning the war.[25] It helped that he shared – and perhaps fostered – the Americans' view of the British. 'Their practice of war is dilatory,' Eisenhower wrote in his diary on 5 January, with evident frustration. The Beaver also persuaded his American friends to divert war material slated for Britain to Russia, in order that Britain could keep the promises he had made in Moscow the previous autumn. This drew a sharp rebuke from Churchill in front of the Americans, which embarrassed and angered Beaverbrook. He retreated to his hotel and immediately submitted a letter of resignation.

Churchill's falling out with Beaverbrook in Washington was about more than resource allocation. Beaverbrook was steadfastly against a landing anywhere except France in 1942: a sentiment he shared with senior American officers. The bone thrown to Beaverbrook and the Americans at Arcadia was the prospect of a descent on the French coast in 1942 (Operation Sledgehammer) if things suddenly went very badly for the Russians, and a firm commitment to land in France in 1943 (Roundup) regardless. This, at the least, gave Marshall and his planning staff a target, and offered the remote possibility of a Second Front in 1942.

Arcadia also established the command-and-control infrastructure of the western Alliance. It was agreed to manage the war from Washington through an Anglo-American 'Combined Chiefs of Staff' (CCS). The new structure included the American Joint Chiefs of Staff (JCS), plus Dill and senior members of the British Joint Staff Mission. The CCS typically met once a week. The British had envisioned a kind of management committee, but Marshall increasingly took charge of the CCS. After the war Brooke lamented that there was 'no reason why at this stage, with American forces totally unprepared to play a major part, we should agree to a central control in Washington'.[26] But it was highly unlikely, given the parochial and xenophobic nature of American military officers, that they would have accepted anything else.

Establishing the CCS also made it easier to limit the number of players involved in the higher direction of the war.[27] With European governments-in-exile loitering around London it would have been difficult to exclude them from decision-making, especially the French. The Anglo-Americans extended this exclusivity to the allocation boards established for the pooling and distribution of war equipment and materials. The latter had little meaning or impact for most junior alliance partners, but it had huge implications for Canada – whose war production was already large and still growing. The Canadians fought a frustrating and largely fruitless action to have a say over the distribution of their production. The Australians arrived in Washington in early 1942 expecting to have a say, too. As Brooke noted in his diary entry for 22 January, he wished them 'Good Luck!'

* * *

There was little good luck in the months following Arcadia. By the end of January, Japanese forces had pushed the Philippine Army and the American garrison onto the Bataan peninsula and the island fortress of Corregidor. Landings in Malaya isolated Singapore, and Japanese troops poured into Burma. Two Australian divisions were at sea in the Indian

Ocean in the midst of all this. They were the last Australian formations withdrawn from the Middle East at Menzies's insistence, and the last available trained and experienced Australian divisions. While Churchill asked the new Australian Prime Minister John Curtin for permission, he ordered the troopships to Rangoon. Curtin was furious, and got the troopships pointed back to Australia. As Manchester and Reid concluded, the incident merely confirmed for Curtin 'the very arrogance he had ascribed to war planners in London'.[28] Instead, the British 18th Division was shifted from India to Malaya, and eventually to Singapore. It was not much.

Worse followed. On 21 January Rommel and his Italo-German desert force counterattacked the tenuous British position in Libya. By 7 February, Rommel, his own supply lines stretched, was finally stopped at Gazala. The rest of February was even more embarrassing. By 8 February, Japanese troops landed on the island of Singapore. Then on 11 February the German battlecruisers *Scharnhorst* and *Gneisenau*, the heavy cruiser *Prinz Eugen*, and six destroyers left Brest and made a dash for home through the English Channel. The British could not stop them. As *The Times* lamented, 'Nothing more mortifying to the pride of sea-power has happened in home waters since the 17th century.'[29]

The sense of calamity was palpable. 'I have during the last 10 years had an unpleasant feeling that the British empire was decaying and that we were on a slippery decline!!' Brooke wrote on the day of the Channel dash. 'I wonder if I was right?' Singapore's ignominious surrender on 15 February stunned the world: 62,000 British, Australian and Indian troops marched into captivity. It was the single greatest military defeat in British history.[30] 'If the army cannot fight,' Brooke lamented three days later, 'we shall deserve to lose our empire.'

The events of early 1942 provoked a crisis of confidence in Churchill's leadership. Britons were fed up with defeats, and tired of news broadcasts that masked the extent of the disasters.[31] Rumours flew that Sir Stafford Cripps, back from service as ambassador to the Soviet Union, would replace Churchill as PM. Churchill was forced to shuffle his Cabinet in mid-February. Beaverbrook became Minister of Production, and Cripps joined the War Cabinet as Lord Privy Seal and Leader of the House in

Parliament. Then, as Churchill was wont to do with his rivals, he sent Cripps overseas – in this case on a mission to settle the India problem.

As for Beaverbrook, he lasted barely twelve days in his new portfolio. Typically, he demanded complete control of everything, including labour (Aneurin Bevan's portfolio) and shipbuilding, the preserve of Lord Leathers. When he did not get it, Beaverbrook resigned on 26 February. Clementine Churchill warned her husband that 'this microbe . . . this bottle imp' would now work against Churchill's interests.[32] Clementine was right. Within a month Beaverbrook – nursing his respiratory problems in the warmth of Florida – warned Churchill that he and his newspapers were poised to open a full-scale campaign against the government's reluctance to provide all support possible to Russia, and to launch 'an expedition to Europe' as soon as possible.[33] The bottle imp was loose – or so it seemed.

* * *

Many in America shared Beaverbrook's estimation of Britain's casual and bungling approach to the war and were content – even in the hour of their ally's gravest crisis – to push the British empire into collapse. Robert Brand, writing in the *Round Table* in December 1941, summarised the problem well. 'Justly or unjustly the British have a hard row to hoe in the United States. The History of American foreign policy is in the main a struggle with the British, and suspicion is more easily aroused against them than any other nation.'[34] In part, the renewed attack on Britain in early 1942 arose from its association with Roosevelt and all that he stood for: bigger government, the New Deal and internationalism. The coming of the war did little to dampen calls to check the rise of the President's powers, get government out of business and social welfare, bring the boys home, and let the world fester in its own corruption.

In early 1942 American dissenters were aided and abetted by a sophisticated Axis propaganda campaign that targeted opposition to the war and anti-British sentiment. The advent of radio, in particular, allowed Axis propagandists to feed American prejudices with considerable accuracy. 'Axis radio is again picking up speeches, editorials and other comment in the United States to show lack of unity in this country,' Donovan warned FDR on 18 February 1942. It 'Recently picked up Senator Wheeler's anti-British and isolationist speech . . . America is unprepared and British have made little use of military supplies from USA.'[35] What Donovan revealed was a feedback loop, in which Axis media used open-source reporting to reinforce its own message to Americans.

The scope and success of the Axis propaganda campaign was tracked by the Canadian Legation in Washington, which began sending Ottawa reports on 'Fifth Column Propaganda' in the USA in early 1942. The fourth report covering the period from 15 February to 1 March noted a sharp drop in American faith in Britain's war effort: down from 65 per cent to nearly 50 per cent. This was attributed to the defeats and humiliations of early February, especially the fall of Singapore. As a result, there were now

> signs of a whispering campaign against Britain reputedly heard in high circles at Washington but circulated also in many parts of the country. This campaign has, as its theme, the contention that the British Empire as such is breaking up . . . there is even evidence of an ambition to relegate Britain, in American eyes, to about the same position as Italy occupies in relation to Germany – a weak vassal of little importance except for her fleet and her strategic position.[36]

The sixth Canadian Legation report covering 8–22 March was more emphatic about the connections between American 'Fifth Columnists' and Axis propaganda. Public attacks on both Churchill, 'the mouthpiece of the Judeo-English villains', and his likely successor Sir Stafford Cripps, followed 'closely the line laid down by the Axis radio during the same period'. 'Britain was portrayed as not only a decadent power, but one which – having bled her dominions and other countries for all she could get – now washed her hands of them and left them helpless.' The 'abandonment' of Australia garnered a great deal of Axis propaganda attention, as did British India. 'What has England ever done for you,' Berlin radio asked Americans on 12 March, 'that you should want to save her from her fate?'[37]

'The greatest and best assets of the Axis', the fifth report concluded, 'continue to be *The Chicago Tribune*, and its cousins *The New York Daily News* and *The Washington Times-Herald*, and the Hearst press'. The *Chicago Tribune* was, of course, Robert McCormick's flagship paper. The *Washington Times-Herald* and the *New York Daily News* were run by McCormick's cousins, Eleanor 'Cissy' Patterson, and her brother Joseph Medill Patterson. Together they acted as a syndicate, swapping stories and editorial content. As for William Randolph Hearst, he 'has long done the work of a fifth columnist' and had recently graduated to 'the class of Axis apologist' in a series of articles suggesting – as the Quakers had done – that America might share some of the blame for starting the war in the Pacific.[38]

None of these major papers, in the end, were as 'dangerous as the reptile press of the [h]interland' – *Social Justice*, the *Galilean*, the *X-Ray*, *Publicity* and others. *Social Justice* was the mouthpiece of Father Charles Coughlin's right-wing movement that modelled itself after Francisco Franco's fascist Catholicism: stridently anti-Semitic and anti-Communist. His weekly radio programme captured 'nearly a quarter of the U.S. population'.[39] On 9 March *Social Justice* wilfully distorted Lord Halifax's recent remarks that Britain was defended by 3 million soldiers, some 2 million of whom were Home Guard who also worked full-time in war industry. *Social Justice* reported this as 2 million soldiers keeping British workers at their lathes and benches. 'Is the English labouring class so riled and dissatisfied that top sergeants and privates with small arms at their belts are required to maintain order and efficiency?'

The focus of much American and British diplomatic and public-relations attention in the winter of 1942 was India. The fact that the Indian Army was the core of Britain's Middle East and Far Eastern military effort simply stoked the American belief that Britain was once again fighting its war to the last colonial soldier.[40] It was not clear that the Congress Party would fight to keep the Japanese out. Worse still, several thousand Indian POWs had joined the fight against Britain, and major defections might follow. Cripps arrived in India in February with a new proposal: complete freedom for India to decide its own fate after the war, which would include the recognition of a Muslim state of 'Pakistan' within the new Indian state. The Congress Party remained adamantly opposed to autonomy for the Muslims, and now refused to cooperate unless it was given a say in how India was to be defended. Talks collapsed in April amid outbursts of violence among Congress supporters.

The fate of India was tracked closely – if not always well – by the Americans. As John Charmley observed, in the late winter of 1942 there was much clamouring in America for Indian independence, and some fear in British circles that the Americans would claim a mandate over India under the proposed United Nations.[41] Lord Linlithgow, the British Viceroy in New Delhi, opined that there was 'no immediate solution' to the Indian problem. As Charmley claims, the Americans assumed that there was a solution to every problem.[42] Roosevelt went so far as to appoint a 'special Representative', Louis Johnson, to help draw up an offer to the Congress Party and mediate the negotiations. When the negotiations failed and FDR proposed that the Americans get further involved, Harry Hopkins had to endure a two-hour 'string of cuss words' from Churchill.[43] Educated Indians were not so naive as to believe the Axis shortwave propaganda, but the British needed to offer more. Then a free and independent India would mobilise and fight.[44]

Americans remained convinced that the British were lying about their intentions in India. Moreover, it was India – more than any other part of the empire – that tainted Britain and the legitimacy of the war itself. If the British had any doubts about where some influential Americans stood, they had only to read the supplement in the April edition of *Fortune* magazine, 'An American Proposal'. The postwar world would be led by the United States: it would be great if the British got with the plan. 'America has a unique chance to redress the shortcomings of the British system,' the article claimed, 'while continuing its best and most liberal traditions.'[45] 'The most vocal representative of this strain of American thought,' according to John Charmley, 'was the Vice President, Henry Wallace.' 'Continued British domination over India, in Wallace's understanding,' the editor of Wallace's diary observed, 'violated the whole purpose of the war.' As Lord Halifax reported in June 1942, Wallace believed that America was 'the chosen of the Lord ... divinely inspired to save the world'. 'Increasingly,' Charmley writes, 'American politicians referred to "imperialism as part of the evils which the United Nations are fighting to abolish".'[46]

The assault on Britain's rule in India by the American liberal press coincided with increasing scrutiny of America's 'negro problem' and clamouring by Americans of colour to be treated in accordance with the Atlantic Charter. In the southern states the 'Jim Crow Laws' effectively denied Black Americans their constitutional rights, while the white-controlled justice system failed to protect them from capricious violence. 'The more I hear,' Lord Halifax said of the 'negro problem' in his diary on 8 March, 'the more I resent their criticism of us in India.'[47] Halifax wanted to hoist the Americans with their own petard. But the politics of the war effort stayed Halifax's hand. Lend-Lease depended on keeping the Southern Democrats happy.

That said, the British scored a notable public-relations victory in March when the amended Foreign Agent Registry Act was signed off by Roosevelt. Once Britain and America were allies in a common cause, much of Adolf Berle's opposition to British information operations in America melted away. Throughout the winter the British were actually invited to participate in redrafting the legislation in ways that favoured their efforts. Even so, anyone who wished to speak on Britain's behalf had to register as an agent of a foreign government. Axis propaganda, run clandestinely through a network of agents, did not have this problem. Nonetheless, the British hoped to build on this small victory. Aubrey Morgan was sent out to run the main BIS office in New York, and soon established a BIS presence in Boston, Seattle, Los Angeles, Kansas City and Denver.[48]

Despite these improvements in the operating environment for the BIS, the British could not count on favourable press in America. One of Robert Sherwood's new duties in early 1942 was to issue weekly press directives to the media encouraging them to spin the news in ways helpful to America's effort. His directive of 11 March 1942 urged the press to 'Play up MacArthur, particularly in British broadcasts, giving all favorable news about his resistance [at Bataan and Corregidor].' Criticism of Churchill was to be avoided, 'but transmit and play up all favourable references to Cripps'. Finally, the brief directive advised American media outlets that 'the British public has developed considerable distrust and irritation at the BBC broadcasts which they suspect of minimizing bad news. American broadcasts to England, therefore, should be exceedingly frank and make no effort to cover up bad news.'[49]

* * *

'I am led to the conclusion,' a prominent Canadian working in Washington warned in early March, 'that there is developing rapidly in the United States a serious disintegration of confidence in the British and Canadian war effort.' The notion persisted that millions of British soldiers and airmen were idle in the UK. 'So long as the large armies which constitute the British and Canadian land and air forces are immobilised in England there is grave danger that the people of the United States will become confirmed in their unfortunate opinion that Great Britain is now willing to fight to the last American man and to the last American dollar.'[50]

It was assumed that these 'millions of men' ought to launch the Second Front and land in France. The public was blithely unaware of the difficulties: the shortage of landing craft, the contested nature of airpower, and the limited number of fully equipped and trained divisions – all of them Anglo-Canadian. Even the creation of a bastion on the Cotentin or Brittany peninsulas, an idea bruited about in early 1942, would have been a disaster. But while the British could not actually conduct a cross-Channel attack in 1942, they could talk about it and posture in ways to deflect public criticism and help the Russians. In retrospect, it seems that what became the whole 'Second Front Now' movement of early 1942 was a vast disinformation and deception operation.

At the heart of the second-front disinformation operation in early 1942 was the First Canadian Army, 'McNaughton's Dagger'. It was already much in the news because McNaughton carried on a very extensive public-relations campaign. His visit to Canada in early 1942 turned into a massive North American public-relations event focused on his unique leadership skills and the key role that he and his little army were about to play in launching the Second Front. A special nationwide CBC radio broadcast covered his arrival in Halifax on 3 February, and he was greeted at the train station in Ottawa at midnight on 4 February by the Prime Minister himself. *Time* magazine covered the triumphant return of the general who soldiers of Canada and elsewhere rated as 'the best officer in the British Empire'. Everywhere he went there were 'scenes of wild enthusiasm'.[51]

McNaughton and a small entourage also flew to Washington on 8 March 1942 to meet Marshall and Roosevelt. No detailed record of either meeting has appeared, but we have some indications. Marshall was primarily interested in a landing in France. McNaughton told him emphatically that the ultimate task of his army was 'a landing and attack on Western Europe'. Roosevelt probed McNaughton about whether his strategic vision really aligned with what the British thought. McNaughton confirmed that it did: the First Canadian Army was already holding German troops in the west and would be launched onto the continent when the time was right. As for the strategic bombing campaign, McNaughton told FDR that it was not going to win the war: German bombing of the British simply hardened their resolve to fight. Someone was going to have to land in France and defeat the German Army.

McNaughton gave the same message to the US Army War Plans Division on 10 March. There he met Brigadier Dwight D. Eisenhower, who expressed his anxiousness to launch a Second Front in France as soon as possible. McNaughton agreed. 'He believes in attacking Europe (thank God),' Eisenhower recorded in his diary. 'He's over here to speed up landing craft production and cargo ships. Has some d— good ideas.'[52] After he left Eisenhower's office, McNaughton stepped out into a mob of forty reporters waiting to hear what he had to say.

McNaughton, like Beaverbrook, stoked American passion for a Second Front. By March 1942 the US Army had rejected the idea that North Africa was even part of the European theatre and Operation Gymnast was off the table. Whatever the Americans could spare was being hurled into the South Pacific. The scheme hatched in Washington a few months earlier to sweep the Axis from North Africa was dead – again, or so it seemed. Marshall and his staff were now focused on getting ashore in France as soon as possible. They also understood that, unless Germany suddenly faltered or the Russians were about to collapse, any attempted landing in France that year, according to Stoler, 'might well end in disaster'. The US Army Plans Department was nonetheless prepared to endorse and encourage such a catastrophe for the British and Canadians as 'a sacrifice for the common good'.[53] McNaughton's visit to Washington inspired Roosevelt, too. Within of hours of McNaughton's departure from the White House the President sent a message to Churchill indicating that he was 'more and more interested in plans for the establishment of a new front on the European continent this summer'.[54]

Marshall and Hopkins flew to London in early April to sell the British on their plan for a landing between Le Havre and Boulogne with forty-eight divisions, codenamed 'Roundup', in the spring of 1943.[55] The British accepted the Roundup concept in principle, although they believed it would likely be late summer of 1943 rather than the spring before the Allies could land in France. Marshall 'foresaw no shortage of troops for the major operation', Churchill wrote later of the London conference of April 1942, 'but he did believe that there would be difficulty in making available the necessary shipping, naval escorts, landing-craft, and aircraft'.[56] He might well have added that weapons and equipment were also needed to outfit America's rapidly expanding army. By early April, Marshall already knew that production plans for 1942 were in disarray and were considered 'unfeasible'. The 215 divisions of his Victory Program were in serious doubt, and the news throughout 1942 would only get worse.[57] So, too, would the shipping and escort situation.

The British also knew that anything proposed by Marshall and Hopkins was a US Army plan, not a fully 'American' plan. The US Navy was completely absorbed by the unfolding crisis in the Pacific. By April 1942 the USN had virtually abandoned the North Atlantic, leaving its operational responsibilities to the burgeoning RCN. As far as Admiral Ernie King, Chief of Naval Operations, was concerned, the strategy was always Japan first. As for Marshall's 'nominal subordinates in the Army Air Force', they considered 'that a large-scale invasion of Europe could not be made before the spring of 1944', and by then their strategic air forces would have won the war.[58]

The British were well aware that the Americans could not agree among themselves on what their strategy should be. Brigadier Maurice Pope, Head of the Canadian Joint Staff Mission, watched this internecine struggle close-up. The US was trying to run a joint and combined global coalition war without either the background or the infrastructure required to develop and articulate strategic planning at a national level. The British empire, Pope noted, had gone through this in the Great War and established the Imperial Defence College (IDC) to provide advanced education on strategic planning to rising senior officers and civil servants. The real work of coordinating that military and strategic planning was then done by the Committee of Imperial Defence (CID), founded in 1902, which brought the services and government together. The

Americans had nothing comparable to either the IDC or the CID. 'On their side,' Pope wrote, 'the U.S. Army and Navy had grown up apart. They had only been drawn together by Pearl Harbor.' British members of the Combined Chiefs of Staff were often obliged to sit quietly around the table while a 'battle royal' went on between US Army, Air Force and Navy officers. 'For weeks,' Pope wrote, 'progress was at a standstill while the United States Joint Planners fought out the issue among themselves.' American Joint Chiefs of Staff meetings were even hotter. One insider confided to Pope that on at least one occasion 'members of this committee were "swinging from the floor" at each other'.[59]

Not surprisingly, the British took American 'plans' at this stage of the war with more than a grain of salt. 'The British had thought the matter over carefully,' Pope reflected later, 'and had come to the conclusion that it would be gratuitously tactless to assume an air of greater experience and bluntly to tell their U.S. friends that nothing could be done that summer.'[60] Instead the British staff in Washington played along, content in the knowledge that London would kill any notions of a Second Front in 1942. They were right. Brooke noted in his diary entries covering Marshall's visit in early April that he was unimpressed with the man and his ideas. All Marshall had to offer by September 1942 for an attack on France was two and a half divisions. The Americans clearly 'had not begun to realize what all the implications of their strategy were!'[61]

The pressure to launch a Second Front as soon as possible was not uniquely American. On 17 March, Beaverbrook warned Churchill that he was about to begin a campaign advocating 'an expedition into Europe'.[62] He had already mobilised his newspapers. 'Here was the beginning of the strange alliance between Beaverbrook, left-wingers, Communists and armchair strategists,' Chisholm and Davie write, 'that became known as the "Second Front Now" campaign.' Prompted by the press, forty thousand people massed in Trafalgar Square on 29 March to support the campaign. More public rallies for Second Front Now emerged over the following months.

In late March, Beaverbrook went to Washington, ostensibly to push the Americans over Lend-Lease and production, and while there was asked by the Newspaper Proprietors of America to address their annual meeting in New York in April. With Marshall's plan for Operation Roundup siting on Roosevelt's desk, Beaverbrook's discussions with FDR and Hopkins quickly turned that speech into an appeal for a Second Front. Beaverbrook believed that any operation not focused on a landing in France in 1943 was a sideshow. That included building bombers when landing craft were needed, and anything to do with the Mediterranean.[63]

Beaverbrook's New York speech on 23 April 1942 was delivered to 'an enthusiastic audience' of press moguls and powerful people in the ballroom of the Waldorf Astoria Hotel, and to a nationwide radio audience. It was designed specifically to support Roundup and to provoke action from the British. 'How admirably Britain is now equipped in weapons of war for directing such an attack on Germany,' Beaverbrook exhorted. The American response was unequivocal: Lord Beaverbrook – confidant of the President and recently a minister in Churchill's War Cabinet – had not only demanded a Second Front now, he claimed that the Allies could launch it in 1942.[64] Admiral Ernest J. King, the staunchest advocate of either landing in France as soon as possible or diverting resources to the war against Japan, was in the audience. He immediately offered Beaverbrook his 'praise and commendation'.[65]

The next morning Beaverbrook pondered aloud, 'I wonder what that fellow Churchill will say?'[66] The effect of his speech, Jamie Farer wrote later, 'was in fact immediate, world wide and profound'.[67] Headlines in North America and the UK trumpeted Beaverbrook's call for action, and it occasioned spirited debate in the British Parliament. Churchill called and offered to put him 'in charge of all the British Missions in Washington'.[68] Taylor claims that this was another attempt to silence Beaverbrook, but it was tantalising enough to put the Beaver on a flight back to England. There he was able to stoke the flames of the Second Front Now appeal to even greater heights.

* * *

The background to Beaverbrook's Second Front Now campaign and the Anglo-America struggle for a viable strategy in 1942 was a war still spiralling out of control. No one seemed able to stop the Japanese. On 4 April, as Beaverbrook slumbered in the White House, five Japanese aircraft carriers and four battleships burst into the Indian Ocean and struck Ceylon. The RN's Eastern Fleet retreated ignominiously to the Maldives and then to Kenya, while the Japanese force raided shipping in the Bay of Bengal. By the time Marshall arrived in London in April for talks, Churchill was worried about the Japanese and Germans linking up in the Middle East. To secure the route through the Indian Ocean the British seized the French colony of Madagascar. A small amphibious force (the equivalent of an infantry division without supporting elements), organised and supported by naval forces assembled from half a world away, took the port of Diego Suarez on 5 May in a matter of hours: it then took six months to subdue the remnant Vichy forces.[69]

Burma fell completely to the Japanese by early May, when they were finally stopped by exhaustion, overextension and the monsoon. On 10 May, American and Philippine troops on Corregidor surrendered, a month after those at Bataan had capitulated. Roughly 90,000 men were captured, more than the British lost at Singapore. But the defence of Bataan and Corregidor was epic, and turned this defeat into a moral victory at a time when good news was scarce. By May the Japanese were also established along the north coast of New Guinea and were probing south-east, along the Solomon Islands chain in an attempt to cut American links to Australia.

Much better news soon followed. On 8 May the US Navy forestalled a Japanese landing at Port Moresby, on the south-east coast of New Guinea. For the first time in history two fleets fought a decisive action without ever coming within sight of one another: carrier-based aircraft did all the damage. The Battle of the Coral Sea was technically a draw, but the Americans did enough to spook the Japanese and they withdrew, landing their troops on the north side of the island. The long and bitter 'Buna Campaign' was then fought largely by Australians to keep the Japanese from marching overland to Port Moresby.

Stung by the intervention of American aircraft carriers in the New Guinea campaign, the Japanese hatched an elaborate plan to trap and destroy them in the mid-Pacific, near the tiny island of Midway. Alerted by superb intelligence work, three American carriers and seven cruisers steamed out to meet a massive Japanese fleet of 145 warships that ought to have overwhelmed them. On 7 June strikes from the American carriers caught the main Japanese carrier force while it was doing a hasty rearmament following an attack on Midway. Within minutes three Japanese carriers were flaming wrecks: the fourth was sunk later in the day. One American carrier was lost. In just a few hours the balance of the war in the Pacific shifted. The Americans had stopped the Japanese not once, but twice. As the Japanese fleet recoiled, the Pacific war settled into a year-long grinding match along the edges of the Japanese defensive perimeter.

In the meantime, the European war burst open once again. In late May, Rommel began his long-awaited assault on the Gazala line in eastern Libya. For nearly three weeks Axis and British forces brawled in the barren wastes of Cyrenaica. In the process British armoured forces once again destroyed themselves in front of superbly handled German anti-tank guns. By 20 June, Rommel was finally on the move. The massive depot at Tobruk fell the next day, as the British retreated to their final position in Egypt at El Alamein – where the space between the Mediterranean and the Great Sand Sea narrowed. There, massed British artillery finally stopped Rommel's advance. By then the German Army in eastern Europe was surging across the southern Steppe, over the Volga River and on its way to the oil fields of the Caucasus. For the moment it seemed that there was little to stop the Germans from reaching the Persian Gulf. And if all that were not enough, May and June were the worst months recorded for Allied shipping losses in the Battle of the Atlantic (more in the next chapter). By the summer of 1942, the Axis was in full cry around the world.

Under the circumstances the need to make the Western Front from the northern tip of Norway to Spain active grew ever more urgent. The Bruneval raid of 27–8 February, which snatched radar information from a French coastal site, was not what Churchill or the Americans had in mind. Nor was the daring and successful Commando attack which destroyed the great drydock at Saint-Nazaire in late March. What Churchill wanted was big assaults to cause general alarm. To meet this requirement, British planners came up with the idea of a division-sized raid to capture the port of Dieppe, codenamed Operation Rutter. Dieppe lay only 70 miles from the airfields in the south of England. Its garrison was believed to be small. No one knew if a port, critical to sustaining any operation like Sledgehammer or Roundup, could be seized by amphibious assault. Air cover would be essential, especially for ships engaged in supporting and withdrawing the landing. The RAF, for its part, hoped to lure the Luftwaffe into a major aerial combat. So Dieppe became the target.

Dieppe would be seized by an assault across the mile-long beach in front of the town between two massive headlands. For the first time tanks would be landed, disembarking from the new and untried 'Landing Craft Tank' (LCT). Supporting attacks on the flanks at Puys and Pourville would take the heights overlooking the main beach, while Commandos attacked gun batteries and radar positions well out on either flank. A huge bombing operation would smash the defences – and much of the town – before the landings. The raid would last for a full day, over two tides, culminating in the capture of the airfield at Arques-la-Bataille 10km inland. Naval-fire support remained to be worked out.

No Canadians were involved in formulating the basic plan for Dieppe. Harry Crerar, acting commander of the First Canadian Army in McNaughton's absence, and Montgomery nonetheless decided that the 2nd Canadian Division, which had done well in recent exercises, would get the nod. Montgomery informed McNaughton that his troops were 'best suited' for this large-scale raid.[70] If anyone could pull it off, the Canadians could. McNaughton agreed.

Meanwhile, public clamour for a Second Front continued unabated. Within days of Beaverbrook's 23 April speech in New York, the *Daily Express* organised a massive Second Front Now rally at the Hippodrome in London. By May, Beaverbrook had fully engaged the British labour movement and its Communist Party in the campaign. Both were fired by the arrival of the Soviet Foreign Minister, Molotov, in London on 22 May, carrying the Russian demand for a Second Front. Molotov went on to Washington to further Soviet demands for action. On 20 June the *Daily Express* reported the Russians' warning to both FDR and Churchill that Germany may well be unstoppable in 1942 without a Second Front.[71]

Rallies for Second Front Now were held across Britain in late June to mark the first anniversary of Germany's attack on Russia. The 'Salute to Russia' in Birmingham drew fifty thousand people, many of whom came to hear Beaverbrook say what everyone wanted to hear: blockade and bombing were the strategies of 'false prophets', he thundered. 'We have been promised a Second Front . . . by the Government.' Britain needed to stop building bombers and start building aircraft to support the army. The British Army 'won the last war', Beaverbrook exclaimed, 'and it will win this war if properly supported!'[72]

American papers – also inspired by Molotov's visit – echoed calls for a Second Front and carried Hopkins's assertion that 'The British can fight'. The *New York Sun* correspondent in Washington, David Lawrence, echoed Hopkins: 'He is right . . . The British can fight. They have demonstrated it again and again.' For Americans, in particular, it was time to get *Britain's* weight in the fight. As Senator Allen Ellender said, they were pretty tired of watching 4 million British troops 'sitting at home on their haunches doing nothing'.[73] According to the *Daily Express* on 25 June, the American view was simple: 'Act, Don't Talk.'

These demands might well have been forestalled had Canadian amphibious training for Operation Rutter gone better on 11–12 June. Launched in darkness in gale-force winds, Exercise Yukon was a disaster.[74] Coordination and communications failed, troops landed miles from their designated beaches, and the LCTs were over an hour late. Another – more successful – exercise was necessary before the raid could take place. The target date for Rutter was pushed back to early July.[75]

Meanwhile Churchill, Brooke and several key staff officers flew to Washington to try to hammer out plans for an invasion of France. The sense that something needed to be done in Europe in 1942 was clear. The meeting was completely overshadowed by disaster in the Western Desert. As Churchill and Brooke met FDR on 21 June, Marshall burst in with news that Tobruk had fallen. The stalwart defence of Tobruk the previous year had been a bright spot in a sea of British gloom. This time it capitulated in a day. It was a profoundly embarrassing moment. Fuelled by the enormous cache of supplies – including some 2,000 new Canadian trucks – Rommel was now on the march to Suez. The President immediately offered 300 Sherman tanks and 100 self-propelled 105mm guns; Marshall offered the 1st US Armored Division (USAD). News of the fall of Tobruk reached Beaverbrook as he mounted the podium in Birmingham. 'On the morning of June 21st,' he wrote later, 'the Second Front was a near certainty, by the evening the odds were 100 to 1 against.'[76]

Now, more than ever, the raiding strategy mattered. On 30 June, Churchill – 'in one of his "black dog" moods'[77] – convened a meeting to discuss the Dieppe operation. He had doubts: Britain did not need another bloody disaster. Brooke urged that Rutter go ahead despite the uncertainties. 'It is just because no one has the slightest idea what the outcome will be that the operation is necessary,' he implored. Churchill retorted that this was not the moment 'to be taught by adversity'. Brooke probably reflected the thoughts of many senior officers then contemplating a return to France when he said, 'no responsible general will be associated with any planning for invasion until we have an operation at least the size of Dieppe raid behind us to study and base our plan upon'. For Brooke, the raid was 'indispensable'.[78]

Montgomery was also convinced the raid was viable. That said, he told McNaughton it would need good weather, 'average luck' and the navy putting men ashore 'in the right places, and the right times'. The second amphibious exercise, Yukon II, went much better, and gave hope that the raid would succeed. On 3 July the go-ahead was given. By then the sound between the Isle of Wight and the mainland was packed with assault shipping. And there they sat for five days, buffeted by wind and wave, waiting for a break in the weather. It says a great deal about the impetuous planning of Rutter that as days slipped away the raid was changed from a two-tide event to a one-tide event.

While the troops waited, a constitutional wrangle erupted between the Canadians and Montgomery. Monty announced that the raid would be 'watched' from the HQ of No. 11 Fighter Group at Uxbridge by himself and Air Marshal Leigh-Mallory: no Canadians were invited. GHQ Home Forces, General Bernard Paget, backed Montgomery. As Stacey observed, 'The British military authorities, in other words, proposed to treat the question precisely as though the 2nd Division had been one of their own formations.'[79] Crerar explained the constitutional niceties of the situation and Monty relented, inviting both Crerar and McNaughton to attend.[80] The Canadian official history concluded that Montgomery got the message. Crerar's biographer – and subsequent events – suggests that Monty never did.[81]

The lack of effort to conceal the amphibious force convinced some Germans that it was all a ruse. Resistance activity in the Dieppe area nonetheless persuaded Field Marshal Gerd von Rundstedt, the German Commander in Chief West, that a raid was imminent. It took him until 7 July to convince the Luftwaffe to launch a strike, and even that was puny: FW 190 fighter-bombers damaged two Landing Ships (without serious casualties). The next day, 8 July, Operation Rutter was cancelled.

That same day Churchill officially declared that Sledgehammer – at least for 1942 – was dead, too. With Rommel at the gates of Cairo, and the Germans driving deep into the Caucasus, the Anglo-Americans suddenly had no plans for fighting the Germans in Europe anytime soon.

CHAPTER 9

JUBILEE TO TORCH

Just because the Americans can't have a massacre in France this year,
they want to sulk and bathe in the Pacific!

Lord Halifax, Secret Diary, 15 July 1942[1]

Fired by news that Sledgehammer was dead, Marshall and King petitioned the President on 10 July to either stick with the American
build-up in Britain for a cross-Channel invasion in 1943, or 'strike decisively against Japan'. Marshall admitted in 1956 that the appeal was a
bluff. Stimson knew it at the time.[2] Roosevelt called it. Marshall and
King were ordered to provide – by that afternoon – 'a full statement of
the Pacific alternative, with estimated times of landings, total numbers
of ships, planes and men, proposed withdrawals of men, ships and planes
from the Atlantic, and the effect of the change on the defense of the
Soviet Union and the Middle East'. As Pogue concluded, 'The service
chiefs had no detailed plan to submit.' Marshall later confided to his staff
that politics had intervened: the President wanted a landing in Africa.[3]

In a year of mid-term elections, FDR needed action in Europe before
November. All 435 seats in Congress and a third of the Senate were up
for grabs. With the catastrophes earlier in the year now behind them,
many Americans 'were struggling to take the war seriously'.[4] The introduction of wage and price controls and, by mid-1942, fuel rationing,
was unpopular. Republicans attacked Roosevelt's management of the
war and his big government in Washington. Moreover, the push for

a Second Front was unrelenting. By July, Roosevelt was getting scores of appeals daily to land in France and end the war.[5] That month forty-three major US papers, from across the political spectrum, ran editorials calling for an immediate Second Front.[6]

So Roosevelt despatched Marshall, King and Hopkins to London on 16 July with orders to get US troops into combat against the Germans in 1942: they had a week to do it. The Americans arrived in a petulant mood. After a day with Alan Brooke, they convened at Claridge's to work on their 'battle plans'.[7] Brigadier General Lucian Truscott, the American staff officer at Combined Operations HQ (COHQ), made it clear that the lower-level planning staff at COHQ believed it was possible to seize the Cherbourg peninsula and hold it.[8] Over the next two days the Americans worked tirelessly to craft a scheme for a lodgement on the Brittany or Cotentin peninsulas in 1942.[9]

They had a weak hand, and the British knew it.[10] Only two American divisions were in the UK, and neither was complete in equipment or training.[11] Two other divisions slated for Britain had gone to Australia on Roosevelt's orders.[12] That left only four divisions in the USA in an advanced state of readiness.[13] Marshall's plan, hatched in Claridge's on 18–20 July, therefore called for an assault by six 'British' divisions and a single American one. Any 'sacrifice for the common good' on the beaches of France in 1942 would be predominantly Anglo-Canadian.

And the British would have to provide the shipping. In 1942 the Americans were in no position to help with that – in fact, they were part of the problem. Prior to 7 December 1941, Roosevelt had diverted 20 per cent of American tonnage to routes in the Indian Ocean, freeing about 1.6 million Gross Registered Tons (a measure of capacity) of British shipping for use in the war zones.[14] The recall of these American ships after Pearl Harbor forced the British to fill the gap in Indian Ocean cross-trades. That cut British carrying capacity by 13 per cent. The ships needed to restore British carrying capacity were expected from American yards under Lend-Lease in 1942. The US Maritime Commission had no interest in the slow, coal-fired, 10,000-ton emergency type being built in America to British design, and eventually dubbed 'Liberty Ships'. They were 'an evil to be avoided if necessary'.[15] For itself, America was building high-speed commercial 'standard' type vessels using high-pressure turbine engines and modern gearboxes: just the kind of ships the USN wanted – and requisitioned – to support its expanding commitments in the Pacific.[16] In January 1942 it had been agreed that all new Allied merchant ships, regardless of where they were built, would be pooled as a common resource and allocated by an Anglo-American 'Combined Shipping Adjustment Board' (CSAB).[17]

Lieutenant General B.B. Somervell, in command of the US Army Service Force (ASF), and USN planners had other ideas. Somervell's job was to meet the army's needs, not those of the alliance. 'He requisitioned shipping without civilian oversight,' Kevin Smith writes, and was prepared to 'cut off food exports to Britain in order to assist military deployments, if need be'.[18] And he was not alone. 'Commanders thirsty for revenge against Japan,' Smith goes on, 'and inexperienced in handling a two-ocean logistics displayed ravenous logistical appetite that fortified a visceral and almost irrational dislike of allocations to sustain the British base for American operations against Nazi Germany. Their Pacific improvisations thereby countered the agreed "Germany First" concept logistically and strategically.'[19] Try as it might, the new US 'War Shipping Administration' and the CSAB could not wrestle allocation of ships from the US Chiefs of Staff. Nor could Roosevelt. Reliance on British shipping data simply fuelled the Anglophobia already rampant in Washington.[20] Meeting British needs would mean curtailing operations in the Pacific. So in 1942 fully 94 per cent of all new merchant ships built in the USA – including those to British contracts – were allocated to the US military.[21]

This might not have mattered had the Americans not bungled defence of shipping along their coast in early 1942. The USN had been the beneficiary of Anglo-Canadian expertise and – perhaps unwelcome – advice on how to defend shipping for over a year.[22] The essence of that advice was convoy and evasive routing. The USN ignored it. In March the USN's Board on East Coast Convoys warned that a weakly escorted convoy system would be disastrous. And so the Americans relied on dispersion of shipping, patrolled 'safe routes', and aggressive hunting of U-boats. Coastal cities also refused to douse their lights because of the possible impact on tourism. As a result, losses in merchant shipping in the first half of 1942 were unprecedented: over 4 million tons, the equivalent of the 1941 total in just six months.[23] In March the Canadians began running convoys in the USN zone, without loss. But the Americans could not be persuaded. Losses peaked in June at 122 ships, again mostly in American waters. In May and June alone losses were roughly equivalent to the yearly average prior to Pearl Harbor.[24]

The official American response to these devastating losses was that they did not matter. 'As far as America is concerned', the press guidance from Sherwood's COI for the week of 1 June 1942 advised, 'the German U-boat threat is embarrassing for us now, because the United States is, first of all, getting ahead with its program of ship construction faster than Germany can build and despatch U-boats to this coast'. American war production would continue to expand, and 'there is nothing the Germans can do about it'.[25] This message seems to have resonated with the American public and down through the decades among American historians. Even Allan Winkler's history of the Office of War Information (OWI), which notes the policy of downplaying American defeats in 1942 so they would not adversely affect the mid-term elections, makes no mention of these staggering shipping losses.[26]

Sherwood's guidance was a lie. The German assault on shipping in American waters cut deeply into Allied carrying capacity, especially the movement of oil from both the Caribbean and Texas to US and British destinations. The loss of tankers threatened American industry and 'impending military operations in Europe, Africa and the Far East'.[27] At one point Admiral King confined US tankers to port for a two-week period.[28] While American tankers sheltered in port, Canadian oil imports – all emanating from the Caribbean – were not affected. From May to September 1942 the RCN ran thirteen tanker convoys through the US zone without loss.[29] In mid-June George Marshall warned King that losses to the US bauxite fleet now threatened aircraft production. Moreover, 'another month or two of this will so cripple our means of transport that we will be unable to bring sufficient men and planes to bear against the enemy in critical theatres to exercise a determining influence on the war'.[30] In mid-July Stimson proposed to Roosevelt that the army take over escort of American military convoys to Europe.[31]

Marshall may also have been aware of the impact which these losses were about to have on the allocation of steel and the development of

America's war industry. Roosevelt's industrial strategy supported an air war in Europe and a naval war in the Pacific: the two combined for some 70 per cent of the output of war industry by 1942. Losses to merchant shipping in the Atlantic and US naval vessels in the Pacific that year, Phillips O'Brien argues, 'pushed shipping construction higher up the priority list'. More ships and aircraft could only come at the expense of Marshall's 215-division army. In 1942 it was decided to curtail the manufacture of armoured fighting vehicles to channel steel into warship construction. The result was the paring back of Marshall's ambitions to an army of roughly a hundred field divisions, and a delay in the equipping of even these.[32]

Finally, historians talk of an attack on American shipping in early 1942, but the majority of ships sunk in American waters were British or under charter to Britain: roughly 58 per cent.[33] The American merchant fleet suffered terribly, as Marshall well knew, but American production would soon cover those losses. The British were not so fortunate. Their new ships were being commandeered to support America's war in the Pacific.

* * *

It was against this backdrop of crisis that a week of gruelling Anglo-American talks began in London on the afternoon of 20 July.[34] The British refused to accept that any lodgement on the continent was worth the effort in 1942. The best the British could lift simultaneously with existing landing craft was 4,300 men and 160 tanks: it would take three weeks to put 132,000 men ashore.[35] When discussion turned to the possibility of attacking North Africa it found no favour with the Americans, who threatened to shift their effort to the Pacific. The argument continued the next day. On Wednesday, 22 July, when Marshall presented a plan to create a lodgement near Cherbourg, he was like a gambler playing with house money. The Americans offered two divisions, some auxiliary troops and one reserve division at a later date.[36] All the shipping, all the landing craft and most of the troops – and the airpower – would have to be British (or Canadian). When the British refused to budge, the Americans said that they would refer the matter to Roosevelt. They also asked to speak to Churchill – which they did. Brooke and Churchill then put the whole matter before the British War

Cabinet. Launching and sustaining such an operation would cost the British three-quarters of a million tons of lost imports at a time when their import programme was already in doubt. The decision was a firm 'No'. Ike lamented to his naval aide, Captain Henry Butcher, it was the 'blackest day in history'.[37] Stimson concluded uncharitably, 'the British have lost their nerve'.[38]

Roosevelt concurred with the decision to land in North Africa the next morning. Marshall was told that the landings should take place no later than 30 October, four days before the US mid-term elections. This was the third time that Roosevelt ordered Marshall and his staff to develop plans for North Africa. Operation Torch was confirmed on Friday 24 July. 'A very trying week,' Brooke wrote in his diary that day, 'but it is satisfactory to think that we have got just what we wanted from out of the USA Chiefs.' It is true – as American historians are wont to complain – that the British also favoured a landing in North Africa. But the ultimate decision for North Africa was about American domestic politics – and American military weakness.

Marshall came home from London a chastened man. Gloomy and disconsolate, he resolved to frustrate and delay planning for Torch in favour of Operation Bolero, the American build-up in Britain for the Second Front. For several weeks both he and Stimson sought ways to obfuscate the planning for Torch. It took Field Marshal Dill to bring Marshall around. 'For good or ill it has been accepted,' Dill wrote in a personal note, 'and therefore I feel we should go at it with all possible enthusiasm and give it absolute priority. If we don't, it won't succeed.' As Lacey explains, Dill's note reminded Marshall that he now had two options: make it work, or resign. Marshall resolved to make Torch a success.[39]

In the meantime, the Second Front Now campaign continued unabated, and so too did the central role of the First Canadian Army in that scheme. The 10 August 1942 edition of *Time* magazine featured McNaughton on the cover and talked about the Canadians' role as invaders. News 'that Canadians will be in the vanguard of the invasion is freshening and heartening to a world which needs good news', *Time* reported. After all, Canadians had done exceptionally well in the Great War, where they had 'kept the sheen of glory' at a time when the word

PRESS CLIPPINGS · GENERAL · LIEUT.-GEN. McNAUGHTON

TIME

THE WEEKLY NEWSMAGAZINE

McNAUGHTON OF THE CANADIANS

His dagger was pointed at Berlin.

(*World Battlefronts*)

6. The cover of *Time* magazine published the week of the ill-fated
Dieppe raid.

had lost its meaning. McNaughton 'is determined to lead Canadians back to France . . . and says often and in many ways that his Canadian Army Overseas is a dagger pointed at the heart of Berlin'.[40]

The public-relations buzz surrounding McNaughton's Dagger and the whole Second Front Now campaign were, it seems, an unqualified success. In the summer of 1942 Hitler estimated that the British might be able to land no less than 300,000 troops over two to three days. According to John Campbell, 'the really quite modest collection' of landing craft lying in the Solent during Exercise Yukon II peaked Hitler's interest. 'On 25 June,' Campbell writes, 'he approved an OKH proposal to convert 23rd ID, already en route from Russia to France, into a Panzer division: while three Panzer divisions already in France (6th, 7th, and 10th) were to remain there, as were the 7th Flieger Division and the Hermann Goering Brigade, which was to receive an armoured component.' Plans were made to transfer even more armour to France, including the SS divisions Das Reich, Liebstandarte Adolf Hitler and Totenkopf to form a Panzer Corps, to be joined later by the Grossdeutschland Division. By August a whole corps of the Sixth Army was to move west after capturing Stalingrad, a grimy industrial city astride the Volga.[41]

But to sell the deception fully required a major raid on the European coast. The cancellation of Operation Rutter on 6 July was followed by a report to Churchill on 7 July that Operation Jupiter – a Canadian assault on northern Norway – was also a no-go. By then it was also clear that Sledgehammer would not happen either. It was, therefore, 'in a mood of semi-crisis' that the planning staff of Combined Operations met on 9 July to decide what to do.[42] Fourteen raids had recently been conceived and planned, and then cancelled. Compared to all these, Campbell concludes, Operation Rutter looked like 'a model of military prudence'.[43] On 11 July COHQ secretly decided to remount Operation Rutter (now renamed Jubilee). Brian Villa, who ultimately blamed Lord Louis Mountbatten for the decision, never found a formal authorisation for reinstating the raid.[44]

So while Brooke wrestled with Rommel's arrival at the gates of Suez and Churchill flew off to Moscow to explain to Stalin why there would be no Second Front in 1942, planning for the raid on Dieppe was revived. Montgomery was opposed and he told General Sir Bernard Paget that it should be abandoned 'for all time'.[45] The RN was not about to risk capital ships in the Channel, and it was decided that a heavy preliminary bombardment by RAF bombers would only kill civilians and clog Dieppe's streets. Success at Dieppe was now predicated solely on a carefully choreographed programme of landings designed to achieve surprise. The margin between success and failure was now razor thin.

The public-relations plan for Operation Jubilee points to the fact that it was both an exercise and 'a sacrifice for the common good'. The meaning of the raid was scripted in advance: success or failure was immaterial. It was 'an essential test in the employment of substantial forces and heavy equipment'. In the event the raid was a failure, heavy emphasis would be placed on individual heroics but the message would remain unchanged: Dieppe was the essential precursor to the Second Front.[46]

Operation Jubilee took place on 19 August and, apart from the success of Commandos and US Rangers on the extreme flanks, it was an unmitigated disaster. Critical timings and landing sites were missed as the raid collapsed into a mad scramble of men against fire. The landing below the towering cliffs at Puys, intended to clear the eastern headland of the main beach, arrived in twilight not darkness. Of the 665 men who landed, over 200 died on the beach: just 109 men returned. The landings at Pourville went better, except that the battalion assigned to clear the west headland landed on the wrong side of the Scie River. Without surprise, heavy weapons or naval-fire support, that battalion remained pinned in the valley. The other battalion at Pourville made a dash inland before receiving the recall order. Casualties at Pourville were comparatively light: 1,026 men landed, 621 came home and only 160 died.

With the Germans in control of the headlands and after only ten minutes of air strikes, the main beach at Dieppe became a charnel house. The two leading battalions landed in a maelstrom of fire and were immediately trapped on the beach and the esplanade. Only a handful of men got into the town. Twenty-nine Churchill tanks of the Calgary Regiment drove off their new LCTs: half got bogged in the chert or trapped by the ditch in front of the seawall. Those that reached the esplanade milled about like angry bees because the engineers who were to blow the barricades blocking streets into the town were soon casualties. Nor could the tanks elevate their guns enough to supress the fire coming from the headlands. Landing the 3rd Canadian battalion at 0700 hours simply added to the carnage, and when the Royal Marine Commandos were ordered in at 0817 hours they refused to go. The decision to evacuate was taken at 0900. Of the 1,844 Canadians who landed on the main beach, only 514 escaped: 438 were killed, the rest became POWs. Fully 68 per cent of the 4,963 Canadians involved in Operation Jubilee became casualties, including 907 killed and 1,874 captured. Eleven US Rangers and 275 Commandos were also casualties. Alan Brooke's response was telling: 'It is a lesson to the people who are clamouring for the invasion of France.'[47]

Media coverage of the Dieppe raid revealed the critical importance of controlling the message and the difficulties posed by the American press. The initial press releases adhered to the media plan: the raid was a success, new equipment and new methods were tried, laying the groundwork for the Second Front. This became the enduring interpre-

7. 'Sacrifice for the common good': the main beach in front of Dieppe on the afternoon of 19 August 1942.

tation. In the immediate aftermath the only accurate reporting on the extent of the catastrophe was German, which of course the Allies denied – for a while. Goebbels naturally portrayed Dieppe as a failed Second Front,[48] something which Allied press guidance had striven to avoid because of its enormous propaganda potential. This was undone by American papers printing banner headlines announcing, 'British and American troops Invade France'.[49]

The American press quite naturally focused on the fifty Rangers who landed. But incomplete and muddled information in the hours following the raid led to accounts which vastly overplayed the Ranger role. 'A large force of American, Canadian, British and French troops swarmed up the beaches with tanks,' Raymond Daniell reported to the *New York Times* late on the 19th. Eisenhower joined the London office of the OWI in protesting against 'overplaying American participation'.[50] In any event, the plan was to kill the story as soon as possible. Only in Canada, where the impact could not be avoided, was Dieppe a long-term public-relations issue.[51]

Nothing appears in the Beaverbrook papers or his biographies about the Second Front Now campaign after 19 August 1942. The British Embassy in Washington, which had tracked American pressure for a Second Front, says nothing more about that after its weekly report of 8 August 1942. The Second Front Now campaign died alongside nearly 1,000 Canadians at Dieppe.[52]

* * *

The press coverage of the Dieppe raid demonstrated two things that would dog the Anglo-American relationship for the rest of the war. The first was the crucial importance of proper 'messaging' to target audiences. The second was the tendency for the American media to overplay any American part in Allied operations. The two were intimately connected. With America now developing its own international propaganda campaign, two contending views of liberal democracy – British and American – were now fully engaged in a struggle for the hearts and minds of the world itself.

In 1942 the British were still out front in this effort. The MOI controlled the official message at home and in the USA through the British Information Services. The message to the enemy and to occupied countries was taken up in earnest by the new 'Political Warfare Executive' (PWE) established in August 1941.[53] PWE sowed doubt and deception, played to enemy fears, countered Nazi propaganda, and determined the spin of the Allies' own media in ways that would weaken the enemy and buttress the Allied war effort. It helped that the BBC was the only global radio broadcaster of consequence.

The British system became the model for America's new propaganda establishment in June 1942. On 13 June, Roosevelt signed the Executive Order creating the Office of Strategic Service (OSS) under Donovan and the OWI under Elmer Davis, a well-known newspaperman and syndicated news radio host. 'Davis was welcome in all quarters,' Allan Winkler wrote of his appointment.[54] Roosevelt's detractors nonetheless saw the OWI as just another domestic propaganda agency designed to consolidate the New Deal.[55] The appointment of Archibald MacLeish, the Librarian of Congress (and its poet laureate) and another Wilsonian liberal, as director of the OWI domestic branch simply confirmed that opinion for many. Robert Sherwood stayed on to run the OWI's Foreign Information Service as America's outreach effort. Under Sherwood, 800 personnel in ten outposts around the world were on a mission to globalise the New Deal and spread Roosevelt's Four Freedoms and the Atlantic Charter to the world.[56]

In time, Davis grew the OWI into a massive information machine – some 30,000 employees by 1945. Winkler concludes that the domestic OWI was largely a failure. Davis got little cooperation from federal departments, suspicion and evasion from the armed services, and was generally ignored by the large and powerful American media. MacLeish soon quit in frustration. Davis could never exert any effective control over American radio and film industries. If Winkler and James Warburg, who was in the OWI at its birth, are right – that the OWI despite its size, scope and 'insider' strengths could not shift the American public consciousness in any appreciable way – then there was never really any hope that the British could do so even with Aubrey Morgan's expanded BIS infrastructure.[57] Nonetheless, for the next eighteen months the foreign service of OWI worked closely with the MOI to shape a common Anglo-American global message. It was imperative that British and American efforts to undermine Nazi propaganda and German morale did not work at cross-purposes. It was agreed that OWI London – soon the 'main foreign office of OWI'[58] – would follow the British lead and British press guidance for the European war. The BBC would also transmit American radio programming into occupied Europe. The British committed to following American guidance in the political and psychological war in the Pacific.

On the face of it the burgeoning Anglo-American campaigns for the world's hearts and minds shared a common purpose: the defeat of fascism and militarism, the liberation of occupied territories, and the expansion of liberal democracy. But the British worldview did not sit easily alongside OWI's Wilsonian liberalism. The fault line is most easily discerned in the handling of India. The weekly report to London from the British Embassy in Washington warned in mid-May that anti-British feeling was 'stronger than it was before Pearl Harbor'. The reason for this was largely the expansion of the war into South East Asia, which highlighted British imperialism in India.[59] The US Foreign Information Service had stoked unrest in India in 1941 by emphasising Roosevelt's Four Freedoms and the Atlantic Charter. The dilemma for the new OWI in the summer of 1942 was that it either had to pursue this line in India or withdraw from the debate over India's future.[60]

The OWI chose to back away. Press guidance for India, issued on 3 August, instructed the press to treat the intransigence of Gandhi and Congress 'more in sorrow than in anger'. Like the British, Sherwood wrote, America was focused on winning the war first, and it trusted British promises of action once the war was won. Reporters were challenged, therefore, not to inflate India's importance to the Allied war effort, 'lest we give them an exaggerated idea of their own bargaining power'. More important for the long-term relationship between the two Great Powers, Sherwood stated emphatically, 'We are not supporting nor attempting to perpetuate British Imperialism.' Sherwood sharpened the approach two months later by pointing out that the present impasse over the future of India was a 'disagreement in matters of timing and procedure rather than in matters of fundamental politics and ideology'.[61]

The establishment of OWI in the summer of 1942 gave America's foreign political and psychological warfare a focus for the first time.

The objective was to dispel the myth, perpetuated in Hollywood films and Nazi propaganda, that America was a decadent land of mongrel races and gangsters, and to showcase 'the American way' as a model for the world. 'For Davis the message was "that we are coming",' John Hench writes, '"that we are going to win, and that in the long run everybody will be better off because we won".'[62]

In 1942 the OWI initiated a massive programme of book publishing with global distribution but targeted particularly markets within the British empire and Commonwealth.[63] There was a demand. Paper rationing, labour shortages, and 20 million unsold books lost in the Blitz[64] led to a sharp decline in the availability of British books. And new books were few and far between. Many British writers went into service. T.S. Eliot and Graham Greene became air-raid wardens; Evelyn Waugh joined the Commandos; and George Orwell worked for the BBC – until he quit in disgust in 1943, describing it as a 'mixture of whoreshop and lunatic asylum'. 'At the M.O.I.,' Angus Calder writes, 'other good writers produced propaganda which often achieved elegance and even distinction.' In the process, British books simply got smaller and fewer in number as the war went on.[65]

American publishers were only too eager to fill the gap. Even the British Army resorted to bulk purchases of American pulp magazines and paperbacks. As American publications poured into Britain and her empire it was clear that securing postwar markets – and not just for books – was a critical objective. British publishers were aware that American publishing and distribution ambitions masked 'a deliberate collective drive towards the economic hegemony of the world'. More importantly for the British, the American drive to capture British imperial markets threatened 'the imperial connection itself'. It was evident, moreover, that the 'freely expressed dislike of British Imperialism' among American book publishers (themselves predominantly Wilsonian Liberals and New Dealers) 'served to mask American imperialism from their consciousness'.[66] As Hench concludes, wartime cooperation between the OWI and MOI never completely papered over this fundamental competition in the struggle for postwar markets and influence.[67]

For their part the British were not idle in the rapidly developing public-relations struggle. Their domination of European – and indeed global – broadcasts, thanks largely to the BBC, was overwhelming. The major problem remained effective penetration of the crowded and cacophonous American market. Following the low point of British fortunes with the fall of Tobruk in June 1942, a major reorganisation turned the British Information Services into what John Wheeler-Bennett described as a business whose job it was to 'sell Britain' to the Americans. The job of the BIS was now to be more proactive, and it was given a mandate to create and distribute material on its own. Moreover, the BIS finally had a clear and simple objective: present Britain 'to the USA as a tough and efficient partner'.[68] Within weeks it generated a pamphlet called *Fifty Facts about Britain at War*, the first of an increasing stream of illustrated popular publications. By November a new glossy magazine titled simply *Britain* had a distribution list of 27,000.

One of the BIS's greatest challenges was to overcome the myth, perpetuated at the time of the Lend-Lease discussions, that America was *the* arsenal of democracy. According to Wheeler-Bennett, the Americans were supposed to make the case about Britain's war effort to their own people but declined to do so for fear of 'stirring up a hornet's nest among isolationist Senators and Congressmen'. 'America's pride in her industrial strength and mass production', Wheeler-Bennett wrote after the war, 'made them unwilling to hear of the industrial prowess of other countries'.[69] He might have added others' military accomplishments as well. OWI domestic press guidance in 1942 painted the war as an almost entirely American effort. If the results of a November 1942 US Army survey of troops serving in Iran are an indication, the OWI campaign was a success: 'Three-quarters of the respondents,' Ashley Jackson writes, 'believed that the Americans were contributing more to winning the war than the other allies.'[70]

In the end, the British had a Sisyphean task in America. 'Anti-British sentiment is affected by the impact of events,' a confidential Gallup poll reported in September 1942. 'After the fall of Tobruk there was a size-able increase in sentiment critical of England's effort.' Gallup speculated that that sentiment might change with 'a series of British successes'. But Americans remained deeply suspicious of 'England'. The legacy of the Great War hung over American attitudes towards Britain like a pall.

American mistrust, even in 1942, had a great deal to do with the unpaid Great War debt. 'Our scepticism regarding England's motives was probably created more by England's non-payment of her First World War debt to us than by any other single factor,' the Gallup Poll of 10 September 1942 concluded. '*And the same attitude is likely to injure Anglo-American relations after the present war* [emphasis in original].'

Gallup revealed that many Americans had no idea what they were fighting for in Europe. Unlike the Great War experience, there was no fear and no hatred of Germany. In part, Gallup reported candidly, this was because 'The German ideas of racial superiority find their counterpart in our own theories of racial and cultural superiority'.[71] That said, the majority of Americans (58 per cent) understood that they would probably have to invade the continent of Europe to settle the issue.

* * *

With the decision for Operation Torch taken, Churchill and Brooke were free to wrestle with the ongoing crisis in the Western Desert. Against Brooke's better judgement, Churchill selected Lieutenant-General William Henry Ewart 'Straffer' Gott, commander of XIII Corps now entrenched at El Alamein, to take over the Eighth British Army. Gott jumped in an aircraft on 7 August and headed for Cairo, only to be ambushed en route by German fighters. It had been carefully arranged by deciphering the careless transmissions of the American liaison officer in Cairo. The Germans knew before the British did that Gott was dead. Lieutenant-General Bernard Law Montgomery assumed command of the Eighth Army on the 13th.

Montgomery fundamentally changed the nature of the Eighth Army, and through that the whole British Army. The Western Desert revealed that its organisation, tactics, doctrine and equipment were all wrong for fighting the Germans. Alan Moorehead, Middle East correspondent for Beaverbrook's *Daily Express*, laid this all bare in March 1942, and repeated it on 2 July with a feature entitled 'How Good is Our Army?'[72] The British Army needed more than armoured brigades swirling around the desert, it needed massed firepower. Moorhead's mantra, 'We have been defeated in detail', became Montgomery's. The British Army needed to get back to fighting the way it knew best, centred on the division, backed by enormous and highly flexible artillery.

With the Germans now fully impaled in Russia, the British finally poured resources into the Middle East, and especially into the Western Desert. By the end of July this included more than 1,600 tanks (nearly half from America under Lend-Lease), some 41,000 vehicles – a large portion from Canada – and British divisions.[73] The army that Montgomery inherited in August 1942 was, for the first time, predominantly from the British Isles. Within a month Montgomery had the basics sorted out: enough to withstand Rommel's final attempt in early September to break through into the Nile delta. This battle, known as Alam el Halfa (or first Alamein), was the beginning of a major change in British fortunes.

While British experience pushed them back to a more methodical and deliberate firepower-based doctrine, the American Army remained mesmerised by German speed and mobility. This fitted well with the American Army's belief in 'quick, decisive action'.[74] American divisions and corps were designed to be light and mobile.[75] 'Defensive' weaponry and specialist units, which tended to bloat their size and restrict their movements, were stripped away. The Americans were also shifting to the smaller triangular division (three regiments or brigades) which many armies – including the British – had adopted at the end of the Great War. All this was much easier said than done. In 1942 it remained unclear what kind of supporting units – such as field and medium artillery, tank destroyer battalions, engineer battalions – would best serve as corps- or army-level assets, and how these might be used to augment infantry divisions. For Lesley McNair, as of March 1942 the 'Army Ground Force' commander, and Marshall trying to impose order and system on their rapidly expanding force was like trying to wrestle a snake. Neither had control over the complete 'Tables of Organization and Equipment' (TO&E) of combat formations because Somervell's ASF marched entirely to its own drum. As formations and supporting units proliferated, Somervell added more drivers, trucks and supply companies to their TO&E. It was not until October 1942 that McNair got control over that critical part of his organisation.[76]

Even so, McNair was unable to sort out the Gordian knot of expansion, equipment, organisation, training and doctrine in 1942, nor could he get his army overseas. He informed the War Department in

April that the thirty divisions slated for deployment to the UK for Operation Roundup in 1943 (virtually the entire available force for 1942) would be ready to go.[77] After that he expected to complete the mobilisation and training of divisions at the rate of two to three per month, and to have 100 combat ready by the end of 1943.[78] But even in April 1942 – before the great carnage of shipping off the US coast – there was not enough shipping to get the Roundup force to the UK in time.[79] Nor were the British sympathetic to the American plight. They complained that US Army equipment allowances were too 'fat', that Americans were reluctant to use other people's vehicles and equipment, and that Americans were not good at 'sweating down' their cargoes.[80]

Not all the US Army's shortfalls in 1942 were self-inflicted. There was a war on, and it had to be fought while striving to create the army. Equipment was still dribbling in from industry, and some of it – like the tanks of the 2nd Armoured Division which Marshall sent to Egypt that summer – was stripped away to support the Allies. Even the 1st Infantry Division, the premier regular-force division, the Big Red One, which arrived in Britain in early August, arrived 'untrained, unhardened and very raw and amateurish'. One British general considered that they would not be 'fit to fight for . . . twelve to eighteen months'. Two months later the 1st US Infantry Division (USID) landed in Africa.

Then there was the vexing issue of landing craft. In April 1942 it was estimated that Sledgehammer – the hasty landing in the event of a German collapse – would require 7,000: the Allies then had about 1,200.[81] A further 1,200–1,500 were on order in the USA, largely to British accounts, especially the new Landing Ship Tanks (LST) and Landing Craft Tanks: most were slated for delivery in 1944. Despite Beaverbrook's efforts, building landing craft was not a priority. Roosevelt ordered production increases in early April and demanded delivery by September. But both the US Army and US Navy designs were too small to carry a mechanised army across open waters and sustain it on a hostile shore. The issue was resolved by British intervention at a special meeting at the White House on 5 May, 'at which the British successfully presented their objections to the American production program'. Roosevelt then ordered that the American programme be switched to larger, more seaworthy British-type designs.[82] By the high summer, the construction of landing craft competed for steel with new merchant ships, a huge expansion in escort shipbuilding, and the US Army equipment programme.[83]

* * *

American enthusiasm for a sacrificial Anglo-Canadian assault on France in 1942 contrasts sharply with their own anxieties about Operation Torch. Their key concern was Spain. Ostensibly neutral, Spain's fascist dictator Francisco Franco was in debt to both Hitler and Mussolini and shared their strident anti-Communism. Franco was also an ardent nationalist itching to recover Gibraltar from the British. The Americans feared that landings inside the Mediterranean might be cut off by Spanish belligerency, or a sudden descent on North Africa through Spain by the Germans. The British could not allay those fears. So the Americans insisted on a landing in French Morocco and then securing a land corridor eastward to Algeria.

The British concept of Operation Torch, in the words of the American history of logistics, 'was much bolder'.[84] Their objective was to sweep North Africa clear of the Axis. Landings outside the Mediterranean contributed nothing to that goal: Tunisia was the prize. Once Montgomery burst out of the El Alamein position in the autumn, Rommel's Italo-German force could be crushed in a vice before the end of the year. By skimping on training and reducing the number of landing rehearsals, the British estimated on 4 August that they could land as early as 7 October. And they preferred to do so well to the east to take Tunisia before the Vichy handed it over to the Germans, or before the winter rains clogged the roads and hampered flying. The unanswered question was how hard the French would fight against a British force. The two-month Syrian campaign of 1941 suggested that their resistance might be fierce. So, too, did a recent assessment of French attitudes in West Africa.[85] Selling the whole thing as primarily an American landing might turn Torch into a victory march.

The Torch operation set the pattern for Anglo-American command and control of major operations in the European theatre for the rest of the war. The commander would be American, in this case to make it more acceptable to the French. Lieutenant General Dwight D.

Eisenhower, recently appointed Commanding General of the European Theater of Operations, US Army (ETOUSA), and still a substantive Lieutenant Colonel, was chosen for the job. It proved an enlightened choice. Although he had never seen combat and never commanded anything larger than a battalion, Eisenhower was a gifted staff officer and diplomat. He had heard first-hand from Pershing, Fox Connor and Marshall of the complexity of coalition warfare and the critical importance of good staff work. Despite his affable character, Ike was reflective and demanding. He worked himself hard and expected others to do the same.

The British also liked and trusted Eisenhower, and his transparent and positive commitment to making the Anglo-American coalition work. Eisenhower's particular skill lay in welding two very different and mutually suspicious armies into a war-winning coalition. His Anglo-American staff did not have to like one another, but they had to get along and make things work. By 1944 a story – believed to be apocryphal – was in circulation of an incident in Algiers between a British and American officer who came to blows. Eisenhower gave the British officer a dressing-down, but the American was sent home. 'I don't particularly mind that you engaged in fisticuffs,' Eisenhower told his countryman, 'you were right in your position ... and I forgive you for calling him a son-of-a-bitch. But I cannot forgive you for calling him a *British* son-of-a-bitch.'[86]

The basic plans for Torch were completed by the end of August. As Rick Atkinson concluded, 'Torch remained breathtakingly bold ... But at a critical moment, the Allies had taken counsel of their fears.'[87] The Western Task Force of 35,000 inexperienced and largely untrained men would come direct from the USA to the beaches of French Morocco. The Central and Eastern Task Forces would leave from the UK. The Central Force of 18,000 men of the 1st USID, supported by elements of the 1st USAD and a battalion of infantry, targeted Oran. British aircraft flying in support from Gibraltar would carry American markings. The Eastern Task Force, under British command, would land 20,000 men at Algiers and lead the 800km thrust to Tunisia.

To secure escorts for Torch, the South Atlantic convoy system and Canadian convoys in the St Lawrence system were suspended. This left all traffic in the South Atlantic, in particular, unescorted, and routed all traffic into and out of the UK via Canada and the main transatlantic convoy route. The longer passages further reduced British carrying capacity, which cut deeply into the import schedule for 1943. The abandonment of the South Atlantic convoy system would prove disastrous.

As the plan finally came together in early September, Roosevelt made one final appeal to Marshall: 'Please make it before election day.' That proved impossible. On 21 September, Eisenhower set the date for Torch as 8 November: five days after the US mid-term elections.

* * *

Anthony Eden, the British Foreign Secretary, watched Torch anxiously. He was not worried about what might happen militarily, but rather how those actions would be portrayed to the wider world. Robert Bruce Lockhart noted in his diary on 28 September that 'Eden [was] a little worried lest the Americans try to claim all the credit for this show'.[88] Eden had every reason to feel anxious. Apart from the defensive victory over Rommel at Alam el Halfa a few weeks before, the British had had little to crow about. Each time since 1940 that they seemed on the brink of a decisive result some crisis intervened and robbed them of it. Now the Eighth Army was poised to try again. Britain could not afford to let its success disappear in an American media frenzy. Good news was vital.

Torch became the first real clash of Anglo-American media cultures. British information flow remained tightly controlled, and the MOI shaped the story. It was no accident that George Orwell's classic novel about information control, *Nineteen Eighty-Four*, was conceived in this era.[89] The British armed forces were particularly reluctant to allow the media meaningful access to their operations. The American media was profoundly different in scale and purpose. It was a highly competitive commercial activity, but also guardian of the public's 'right to know', and an integral part of American governance and political process. In 1942 the clamorous American fourth estate descended on Britain, and in November on the British preserve of the Mediterranean and North Africa. Government agencies and the military could control reporters by limiting their accreditation in the operational area. But they could not control the 'spin' that press editors and radio producers put on the stories once they were filed.

Eden was well aware of the major restructuring of the BIS now underway in the USA, and the new focus on selling Britain as an efficient, effective and trustworthy ally. He also knew that the British Treasury and the US Treasury Department were in the midst of economic planning for the postwar world. In this backroom struggle for power Britain held a very weak hand. By 1942 two-thirds of the world's monetary gold was in American vaults, and through Lend-Lease the Americans controlled much of the finance and economy of the British empire. In March the Under-Secretary of the Treasury, Henry Dexter White, completed the first draft of his 'White Plan' for the postwar world. 'Arrogant and bullying', and highly insecure, in Benn Steil's words, White 'had a vision of the post-war order antithetical to long standing British interests, particularly as they related to the Empire'.[90] Discriminatory trade practices, such as the sterling bloc of the British empire, would be outlawed. So, too, would debt default – a legacy of the Great War that still haunted Anglo-American relations. In the process the new international standard currency would become the American dollar.[91]

The British response, developed by the wunderkind of contemporary economic theory John Maynard Keynes, took shape as the final arrangements were made for Torch. The essence of the Keynes postwar economic plan was debt management through an 'International Clearing Bank' for currencies, to which all economies contributed deposits according to their wealth. Trade balances would be managed through a notional currency he called 'Bancor'. By late 1942 two contending visions for the postwar economic order were in play. The only leverage the British had in this struggle, according to Benn Steil, 'was the power to disengage'.[92] This they could not afford to do. So the struggle to win respect from America was critical, and the coverage of the Dieppe raid suggested how challenging that would be.

The launching of Montgomery's great offensive at El Alamein in October therefore came at a critical moment. For the first time in the Western Desert, half of the divisions engaged were British. Among the latter were units recently re-equipped with Sherman tanks. The British had asked for aircraft, too, and sent personnel (including Canadians) to the Middle East to man them. The Americans sent USAAF squadrons instead: by October about one-eighth of the squadrons deployed in support of the Eighth Army were American. The build-up was massive, including trucks from 'North America',[93] a polite way to mask the fact that they were largely from Canada.

Montgomery's great attack – like all his subsequent set-piece battles – was conceived in three phases: a break-in, a dog-fight and a break-out. The objective was to destroy the Axis forces in situ before launching a pursuit, and to ensure that any move westward did not end again with a spent British force at El Agheila. The break-in commenced on the night of 23–4 October with a massive fireplan and an Australian infantry assault. As in 1917–18, the idea was to capture a defensible position and destroy the German counterattack. The plan worked. This phase lasted longer than planned, but all of Rommel's counterattacks were crushed by British fire. When the New Zealanders and the 51st Highland Division broke through on 2 November, followed by the armour of X British Corps, Rommel faced annihilation. He ordered a retreat, and with that the final phase of the campaign in the Western Desert began.

This British attack got fair press in America, although the presence of USAAF squadrons brought echoes of the Dieppe coverage. From 25 October until 8 November, when the Torch landings captured the headlines, the El Alamein story was front page, above the fold in the *New York Times*. The banner at the top of the 25 October edition read 'Allies Gain in Big North African Offensive'. In this case 'Allied' meant British Commonwealth and empire, along with some Poles and Free French, and American squadrons. In the early days of the operation – always a press problem because details were so thin – reporting tended to emphasise the air campaign, and that allowed the modest American role to be highlighted. The lead story on 26 October, filed by the *New York Times* reporter James Macdonald from London, highlighted the American role. 'With United States, British, South African and Australian fighters and bombers playing a prominent part', supporting 'the Allied force of toughened desert fighters', bitter fighting was underway. 'Today's attacks', Macdonald reported, 'were marked by close teamwork between the United States Army Air Forces, the Royal Air Force and the South African Air Force'.[94]

There was little in the grinding down of Axis strength that sparked American media interest – a pattern that would follow for the rest of the war. 'It remains a slow, intense fight like those of the First World War in which large groups of men were obliged to make heroic efforts to move forward a few miles or even yards,' the *New York Times* reported on 28 October. 'It has not met any spectacular successes, for none could have been expected considering the nature of the Axis defenses and the narrowness of the front.' The report went on to explain that so far tanks had been used sparingly. Massed tank attacks would come when the infantry dealt with the guns: 'that is what is being done'. This was not lightning war as the public hoped, or as the US Army imagined it.

Three days later the *New York Times* reported that fighting along the front, 'under the cover of United States and other aircraft', remained 'a dogged, hard struggle with the Germans repeatedly launching counterattacks despite huge losses from British artillery and machine guns'.[95] After much talk of 'imperials', Australians, New Zealanders and South Africans, and British armour, the front page story on 3 November acknowledged that 'English and Highland regiments have done excellent work'. They had been launched into the attack on the night of 1–2 November, alongside the New Zealanders, to finally rupture Rommel's position and precipitate his retreat. Mid-term election results dominated the *New York Times* front page the next day, 4 November, but in the top left of the front page – just under the headlines about the election – was a feature headline which read 'Rommel's Tanks Retreat in Egypt: Imperial Forces Break the Axis Line'. The War News Summary in the *New York Times* that week credited 'British forces' with winning a major battle.

For the next three days – 5–7 November 1942 – the *New York Times's* banner headlines finally trumpeted the *British* victory over Rommel and ran feature photos of British troops in combat. Over those same days it was reported that the Eighth Army victory was but part of a much larger 'African-Mediterranean Allied Strategy', and that there were reports of troop movements throughout the region. The German shortwave radio service, DNB, talked about the possibility of an American landing in French North Africa, but suggested that the great movement of ships through the Straits of Gibraltar noticed on 6 November was just another futile attempt to reinforce Malta.[96]

For the moment, however, and for the first time in the whole course of the war, a British Army victory captured the world's headlines. British publicists, especially those in the BIS in America, had longed for something like El Alamein for two years. However, before too much could be made of it, news broke that the Americans had landed in North Africa.

CHAPTER 10

TORCH TO SPARTAN

It was obvious that the British, after their long struggle to keep alight
the flame of European liberation, would hardly relish the spectacle of
the Americans suddenly becoming the noble Liberators of Europe.

Robert Sherwood, *Roosevelt and Hopkins*[1]

There was a political cost for the delay in launching Torch the week
after the November mid-term elections. The Democrats retained
control of both the House and the Senate, but their majority in the
House remained razor thin and threatened by 'dissident Southern
Democrats and resurgent Republicans'.[2] And since Lend-Lease was
reviewed and renewed annually by Congress, the outcome had implications for Britain, too. The British Embassy reported that the new
Congress was 'somewhat less friendly to Britain than its predecessor'
and was expected to 'echo current criticism of our policy in India and
be affected by anti-imperialist cry'.[3]

The assault on French North Africa, which began in the early hours
of 8 November 1942, was nonetheless enormously successful. In virtually every case, the navy got the landing force at the right beach at the
right time. But as a demonstration of Allied amphibious capability and
the state of the US Army, Torch revealed just how far removed the Allies
were from making a successful landing in France itself.

The largely British landing at Algiers met little resistance from the
French,[4] but was attacked at dusk by German and Italian aircraft. The

aircraft came back the next day, and by then enemy submarines had arrived. Several ships, including the 16,632-ton troopship *Nakunda*, were sunk.[5] The landings of II US Corps around Oran and the French naval base at Mers-el-Kébir went well enough. The Americans had to seize the ports and airfields, and then prepare to move west into Spanish Morocco, or to French Morocco if necessary.[6] Getting men and vehicles ashore took hours of hard work. A modified Lake Maracaibo tanker able to carry twenty-two Sherman tanks – the prototype 'Landing Ship Tank' (LST)[7] – struck a sandbar 100 yards offshore and it took four hours to build a pontoon bridge to the beach. The only resistance came from the coastal battery at Fort Stanton, which the British battleship *Rodney* silenced – several times.

Unfortunately, the attempt to seize the naval dockyard at Mers-el-Kébir ended in tragic failure. HMS *Walney* and *Hartland*, loaded

8. America joins the fight: troops landing at Arzeu, east of Oran, 8 November 1942.

with 393 men from the 1st USAD, entered the port in darkness flying massive American flags, to secure it by a coup de main. Both were shattered by concentrated French fire and sunk with heavy loss of life.[8] When French destroyers escaped and tried to attack the landing forces British ships eventually drove them aground outside the harbour. Oran also included an air assault by the 2nd Battalion of the 503rd Parachute Infantry Regiment. They left Cornwall, England, in thirty-nine Douglas C-47 Dakotas. 'The operation demonstrated a breathless readiness to accept risk,' Vincent O'Hara wrote, 'but it contributed nothing to the battle's outcome.' Six C-47s were lost en route, while the remaining transports landed and the paratroopers marched to their objective. The good news was that USAAF Spitfires arrived from Gibraltar at 1700 hours, and they helped the next day as fighting continued around Oran.

Meanwhile, the all-American Task Force 34, two and a half divisions led by George Patton, targeted the Atlantic shoreline of French Morocco. Patton's troops were a garrison force, sent to guard against a Spanish intervention and to train. 'Hundreds of new soldiers had been virtually press-ganged for the invasion,' Rick Atkinson writes; 'sergeants taught them how to load, aim and fire a rifle from the fantail' on their way across the Atlantic.[9] The objective at Port Lyautey, north of Casablanca, was the airfield a few miles up the muddy Wadi Sebou. French Moroccan troops chose to fight, which left the 60th Regiment 'shaken'. It took three days to capture the objectives. 'The real problem,' O'Hara concludes, 'was American inexperience.'[10]

The largest landing was at Fedala, just north of Casablanca, where a division, an armoured battalion and supporting troops went ashore. This was the most perilous Moroccan landing. Several field units of the French Colonial Army, including tanks, garrisoned the area, and there were two powerful coastal batteries. The landings went well, and the local Senegalese regiment declined to fight. The gravest threat came from the French Navy. At Casablanca lay the unfinished battleship *Jean Bart*, with nine fully operational 15" guns, along with seven destroyers, a light cruiser and five operational submarines. American bombs, and shells from the USS *Massachusett*s, eventually silenced the *Jean Bart*. Meanwhile, the French destroyers raced for the American landing craft.

It took until noon to destroy the French squadron. The naval Battle of Casablanca – generally overlooked in the literature – was the only time in two world wars that the USN engaged in a fleet action in the European theatre.[11]

One-hundred and thirty-five miles south of Casablanca, protected by the battleship *New York* and several cruisers, a small force of infantry and tanks landed at Safi. The attack went according to plan. The port and its heavy cranes were seized undamaged. As three battalions of infantry scrambled ashore, the railway carrier *Lakehurst* came alongside to discharge fifty-four Sherman tanks. By the time the Shermans reached Casablanca on 11 November an armistice was in the wind.

The Americans had hoped that General Henri Giraud, Commander in Chief of French North Africa, would deliver the area to the Allies without a fight. He proved to be an arrogant martinet. Eisenhower then cut a deal with Admiral François Darlan, the Commander in Chief of Vichy military forces, who happened to be in Algiers. Darlan was the epitome of Vichy collaboration, and dealing with him proved politically disastrous. 'It seemed to confirm the impression,' Sherwood concluded, 'that, while Americans talked big about the principles of the Four Freedoms and the Atlantic Charter, they actually knew nothing about Europe and could be hoodwinked by any treacherous gangster who offered them collaboration.' The British supported their American allies through the crisis that followed, but as Sherwood observed, 'The British Foreign Office derived a certain private satisfaction from the embarrassment of the U.S. Government throughout the Darlan affair and its ridiculous aftermath.'[12]

By any objective measure, Torch was a success and Eisenhower's Faustian deal ended the senseless fighting. 'Franco-American amity – part of the natural order, in Yankee eyes,' Rick Atkinson wrote – 'was quickly re-established.'[13]

* * *

The reaction of the Vichy government to Torch was visceral: France had been attacked. The fleet at Toulon readied for sea, and by late afternoon on 9 November the 5th German Parachute Regiment had seized El Aouina airfield outside Tunis. When local officials wanted to contain the Germans they were told to stand down. 'It is not us or the Germans who have begun war in French Africa,' they were told.[14] When Hitler ordered the occupation of Vichy France, the fleet at Toulon scuttled itself – as Darlan promised it would. The race for Tunisia was now on. Hitler's decision to reinforce North Africa changed the whole dynamic of the war in the west in ways that Marshall and his American colleagues feared. The Mediterranean now became a great vacuum, sucking in resources that Marshall wanted to assemble in Britain for the Second Front.

The British had wanted to take Tunisia quickly by landing as far east as possible. American anxiety reined them in. And so while roughly 100,000 American troops secured French North Africa and watched Franco's forces, elements of two British divisions and two Royal Marine Commandos began the arduous 800km trek from Algiers to Tunis. With help from parachutists, naval units creeping along the coast, Allied air forces, and the French Colonial Army, this notional '5th British Corps' initially made quick progress. By 22 November the spearpoint was poised to seize Tunis and the port of Bizerta when it ran into Germans.[15] John Downing, a young American liaison officer attached to the British, 'was amazed at the small number of Allied troops in Tunisia' by early December.[16] British battalions were down to a few hundred men, and French colonial forces lacked modern equipment. Stalemate – and the rains of winter – lay ahead.

Meanwhile, Montgomery's pursuit of Rommel across North Africa turned into a protracted campaign, proof to some that the British were plodding and methodical. But the advance from El Alamein to Tripoli was the longest by any western army in the Second World War, over 2,000km – further than the distance from Berlin to Moscow. Montgomery had no intention of arriving at El Agheila, as the British Army had done twice before, exhausted and beyond effective logistical support. So the Eighth Army's march was deliberate, with rail lines, roads, ports and airfields developed as they went. Road transport 'was more flexible, readier, and more quickly extensible than rail or sea', the British official history observed, 'and was therefore the maid-of-all-work'.[17] The workhorse of that crucial system was the ubiquitous Canadian-built truck. It turned a tactical victory into a strategic success. They were fuelled by USAAF C-47s flying in drums of gasoline.

On 23 November, Rommel's tired army tumbled into the El Agheila position pursued by the 7th British Armoured Division. There the two exhausted armies paused for nearly a month. Montgomery needed time to assemble an assault, and to develop the port of Benghazi. Between it and Tripoli, along 1,000km of the Gulf of Sirte, there was scarcely a port worthy of the name. The final push to Tripoli would have to be supported almost entirely by road. Rommel was not so lucky. Allied air attacks and depredations by British submarines savaged his supplies. His retreat from El Agheila needed to be finely timed. When Rommel left for Berlin on 28 November to explain the situation, preparations were underway for a withdrawal to Buerat, halfway to Tripoli.[18] As it was, an attempt by New Zealand forces to swing through the desert and trap the Axis army missed by a matter of hours. It was a much-attenuated Eighth Army that finally reached Tripoli on 23 January, extinguishing the Italian empire in Africa.

A week later, as Montgomery's lead elements reached southern Tunisia, what was left of the Sixth German Army surrendered at Stalingrad. But even as 200,000 Germans went into captivity in Russia, troops and supplies poured into Tunisia. By early 1943 a quarter of a million Axis troops were dug into that small corner of Africa. No one who lobbied for a Second Front in 1942, or for Operation Torch, could have imagined that North Africa would deliver that windfall.

* * *

The short pause between victory at El Alamein and Torch did not serve Britain's public-relations campaign well. The OWI Central Directive for the week of 6–13 November had urged the US media to 'Play heavily and steadily on British Commonwealth victory of the Eighth Army' without (of course) neglecting the American contribution in airpower and equipment. Two days later, in light of the 'anti-British hate campaign' being revived by Goebbels' propaganda ministry, OWI broadcasts to Germany were instructed, 'Do not exaggerate American role in El Alamein . . . Surveys of the North Africa victory,' the directive of 8 November 1942 advised, 'should stress the fact that British infantrymen by frontal assault won victory against the strongest prepared positions defended by the German Army.'[19]

But victory at El Alamein was now overshadowed by America's entry into the European war. Special guidance for Torch issued by OWI on 7 November, in conjunction with Roosevelt's press release announcing the imminent landings, naturally championed America's new role. 'Emphasize the far-seeing, global strategy of President Roosevelt and the American high command,' the directive instructed. 'We are fighting not merely a European war, not merely an Atlantic war, but a world war. The United States has the size and power and the energy to do this.' OWI press guidance, and newspaper coverage in the early days, made it clear that Torch was an American operation, with the British playing a supporting and cooperating role. Even the advance to Tunisia, largely British, was sold on OWI broadcasts as an 'American drive'.[20] Hoping to forestall French resistance, nothing was to be said of the British combat role until official communiqués revealed the truth.[21]

'There was no doubt that, in the first place,' Robert Sherwood reflected later, 'Churchill and his colleagues were not happy about Roosevelt's insistence that the North African operation should be proclaimed an entirely American affair, even to the extent of putting American insignia on aircraft of the R.A.F. and American uniforms on British troops. It was obvious that the British, after their long struggle to keep alight the flame of European liberation, would hardly relish the spectacle of the Americans suddenly becoming the noble Liberators of Europe.'[22] British Commonwealth forces in the region vastly outnumbered the Americans, and the assault fleet and covering forces for the landings inside the Mediterranean were overwhelmingly British. In the weeks immediately following the landings the bulk of the American Army in French North Africa sat idle, while a small British force clawed its way towards Tunisia. By December increasing numbers of US troops were drawn into the battle for Tunisia, but the story was that America had started the liberation of Europe with the British playing a supporting role. Eden's anxiety proved well founded.

Torch threatened Britain's viability as a global power in other ways, especially her merchant shipping. Prior to 1942, lost carrying capacity was largely offset by new construction in the UK and British Commonwealth, shipping from occupied European nations and purchases from neutrals. By 1942 American new construction was supposed to cover losses.[23] As early as July 1942 Churchill had appealed to Roosevelt to give Britain priority in the allocation of new merchant ships: new construction was overwhelmingly American, while losses were overwhelmingly British. By late 1942 there was plenty of new shipping available, but as Chris Bell has written, 'the immediate cause of shipping shortages was the excessive demands being made by the American armed services, particularly for the Pacific'.[24] British imports for 1942 were pegged at 25 million tons, barely half their 1939 rate, and those for 1943 just 27 million. By November even those figures looked optimistic.

Torch exacerbated the crisis. Longer voyages into and out of the UK via North America reduced carrying capacity. And without escorted convoys in the South Atlantic, losses there reached a wartime high. By November 1942 Britain was again haemorrhaging shipping at an alarming rate. That month Allied shipping losses peaked at 729,000 tons – second only to the disastrous month of June.[25] And if all that was not bad enough, Operation Torch put an unexpectedly high demand on British shipping and war reserves. It was estimated that the campaign would need sixty-six ships per month for the first three months: the average was 106, with a proportionally higher drain on British reserves, especially oil.[26] By late 1942 the British were consuming 250,000 tons of oil per month more than they were importing, partly the result of heavy tanker losses over the year.[27] Tankers on the scale required could only be secured from America. By late 1942 Britain faced her gravest import crisis of the war.[28]

The Americans were unmoved by the British shipping and import crisis. On 18 December, in response to a plea from Churchill, Roosevelt pointed out that the UK had much greater oil reserves than 'other combatant areas . . . such as Australia, Greenland, Noumea and Newfoundland'. Churchill was flummoxed. In one of his famous 'pray' memos he asked rhetorically of the Minister of War Transport and the First Sea Lord what the purpose of this American slight might be to 'the heart of the whole resistance to the enemy'.[29] It turns out that Roosevelt could not persuade his Chiefs of Staff to release new merchant ships to the British – and he would not order them to do so.[30]

And then there was the Canadian problem. The Canadians had taken over America's escort responsibilities in the north-western Atlantic and it had stretched them thin. They escorted all convoys between New York and the Grand Banks, helped escort American convoys between New York and the Caribbean, ran their own network of coastal convoys, and had sent escorts to help with Torch. The Canadians were also still guarding the majority of slow convoys across the mid-ocean Atlantic, where they provided 35 per cent of the escorts. In late 1942 the U-boats preyed on these Canadian escorted slow convoys in the mid-ocean, and launched a major attack on shipping in Canadian waters. In fact, Canada bore the brunt of the U-boat campaign in the last six months of 1942.[31] The British were quick to attribute the resulting heavy losses to Canadian bungling. So 'fixing' the problem of merchant ship losses included fixing the Canadian problem.

The RCN was well aware of its shortcomings and was increasingly frustrated by Anglo-American meddling in its efforts to address them. The Canadians wanted a force of destroyers established in Newfoundland to support convoys in the fog-shrouded waters of the Grand Banks, where the Germans operated with impunity. When the RCN used its own operational training group there as a support force, it brought a sharp reprimand from the US Admiral at Argentia forbidding 'freelance operations'. Then, when the Anglo-Americans finally acted on a support force for the western Atlantic, they redeployed Canadian destroyers without consultation. The RCN demanded that its destroyers be returned, and that its corvettes operating between New York and Cuba be sent home. And it asked for more destroyers to help escort slow convoys across the Atlantic.

In the meantime, the Americans demanded that the RCN stop promulgating intelligence to Canadian warships. That responsibility, the Americans claimed, was theirs. But everyone knew that the RCN had provided effective naval intelligence in the western Atlantic since 1939.[32] In fact, Canada controlled shipping and convoy routing in the western hemisphere until July 1942, when the USN finally took over. Compliance with the USN demand would prevent the Canadians from providing vital information to their own ships even in Canadian territorial waters. This was more than the RCN could abide. In December 1942 the Canadians began to rationalise their command-and-control arrangements in the north-west Atlantic, and started a campaign of obstruction directed at the American Admiral in Argentia.[33]

Then, on 17 December – Mackenzie King's birthday – Churchill sent a personal telegram to the Canadian Prime Minister blaming recent heavy shipping losses squarely on the RCN and asking Canada to remove its escorts from the embattled mid-Atlantic.[34] The request was met with anger and a sense of betrayal. The RCN had stretched itself to breaking point covering for the Anglo-Americans in the North Atlantic and was now blamed for recent shipping losses. While the Canadians mustered their case, Admiral Ernest J. King entered the fray. He objected to the transfer of a significant part of the *Canadian* Navy away from him without discussion. So the British and Americans arranged to meet in Washington to sort out the allocation of Canadian forces in the North Atlantic. The Canadians were not invited.

The RCN found out about the meeting and promptly despatched three officers to Washington. The meeting was already underway when they arrived. Captain Harry DeWolfe, the RCN's Director of Plans, immediately reminded his Anglo-American counterparts that only the Canadian government could make decisions about the deployment of Canadian forces. He also reminded them that it was the RCN's efforts to establish convoys in 1942 – including in American waters – that saved countless Allied ships.[35] Canada would agree to the proposed withdrawal of the Canadian groups from the mid-ocean if it was clear that they would return to that role. No further transfers of Canadian ships would occur until RCN forces at home and in Newfoundland were up to strength. De Wolfe also made it clear that the current command arrangements in the north-west Atlantic, in which a USN Admiral with no ships of his own commanded virtually the entire Canadian Navy, were unacceptable. On 9 January 1943 the Canadian War Cabinet agreed to the transfer, and both the government and the RCN resolved to look after their own interests first. The incident was hushed up and remained unknown until 1980.[36]

Mackenzie King's government had invested heavily in the RCN, and by late 1942 that effort had earned nothing but a rebuke from Canada's allies. Colonel J.L. Ralston, the Minister of National Defence, cut to the nub of the matter during the Cabinet discussion of Churchill's request on 24 December. 'If the war ended now,' Ralston lamented, 'we would have to hang our heads in shame.' His comment stunned

Mackenzie King and the Cabinet. The Naval Minister, Angus L. Macdonald, pointed out that what mattered was not the commitment of treasure, but the blood sacrifice, and 'our effort in fighting may have been less than that of the other Dominions and [the] U.K'.[37] In 1943 Canada needed to get control over its war effort, get more international recognition for it, and finally get the army into the fight. These efforts would help shape the assault on France.

As for the shipping crisis, the solution lay in American hands, and try as he might, Roosevelt could not pry new construction from the clutches of his service chiefs. And so the British shipping and import crisis lingered through the winter.

* * *

In the aftermath of Torch Churchill urged that planning for Roundup go ahead with speed. Tunisia was expected to fall by Christmas, and with that Italy might capitulate. The collapse of their southern Allies was precisely how the German defeat unfolded twenty-four years earlier, and some believed that a similar process was possible again.[38] As late as mid-December, George Marshall remained confident that his divisions would soon be gathered in Britain for a cross-Channel attack. Over dinner with Lord Halifax on 15 December, Marshall candidly revealed his ideas for the next phase: what was now the British First Army in Tunisia could remain in North Africa to threaten Italy, while Montgomery's Eighth Army shifted to Syria to secure that area and encourage the Turks to enter the war. Meanwhile, the Americans would land in France and win the war.[39]

The failure to take Tunisia in late 1942 and the German decision to hold there put paid to Marshall's fanciful scheme. The only two American combat divisions that had been in the UK, the 1st USAD and 34th USID, combined as II US Corps – the corps that had fought in the BEF during the Great War – were soon locked in a campaign of attrition in North Africa. The best divisions that had been available in the US, the 2nd USAD and 3rd USID, were still finding their feet in Morocco. By early 1943 the burden of launching Roundup and Sledgehammer once again fell to the Anglo-Canadians. The First Canadian Army, now well organised and nearly complete with a high level of mechanisation, would lead the charge if Sledgehammer was necessary.[40] But the issue of

Roundup and Bolero, the American build-up in Britain, needed to be resolved, and a decision had to be made about what to do after Tunisia. None of this could be fully addressed until the shipping situation and the Battle of the Atlantic were sorted out. On 21 December 1942 Roosevelt and Churchill agreed to meet at Casablanca.

The Americans hoped that the long lead-time before the meeting would help them clarify their strategy.[41] It did not. The Joint Chiefs of Staff and the President met on 7 January and could not agree on what to do next. Marshall preferred landing on the Brittany peninsula. Seizing a beachhead there would be costly in troops, but he reasoned coldly that 'we could replace troops whereas a heavy loss in shipping . . . might completely destroy any opportunity for successful operations against the enemy in the near future'.[42] His logic was unlikely to win him any British support. The American delegation left for Casablanca still divided. All they knew with certainty was that the British would be well prepared.

They were. General Hastings 'Pug' Ismay, Churchill's Military Assistant, recalled that the British knew 'exactly what they wanted' at Casablanca: to clear North Africa and capture Sicily to open the Mediterranean to shipping. Given the huge British shipping losses in 1942 and the intransigence of the Americans over allocation of new construction, it was the only way to increase carrying capacity. A follow-up landing on the mainland of Italy would likely knock that Axis power out of the war, forcing the Germans to occupy not only Italy but also the Balkan peninsula. The British also wanted to resolve the U-boat crisis in the North Atlantic, increase the tempo of the bombing campaign over Germany, and re-invigorate Operation Bolero and planning for a cross-Channel assault.[43]

The Casablanca conference was characterised by eleven days of almost endless meetings. Marshall, anxious about the lack of agreement among his own countrymen and certain that the British would present well-articulated plans, brought Field Marshal Sir John Dill along as the 'broker' – in Alex Danchev's word – between British desires and American dreams.[44] American indecision was apparent. Marshall's push for an assault on Brittany got only passing support from his fellow Americans. Admiral King was focused on the Pacific war. The only thing the Americans agreed upon was that the British should attack into southern China to open the supply route to the Kuomintang. Brooke's diary for these days reflects frustration. It was plain to the whole British delegation that the Mediterranean was the necessary precursor to any direct cross-Channel assault. It was, in modern military parlance, a 'shaping operation'. Moreover, fighting in the Mediterranean was what they could do with the resources to hand.

Marshall eventually accepted Sicily as the logical next step, but for most in the American camp that represented a defeat. After the conference Albert Wedemeyer, who had come to Casablanca as Marshall's lone staff planner, dashed off a letter to General Thomas Handy, head of the US Army Operations Division, explaining how things had gone. 'They swarmed down on us like locusts,' Wedemeyer wrote. The British had arrived 'with a plentiful supply of planners and various other assistants, with prepared plans to ensure that they not only accomplished their purpose but did so in stride and with fair promise of continuing in the role of directing strategy for the whole war'. The British, he admitted, were polished: 'we were confronted by generations and generations of experience in committee work, in diplomacy, and in rationalizing points of view'. His admiration was tainted with more than a slight hint that the British were snake-oil salesmen, selling a dead-end strategy for their own nefarious purposes. In sum, Wedemeyer said, 'We came, we listened, and we were conquered.'[45]

The Casablanca conference reaffirmed the Germany-first strategy. Sicily was the next target, then probably Italy. Operation Bolero would be revitalised, and a planning staff established to launch Roundup in 1944. The Americans would expand their role in what was now called the 'Combined Bomber Offensive' against Germany. And resources would be found to win the Battle of the Atlantic. The Anglo-Americans also agreed that there would be no negotiated peace with the Axis: the Allied objective was unconditional surrender.

The decision to continue fighting in the Mediterranean meant that the war in Europe would still be run by the British, but with an American twist. As Montgomery's army closed up to the southern border of Tunisia the two campaigns were fused. Eisenhower became Supreme Commander, Allied Expeditionary Force (SCAEF), with his headquarters in Algiers. His naval, air and ground-force commanders were all British. The ostensible reason for establishing SCAEF, Brooke wrote, was 'to restore the necessary drive and coordination which had been so seriously lacking of late!'[46] The real reason was maintaining British control over the development of Allied strategy. America was in the war, but her weight was not yet being felt in Europe.

* * *

The decision to pursue a Mediterranean strategy effectively killed any hope of an assault on France in 1943. Only some 70,000 Americans – few of them combat troops – were left in the UK by January 1943.[47] The 295,000 Americans now in North Africa would not have been enough to launch a Second Front in 1943, but the Americans would never have gone to Brittany alone. There already was a force of nearly 250,000 trained and equipped combat troops assembled and waiting for the cross-Channel attack: the First Canadian Army.

By McNaughton's estimate, his army would be complete by 31 August 1943: three infantry and two armoured divisions, three armoured brigades, and supporting forces totalling 239,000 of all ranks. It would be backed by three months of reinforcements totalling a further 44,550 officers and men, bringing the total to just under 300,000.[48] Between them, the Americans and the Canadians might well have put 500,000 men ashore in the second half of 1943. What the British could have added is unknown, but the total available for Roundup in the late summer of 1943 would have approached the 875,000 men who were ashore in Normandy by the end of June 1944.[49] The inclusion of McNaughton's Dagger in the mix adds an element of plausibility to Marshall's ambitions for Roundup in 1943 which historians have missed. The problem for Marshall was that his field army was now stuck in North Africa. As for McNaughton, he was actively discouraged from working with the Americans.[50]

In the meantime, McNaughton was not opposed to sending a division off for combat experience, which his army desperately needed. In early January it was intimated to McNaughton that one Canadian division could be included in the proposed invasion of Sardinia.[51] Any formation sent out to the Mediterranean had to conform to British Army War Establishments in order 'to simplify loading and landing tables' for amphibious assaults.[52] On 10 January 1943, the First Canadian Army began to reorganise to make it deployable. McNaughton was assured that any division deployed to the Mediterranean would be returned to Britain 'in time for possible operations on the continent of Europe' – now estimated to be around 31 August.[53] The Chief of the Canadian General Staff, Lieutenant-General Ken Stuart, was also assured in March that the First Canadian Army would be kept intact for the invasion of the continent – then expected in September.[54]

Meanwhile, planning for an assault on France entered a new phase. The task initially belonged to the Commander in Chief of Home Forces, General Sir Bernard Paget. In early 1943 Paget handed the job to Major-General Freddy Morgan, commander of I British Corps.[55] By February 1943 Morgan's officers were working on two schemes. Sledgehammer – a landing to push a crumbling Germany over the edge – was to be a First Canadian Army operation, with I British Corps under command. The break-out would be conducted by the I and II Canadian Corps.[56] A major exercise to test this Canadian break-out role was slated for early March (of which more below). Once the bridgehead was expanded, two British armies would come into line on either side of the Canadians.

The other task for Morgan and his planners was Operation Roundup: an assault against an unbroken Germany. Morgan assigned the task of developing this a plan to his Brigadier General Staff (Plans), Charles F. Loewen. A Canadian who remained in the British Army after the Great War, Lowen later said his job was 'to make an assessment of the minimum resources necessary for an invasion of the continent'.[57] By 13 March 1943 Loewen had completed plans for Operation Skyscraper, a lodgement between the Orne and Vire rivers in lower Normandy. Skyscraper called for four divisions in the initial assault, four airborne divisions and Commandos on the flanks, with six in the immediate follow-up. The British Chiefs of Staff Committee considered Skyscraper too ambitious and shelved it. Morgan would have to come up with a more modest plan.

Morgan's planning cell gained new status on 12 March when he was designated the 'Chief of Staff, Supreme Allied Commander' (COSSAC) and ordered to have a tentative plan ready by August. In the meantime,

238

COSSAC was to support deception operations intended to maintain the illusion of a possible attack in 1943. Knowledge of his work was sharply restricted. 'Allied Military Staffs (other than British and American) will not be brought into planning at present,' his orders read.[58] Morgan did not allow his injunction to exclude the Canadians, who had a central role in all of his planning.

* * *

While Morgan got down to planning, the First Canadian Army trained for the break-out from the beachhead. The ostensible reason for Exercise Spartan was to test the Canadians' ability to make the transition to mobile warfare. Spartan was also a test of Andy McNaughton as an army commander. As John Rickard observed, 'McNaughton did not have to exhibit Napoleonic brilliance, but a solid performance would have gone a long way to solidifying his position as commander of First Canadian Army'.[59] By March 1943 the assassins were already gathering. Brooke, Lieutenant-General Ken Stuart, the Chief of the Canadian General Staff, Lieutenant-General Harry Crerar, the commander of I Canadian Corps, Colonel Ralston, the Minister of Defence, and 'other Brass Hats' were convinced that McNaughton was not fit to command. McNaughton was already suspicious that Crerar, in particular, was working against him. He was right. 'Spartan', Paul Dickson wrote, 'became the catalyst for destroying McNaughton's position'.[60]

Spartan was one of the largest military exercises of the war in Britain. It spanned south-eastern England, from London, west and north-west over the Chiltern Hills to the edge of the Cotswolds and reaching north of Banbury. This whole area was defended by the 'German' Sixth Army composed of four divisions under Lieutenant-General J.H. Gammel. McNaughton deployed three corps. I Canadian Corps under Crerar was his best: its divisions and staffs were well trained. So, too, were the divisions and staff of XII British Corps. McNaughton grouped his two armoured divisions, the Guards Armoured and the 5th Canadian Armoured divisions, in II Canadian Corps. Its HQ was new, inexperienced, deficient in communications equipment, and its commander, Lieutenant-General E.W. Sansom, had no experience handling armour. McNaughton reasoned that since it was a training exercise, and ones on the scale of Spartan were rare, it was best to get everyone in.

McNaughton's opening move on 4 March was fast and decisive: Gammel was forced to retreat. Then McNaughton seemed uncertain of what to do next. His thought processes were probably not helped by a steady procession of high-ranking visitors. As John Rickard writes, 'McNaughton's subsequent decision based on the captured orders was the key factor in his eventual relief from command of First Canadian Army'.[61] With Gammel's army falling back north of London, McNaughton decided to shift his armour east, to cut Gammel's line of communications. He gave Sansom only twenty-four hours to affect the move, and his engineers a day to build the bridges. Worse still, II Corps would have to cross I Corps' line of communications, potentially tangling both in a traffic jam.

Sansom was still struggling to execute McNaughton's order the next morning when Brooke arrived for a visit. What he saw confirmed his belief that McNaughton was 'quite incompetent to command an army! . . . and was tying up his force into the most awful muddle'.[62] Shortly after Brooke left, McNaughton countermanded Sansom's orders and turned his armour west again, for the good tank country between Oxford and Banbury. The Canadian Army official history could find no clear reason for the change, but Rickard speculates that Brooke had something to do with it. Failed communications – Sansom was out of touch for fifteen hours on 7–8 March – inexperienced staffs and a major traffic jam compounded the muddle. II Corps was not ready to move against Gemmel's right flank until 10 March, and then Sansom paused to reorganise his divisions into two battlegroups, one infantry and one armoured. II Corps was still immobile when Spartan was halted on 12 March.

The official report on Spartan by Paget's office suggested no failure of leadership by McNaughton.[63] This may be because, as Brooke noted in his diary entry for 7 March, Paget was 'quite incapable of realizing how bad Andy McNaughton is'. The fact that Spartan was McNaughton's debut in command of an army in the field does not seem to have entered the calculus. It was assumed, of course, that commanding an army on exercise was much easier than doing the real thing. Not everyone agreed. Shortly after Spartan Brigadier Guy Simonds visited the Eighth Army in North Africa and had a chance to watch it in battle. 'There is an appreciable difference in tempo at an Army or Corps HQ during an exercise and during a real battle,' Simonds observed. 'The slowing effect of fire is never felt in exercises . . . Situations do not develop or change so quickly under real conditions as when they hinge on the instantaneous decision of an umpire.'[64] Spartan was a pressure cooker.

On 31 March, Brooke invited Crerar to dinner and had 'a long chat with him as to which was the best method of having McNaughton recalled back to Canada'. Brooke had tried to get McNaughton appointed to the British Chiefs of Staff as the Canadian representative, an idea McNaughton rejected. The fall-out from Spartan and the campaign to remove McNaughton would have long-term implications for planning the Second Front and indeed the conduct of operations in Normandy.

* * *

The 'problem' of McNaughton was tied up in increasingly complex Anglo-Canadian relations by early 1943. This stemmed from the enormous growth of Canada's role in the war, and frustration over both control and recognition of that effort. Canada was a democracy, too, and the fate of Mackenzie King's government depended on public support for its war effort. Although the Canadian government never pressed – as the Australians did – for permanent representation on military staffs, it did push for memberships on various Allied munitions and production boards. When the Anglo-Americans refused to allow a Canadian to sit on the Munitions Allocation Board, Canada simply retained control of its substantial munitions production through a 'Canadian Munitions Assignment Committee'. Getting a seat on the 'Combined Product and Resources Board' was accomplished by November 1942. But as a major exporter of food, especially wheat – which even the Americans were forced to buy in 1942 – Canada was, in Charles Stacey's words, 'treated as though she did not exist'. The Allies finally let Canada onto the Combined Food Board in October 1943.[65] The struggle to get a seat on two other allocation boards that drew heavily on Canada continued until the end of the war.

It is possible that Brooke and the British Chiefs of Staff knew little and cared less about these Canadian contributions to the Allied war effort. But they would have known that Montgomery's defeat of

Rommel in the Western Desert, and the pursuit to Tripoli, owed a great deal to Canadian guns, ammunition and especially transport. Montgomery was asked to give a statement on the role of these in his victory for use in the 4th Canadian Victory Loan drive in 1943. Much of this critical support had been acquired through a gift of $1 billion (Canadian) to the British government in 1942. By the end of that year Mackenzie King's government was discussing the idea of doing that again in 1943. That second gift morphed, due to political pressure in Canada, into a 'Mutual Aid' programme for all the Allies. The veneer of universality allowed the $1 billion Mutual Aid Bill smooth passage through the Canadian Parliament in May 1943: some 80 per cent of it went to Great Britain, as intended.

The counterpoint to all this generosity was that the Canadians wanted some say in how their armed forces were used, and they wanted public recognition of Canada's war effort. Brooke was certainly aware of that. His diary entry for 21 July 1943 opined that the Canadian 'government had already made more fuss than the whole of the rest of the Commonwealth concerning the employment of Dominion troops!' That fuss was not limited to McNaughton's army. The British Commonwealth Air Training Plan proved to be an enormous success, and it now needed to be expanded to support the growth of the bomber offensive. The Canadian role in training aircrew was so strong that the RCAF simply rejected a proposal by the USAAF that the British and Canadians come to Washington in April 1942 to sort out Allied air training in North America. If the Americans wanted to talk they could come to Canada for a meeting in May. They did, and so too did the British and a dozen other countries. The result was the consolidation of British Commonwealth and Allied – but not American – air training in Canada. The Canadian government now took over funding the scheme, with the British providing roughly 50 per cent in-kind support through materials provided from the US under Lend-Lease. Canada now became, in Roosevelt's phrase, the 'aerodrome of democracy'.[66]

The BCATP poured tens of thousands of Canadians into the RAF, as British authorities showed little interest in funnelling Canadians into Canadian units. In the first six months of 1942 a smattering of Canadians went into twenty-two new RCAF squadrons, while most

Canadian aircrew ended up in British squadrons.[67] The inability of Mackenzie King's government to tell Canadians where their sons were was a source of embarrassment. Canadian fighter pilots sent to Egypt in 1942 to man aircraft in support of Montgomery's offensive went missing for nearly a year: they were eventually found in Khartoum doing guard duty.[68] The RAF also declined to promote Canadian pilots serving in British squadrons to Flying Officer because British policy restricted the number of commissioned pilots. The Canadian Air Minister, Charles 'Chubby' Power, told the Acting British High Commissioner, Sir Patrick Duff, that he would have the British Air Council charged with treason for 'disputing the orders of the King in Canada . . . Without cracking a smile Duff replied that the British Parliament would pass an Act of Indemnity' which would protect the RAF from Canadian 'pains and penalties'. The pilots in question were moved into RCAF squadrons, where their commissions were recognised. As Power observed, none of this fostered good relations.[69]

Buoyed by their new role as an emerging airpower, both the RCAF and the Canadian government grew increasingly frustrated throughout 1942 by the slow march to 'Canadianisation' of overseas squadrons, and by the lack of press that Canada's air war was getting. The latter stemmed from the RAF press policy of anonymity: no names and all operations generically described as 'RAF'. 'The British fondness for reticence vexed the Canadian Air Minister,' Charles Stacey observed. When 'nothing was said to particularize the participants in an action the Royal Air Force automatically got all the credit and the Royal Canadian Air Force or other national components got none'.[70] Power broke the logjam on public relations during a visit to London in August 1942. The two RCAF public-relations officers stationed in London gained access to Canadian flyers and squadrons, and five more were sent to help. By September communiqués describing Canadian raids on Germany reached Canadian newspapers. When the first stories appeared in the British press – something that was not supposed to happen – they embarrassed the RAF. But they also made the point when one London paper asked if this was the first time Canadians had flown over Germany (they had been doing so since June 1941). 'For the first time some effective means existed of informing the public in Canada, the

United States and Great Britain that Canadians were in fact playing a large day-to-day part in the air war.'[71]

It remained to concentrate and define a clear role for the RCAF in the war. This proved difficult to achieve. Canadians hoped to get there by building up the number of RCAF squadrons overseas and ensuring that they were manned by Canadians. The British resisted strenuously. Air Vice Marshal Sir John Slessor, Air Officer Commanding, No. 5 Group, RAF Bomber Command, spoke for many when he tried to persuade senior RCAF officers and Chubby Power that mixed Commonwealth aircrews were an 'invaluable opportunity for cementing the Commonwealth' together. 'I was on a bad wicket,' Slessor wrote in his memoir: the Canadians 'would not have been satisfied with anything less than their own Canadian squadrons fighting in the forefront of the battle'.[72]

The RCAF pressed the case for Canadianisation hard in late 1942, and established their own operations room in London, and elevated Air Marshal H. Edwards, RCAF, to the exalted status of 'Air Officer Commanding, RCAF Overseas' to emphasise the point. Edwards had nothing to command, and senior RAF officers considered Edwards's HQ as 'a piece of nationalistic window dressing'.[73] But Edwards would not be trifled with, and the knowledge that ten more 'RCAF' squadrons had been formed since June with few Canadians in them pushed him even further. The first ever Canadian 'Group' was established on 1 January 1943, No. 6 Group, RCAF of Bomber Command. When two new RCAF squadrons were formed with less than 33 per cent Canadian air crew, and command of four new Canadian squadrons was given to British officers, Edwards finally exploded. On 22 January he sent a 'strong letter' to the Air Ministry excoriating the lame British efforts at Canadianisation, charged them with employing the best Canadian flyers in RAF squadrons, and sticking strictly to seniority when selecting commanding officers for new RCAF squadrons. 'Only 585 aircrew are required to complete Canadianization of our squadrons,' Edwards charged, 'and yet there are 8,515 RCAF aircrew in the U.K.' Edwards threatened to cancel all existing agreements and take charge of posting Canadian aircrew.

Edwards's missile 'exploded very loudly both in the Air Ministry and Ottawa'. The Canadian High Commissioner, Vincent Massey, noted a week later that Edwards 'is having a pitched battle with the Air Ministry on the subject of postings to Canadian squadrons'.[74] The RAF's Chief of the Air Staff, Air Chief Marshal Sir Charles Portal, arrived home from Casablanca in the midst of the battle. He cabled his Canadian counterpart, Air Marshal Lloyd Breadner, RCAF, who flew to London immediately. The two air chiefs resolved the issue, and on 19 February a missive went out from the Air Ministry stating that 'Canada is a Dominion and as such is no less entitled to a separate and autonomous Air Force than is the United Kingdom'.[75] The struggle for Canadianisation was not over, but the way forward was clearer to all.

Brooke was probably aware of the battle with the RCAF, if only from Portal's bewilderment over whose side the Canadians were on.[76] But that was not the sum of the Canadian push-back in early 1943. Senior RCN officers were fighting a campaign to control their own forces and to get Anglo-American recognition for Canada's critical contribution to the war at sea. It was a tense time in the Atlantic war. In early 1943 Germany had 100 U-boats in the mid-ocean air gap, and in January Admiral Karl Dönitz, the architect of the U-boat campaign, took over command of the Kriegsmarine. Britain's only lifeline to the outside world was now truly under siege. In the circumstances it was not surprising that the number-one priority coming out of the Casablanca conference was winning the Atlantic war.

Part of the problem was the divided command and control in the North Atlantic. Britain's Western Approaches Command controlled convoy and anti-submarine operations to the Change of Operational Control (CHOP) Line at 40 degrees west. West of that line chaos reigned. Between the Grand Banks and New York four naval commands and five air commands of two countries conducted convoy and ASW (Anti-Submarine Warfare) operations. The Americans controlled most of these even though virtually all of the escort forces north of New York were Canadian.

In January 1943 Vice Admiral Percy W. Nelles, Chief of the Canadian Naval Staff, made it very clear that the Canadian objective was command of convoy and anti-submarine operations in the north-west Atlantic.[77] The Canadians were already consolidating their own command system around an Area Combined HQ in Halifax patterned on Western

Approaches Command.[78] It was time to push the Americans out. Nelles pressed for a conference to resolve the complex command-and-control issues affecting the Atlantic war. Admiral King convened that conference on 1 March and immediately recommended that the Admiral at Argentia relinquish his command of convoy operations to the Canadians.

The urgency to resolve the problem of the Atlantic war heightened the day the Washington Convoy Conference convened, when the Germans introduced a fifth rotor for their U-boat Enigma machines. For the next twenty-days every North Atlantic convoy was intercepted, over 50 per cent were attacked and some 22 per cent of ships in those convoys were lost.[79] The solution to the problem of Wolf Packs in the mid-ocean air gap was evident: eliminate the gap by assigning Very Long Range (VLR) aircraft to the Atlantic war and reinforcing the struggling escorts. Regaining access to the U-boat signal traffic again would not win the Atlantic war, but it would make victory possible.

The path to that victory was shaped at Washington in early March. Naval and air reinforcements, including escort aircraft carriers and VLR aircraft to close the mid-Atlantic air gap, would be committed. The command arrangements were thoroughly revised. The strategic division of the North Atlantic between the Anglo-Americans remained, but control over transatlantic mercantile convoy operations reverted to the Anglo-Canadians. A new 'Canadian Northwest Atlantic' command was established between the Gulf of Maine and the Grand Banks: the only Allied theatre of war commanded by a Canadian. Canadian escort groups transferred out of the mid-ocean for retraining would be returned immediately, new destroyers were found for the RCN and the nominally American escort group A3 – which was largely composed of Canadian corvettes – converted to a fifth RCN group. The British got what they wanted, too: operational control over the mid-ocean battleground.

With the freedom to run the Atlantic war the way they wanted, the British used the re-penetration of the U-boat cypher after 20 March and a massive infusion of reinforcements to win the Battle of the Atlantic. In April the weather improved, small escort carriers and support groups arrived, and superb intelligence allowed it all to be applied with devastating effectiveness. In May the expansion of VLR airpower, including the allocation of B-24 Liberators to the RCAF, eliminated the air gap completely. In that month alone forty-seven U-boats were sunk, and the mystique of the Wolf Packs was destroyed.

* * *

If the larger objective of Churchill's war effort was to preserve the unity of the empire and Commonwealth, allowing Britain to retain its position as a Great Power, the handling of the Canadians over the winter of 1942–3 did much to undermine that cause. Malcolm Macdonald, the British High Commissioner to Canada, saw this clearly at the time. In a lengthy memo in February 1943 he compared Australia's bitter discontent with British treatment to the more staid Canadian response, but noted that the result was much the same. 'The Canadians,' he wrote, 'remained steadier, and avoided recrimination even when their troops in Hong Kong were lost to a man. But other developments began to shake their confidence in Britain.' MacDonald noted especially the Anglo-American exclusion of Canada from 'a series of Combined Boards' without any warning or consultation. 'Responsible Canadians resented this,' he observed.

He might have added the contretemps over the Canadianisation of RCAF squadrons, or the cavalier way in which the Anglo-Americans argued over the deployment of the Canadian Navy. The Canadians, he said, 'felt that non-consultation in matters which might be of great concern to them was a breach of the constitution of the British Commonwealth of Nations'. He was right. 'All the trouble which arose afterwards could have been avoided if Canada (and the other Dominions) had been taken into our confidence beforehand.'[80] Reflecting on this period many years later, McNaughton told his biographer that by the middle of 1943 'Canada had become a big organization, "not amenable to being pushed around on exercises" & Churchill & others didn't like it.'[81] He had reason to know.

For the moment, 'McNaughton's Dagger' remained the subject of media attention, and a key component of the rhetoric over the looming Second Front. In mid-February McNaughton told a press conference that the Canadian Army was now technically superior to the Germans: 'we have a higher fire-power ratio, and better equipment'. These were the key characteristics of the highly modern, highly mobile, hard-hitting Canadians. As he told a staff meeting a few days later, 'when the time comes all available Canadian troops must be used for a knock out blow against the enemy'. The image of his beloved Canadian Corps of 1918 smashing through the Hindenburg Line and defeating scores of German divisions was never far from McNaughton's imagination. At the end of the month the BBC featured McNaughton in a special broadcast to Germany.[82] As in 1918, the final assault was coming, and once again it would be led by the Canadians.

COSSAC

I realize that the seeds of discord between ourselves and our British allies were sown, on our side, as far back as when we read our little red school history books.

General Dwight D. Eisenhower to General
George Marshall, 5 April 1943[1]

On 2 February 1943 Field Marshal Friedrich von Paulus surrendered what was left of his Sixth Army at Stalingrad. It was a catastrophe of Wagnerian proportions. The vast power of Euro-Asia had swallowed nearly half a million men. For the first time the Anglo-Americans faced the possibility that the Russians might 'liberate' Europe before they could land. At the end of January 1943 the Japanese Military Attaché in Turkey warned his government that Germany's eastern strategy was on the brink of collapse. In these circumstances, the 'British and Americans, who are at their wit's end, may any day now finally move to take advantage of such a grave stalemate'.[2]

That was certainly what the western Allies wanted the Axis to believe. The target date for a landing in France was still August 1943, but Marshall's combat forces were stuck in North Africa. In December II US Corps under Major General Lloyd R. Fredendall was drawn eastward to support the right flank of Lieutenant-General Kenneth Anderson's stalled and exhausted British First Army. Anderson scattered Fredendall's two divisions along an outpost line guarding the approaches along the southern face of the Western Dorsal of Tunisia at Kasserine and the road to the Allied mainline of defence at Sbiba. 'By early February the II Corps controlled only two battalions of the 168th Infantry of the 34th Division,' Christopher Rein wrote – the rest was under British command.[3] To General George Patton, weaned on Pershing's fight to keep American forces unified under American command, the assignment of II US Corps to Anderson was a sell-out. But Fredendall, anxious about the delicate relationships now building with the British, did not protest loudly. Nor would Fredendall have received a very sympathetic response from Eisenhower, who thought little of Fredendall as a corps commander.[4]

By the end of January the Fifth Panzer Army, 100,000 men and growing, under General Von Arnim, faced Anderson's forces. Meanwhile, Rommel straggled into southern Tunisia with about another 90,000 troops, including 50,000 Italians.[5] Both Rommel and Von Arnim thought that the Axis should evacuate Tunisia. Hitler promised more men, tanks and equipment. So Rommel hatched a scheme to strike the novice Americans, drive them back and threaten Anderson with a flanking manoeuvre. He would then switch his armour south to destroy the Eighth Army. Fredendall's bright intelligence officer Colonel Dickson predicted the attack on II Corps. Anderson doubted the 'alarmist' Americans but sent Fredendall a battalion of tanks from the 1st USAD anyway.

Two of von Arnim's Panzer divisions fell on the Americans at Faid Pass and Gafsa on Valentine's Day 1943. 'Sidi Bou Zid quickly turned into a first-class military disaster,' Carlo D'Este writes, 'as American positions were surrounded, attacked, and eventually overrun'.[6] At Faid, ninety American tanks were soon blazing and abandoned.[7] Then on 19 February Rommel launched a mixed German-Italian battlegroup on the hastily reinforced Americans holding Kasserine Pass. The Americans held the valley floor – in Omar Bradley's words – 'as if to halt a herd of cattle'.[8] The Germans took the high ground and virtually annihilated the American force: by some estimates, 6,000 killed or wounded and 3,000 captured.[9] By the time Rommel broke through, British forces backed by American artillery had stopped von Arnim's thrust short of Thala. Rommel abandoned his attack in the face of rain, faltering logistics and the arrival of the British Eighth Army in southern Tunisia. Montgomery anticipated Rommel's plan to now switch to his front. His massed tanks, artillery and anti-tank guns at Medenine destroyed a third of Rommel's tank strength: British losses for the day were 130 killed.[10]

The debacle at Kasserine, and the contrasting British victory at Medenine, came as a rude awakening for the Americans. As Atkinson observed, 'Those who had seen American tank shells punch through the French Renaults [in Morocco] swaggered through their bivouacs with helmets full of Algerian wine, crowing "Bring on the Panzers" . . . They believed they had been blooded . . . they believed they had actually been to war.'[11] Fredendall blamed Anderson for micro-managing II US Corps and deploying its units piecemeal. Most historians, including the British official history, agree. Anderson was shuffled sideways to command the British First Army on 20 February and General Sir Harold Alexander was put in command of the overall campaign in Tunisia. Fredendall was promoted and sent home to train troops. Eisenhower, in his first serious test of command, was seen to dither and tinker. Even his presidential biographer, Stephen Ambrose, was sharply critical of Eisenhower's first test as a battlefield commander.[12] 'To the American people the event [Kasserine] was incredible,' Ambrose wrote. 'It shook the foundations of their faith, extinguished the glowing excitement that anticipated quick victory, and, worst of all, it raised doubt that the righteous necessarily triumphed.' It also shook British faith in their ally, 'our Italians' as some Brits dubbed the Americans. 'The inescapable conclusion after Sidi Bou Zid and Kasserine,' D'Este writes, 'was that had the arguments of Marshall and Eisenhower for Sledgehammer prevailed in 1942, an even greater disaster would have occurred.'[13] Bradley agreed.[14] After the war Marshall conceded that North Africa had been the necessary learning experience for America's army.

* * *

If there was a major media buzz in America in the late winter of 1943 it was the speaking tour by Madame Chiang Kai-shek, and Churchill's seemingly trite dismissal of China as a Great Power. Madame Chiang's tour united Pacific Firsters, isolationists, pro-Chinese, anti-British and Protestant churches, led by the Hearst newspaper chain, into a solid anti-Roosevelt bloc. The administration in Washington, Lord Halifax observed, might be 'fighting the Axis' but 'the Republican Party is fighting Japan'.[15]

The British had no interest in China. On 20 March, Churchill made this clear in a broadcast to the world. America, the Soviet Union and Great Britain would be the guarantors of global peace and security. America was listening. Isolationists used Churchill's words to attack a bipartisan bill in Congress committing America to postwar rehabilitation and international security. One Republican Congressman warned on 24 March that nothing in Churchill's speech indicated a commitment to the 'spirit and letter to the provisions of the Atlantic Charter'. Moreover, Churchill's assertion that 'Britain for the second time had saved civilization' made it clear that America would get no 'credit for their contributions of men, money and materiels . . . There are many Americans who believe that we were the ones who saved civilization in the first world war, and America will have to contribute the balance of power to save civilization this time.' A belief that Britain would partially demobilise after the war in Europe, and contribute little to the war against Japan, confirmed Britain's perfidy: they would fight the war to the last American soldier. Harold Callender, writing in the *New York Times* on 28 March 1943, expressed alarm that these sentiments could even be expressed openly. It was, he wrote, 'a sign of the proportions of the mental barriers between Americans and British, and between official Washington and official London, that even now remain to be overcome before cooperation of the two powers can be based upon anything like real mutual confidence'.[16]

And, of course, the British empire would have to be dissolved. By 1943 Americans had insinuated themselves into talks in New Delhi on the future of India.[17] The British said little about this American meddling, but Canadian newspapers found Americans 'hopelessly uninformed and naïve' about India. This ignorance of and enthusiasm for dismembering the British empire gave great comfort and support to isolationists, Anglophobes and pro-Nazis.[18] McCormick's musings about taking over the British empire were picked up by Nazi propagandists in July and used 'to create dissension between Britain and the United States'.[19] An editorial in the *Vancouver Province* on 9 March captured Canadian frustration: 'repeated suggestions from the United

States that the end of the war should see an end of the British empire are becoming exceedingly tiresome. If victory follows Allied arms, it will be in no small degree because the British empire was able to hold the breach while Russia and the United States were considering the pros and cons.'[20] Even Roosevelt displayed that curious American Janus-faced attitude of being pro-British but anti-British empire.[21] He suggested to Eden in March that as a gesture of good will Britain surrender Hong Kong to China after the war. When Eden asked what territories the USA was willing to give up, Roosevelt offered no reply.[22]

Roosevelt's suggestion of a gesture towards China was not incidental. The American worldview was of a Four Power pact: the US, the USSR, Great Britain and China. Cordell Hull, the Secretary of State, told Eden that 'Churchill has made a serious mistake in his speech ... by not mentioning China'. Worse still, Roosevelt was drifting towards a notion that America and Russia would rule the postwar world. All it would take, George Kennan wrote, was the exposure of Stalin 'to the persuasive charms of someone like F.D.R. himself' and everything would work out fine.[23] Eden found Roosevelt's musings about the postwar world 'alarming in their cheerful fecklessness'.[24]

Typically, Eden ended his March 1943 visit to America with a quick stop in Ottawa. If Britain was to remain a Great Power after the war, keeping Canada on side was critical. Eden brought news that there would be no invasion of Europe in 1943, which put the Canadian Prime Minister in a difficult spot. Building a huge war industry and fighting in the air and at sea had not been enough. Canadians identified real fighting with their army, which had been sitting in England since 1939. Colonel Ralston had already warned that failure to get the army into the fight would be a national embarrassment. The Clerk of the Privy Council, Arnold Heeney, shared that sentiment. He reminded his Cabinet colleagues in January of the epithet hurled by the French king Henri IV in 1597 at one of his noblemen who was too late for a battle: 'Hang yourself, brave Crillon, for we have fought at Arques and you were not there.'[25]

* * *

The meeting at Casablanca has been judged one of the most important of the war, but it would have been hard to convince the British Chiefs of Staff of that in the weeks that followed. 'Am worried by the way in which Americans are failing to live up to our Casablanca agreements,' Brooke confided to his diary on 28 February 1943. 'They are entirely breaking down over promises of American divisions to arrive in this country.' Brooke, it seems, was unaware that Marshall did not have the divisions to send, and that the entire US Army plan was now seriously in arrears due to shortages of both manpower and equipment, and shortfalls in America's industrial planning.[26]

Shipping remained a major problem: there was just too little of it. When Britain's House of Commons and House of Lords were briefed on the situation in late March, both reacted angrily. Churchill admitted that losses were high enough to impede the development of Allied strategy and to erode Britain's reserves of food and raw materials. His assertion that new construction now outpaced losses – the case made to the American people in 1942 and again in the spring of 1943 by OWI[27] – was described as 'a counsel of despair'. A lengthy anonymous document, running to some thirty foolscap pages, circulated privately in April 1943 excoriating the government for its handling of the U-boats and shipping.[28]

If this was not bad enough, a lengthy appendix to this document revealed that the bulk of Allied shipping losses were British or British-controlled, while the new construction was primarily American. It was supposed to be that way. Roosevelt had argued persuasively that America ought to be the shipbuilder for the alliance, freeing British yards to build and repair warships. Now those American-built ships were being requisitioned by the US armed forces. The long-term implications for Britain's shipping situation were dire, not least because 'the United States is rapidly becoming the dominant shipping nation in the world'.

Roosevelt had promised in November that Britain's import projections for 1943 would be met. The British assumed that this meant the allocation of new ships: General Somervell apparently assumed that Roosevelt meant cargo delivered. As Leighton and Coakley note, the British expected the Americans to deliver some 7 million of their required 27 million tons in 1943. Somervell planned to send only about one-third of that,[29] and also expected the British to carry 1.6 million tons of American military cargo to Britain. No one knew where the ships would come from to carry all this. When pressed on this matter in the late winter, American senior planners revealed that they were reluctant to allocate new ships to Britain because it would interfere with their military plans. Some even believed that British imports for 1943 should be slashed – by the Americans – to 16 million tons, so they could get on with deploying and supporting US forces overseas.[30] As Somervell observed, American shipping for British imports should be provided only 'to the extent that the United States thinks is necessary'.[31]

Throughout the long winter of 1943 the British displayed remarkable forbearance with America on the subject of shipping allocation, perhaps because Roosevelt had promised it would be fixed. British shipping losses, and lost carrying capacity because of Torch, had been catastrophic. By March 1943 Britain's net deficit of available ocean-going ships (losses against new construction) was over 1,500. During the same period the United States had a net gain of 4,391 ships.[32] 'The Americans are letting us down,' Brooke opined to his diary after a 'long and difficult' Chiefs of Staff discussion of the shipping situation on 2 March 1943, 'and we cannot find the shipping for all our enterprises.'

Perhaps at no other time of the war was the failure of the United States to develop a coherent and unified national strategy more in evidence than during the shipping crisis of 1942–3. Even Roosevelt could not pry ships from the hands of his military chiefs. In an attempt to cover the gap in their 1943 import programme, the British stripped the Indian Ocean of 'surplus' tonnage – fifty-two of the ninety-two ships supporting British forces.[33] Even so, the British had no surplus capacity to meet their 1.6-million-ton commitment to Bolero, and the projections for imports during the year were grim. And the sharp reduction in shipping in the Indian Ocean contributed to a famine in Bengal that eventually claimed a million lives or more.

At the end of March 1943 Roosevelt – apparently – suddenly realised that the US Chiefs of Staff had not only failed to act on his orders from November, but 'had repeatedly exaggerated its requirements and had wasted shipping as floating depots in the South Pacific'. There was also the dawning realisation that 'Further delay in assisting British imports would weaken Britain's economy, and thus threaten its utility as a staging area for cross-Channel operations'. Roosevelt, 'despite furious Army objections', ordered that securing the British import programme for 1943 was now to be America's number-one priority. But since he could still not pry new American-built merchant ships from his own Chiefs of Staff, Roosevelt bought ninety new Liberty-type ships from Canada and allocated them to Britain under Lend-Lease.[34]

Over the same period the British fought a similar battle over securing VLR aircraft to eliminate the mid-ocean air gap, where U-boat Wolf Packs operated with impunity. The best aircraft available for this task, the Consolidated B-24 Liberator four-engine bomber, was tied up in American interservice politics. The USAAF wanted them for strategic bombing, while the USN was using 260 in the Pacific for long-range patrols. Eliminating the North Atlantic air gap required about fifty B-24s. By the late winter the British had secured a monthly allocation of twenty, but the Americans refused to allocate any B-24s to the Canadians. So at the end of March the RAF agreed to divert five per month from their allocation to the RCAF.[35] It would be June before these RAF and RCAF aircraft eliminated the mid-Atlantic gap in air support for convoys. In the meantime, Churchill had to bear the charge of gross mismanagement of the Atlantic war.

* * *

It is likely that in early April Eden carried home with him from Ottawa the full weight of frustrated Canadian ambitions. To these could now be added the rejection of Mackenzie King's plea in March to send a Canadian division to North Africa, and the bumping of troop movements needed to complete the First Canadian Army in favour of US air-force personnel.[36] Wooing Mackenzie King and drawing Canada back into the imperial fold became one of Churchill's objectives over the next year. He started by sending Mackenzie King a cable on 4 April promising to, in Mackenzie King's words, 'proclaim Canada's contribution to the common cause, probably on Empire Day'. Then he got to the nub of the issue: Churchill wanted an 'Imperial Conference' in 1943 'to show the whole world the strength and union of what we should call in the future the British Commonwealth and Empire'.[37]

Mackenzie King did not respond to Churchill's suggestion. Over the next week someone got to Churchill and he changed his tune. On 13 April he cabled Mackenzie King again, this time suggesting a 'Prime

Ministers' Conference'. Before he accepted the invitation, Mackenzie King sought the assurance of the Secretary of State for Dominions Affairs in London that he would resign before he accepted any back-tracking on 'the conference of 1926 and the Statute of Westminster'. The secretary agreed that 'an Imperial Conference would have been a terrible mistake'. With that, Mackenzie King agreed to attend a meeting of Prime Ministers. Over the next few days Churchill was reminded of why he needed Canada. On 15 April the agreement for Canada to fund the BCATP to the tune of $350 million was signed in London.[38] And the Canadian Mutual Aid Bill, which promised Britain access to $1 billion for war purchases, was about to become law.[39]

All this may explain why, on 23 April, McNaughton was suddenly summoned to Brooke's office to be told that 'the Prime Minister had given him directive that Cdn participation in the next operation was to be arranged'. This was an abrupt departure from Churchill's position just a month earlier. As Brooke said, slipping the Canadians in at this late date was a 'great inconvenience to the British Army', and it was undertaken despite the opposition of his War Office staff. Brooke told McNaughton that he made the decision himself because his staff 'did not fully appreciate the need' to get Canadians into the fight.[40]

While the British handled the prickly and sensitive Canadians, a more serious Allied falling out was occurring in North Africa. There, over the winter and spring of 1943, the struggle over the prestige of British and American forces – the bane of Anglo-American public rela-tions throughout the war – had begun to play out. In mid-April Marshall admonished Eisenhower to do a better job of tracking the press. Patton's excellent action at El Guettar, in which II US Corps moved forward to link up with Montgomery's Eighth Army, got little coverage. But the apparent failure of the 34th USID to cooperate effectively with the British at Fondouk Pass further north had allowed Rommel's forces to escape into the final siege lines around Tunis and Bizerta. Or so it seemed. British General John Crocker's mishandling of the attack on Fondouk was compounded by his subsequent careless talk to reporters, in which he blamed everyone in the 34th USID from Major General Ryder on down for the failure.

By mid-April the prevailing mood between the two armies was caustic, and even the lowly British Tommy was not beyond chiding the Americans for failing to live up to their hype. After Fondouk one British gunner was overheard commenting to a passing American convoy, 'Going to fuck up another front, I suppose?'[41] Ryder wisely declined to be goaded into responding to Crocker's charges, saying diplomatically that 'The British were damned good'. The American media had already commented on the relief of General Fredendall at the end of March as evidence of American failure.[42] On 19 April *Time* ran with Crocker's indiscretion, alleging that American performance at Fondouk was 'downright embarrassing' and that the British had saved the day.

It's hard to do better than Rick Atkinson's summary of the pressure on Anglo-American relations by April 1943; 'however many months or years it took, the task of keeping the Allied coalition unified in pursuit of a common goal would remain among the great military challenges of modern history. Chauvinism, vainglory, frustration and grief – all these were centrifugal forces, pushing the alliance apart.'[43] Eisenhower deflected vainglory and soothed egos, and ensured that his press censors got out the good news and minimised the bad. He also reported to Marshall on 15 April that senior British officers understood the importance of maintaining American prestige.[44] Patton's success at El Guettar eventually got full coverage in Ralph Ingersoll's gripping account, *The Battle is the Payoff*, published in October 1943. In the meantime, even the OWI issued a caution against claiming too much and being too negative. 'Report from General Eisenhower and General Alexander have thrown the contribution of the American ground forces into proper relation with the whole campaign', the directive of 23–30 April said. 'We must continue to avoid both the exaggerated boasting and the apologetic belittling.'[45]

But Eisenhower also intervened to ensure that the American effort was not sidetracked. Alexander originally planned to take Tunis with a pincer movement of the British First Army in the north and Montgomery's Eighth Army in the south that would squeeze out George Patton's II US Corps in the centre. Eisenhower reminded Alexander that 'the bulk of the ground forces required by the Allies to defeat Germany would have to come from the United States. The need for battle training on a large scale was evident.' Success, Eisenhower wrote after the war, 'would make the unit, and it would give a sense of accomplishment to the American people that they richly deserved'.[46] To his credit Alexander agreed 'instantly'. Patton's II Corps was shifted north for the final push. Tunis fell on 7 May, ending the Axis presence in North Africa.

The squabbling in Tunisia between the British and the Americans reflects the clash of expectations and power in an uneasy coalition in its formative stages. Both Great Powers were democracies, both needed good press to sustain their governments and motivate their people. In Tunisia the British also had some reason to be smug. For nearly four years they had oscillated between glorious defeat and catastrophic embarrassment. They were ridiculed by the German and American press in equal measure, and even the British themselves harboured doubts about their ability to win. And now their new American allies – the people who claimed to have won the Great War when the British and French were too incompetent to do so – had stumbled badly in their debut in Tunisia.

The defeat of the Axis in Africa was, in the end, an overwhelmingly British effort. The evidence of that reality was the victory parade in Tunis. It took an hour for the French to march past in a contingent vastly inflated to impress their colonial subjects. Then the 34th USID's 135th Regiment, their soft-soled boots slapping the pavement, shuffled by. They were all in new wool uniforms, buttoned up tight with helmets shadowing their faces. The crowd cheered them wildly, but General Harmon thought they marched like 'Arkansas backwoodsmen'. Patton was not impressed. Behind the Americans came the British, 14,000 strong, marching nine abreast to the skirl of pipes and drums: Scots, Maoris, Aussies, Sikhs, Coldstream Guards, South Africans and English county regiments. 'They were gleaming,' Rick Atkinson writes. 'The men wore shorts and knee socks, with berets or forage caps, and the blouses were open at the throat and [sleeves] rolled to the elbow to give an effect of sinewy limbs and tanned faces.'[47] It was the empire on parade and perhaps the British empire's finest moment of the war. Eisenhower was moved to tears at the thought he had commanded such men. Bradley and Patton, sitting among French civilians and other

9. The empire on parade: the Scots Guards march past General Eisenhower, Tunis, 20 May 1943.

'inconsequential military officers', were just embarrassed by the whole affair.[48]

It was imperative that Americans, too, see themselves as victors in North Africa. This was very much Roosevelt's ambition, supported by Sherwood and OWI. North Africa became – for Americans at least – an American campaign and an American victory. As George Patton confided to his diary after the Tunisian campaign, 'The U.S. must win – not as an ally, but as a conqueror.'[49]

* * *

By mid-April Brooke despaired that everything accomplished at Casablanca had lapsed. The American Chiefs of Staff had lost their focus: US troops were not coming to Europe. 'Their hearts are really in the Pacific,' he lamented to his diary on the 15th. Meanwhile, Roosevelt was wholly absorbed in domestic politics. The process of selecting a Republican candidate for the 1944 presidential election was underway. Many Republicans, like Henry Luce, publisher of *Fortune*, *Time* and *Life* magazines, expected General Douglas MacArthur – at that moment Commander in Chief of the Southwest Pacific Area – to get the Republican nomination for President and lead them to a landslide victory. Beaverbrook's conclusion about America's real strategic objectives from this cursory survey was simple: 'The volume of opinion in favour of the Pacific War is immense.'[50]

It was in this climate that Churchill pressed for another high-level meeting, which became the 'Trident Conference' of May 1943. Churchill and his entourage were still at sea when Bizerta and Tunis fell on 7 May. There is little evidence in Brooke's diary that this brightened his mood. 'Casablanca taught me too much,' he wrote on 4 May as *Queen Mary* ploughed her way westward. It seemed that the battle for a Germany-first strategy was not yet won. 'Agreement after agreement may be secured on paper but if their hearts are not in it they soon drift away.' Travelling in the train from New York to Washington on 11 May, Brooke scribbled, 'I shudder at the useless struggles that lie ahead.' For his part, George Marshall was resolved not to get 'beaten' again by the British as he had been at Casablanca. At the next conference the Americans must 'be *together* and *ahead* of them'.[51]

The Trident Conference came too quickly to effect much change in American planning coordination. The British brought an army of key staffers ready to fight the paper war. They also brought key commanders from India, to meet with America's Far Eastern generals who had remained in Washington to participate in the conference. In the end, the Trident Conference was the 'largest gathering of high ranking official and officers that had yet taken place in the war'.[52] The American objective was to pin down an invasion date. The British objective was to knock Italy out of the war. Over it all hung the issue of the war in China and the Far East.

Churchill spoke first, alluding to 1918, when the collapse of the Balkan front in the late summer precipitated the German request for an

10. En route to Washington aboard the *Queen Mary*, May 1943. From left to right, Air Marshal Sir Charles Portal, Admiral Sir Dudley Pound, General Alan Brooke, Churchill, and his military assistant 'Pug' Ismay.

armistice. The benefits of a continued Mediterranean thrust were therefore only too obvious. Knock Italy out of the war, and then turn the Balkans into a major front. The whole thing, Churchill assured the Americans, would 'cause a chill of loneliness over the German people, and might be the beginning of their doom'.[53] Roosevelt did not completely disagree, although he feared that the Germans might simply abandon Italy and achieve an economy of force as a result. Rather, he pushed gently for sending all surplus manpower to the UK (Operation Bolero), with an eye to a major assault on France in the spring of 1944. The most effective way, FDR said, 'of forcing Germany to fight was by carrying out a cross-Channel operation'.

The next two days were spent sparring over global strategy, with the Americans focused on China. The conference reconvened on Monday

18 May to consider the American staff paper on the war in Europe. It was not ready, and the American chiefs confessed that they had not fully digested the British position paper. 'We therefore accomplished nothing!!!' Brooke wrote in his diary. The tone of discussion nonetheless made it clear that the Americans still considered the Mediterranean a dead end, and that the British were dragging them to Sicily. Might the Balkans be next? Brooke's long postwar notation on this day laments the fact that the Americans 'still failed to grasp how we were preparing for a re-entry into France through our actions in the Mediterranean'.

The next day, 19 May, was the toughest, when the position papers on Europe were debated. When things got hot and reached an impasse, the room was cleared of everyone except the two senior staffs, the recording secretary, Admiral Leahy (Chairman of the American COS) and Field Marshal Dill. Freed from their myriad minions, and mediated again by Dill, the two sides 'at last found a bridge across which we could meet!' Brooke described it as 'Not altogether a satisfactory one, but far better than a break up of the conference!' The essential points were two: France would be invaded in the spring of 1944, with a target date of 1 May, and in the meantime pressure would be kept on Italy with the hope of driving her out of the war. So both sides 'won'. In the meantime, the Mediterranean was not to further impede the build-up for the invasion of France in 1944.

Mackenzie King arrived at the White House on 18 May to troll the periphery of the Trident Conference. He was anxious about the evolving rift between Canada and the UK over the future of the Commonwealth and empire and the fate of the First Canadian Army, and he wanted public Anglo-American recognition of Canada's war effort. Throughout the winter and spring of 1943 he had sought to buttress his government's position by talking about Canadian victories over the enemy. There was not much to crow about. Bombing German cities was not 'fighting' the enemy in ways that Canadians identified with, and the army was idle. So all the drafts of his speeches in the spring of 1943 contained 'fill in the blanks' sections about the latest Canadian sinking of U-boats, but there were none. When Canada's mid-ocean groups returned to the transatlantic convoys in April, the British routed them clear of danger – and U-boats. Mackenzie King was reduced to vague generalities about the scale and importance of Canada's contribution to the Atlantic war.[54] Canadians were unimpressed. Mackenzie King needed the Anglo-Americans to say something good about Canada's war effort.

Churchill was busy preparing his speech for Congress when Mackenzie King sauntered into his room at the White House. The Canadian PM commended Churchill for finally sending *British* formations to Africa and suggested that the presence of Canadians in the UK allowed that to happen: 'he immediately replied that that was true', Mackenzie King wrote in his diary. Churchill made it clear that the plan for 1943 was Sicily then Italy, and then perhaps on to the Balkans to link up with the Russians. The Americans, he confided, had not yet bought into that plan, but they would. As for an assault on France, that was off for now. Churchill 'did not want to see the beaches of France covered with slain bodies of Canadians and Americans', and if they tried anything in 1943 'there might easily be many Dieppes in a few days'. To help clarify all this, Churchill invited the Canadian Army general staff and Colonel Ralston, the Minister of Defence, to Washington to meet with their British counterparts: they were soon on their way.

When Mackenzie King read through the draft of Churchill's speech that evening he took exception to Churchill's use of 'we' as meaning only the forces of Great Britain and the USA. He told Churchill's private secretary that this was unacceptable. In any event, in the British case 'we' really meant 'all the forces of the different Dominions as well as the British Isles'. Churchill's speech to Congress the next day ignored all of Mackenzie King's recommendations. Churchill attempted to disarm the Canadian Prime Minister by singling him and Canada out for special praise, which brought enthusiastic applause. But Mackenzie King lamented in his diary that the Allied war effort remained solidly 'Anglo-American'. The next morning, 20 May, Roosevelt, Churchill and Mackenzie King sat down for a long chat. When discussion drifted around to the elevation of the Canadian Legation in Washington into a full embassy, FDR feigned ignorance of the constitutional development of the British Commonwealth. He observed that Canada would, of course, have to obtain permission from King George to establish an embassy (done at the end of 1943). This allowed Mackenzie King to explain – presumably to Churchill – that Canada had 'a perfect equality in status, not stature [with Great Britain], in all that pertains to our domestic and external affairs'.

Late that afternoon, 20 May 1943, Churchill and Mackenzie King met with the Canadian and British Chiefs of Staff, along with representatives from Australia, New Zealand and India, Lord Halifax, and Colonel Ralston in the dining room of the White House. It was, Mackenzie King observed, a 'remarkable event': the brain-trust of the Commonwealth and empire all 'right in the very centre of the White House'. The meeting was more than just theatre. Churchill made his most impassioned plea yet for imperial unity, using 'British Commonwealth' and 'British empire' synonymously, which made Mackenzie King uneasy. Perhaps more importantly, Mackenzie King said plainly, 'we wanted it known that we were prepared to have our men serve wherever they could be the most helpful in the winning of the war. That we were prepared to have them fight as one great army. We were equally [prepared] to have the force divided up.'[55] The next day, Mackenzie King reiterated this point to Churchill.[56] If Brooke needed a carte blanche to deal with McNaughton, this was it.

Upon return to Ottawa, Mackenzie King warned his Cabinet colleagues that Churchill was 'determined, if possible, to effect, and insofar as possible, centralize the direction of Empire affairs'.[57] As a result, Churchill 'was clearly determined not to make special mention of the Dominions when referring to efforts in which the British forces and the U.S. were engaged'. This policy was already starkly in evidence. The British documentary *Desert Victory*, released in March 1943, highlighted Britain's great victory at El Alamein and the march across North Africa. The film remains one of the classics of the war. Its main theme was how British and American production made that victory possible. As a sop to American hubris it worked. Marshall ordered that the film to be played in every American defence plant. Mackenzie King, too, was deeply impressed by the film. He might well have noted that Canadian industry had played a critical role in that victory. At the time of El Alamein, just 10 per cent of supplies for the Middle East came from the UK, while 30 per cent came from 'North America', a clever choice of words that – whether deliberately or not – effectively masked Canada's significant contribution.[58] The most that Mackenzie King got from his trip to Washington in mid-May was an admission from Lord Cherwell, Churchill's scientific advisor, 'that the British had got as much help from Canada to date as they had from the United States'.[59] Apparently, nothing could be said about that.

Mackenzie King also got nothing from Canada's crucial role in Allied victory in the North Atlantic by the end of May. When Churchill announced the defeat of the Wolf Packs at the Guildhall in London on 1 July he tallied the destruction of U-boats – which was primarily a British accomplishment – as the crucial metric of victory. Half of the Allied escorts and about a quarter of the airpower involved had been Canadian. Nothing was said about that at the Guildhall, or in the joint Anglo-American press release on the Atlantic victory on 9 July. Mackenzie King protested: Churchill pleaded ignorance.[60]

There was, nonetheless, reason to hope for a little bump in public notice of Canada's military effort a week later, as the assault convoys approached Sicily. One of these carried the 1st Canadian Infantry Division and First Canadian Army Tank Brigade. When Mackenzie King learned on 7 July that the draft communiqué for Operation Husky made no mention of Canadians he immediately protested to London. Vincent Massey, the Canadian High Commissioner, replied that there had been no mention of Canadians for reasons of security. Mackenzie King's response was indignation. He immediately phoned the White House: Hopkins answered the call and promised action. Lester Pearson, from the Canadian Legation, went to the White House to make the case: Roosevelt agreed. When Eisenhower refused to amend the official communiqué, the White House prepared and issued its own 'news flash' on 10 July announcing that American, British and Canadian troops had landed on Sicily.[61] That news flash was carried on the front page of the *New York Times* that day.

Mackenzie King felt enormous relief that Canada had garnered some recognition thanks to the Americans, but he was livid over the British reluctance to acknowledge Canada's role. The incident did little to ease Anglo-Canadian tensions. 'Was it any wonder that our people began to like the Americans,' Mackenzie King scribbled in his diary, and 'were antagonized at the English.' The contretemps over public acknowledgment of the Canadian role in Operation Husky would later shape how the Normandy campaign was reported.

* * *

The rejection of Skyscraper in March, and orders to find a way forward with just three divisions in the assault phase, put COSSAC in a tough spot. Morgan fell back on the plans for Sledgehammer, an assault by I British Corps, as part of the First Canadian Army.[62] So Morgan invited McNaughton to appoint a Canadian Personal Assistant to himself and a dozen officers to the COSSAC staff. McNaughton also wanted one senior Canadian officer appointed as direct liaison with COSSAC.[63]

McNaughton chose Major General G.R. Turner to represent Canada on the COSSAC staff. Turner, too, was an old friend of Morgan, 'since the days when I had served in the Canadian army in France from 1915 to 1917'.[64] It was soon discovered that Morgan had exceeded his brief. Despite their task as the lead army, the Canadians were to have no formal role in planning for the Second Front. Prohibiting the commanding officer of the assault army from having any role in the planning of the operation was extraordinary and unprecedented. This was probably Brooke's doing as a way of excluding McNaughton. No British or American would have abided it. Brooke allowed Turner to serve as an observer in a 'private and unofficial arrangement' between General McNaughton and Morgan in recognition of McNaughton's role as a representative of the Canadian government, not as Commander, First Canadian Army. Turner got an office at Norfolk House, but no place on the COSSAC organisation chart – not even a dotted line. On 26 April, McNaughton took the issue up with Brooke, only to be told that 'the planning to be carried out under General Morgan's direction would be too particular for General McNaughton's purpose'. Turner continued to attend COSSAC meetings and report on progress until December (more below).[65] His fourth report, forwarded on 24 April, proposed another reason for excluding the Canadians: it was necessary to maintain the fiction of an Allied descent on the French coast in 1943, and that threat had to be maintained by the First Canadian Army.

Meanwhile, the 1st Canadian Division and First Canadian Army Tank Brigade prepared for Operation Husky. When Montgomery returned to England on 17 April, McNaughton summoned him to explain his plan. Monty did so, and promised not to break up Canadian formations in the field – which well suited his views about divisions fighting as divisions. McNaughton, in turn, declared Monty's plan strategically and tactically sound and authorised Canadian involvement.[66] What Montgomery thought of the summons and having to justify his plan to McNaughton we will never know, but given Monty's prickly character one can imagine. But Montgomery did invite McNaughton to visit the Canadians once they got into action. While at the War Office that day McNaughton also met briefly with Paget, who assured him that the deployment to Italy did not affect the leading Canadian role in launching the Second Front. The next day McNaughton was told that the First Canadian Army was to be ready by 1 April 1944.[67]

On 9 June COSSAC was ordered to plan a nine-division assault, carried by 4,657 landing craft, most of them British. Five divisions would be afloat – three in the assault, two in reserve – supported by two airborne divisions. Two follow-up divisions were to be landed in the next week. Twenty divisions would be available for the 'build-up phase', making for twenty-nine in all organised into two AGs, one Anglo-Canadian and one American. Among these would be at least seven veteran divisions from the Mediterranean and perhaps one French division.[68] Morgan had his marching orders for what was now dubbed Operation Overlord. A detailed plan was to be submitted to the British Chiefs of Staff by 1 August 1943.[69]

The only Overlord force that was ready to go in June 1943 was the First Canadian Army. On 12 June, Lieutenant-General Sir Archibald Nye, the VCIGS, confirmed that Canadian formations committed to Husky would be 'returned to the U.K. in the late Fall of 1943'.[70] By then the British were expecting the British Second Army to be assembled from divisions also brought back from the Mediterranean. For the moment, American forces remained notional. The whole Overlord force, First Canadian, British Second and the two American armies, would form the 21st AG under General Sir Bernard Paget.[71]

While McNaughton worked to ensure that the deployment to the Mediterranean would not shatter his army, Brooke acted on what he saw as carte blanche given by Mackenzie King at Washington on 20 May to deploy the Canadians as he saw fit. On 17 June, Paget informed McNaughton that Brooke had ordered a Canadian division be assigned to I British Corps for amphibious assault training. McNaughton selected the 3rd CID. The next day General Nye confirmed that bringing the Canadians back from the Mediterranean was still the plan, but cautioned that plans were subject to change and there were now no guarantees. McNaughton's Dagger was starting to wither. McNaughton then asked Nye to make arrangements for him and Lieutenant-General Ken Stuart, the Canadian CGS, to fly out to visit Canadian forces in Sicily – on Montgomery's invitation. Nye called Brooke, who agreed to the visit, and then asked Nye to tell McNaughton that 'the numbers from Cdn Army to go to North Africa could be greatly increased with advantage'.[72] There was nothing ominous in Brooke's remark. In McNaughton's notes it appears as little more than a statement of the obvious: the Allies could use more Canadians in the fight.

Operation Husky began shortly before dawn on 10 July. The Seventh US Army landed along the arc of Sicilian coast stretching from Cape Scaramia in the east to Licata in the west. The best of the Axis garrison lay in front of them. The Anglo-Canadian assault fell on the very south-eastern tip of Sicily, either side of Cape Pessaro, the Canadians on the west and the 50th British Division on the east, supported by Commandos and the 231st Malta Brigade. The 5th BID of XIII British Corps landed south of Syracuse.

On 10 July, McNaughton, Lieutenant-General Ken Stuart and four staff officers flew out to visit the 1st Canadian Division in Sicily. When they arrived at the advanced HQ in Malta, Alexander said that he was flying to Sicily in the morning and would confirm the visit with Montgomery. At noon word came that Montgomery denied McNaughton and his party permission to visit, ostensibly because there was no transportation available on the island to move the Canadians around. Worse still, Montgomery now threatened to have McNaughton arrested if he turned up without permission.[73] It was Montgomery at his petulant and vengeful worst.

Montgomery later claimed that Major-General Guy Simonds, in command of 1st Canadian Division, did not want McNaughton to visit. But as Nigel Hamilton points out, Montgomery framed the question 'in such a way that Simonds was encouraged to say no'. In any event, it was not Simonds's – or Montgomery's – call.[74] McNaughton appealed to Alexander, who backed Montgomery. That evening the

Canadians hopped a ride on a flying boat back to Eisenhower's HQ in Carthage. Captain Harry Butcher, USN, Eisenhower's personal aide, suggested to Ike that they load McNaughton and a jeep into a C-47 and land them in the US sector and tell Alexander and Montgomery what they were doing. When Alexander got wind of the scheme he rejected it, saying that if McNaughton had been a junior officer he, too, would have him arrested. Eisenhower protested, as McNaughton had already done, that the incident had all the makings of a public-relations disaster. Alexander remained unmoved.[75] The incident left the Americans dumbfounded. That evening when Eisenhower protested – quite rightly – that 'Alexander was not giving sufficient weight to the problem of a democracy conducting a war', his British Deputy Chief of Staff, Major-General Whitely, retorted that McNaughton 'would just be a nuisance', and that he was 'just being naughty'. Butcher captured the moment best: 'I ventured a query as to how the British had ever succeeded in holding together an Empire when they treat the respected military representative of its most important Commonwealth [sic, Dominion] so rudely.'[76] Good point. The Americans would find British treatment of the Canadians equally troubling in the run-up to Overlord.

Not surprisingly, McNaughton's meeting with Brooke on 20 July did not go well. Brooke recorded that McNaughton 'was livid with rage'. The tension deepened quickly when Brooke – in the words of McNaughton's biographer's notes – 'expressed the view forcibly and with some passion, that I had no right to visit Canadian troops'. When McNaughton reminded Brooke that he was wrong, Brooke apologised. The mood eased during a discussion of the general war situation, but then in a Freudian moment Brooke revealed the real problem. He reminded McNaughton that at Passchendaele in 1917 General Sir Arthur Currie overrode Brooke's advice as Chief of Staff (Artillery) of the Canadian Corps and brought in 'the Cdn Hy Artillery at great inconvenience, so that the Corps could fight as a unit' instead of drawing on local British guns. 'In this part of the conversation,' McNaughton recorded, 'very little sympathy was expressed for the Cdn Army and their difficulties . . . At times, the atmosphere of the conversation became somewhat tense, and General Brooke was obviously disturbed and anxious.' McNaughton reiterated his point about access to Canadian troops, telling Brooke that it was all about winning the war. They shook hands and McNaughton left convinced that he had won the day.[77]

Brooke's diary suggests otherwise. His postwar annotation about this is revealing.

The McNaughton incident was an excellent example of unnecessary clashes caused by failings in various personalities. In the first place it was typical of Monty to try and stop McNaughton for no valid reason, and fail to realise, from the Commonwealth point of view, [the] need for McNaughton to visit Canadians under his orders, the first time they were committed to action. Secondly, it was typical of Alex not to have the strength of character to sit on Monty and stop him being foolish. Thirdly, it was typical of McNaughton's ultra political outlook always to look for some slight to his position as a servant of the Canadian government. The troubles we had did not, I am sure, emanate from Canada, but were born in McNaughton's brain. He was devoid of any kind of strategic outlook, and would sooner have risked losing the war than agreed to splitting the Dominion forces.

Brooke's final comment is disingenuous: McNaughton was never opposed to employing individual Canadian formations so long as the army remained intact. The fact that Brooke raised enduring frustrations from the Great War – not just with McNaughton but with the Canadians in general – suggests that the problem did not lie exclusively with McNaughton.

In the event, there was no public-relations disaster arising from McNaughton's failed attempt to visit his troops in Sicily. On 21 July *The Times* announced blithely that 'McNaughton has been at the Sicilian front to see Canadians in action'.[78]

What McNaughton did not know was that his status was already being undermined by his Canadian colleagues. When Brooke raised McNaughton's unsuitability for high command over lunch with the Canadian High Commissioner, Vincent Massey, on 14 July, Massey cautioned him that the removal of McNaughton 'would be a tremendous shock to the Canadian people with whom he has very great prestige'. Brooke was clear that it had to be done, to ensure 'the success of the operations concerned'. Massey noted that Ralston was due in the UK soon; Brooke should talk to him.[79] On the afternoon of 27 July Lieutenant-General Stuart dropped in on Brooke. 'He suggested splitting the Canadian force between Home and the Mediterranean so as to dispose of McNaughton as an Army Commander!' Brooke wrote with some enthusiasm in his diary. 'He is right. It is the only way to save the outfit.' This took four months to accomplish.

In the meantime, Freddie Morgan and his COSSAC staff presented a draft plan for an assault on France to the British Chiefs of Staff on 14 July 1943. The ultimate objective was to create conditions to insert a force of perhaps eighty-five American divisions into continental Europe.[80] Operation Overlord would be a vast conduit funnelling American power from San Francisco to Berlin. Marshall's army was coming to win the war.

CHAPTER 12

UNCERTAIN TRUMPET

If the Allies invade southern Europe, 'the Germans will tend to discount the possibility of an Allied invasion from the United Kingdom in 1943'.

Report on German Strategy, UK Intelligence, 5 July 1943[1]

The Sicilian campaign lasted thirty-eight days. In the process the Allied command team which would execute Operation Overlord was assembled and tested, and the stereotypes and myths that would haunt the rest of the Anglo-American war effort and the postwar literature were sharply defined. On 22 June, Alexander told Patton that 'we are foreigners to each other'. Patton agreed, and wrote in his diary that 'the sooner everyone recognized it the better'.[2] It fell to Eisenhower over the summer and autumn of 1943 to weld these suspicious strangers into a winning coalition.

The underlying theme of much postwar history is that capturing Sicily, including its garrison, ought to have been easy. Rick Atkinson reflected that tone when he observed that 'barely fifty thousand Germans had overcome Allied air and naval supremacy, and the virtual collapse of their Italian confederates to hold off an onslaught by nearly half a million Anglo-Americans for five weeks'.[3] In fact, both the Italians – about 150,000 troops – and the Germans were prepared to fight for Sicily. On the morning of 11 July the American beach head at Gela was struck by the Hermann Goering Panzer Division and the Italian Livorno Division. The attack nearly penetrated to the sea. When George Patton, commander of the Seventh US Army, waded ashore that morning it was assumed by the American press that his personal intervention saved the day. Newspaper headlines from New York to Los Angeles trumpeted his leadership. Eisenhower was forced to award him a DSO. But as Patton's most reflective biographer, Carlo D'Este, observes, it was all a complete fabrication: Patton came to watch. He let his subordinates fight their battle at Gela.

Sensing a total lack of grip on the campaign by Alexander, on 12 July Montgomery concocted a scheme to win the Sicilian campaign. Commandos would capture the Malati bridge at Lentini, and a parachute brigade would snatch the Primosole bridge over the Semieto River. Then Lieutenant-General Miles Dempsey's XIII British Corps would 'blitz' its way to Messina and trap the garrison. Meantime, XXX British Corps would strike out for the north coast and cut the island in half. Patton's army would eliminate all resistance in the western part of the island. To make this happen Montgomery needed to move the army boundary west. As Nigel Hamilton said, 'the stage was set for the historic rivalry between Patton and Montgomery that would become an almost manic obsession with Patton, as well as spawning books and films for decades'.[4] However, it 'is worth remembering', Lee Windsor observed seventy years after the event, that Monty's plan for a thrust to Enna 'made sense on 12 July'.[5] Montgomery bullied Alexander into accepting his plan. He did not take much persuading. Alexander was already convinced that the Americans would play a secondary role, and his light hand on the tiller – and especially on Montgomery – stoked Patton's anti-British fury. 'The boundary line contretemps,' Carlo D'Este writes, 'left Patton determined to alter the course of the campaign on his own.'

Montgomery's plan quickly failed. Commandos landing near Lentini on the night of 13–14 July seized the Malati Bridge, but the landing of the 1st Parachute Brigade at the Primosole Bridge was a shambles. Everything went wrong. Allied anti-aircraft fire shot down four C-47s and sent nine back with damage. The Axis shot down thirty-seven more, and most of the gliders. Only thirty-nine aircraft and four gliders found the drop zone. They arrived to find German paratroopers had deployed at Primosole just hours before.[6] By the time the vanguard 50th British Division arrived at Primosole in the early hours of 15 July the British paras had retreated to high ground to the south. The British recaptured the bridge and pushed out to about 3,000m beyond before fierce resistance stopped them.

A new directive from Alexander on 16 July shifted the Eighth British Army's efforts north, towards Adrano and the north coast, and tasked the Americans with a continuing support role. Patton was 'mad as a wet hen' when he got the news.[7] The next day Patton and Brigadier General Albert Wedemeyer flew to Alexander's HQ in Tunisia to make their case for turning Patton loose to capture Palermo and sweep up the remaining Axis formations in the west. Patton wanted to capture Palermo as a public-relations coup, but he planned to drive into Messina himself. Alexander gave him the go-ahead, he really had no other choice: Patton was going to go anyway.[8]

Patton established a provisional corps under Major General Geoffrey Keyes led by Lucian Truscott's 3rd USID and General Maxwell Taylor's 82nd Airborne, supported by the 2nd USAD. While Taylor went west, on what he later described as a 'pleasure march', Truscott's infantry scrambled across central Sicily in three days and entered Palermo on the 21st. Patton arrived on the 23rd to bask in the glow, but he never took credit for capturing Palermo – that belonged to General Keyes. However, Patton was hardly modest about the accomplishment. His army had 'exceeded anything the Germans had ever done', and confided to his diary that future staff college students 'will study the campaign as a classic example of the use of tanks'.[9] With the collapse of western Sicily the Allies expected the Axis to abandon the island. But the Germans once again resolved to fight, this time hoping to keep Italy in the war. If all went well, the new 'Etna Line' would hold until the rains of winter stalled the Allied advance.

While Patton's five divisions clustered around Palermo and Trapani, the British were trying to find a way onto the Plains of Catania. That left the 1st Canadian Division, the 231st Malta Brigade, and the 1st USID in isolation in the centre of the island. The Canadians and Americans organised themselves into what Lee Windsor describes as a provisional corps, advancing towards the critical road junction at Enna. Together they winkled out German rear guards using manoeuvre and surprise. One German report complained of Canadian and British 'Indianerkrieg . . . field craft superior to our own troops'.[10] By 21 July the Canadians and British were pushing against the outer works of the Etna Line.

Meanwhile, the 1st USID had captured Enna and was pushing north towards Nicosia against strong opposition. The capture of Enna occasioned something of an international incident, when the BBC announced that it had fallen to 'British' troops. This piled insult upon injury. The day before the BBC had announced that the 'Seventh Army had been lucky to be in western Sicily eating grapes' while the British fought pitched battles along the Simeto. It was, as D'Este describes it, a snide remark. There was, however, a modicum of truth in the 'British' claim about Enna. A Canadian patrol of four men and a commandeered donkey were nearly at the top of the long climb into Enna when they were picked up by the Americans and carried into town on a jeep. As for the BBC, a sharp rebuke from the Prime Minister's office and a reminder that its Mediterranean broadcasts went to everyone brought the news coverage back in line.[11]

On 23 July, Alexander changed the strategy of the campaign to engage Patton in the drive for Messina. The inter-army boundary was bent eastwards, just south of Troina, allowing Patton's army to drive along the north coast. 'In other words,' the US Army official history observed, 'Messina was now up for grabs.'[12] On 25 July, Montgomery invited Patton to his HQ in Syracuse where he suggested that Patton's Seventh Army should capture Messina. 'Patton was certain that Montgomery had some ulterior motive,' but D'Este found nothing disingenuous in Monty's offer.[13] 'Montgomery's reasons were quite uncomplicated.' The British were locked in 'savage' battle south of Catania. Trying to reach Messina that way would simply cost too much blood. 'For all his outward arrogance, which so infuriated the Americans,' D'Este concludes, 'Montgomery was first and foremost an honourable professional soldier . . . [who] would not jeopardize the Allied effort for the sake of personal glory.' Patton, who *was* driven by a quest for personal glory, did not believe that Montgomery was sincere. Thus was born the myth of a race for Messina – and the genesis of a small postwar industry of books and films. 'The truth is that this misunderstood and historically distorted incident was largely a myth: The only rivalry,' D'Este says, 'was in the mind of Patton.'[14]

Patton was a showman and a media hound. D'Este describes his movements in Sicily as having a 'carnival atmosphere'. According to Bradley, Patton 'steamed about with great convoys of cars and great squads of cameramen'. 'Patton's profanity and theatrics irritated Bradley,' D'Este claims. Moreover, Bradley 'believed that Palermo, and now the fixation with Messina, were thinly disguised ploys for headlines and personal glory at the expense of his troops'.[15] Patton's subsequent behaviour in Sicily supports that claim.

On 25 July, Mussolini was arrested and Marshal Pietro Badoglio assumed power in Italy. Badoglio renewed Italy's commitment to the Axis and the war, but he was known to be anti-German. Hitler certainly took no chances. In July there were seven German divisions in the country: four on the mainland, two in Sicily and one in Sardinia.[16] Over the next month that number rose to thirteen, all of them first-rate, combat ready and disproportionately Panzer, mechanised or SS. German troops were also sent to backstop the four Italian divisions guarding the Mediterranean coast of France.[17]

Mussolini's fall prompted Hitler to order plans for the evacuation of Sicily.[18] That day (25 July) Montgomery flew to Patton's HQ in Palermo to finalise the Allied plan. He might have died when his personal B-17 crashed on landing, but he walked away. Patton laid on a guard of honour, a band and a sumptuous lunch at his palace HQ. Monty renewed his insistence that Patton must have the honour of taking Messina, and Patton remained no less sceptical. The next day Patton told Major General Troy Middleton that 'the prestige of the US Army is at stake. We must take Messina before the British.'[19]

And so the race was on.

Patton's options for a rapid advance were severely limited. Route 113 along the coast runs in the narrow space between the sea and the Caronie mountains, through a seemingly endless series of good defensive positions. The road eastward behind the Caronie mountains, Route 120 through the foothills of Mount Etna from Nicosia and Troina to

Randazzo on the northern slope of the volcano, was exceedingly narrow and winding, with sharp switchbacks. Moreover, the shortest way into Messina from Randazzo lay along Route 114, the road which the Eighth Army hoped to take. There was, in fact, no easy way for the Seventh US Army to get to Messina.[20]

In the last week of July the 3rd USID came into the line to carry the fight along the north coast to Messina. Further south, the 1st USID swung east to begin the push along Route 120, taking Nicosia in the toughest fight the Big Red One had experienced so far. Beyond it lay an even tougher nut, Troina. South of the Big Red One, across the inter-army boundary, the 1st Canadian Division 'cleaved a wedge into the seam between the two wings of the Axis line'[21] along the north side of the Dittaino valley, taking Nisoria and Agira. By 31 July the Canadians and the 231st Malta Brigade were threatening to take Regalbuto.

The Battle of Troina was the toughest American fight of the Sicilian campaign. The town sits on a rise in a wide bowl of surrounding hills. The approaches are steep, the road winding, and it is all overlooked by a series of low hills backed by even higher ones. German observation was excellent, and their guns well hidden further up the valley. Getting at Troina was like sticking your head in a wasps' nest. Major General Terry Allen was told that Troina was 'lightly held', and that the Germans would quickly retreat to Cesaro.[22] In fact, Kampfgruppe Rodt (a 'fighting group' of readily available troops named after its designated commander) and four Italian battalions were ready to fight. Support was expected from the 29th Panzer Grenadier Division to the north and the Hermann Goering Division to the south. On 31 July, Allen launched the first of a series of attacks over four days that all ended in failure. Kampfgruppe Rodt might have held on a little longer at Troina, but they were in danger of being trapped when the 231st Malta Brigade took Regalbuto. The Eighth Army, which had finally taken Catania on 4 August, was already advancing towards Messina.[23]

On the day the Eighth Army began to move onto the plains of Catania, the 3rd USID reached the main Axis position on the north coast at San Fratello. The position was formidable. Here the Furiano River created a wide, fan-shaped estuary between low, rolling hills over-looked by the 2,200-foot-high Monte San Fratello. German observation and fields of fire were excellent, and their position was also heavily fortified.[24] Attempts on 4 and 6 August to cross the lower reaches of the river and to outflank the position inland failed. On 6 August, Truscott hatched a scheme to put Lieutenant Colonel Lyle A. Bernard and 650 men ashore down the coast to cut the road and trap the defenders. When a rare attack by the Luftwaffe hit the key LST of the landing force, Truscott had to delay the landings for a day.

Bernard's task force – ten landing craft supported by two cruisers and six destroyers – landed near the Rosmarino in the early hours of 8 August and achieved complete surprise. A chance encounter with a German half-track alerted the defenders and Bernard's force was soon pinned to its small beachhead. As it turned out, the Germans were already retreating from the San Fratello position, and most units had passed east of the Rosmarino River before Bernard's force came ashore.

By 9 August, Truscott's division had closed up on the Germans' next delaying position at Cape Orlando. Anxious about a further delay, Patton summoned Bradley and ordered him to launch another amphibious landing behind the Germans. 'I want you to get into Messina just as fast as you can,' Patton told Bradley. 'I don't want you to waste time on these manoeuvres even if you have to spend men to do it. I want to beat Monty into Messina.' Bradley later observed that 'To George, tactics was simply a process of bulling ahead. He never seemed to think out a campaign. Seldom made a careful estimate of the situation. I thought him a shallow commander.'[25]

Patton's impatience exploded the next day when Truscott had asked for a twenty-four-hour delay in his next attack. His artillery was not in position, and the amphibious force had lost another LST to air attack. Patton's Deputy Commander, Major General Keyes, urged no more delays, 'especially', D'Este writes, 'since there would be correspondents accompanying the task force'. According to the US Army official history, 'Patton wanted no unfavorable publicity for the Seventh Army.'[26] Regardless, Bradley granted the delay. Within an hour Patton descended on Truscott's HQ, 'giving everyone hell from the Military Police at the entrance on through until he came to me'. Patton told Truscott he would be relieved if he was unwilling to fight. Truscott told him to go ahead. 'But I will tell you one thing,' Truscott said in a very

11. General George Patton confers with the intrepid Lieutenant Colonel
Lyle Bernard near Brolo, Sicily, August 1943.

telling reply, 'you will not find anyone who can carry out orders they do
not approve of as well as I can.'[27]

The amphibious assault at Brolo – led again by the intrepid
Lieutenant Colonel Bernard – landed on a narrow strip of coastal plain
in the early hours of the 11th. Again, a chance encounter alerted the
Germans and the fight began. Bernard needed fire from the cruiser
Philadelphia and air support to get through the day. By late in the afternoon Bernard's force had assembled on Monte Cipolla for what seemed
a last stand. Only naval gunfire and support from 155mm 'Long Toms'

firing at maximum range saved his small force. By the time contact with Bernard was made the next morning the Germans were again in full retreat. Patton insisted on yet another amphibious landing at Cape Milazzo. Truscott protested that his troops were already beyond that point. No one wanted to tell Patton that, so the landing went ahead anyway: Truscott and his staff were on the beach to greet the assault.[28]

A patrol from the 3rd USID entered Messina late on 16 August. That evening an American reporter caught up with Lieutenant Colonel Bernard as he was about to lead his men into the town. While they chatted a jeep drove up with news that some Germans were holding out along the north road: Bernard was ordered to take them on. The disappointment on his face could not be masked.[29] Truscott had no interest in being the first into Messina, and Bradley wanted nothing to do with it. When the Messina garrison commander arrived at Truscott's HQ to surrender he declined to accept it: Patton was on his way. At 1000 hours Patton rolled triumphantly into Messina's central piazza at the head of the American column. Waiting for him was Brigadier J.C. Currie, commander of a small force of British tanks and Commandos, which had landed south of Messina just hours before. Currie conceded the race to Patton and congratulated him. Patton thought Monty had sent Currie in to 'steal the show'. He may have been right.

On the 18th the *New York Times* ran a banner headline: 'Sicily Conquered as Americans Win Messina'. There was no mention of George Patton. By then the press had got news of his scandalous behaviour when visiting wounded soldiers. On 3 August, Patton had verbally abused and slapped a soldier whom he found in a field hospital suffering from shell shock. A week later he assaulted another soldier at the 93rd Evacuation Hospital, calling him a 'Yellow Bastard' and ordering the hospital not to admit him. He then pulled his pistol, waved it in the young man's face and threatened to shoot him. The hospital's commander was unable to deflect Patton's rage, and he twice returned to slap the soldier. News of this second incident could not be contained. Eisenhower received a report the day before Patton entered Messina, followed by a delegation of reporters led by Quentin Reynolds. The press corps offered to kill the story if Eisenhower sacked Patton. There were, Reynolds told Eisenhower, 'at least 50,000 American soldiers on

Sicily who would shoot Patton if they had the chance'.[30] They had to settle for a public apology.

It was critical, in the aftermath of the North African campaign, that the capture of Messina be sold as an American victory. The anti-Roosevelt media was prepared to use even the hint of failure on the battlefield – or alleged toadying to the British – to gnaw away at the President. In 1943 the odour of association with Britain was so pervasive, and potentially politically damaging, that Roosevelt's administration failed in its commitment to tell Americans about Britain's role in the war. Edward Stettinius, the administrator of the Lend-Lease programme, made an effort to inform Americans of the enormous benefit which the US derived from 'Reverse Lend-Lease' – the provision of materials, bases, supplies and equipment to American forces overseas from British resources – but Americans were just not interested.[31]

* * *

On 6 August, just as the final push to Messina began, Alan Brooke read Freddie Morgan's plan for the invasion of France. It had been submitted to the British Chiefs of Staff on 15 July and approved in principle. 'It's a good plan,' Brooke noted in his diary. Morgan also admitted that it was 'not by any means entirely original work'.[32] It owed much to Charles Loewen and his Operation Skyscraper. The purpose of Morgan's plan was not to *win* the war: it was to create a conduit to pour American power onto the continent.

Postwar historians have largely ignored Morgan's plan. David Reynolds dismisses it tritely as 'little more than a staff exercise'.[33] That, at least, is what Montgomery wanted everyone to believe. But Skyscraper was more ambitious than even Monty's plan for Overlord, and Morgan's original concept in March 1943 was for a five-division landing. He remained committed to expanding the assault if more resources were allocated. Moreover, the basic concept of Operation Overlord and the development of the subsequent campaign remained as outlined by COSSAC in July 1943: only the details changed.

The COSSAC plan recommended a landing along the southern shore of the Baie de la Seine north of Caen. These beaches lay within range of fighters based in England, had excellent capacity for offloading across the beach, excellent terrain for airfield construction, and the ports of Cherbourg and Le Havre lay close at hand. The Americans would land at the Colleville–Vierville area in the west (later dubbed Omaha beach), the Canadians at Saint-Côme-de-Fresné and Mont Fleury in the middle (Gold beach), and the British at Mont Fleury and Bernières-sur-Mer in the east (Juno beach). In 1943 all these beaches were weakly defended. An airborne division would capture Caen on D-Day, while Commandos and Rangers secured the flanks of the landings. If a fourth division could be added to the beach assault Morgan would put it ashore west of the Vire River (Utah beach), directly onto the Cotentin peninsula.

The plan anticipated an easy entry and a quick build-up of forces. In the second phase Anglo-Canadian forces would drive deep, to the line of the Dives River, in order to meet and defeat German reserves. The Americans would assist in this, but their primary focus was Cherbourg. By D+14 Morgan expected to have a lodgement from Deauville (east of Caen), south to Alençon and west to Mont-Saint-Michel (south-west of Avranches). By then eighteen Allied divisions organised into three armies would be ashore: an American army of seven divisions holding roughly 30 miles of front east of Mont-Saint-Michel; a Canadian army of five divisions holding 80 miles of the line in the centre (including the apex of the Allied lodgement at Alençon); and a British Army of six divisions holding the last 50 miles between the Canadians and the sea at Deauville. The plan envisaged a gradual expansion of this lodgement over the next thirty-five days until it reached the line of the Seine just west of Paris, then south to the Loire River and west along the Loire to the Biscay coast. The American task in this phase was opening ports in the Brittany peninsula and the Bay of Biscay to facilitate the rapid growth of their forces direct from the USA. For this reason, by D+50 the Americans would hold only a slender section of the lodgement frontage, about 30 miles. The vast bulk of the lodgement frontage, roughly 150 miles, would be held by the First Canadian Army. The Canadians would control the critical apex of the lodgement in the Coteaux du Perche area, using two armoured corps (one Canadian, one British), backed by a Canadian infantry corps. The line of the Seine from Paris to Honfleur, about 80 miles as the crow flies, would be held by the British.[34]

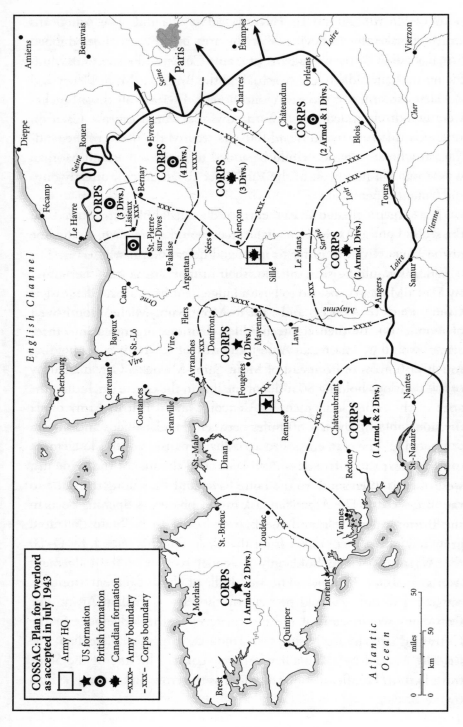

2. COSSAC: the plan for Overlord as accepted in July 1943.

By D+90, with American divisions arriving in increasing numbers, and the break-out imminent, COSSAC's mandate was complete. The First Canadian Army would hand over its front to the Americans and line up with the British along the Seine west of Paris. The leading edge of Marshall's army would then be poised to sweep east, south of the Ardennes, through their Great War battlefields and into Germany. The Anglo-Canadians would attack north-east, also across their old Great War battlefields, over the Somme, towards Belgium and onto the plains of northern Germany.

The COSSAC plan was comprehensive and included other elements which Morgan's planners deemed essential. Among these were two inherently contradictory views. One was the need to draw in and tie down German forces in the west through a threat of imminent invasion in 1943. The other was that there should not be more than twelve battle-ready first-rate German divisions in France and the Low Countries at the time of the actual attack. The fixation on 'no more than twelve' remained – for some – the threshold for abandoning the attack. There also needed to be a specific cover plan to keep the Germans focused on the Pas-de-Calais, and an ability – in the event of a German collapse – to launch an immediate assault.

* * *

The possibility of a German collapse seemed increasingly likely as the summer of 1943 wore on. For the Germans, the news was bad from every front. The U-boat offensive in the Atlantic was defeated in the spring amid staggering losses. The German effort to re-establish the initiative on the Eastern Front, Operation Citadel (also known as the Battle of Kursk) – one of the largest battles of the war – broke on the Russian defences in a matter of days. The Russians followed it with a relentless series of hammer-blows that kept the Germans reeling until the autumn. Disaster in Tunisia was followed by the Allied landing in Sicily and the looming defection of Italy, with all that that meant across the whole Mediterranean front.

And the Allied air offensive over Germany was growing ominously in strength and destructiveness. Almost every night 500 or more British heavy bombers pounded the Reich. By 1943 American daylight raids were increasing in size and intensity. Anecdotal evidence from Germany, and reports in Swedish newspapers, told of growing discontent arising from the bomber raids. One Swedish newspaper reported speculation that the air campaign alone might end the war – just what strategic bombing enthusiasts wanted to hear.[35]

In the high summer Allied airmen seemed to have found the winning formula. In a series of raids lasting nearly a week in late July and early August, RAF and USAAF bombers unleashed a firestorm on Hamburg that destroyed 20 square miles of the city. The intense heat melted metal, glass and pavement, and generated hurricane-force winds. 'Air raid shelters became vast crematoria,' Max Hastings wrote, '42,000 Germans are estimated to have died. A million refugees fled the city.'[36] The effect was apocalyptic. Gangs of concentration-camp prisoners sent to recover the bodies were led by flame-thrower teams to burn a way through the clouds of flies. Even Goebbels was driven to despair.[37] Not surprisingly, selling the bomber offensive as a relentless and increasingly effective campaign became a central focus of British and OWI propaganda in the summer of 1943.[38]

But success in the air came at a price, and Goebbels found comfort in the enormous cost of the bomber offensive for Great Britain especially. Over the previous year some 2,200 British bombers – state-of-the-art instruments of war, built by thousands of hands at tremendous cost, and crewed by the best and brightest – had been lost. In the year prior to the Hamburg raid, 18,000 aircrew flying with the RAF died on operations or parachuted into captivity. By 1943 Bomber Command aircrew losses averaged 600 a week.[39] The upside of this 'Second Front' in the sky was that it stripped German airpower away from both the eastern and the Mediterranean fronts, where the Allies obtained air superiority. It also tied down a million Germans in the air defence. In all, the western Allies engaged virtually all the Luftwaffe, all the Kriegsmarine and kept fully one-third of the Wehrmacht – ninety divisions – busy in the west. Stalin was not prepared to admit that all this mattered, but it did.

By the high summer many senior Allied officials believed that Germany was on the verge of collapse. The OWI Central Directive – taking its lead from the British – stressed the comparison to 1918.[40] A report from the Joint Intelligence Committee (JIC) in late August did the same: Germany would quit – again – before it let the war sweep into its territory.[41] Allied intelligence also believed the Germans were at the limits of available manpower.[42] Optimism over an impending German collapse increased over the late summer.

The unravelling of the Axis, Churchill's renewed enthusiasm for the Mediterranean and American anxiety about what it all meant for Operation Overlord prompted a series of high-level conferences in late 1943.[43] Henry Stimson, the US Secretary of War, spent several weeks in London and the Mediterranean in July. He tried his best to make Churchill understand that American popular interest in the war in Europe was entirely 'intellectual', crafted politically because of a need: Americans felt no animus towards Germany, but they truly hated the Japanese. As for the Italians, they were 'a joke as fighters', while a foray into the Balkans, Greece or the Middle East would be 'a serious blow to the President's war policy'. Stimson came home convinced of two things: the British would go ahead with Overlord if pressed, but Churchill had his eye fixed firmly on Italy and the possibilities of an Italian capitulation.[44] He was right on both counts.

Roosevelt was well aware of Churchill's Mediterranean interests. His 'insider' source was once again Beaverbrook. The Beaver's profile had diminished since the collapse of the Second Front Now campaign in August 1942, and historians have ignored him as an agent provocateur in Anglo-American relations. But Beaverbrook still travelled with the Prime Minister, typically now staying well away from the White House in a New York hotel. He remained an information broker and a political manipulator, and also Churchill's friend, mentor and late-night drinking partner.

And Beaverbrook remained a confidant of the US President. At the Trident Conference Churchill refused to allow him to attend any of the military sessions, and even tried to exclude him from a weekend retreat with FDR. 'In Washington,' Beaverbrook's biographers contend, 'Churchill certainly seems to have feared that Roosevelt and Beaverbrook would combine against him over his Mediterranean strategy.'[45] He had reason to be suspicious. Beaverbrook remained an unrepentant advocate for a Second Front and help for Russia. Before he returned to the UK in late June 1943 Beaverbrook passed a lengthy memo to Hopkins reviewing the case for a Second Front. Britain and the USSR, Beaverbrook claimed, had reached their peak of power. Only the United States 'in a year's time . . . will be more powerfully armed' than it was at present. Beaverbrook did not see much benefit from the capitulation of Italy, certainly not 'decisive results'. There were, in the end, only two real possibilities: bring Turkey into the war and establish the Second Front on the Danube plains, or land in France. Given the diminishing power of the British, the time to act was now.[46]

Beaverbrook had flown back to the UK with the American ambassador, Averell Harriman, arriving on 30 June, and the two went straight into dinner with Churchill. They spent the evening arguing over 'fundamental disagreements'. By the time Beaverbrook retired at midnight Churchill was clearly 'upset', but Harriman carried on for another two hours, conveying Roosevelt's messages. The most important were two: Roosevelt wanted a meeting of the big three – himself, Churchill and Stalin – and, second, such a meeting could not take place in the UK. 'I explained the difference in public reaction in the United States to a personal meeting of two,' Harriman reported later to Roosevelt, 'as compared with a three-cornered meeting on British soil in which it would appear that he, Churchill, had been the broker in the transaction.'[47] Since Roosevelt also hoped to visit Alaska soon, the Americans suggested a date in early September.

Churchill wanted to meet much sooner, in August, and Roosevelt suggested Quebec City. He probably thought he was doing Mackenzie King a favour. But the prospects of hosting the two men whom even Canadians thought of as their war leaders caused a small tremor of anxiety in Ottawa. Mackenzie King fancied himself in that role, too. The request also came in the midst of a spat over the failure of the initial Operation Husky press release to mention Canadians. When asked about this in the British Parliament, Churchill lied, saying that the failure to acknowledge the Canadians was an oversight caused by problems of distance and time. Mackenzie King was livid and called Churchill out on his lie in Canada's Parliament a few days later. The revelation put Churchill in a delicate spot: lying to Parliament usually obliged resignation. When Churchill appealed to Mackenzie King to help him out with the embarrassment, he considered Churchill's request 'somewhat insolent' and refused. The British High Commissioner, Malcolm Macdonald, was told that if Churchill pressed the matter Mackenzie King would dissolve Canada's Parliament and call a general election over 'the degree to which Britain was taking credit, exclusively to America and herself, and deliberately leaving Canadians out of the picture'.[48] Churchill apologised and the whiff of scandal blew over – for the time being.

Mackenzie King agreed to host the Allied conference. It would be, as Churchill demanded, an Anglo-American conference held in Canada. Churchill did himself – and the cause of Commonwealth unity – no service by explaining that if the Canadians attended as a formal partici-pant, the Americans might ask that Brazil be included.[49] The Canadians could hover around the edges and bask in the glow. And there would be occasion for joint military staff meetings with the British to discuss the question of the First Canadian Army's role in the war, especially in the launching of the Second Front.

The potential Canadian role in Operation Overlord was very much on British minds, especially Brooke's. Colonel Ralston and the Chief of the Canadian General Staff, Lieutenant-General Ken Stuart, had recently been in London lobbying hard for increased Canadian involve-ment in the Mediterranean. By August 1943 Ralston's anxiety to get more Canadians fighting was almost pathological. It hurt that Australian liaison officers were overheard snorting derisively in an Ottawa wash-room about Canada's 'boasting and bragging about one Division'.[50] The issue of what to do next with the First Canadian Army was suffi-cient to put Brigadier Maurice Pope, Canada's senior army officer in Washington, on a plane to London at the end of July. Pope had no influence on any of it, but he had access to people who did. In the high summer of 1943 Pope was grumpy and confused, and he was not alone. The British staff in Washington and London were agitated about the Americans trying to hold the British to a rigid plan while they dissi-pated their own effort around the globe. Pope had recently toured Alaska, where he and fellow Canadian officers were astounded at the number of troops deployed. The remaining 5,000 Japanese soldiers on the remote Aleutian island of Kiska – 2,500km west of Anchorage – were described by one Canadian officer as a 'beautiful example of the value of a detachment'. This small force held down 120,000 US troops. In the meantime, the British were trying to figure out why General MacArthur had 340,000 US troops in the south-west Pacific (in addition to Australian divisions), and why America was now equipping 250,000 French troops in North Africa, 'in some respects . . . at the expense of the British' and limited Allied shipping.[51] If the Americans were so keen on Overlord, where was the proof?

Before leaving Washington, Pope asked Lieutenant-General G.N. Macready, commander of the British Army Staff Mission in Washington, about the odds for a landing in France next spring: 'three or four to one against' was the reply. Pope got a slightly more certain message in London in early August. The campaign in Sicily was all but won, and the Italians were talking. Eisenhower had been ordered by the Combined Chiefs on 26 July to plan a landing near Naples.[52] The consensus in the War Office was that Italy would be occupied quickly as far north as the Po River, where the Germans would stand. The Allies would make no effort to dislodge them because there was nowhere to go. As for the chances of a landing in France in the spring of 1944, Brigadier W. Porter, Director of Plans at the War Office, odds were even for a spring 1944 landing: he urged the Canadians to 'stay put' in England. So, too, did Lieutenant-General Sir Archibald Nye, the VCIGS, although Nye suggested that a better date for Operation Overlord would be 1 September.[53]

It was clear that the British wanted the Canadian Army to remain intact, and in the UK. Ralston was not persuaded. The previous week Mackenzie King's Liberal party had suffered terrible defeats at the polls. George Drew's pro-empire, pro-conscription Tories won a minority government in Ontario, where the Liberals finished a distant third behind the surging social democrats of the 'Co-operative Commonwealth Federation' (CCF). By-elections for the federal Parliament on 9 August went no better: Mackenzie King's government lost all four. 'The use of our army will help matters,' the Canadian Minister of Munitions and Supply, C.D. Howe, confided to Beaverbrook the next day. 'We hear too little of the operations in Sicily and they are hardly of sufficient magnitude to capture the imagination of our people.'[54] Public opinion of Mackenzie King's management of the war was now also riding on the

12. The Quebec Conference, Quebec Citadel, August 1943:
Mackenzie King basks in the glow while Roosevelt and Churchill chat.

imminent American–Canadian landing on Kiska, where a brigade of
home defence conscripts would soon be in action against the Japanese.
That might slake the blood lust.

The Quebec Conference tied up the senior British staff and Churchill
himself for nearly a month. The plan, clearly, was to confirm the
commitment to Overlord, but leave open all options for exploitation of
an Italian collapse. When Pope enquired what this might mean for the
First Canadian Army, Macready told him not to worry. The Americans
would never stand for a reduction of strength in the UK, and no one
would support an 'interchange of British and Canadian divisions just to

please us'. When Pope suggested – as Nye had done – that the pressure was off anyway because Overlord would not happen until 1 September 1944, Macready shot back: 'My God, you must not say that, the Americans will explode if they heard such a thing! Rather, we must talk of the beginning of good weather next spring.'[55]

George Marshall worried constantly that the Mediterranean was a great vacuum, sucking in resources. He was right, but the vacuum pulled strongly on Germany's declining resources, too. For the British, that was the whole point. At the very least the Germans would have to back-fill for their defecting ally. The Italian Field Army was notionally sixty-two divisions, including thirty deployed in the Balkans.[56] If the Italian Army switched sides the Allies would have a massive infusion of strength, a new front and a possible link-up with the Russians. With the Bosphorus open there would be no need for convoys to the Arctic. In the late summer and early autumn of 1943 the wider implications of an Italian defection underlay much of Allied strategic discussion and planning, including options for a very different kind of Second Front. This was just what the American feared.

* * *

Before the conference Churchill spent several days at Hyde Park in discussion with Roosevelt. They agreed that Overlord would be commanded by an American. Ostensibly Churchill capitulated because the vast bulk of Allied forces in north-west Europe would eventually be American. In exchange, supreme command in Italy, the Mediterranean, the Middle East and South East Asia would be British. These were all places where British forces predominated, so it seemed a fair swap. The more suspicious believed that Churchill had a deeper motive. As Manchester and Reid write, 'if the agreed upon conditions for under-taking the invasion of France were not met, there would be no invasion, leaving the Americans with command of a nonentity, while Churchill held the rest of the marbles'.[57]

The spare days in Quebec for the British staff were taken up with briefing the Canadian General Staff, conferring with the Washington Mission and fishing for trout. Brooke also read the American Staff Appreciations – ready in advance this time – and expressed himself 'delighted . . . at last they are beginning to see some daylight in the problems confronting us'.[58] Prior to the plenary session on 15 August Churchill took Brooke aside to break the news that George Marshall would command Operation Overlord. Eisenhower was to replace him in Washington, allowing Alexander to become Allied Supreme Commander in the Mediterranean. Command of the ground component of Overlord would be given to Montgomery. Brooke would have to soldier on as CIGS. Churchill's news left Brooke 'swamped by a dark cloud of despair'.[59]

The rest of this 'gloomy and unpleasant day' Brooke spent trying to convince Marshall – again – that there was an important relationship between the Mediterranean and a successful landing in France in 1944. After three hours of seemingly fruitless endeavour, both sides were exhausted and frustrated. Brooke went off for a private dinner while Dill met with Marshall, whom he found 'unmanageable and irreconcilable'. Dill and Brooke then chatted until midnight trying to find a way forward.

The next day began with a buzz of excitement about negotiation with the Italians, which had started secretly in Lisbon. The British, mindful of the perilous nature of the Italian initiative and the possible windfalls from Italian belligerency, wanted these talks conducted by diplomats and politicians. Roosevelt insisted that his generals handle them. Eisenhower's deputy Bedell Smith and a British staff officer, Brigadier K.W.D. Strong, met the Italians, and were given no scope to offer anything except unconditional surrender. The Italians would have to surrender before any offer of co-belligerency could be discussed. The Americans were also deeply suspicious of constitutional monarchies and wanted nothing to do with the Italian king. For their part, the Italians were clearly looking for flexibility, and the delay in settling things proved critical.[60]

Meanwhile at Quebec, on Monday 16 August the attending staffs, secretaries and planners were again cleared from the room so the senior officers could speak candidly. Brooke hit it right when he started by saying that the two staffs did not trust each other, and that the Americans had no faith in the British commitment to Overlord in the spring of 1944. For the next three hours the gloves came off, as Brooke once again made the case for pursuing the attack on Italy as a way of drawing the Germans into the theatre and helping to create conditions for

Overlord. He concluded his diary for that day with an exhausted lament: 'I do not feel that I can possibly stand any more!'

He did. When the Combined Chiefs met the next afternoon the deadlock over European strategy broke. 'To my great relief,' Brooke wrote in his diary, 'they have accepted the proposals for the European theatre so that all our arguing has borne fruit and we have obtained quite fair results.' The Americans thought so, too. Dill had worked his magic again. The Americans agreed to a direct attack on Italy, in the expectation that the Germans would retreat to the north, abandoning Rome and good airfields in the south – and leaving the Allies free to concentrate on Overlord. Given that the bomber offensive had 'the highest strategic priority'[61] in Europe, capturing the Italian airfields at Foggia made good sense. What Marshall squeezed out of the British was agreement to limit the total number of Allied divisions committed to Italy by the spring of 1944, a firm commitment to Overlord, and agreement on an additional landing in the south of France to coincide with Overlord.

The Quebec conference went on for six more days, with intense debate over strategy for the war against Japan, especially over British 'foot dragging' in Burma. The American engagement in what was overwhelmingly a British theatre of war was a courtesy not extended to the British over their Pacific war. The British had a vested interest in MacArthur's SWPA, where a large number of British, colonial or Dominion troops were engaged. Prior to Quebec the British staff in Washington had suggested shutting down SWPA and Burma and concentrating on a combined amphibious drive through Sumatra, to Singapore and Malaya and then eastward using British naval strength released by the Italian capitulation. At Quebec, Pope enquired if this scheme was to be discussed. It was not. The Americans had flatly rejected it because it might lead to MacArthur's resignation and the Republican nomination for President. Dill had already warned Alan Brooke of that possibility in June.[62] As Pope lamented, this was not 'a very good military reason' for not discussing strategy in the south-west Pacific.[63] 'It seems,' Pope noted in his diary, 'as if the Americans want the entire Pacific to themselves.'[64] For the British the Pacific war remained almost as enigmatic as the Russian front.

Churchill emerged from Quebec content. He had secured British supreme command over just about everything except Overlord, and he was not convinced that the Second Front in France would even take place. The Mediterranean offered too many tantalising potentials, and the beaches of France too many perils. In any event, the Americans still had only two divisions in the UK. Where was Marshall's army?

As for Roosevelt, he was increasingly focused on planning for what was to happen postwar. Roosevelt and Churchill agreed that the next meeting would have to include Stalin. An invitation was sent on 18 August.[65] When, over drinks late in the evening on 21 August, Churchill suggested that the planning of the UN could wait, Roosevelt said no. He needed to get something out before the other candidates for President in 1944 did. Mackenzie King lamented to his diary that 'the embarrassment of a fixed time for the election lay in part at the root of the discussion'.[66]

The uncertain trumpet calling out from Quebec muddled planning for Overlord, too. While the Americans were clearly 'in', there was no great rush of formations and headquarters to the UK to make it happen. Given the lack of American commitment the British remained sceptical that Overlord would happen. So, too, were the Canadians. Ralston, Stuart and many others – like Maurice Pope – hoped that the landing on Kiska would capture public imagination in Canada. The battle for nearby Attu in May had been a long and bloody affair, during which the Japanese garrison fought virtually to the last man. It was estimated that 10,000 Japanese – three times the Attu garrison – were holding Kiska.[67] Among the 34,000 troops slated to land on Kiska on 15 August were some 5,200 Canadians. Most of them (4,800) were conscripts who found out in July that home defence included remote and desolate American islands closer to Japan than Vancouver. The new and untried American–Canadian '1st Special Service Force', a 3,000-man elite unit especially trained in mountain warfare, was also slated to land.[68]

Word quickly trickled back to Quebec that the Kiska landing was unopposed. By 17 August, Pope, and probably a few other senior Canadian generals, were getting anxious. 'If the Japanese have completely abandoned ship,' Pope wrote that day, 'it will be a case of very bad luck for us.' The next day they learned that the Japanese had fled, 'and more's the pity'. Historians have treated the Kiska operation as a bit of a joke. It all seemed much ado about nothing. But the flop on Kiska echoed in the distant corridors of power. Had Kiska been a hard fight the political urgency to get more Canadians engaged in the Mediterranean might have been assuaged. But three days after the news from Kiska was confirmed, Macready confronted Pope at Quebec about rumours of another Canadian division headed to the Mediterranean. Pope professed his ignorance: Macready urged him to resist. The Canadians would end up as occupation troops in northern Italy. As Pope exclaimed in his diary, the Americans were going to France 'in eight months' time!'[69]

Over lunch with Mackenzie King on 31 August Churchill made it clear that 'he was not at all averse to having another [Canadian] division going from Britain to Sicily and Italy for battle experience: not averse to Canada having an army corps in Italy'. If this happened, however, it would be necessary to bring British divisions back from the Mediterranean in order 'to keep faith with the Americans' in the Overlord planning.[70]

* * *

While Brooke relaxed fishing trout in Quebec, Eisenhower and his staff prepared for the invasion of Italy. Increasingly it seemed that the Germans were not going to give up Italy without a fight. 'It is becoming increasingly apparent', Butcher wrote, 'that the Germans intend to defend their European Citadel as far from Germany as possible and will make Italy a battleground whether the Italians cooperate with them or not'.[71]

On 29 August, Eisenhower and Montgomery motored to Messina to look at the Italian mainland. The preliminary bombardment for Operation Baytown was already underway. In a few days the 5th British and 1st Canadian Infantry divisions would land on that opposite shore. Monty could not help but comment that he had been kicked off the continent at Dunkirk. Now, as Butcher recorded the moment, 'Montgomery's British and Canadian troops' were poised to go back, to become the first to 'invade the Citadel of Europe'.[72] It was all true. But historians are wont to forget that the 1st Canadian Division had been chased out of France in June 1940, too. They were also anxious to get back.

CHAPTER 13

DOMINOES

The Balkan domino thesis was how Churchill explained victory in 1918, but Washington believed the critical factor of the collapse of Nazi Germany, as of the Kaiserreich twenty-five years before, would be the arrival of a massive American army on the Western Front.

David Reynolds, *In Command of History*[1]

On 3 September 1943, the day British and Canadian troops landed at Reggio de Calabria, Badoglio's government secretly signed the articles of surrender. But Badoglio wanted fifteen Allied divisions to land before he would change sides. Frustrated by the dithering, on 8 September, Eisenhower announced the Italian capitulation. It was, Shelford Bidwell and Dominick Graham concluded, 'one of the few political miscalculations of his career'.[2] The Germans immediately began disarming Italian troops, while the Italian government disintegrated and fled. Italy and its armed forces were now without leadership or direction.

The essential question was: what would the Italian Army do?[3] In July, Todman writes, 'reports started to reach Cairo that Italian occupation forces in the Balkans were ready to come over to the Allies if they could be guaranteed protection from the Germans and from the local inhabitants'.[4] The implications of an Italian defection were hardly a secret. Seventeen German divisions were in the Balkans by early

September, and as many as twenty in Italy itself.[5] A force roughly the equivalent of AG North on the Russian front had been drawn in by Allied Mediterranean operations.[6] The Italians still vastly outnumbered the Germans in the region, but no one believed that they could defeat them.

Moreover, it was unclear what the Germans would fight for. Most believed that they would abandon Italy south of the Pisa–Pesaro line, which was in fact Hitler's original intent. Some senior British officers hoped, however, that the Germans would contest every inch of the Italian boot. Field Marshal Dill was among them. He told Maurice Pope on 3 September that 'he hoped that the Italians would cry for help from the Germans', adding that 'if they are going to double-cross the Hun it would seem appropriate that they make a complete job of it'.[7]

* * *

Dill got his wish. The German military commander in Italy, Field Marshal Albert Kesselring, thought the Anglo-Americans could be held south of Rome. Typically, Hitler resolved his strategic dilemma by having it both ways. He gave Rommel command of forces in northern Italy, and Kesselring command of the nascent Tenth Army south of Rome. Kesselring began to build a fortified line across Italy's narrowest part, from the mouth of the Garigliano River in the west to Ortona on the Adriatic. If he could prove to Hitler that the Anglo-Americans were 'soft, feared close combat and soon gave up', Italy's geography would allow him to stall the Allies indefinitely.[8]

Command of the main Allied assault headed for Salerno fell to General Mark Clark of the newly created US Fifth Army. Many of Clark's contemporaries and subsequent historians agreed that his plan for Operation Avalanche was flawed. Three divisions landing along a 30-mile stretch of beach astride a major river obstacle was a poor start. George Patton, in command of the reserve and the back-up for Clark should anything happen to him, was sharply critical of the plan, especially the wide gap between the British and American landings. Patton figured that if he could see the flaws, so could the Germans. The British certainly did. But Avalanche was an American operation and, in the tradition of the US Army, no one questioned the General's plan.[9] Only the US Navy recommended a change, suggesting a preliminary bombardment. Clark declined. Consequently, the only fire support from the sea occurred during the British assault, where 'a large number of special landing craft, fitted to fire mortars and rockets as well as guns' were deployed.[10]

The landing at Salerno took place in the early hours of 9 September, shortly after Eisenhower and the BBC broadcast the news of the Italian surrender. The main assault by two British divisions and one American, and the advance inland, went well. Then counterattacks by the 16th Panzer Division contained the landing while reinforcements were despatched. Soon most of six Panzer or Panzer Grenadier divisions surrounded the Salerno beachhead, outnumbering the assault forces by at least two to one. This was the scenario which all Allied amphibious planners feared.

The German assault on the beachhead began in earnest on 12 September. Over the next three days the Anglo-Americans recoiled, but did not break. In the US sector the Germans got within 2 miles of the beach, which came under German artillery fire. Relentless firing by Anglo-American artillery, attacks by tactical airpower and support from British and American warships, and eventually the British battleships *Warspite* and *Valiant* helped to hold the line. By the 15th, the German effort was spent.[11] Allied reinforcements were also arriving. It helped that the leading elements of Montgomery's Eighth Army were closing on Salerno from the rear. The Germans were now at risk of encirclement. In any event, Kesselring had made his point: the Germans would defend south of Rome.

On the Allied side recriminations for shortcomings on both the American and British part were already well underway. 'In this,' Graham and Bidwell aptly conclude, 'they resembled two whores upbraiding each other for lack of chastity.'[12] Once again, Montgomery was in the thick of it. During the crisis at Salerno, Alexander had urged him to push the Eighth Army harder. Montgomery refused. He had long since exhausted his engineering stores, especially bridging equipment, and was moving as fast as he could. To deflect the Germans' attention away from Salerno, Alexander suggested to his media entourage that they nonetheless highlight the rapid advance of the Eighth Army. In the midst of all this a group of reporters travelling with the Eighth Army slipped through to Clark's HQ on the 15th. If the press could get through, why not Monty? In the end, Salerno did much to confirm national prejudices. For the Americans Montgomery was a plodder – as he had been after El Alamein, in southern Tunisia, and on the plains of Catania. For the British, only Montgomery's timely arrival had saved Clark's army from annihilation. Either way, Graham and Bidwell conclude, 'Clark's vanity was badly scarred, and he was convinced that the British as a matter of policy were determined to steal the publicity for victories gained by American valour.'[13]

* * *

The day after Clark's army landed at Salerno, Anthony Eden confided his latest frustration to his diary. He had been trying to arrange for a high-level meeting involving the Russians. It was hard to do with Churchill lingering in Washington under Roosevelt's baleful influence. Roosevelt's 'determination not to agree to a London meeting for any purpose, which he says is for electoral reasons, is almost insulting considering the number of times we have been in Washington', Eden wrote on 10 September. 'I am anxious for good relations with U.S. but I don't like subservience to them and I am sure that this only lays up trouble for us in the future. We are giving the impression, which they are only too ready by nature to endorse, that militarily all the achievements are theirs, and W., by prolonging his stay in Washington, strengthens that impression.'[14]

In the aftermath of the formal Italian surrender Churchill still hoped to open a new front in the Balkans based on Italian resistance and Turkish belligerency. The growing power of the Soviet Union made both Churchill and Eden anxious about Russian control of vast tracts of Europe. The possibility of beating the Russians into eastern Europe may have been a thin reed to grasp, but from Churchill's perspective it was worth the effort.

And so the British began their own campaign to jump-start the Balkan war. Control of the Italian-controlled Dodecanese Islands in the eastern Aegean was a possible key to luring Turkey, and its forty divisions, into the war, and opening a short and direct route to Russia. Special forces were already active in the islands. The Italians were known to be disaffected, and so on 8 September, Major Lord Jellicoe parachuted onto Rhodes to persuade the 30,000-man Italian garrison to switch sides. Instead, they surrendered to the 7,000 Germans on the island. At Churchill's urging Middle East Command then despatched 4,000 men to occupy nearby Kos, Leros and Samos. Beaverbrook had warned the Americans in June that the Dardanelles was once again a draw for Churchill. In September events seemed to be bearing this out.[15]

The potential benefits of the Italian capitulation slipped away quickly. As early as 13 September, Robert Lockhart lamented that 'all the optimistic effect of the armistice has been destroyed'. Our 'soldiers', he wrote, had pinned their hopes on the Italian Army and 'reckoning them a real gain'.[16] Within two weeks of the capitulation that army had virtually disappeared. Of the sixty-two Italian field divisions believed to exist on 8 September, the Germans disarmed about forty-five of them. Pro-German partisans in the Balkans disarmed half a dozen more, and two or three stayed loyal to the fascist cause. Only a handful of Italian divisions fought it out, and they could not be helped.[17] The news was not entirely bleak. The Italian collapse freed large areas for partisan forces, and recapturing it proved hard. By October five German divisions, and elements of five more, were trying to pacify Yugoslavia alone.[18]

The partisan war in the Balkans burned brightly enough to sustain Churchill's ambition in the region. In late September he silenced one of the major public critics of his Mediterranean strategy when he brought Beaverbrook back into his government as Lord Privy Seal – essentially a minister without portfolio. Churchill gave him a task: champion Britain's position in the emerging struggle with the US over postwar international air travel. Beaverbrook grasped the challenge with both hands and was off.[19] Those closest to Churchill, like Eden and Bracken, were content that Beaverbrook was back in the tent, and available to deflect Churchill's wilder urges. 'He told Max practically everything,' Lockhart confided to his diary. 'It was therefore better to have him inside government than outside it.'[20] Dill sent Brooke his condolences.[21]

With Beaverbrook silenced Churchill now took counsel on his Mediterranean ambitions from the South African Prime Minister, Field Marshal Jan Smuts. By 1943 Smuts, who as a young man had fought the British and once captured Churchill, was a deeply revered elder statesman and a staunch supporter of the empire.[22] He arrived in London in October, just as Roosevelt emphatically rejected Churchill's Balkan ambitions.[23] On the 14th Churchill and Smuts had dinner with King George, whom Churchill was trying to draw into his Balkan scheme. According to Reynolds, Churchill told the King that there was no reneging on the Overlord commitment but that there should be enough resources for both. More importantly, Churchill wanted to be 'masters of our own destiny' and not bound by what the Americans wanted. His secret staff study of the benefits from a Balkan initiative was reviewed on 19 October by the British Chiefs of Staff. 'I am in many ways entirely with him,' Brooke confessed later that day, 'but God knows where that may lead us to as regards clashes with Americans.' Later that evening when the War Cabinet met to discuss the study, Churchill's position was, in Reynolds's words, 'now more extreme . . . Others present [including Brooke] joined in attacking the rigid commitment to Overlord at a time when southern Europe seemed so promising.' Smuts' position seemed to sum up the general view of the War Cabinet: southern Europe now presented 'a clear run in to victory . . . provided we did not blunder'.[24]

While the British hardened on the merits of a Balkan strategy, Dill wrote to Brooke urging restraint. 'I do not believe that it was ever possible to make the Americans more Mediterranean-minded than they are today,' Dill said in a personal note dated 16 October. 'The American Chiefs of Staff have given way on our views a thousand times more than we have given way to theirs.' Things were going well, but the politics of dealing with the Americans grew ever more perilous. 'Our difficulties with the Americans are going to increase,' Dill warned, 'rather than diminish with their growing strength and a presidential election approaching. The President's enemies attack him through us and so his advisors feel that they must do everything to prove that they are not in our pockets.' Dill flatly warned Brooke that he could not afford to lose Marshall: everyone in Washington trusted him and he was non-political. The perils of dealing with America were evident, Dill observed, in how the Americans viewed Churchill. At the moment the Prime Minister was 'the most popular foreigner America has known'. But it would take just one or two ill-advised remarks and the anti-FDR press would turn on him.[25]

There is no evidence that Dill's warning was heeded. In mid-October 1943 the British intended to pursue a Mediterranean strategy regardless of the Americans. Churchill wanted the whole thing presented to them as soon as possible. It seems that Brooke, too, was on side. By late October the Italian theatre was stagnating, strangled by diminishing resources. On 1 November Brooke wrote a long lament in his diary over his inability to get the Americans to see the merits of a full-out Balkan offensive instead of diverting forces for a 'nebulous 2nd Front'. Had he succeeded, the Balkans would be 'ablaze by now, and the war might have been finished in 1943!!' Brooke's postwar annotation for 18 November captures the mood. 'First of all the new feelings of spitefulness which had been apparent lately with Winston since the strength of the American forces were now building up fast and exceeding ours. He hated having to give up the position of the dominant partner which we had held at the start.' According to Brooke, this petulance led Churchill to make strategic proposals 'which he knew were unsound purely to spite the Americans . . . There lay, however, in the back of his mind the desire to form a purely British theatre when all the laurels would be ours.'[26] Brooke remained convinced that the 'American failure to realize the value of exploiting the whole Mediterranean situation' extended the war by at least six months.[27]

The Germans also saw the failure to aggressively follow up on the Italian capitulation as a major strategic error. 'Seen from today,' Heinz Magenheimer wrote in 1998, 'this strategic compromise between Allied leaders was a serious mistake.'[28] Reynolds claims that the scope and the intensity of this British effort to pursue a Balkan strategy in the autumn of 1943 was simply erased from history after 1945. Churchill's 'cover-up of this in *Closing the Ring*', he writes, 'is one of the most blatant pieces of distortion in his six volumes of memoirs'.[29]

* * *

Churchill reacted strongly to rising American power in late 1943, and with good reason. America was not only finding its feet in the struggle for hegemony, it was also finding its voice. The OWI and the British MOI had agreed in 1942 to share a common directive for propaganda in Europe, but by 1943 – in the words of the in-house history of OWI – 'large scale planning for the "Projection of America" in the Liberated countries after the fighting' was well underway.[30] This went well beyond what the Psychological Warfare Division of Supreme Headquarters, Allied Expeditionary Force, was preparing. British aircraft operating for OWI dropped 24 million leaflets on France in the aftermath of Torch. In the summer of 1943 the USAAF took on that task with two dedicated B-17 squadrons. By early 1944 they were dropping 300 million leaflets a month.[31]

American radio broadcasts to Europe were also rapidly developing. So long as 'Voice of America' (VOA) was broadcast from New York it reached only 'a relatively small minority of Europeans'. Coverage improved dramatically when the BBC agreed to rebroadcast VOA, but by 1943 that – in the words of the OWI history – 'did leave a certain aftertaste of American dependency on a British medium'. So the decision was made to build a dedicated 'American Broadcasting Station in Europe' (ABSIE) in time for Overlord and have it ready to carry America's message direct to Europe.[32]

By late 1943 OWI had, for the most part, also sorted out how to 'sell' America to the British themselves. This was no easy task, although the existence of a single, centralised radio broadcasting system – the BBC – made the task much less complicated than what the British faced in the USA. The directive governing OWI propaganda in the UK for the last two years of the war was issued in April 1943. It consisted of four basic themes: respect for the fact that the British had been at war for (then) three long years; no overplaying the American contribution; efforts to allay British anxiety about American troops in their country – who were better clothed, better fed and better paid – and reassurance that America was not going to abandon Europe as it had in 1919–20. The wording of the directive is revealing: 'In dealing with America's part in the post-war world, we must lead the British people to keep their faith in us, and yet not lead them to expect more from us in positive commitments than we shall be willing to accept.'[33]

The latter may well be an oblique reference to America's ambition to use its military, cultural and economic might to recast the world in its own image. This was the object of much public discourse by 1943.

Journals such as *Foreign Affairs* and *Fortune,* and major newspapers in all the Allied countries, carried extensive discussion of what the arrival of America on the global stage would mean. Even the Canadian Minister of Munitions and Supply, C.D. Howe, warned Beaverbrook at the end of September 1943 that the looming appointment of Edward Stettinius to the State Department 'is a definite indication that the United States is going out after post-war trade in a big way'.[34]

Howe was right, but Stettinius was merely the tip of the iceberg, and the British were already well aware of who the primary victim of America's ambition would be. On 15 September Mr Robert Brand, Chairman of the British Food Mission and well-known international banker, spoke to the War Services Committee of the American Bankers Association on the subject of postwar international trade. By that stage the British, Americans and Canadians had all circulated plans for achieving postwar economic stability. The objective was to avoid bilateral arrangements of debtor–creditor nations which often became adversarial, and to create a global system whereby nations could balance their debts against the credits owed them, and where loans could be obtained to support economic activity. By 1943 the sticking point between the British and Americans was how generous the credit reserves should be: the British wanted more, and more generous terms for borrowers.

On that September evening in New York, Brand said nothing specific about the lingering Anglo-American tension over Britain's Great War debt. But the notion of balancing what was owed to foreign nations against what was owing from them was an important element of Britain's case about its Great War debt to the US. It will be recalled that the debt owed to Britain by other nations, which proved largely unrecoverable, offset that which Britain owed to the Americans. By 1943 that scenario was playing out once again. Deficits, Brand asserted, were no more evidence of 'wrong doing' than surpluses were evidence of 'virtue . . . as they are evidence of different stages of development, or at this moment of time, of temporary poverty due to war sacrifices'.

The essence of Brand's talk was about convincing American bankers of the need to help keep Britain economically viable. This was, he observed, very much in America's own interest. To buy American goods other nations needed to sell things to America to earn either gold or US dollars. Postwar economic revival required investment. Failing that, nations would have to borrow or run budget deficits, either of which would have to be serviced, thereby driving the debt spiral. As Brand warned, Britain's total war effort was only possible because of 'your Lend-Lease and by Canadian Mutual aid . . . since we have thrown all our normal means of international livelihood into the common pot'. Brand warned that, 'when the bugles blow for peace', Britain would not 'immediately be able to pay our way'.[35]

The response of Brand's audience was overwhelmingly positive. But Brand had pulled his punches on the dire state of Britain's economic forecast and its relationship to the American plans. Writing to his old friend Frederick Marquis, now Lord Woolton, Minister for Reconstruction, Brand was much clearer about the urgency of the American threat. Since 1939 Britain had accumulated a US$10 billion trade deficit, with more to come as the war dragged on. Britain received about US$1 billion per year of food aid from the US and Canada. When the fighting ended, the food would have to be paid for and the debt serviced, while British industry needed money – from somewhere – to transition to an export economy. As for the Americans, their domestic economy remained large enough, Brand asserted, to prosper as it always had done through its own internal trade. In contrast, to Britain exports remained a 'vital necessity'. As a consequence, US global trade would 'slap up against our competition all over the world'. This, Brand warned, would lead to 'a great deal of misunderstanding and hard feeling'. Americans knew little about Britain's economic plight, but 'They will know that they Lend-Leased to us billions of dollars and that in return we are facing them with severe competition everywhere.'[36]

The backdrop of Brand's speech to American bankers was the ongoing negotiations between the treasuries of Britain and the US to find a solution to economic stability in the postwar world. Their plans (and the Canadian one as well) had been made public in early 1943, and the arguments about how to reconcile them had raged ever since. Henry White, the US Treasury Department official charged with working out the details with Britain's John Maynard Keynes, won just about every round. He had outflanked the British by enlisting the support of other European countries, drawn to the American plan because the US had all the gold and the money. White proposed using gold and the US dollar as equivalents, leaving British sterling – long the world's international standard – as just another currency. Lengthy discussion in Washington in September and October between Keynes and White designed to achieve a joint plan faltered. For the moment they agreed only that there would have to be what Keynes now dubbed an 'International Monetary Fund' to manage the global economy, and a major international conference to settle the details. White wanted the conference early in the spring of 1944 so the Democrats could build the new global economic order into the presidential election campaign.[37]

Churchill seemed little concerned about the implications of Lend-Lease. He preferred to see it in the same terms as the American loans of the Great War: treasure sacrificed to spill British blood. This may explain why the MOI effort in America was so paltry. By 1943 the entire American Division of the MOI in London still consisted of just thirty-nine people, most of them clerks. They compiled material for the regular 'Saturday Bag' to New York. A proposal in June 1943 pointed to the need to expand the MOI effort in America in order to increase American awareness of Reverse Lend-Lease, the nature and purpose of the British empire and Britain's resultant India policy, and to demonstrate Britain's commitment to postwar planning. All of this was tied to the need to improve Britain's image in the US before the 1944 presidential elections. The result was the addition of just three staff to the American Division: one to cover an impending departure and two to bring the division staff back up to what it had been in 1942, forty-one in all.[38]

By 1943 the BIS in New York finally had British victories to crow about, but they were stymied by both Roosevelt's own administration and the tiny American Division in London. FDR's office had wilfully failed to champion Reverse Lend-Lease because to highlight the British effort ran counter to their PR message that America was 'the' – instead of 'an' – arsenal of democracy.[39] The inadequacy of the American Division of the MOI itself left the BIS scrambling in late 1943 to find the latest information to distribute in the US. The BIS was told to rely on the various British missions in Washington, including the Joint Liaison Committee which handled public relations for the three British services. But the JLC worked for the armed services, and information proved difficult to obtain.[40] The surviving documentation suggests that the MOI was just not very interested in what Americans thought; its main objective was to unite the empire.

* * *

In late 1943 the British could still dream of winning the war before George Marshall's army arrived. As late as August there was still only a token American combat presence in the UK, the 29th and the newly arrived 5th US Infantry divisions. If the Allies were to invade France in eight months' time, where were the Americans? The popular consensus for the delay, at least among Americans, was that the devious and skilful British had distracted the power of the United States into the Mediterranean morass. Few recollect that the decision to attack French North Africa was Roosevelt's, and that he wanted it timed to help with the 1942 mid-term elections. Or that the request for 160,000 additional troops – and the shipping required to move and support them – for Operation Husky came from Eisenhower.[41] Marshall was right: the Mediterranean campaign developed its own logic and momentum. But America was deeply implicated in the evolving strategy, and operations there were not devoid of results important to the outcome of the war. The eradication of the Axis from Africa, the opening of the Mediterranean to through shipping, the destruction of the Axis air force in the region, knocking Italy out of the war, the establishment of airfields from which to bomb Germany, and drawing of German combat power into the region all benefitted the Allies enormously.

The traditional view of the American response to being 'forced' to fight in the Mediterranean is a petulant shifting of resources to the Pacific. If Phillips O'Brien is right, this was already secretly underway in 1942 with the diversion of US steel production into naval vessels rather than tanks and vehicles for Marshall's army. The result was both a contraction of US Army plans and a delay in building up that smaller army.[42] Moreover, in the summer of 1943 the US Army was still wrestling with some very fundamental questions: how big an army to send to Britain, how to get it there, what needed to be sent to hone combat divisions in the UK for an assault on the continent, and what portion of the US Army would eventually go directly to France.

For a variety of reasons, not the least of which was the very low priority given to completing the mobilisation of ground-combat troops, the US Army was simply incapable of building up its forces in the UK in the first half of 1943. Torch was a distraction, but the critical shortage of shipping in early 1943 profoundly influenced American mobilisation and planning – and eventually the very shape of the US Army – during those crucial months. US Army official histories treat the shipping shortage as if it was an act of God, something inflicted on America by the vicissitudes of war. In fact, as noted above, the shipping crisis owed much to America's failure to defend merchant ships in its own waters in 1942.[43] Marshall had protested to Admiral King in June of that year that American losses alone 'threaten our entire war effort'.[44] He was right. OWI buried that story deliberately and so deeply that the American literature dealing with the 1943 shipping crisis acknowledges no American culpability in helping to create it.

The shipping crisis ultimately affected the kind and quality of army that the USA put in the field. At Casablanca the Anglo-Americans agreed that Operation Bolero, the build-up of US Army combat troops in the UK for the Second Front, would be a priority in 1943. As Brooke noted, that commitment slipped the moment the ink was dry on the minutes. In the first five months of 1943 the air war had priority. The USAAF therefore grew quickly from 150 aircraft in Britain in April to 4,618 aircraft by the end of 1943.[45] Aircrew and ground personnel could be moved en masse on troopships, while aircraft were increasingly flown across. Of the 160,000 American troops who disembarked in the UK in the May to August period, 100,000 were air force.[46]

Ground-force troops could be moved swiftly, too, but they needed guns, tanks and hundreds of vehicles. The decision to equip eleven Free French divisions in North Africa diverted a great deal of equipment which Army Ground Force units needed for training, pushing back readiness dates throughout the year.[47] When some 150,000 tons of shipping suddenly became available to the US Army in February and March, Lieutenant General Frank Andrews, ETOUSA commander, recommended using this windfall to simply stockpile equipment in the UK. That suggestion then occasioned a long debate over whether to ship equipment specifically earmarked for formed units (the 'type-specific' method), or to create overseas depots. Andrews lost that battle when it was decided to ship type-specific loads of equipment.

That decision, however, did not solve the problem. If the equipment was to be despatched specifically for formed units, logistics planners needed to know how many and what kind of divisions the Army Ground Force intended to send to Britain – what the US Army called its 'Troop Basis'. This included support and depot troops of the Services of Supply.[48] In short, before it could send 'type-based' cargo loads, the US Army needed to figure out how many combat formations would be based in Britain for Operation Overlord, how many would then stage through the UK en route to the continent, and how many would later go direct into France?

As it turned out, in early 1943 the US Army had not yet finalised what kind of army it wanted – or more importantly, it was able – to send overseas. American industry, the Army Service Force (ASF) and the USAAF took an increasing toll on available resources and manpower. By the end of 1943 the ASF was actually larger than the Army Ground Forces (2.74 million compared to 2.45 million) and the air force had grown to 1.8 million. It looked increasingly like the army would max out at ninety divisions. How many of these would be infantry and how many armoured was still unclear. Armoured and motorised divisions required more shipping than infantry divisions. The solution, in 1943, was to reduce the number of armoured divisions, eliminate the motorised divisions and concentrate on completing standard infantry divisions.[49] This was a major concern. Arthur S. Nevins, who joined the COSSAC staff in the summer of 1943, pointed out at the time that exploitation of a breakthrough in France would require mobility and armour. 'In this connection,' Nevins observed, 'it is to be remembered that the British armies are very strong in armor.'[50] They were also very strong in vehicles of all sorts, including specialised armour. The problems of mobilisation, planning, equipping and deploying Marshall's army for Operation Overlord eventually produced a comparatively light combat force.

For much of 1943, therefore, Bolero was delayed while the US Army figured out what it was going to look like and how and where it was to deploy. As late as the Quebec Conference in August, Bolero was in eighth place on the priority list, behind the Mediterranean, two Pacific theatres, the USAAF build-up, rearming the French and other priorities; 'advanced shipments to the theatre' rated even lower. As Ruppenthal writes, despite the protests of both ETOUSA and the Army Service Force, 'no action was taken to change priorities, and in September and October [1943] sufficient cargo was again lacking to fill available shipping space'.[51]

The discussion over Operation Bolero in mid-1943 revealed yet another snag: Britain lacked the labour, transportation and accommodation to handle a sudden influx of the 2.5 million tons of war supplies and 1 million American troops. Troops could be accommodated, but offloading and distributing their supplies and equipment represented a considerable challenge. Britain was already desperately short of labour, and its longshoremen were largely men too old for military service. The British curbed the worst abuses of the trade unions and stevedoring companies that often impeded efficient offloading, and cleared the way for US Army Port battalions to handle American cargo. Getting the equipment away from the ports on Britain's 'crooked' roads, its 'Lilliputian' railway system and its 'tiny' rail equipment had been a worry for some time. By 1943 fifty purpose-built locomotives, plus rail cars, were arriving in Britain each month to help alleviate the problem.[52]

The British never understood the problems afflicting America's mobilisation of ground-combat forces and the delay in deploying them overseas. 'The Americans had mobilized already six and a half million men,' Lockhart wrote in his diary on 12 February 1943, 'but they had only five divisions ready. They had promised us seven in North Africa: they had only two [ready for combat]'.[53] Marshall was bent on the US Army taking the field combat ready. But the exigencies of war and the hard reality of the limits of America's manpower and industrial might occasioned constant readjustment.[54] The authorised Troop Basis for 1943 was 100 divisions, with a strength of 7.533 million men.[55] The actual size of the US Army by the end of 1943 was 7,482,434 personnel and ninety divisions.[56] By September this enormous force provided just seven divisions in the ETO and four in the UK.[57] It was not much. The US Army planned to have perhaps twenty-nine divisions in the ETO by the spring of 1944. This was enough to give Overlord a fighting chance. But they would have to arrive soon if Overlord was to launch on 1 May.[58] American mobilisation problems may explain why the British believed that September 1944 was a better bet for Overlord than May. Moreover, the painfully slow development of Bolero provides important context for Churchill's initiative in the Balkans and British enthusiasm – generally – for the Mediterranean in the autumn of 1943.

* * *

The Balkan distraction also shaped the plan for Operation Overlord. On 15 September, Brooke had dinner with his old friend Harry Crerar, the designated commander of I Canadian Corps. Crerar was the only person whom Brooke entertained with some frequency. On that September evening Brooke found Crerar 'in a very despondent mood about the Canadians not being sufficiently in the limelight, and the fact that the Americans, although late to enter the war, were playing a greater and more conspicuous part. He made me quite angry with some petty criticisms and remarks,' Brooke recorded.[59]

Brooke's irritation with Crerar was understandable. Despite his uneasy relationship with McNaughton, Brooke had always been a supporter of the First Canadian Army.[60] It had been at the heart of planning for a return to France for two years, and by the summer of 1943 it was central to the COSSAC plan. The Canadians had also recently been given the important task of developing plans for an assault on Antwerp – where the British had gone ashore in September 1914 in a failed attempt to save Belgium.[61] This would, in time, become an important part of the Overlord deception scheme. Now, for domestic political reasons, the Canadian government wanted to break it all up. For Mackenzie King's Minister of Defence, Colonel Ralston, the solution to Canada's domestic political crisis – and to establishing its status postwar internationally – was to get the army into the fight. Another idle year in Britain was more than Ralston and many in the army could abide.

Brooke and the War Office successfully resisted Canadian pressure at the Quebec Conference to send another Canadian division to Italy. They had done so, in part, because they needed to demonstrate 'British' commitment to Overlord. Even Field Marshal Dill had advised against the move. Just before the Quebec Conference Dill told the Canadians that the Mediterranean effort would soon be scaled back, so there was no need for more troops there. But Mackenzie King and Ralston were not deterred: they wanted the army headlining Canadian newspapers. After talking to Churchill, Mackenzie King feared that Overlord would be a blood bath. 'The more of our men participate in the campaign in Italy,' he confided wistfully to his diary at the end of August, 'the fewer there are likely to be who will be involved in the crossing of the Channel which, as Churchill says, will likely be a tough business.'[62] On 31 August, Churchill conceded to the Canadian War Cabinet that a second division might, after all, be sent to Italy.[63] That day Churchill asked the British Chiefs of Staff to 'Pray let me know as soon as possible what can be done'.[64]

Within days McNaughton was in General Nye's office making the case – with as much fervour as he could muster – to send more Canadians to Italy. Nye told him that the British had already bumped the 1st CID from the list of those returning from the Mediterranean for Overlord.[65] There was no point in sending out another one. McNaughton sent a memo to Canada on 14 September confirming that the division would not be coming back for Overlord, and that a second division would not go out. If Overlord was delayed to 1 September 1944, the 1st CID might get back in time to join the campaign.

In the heady days following the Italian capitulation, and the wild speculation of an imminent German collapse, Canadian generals and politicians were not prepared to wait for Overlord. In mid-September Mackenzie King made the issue political, drawing in the Canadian High Commissioner in London, the Secretary of State for Dominion Affairs, the British High Commissioner in Ottawa and other senior intergovernmental officials.[66]

Brooke's intent in all this was to replace McNaughton, not break up the First Canadian Army. It was, after all, the most battle-ready field army in the UK, with the most fully developed Army HQ. It also repre-sented a fair portion of deployable 'British' divisions in the UK. British manpower was stretched to the limit, and the wastage rate was soon expected to exceed enlistment. The First Canadian Army, with five actual divisions and several armoured brigades, was rated as six equivalent divisions. That left the British to find only nine divisions to meet their obligations for Overlord. Freddie Morgan confided to McNaughton in May that the idea of maintaining even nine British divisions ready for

Overlord was 'fantastic'.[67] Moreover, the Canadian Army was generally more highly mechanised than its British equivalent. This had always been McNaughton's vision. By mid-1943 the First Canadian Army was the single most powerful force in the empire and Commonwealth not yet committed to battle. Brooke was not interested in shattering it.

* * *

While the US Army scrambled to deploy divisions and their equipment overseas, Roosevelt could not make up his mind about who should command Overlord. It says a very great deal about America's ambitions that Roosevelt was soon talking about Marshall as Supreme Allied Commander of all Western Europe. The idea derived, in part, from the storm of opposition that met Roosevelt's plan to send Marshall overseas to command the Second Front. The anti-Roosevelt press quickly concluded that politicians were working to have Marshall 'kicked upstairs'. The solution, floated in early October by Harry Hopkins, was to appoint Marshall to Europe as *the* Supreme Allied Commander. It made sense, Hopkins argued, to have one overriding commanding officer for the Anglo-American war in Europe. The sop to the British – who would still outnumber the Americans – would be to appoint Montgomery to command Operation Overlord.

The idea was dead before it reached London in early October.[68] The British knew, from Dill, that Marshall wanted to command Overlord, nothing more.[69] But the idea of Marshall as a modern Foch refused to die. Over the autumn the idea elevated Marshall's public image. Drafts of an embarrassingly flattering profile in *Collier's Magazine*, slated for early December, portrayed Marshall as the architect of the Allied success on all fronts – including the Eastern Front, where American supplies propelled Russian victories.[70] Churchill informed Dill that if Marshall became the European Supremo 'there would be an explosion' in Britain.[71] The Americans quietly let the idea die. In the meantime, no one commanded Overlord.

Meanwhile the Americans were unhappy with British domination of COSSAC, which became the de facto operational staff of Overlord Supreme Commander on 7 September.[72] With so little American presence in the UK there was nothing much they could do about that. Lieutenant General Jacob Devers, the ETO commander, appealed for the establishment of an American Army HQ in the UK.[73] Morgan and Brooke also appealed for one, if only to add credence to the ongoing deception operations. Marshall refused. Even after Quebec, he would not be moved. Not surprisingly on 14 September Marshall also rejected a proposal, backed by the British, to establish an American AG HQ.[74] In Marshall's view these would all emerge organically as the size of US forces in the UK expanded. The only American higher formation HQ in the UK until mid-October 1943 was V US Corps. It contributed to the COSSAC deception schemes, and on 12 September started working on Overlord itself.[75]

With George Marshall as the designated Overlord commander pro tem, the Americans were not content with the idea that a British formation would lead the assault.[76] The case for an American-led assault was made in late September in a memo likely written by Devers. It accepted that the preponderance of the initial assault forces would be Anglo-Canadian, and that it therefore made sense that the Army Group in command would be the British 21st AG. 'It is immaterial,' Devers claimed, 'which army headquarters is the leading army headquarters, but to be equitable it should be First U.S. Army.'[77] That army already existed as a formation HQ in New York, and much of that was soon on its way. When Omar Bradley arrived in the UK from Italy in October to command it he brought with him thirty staff officers from II US Corps. These men were America's best planners and operators, and were veterans of two amphibious assaults, and two campaigns.

Freddie Morgan also supported the shift to a US-led assault. On 7 October he and Major General N.C.D. Brownjohn set off for a five-day visit to Washington to sort out the details of America's role in Overlord. Morgan was warned not to be seduced by American hospitality. It proved impossible to resist. He and Brownjohn were 'wafted into what seemed like paradise' at Fort Meyers, into quarters especially redecorated by Mrs Marshall.[78] He protested after the war that it all seemed 'utterly genuine'. 'But the fact remained', Morgan wrote in 1947, 'that if COSSAC was, as seemed clearly indicated, to regard itself and be regarded as in some measure an agency of the United States Government', then a closer examination of that government was clearly desirable. Morgan and Brownjohn stayed for six weeks.

Morgan was impressed by both Marshall and America. Marshall paid weekly visits to his old mentor General 'Black Jack' Pershing, who – as Morgan noted – had held the fort in 1918 against attempts by the British and the French to 'use the United States divisions as transfusions of blood into their war-tried but almost exhausted veteran French and British formations'. 'As General Marshall put it,' Morgan wrote, 'had either Sir Douglas Haig or General Foch been given the opportunity that was now mine, of visiting the United States and getting some idea of its vast size and potentialities, how different it all might have been.'[79]

While Morgan was away, his American Deputy, Brigadier General Ray W. Barker, reorganised COSSAC along American staff lines, and introduced an operations staff. This resulted in a shift from the British staff system of 'branches' (e.g. 'Q' for logistics [quartermasters], 'A' for Administration, etc.) and command by committee of three service heads all notionally equal, to the American (actually, Napoleonic or continental) system with five key staff officers: G1 for Personnel, G2 for Intelligence, G3 for Operations, G4 for Logistics and G5 for Plans. Each of these key COSSAC staff positions eventually had an American or British officer as the head, with the deputy from the other country.[80] Over the autumn of 1943 a steady stream of American officers – hand-picked by Marshall to work with him as commander of Overlord – arrived in the UK to fill out Morgan's staff.[81] The agreement that the First US Army would lead the assault put the issue of the first follow-on army into question. So, too, did the Canadian government's insistence on sending another Canadian division and a Corps HQ to Italy.

The dismemberment of the First Canadian Army was accomplished by intense Canadian political pressure in the face of resistance from Brooke and the British Chiefs of Staff. The logjam was finally broken in early October when the British decided to bring XXX Corps HQ and the 7th BAD home from Italy for Operation Overlord. To reduce the strain on shipping the Canadians would just take over the vehicles and equipment of the British units going home. McNaughton informed his government of the new British proposal on 7 October and five days later the deal was done: I Canadian Corps HQ, assorted corps-level units and the 5th Canadian Armoured Division were now destined for Italy. It was agreed that Harry Crerar, now being groomed to take over the First Canadian Army from McNaughton, would go to Italy to command the corps.[82]

The Canadians arrived in early November. Eisenhower had 'made clear in advance that necessarily there will be considerable delay in equipping the Canadians and bringing them to action'.[83] The equipment of the departing British units had been picked over, and every piece of junk in the Eighth Army assembled for the Canadians. McNaughton feared that this would happen.[84] He arranged an emergency shipment of 3,550 Canadian vehicles – and provided a similar number to XXX Corps in England. I Canadian Corps and the 5th CAD did not reach the 'local standard' of issue until the end of January 1944: some artillery regiments were not complete until April – six months after arriving. McNaughton remained bitter about this to his dying day.[85] Crerar returned to England in March without ever having fought a corps-level battle.

By October 1943 it seemed that the First Canadian Army was dead.[86] Between the forces committed to Italy and the transfer of the 3rd CID and the 2nd Canadian Armoured Brigade to I British Corps for the Overlord assault, McNaughton's Dagger was down to two divisions. On 18 October, Morgan and Paget visited McNaughton to discuss the fate of what Paget now called the 'Anglo-Canadian Army'. This, of course, was not what Colonel Ralston, senior Canadian generals or Brooke had wanted. They hoped that by sending more troops to Italy McNaughton could be goaded into resignation.[87] That plan had clearly failed. Ralston and Ken Stuart, the Canadian Chief of the General Staff, made plans to fly to the UK that day.

Ralston and Stuart arrived in England to salvage the army for Canada – and for Harry Crerar. In this they had Brooke as an accomplice. At a tense meeting with Ralston and Stuart on 6 November, McNaughton protested against the decision to send more troops to Italy: nobody wanted them there. More importantly, by abandoning its field army Canada had given up any pretence of operational control over its formations, the opportunity to be inside the strategic planning circle, and 'the right to look into proposed campaigns in advance'. Ralston and Stuart naturally disagreed, noting that all Canadian commanders retained the right of appeal to their own government. This was not McNaughton's point, as Ralston would soon discover: no army, no seat at the table.[88]

Ralston and Stuart went on to meet Brooke, who was asked point-blank whether he and Paget had faith in McNaughton's ability to command. The answer was a firm 'No'. But Brooke had faith in his old friend Harry Crerar. Once Crerar got command experience in Italy, he would take over the First Canadian Army. Brooke told his Canadian visitors that the HQ and title 'First Canadian Army' should remain. 'It was working well and the British had not the means to create another such structure.' It was now up to Ralston and Stuart to wield the knife.[89]

On 8 November they broke the news to McNaughton: they blamed Brooke and Paget. By all accounts McNaughton took it calmly. But the next day when McNaughton strode into Paget's office there was no exchange of pleasantries, just a blunt statement: 'You know why I am here.' Two very conflicting views of this brief encounter were recorded. McNaughton recalled that Paget blamed it all on Ralston and Stuart. Paget claimed that he was very clear to McNaughton that both he and Brooke wanted him gone. Given that both Ralston and Stuart bore personal grudges against him, and had for some time, McNaughton concluded that his Canadian colleagues had done him in. He appealed immediately to Mackenzie King to make the choice: the Prime Minster demurred. For Brooke, overwhelmed with preparations for Anglo-American conferences in Cairo and Tehran, the whole affair was wearisome. McNaughton had given a completely 'erroneous interpretation of his meeting with Paget' to the Canadian PM, and it looked to Brooke 'as if McNaughton is going completely off his head!'[90]

On 13 November, Paget sent McNaughton a firmly worded memo that contained 'two frank statements'. The 'first is that I do not consider you [McNaughton] fitted to command First Canadian Army in active operations', and the second was that 'it was not General Stuart nor Mr Ralston who inspired this opinion, it is one to which the C.I.G.S. and I have been coming for some time'. McNaughton later told Stuart that Paget had 'probably acted under instructions of a higher authority'.[91] He was right. Brooke later confided that he had contrived to have McNaughton removed.[92] The next day McNaughton agreed to carry on until the new commander was appointed.

Plans for Operation Overlord were now in a state of flux. The Americans had shouldered their way into leading the charge, but their army had not yet arrived in England. Now the army that was supposed to lead the break-out from the beachhead had been destroyed through the machinations of its own government. And Roosevelt had still not appointed a commander for the whole operation. Overlord, still slated for 1 May, was barely five months away.

There was much to be done. In the wee hours of 17 November, Brooke took off for Cairo and ultimately Tehran to settle the issue of a commander for Operation Overlord, the fate of Britain and eastern Europe, and the arrival of America as a Great Power.

CHAPTER 14

THE AMERICANS ARE COMING

The Americans, Stalin had every reason to conclude, would in all likelihood retire from the international scene at war's end, just as they had after World War I . . . Churchill's nightmare was Stalin's dream . . . Europe at war's end would lie prostrate and hopeless before Soviet power.

David Kennedy, *Freedom from Fear*[1]

The Americans saw Churchill's Balkan gambit in the fall of 1943 as the British playing the Great Game: it had nothing to do with winning the war. In the final volume of his trilogy about Roosevelt as war leader, Nigel Hamilton skewers the British as misguided and self-serving. According to Eisenhower, Hamilton asserts, Churchill's ideas were often 'outside the scope of the immediate military problems'.[2] Hamilton's glib dismissal of the British case for a revised strategy in 1943 misses the point: there was much more at stake than British power or hubris.

When Brooke arrived in Malta on 17 November he found the Prime Minister in a petulant mood, annoyed at the Americans and dismayed at Britain's declining power. Nothing over the next month altered that mood. Even the brilliant yellow of the sand and the contrasting deep blue of the sea was not enough to lift Brooke's spirits as they flew on to Cairo. 'I wish our conference was over,' he penned in his diary during the flight. 'It will be an unpleasant one.' In the lead-up to the conference the British Chiefs of Staff sharpened their rationale for a new push in the Mediterranean. The Americans were resolved to crush this Mediterranean distraction finally. They would control the agenda in Cairo by inviting Generalissimo Chiang Kai-shek to come early so the war in China would dominate the discussion. Then, in Tehran, Roosevelt would use Stalin to cow and outvote the British. Roosevelt was certain that he could charm the Soviet dictator, and ultimately work with him to secure peace and stability in the postwar world. What FDR wanted most from the Russians was support for his UN plan. Once the two superpowers had arranged things, the British would have to tag along.

This time the Americans were prepared. America's newest battleship, USS *Iowa*, carried the President, plus Marshall, Arnold, Somervell, Admiral King and over a hundred planning staff. The passage to Mers-el-Kébir allowed them to hone America's strategy. At the top of the agenda was securing Soviet endorsement of the United Nations, and getting the British to focus on Overlord. The Americans understood that British power was ebbing, and that they needed to conserve strength – including manpower – for after the war. A bloodbath on the beaches of France, or a long battle of attrition once ashore, threatened to sap Britain. Dill had made this very clear to the Americans before they left for Cairo.[3] So the plan, in Hamilton's words, was to use the Russians to 'help put iron back into the soul of the faltering British'.[4]

All that said, the Americans were not entirely unsympathetic to the British plight. When the subject of a Supreme Commander for the Mediterranean theatre was discussed aboard *Iowa* on 19 November, most – including FDR – objected to appointing a British officer. But Marshall claimed that the current arrangement, with Eisenhower commanding the west and central Mediterranean, including the Italian campaign, and the British commanding the Middle East, was a weakness. Given the preponderance of British forces in the area and the acceptance of an American to command Overlord, it made sense that the Supreme Allied Commander in the Mediterranean was British. When Roosevelt and others protested that the British might use American forces in the Balkans or Turkey, Admiral Ernie King pointed out the obvious: any employment of US forces would have to be approved by the JCS and the President.

Finally, Roosevelt made it clear that America would have nothing to do with sorting out Europe's postwar problems. American troops would stay for a year or so, and then leave Europe to the British and Russians. Roosevelt had no time or sympathy for the French: they were to be stripped of their empire and left to the British to sort out. As for Germany, the American people still believed that the Germans had been bullied into the war by the Nazis. Even so, Roosevelt favoured some kind of partition, and perhaps punitive action. So as the leadership of the western Alliance descended on Cairo, competing visions of how the war would end and how the postwar world would be shaped were starting to coalesce. Roosevelt held the whip, and he planned to use it.

At Mers-el-Kébir on 20 November 1943 FDR was met by Eisenhower, who had just met with Churchill in Malta and was well aware of the British mood. When FDR and Eisenhower lunched near a recent battlefield the next day, Roosevelt reminded Ike how disappointed he was that Torch occurred after the 1942 mid-term elections.[5] That election left FDR with a quarrelsome Congress. It is doubtful that Eisenhower needed to be reminded that 1944 was a presidential election year: there could be no delay in opening the Second Front. Roosevelt flew on to Cairo on 22 November, the day Chinese arrived. Averell Harriman soon brought news that the Tehran conference would start in five days, and all Stalin was interested in was Overlord. He would – in Hamilton's words – 'happily act as the President's "enforcer" in Tehran . . . If this sounded unkind or underhanded toward the British, it was.'[6] Churchill would be outvoted.

The British came prepared to make their case for a revised campaign in the Mediterranean, and more importantly they wanted a solid Anglo-American front before meeting Stalin. But Chiang and the Chinese set the agenda, just as Roosevelt had planned. The afternoon of 23 November was spent discussing the war in China and Burma, with Madame Chiang providing the translation. The whole affair made Brooke fidget, although he was careful to write down a long and detailed description of Madame Chiang's form-fitting black silk dress with a cut revealing a very attractive leg. Apart from that, the meeting had no redeeming quality for Brooke. When it ended he turned to Marshall and vented, 'That was a ghastly waste of time!' Marshall apparently agreed.

The next morning FDR joined the British delegation to hear Churchill make the plea for a revised European strategy. The meeting was tense. Churchill was not opposed to a landing in France, but German power needed to be sharply eroded before that happened. A bloodbath or a stalemate in Normandy, Dan Todman wrote, 'could only diminish British power in the Grand Alliance and the country's influence over the settlement of the peace'.[7] None of this was Roosevelt's concern. The President had promised Chiang a reopening of the Burma Road and the British capture of the Andaman Islands, Operation Buccaneer – which Chiang demanded as a prerequisite for helping in Burma. The afternoon was spent with the American JCS and the Chinese Chiefs of Staff in what Brooke described as a 'lamentable fiasco'. The British protested that the resources for Buccaneer would be better used to land six divisions behind the German line in Italy. Roosevelt had rehearsed his response. In 1944 the British empire and Commonwealth would field 4.5 million men, he said, while America's military strength would peak at 11 million. American industrial power would also peak in 1944.[8] According to Manchester and Reid, the conference simply went downhill from there.[9]

It was not until 25 November that the British were able to actually make their case. The Americans listened and said little. 'We did not meet with half the reaction we were expecting,' Brooke confided to his diary. But the battle was not yet joined. That came the next day, over American insistence that the British launch Operation Buccaneer. The British had no interest in dissipating their strength in the Andamans, or in helping Chiang. The advice from Roosevelt's own China specialist, General Joseph 'Vinegar Joe' Stilwell confirmed the British opinion. Chiang led a 'rotten regime', Stilwell told FDR, 'a one-party government supported by a Gestapo and headed by an unbalanced man with little education.'[10] The Chinese really did not matter.

According to Dallek, FDR needed to 'foster the image of China as a Great Power in order to use it as a surrogate for US designs in postwar Asia'.[11] So he bullied the British into supporting China, and therefore America's postwar international ambitions. Chiang went away with the promise of a British assault on the Andamans and a Burma offensive, while the Anglo-Americans settled on an anodyne declaration about their objectives in the war against Japan. They flew off to Tehran on 27 November without any agreement on a common front to meet Stalin. So far, everything was going according to Roosevelt's plan.

The five days of the Tehran conference are celebrated as the first meeting of all three Great Powers engaged in the war against Nazi Germany, and for two important decisions: the agreement to establish the United Nations and a final commitment to Operation Overlord in May 1944. The Americans and much of the western press were almost giddy over the meeting with the Soviet dictator. For his part, Roosevelt was confident that his charm and guile would overwhelm Marshal Stalin, and that together they would shape a postwar world free of empires and governed by peace.[12] The vehicle for that brave new world would be the United Nations, run by the Great Powers as world policemen. The President already knew, from the October conference of foreign ministers in Moscow, that the Soviet Union would sign up to the UN plan, and he also knew that Stalin would back the American demand that Overlord go ahead in the spring of 1944. The remaining question for FDR at Tehran was whether 'Uncle Joe' was a man he could work with.

So at Tehran Roosevelt played suitor to Stalin's Russia. There was no hesitation about moving into the Russian compound from the distant American Embassy when the Russians played on American assassination fears. The Soviet Embassy was the site of the conference in any event, and the Americans accepted that their suites were bugged.[13] When Churchill suggested that he and FDR meet privately before meeting Stalin, Roosevelt declined: he did not want any appearance of the Anglo-Americans ganging up on the Russians. Rather, FDR met Stalin first and alone on the 27th, anxious to get the measure of the man. He found Stalin cool to the idea of the UN, and to the inclusion of China among the Great Powers, but otherwise the two great 'anti-imperialists' got off to a good start.

Roosevelt chaired the meetings that followed. The American and British staffs met early on 28 November but came to no agreement on the main points for discussion. The first plenary session with the Russians began at 4.00 p.m. After a presentation on American operations in the Pacific, Roosevelt cut to the nub of the conference: Operation Overlord. The American proposal was to shut down Italy, land six divisions in the south of France in April and launch Overlord on 1 May. Stalin agreed. He had no interest in opening the Dardanelles now that the Murmansk convoys were running again,[14] and the Balkans were – as the Americans believed – a strategic dead-end. The best thing the Anglo-Americans could do, Stalin said, was to land in France as soon as possible. However, Stalin chided the Anglo-Americans for failing to name a commander for Operation Overlord. Without a designated Commander in Chief there really was no operation.

Brooke watched Stalin like a hawk and added a lengthy postwar annotation to his diary lauding Stalin's skills. 'Never once in any of his statements did he make any strategic error, nor did he ever fail to appreciate all the implications of a situation with a quick and unerring eye.' In this, Stalin was clearly the best of the three war leaders. Of the meeting on the 28th Brooke reflected, 'We were reaching a very dangerous point where Stalin's shrewdness, assisted by American shortsightedness, might lead us anywhere.' Hastings Ismay, Churchill's military advisor, simply found Stalin 'inscrutable'.[15] It was clear that Stalin already had designs on the Balkans and was content to allow the Anglo-Americans to concentrate their effort as far west as possible: two landings in France was ideal.

On the 29th Roosevelt went from bullying Churchill to humiliating him. When the British suggested that the Balkans offered opportunity, they spent the afternoon – in Todman's words – 'answering American and Soviet accusations that Britain was cynically pursuing post-war objectives'. Great Britain's effort – unstated but implied – in keeping Russia out of as much of Europe as possible was seen as British self-interest. Roosevelt summarily dismissed the Mediterranean as a distraction. Stalin took the cue and demanded that Churchill say once and for all whether Britain was committed to Overlord. Manchester and Reid describe that moment as 'one of the most brutal contrivances of public embarrassment recorded in diplomatic history'.[16] Brooke's diary noted later that after an afternoon defending British interests from the Russians and Americans he felt like 'entering a lunatic asylum' to get away from the madness.[17]

If the bullying and humiliation of Churchill and the British had been Roosevelt's only misstep at Tehran it would have been bad enough.

But Roosevelt's private revelations to Stalin of America's postwar plans for Europe, and his failure to present a common Anglo-American front against the Russians, gave Stalin a carte blanche. When Churchill met Stalin to discuss the future of Poland, Roosevelt declined to go. Churchill and FDR had already agreed to abandon Poland and the Baltic states to Russia's tender mercies, but the failure to support the British was telling. Instead, the President met Stalin separately on 1 December to discuss postwar Europe. France would be stripped of its empire, Germany ought to be dismembered, Poland could move west and the Russians could re-occupy the Baltic states. He could say none of this publicly, FDR warned Stalin, because, as Todman wrote, 'of the number of American voters with an interest in Eastern Europe'.[18] It was an astonishing admission to make to the Soviet dictator. Roosevelt's only concern was that Europe was stable and no longer a source of conflict.[19] Stalin of course agreed with FDR's ideas for Europe and admitted that he now thought the UN was a good idea. Roosevelt believed that he had got his man.[20]

Roosevelt paved his path to victory at Tehran by bulldozing and abandoning the British, and by humiliating Churchill.[21] Evidence of that was plain at the final dinner at the British Embassy on 30 November, Churchill's sixty-ninth birthday. When Stalin said he would solve the German problem by shooting 50,000 of Hitler's followers, FDR's son Elliott announced that the US Army would support such a plan. Mindful of the recent revelations about the Katyn massacre, in which the Russians solved the Polish 'problem' by shooting 9,000 officers, Churchill was incensed and left the room. Stalin and Molotov brought him back. 'Afterward', Dallek writes, Churchill 'vented his anger and frustration, seeing nothing but disaster ahead – another bloody war and "impending catastrophe" with an end to civilization and a "desolate" Europe'.[22] 'Toast followed toast,' according to Manchester and Reid. And then Stalin toasted America, without whose industrial production 'the war may have been lost'. 'This facile salute,' Manchester and Reid note, 'ignored the fact that for almost two deadly years, while America prepared for war and Stalin avoided war, Churchill and Britain alone had fought the war.'[23] Or that aid from the British empire and Commonwealth had helped stop the Germans at the gates of Moscow in December 1941.

Churchill expressed himself content with the evening, but historians say otherwise. 'He had been humbled and made fun of in a situation in which he could not directly fight back,' Todman concludes. 'More severely, he faced the failure of the strategy that he had pursued since the USSR and the USA had been dragged into the war. Britain had not produced its own decisive military victories quickly enough to maintain influence with the Grand Alliance.'[24] For his part, Roosevelt sold out his best ally, gloating to his staff on his return to Washington that he had baited and humbled the British Prime Minister in a triumph of American diplomacy and power. The 'Fate of Britain', General A.G.L. McNaughton told his biographer in March 1966, was 'settled at Tehran'.

The same was true for Europe – precisely what British diplomacy had sought to avoid. Charles Bohlen, the recently appointed Assistant Chief of the Russian Section at the State Department, felt that way at the time. 'I did not like the attitude of the President,' he wrote of that last dinner at Tehran and of the Churchill-baiting, 'Roosevelt should have come to the defense of his close friend and ally.' Bohlen felt strongly that it was a mistake for Roosevelt to confide in Stalin his electoral difficulties with Polish voters. He told Ambassador Harriman in Moscow that the United States sold out Europe at Tehran, where a strong Anglo-American front was needed. 'The result would be that the Soviet Union would be the only important military and political force on the continent of Europe.'[25] Roosevelt left the impression at Tehran, David Kennedy writes, that the US 'would in all likelihood retire from the international stage at war's end just as they had after World War I'.[26]

Roosevelt also got confirmation that Overlord would launch in the spring of 1944, and would now be supported by a landing in the south of France, Operation Anvil. The Russians would launch a major summer offensive in support. The British won some concessions for Italy: operations to capture Rome and move north would continue. Anglo-American meetings to resolve how all this would be accomplished began back in Cairo on 3 December. Roosevelt, magnanimous in victory, now announced that he would support expanded operations in the Mediterranean if Turkey joined the alliance. If nothing else, opening a passage through the Dardanelles to Russia would have been a great saving to Britain in men, ships and materiel. The Turks refused to move without massive Allied support.[27]

Putting the decisions of Tehran into action absorbed four days of intense discussion back in Cairo. It was agreed that Overlord and Anvil were the two 'supreme operations' of 1944.[28] Churchill remained anxious about Overlord. The literature links this to his enduring phobia about another 'first day of the Somme' event. But historians make far too much of this connection. The real problem was that – as then planned – both Anvil and Overlord were pitifully small: Anvil would land parts of just two divisions about the same time that three divisions crossed the beaches of Normandy. As Churchill pointed out, five divisions landing 1,000km apart seemed like a recipe for disaster. In any event, there were not enough landing craft to do both.

Finding the resources to land in France led to heated discussion of Roosevelt's promises to Chiang for Buccaneer and an offensive in North Burma. On 5 December, Roosevelt huddled with his senior staff to talk about these. He cut his losses and called off Buccaneer. That freed more landing craft – especially LSTs – for the Mediterranean, allowing Anvil to land two full divisions.[29] The British had their own plans for an offensive in north Burma which Chiang refused to support. These decisions effectively ended China's high-profile role in the war.

That same day – 5 December – FDR announced to his American staff that General Eisenhower would command Operation Overlord. Marshall accepted the decision 'without demur'. The news was passed to the British and Russians on 6 December. This cleared the way for a shuffling of command arrangements in the Mediterranean, appointing British General Maitland 'Jumbo' Wilson as Allied Supreme Commander, with General Alexander in command of Italy and General Sir Bernard Paget sent out to command the Middle East.[30]

* * *

On 29 November, Morgan forwarded a new basic Overlord plan to the 21st Army Group. It was largely unchanged from the summer except for one crucial detail: it would be led by the First US Army.[31] A 'Summary of the COSSAC Outline Plan' revised on 13 December, and 'Instructions to Armies' drafted on the 15th, elaborated on the deployment of follow-up formations. I British Corps would assume command

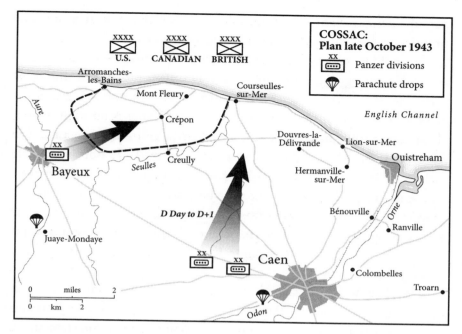

3. COSSAC: the plan in late October 1943.

of the initial Anglo-Canadian formations. As more Anglo-Canadian divisions landed, II Canadian Corps HQ would arrive to command them. Once these two Anglo-Canadian corps were settled, the First Canadian Army HQ would take charge of the Anglo-Canadian front. As the draft instructions of 15 December stated, 'British Second Army will follow the First Canadian Army' at some later date.[32]

Given that the HQ of the First Canadian Army was well developed and ready it made sense to keep it in a leading role in Overlord. Moreover, its air support was in an advanced state of readiness. Since the summer the RCAF and the RAF had worked to build No. 83 Group into a Canadian formation specifically to assist the First Canadian Army in the early stages of Overlord. During the autumn Canadian personnel were concentrated in the group's headquarters, repair and salvage, air stores, casualty evacuation 'Wings' and the group's field hospitals. RCAF fighter squadrons were transferred in, including six from Canada – veterans of the Aleutian campaign. It proved impossible to create a totally Canadian group, but by June 1944 fifteen of No. 83

Group's twenty-eight squadrons, six of its ten operational wings and about half of its support units and personnel were Canadian.[33] Canada's army would be supported by its own air force, and both would lead.

McNaughton was supposed to stay in command of the First Canadian Army until Crerar returned from Italy in the spring. But the stress of his betrayal took its toll. On 26 November McNaughton was diagnosed with exhaustion and prescribed three months of leave. On 10 December, McNaughton asked to be relieved of command.[34] He unburdened himself two days later in his last meeting with Freddie Morgan. The goal had always been to keep the army intact 'for employment in the decisive theatre of N.W. Europe, at the decisive time'. The First Canadian Army was now 'unbalanced', and it would soon be leaderless.[35] It was agreed to appoint Ken Stuart in an acting capacity pending Crerar's return.[36]

The disarray in the Canadian camp by December was mirrored in Freddie Morgan's own COSSAC staff. The prospect of the Germans crushing the tiny Allied landings proposed in the COSSAC plan had driven Morgan's planners and the staff of the 21st AG 'to frank defeatism' by late 1943.[37] With the appointment of General Erwin Rommel to command the coastal defences of western Europe, German preparations went into high gear from the Netherlands to the Biscay. An assault by three divisions now seemed totally inadequate. The recently appointed commanders of Overlord, Eisenhower and Montgomery, agreed. On 27 December, four days after getting the news of his appointment, Montgomery flew to Tunisia to discuss Overlord with Eisenhower. Both were unhappy with the plan and told their Chiefs of Staff to recommend changes.

The announcement of McNaughton's departure from command of the First Canadian Army on 26 December was covered by the international media. It was timed to coincide with news that I Canadian Corps was in Italy and that the Canadians were engaged in a bitter battle for the Italian city of Ortona. Most media outlets simply ran the press release: Canada was finally in the fight, and Andy McNaughton was worn out and was going home. But not everyone bought the official line. The *Yorkshire Observer* lauded McNaughton as at one time the likely ground-force commander for the Second Front. But the speed of Monty's exploitations in Sicily and Calabria, the paper concluded, 'compared with the relative slowness of McNaughton's development of a similar situation on that occasion [Exercise Spartan] may have something to do with it'. A few days later the *Bath Chronicle and Herald* ran with a story from the *Windsor Daily Star* in Canada that claimed once Montgomery was appointed ground-force commander, McNaughton had to go. 'Montgomery was not an easy man to get along with,' John Marshall reported, and a clash of temperament between the two had 'existed for years'.

The Germans noticed, too, and commented on McNaughton's departure on their shortwave service. 'During the past few years, ever since there has been talk about a Second Front, McNaughton was put down as the favourite for the post of Commander in Chief of the invasion forces,' the Deutsches Nachrichtenbüro reported on 29 December. Now that Eisenhower was named, McNaughton had quit because he had no desire to 'command Canadian troops under an American superior, and to have them slaughtered by a foreign general as had happened so often with the British'.[38] The German expectation that Canadians remained involved in the main assault on France soon became an important part of the wider Overlord deception operation.

The significance of the dual announcements on 26 December – half the army now fighting in Italy and McNaughton retiring – to Canada's role in future operations was not lost to the media either. On 27 December, Ross Munro filed a long story noting that the Canadians had been moulded and trained 'to hit the coast hard in the campaign in northwest Europe'. 'The complicated question of whether the army should fight as a whole or in packets of divisions and corps has been a contentious and tangled one,' Munro noted; 'this has been the big issue in the past year . . . and now it is settled.' British newspapers echoed Munro's sentiment. The *Manchester Guardian* commented on 29 December that the Canadians will now go to France as a corps, with the army organisation modified to include British and Allied troops. A British United Press story datelined Ottawa cut to the essential point: the removal of McNaughton marked the 'integration of Canadian troops within Empire units under Generals Montgomery and Alexander'.[39] And so it did.

Ralston and Stuart hoped and believed that this was not the case. But they soon discovered what McNaughton – and Sir Arthur Currie a generation earlier – understood: fielding divisions, and now even corps, did not get you a seat at the table. The diminished role for the First Canadian Army quickly led to the removal of Major-General Turner as an *ex-officio* member of the Overlord planning staff. The Canadians, as McNaughton informed Freddie Morgan in mid-December, would now have to work through the chain of command to find out what was going on.[40] By February 1944 Ralston was forced to tell Mackenzie King that he knew nothing of the Overlord plan or the Canadian role in it. It appears, Ralston told his PM, 'that we have to and do rely on the judgement and efficiency of the [division] commanders' to look after Canadian interests. This was not enough for Mackenzie King. Three days later Ralston appealed to Ken Stuart, still Acting Commander in Chief of the First Canadian Army, to find out what was happening. But Stuart had no standing and was in the dark, too. 'I am sure that I am the last one to raise an abstract question,' Stuart wrote, but the Canadian staff and the Canadian government needed 'to be in a position to exercise their judgement for the benefit of the Canadian troops whom they are responsible to Canada [for]'.[41]

By early 1944, however, the Canadian government had lost any semblance of control over the operations of its army. By all accounts no Canadian ever saw the final plans for Operation Overlord, and even Canadian historians were not allowed full access to Overlord documents after the war. The Canadians had been reintegrated into the imperial army and would soon be written out of the Overlord story.

* * *

Operation Overlord is such a dominant feature of the Second World War story that its inevitability is taken for granted. But in December 1943 even senior planners were not sure it would happen. On 7 December the senior Anglo-American staff officers, along with Churchill, Eden, Smuts, Dill and several others, met for dinner in Cairo. It was a boisterous, congenial affair. Churchill asked them all to guesstimate when Germany would fall. 'Marshall predicted March and if not then November. Dill gave even money on March.' Brooke himself 'gave 6 to 4 for March'. That evening in Cairo everyone seemed reasonably convinced that Germany would capitulate before the winter ended.[42] The reason for their optimism was the dramatic spike in the power of the Allied strategic bomber offensive.

The 'Casablanca Directive', issued on 4 February 1943, set out to achieve nothing less than destruction of Germany's ability and will to fight through aerial bombardment.[43] Germany was to be bombed around the clock: by RAF Bomber Command at night and the US VIII and XV Air Forces by day. The emphasis of the air campaign sharpened in June when the Pointblank Directive from the Combined Chiefs of Staff ordered bombers to concentrate on German transportation systems and on aircraft production in order to secure the command of the air needed for an assault on France. The CCOS assumed that the final defeat of Germany depended on landing an army and marching to Berlin.

The bomber barons had other ideas. Air Marshal Arthur Harris, commander of Bomber Command, was already bent on a general assault on German urban/industrial targets – de-housing as some called it. By 1943 the RAF was fully committed to an 'area bombing' campaign that relied on a rapidly growing fleet of four-engine bombers, electronic navigation methods, and countermeasures to get bombers through to a target big enough to find in the dark. All that, and plenty of incendiaries. The raids became increasingly malevolent in their orchestration. High explosives 'opened up' buildings for the incendiaries that followed. Once firemen were in the streets, they could be killed by later waves of high-explosive bombs. Time-delay fuses added to the misery and death.

In the spring and early summer of 1943 Harris concentrated on the industrial area of the Ruhr, on places like Düsseldorf, Essen and Cologne. The RAF also conducted the famous dams raid, using unique bombs and equipment to breech the electric power dams in the Mohne and Eder valleys. The impact of these raids on German production and morale was marginal. On 20 July one German official dismissed them all as minor.[44] Four days later Harris launched Operation Gomorrah, an effort to smash Hamburg.

On the evening of 24 July, 791 of Harris's bombers headed out across the North Sea. German radar, suddenly jammed with static from aluminium foil dumped into the sky ahead of the bombers, revealed little of the raid's size and direction until it burst out of the cloud. In less than an hour 2,284 tons of bombs fell on the centre of Hamburg. Damage was heavy. When 121 USAAF bombers arrived the next afternoon to attack a diesel-engine factory, the city was cloaked in dense smoke: the fire burned for days. On 26 July the Americans returned to Hamburg, only to abandon their attack due to persistent smoke. But smoke – and darkness – did not constrain Bomber Command. On the night of 26–7 July it returned to Hamburg in force, dropping 2,326 tons of bombs – just short of half of them incendiaries.

No one planned what happened next. The summer had been dry and the day was hot and still. The new fires quickly coalesced into a firestorm. Flames soared 2,000 feet into the air, driven by winds that reached at least 150mph. 'At its height,' W.G. Sebald, wrote, 'it lifted gables and roofs from buildings, flung rafters and entire advertising billboards through the air, tore trees from the ground and drove human beings before it like living torches.'[45] Temperatures reached 1,000 degrees centigrade, glass melted, pavement liquified, air-raid shelters became crematoriums and the fire sucked so much oxygen from the air that many simply suffocated. Max Hastings summarised the results: '40,385 houses, 275,000 flats, 580 factories, 2,632 shops, 277 schools, 24 hospitals, 58 churches, 83 banks, 12 bridges, 76 public buildings and a zoo had been obliterated'.[46] An estimated 40,000 people perished. Twenty-two square miles of Hamburg were destroyed.

The Hamburg raid shook the German leadership and people. Goebbels was heard to opine that it was 'a catastrophe, the extent of which simply staggers the imagination'.[47] If the British could do this three or four more times the war would be lost. An estimated 1.2 million refugees fled the city, carrying the news to the far reaches of the Reich. In late August a woman's suitcase burst open on a train platform in Bavaria, spilling out 'Toys, a manicure set, singed underwear. And last of all, the roasted corpse of a child, shrunk like a mummy, which its half-deranged mother has been carrying about with her.'[48] When concentration-camp inmates went to Hamburg weeks later to bury the dead they were driven back by swarms of flies: rats were everywhere. Military engineers with flame-throwers had to clear the way.[49]

The shock of Hamburg combined with the defection of Italy, the Allied landings on the Italian mainland and the relentlessness of the Russian offensive raised hopes that the Germans would fold. Swedish diplomats, industrialists and news media all suggested that German morale was on a knife-edge in the autumn of 1943. And the Allied air offensive was just getting started. In May 1943 the USAAF deployed sixteen operational groups totalling 1,260 aircraft: only ten of these groups were heavy bombers. By December the USAAF had over thirty-seven groups operating 4,618 aircraft, more than half of which were heavy bombers.[50] But the USAAF was not done: the target for operational aircraft from British bases by 1 July 1944 was 6,779. By then the RAF was hoping to have 4,014 bombers operational. In 1944 the Germans would reap what they had sown.

The Americans fully committed to precision daytime bombing using heavily armed aircraft. They also flew very high, up to 30,000 feet, in self-defending formations, with squadrons and bomb groups arranged to provide overlapping and mutually beneficial fields of fire. The Germans soon learned how to fight them. In 1943, they could simply bide their time and attack when the bombers' short-range escorts peeled away. Fighters with heavier firepower – including 20mm cannons – were also needed.[51] The Germans eventually learned to attack American formations from head-on, where defensive firepower was weakest. This also allowed German fighters to slice through the bomber formation at a much higher relative speed, making it tough for gunners to engage them.

It did not take long for the perils of unescorted penetration of enemy air space to be revealed. On 1 August 1943, 178 B-24s set off from Libya to attack the Romanian oil fields. The targets had been hit the year before by a small force without loss. By 1943 the air defences around Ploesti were fully developed. The B-24s were swarmed by German, Romanian and Bulgarian fighters: fifty-five were totally lost, while damaged aircraft scattered onto airfields across the eastern Mediterranean. It was a gallant and ultimately futile effort: Ploesti's production was not affected.

Worse was to follow. On 17 August 1943, VIII AF based in Britain despatched two missions deep into Germany. In the morning 146 B-17s set off for the aircraft factories at Regensburg in Bavaria. Fifteen were lost before the force reached the target, at which point the German fighters miraculously disappeared – it turns out that they were refuelling and rearming to meet the second raid now building over East Anglia. Those 230 B-17 Fortresses were headed for the ball-bearing plants at Schweinfurt, also in Bavaria. The Germans launched a full-scale assault on the Schweinfurt force as soon as it crossed the Dutch coast. For a while it seemed that the leading groups would be annihilated: twenty-two B-17s went down en route. On the return trip the Germans preyed on the damaged and vulnerable. In the end, thirty-six B-17s were lost and of those that returned thirty-seven never flew again.[52] These losses crippled VIII AF for weeks. German ball-bearing production was briefly cut by 30 per cent, not enough to impact engine production, and the factories were quickly repaired.

In the autumn of 1943 the notion gradually emerged that an aerial war of attrition might be waged successfully if fighters could support bombers deep into Germany. Attacks on the aircraft industry and transportation systems would force the Germans to fight a battle with America's vast and growing aircraft industry which they could not win. This was precisely what the Germans had long feared.[53] The trend was clear. During a raid on Kassel on 28 July, American P-47 fighters, using drop tanks for the first time, pushed 30 miles deeper into Germany than ever before. In August P-47s appeared over Hamburg and Frankfurt – nearly 400 miles from their English bases.[54]

The Luftwaffe's solution to the growing American problem was to largely abandon its air effort in the Mediterranean and Russian fronts and concentrate on air defence of the Reich.[55] The growth in fighter strength and sophistication over Germany was demonstrated dramatically on 14 October, when 291 USAAF bombers set off to attack Schweinfurt again. The Luftwaffe threw everything they had at them, even night-fighters. Sixty B-17s were shot down. 'Of the men,' Alan Levine writes, '605 were missing or dead, and 43 wounded. Morale at American bomber bases hit rock bottom.'[56] After Schweinfurt II, deep raids into Germany were abandoned until the escort problem could be solved.[57]

The solution was en route. The twin-engine P-38 fighter, equipped with drop tanks giving it a range of over 500 miles, was ready in November. The early versions were unheated, had no windshield defrosters, and their combat performance – excellent below 25,000 feet – slipped noticeably at 30,000 feet. But they were a welcome addition. Larger drop tanks on the P-47s pushed their range further into Germany as well, and so with a relay of fighters, escorts could range well beyond

Schweinfurt, and as far as Berlin, by December 1944.[58] An even better long-range fighter, the fast and nimble P-51, was on its way for early 1944.

Marshall was well aware that VIII AF had turned the corner by the end of November 1943. Both the American and British Chiefs of Staff also knew Arthur Harris was bent on winning the war himself over the winter. On 3 November 1943 Harris had made his case to Churchill. Bomber Command had already laid waste to at least nineteen German cities, and now planned to attack a series of target 'complexes'. The destruction of these, Harris claimed, is 'more than half completed already'. The critical target now was Berlin – which Bomber Command could now reach completely under the cover of darkness. 'We must get the USAAF to wade in in greater force,' Harris told Churchill. 'We can wreck Berlin from end to end if the USAAF will come in on it. It will cost us 400–500 aircraft. It will cost Germany the war.'[59]

Harris, like many others, preferred to believe that German morale was brittle, and that the Nazi regime terrorised and enslaved even its own people. Intense bombing would break them. The reality was rather more complex. Their defeat in the Great War and the even greater humiliation of Versailles had bred a sense of resentment and entitlement that was widely shared among the German people.[60] The Nazis fed off that, nurtured it and co-opted it. They then raised the morale and living standards of Aryan Germans at the expense of those deemed enemies of the German Volk both at home and eventually abroad. As Götz Aly writes, in the late 1930s the Germans accepted the Nazi agenda 'as a difficult, even tortuous process toward national unification of a linguistic and cultural community, not unlike what had taken place in other European states'.[61]

By 1943 the German people were wilfully complicit in the war and in the genocide of their neighbours, because life was good under the Nazis. Germans were well fed, consumer goods were available, taxes were low, the social safety net was efficient, and Germany was asserting its natural place in Europe.[62] 'National Socialism' really did mean a welfare state for ordinary Aryan Germans. The Nazis created a sophisticated financial system in which the occupied countries paid for the occupation forces, helped to finance the war, and had their wealth sucked out through a system of scrip and occupation currency. Systematic looting of consumer goods, clothing and food followed as the material wealth of occupied Europe flowed into Germany. 'Free' personal effects confiscated from French Jews were provided to those dispossessed by bombing. In 1942 Hermann Goering shipped 2,306 freight cars and several river barges of 'cosmetics, toys and general gift items' from France to heavily bomb-damaged parts of Germany: a small part of the 18.5 billion francs spent by the German high command on its 1942 Christmas purchasing spree in France.[63] 'They didn't take anything away from us by force,' Pierre Arnoult wrote in 1959, 'they purchased everything correctly – with money they took from us.'[64]

In the circumstances, there was little cause for Germans to rebel against the Nazis in 1943 – or later. Well-thought-out propaganda was convincing: the war was being won. Everyone knew that the Jews, Socialists, Communists and other dissenters were being swept up and would not be coming back. And they knew that the Eastern Front was a racial war of extermination against the Slavs. Letters home from ordinary Wehrmacht soldiers explained the brutal necessity of slaughtering the Slavic population in the east: they could not be redeemed and they often resisted.[65] If Nicholas Stargardt is right, the German people bought into all this because it was right: it was the path to Germany's destiny.[66] Wolfram Wette described the mindset as a 'thoroughly militarized German *Volksgemeinschaft* whose armed members consisted overwhelmingly of conscripts with no option than to serve', who nonetheless 'fought to the bitter end, and failed to revolt as their fathers had in 1918'.[67]

Much of this remained for postwar analysts to determine. Certainly, Sir Arthur Harris believed that he could break German morale and force an end to the war by March 1944. In many ways, however, Bomber Command had already made its greatest contributions to winning the war even before Harris launched his Battle for Berlin. Bomber Command had forced Germany to develop a huge air-defence system that was effectively a Second Front in the air by late 1943. In 1940 Germany employed 791 heavy anti-aircraft batteries, each equipped with four to six powerful 88mm guns, in defence of its cities. By the end of 1943 that number had risen to 2,132 heavy batteries: roughly 10,000 88mm guns. The whole Reich air-defence system was manned by 1.8 million men, and it consumed an enormous amount of ammunition. It was estimated that to bring down one 'British' bomber the Germans expended an average of 16,000 rounds of 88mm ammunition. The figures are staggering, and none of it was pointed at the Russians. However, the real measure of Bomber Command's accomplishment by 1943 was, as Williamson Murray describes it, a 'fundamental distortion it caused in German armaments production'. Unable to match British aircraft production, the Nazi regime turned to *Vergeltungswaffen*: reprisal or retaliation weapons, V-weapons. These included both the jet-propelled, winged missile, the V1, and the ballistic missile V2. These projects sucked wealth, resources and labour out of other efforts – like aircraft production – that would have proved better investments. All this had been done before the American bombing campaign really got started.

By late 1943, the final destruction of Germany's airpower was the objective of the American bombing campaign. Once the P-51 with drop tanks deployed in significant numbers, there was no safe airspace over Germany in which to even train pilots. The Luftwaffe was, in effect, now trapped in a death spiral. If the airmen were right, there would be no need for Operation Overlord.

* * *

Colonel Ernest Dupuy, the American officer in charge of SHAEF press coverage, described Overlord in early 1944 as 'The Biggest Story in the World'.[68] It was very much an open secret. On 1 December a *US News* story datelined Tehran predicted the opening of the Second Front in the spring of 1944. It would be preceded by a bombing campaign and supported by diversionary landings. Most importantly, it reported that in the main operation across the Channel '*two thirds of those landing* [my emphasis] probably will be Americans'. Then Senator Edwin C. John of Colorado, a member of the Military Affairs Committee, let it slip that the United States was committing 73 per cent of the forces to the invasion of Europe.[69]

Roosevelt arrived home from Tehran amid a storm of protest from the isolationist and anti-British Senate caucus over the Overlord plan. Barton Wheeler, Montana's notoriously anti-British senator, opined that 'The proposed percentage is too great'. However, he concluded, since the British believed that an assault on France would likely be costly, 'and, since the United States is demanding it, the United States must furnish the greater percentage of troops'.[70] The Democratic senator from Kentucky, Albert B. Chandler, agreed, describing America's commitment as 'little short of murder'. German shortwave radio chimed in, taunting Americans listeners that 'British blood was too precious to spill'.[71]

What the now Canadian Embassy reported that efforts by the JCS and even Secretary Knox of the Navy Department to stop 'that stupid and unpatriotic falsehood' had some success.[72] By early January the message, if anyone was ready to hear it, was more nuanced. As *Time* reported on 3 January, the initial attack was likely to be balanced: 50–50 US–British. Other periodicals carried the same message, and reiterated that so far the British had carried the burden of the war in Europe.[73] How many Americans were receptive to these clarifications remains unknown. But the enduring myth in America that Overlord was primarily an American operation probably had its origins in December 1943.

Open discussion of the Second Front, including its details, was not limited to the United States. The Germans were talking about it, too, and waiting anxiously for the landings. 'Second Front in 90 Days' became the catchphrase of German propaganda by January 1944.[74] The public-relations campaign to prepare Germans for the Second Front extended to the appointment of Field Marshal Erwin Rommel to oversee the defences along the coast. Goebbels portrayed him as an unfailingly successful battlefield commander, while the British attributed much of their trouble in Africa to his genius. Even Churchill had masked British defeats in the Western Desert by claiming they had been 'out generalled' by the Desert Fox.[75] The Americans, only too ready to believe in the incompetence of British generals and culturally prone to focus on great men, bought into the Rommel myth as well.

By early 1944 most Germans saw the invasion, in the words of the German official history, as 'a unique opportunity to turn the tide of the war in Germany's favour'.[76] With the invasion defeated, scores of divisions would be freed to stem the Russian tide. As one historian of German public mood explained, 'a majority of Germans had daily expected and yearned for this operation for weeks and months'.[77]

Rommel played to that theme. 'He has an old score to settle with the British and Americans,' Goebbels announced in April 1944, and 'is on fire with anger and hate, and has put all his cunning and intelligence into perfection of the defensive works . . . Rommel is the old fighter again'.[78]

While a German propaganda unit followed Rommel around and reported on his efforts,[79] the British championed their own hero, Bernard Law Montgomery, the man who defeated the Desert Fox and driven him out of Africa. The 'relentless British press campaign that elevated Montgomery to the station of Britain's greatest since Wellington', in D.K.R. Crosswell's words, grated on the Americans, especially Eisenhower's Chief of Staff, Bedell Smith.[80] Patton, himself the consummate showman, understood what was going on. Monty 'is an actor but not a fool', Patton confided to his diary on 11 February 1944. It hurt, nonetheless, that Montgomery assumed the airs of the Overlord commander and 'correspondingly denigrated Eisenhower to affable chairman of the board'. Moreover, by February it was dawning on many Americans that although Ike was Supreme Allied Commander, the British had insinuated themselves into all three operational commands: Admiral Bertram Ramsay at sea, Air Marshal Leigh-Mallory in the air, and Montgomery in command of the armies.

This was at least in keeping with the original COSSAC concept that the creation of the lodgement was to be a largely Anglo-Canadian effort. It will be recalled that COSSAC's original phase lines to D+50 had the whole front from the mouth of the Seine sweeping west of Paris and along the Loire almost back to the Bay of Biscay held by British and Canadian armies.[81] The main American task was to clear Cherbourg and Brest, and open access to Biscay ports, especially Quiberon Bay. But securing the rear and its ports was not how the Americans saw their role. The plan that they were working on by the spring of 1944 placed the largest portion of the final lodgement under American command. By D+50 the US Army planned to hold the line of the Loire as far east as Tours, and from there north to Le Mans.[82] The Anglo-Canadians would be squeezed into the line of the Seine west of Paris. The Americans meant to be in charge from the outset, and their media campaign (discussed in the next chapter) sought to illuminate that.

The whole open public discourse on the looming assault on France was a source of great anxiety to senior British officers. Britain had only one deployable army left, and it was committed to Overlord. Its destruction would seriously weaken Britain's position as a Great Power. While historians have often quoted Churchill's nightmare of another 'first day of the Somme' on the sands of Normandy, the public nature of the whole Second Front scheme reminded Alan Brooke of an even greater disaster. Sir John Kennedy, at the time Director of Military Operations in the War Office, recalled that in January 1944, 'Brooke remarked to me that all this, and the political influences which came into play, made him shiver and reminded him of the prelude to the disastrous Nivelle offensive of 1917.'[83] General Robert Nivelle, appointed Commander in Chief of France's armies on 12 December 1916, promised to blast the Germans out of his country in the spring of 1917 with concentrated and sophisticated artillery fire. The plan was so simple, and Nivelle so confident, that it was the object of public discussion for months, including extensive coverage in the French and British press. Well warned, the Germans simply withdrew from most of their forward positions, and Nivelle's powerful barrages fell into space. French infantry surged across the empty battlefield, outran their guns and were slaughtered on the new German positions. Mutinies followed and France balanced on a knife edge for the rest of the year. Might Overlord suffer the same fate?

CHAPTER 15

NO QUITTING

By God, you tell that bunch that if they can't get together and stop quarreling like children, I will tell the Prime Minister to get someone else to run this damn war! I'll quit.

Eisenhower to Tedder, April 1944[1]

Montgomery was clearly not happy with the COSSAC plan as it stood by late December 1943. At a minimum the scale was simply too small, and – although historians do not comment on it – the British role was tertiary, following ashore behind the First US and First Canadian armies. His initial reaction was to propose something radically new, which he revealed to Major-General Sir John Kennedy, the Director of Military Operations at the War Office, on 2 January 1944: landings on the Calvados coast would be entirely British, while the Americans landed on either side of the Brittany peninsula at Saint-Malo and Saint-Nazaire.[2] Kennedy suggested that the Americans were not going to be pushed off to the rock-bound coast of Brittany – although de Guingand claims it was studied.[3] After lunch Monty returned with a less radical scheme: cancel Anvil and put everything into Overlord. Eisenhower's Chief of Staff, Walter Bedell Smith, agreed, and so too did the British Chiefs of Staff.[4] It is an article of faith nonetheless in the existing literature that the Americans had to bully the British into doing Overlord, but in early 1944 the biggest impediment to the launching of a Second Front was the Americans themselves.

343

By the time Montgomery and Eisenhower returned to Britain it was still not clear just how the Overlord force was to get to France and stay there. Operation Neptune – the escort, covering, landing, bombardment and naval responsibilities of Overlord – was British. To mount the existing COSSAC plan, the Royal Navy paid off battleships, cruisers, armed merchant cruisers, minelayers and forty ageing destroyers to find the 45,000 personnel needed.[5] The Canadians helped by crewing new British warships, and providing two Landing Ships (Assault), three flotillas of Landing Ships (Infantry, Large) and a fleet of ASW vessels and minesweepers. All this was barely enough for the three-division attack. Initial appeals to Admiral King for help from the USN were simply refused.[6] King would not release American LSTs beyond what was already agreed for the European theatre. The bulk of new LSTs were destined for the Pacific, where Nimitz's central Pacific drive was slated to start. Overlord was a British show: they would have to find the resources. Adding a fourth division to the COSSAC plan was only possible if Anvil could be scaled back, or delayed.

On 21 January 1944 Montgomery made the case for a five-division assault spanning lower Normandy from the Orne to the Vire rivers, with supporting airborne landings to secure either flank. The merits of significantly expanding the landings were covered in a SHAEF document circulated on 23 January. No author is identified, but there is evidence of Morgan's hand. The issue came down to a fundamental question of objectives. In 'Plan I', a four-division landing, there were three initial objectives to be achieved in sequence: capture Caen, defeat the Panzer counterattack, then capture Cherbourg. Given the importance of Caen as the first objective, the memorandum favoured landing the fourth division – another British division – north of Caen at Ouistreham. In 'Plan II', Monty's five-division assault, all three objectives were to be pursued simultaneously. However, the memorandum strongly dismissed Plan II as too risky. It would reduce 'our degree of superiority over the enemy in the CAEN bridgehead during the critical first week' and might result in the failure to capture both Caen and Bayeux, which 'may lead to a penetration of the bridgehead and the defeat of the US and BRITISH forces in detail'.[7]

On 31 January 1944 COSSAC issued an appreciation of likely enemy responses to Monty's expanded plan. Morgan's estimates remained largely unchanged from the autumn of 1943. The Panzer division known to be at Lisieux would either attack down the east bank of the Mue towards Douvres and seize the high ground north-west of Caen, or attack west of the Mue River towards Crépon, Banville, Bazenville. The scenario for D+2 was for the Germans to secure the Bayeux pivot and then radiate attacks with three divisions on the assault beaches from Port-en-Bessin to Courseulles-sur-Mer along the Sommervieu–Bazenville ridge.[8] For COSSAC, at least, the expanded assault did not change the fundamentals of geography or the German response: rapid Panzer thrusts across good tank country north and west of Caen to split the Allies and destroy them in detail.

On 24 January, Eisenhower visited Brooke to explain the expanded plan and his desire to mount it using even more resources drawn from Operation Anvil.[9] Brooke 'entirely agreed'. At that moment an example of what happens to a weak landing was playing out in Italy. On 22 January a small Allied force of just two divisions landed west of Rome near the town of Anzio. Its task was to unhinge the German position at Cassino and open the road to Rome. The Germans reacted with unanticipated ferocity, and the Anzio landings were soon trapped in a small bridgehead and under siege. The unfolding story of the Anzio landings exerted a powerful influence on the evolving Overlord plan.

On 1 February 1944 Montgomery issued his 'Initial Joint Plan' (IJP) for a five-division assault across the whole lower Baie de la Seine. It is assumed in the literature, because this plan was ultimately successful, that it was the natural and obvious one to adopt. Morgan was not convinced, nor initially was Omar Bradley. Caen was too far away from the American objective – Cherbourg – for Bradley's liking. Moreover, between the Americans and Cherbourg lay 'an intricate jungle of rivers and swamp that almost severed the neck of the Cotentin peninsula'.[10] A division landing west of the Vire needed to get off the beach and across several narrow, raised roads over low ground quickly. Bradley wanted an airborne landing to ensure that the seaborne division was not trapped. He was also anxious that the beach exits from what became Utah beach could handle the traffic and feared that one road in particular might contain pockets of silt under a veneer of sand. After musing about this he was visited several days later by

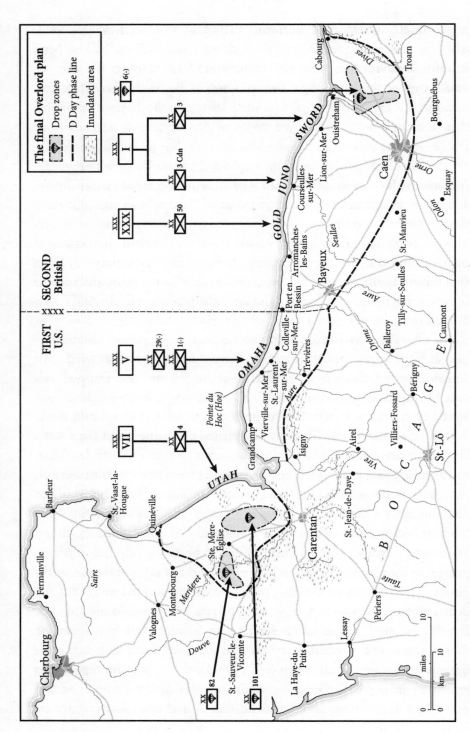

4. The final Overlord plan.

a young Royal Naval officer who presented him with a long glass vial full of sand. Two nights previously the officer had slipped ashore from a submarine, visited the spot questioned by Bradley and retrieved a core sample. 'The shingle is firmly bedded on rock,' the young man explained. 'There is little danger of your trucks bogging down.'[11]

There were other reasons why Plan II was desirable. The 'expanded' COSSAC Plan I added one British division landing on what became Sword beach to ensure the capture of Caen. In this scenario the First US Army would then command an assault of one American and three Anglo-Canadian divisions. At this stage it would have been inconceivable to turn command of the assault back to a British or Canadian army. However, adding a British division at Ouistreham and an American landing west of the Vire meant that Overlord could become a two-army landing: the First US Army in the west and the Second British in the east.

So Montgomery's expanded plan resolved not only an operational problem, it also nicely handled a delicate political one as well. The knock-on effect was even better for the British. With two armies landing side by side, coordination and command of the Overlord assault now switched from the First US Army to the 21st Army Group, and therefore to Eisenhower's Land Force Commander, General Montgomery. 'It must have been disappointing to many of them [Americans],' de Guingand wrote years later, 'for according to the original proposals an American and not an Englishman would be commanding the assault.'[12] Once again, the devious British had outfoxed the naive Americans.

The decision to assign the British Second Army a leading role put the air-support plans on the horns of a dilemma. The RCAF had poured resources into No. 83 Group on the understanding that it would be the first tactical air group ashore and in support of the First Canadian Army. When news of the change was revealed, senior RCAF officials quickly concluded that they would not surrender their lead role. The Canadians would now support the British Second Army, and the RCAF continued to pour resources into 83 Group.[13] No. 84 Group, with its mixture of British and Allied squadrons, switched to support of the First Canadian Army.[14] There is nothing in the Normandy literature pointing out that the British Second Army was supported by a largely Canadian tactical air group, but Canadians were well aware of it.[15]

Much of the next two months was spent trying to find the resources to make a five-division assault happen, and during that time the British became the driving force behind Operation Overlord. At the operational level five things needed to be resolved: allocating additional assault divisions, securing additional landing craft and naval support, sorting air support, and arranging additional logistical support for an expanded force once ashore.

Of all these, designating two other divisions to join the assault wave was the easiest. The British 50th Division, just back from Italy, got the nod. It would land on Gold beach (north of Bayeux) as the leading wave of XXX British Corps, and began intensive amphibious training with its naval landing force in mid-March.[16] The British Second Army's other two assault divisions, the 3rd British and 3rd Canadian of I British Corps, had been undergoing intensive amphibious training with their assigned naval landing forces since the summer of 1943. For the new landing west of the Vire (Utah) Bradley chose the 4th Infantry Division, just off the boat from the USA at the end of January. The 4th USID had trained intensively in amphibious warfare before leaving the States.[17] That training continued in the UK as every regiment went through the US Assault Training School.[18]

The logical choice for Omaha beach was the 29th USID: it had been waiting in the UK since 1942 and simply assumed that it would go in the assault wave. The whole 29th Division went through the assault school, but it had no combat experience. So the decision was made to add the 1st USID to the assault on Omaha. The Big Red One had plenty of combat experience, and it had already made two amphibious assaults. For that reason it was largely excused additional training in the UK after it arrived from the Mediterranean in early November 1943.

Finding the landing craft to get these divisions ashore, and to sustain them, was much harder. The expanded plan required a further six assault ships, two more HQ ships, forty-seven LSTs, seventy-two large Landing Craft (Infantry, Large) (LCI(L)), capable of landing a full battalion, and 144 LCTs. Half of these might be found by further cutting Anvil, which was now slated to launch on the same day as

Overlord. But Anvil was an American operation and they retained a firm attachment to it. Not only had they promised Stalin a landing in the south of France, but they had put considerable effort into rebuilding the French Army in North Africa. Without a southern gateway into France, Marshall opined, 'all our French investment will have been wasted'.[19]

A decision in early February to delay Overlord until late May allowed British new construction to make up some of the shortfall of LCTs, while an agreement to free even more landing craft from Anvil seemed to close the gap. At least that's what American planners in Washington believed. The real problem, they claimed, was SHAEF's faulty calculations of loading capacity and serviceability. 'With no more effort than that required to punch the key of an adding machine', Leighton and Coakley wrote, planners in Washington resolved Overlord's landing-craft problem by simply putting more men into each vessel. It was possible, they claimed, to pack 1,400 men into each LCI(L), significantly more than the figure of 960 – a battalion – that the British employed.[20]

Washington planners also increased the carrying capacity of the Overlord landing force by waving 'the magic wand of high serviceability'.[21] British projections of 90 per cent serviceability rate for LSTs and 85 per cent for LCTs were agreed to at Quebec.[22] Recent US experience, Washington argued, suggested a serviceability rate of 95 per cent for all landing craft. The British countered that their congested ports, busy dockyards and labour shortage made the lower figure a safer bet. The staff in Washington disagreed and turned Overlord's landing craft deficit into a surplus – even allowing lower serviceability estimates for British landing craft. None of this was a comfort to Overlord planners. The basic requirement was to get ashore safely and stay there. Both Bradley and Montgomery were utterly opposed to packing landing craft with as many men as possible.[23] The initial assault needed to be tactically loaded.

The battle over landing craft carried on throughout February, clarified slightly in the middle of the month when Major General John E. Hull, from War Department Plans, and Rear Admiral Charles M. Cooke, USN, arrived. The USN put twenty more LSTs on the table from its spring production. This would mean that about half of the world's supply of LSTs was now committed to Overlord.[24] American Overlord planners also accepted a 95 per cent serviceability rate for their own LSTs. On 18 February the 21st Army Group capitulated and dropped its estimated requirements by seven LSTs and thirty LCI(L)s. This reduced the draw-down on Anvil landing craft to twenty LSTs and twenty-one LCI(L)s. To achieve this, however, the British paid an enormous price: they agreed to find sixty-four 'more' cargo ships (no figure for the existing British commitment of cargo vessels to Overlord appears in the literature) for the Overlord build-up – with serious implications for their 1944 import schedule (more below).

The February conference also broke the logjam over American naval support for the expanded plan. At a dinner for Cook and other senior American sailors hosted by Admiral D.P. Kirk, the Western Task Force Commander, Rear Admiral John Hall, commander of the amphibious force slated to land troops at Omaha, 'sounded off in no uncertain terms about the want of gunfire support' for his beach. Hall had every reason to be upset. Omaha lay deep in the Baie de la Seine, brooded over by German coast batteries on the Cotentin peninsula. Cook took exception to Hall's candour, but he agreed to fix the problem.[25]

Finding enough landing craft to give Overlord a margin of insurance was not fully resolved until the end of March. Events in Italy played a huge role. Marshall informed Eisenhower on 7 February that if they were still fighting south of Rome on 1 April, 'then Anvil would of necessity be practically abandoned'.[26] It was the Germans who made the case for continued fighting in Italy. In mid-February they hurled ten divisions at the Anzio beachhead, their largest attack in the west since 1940. The Allies were well informed of the German intent by Ultra, the intelligence derived from the highly secret ability to read German codes, which allowed them to check the main thrusts.[27] But the fighting was intense and deadly: by the end of February there were about 19,000 casualties on either side. The struggle for Anzio suggested what any landing in France could expect.

The British always believed that the Germans would never abandon Italy, and that fighting them there was better than a small landing in the south of France. Marshall (and the planners in Washington) remained unconvinced. He was not alone. The Allied Forces HQ in Algiers (AFHQ) was dominated by Americans – British senior officers in the Mediterranean regarded it 'as a second capital of the Daughters of the Revolution'[28] – and held fast to the view that the Germans would simply abandon Italy and throw everything they had at the landings in north-west Europe. All this was laid out to Eisenhower in a telegram on 16 March, but Marshall left the final decision to Ike. Two days later Ike replied that it was now too late to mount Anvil to coincide with Overlord, and besides he needed all available landing craft for Overlord.[29] The compromise finally reached was that Anvil would be postponed until July.

It took until April 1944 to finally get the USN fully on side for Operation Overlord. A surfeit of new construction eased the LST crisis in April, when the USN finally relented and allocated more. For their part, the British had been unstinting in the allocation of UK-built LCTs: of the 900 on D-Day, 664 were British-built.[30] In the meantime, Rear Admiral Cook worked his magic and in April three old US battle-ships and one destroyer squadron arrived in the UK to assist with fire support for the American beaches. More American warships were on the way. In the end the USN sent more help than the British asked for.

Despite these increments of American support, the 'Neptune' portion of Operation Overlord remained overwhelmingly British. By one estimate, Overlord employed some 7,000 vessels of all types, from small landing craft to battleships. Of those, some 950 vessels were American, the rest – including large parts of Admiral Kirk's Western Task Force – were British or Allied ships. The battle with the Americans over landing craft also forced the British to shift 1 million dead-weight tons – roughly half of their coastal shipping – to logistical support for Overlord. 'No merchant ships need have been employed,' Cynthia Behrens opined, 'if there had been enough of those landing-ships and landing craft . . . In the early, crucial stages of the operation the burden of providing shipping fell mainly on the British.'[31] Once again, the Americans assumed that Britain would simply tighten its belt for the common cause, as it had done over the winter of 1942–3. Exhausted and war-weary in this fifth winter of the war, Britain was certainly doing its best to get Marshall's army into the fight.

* * *

The struggle to get the USN engaged in Operation Overlord ran parallel with an even tougher fight to get the air forces on side. Both the First US and British Second Armies had tactical air forces assigned to support them, but the Anglo-American Bomber Barons refused to allow Air Marshal Leigh-Mallory – the commander of the Allied Expeditionary Air Forces – to command strategic bombing forces. As Carlo D'Este writes, the key Anglo-American air-force commanders 'all subscribed to the almost sacrosanct big-bang tenet that the war could be won on the basis of airpower alone'.[32] Harris was going to win it over the winter by bombing Berlin into rubble, while General Carl 'Tooey' Spaatz, commander of US Strategic Air Forces in Europe, predicted that the intensification of bombing resulting from improved weather in the spring of 1944 meant that 'Germany will give up in three months'.[33]

By the winter of 1944 the RAF's Bomber Command and the USAAF's VIII and XV Air Forces were deeply into their 'decisive' campaigns. Between the night of 18–19 November 1943 and the end of March 1944, Bomber Command launched raids on 100 nights. Thirty-two major raids struck distant targets: Berlin was hit sixteen times. The German response was ferocious. By the end of January 1944 Harris had lost 384 four-engine bombers.[34] The withdraw of his vulnerable low-flying Stirlings from the campaign simply opened up the under-powered Halifax Mk II and V bombers to concentrated attack. After the raid on Leipzig on 18–19 February, when the losses among Halifaxes hit 16 per cent in one night, the Mk II and Vs were also withdrawn.[35] 'The story of the Battle of Berlin,' Martin Middlebrook and Chris Everitt wrote, 'is of a steady deterioration of effectiveness by the bomber forces at increasing cost.'[36] Production of Lancasters and Halifax Mk IIIs was just able to cover the loss rates – if not the wholesale withdrawal of obsolescent types.

Harris persisted. Path Finder Group marked targets with increasing accuracy, while Master Bombers, orbiting the target at great height, orchestrated the attacks. A new electronic warfare support group, No. 100, established in early 1944, jammed and spoofed German night-fighter, searchlight and gunnery control radar.[37] And increasingly Mosquito night-fighters attacked their German counterparts, increasing losses among German night-fighter pilots in February and March.[38] Better organisation concentrated bombing into just a twenty-minute window. As grim and as costly as the 'Battle of Berlin' was for Bomber Command, by February 1944, Harris was not ready to concede that he was wrong – or that Overlord was necessary.

What Harris did not know was that his campaign drove Hitler into launching the 'Baby Blitz', with important ramifications for Overlord. Frustrated by the delay in deployment of V-weapons, in January Hitler ordered the Luftwaffe to strike back. The Germans assembled their remaining bombers, 550, in France, and on 21 January they renewed night-time attacks on Britain – primarily London. Over the course of the next three months the remnant of the German bomber force was destroyed in what were little more than nuisance raids.[39] The Germans wasted an irreplaceable asset which ought to have been held in reserve for D-Day.

The reason that German bombers were irreplaceable by 1944 was because they were too busy building fighters. The Pointblank directive tasked the USAAF with the destruction of the German aircraft industry and, in the process, shooting down whatever the Germans put into the air. By January 1944 the USAAF could deploy enormous swarms of fighters each day: the 552 bombers sent to attack V-weapon sites in the Pas-de-Calais on 14 January were escorted by 645 fighters.[40] Among these were the new P-51 Mustangs, a high-performance fighter which, when equipped with drop tanks, could operate to Berlin and beyond.

It proved difficult to apply this military power over the winter of 1943–4, as American bombing doctrine collided head-on with the short days and abysmal weather of a European winter. Weather over the UK often disrupted the assembly of bomber formations before they even headed east, while targets could not be found through the cloud. As early as November the VIII Air Force was experimenting with 'radar bombing', dropping their payloads based on radar estimates through solid cloud. The 'practice' raid on Wilhelmshaven on 3 November was encouraging enough to base operations on radar for the next three months. From 'mid-October 1943 to mid-February 1944', the USAAF official history states, 'the story of daylight strategic bombing from the United Kingdom is essentially the story of an experiment in radar bombing'.[41] The equipment was not yet perfected and the radar crews of the new Pathfinder forces were not fully trained. 'The aiming point', according to Craven and Cate, 'became highly theoretical'.[42] But they learned by doing and in December the VIII Air Force dropped more tonnage on Germany – through cloud – than the RAF.[43]

Little of that bombing contributed to the overall American objective. The need to use easily identifiable ground features, like rivers and coastlines, for radar-directed bombing meant that raids often struck ports rather than the German aircraft industry.[44] Dropping leaflets and attacking targets in northern France, which characterised much of VIII AF's activity in late December and early January, contributed little to the defeat of the Luftwaffe.

The only opening during those dreary mid-winter weeks came on 11 January 1944, when a patch of clear weather allowed VIII AF to attack the FW 190 plant at Oschersleben, the Junkers plant at Halberstadt, and several factories in the Brunswick–Osnabrück area making parts for the ME 110. These were deep penetrations, and the fighter escort was not large: just 221 for the Oschersleben strike and 371 for the Brunswick–Osnabrück bombers.[45] Sixty of the 238 bombers were shot down.[46] The raid confirmed that the Germans would fight to defend their aircraft industry. After 11 January, however, the weather closed in again – even worse weather for the XV AF bombers based in Italy trying to cross the Alps to get at southern Germany.

By then the merits of the Combined Bomber Offensive (CBO) were being hotly debated by senior Allied staff.[47] The British agreed that the Luftwaffe remained the prime target, although operational conditions precluded easy cooperation with the Americans.[48] In any event, Harris remained convinced that Bomber Command could win the war itself by 1 April 1944 by 'de-housing' the citizens of thirty-eight key German cities.[49] 'The debate was ended on 13 February 1944', Craven and Cate claim, 'in the issuance of a new directive' for the CBO. For Americans the objective remained clear: 'the material destruction of German air combat strength'. However, the preamble in the 13 February directive gave Harris all the leeway he needed. The objective of the CBO was now 'The progressive destruction and dislocation of the German military, industrial and economic systems, the disruption of vital elements of lines of communications *and* the material reduction of German air combat strength.'[50]

It was in the spirit of a re-energized (and soon to be intensified) CBO that Air Marshal Leigh-Mallory convened a meeting on 12 February to lay out the SHAEF plan for the use of strategic bombers in support of Overlord.[51] SHAEF proposed to destroy the railway network of northern France – in fact all of north-western Europe – in order to isolate Normandy and reduce the likelihood of rapid German reinforcement. This became known as the 'Transportation Plan'. The Bomber Barons opposed it as impossible both because of the requirements for accuracy, and because it was a major distraction from winning the war through airpower. 'Even at this late stage', Max Hastings writes of Harris and Spaatz, 'neither officer had renounced his private conviction that Overlord was a vast, gratuitous, strategic misjudgement, when Germany was already tottering on the brink of collapse from bombing'.[52]

Harris and Spaatz were not alone in their opposition to the Transportation Plan. The British air ministry, Churchill, Eden, Doolittle (now in command of VIII AF), Brooke, the Joint Intelligence Committee, the British Ministry of Economic Warfare, the British Cabinet, and a myriad of others were all opposed. The opposition stemmed from the estimates of French and Belgian civilian casualties which ran to 80,000–160,000 killed, wounded or missing. When Montgomery 'insisted' to Churchill that the bombing must go ahead, Churchill flew into a rage.[53] Air Chief Marshal Tedder, Eisenhower's deputy commander, took over the Transportation Plan file for the two-month battle which followed (more below).

Meanwhile, Harris and Spaatz pressed on with 'winning the war'. Over February and March even the Americans took to bombing Berlin as a way of drawing the Luftwaffe into battle. It all started with 'Big Week', 19 to 26 February 1944, a prolonged patch of clear weather. This was the moment the Americans had been waiting for. On 20 February, Spaatz launched 689 bombers at the ball-bearing and aircraft plants around Brunswick and Leipzig, and 314 at the aircraft factories near Tutow north-east of Berlin. As expected, the Germans concentrated on the main force, which was escorted by no less than 835 fighters. The targets were heavily bombed at a cost of twenty-one bombers. Escorting fighters claimed sixty-one victories for the loss of only four of their own. Four more major USAAF raids followed on the 21st, 22nd, 24th and 25th, to Brunswick, Schweinfurt, Augsburg and Stuttgart, supported at night by Bomber Command attacks. By the time the weather closed in again, the USAAF had – it seemed – inflicted a stunning defeat on the Luftwaffe. Contemporary estimates put German aircraft losses at 2,500: 1,000 aircraft destroyed on the shop floor, 1,000 aircraft 'not built' because of the two-month hiatus in production, and 500 shot from the sky.[54] The figures are guestimates. The postwar US Strategic Bombing Survey challenged them, noting that the Germans were adept at getting aircraft assembled. But there was no gainsaying the impact of Big Week. The Germans could replace aircraft, but not pilots. In January they lost 292, and in February 434 pilots in all theatres.[55] The air defence of the Reich was now a war of attrition which the Germans could not win: pilots flew until they were killed or maimed. Big week, Richard Overy concluded, 'finally undermined an already demoralized and weakened Luftwaffe'.[56]

In March the Americans struck hard at Berlin because they knew that the Germans would fight to defend it. Swarms of P-47 and P-38 fighters squired the bombers into Germany, where hundreds of P-51s took over to shoot down the defenders. It was now the turn of American bomber crews to suffer a decline in morale, as their losses mounted. There was no darkness in an American operation to mask the rain of wings, engines, smoking fuselages, and aircrew cascading down through the bomber formations. 'One B-17 pilot recollected bitterly,' David Kennedy wrote of this period, that 'the realization sank in that "we were expendable . . . we were bait".'[57]

Meanwhile, Bomber Command pressed on with the so-called Battle of Berlin. The last major attack on the city, 15–16 February 1944, was the largest yet, with 891 aircraft inflicting heavy damage for the loss of forty-one of their number. After that Harris shifted targets of lesser importance as part of his de-housing campaign, but that did not ease the losses. By the end of March 1944 Bomber Command had lost 1,117 bombers in the Battle of Berlin: more than twice what Harris predicted in November, and the Germans were no closer to surrendering.[58]

In March, Harris was ordered to test the feasibility of the Transportation Plan to determine whether railways could be hit with any accuracy and if the collateral damage was acceptable. He was doubtful, but Harris had a large number of Stirling and Halifax Mk II and V squadrons which were no longer effective over Germany. According to the Canadian official history, 'fully half of the crews taking part in these experimental attacks would come from RCAF squadrons'.[59] Eight targets were selected by the RAF Air Staff, and Harris added a ninth at the end of March.

The first target on the night of 6 March was the rail junction at Trappes south-west of Paris, attacked by 261 Halifaxes from Nos 4 and 6 (RCAF) Groups. With no flak and or fighters to face, the Halifaxes bombed from 13,000 feet. Visibility was good, the target well marked and 'enormous damage' was inflicted on rolling stock and infrastructure.[60] The next two raids, both on the rail junction at Le Mans, were also successful, although heavy cloud led to dispersion, and seventy-nine civilians were killed. Two raids on Amiens followed on the 15–16 March and 16–17 March, again with evident damage to the railyards and civilian deaths (eighteen each night). In both cases, the failure of the Path Finder Force to properly mark the target was the cause of errant bombing. The attack on Laon on 23–4 March was conducted in clear visibility with a well-marked target, but the Master Bomber directing the attack called it off halfway through when bombs drifted into the nearby homes: seven people died.

The last raid ordered by Portal was on Aulnoye, a rail junction on the Belgian border near Mauberge. The weather was clear but for some reason the Pathfinders were unable to find the railyard. The bombers milled around the target area for nearly half an hour until they found it, then they bombed from just 7,000 feet. Harris added the railyard west of Paris at Vaires to the target list. Seventy-nine Halifaxes, most of them RCAF, attacked it on the night of 29–30 March with great accuracy. The raid detonated two ammunition trains and killed a reported 1,200 German soldiers.[61]

This series of raids was, as the Canadian official history concluded, an 'outstanding success'. They tipped the balance in support of the Transportation Plan. Harris admitted he had been wrong. The Stirling and Halifax crews demonstrated, in the words of a Bomber Command Operational Research Report in May 1944, 'an accuracy and concentration far exceeding that achieved by American heavies by day'.[62] Harris was certainly surprised, but that accolade needs to be tempered by the lack of any opposition, and the ability to bomb at low altitudes and to linger over the target until it was identified. Things would not always be that easy.

By the end of March the struggle to control the strategic bomber force in support of Overlord had become a battle of all against all. Churchill and many others remained opposed to the Transportation Plan because of the fear of civilian casualties; Spaatz now wanted to concentrate bombing on oil production; Harris was opposed to all 'panacea' targets and wanted to level German cities; Eisenhower and Tedder wanted the bombers shifted to support of Overlord; and everyone agreed that Leigh-Mallory should not command the heavies. Harris was prepared to allocate his Stirling and Halifax Mk II and V squadrons, and some of his Halifax Mk III aircraft which had limited range, to help with Overlord, but not his frontline Lancaster squadrons. For his part, Spaatz wanted nothing to do with Overlord. With barely two months to go before D-Day Eisenhower's frustration reached a boiling point. ' "By God," he declared to Tedder in early April, "you tell that bunch that if they can't get together and stop quarrelling like children, I will tell the Prime Minister to get someone else to run this damn war! I'll quit".' He warned Marshall of his intention to quit as well.[63]

The quarrelling went on, nonetheless, until May, and included what D'Este describes as a 'furious confrontation' between Eisenhower and Spaatz. With improved weather in April the VIII and XV Air Forces pressed their campaign over Germany. Spaatz was not going to start bombing railyards unless he was certain that Harris would not win the war over Germany in the meantime. Moreover, American bombers, Alan Levine writes, 'served as the anvil on which the escort fighters hammered the Luftwaffe fighter force'.[64] That month 447 German pilots died in the air. But the anvil got hammered, too. The VIII AF loss rate was the highest of the war in April 1944: 512 aircraft, of which 361 were four-engine bombers.

Tedder's intervention finally brought both airmen in line, not least because of the increasing urgency to bomb V1 sites sprouting along the

French coast. The experimental raids of March also allowed the figures for potential civilian casualties to be revised sharply downward, to perhaps 20,000. Roosevelt considered this acceptable. So, too, did the French. Major-General Pierre Koenig, commander of Free French Forces in the UK, said plainly 'we would take twice the anticipated loss to be rid of the Germans'.[65] Like the endless rows of unknown dead from the Great War, their sacrifice would be remembered: 'Mort pour la France'. Churchill went along, but he was not happy.

The Transportation Plan was approved just a month before D-Day, and a large part of the task fell to Harris's bombers. 'The fears of USSTAF [US Strategic Air Force] that it would have to bear the burden of transportation attacks did not prove correct,' Forest Pogue writes. 'Bomber Command struck at a greater number of targets and dropped a larger tonnage of bombs on the occupied areas in the pre-D-Day period than did the United States Eighth Air Force'.[66]

* * *

The Transportation Plan was also part of Operation Fortitude, the largest and most complex deception scheme ever conceived and operated. Since it was an open secret that France would be invaded in 1944, where and when were the only crucial questions. These were not hard to discern. Describing an arc of effective fighter cover from English air bases limited the potential landing sites to two: the Pas-de-Calais and the beaches of lower Normandy. Timing was a little more problematic. A full moon would be necessary for parachutists and gliders, and it would also produce a higher tide to carry the landing craft closer to beach defences.

The task of trying to deceive the Germans fell to the London Controlling Section (LCS) of Britain's Psychological Warfare Executive. LCS began working on deception for Overlord in earnest in July 1943, shortly after the initial COSSAC plan was submitted. From the outset, the Overlord deception was conceived as a Europe-wide plan for 1944. A comprehensive deception scheme for western Europe coded named JAEL was submitted to the CCS in late September 1943, providing guidance for every deception operation from the Balkans to Norway.[67] Among these was Operation Fairlands, built around General George Patton's notional Seventh Army in Sicily. It was to descend on the

Italian coast around Livorno with twelve American, British and French divisions. Meanwhile, the British kept the Germans guessing about landings in the Balkans and on the Island of Rhodes.[68] The threat of an invasion of southern France stoked genuine fears among the Germans.[69] When Overlord was confirmed at Tehran in December, it became necessary to devise a scheme to keep German attention away from lower Normandy. At that point, the Pas-de-Calais became the focal point for a major Allied feint.

By 18 December 1943 the LCS produced its first version of 'Plan Bodyguard', basically a revised JAEL with schemes to fix German attention on the Pas-de-Calais. Given the scope and breadth of the whole Bodyguard operation it was imperative to supervise it tightly and maintain its integrity. That task fell to Sir Findlater Stewart, the British Minister of Home Security, and both MI5 and MI6 of the British Secret Service.[70] Overall strategic direction – subject to oversight from various parties – remained with LCS. The effort was staggering in its scope and complexity. Ralph Ingersoll, the American journalist turned soldier, saw this deception operation from the inside in the winter of 1944. He concluded that it was 'brilliantly conceived by the British' and made the difference between success and catastrophe.[71]

As part of the long-term plan to return to the continent, the British had turned all German agents operating in the UK by 1941, and carefully husbanded them to support the Second Front. They also fed disinformation to the Germans through neutral embassies and legations in London, through diplomats abroad, and through false information in letters to British POWs.[72] The British also crafted information for the Germans to discover themselves, what was known at the time as 'Special Means'. This work ultimately fell to military staffs at SHAEF and the 21st AG. In late December 1943, Colonel N. Wild arrived at SHAEF to lead the deception staff, and SHAEF assumed responsibility for Special Means on 12 January 1944.[73] While the LCS tracked the long-term strategic direction of the deception, Wild and his staff at the 21st AG worked on wireless signal traffic and visual deception.[74] The 21st AG was never fully enamoured of camouflaged dummy camps and depots but the effort was prodigious. German aerial reconnaissance was virtually non-existent. There was, in any event, enough going on should the Germans care to look, not least the increasing concentration of shipping in the UK's western county ports.

By the end of February, the 21st AG had largely abandoned visual deception[75] and shifted to dummy signal traffic carefully coordinated to support and confirm agent reports. No. 5 Wireless Group, using pre-recorded wireless messages to fake the signals of an entire division from the back of one truck, simulated British Army traffic. American signal traffic was generated by No. 3103 Signals Service Battalion, which arrived in March. The battalion could simulate an Army Group HQ, an Army HQ and three corps composed of nine divisions. The Fourth Army, in Scotland, took care of signals traffic for Fortitude North, while the Admiralty's 'CLH' network simulated naval wireless traffic.[76] Although the official history of Operation Fortitude fails to mention it, the First Canadian Army also engaged heavily in the wireless deception scheme (discussed below).

With Bodyguard approved (by the British Chiefs of Staff – BCOS) on 25 December 1943 and the JCS on 19 January 1944, it became necessary to protect the deception operation as much as Overlord itself. Everything had to be carefully choreographed: the granting of leave, civilian movements, call-up notices, troop movements, the press and even diplomatic mail and telegrams, and the movement of diplomats (which was curtailed on 17 April 1944). All civilian travel to and from the Republic of Ireland was suspended on 9 February, and movement in coastal areas from southern Scotland, down the east coast and around to Land's End was curtailed.[77] Everything that the Germans might discover had to conform to a tightly scripted plan. By January 1944 this included a major assault on Norway, a landing in the south of France, attacks in the Balkans and a major Russian offensive all prior to the main Overlord landings at the Pas-de-Calais – still slated for late summer. Idle specula-tion in the press about when and where Overlord might happen was strictly prohibited. Basil Liddell Hart, the military analyst and historian, stunned the security and intelligence community in early January by circulating a critique of the Allied plan as he understood it. Liddell Hart's particular bête noire was the idea of landing in the Pas-de-Calais – the 'direct approach', which the Germans were bound to focus on. He preferred, instead, the 'line of least expectation', a landing between the

Loire and the Gironde, along the Biscay coast.[78] The last thing the deception planners wanted was an open airing of why landing in the Pas-de-Calais was a bad idea. His document was seized and an investigation by MI5 was launched to determine Liddell Hart's sources. Churchill wanted him jailed, and he was not alone. It was decided not to give notoriety to Liddell Hart's claims. To protect the deception, the Pas-de-Calais had to remain the obvious choice for Overlord.

On 23 February 1944 the Canadian Minister of Munitions and Supply, C.D. Howe, let it slip that he was keeping open an expensive shipyard because of 'most urgent cables for help in delivering to Britain 4,700 ton ships, which will be urgently needed for . . . Major Allied military operations within the next three or four months'. Howe's indiscretion was picked up by the Toronto *Globe and Mail* and arrived in the UK in time to appear in the *London Evening News*. What German military intelligence (Abwehr) made of it remains unknown, but cables flew between Ottawa and London to forestall any further breach of security.[79]

Curtailing American media speculation was not so easy. Bracken's Ministry of Information appealed to American authorities in late December to ensure a blackout on idle speculation about the details of Overlord in the press. This did not stop the media from printing the US Under-Secretary of the Navy's comments in early January 1944 that an increased tempo of construction of landing craft was required because the dates of the major amphibious operations of 1944 had been set. Churchill was informed on 14 January that the British request for a press blackout had been ignored in America: 'apart from feeble bleats about America's domestic difficulties no reply has been received'.[80]

The MOI and SHAEF both had reason to fear the unbridled nature of the American media. In January 1944 *Time* celebrated the launch of a Swedish edition. As the publisher, P.I. Prentice, observed, now German agents in Buenos Aires did not have to summarise the contents into a 2,000-word telegram, or 'Air Express' each issue of *Time* to Berlin. The Swedish editions, Prentice wrote, 'are quickly placed on sale at 2,000 newsstands from Malmo (where you can smell the smoke of burning Berlin when the wind is from the south) to Boden, 50 miles from the Arctic circle'. The Swedes embraced *Time* enthusiastically, and Prentice hoped that visiting Germans would, too.[81]

It was not just the Swedish edition but also the push-back by *Time's* publishers on the US Army's attempt to control what was printed that raised concern. A recently released *Guide to the Use of Information Materials* reminded the American press that 'In time of war the armed forces themselves are creators of news and have therefore a vested interest in the way it is reported by the information services'. *Time* was not buying that: the 'statement was a shocker ... The new Army doctrine means, if words mean anything, that the Army may now (by its "vested interest") definitively prescribe what news may be printed in wartime and what not. Seldom in democratic countries had a servant of the people gone so far before.'[82] The last sentiment was pure hyperbole: American press censorship in the Great War had been draconian by comparison. In this context, Eisenhower's somewhat controversial injunction to the press at SHAEF on 18 January 1944 that he regarded them 'as part of his staff' was intended not only to grant them special status, but to bind them to the army PR and to the deception plan.

The deception operation for Overlord coalesced into Operation Fortitude and was approved on 21 February 1944.[83] It had two major components. Fortitude North covered the ongoing threat of a descent on Norway – a key source of German anxiety. By stroking these fears the Germans kept 200,000 more troops there than necessary.[84] The purpose of Fortitude South was to achieve an acceptable level of operational and tactical surprise in lower Normandy, and to keep the initial rush of German reinforcements at bay.[85] The primary focus was on the Pas-de-Calais, which the Germans saw as the simplest and most direct route for any major assault on Fortress Europe. Not only was it heavily fortified, but also nineteen divisions of the German Fifteenth Army garrisoned the region. To help keep the German focus northward other threats were nurtured, including a possible landing in the Scheldt estuary (of which more later).

An essential part of Operation Fortitude was therefore convincing the Germans that the Allies were capable of several, virtually simultaneous, large-scale landings. In January the plan was to threaten the Pas-de-Calais with V US Corps and I British Corps – two of the key components of the actual Overlord assault. But it was not clear how the threat could be sustained once these formations drifted westward to their departure ports. The solution arrived at by the 21st Army Group by March was to structure the deception operation around the new, still skeletal, First US Army Group (FUSAG). FUSAG would be 'given armies' and set astride the Thames estuary as a direct threat to the Pas-de-Calais.

The decision on which armies to assign to FUSAG was fairly easy. As Roger Hesketh noted, the First Canadian Army, with II Canadian Corps under command at Dover, was already in Kent and therefore 'ideally placed for their role'.[86] It helped that the Canadians now had their long-awaited commanding officer, General H.D.G. Crerar, who assumed command on 20 March.[87] Crerar's army also assumed 'command' of the US VIII Corps, notionally headquartered at Folkestone. It was a shadow force, with the 79th and 83rd USIDs just arriving in the UK and the 28th USID still in the USA. But the Germans had no way of knowing that. Double agents informed Abwehr that the First Canadian Army had no less than thirteen divisions under command. With a straight shot from Kent to the beaches of Calais, II Canadian Corps was tagged as FUSAG's assault force.[88]

North of the Thames estuary, in Essex and Suffolk, the Third US Army 'assembled'. It was commanded by General George Patton, who arrived in England from the Mediterranean at the end of January. Officially, Omar Bradley was in command of FUSAG. Patton commanded the 'build-up' army which would follow the Canadians ashore. The divisions of Patton's XX US Corps were already in the UK, but those notionally assigned to XII Corps had not yet arrived. The 3103rd Signal Battalion simulated their presence north of the Thames while the real formations maintained radio silence.[89] The final order of battle for FUSAG was agreed to at a 21st AG conference on 30 March 1944.

FUSAG changed the nature of the Fortitude story. Throughout February and March, Overlord had been masked by trying to sell a late summer landing. By the spring of 1944 it was possible to sell the idea of two almost simultaneous landings: a feint, followed quickly by the 'main assault' on the Pas-de-Calais. By then German intelligence had been led to believe that the Allies had over fifty combat-ready divisions in Britain and enough assault craft to lift fifteen at a time.[90] But the key to operational surprise for Overlord was to ensure that the meaning of the initial landing in lower Normandy was unclear. Settling on the two-

Army Group concept and the order of battle for FUSAG 'provided a firm foundation for the operation, on which the wireless programme and the Special Means could now be built'.[91] This revised Fortitude South plan also put the First Canadian Army back where it had been for years – as the lead formation of the 'main' assault on France. McNaughton's Dagger would play a role yet.

* * *

In February 1944 the defences of lower Normandy, both mobile and static, were still modest. It was assumed that the organisation, doctrine and equipment of the Allied armies were adequate for the task ahead. That said, George Marshall was only too mindful that he was sending divisions to the UK in haste, short of trained officers and NCOs and padded with thousands of men stripped from divisions further down the pipeline. On 10 February 1944 he warned Stimson that reassigning trained men from operational formations to make up shortfalls of 2,000–3,000 men in divisions going overseas 'necessitates a revamping of training and in effect lowers the efficiency of divisions'. This was not how it was supposed to be. 'The training of troops for the assault was never a primary responsibility of the theatre,' Gordon Harrison wrote in *Cross-Channel Attack*. 'It was assumed that divisions would arrive in the United Kingdom fully schooled in their tasks.'[92]

In the late winter of 1944 the state of America's hastily assembled Overlord army was a cause for concern. As Stimson's memoir noted:

They had argued for this campaign in the conviction that a properly equipped and well-trained Army could fight on equal terms with the best forces of the enemy in its first battle – most of the invasion divisions would have no battle experience. More than that, the whole theory of victory by ground force superiority – supported by air mastery – was one in which the War Department had been a lonely advocate. The victories of North Africa and Italy had not dispelled the caution with which many Allied officers looked at the new American Army, nor were there many Americans outside the General Staff and the Ground Forces who wholeheartedly believed that the army could produce explosive victories against battle-tested Germans.[93]

These concerns were not allayed by grumblings from Italy that the Germans had better tanks, artillery, mortars and machine guns, and that this was having an impact on morale.[94] Eisenhower, too, expressed himself 'a bit uneasy about our failure to get a great leaven of combat experience among our divisions' brought back from the Mediterranean for Overlord. Only two were 'battle tried infantry divisions'.[95] As Stimson confided to Marshall in early May, 'It has been our fate in two world wars to come in as the final force after the other combatants have been long engaged. Our men thus come to the field untested, even when well-trained, to fight veteran enemies. Such conditions make the appearance and possession of overwhelming strength on our part important both tactically and psychologically.'[96]

In the scramble to build a massive expeditionary force, America had compromised on a great many things. The Sherman, at 30 tons, was a good medium tank with a good 75mm gun. It was optimised for mass production – and for the 1940–1 battlefield. So, too, were the US Army's anti-tank capabilities. Technological inexperience and a mistaken belief that 'the tank threat faced in France in 1944 would be essentially the same as that encountered in Italy in 1943', Steve Zaloga writes, meant that the US Army was unprepared for the tanks they would meet in Normandy.[97] The British 17-pounder anti-tank gun, demonstrated to the Americans in 1943, had much greater penetrating power than the American 3" then being fitted to M10 tank destroyers and employed in a towed version. But a higher muzzle velocity and a much larger propellant charge shortened barrel life and, in any event, the US Army was unconvinced of the need for such a powerful gun.[98]

While America standardised in order to equip a massive army, British industry adapted much quicker to changes in tactics and equipment. By the spring of 1944 they had developed a discarding sabot round for the 6-pounder anti-tank gun which greatly increased its lethality. The American version of the same gun, the 57mm, could not chamber the new round. The British had also redesigned the 17-pounder to fit in a Sherman tank, and were producing a whole series of specialised armoured vehicles to support the assault on France. These included 'Flail' tanks, with chains attached to rotating drums to clear minefields, flame-throwing tanks, specialised Churchill tanks with bunker-busting spigot mortars, fascines (bundles of sticks) to lay in gaps, bridge-layers, and beach-recovery vehicles. 'British factories do not produce as rapidly as American,' US labour-union leaders reported in April 1944 after an exchange visit to the UK, 'but can convert more easily to changes in design.'[99]

The US Army was not unaware of these British developments. They had readily adopted the Duplex Drive (DD) swimming Sherman tank: '30 tons of steel in a canvas bucket'. The Americans were prepared to adopt other specialised British armour to help them across the beach: flails, mine-ploughs and Sherman 'Crocodile' flame throwers. But British industry was so stretched that it could barely meet British orders. As Zaloga noted laconically, the War Office simply 'refused to forward the U.S. Army request [for Sherman Crocodiles] to the Ministry of Supply since it interfered with delivery of Churchill Crocodiles to the British Army for Overlord'.[100]

The Anglo-Canadians planned to land a very heavily mechanised force, with plenty of armour and self-propelled artillery. This reflected both years of fighting the Germans and the anticipation of an early and sustained battle with counterattacking Panzers. Overlord had to succeed, and the British were determined to see that it did.

CHAPTER 16

SHAPING OPERATIONS

There will be plenty of credit for all when the war in Europe is won. There will be little ground for postwar argument and bitterness over who did most. Effort to stir up the argument has already begun.

US News, 7 January 1944[1]

Brigadier General Robert McClure, who handled Eisenhower's psychological warfare and press office in Algiers, assumed when he took over the same duties at SHAEF in late 1943 that he would have thirty or so reporters to wrangle. On 6 June 1944, 461 reporters were accredited to SHAEF.[2] Even as they worked together to craft a common military effort to liberate Europe, the Anglo-Americans clambered to highlight their own national role in the great enterprise. 'Apparently,' Colonel William Abel, the Deputy Director of Public Relations for the Canadian Army in London wrote on 7 January, 'the feeling is that as the war comes to an end, everybody is looking for all the kudos they can get in a world press.'[3]

But the issues went well beyond bragging rights. The fate of Europe hung in the balance. New governments would be established, and each of the Allies had very different ideas about how that should go. Forestalling Communist governments and creating a liberal democratic Europe were the primary British objectives. This much had been recognised when the OWI accepted in 1942 that their weekly directives would follow the

British lead in Europe. The Americans were, nevertheless, opposed to monarchies, constitutional or otherwise. By early 1944 Roosevelt's objectives for Europe – other than that it was a British 'problem' – remained Wilsonian: national self-determination, an end to empires, and world peace governed by a new League of Nations.

The American military also had its own agenda: win the war and then let the politicians sort things out. Under Eisenhower in the Mediterranean, the Psychological Warfare Branch (PWB) in Algiers was focused entirely on battlefield- and theatre-level impact. Propaganda was manufactured close to the front and used for immediate military purposes. British psychological warfare agents in Algiers did their best to broaden the scope of PWB's work. As Charles Cruickshank later wrote, they thought 'that propaganda should be used to help win the peace as well as the war'.[4] With 360 Americans and sixty British on McClure's staff, the American view predominated.

Given the ill-defined nature of America's foreign policy and the US Army's focus on battle, the last thing the British wanted from Overlord was another Darlan-style political disaster in France. The British championed Charles de Gaulle and his Comité Français de Libération Nationale (CFLN) as France's logical post-liberation government.[5] The Americans still preferred de Gaulle's rival and founding co-president of the CFLN, Giraud. 'Roosevelt's policy towards France,' David Kennedy writes, 'was a tangled skein of contradictions shot through with an unreasoning disdain for De Gaulle whose ultimate sources are not easily located.'[6] The tension over the future of France highlighted the fact that it was not Eisenhower's writ to establish post-liberation governments in Europe. What, then, was the message to be sent to these people in advance of their liberation? Whose message would it be, and who would send it? And what would the world be told of the desperate fighting and sacrifice about to unfold? To whom would Europeans ultimately credit their liberation? And – most challenging of all – how could Americans be convinced that Britain was a postwar ally worth supporting when it was all over?

The British understood that they would need American help in the final phase of the propaganda war. As David Garnett's secret history of PWE noted, only the Americans 'could supply the men and the machines necessary for propaganda in the field and in the Liberated areas'. That said, the British had every intention of controlling the message. 'PWE hoped to supply the political experience and political doctrine necessary,' Garnett writes, 'by taking the Americans into complete partnership.'[7] The first British success in this struggle may well have been their last. In August 1943 the Americans proposed to make Washington the 'Central Authority' for political warfare around the globe. The British sensed that the Washington committee would be controlled by the military, not by civilians with an eye on international relations and politics. Churchill would not have it. 'In Britain there is a well coordinated propaganda machine under civilian control, and long may it remain thus,' Churchill protested on 5 September 1943. And then he drove the point home. 'All the great propaganda gaffes have been made as a result of soldiers interfering in publicity matters.'[8]

The British proposed instead three Allied regional political warfare centres: London for Europe, Washington for the Pacific and New Delhi for South East Asia. The New Delhi committee was a non-starter because the Americans declined to be 'tarnished' by association with British India. The burden for both Europe and South East Asia therefore fell to the 'London Political Warfare Co-ordinating Committee'. Its job was to coordinate a systemic and combined Anglo-American attack on the will of the German people to support the war effort, on the willingness of Axis soldiers – especially Poles, Czechs, Slovaks, Croats and men recruited from POW camps – to continue the fight, and to encourage satellite states to abandon the war. OWI was also specifically tasked with selling the idea of the United Nations as a cure for the world's ailments.[9] In addition to a pamphlet campaign, both the BBC and the ABSIE (due to start operations in April) were to play a key role.

The London Political Warfare Co-ordinating Committee failed almost immediately. Robert Lockhart lamented in his diary as early as 6 December 1943 'that the Americans had packed the London Co-ordinating Committee'. Word was already out that Eisenhower – just announced Supreme Commander – would bring McClure to London to be 'Head of Propaganda and Press Section' of SHAEF.[10] Once that happened, McClure would take the lead – supported, certainly, by the coordinated political work of PWE and OWI. That put the military squarely in charge of work which the British not only believed was the prerogative of civilians, but work that they claimed a proprietary role in. In the meantime, PWE and OWI were tasked to devise a joint Political Warfare Plan for Overlord.[11]

The objective of the joint PWE–OWI plan by early January 1944, in Garnett's later words, was the 'greatest degree of Anglo-American integration which was compatible with efficiency'.[12] By then Robert Lockhart – the driving force and steady hand behind PWE's efforts – was on extended sick leave with another raging bout of eczema: he was gone from London for two months. In the interim, oversight of PWE passed to the benighted hands of Brendan Bracken, the Minister of Information. Bracken was not well briefed on PWE, and the staff did little to ameliorate that. By the end of January 1944 word reached Lockhart that Bracken 'is driving P.W.E. nearly dotty'.[13]

Bracken wanted no truck or trade with the Americans. 'The people who control this organization [the OWI],' he wrote on 10 January 1944, 'are incompetent, shifty and hare-brained.' The Americans will pump out 'silly stuff' and when the joint plan is seen in America to go adrift, the British would be blamed. America has no 'consistent policy . . . The content of their hectic output depends on American electoral considerations. The Polish vote, the Balts vote, the Jewish vote, the German vote' all 'slant' their thought. He warned PWE, 'Do not take any responsibility for their actions. For if you do they will surely try to make you wallow with them in the squalid mess they have created in America and wish to reproduce here.' The result of Bracken's memo, according to Garnett, was 'a temporizing policy' towards OWI and the Americans 'which became increasingly difficult to maintain'.[14]

Bracken knew that OWI, as a reliable partner of PWE, was on its last legs. It was known to be staffed by 'New Dealers', and so conservative Americans objected to its domestic propaganda activities from the outset.[15] At the end of 1943 Congress stripped OWI of much of its funding and reshaped its domestic role. The new director of OWI, the former CBS newsman Elmer Davis, believed that Americans should be fed propaganda as a form of entertainment. He secured the resignations of senior OWI officials including Sherwood's deputy in London, James Warburg, and then turned OWI into a news arm of the American war effort.[16] Sherwood,

Director of the OWI Overseas Branch, protested against the evisceration of OWI, but FDR declined to get involved. This shift is borne out by the nature of the OWI directives issued in the late winter and spring of 1944, which are heavily focused on American operations – especially in the air.[17]

On the eve of Overlord 'The OWI was officially depoliticized,' Gerd Horten wrote, 'no longer disseminating high-minded political appeals that might favor specific political ideas or emphasize democratic obligations and civic duties. It was now in the hands of advertisers and their corporate clients, who could inscribe this propaganda with private, commercial and – supposedly – apolitical appeals.'[18] By early 1944 OWI had become part of the media itself. Despite some continuation in links between PWE and OWI, the two organisations drifted apart – in both London, as well as with the parent OWI organisation and the British Political Warfare Mission in Washington. The British did little to stop the drift. When OWI wanted to develop a joint radio broadcasting scheme based on the BBC's extensive coverage of occupied Europe, Bracken rejected the idea out of hand. The British were unimpressed with 'inexpert American output'. It was generally accepted that few Europeans listened to American broadcasts anyway,[19] and that 'BBC output would suffer in quality had amalgamation taken place'.[20] This left the Americans free to develop their own radio programming, which would soon reach across Europe through ABSIE.

Not only did the pretence of Anglo-American cooperation in media messaging collapse while Bracken was in charge, PWE itself almost lost its way. Many of its key London personnel drifted into McClure's expanding SHAEF psychological warfare branch, where the action was. PWE also struggled to produce its weekly Central Media Directive because the military was no longer briefing the MOI on the latest developments. Apparently this went on throughout the winter and right up to the eve of D-Day.[21] The BBC experienced so much trouble acquiring material from the British forces that by April it received complaints from Australia that there were too many American voices in the BBC broadcasts. The Assistant Director of Overseas News Talks, H. Rooney Pelletier, explained that they had tried to get British material, and sought to keep the coverage balanced, but it was just too 'easy to get

American material'.[22] This was an old complaint from the British media and MOI, and it would not be the last.

PWE continued its important work with British agencies, like the BBC and SOE, and as a major source of information for McClure's PWB at SHAEF. PWE also worked closely with the Americans to attack the morale of German troops in the west. This included the establishment of fake German radio stations like Soldatensender Calais, which mixed false news with – for the Germans – verifiable news and laced the programming with jazz which the Nazis forbade. Over the winter PWE also wrote, translated and published a series of small books 'designed to boost Britain . . . at the earliest possible moment after liberation'. These basically told Europeans how Britain held the line (*Britain – Citadel of Liberty* and *The Battle of Sea Communications*) and fought back (*The Battle of Britain* and *500,000,000 People: Britain's Empire at War*). Manuals and guidebooks for both advancing soldiers and newly liberated civilians were also produced.[23]

The prospect of the Second Front also opened up serious gaps between the British and Americans on how the operations would be reported to their own people and to the wider world. Here, too, Americans assumed the lead. In mid-December 1943 Colonel Ernest Dupuy arrived at COSSAC HQ from Washington to handle press censorship. Dupuy had left the *New York Herald* in 1927 to help the US Army manage its press relations. He brought his own, uniquely American, ideas about managing the media to Overlord. Dupuy's job, first and foremost, was to facilitate press access to military operations: the American Army was 'a people's army', and the people had a right to know what their army was doing. His second guiding principle was that the media had hard deadlines for filing stories and it was the duty of SHAEF to create an organisation that allowed those deadlines to be met.[24]

Dupuy quickly assembled a team of British, Americans and Canadians, so it could not be said that SHAEF public relations was an American fiefdom. Among the first to join was Brigadier W.A.S. Turner, RA, who had handled War Office Press Relations since 1939, and 'really understood' the British press.[25] Major Fred Payne, 'a smart Canadian newspaperman', joined Dupuy's censorship staff early on, and by March Major S.R. Pawley, formerly of the Royal East Kent Regiment, the

Buffs, headed the British side of his shop. Pawley was a former news-paperman as well, but also an officer with combat experience: 'a good sort', Dupuy noted in his diary.[26]

Despite the integration of staffs and the evident good will prevailing, the greatest challenges facing SHAEF Public Relations were rising Anglo-American tensions. American newspapermen were suspicious of the British and of Americans whom they believed were anglophiles. Some of the 'prima donna' reporters were also personal friends of senior officers, following them closely during the day and dining with them in the evening. Dupuy claims that these favoured reporters turned 'gossip to their own account regardless of the effect on international relations . . . they did a vast disservice to the Allied cause'.[27]

In large measure the tension in the Allied press camp over the winter of 1944 arose from the difficulty of trying to sell Overlord to the American people. The problem was the predominant role of the British in the operation.

The one and only 'Monty' was Britain's idol. He would have to be identified when the assault started. Bradley would be subordinate to him as commander of First U.S. Army, although in reality coequal even now as commander FUSAG, and eventually coequal in the field when the 12th Army Group materialized.

When that happened, would Britons consider this a slur on Monty? Would British popular opinion consider that Ike, being an American, was now building up another American at the expense of the British hero? In the meantime, would American public opinion, restive at the idea of American troops being under British command, create such a rumpus as to engender bitterness between the two nations during the initial assault? Further potential friction point was the fact that although in the beginning the distribution of empire and U.S. forces was approximately equal, America's potential strength of forces disposable in Europe was much greater than that of the empire and would in reality be overwhelmingly greater in actual numbers as soon as we all got going.

To tell the story in advance would have solved all our trouble so far as Anglo-American public relations was concerned.[28]

The requirement for security left plenty of room for speculation, not all of it helpful to Anglo-American relations. The 15 May edition of *Life* magazine, for example, carried a photo-essay on the massing of American troops in England, highlighting Eisenhower's role as the Allied Supreme Commander. But the featured article, and cover photo, was about Montgomery. The cover photo captured Monty's calculated eccentricity: trademark black beret with two badges, hand-knitted white woollen sweater and a bomber jacket. The article extolled his concern for his men, deliberation in planning and success on the battle-field. But there was no suggestion that any Americans might serve under him. The title of the piece says it all: 'The "Monty" Legend: General leading British Wing [*sic*] of Invasion Builds Troop Confidence on his Past Successes'. Apparently, no one at *Life* magazine had the heart to tell Americans that Montgomery commanded both 'wings' of the coming assault.

The US Army was intent on having a media plan for Overlord that allowed it to highlight its role. Media coverage in the Mediterranean had very much followed the British lead. Press stories were tied closely to the daily communiqué issued by AFHQ. Stories outside the focus of the communiqué were either much delayed or killed by censors. Access to the front was also regulated, especially in the British zones. The British provided a jeep, a driver and an escort officer to take reporters out to the scene of action, and then return them to the media pool where their stories could be cleared by the censors and filed. American reporters were much less restricted in their movements, although subject to the same scrutiny from the censors.[29] In the Mediterranean, reporters generally wrote about what the military wanted them to write. And all media moved through London.

Dupuy set out to change this. First, he de-coupled press reporting from the daily communiqués, which got immediate push-back from the British military services. It will be recalled that the British Information Services in the USA and the MOI in London complained as early as 1942 that the British military were proprietorial about their media coverage, wanting to limit and control it (hence the practice of escorting officers for journalists). Nothing had changed by 1944. The RN claimed that no land lubber could possibly censor naval stories, and both the USAAF and the RAF did not want non-airmen messing with their press coverage. And as for the British Army, Dupuy claimed that it was 'quite sniffy about the ability of anyone else to blue-pencil its section'. The US Army, in contrast, was intent on massively expanding press coverage. In November 1943 it established the 72nd Publicity Service Battalion, complete with twenty jeeps and trucks, field kitchens, mess teams, orderlies and communications links to facilitate media coverage.[30] The press would be allowed to tell the story as they found it, free of the constraints of the official communiqués or escorting officers, and Dupuy's censors would just have to handle the work. The Americans were 'fine' with Dupuy's press plan for Overlord, and SHAEF adopted it.[31] American control of SHAEF Public Relations ensured that the American effort in Overlord – at least – was wide open to the press.

The British hope that they could somehow play the role of senior partner and shape the political and psychological war unleashed on Europe in 1944 was laid to rest at the end of March. When David Bowes-Lyons, Director of PWE in Washington, returned to London for briefings he brought with him 'a gloomy view of Anglo-American relations which he said had now reached their lowest level'. There were no particular reasons for this, Bowes-Lyons cautioned when he met Lockhart on 28 March. Worse still, the slump in Anglo-American relations was not temporary, nor was it caused by the looming election. The reason was fundamental: 'The Americans now realise their immense power in production and on land, air and sea. They were becoming intensely national and were determined to use their power. The British had pushed the world around for the last hundred years and now the Americans were going to do it.'[32]

Lockhart encountered a similar mood within McClure's Psychological Warfare Branch at SHAEF two days later. The Americans remembered and resented every condescension inflicted on them by the British over the previous two years. 'I am beset by difficulties,' Lockhart lamented, 'in the task of trying to ensure effective partnership with P.W.B. who are now much under the influence of the rapidly growing American power consciousness (see also U.S. imperialism) and of American resentment (especially in the American air force) of the patronizing tone adopted towards American forces at the beginning by our soldiers, sailors and airmen.'[33] Lockhart was an astute observer, and he closed his diary entry for the day with a profound insight into both the handling of the war and the management of its information flow to various media. The Americans, he wrote, 'act first and think later', but at least they act and that 'keeps things moving'. In contrast, the British 'think and don't act – or, perhaps better, take a long time to act. The thinking is good, but there is a danger of postponed action and, often enough, of no action at all.' The selling of Overlord would be the ultimate example of American risk-taking and British caution.

* * *

With the exception of the Transportation Plan (of which more below) the vast literature on Operation Overlord largely skips over the 'shaping operations' that created the conditions for its ultimate success. In the case of naval operations this may be because the British official naval history, *The War at Sea*, handles these operations in a separate volume.[34] It is equally likely that the effort to secure the English Channel prior to D-Day is omitted from the Overlord story because there were few – if any – American forces engaged. These naval and air operations, and the subsequent support of operations ashore, are the great unheralded British accomplishments of the campaign.

In early 1944 the English Channel was contested waters.[35] A half-dozen flotillas of 'Schnellbooten' (E-boats to the Allies) operated between Cherbourg and the Netherlands. These were big, powerful and enormously fast motor-torpedo boats, able to sustain speeds of over 80kph. They were supported by two flotillas of small 1,330-ton destroyers dubbed 'Torpedo Boats' (T-boats) in German service, escorting convoys and covering minesweeping and laying activities between Cherbourg and Le Havre. Four of Germany's big 'Narvik'-fleet-class destroyers were based on the French coast as close as Brest. These 3,600-ton vessels, carrying four 15cm (5.9") guns and four torpedo tubes, could reach 36 knots (some 67kph), and could not be allowed to run amok in the invasion anchorage.

The threat from U-boats was the hardest to measure, and the most difficult to tackle. By this stage the Germans had almost perfected their new 'schnorkel' breathing device for submarines and had begun to retrofit the fleet. These U-boats no longer had to run on the surface to recharge their batteries, and the small schnorkel head – covered in radar-absorbing rubber – was all but invisible. Schnorkel boats could easily penetrate the central Channel. So, too, might a large wave of conventionally powered U-boats, although their losses would be high. Finally, the Germans were testing a new type of hydrogen-peroxide-driven U-boats, the so-called 'Walter Boats' (W-boats). They did not need to surface at all and had an estimated speed of 40 or 50 knots. A large number of W-boats was apparently under construction.[36]

At the end of March the Admiralty's Anti-U-Boat Division issued a gloomy forecast of the U-boat threat to Overlord. If the Germans sent 170 into the channel and if only 20 per cent of their torpedoes hit, losses might reach 240 ships a week. Naval and air patrols could not possibly stop them all, and there was no clear solution to the fifty W-boats expected to be within range by June. The Germans had the potential to sink 800 ships a month.[37] Even the Admiralty's more sanguine views estimated that the Germans could put at least sixty-five U-boats in the assault area in the first week. To secure Overlord against this danger, the British had to mount an enormous anti-submarine operation.[38]

The campaign to control the English Channel began in February 1944. The objective, as Stephen Roskill wrote, was 'to ensure that, when the invasion fleet set sail for France, the Germans would not be in a position to molest them seriously'.[39] Four Canadian and two British Tribal-class destroyers, along with the light cruiser *Black Prince*, of the 10th Destroyer Flotilla (DF) were deployed to sweep the English Channel of German surface forces. The 10th DF, reinforced by more British and Polish destroyers, was at sea almost constantly throughout the spring of 1944, prowling the channel by night, looking for trouble.

In late April they found what they were looking for off the northern coast of Brittany: German destroyers. On 26 April HMCS *Haida* sank *T-24*. Two nights later while covering minelaying operations, *Haida* and HMCS *Athabaskan* went after two more T-boats. The Germans sank *Athabaskan* but *Haida* beat *T-27* into a blazing wreck and drove it ashore. Meanwhile, Allied motor torpedo boats prowled the Channel at night, looking for E-boats and covering an intense minelaying programme designed to destroy ships and inhibit German movement. Over April and May 1944 the Royal Navy laid nearly 3,000 mines along the Normandy coast. The RAF laid three times that number. About a hundred German ships were sunk by these mines.[40]

Evidence of the contested nature of the Channel came on the night of 28 April 1944 when E-boats operating from Cherbourg attacked an American landing exercise at Slapton Sands, in Lyme Bay. Two LSTs were sunk with heavy loss of life (over 750 sailors and soldiers). The incident was hushed up, and even the Germans failed to make much sense of it. These LST losses stripped Eisenhower of his tiny reserve of LSTs for the whole Overlord operation.[41]

The net result of the naval and air effort was a serious weakening of German surface power in the Channel. Moreover, virtually all German efforts to replace or even expand minefields in the Baie de la Seine – where the German Navy was convinced the landings would occur – failed either because the mines were not delivered (thanks to the Transportation Plan) or because the minelaying force was destroyed. These shaping operations were so successful that Gordon Harrison dismissed the Kriegsmarine threat to Overlord as irrelevant.[42]

However, the U-boat remained the one naval threat to Overlord that was unresolved on the eve of D-Day. Throughout April and May the British gathered anti-submarine vessels to create barrier, hunting and escort forces to cover the assault. These were shaved from existing British commitments, and bolstered by a major effort from the Canadian Navy.[43] By the time they were done, the British had assembled 286 ASW vessels to shepherd and secure the landings. When Stimson visited Normandy in July 1944 he was amazed at the smoothness and safety of shipping movements to and from the beachhead. That was no accident. It was the result of months of hard fighting by America's allies.

* * *

The major Overlord shaping operation which has long been part of the Overlord narrative was the Transportation Plan. Eisenhower did not get formal control of the Allied strategic air forces until 14 April, the official starting date for the attack on the rail system. But as noted above, the attack was already underway. Encouraged by the success of these early raids – and chastened by its heaviest ever single-raid losses of the war over Nuremberg on the night of 30–1 March (sixty-four heavies, a rate of 11.9 per cent) – Harris committed his whole command to the Transportation Plan.[44] By then IX Bomber Command of the IX US Air Force – the tactical air force assigned to the First US Army for Overlord – had also started attacking approved targets.[45] Perhaps because of lingering anxiety over French casualties, final approval for a full-out assault on the rail system was not obtained until early May.

In the meantime, the VIII and XV USAAF continued the destruction of the German air force. Along with securing command of the Channel, this was the most important of all shaping operations. The Allies needed command of the air not simply to launch the attack, but for the subsequent resupply and build-up as well as the ability of battleships and cruisers to provide devastating fire support inshore; all was dependent on Allied air superiority. So while the Americans crushed the Luftwaffe, RAF Bomber Command began pounding French rail yards on the night of 5–6 April. Of the 133 major Bomber Command raids over western Europe in April and May, eighty were directly linked to Overlord, including fifty on the thirty-nine Transportation Plan targets assigned.[46] Of the 71,000 tons of bombs dropped by Allied strategic bombers as part of the Transportation Plan, 46,000 tons were delivered by British and Canadian squadrons.[47]

The IX USAAF carried the burden of the American role in the Transportation Plan throughout April and the first half of May. By mid-April attacks by medium bombers were supplemented increasingly by strafing and dive-bombing by P-47s and P-51s, and by rocket-firing Typhoon fighter-bombers and Mosquito bombers of the RAF's 2nd Tactical Air Force (TAF). By the end of April, according to Craven and Cate, 'it was evident that enormous damage was being done'.[48] It was noticed with some alarm, however, that the Germans were highly effective at making repairs, at routing traffic around the damage and at ensuring priority for their military traffic. And they began to move night-fighters into France and Belgium to counter the attacks.

In May the Transportation campaign intensified. By the middle of the month it was estimated that the pre-D-Day 'rail centre program was close to completion'.[49] At that point, VIII AF finally shifted its focus to direct support of Overlord.[50] During the last three weeks before

D-Day the VIII dropped 13,000 tons on its twenty-three assigned targets, wrecking fifteen.[51]

Craven and Cate speak glowingly of the success of the air assault on French transportation, and of the IX USAAF claims to have perfected bridge bombing, using a mixture of aircraft to destroy every bridge on the Seine below Paris.[52] Most of those bridges were certainly down, but the IX USAAF remained a blunt instrument. Over nine days in late May and early June, it launched nearly 500 sorties against the three bridges at Rouen. By the eve of D-Day only two were wrecked. Stephen Bourque concludes that the medium bombers and fighters of the IX, which were supposed to be more accurate than the heavies, 'were both inaccurate and ineffective'.[53]

Anglo-Canadian bombing at night was generally better, and pains were taken to keep it as sharp as possible. Pathfinders marked the targets, and Master Bombers ensured that bombing was concentrated on the target.[54] Accuracy became more difficult when the Germans moved night-fighters into France. During the attack on the German military base at Mailley-le-Camp on the night of 3–4 May bombing was delayed because of communications problems between the lead marker and the main force. During the delay the German night-fighter force arrived. The bombing was well concentrated, but the British lost forty-two Lancasters: its single greatest loss of the campaign over France in the spring of 1944.[55] Air Marshal Harris nonetheless took great pride in Bomber Command's effort and its accuracy during the pre-Overlord bombing campaign. 'The U.S. air forces,' he wrote to his crews at the beginning of May 1944, 'who specialize in precision visual attacks by day, are particularly astonished at the result.'[56]

By late May massive fighter and fighter-bomber sweeps, mostly American, began to target the rail system as far east as the Rhine. On 21 May the Americans sent out over 1,200 fighters to shoot up trains across France, Belgium and western Germany. Although in the end 98 per cent of trains actually destroyed were struck by heavy bombers, by 26 May the Germans had sharply curtailed daytime movements.[57] Then, in the final week before D-Day, the concentration of bombing shifted to the coast, to gun batteries and defences, especially around the Pas-de-Calais, and finally to the bridges over the Loire.

The pattern of bombing for the Transportation Plan reflects its other – perhaps equally important – purpose: deception. When Operation Fortitude entered its final phase in late April (of which more below), the message – in Bourque's words – 'was simple: for every pound of bombs you drop in the actual landing area, make sure you drop two in the north'. He then goes on to quote the after-action report of VIII AF submitted in early June: 'The idea of deception was paramount and outweighed the recognized factor that actual damage to coastal defences would be for the most part negligible.'[58] The same might be said for the whole Transportation Plan. The Germans tracked Allied bombing, and by late May concluded that, 'the neutralization of the south flank between Rouen and Paris might be held to indicate the North-West of France as the objective'.[59] This and the disinformation campaign launched by the Allies in late April to sell FUSAG as the main threat were mutually reinforcing.

* * *

There was one final Overlord shaping operation underway in the spring of 1944: a major offensive in Italy. In February, General Henry Maitland Wilson, Allied Commander in Chief Mediterranean, was given the go-ahead to drive for Rome. The Americans remained unconvinced of its merits. By late March they were still committed to Anvil as the best supporting operation for Overlord, although Eisenhower had advised Marshall on 21 March that it was too late to launch it by early June.[60] Marshall pushed back, saying that he would release additional landing craft (already allocated for the Pacific) for Anvil if it was done simultaneously with Overlord. Marshall's revelation went off like a bomb in London. Overlord planners had fought tenaciously to secure enough lift for the expanded Normandy scheme. The British found it by mortgaging their import plan for 1944 and stripping their coasts of a million tons of shipping. Now the Americans had apparently found landing craft needed to launch Anvil anyway.

Eisenhower's senior staff, all British except Bedell Smith, were joined by Brooke and Churchill's military advisor, General Hastings Ismay, on 27 March to discuss Marshall's revelation. Brooke's frustration emerges in the minutes of the meeting. The diversion of American resources to the Pacific had already resulted in a setback of 'approximately six months in the defeat of Germany', Brooke claimed, and the 'lack of sufficient landing craft and other resources in the Mediterranean resulted in our failing to take full advantage of the fall of Italy'.[61] Eisenhower was inclined to agree with Brooke. As Ike told the meeting, 'he had been pleading for the past two years the transcending importance of whipping Germany first'. The problem was that the American public was not interested in the war in Europe, and 'public opinion in the United States . . . had to be reckoned with'. The pressure in Congress was for an 'all out Pacific offensive'.

That offensive in the Pacific was now well underway. It had started, bloodily but successfully, in November 1943 at Tarawa in the Gilberts. By the end of February 1944 the Marshall Islands had been breached and the great Japanese base at Truk crippled. The going had been surprisingly easy despite the heavy casualties among the assault troops: Eniwetok fell six months ahead of schedule. The whole push could be advanced, with the Marianas – the inner ring of defended islands – targeted for June rather than September. Not to be outdone, MacArthur launched his own campaign through the Solomons, and along the north coast of New Guinea. By March he was four months ahead of schedule and driving hard for the Japanese base at Hollandia.[62] America, it seems, was suffering from its own version of 'victory disease'.

In the circumstances, Brooke argued on 27 March, the best bet in the west was to drive for Rome. Bedell Smith noted that the US Joint Chiefs of Staff believed that the best way to hold 'the maximum number of German divisions was the establishment of a line from which we could not be driven back'. Brooke pointed out that going onto the defensive in Italy put no pressure at all on the Germans just as Overlord launched. Rather, Brooke argued, 'an offensive for the capture of Rome was the best method for containing the maximum number of German forces'.[63] He might have mentioned – although it does not appear in the minutes of this meeting – that the Germans had already invested heavily in fortifications south of Rome. Kesselring had staked his reputation on the ability to hold the Allies: he was not going to retreat. Eisenhower told Marshall that Anvil was off – for now. The Allies would fight in Italy in the spring. To sweeten the decision for the Americans it was agreed on 2 April that the objective of Mark Clark's US Fifth Army was Rome.[64]

Clark was not convinced he would get to Rome anytime soon. Attempts by his army to force its way into the Liri valley and on to Rome in January and February were bloody failures. The January effort, executed in some haste to get ahead of the Anzio landings, called for X British Corps to force a bridgehead over the Garigliano to the south, which Clark hoped would draw off German reserves. Then II US Corps would cross the swollen Rapido River in front of Cassino and open Route 6 to Rome. The British established what became known as the Minturno bridgehead, but the gallant efforts of the 36th USID to cross the Rapido were no match either for the Germans or for nature. 'Bloody River' was characterised by desperate and heroic attempts to cross a wide river in full flood under direct observation and fire from a skilled enemy. For political reasons – not least his dislike and distrust of the British – Clark declined to exploit the British success at Minturno.[65] February went no better, as the British tried to claw their way along the high ground behind Monte Cassino, efforts that led to the pointless destruction of the ancient Abbey of Cassino – thought to be in use by the Germans for observation.

General Alexander concluded from all this that the only way to break through to Rome was through a massive application of firepower and force. In early March the Eighth British Army took over the whole Cassino front, reducing the frontage held by the US Fifth Army to a short 10-mile stretch between the lower Garigliano and the sea, and the Anzio bridgehead. Alexander concentrated nine divisions around Cassino and planned to crush the Germans with overwhelming force. The ultimate objective was to fix the enemy to his front, prevent him bolting for the safety of northern Italy, and then launch Clark's army out of the Anzio bridgehead and trap the right wing of the German Tenth Army in a double envelopment. Once that was done, Clark was clear to march on Rome.[66]

The British had their own reasons for wanting to take charge in Italy. While American support for the campaign had been tepid at best, they had claimed the effort as their own. American failure to publicly acknowledge the British contribution to the US Fifth Army became a sore point. The previous September the Americans had celebrated the landing at Salerno beachhead as a 'wholly American victory'. It was only in late 1943, the magazine *Nation* admitted, that 'we now learn that the initial landing on that bloody beach was made by two British divisions and one American'. *Foreign Affairs* backed up this view by pointing out that the British actually held the 'hotter sector' at Salerno, and in any event they had most of the troops in Italy and even made up half of Clark's 'American' army.[67] In late February 1944 Churchill tried to rename the force at Anzio the 'Allied Bridgehead Force' to get a little press for the British role. Clark would not have it: the British were not going to enhance their prestige at the expense of the Americans.[68]

The British appealed to Marshall and the JCS in early April to sign off on Wilson's plan. The Americans reluctantly accepted that an attack in Italy was probably the best option, but told the British to set a date immediately for Anvil or they would divert no more landing craft to Europe. A frustrated Brooke vented in his diary on 8 April 1944: 'This is typical of their method of running strategy. We agree on Europe first, but if they don't get their way they use their resources as bargaining chips.' Postwar historians were more blunt: Brigadier W.F.G. Jackson called it simply 'blackmail'.[69] In this instance the British refused to budge. The Americans had been promised the prize, Rome, but that was not enough. Marshall responded by pleading that America's 'sacrifice in the Pacific can be justified only with assurances that we are to have an operation in the effectiveness of which *we can have complete faith*'. Unless the British fixed a date for Anvil the promised landing craft would head to the Pacific. On 17 April the British ordered Wilson to proceed with Operation Diadem without American concurrence.[70]

The contretemps over Anvil and landing craft was resolved in a series of meetings between 3 and 6 May. The Americans signed off on the Mediterranean strategy on 8 May and the landing craft – nineteen LSTs each carrying an LCT as deck cargo – were eventually despatched.

* * *

The struggle over strategy in the late winter and spring of 1944 reflected the changing dynamic between the two Great Powers – a natural progression from the bullying and condescension which Churchill and his colleagues had received from Roosevelt at Tehran. As Dill had warned Brooke in October 1943, America's power would be fully manifest in 1944. The looming presidential election coloured everything. In particular, by 1944 Britain's financial and economic situation was headed for a postwar collapse if no arrangements (discussed in the next chapter) could be wrung from Washington. And the empire and Commonwealth needed to be strengthened and unified under British direction in order to maintain Britain's standing as a Great Power.

Senior British statesmen and politicians were deeply mindful of their plight. They also knew that early 1944 would be the last period of the war that British military and industrial power dominated the European war. Italy and the Mediterranean remained an overwhelmingly British theatre, and the burden of mounting Operation Overlord – land, sea and air – fell heavily on Great Britain. Anthony Eden had warned at the time of Torch in 1942 that any American involvement in a campaign automatically turned it into an American operation in the US media. Italy proved the point. At the end of January 1944 Eden unburdened himself in a telegram to Lord Halifax in Washington. 'Americans have a much exaggerated conception of the military contribution they are making in this war,' he wrote.

> They lie freely about this, e.g. figures of percentages of forces for Overlord and their share of sunken U-Boats, and we are too polite to put them right, or it may be difficult to do so without giving information to the enemy. The result of all this is that the Americans advocate claims of Washington as the capitol of the country making the major fighting effort, which it is certainly not. The moral of all this would seem to be that we must blow our own military trumpet rather more, and this we plan to do.

Halifax's response two weeks later did little to ease Eden's anxieties. America's inflated view of its military contribution was because 'practically every newspaper writer and radio commentator consistently exaggerates American prowess and achievement'. Even accounts of the US Fifth Army, which at this point was half-British, neglected Britain's role. 'The reader therefore gets a vivid impression that the Americans are fighting hard and a vague impression that there may be some British troops somewhere about.'[71] Evidence of this was not hard to find. In March 1944 James Hodson, on the final leg of his cross-country tour tracking what Americans thought of the British, met a Political Science class at William and Mary College in Williamsburg, Virginia. The Chair of the department cautioned him about the results of a recent survey of his students asking them to mark places where the US was fighting all on its own: many circled Italy, Burma and New Guinea.[72]

Halifax admitted that the British were doing a poor job of selling their story. While the BIS in New York, with a staff of 412, tried to give Britain a voice, the British military public-relations staff in Washington consisted of six people. Dill informed Churchill in February 1944 that the success of the military PR staff depended on Air Vice Marshal MacNeece Foster's relationship with Major-General Alexander Surles, Director of the War Department's Public Relations, and the Joint Liaison Committee. The latter was tasked 'to do all it can to see that the best views of Britain appear in the Press and are put over by commentators and by personal contacts to prevent the publication of evil tales'. But Foster had been recalled to the UK, leaving the six British PR officers to struggle on 'worm-like'. Liaison with Surles was a job for a senior officer. Something needed to be done: '1944 is, as you are well aware,' Dill warned Churchill in late February, 'going to be a difficult year for Anglo-American relations.'[73]

There was no better opportunity to sell Britain as a valuable ally and partner in shaping the postwar world than Operation Overlord. In early 1944 media from around the world, Allied and neutral, drifted to London to cover the opening of the Second Front. But if the MOI and the Foreign Office planned – as promised at the end of January – to do something about American ignorance of Britain's war effort, it is difficult to find evidence of that effort. Over the winter of 1944 the British printed hundreds of thousands of pamphlets and booklets outlining what Britain had done to stave off defeat and keep the prospect of a Liberated Europe alive. But these were primarily targeted at Europeans and the empire, not America. Some of these MOI publications, such as *What the British Empire Has Done 1939–1943* issued at the end of January 1944, seemed ideally suited to sway American popular opinion. The surviving distribution list for the 101,930 copies printed of *What the British Empire Has Done* (25,385 in French) shows that all the French copies and 50,000 English versions were shipped to Canada. Just 100 went to America. A variation on this publication, *What the British Empire Has Done*, published in March, was also targeted at the empire: nearly half of the 40,921 copies went to India and Ceylon. Apparently none of *Britain's Industrial Achievement* (69,940 copies), *50 Facts About India* and *What the British Empire Has Done* went to the USA either. Only the eight-page illustrated pamphlet *Mutual Aid* (10,000) went to America. It outlined British help given to all the Allied nations, with particular text and photo emphasis on the USA.[74]

That said, the BIS prepared for an Overlord media blitz, and it got help from the MOI. According to John Wheeler-Bennett, the BIS received 'a remarkable study of pre-invasion and background material entitled "Index for Invasion" which had been prepared by the Reference Division of the Ministry of Information'. The BIS also worked out 'elaborate arrangements' with American newspapers for distributing a series of 'Fighting Packages' being prepared in London outlining the background to Overlord. These packages were intended to fill the global media gap between the landings and the arrival – about four days later – of the first in-depth print and film coverage. Subjects included planning, training, concentration prior to boarding assault shipping, logistics, etc. Each package included seven or eight pages of text and approved photographs. Five hundred copies of these Fighting Packages were ready for global distribution by the end of May.[75] Their highly controversial fate is discussed below. According to Wheeler-Bennett, the BIS was able to 'run a highly comprehensive daily service covering Overlord, which was widely used by the American press and radio'.[76] As will be discussed, the British view from Washington was markedly different.[77]

Apart from these tantalising morsels, the lack of evidence of a British PR offensive in America in early 1944 speaks of failure at a critical moment in the PR war. This researcher was never able to find the files of the American Division of the MOI, nor the appendix on PR plans for D-Day prepared for Wheeler-Bennett's 'History of British Information in the U.S.A.'. Research notes from 2011 observe laconically, 'The MOI files for 43, 44–45 are apparently closed!'[78] Personal papers, memoirs, biographies or histories related to the MOI during this critical period are barren. Ian McLaine's *Ministry of Morale* focuses on the Home Front and says nothing of Overlord. The two biographies of Bracken and Halifax's biography have little to say about 1944 at all, and even the Halifax Papers (and his personal diary) are silent on the matter. Something ought to have been in the Bracken Papers at Churchill College. However, these contain only one very thin file on the Second World War. Bracken's instructions to his executor were clear: burn everything immediately after my death. Apparently this was done with commendable thoroughness.[79] In the end, what survives in the record of the effort to sway American opinion in early 1944 suggests a colossal failure at a critical moment in the Anglo-American relationship and Britain's retreat from power.

In contrast, the American effort, as channelled through SHAEF, was clear and powerful. The objective, as stated in the SHAEF public-press plan circulated on 1 May 1944, was simple: 'Complete, equitable, and expeditious news, pictorial and broadcast coverage of Operation OVERLORD.'[80] Although, as noted above, the British were well represented in the PR Division of SHAEF, its driving force was American. This remained so even when, in mid-April, press relations were removed from Brigadier General Robert McClure's Psychological Warfare Division and established as its own SHAEF division under another American, Brigadier General Thomas Jefferson Davis.[81]

When Davis took over the new PR Division of SHAEF on 14 April 1944 there was much to do, not enough staff and no easy access to teleprinters and wireless communications. Within days Brendan Bracken offered SHAEF PR space at the MOI's headquarters in Senate House. The move gave Davis's organisation space and access to resources, and served to consolidate the MOI at the centre of Overlord PR. For SHAEF's PR division, Senate House was a dream come true. The MOI was already the heart of a global communications system, with links to all major Allied HQs and formations, and a 40kW transmitter routinely used to send material to the USA. Under the SHAEF press plan, Senate House was to be the first and primary recipient of all media forwarded from France for at least the first three weeks. Only when the lodgement in Normandy was well established would direct radio links between France and the USA become operational. Chancellor's Hall – nearly 100 feet long and 35 feet wide – was set up as a large media-briefing room. Staffed twenty-four hours a day, the hall was 'equipped with maps and charts, reference books and other material to assist correspondents to carry out their work'.[82]

The BBC, Britain's unrivalled global broadcaster, was at the heart of the Overlord PR plan – at least outside of America. 'There was little listening [by Europeans] to American broadcasts,' Asa Briggs claims, 'some to Swiss broadcasts and more, particularly in the north, to Russian broadcasts. Yet it was the BBC which counted for more than the rest put together.' The French listened to London over other stations, and many French and Belgians preferred the BBC British Home Service, from which they 'got accurate facts without any embroidery: no encouragement, but truth'.[83] In Belgium it is estimated that eight out of ten English speakers tuned into the BBC Home Service. The European News Service, broadcast in English to add legitimacy to the message, was available more widely, although it was often jammed.[84]

Because of its large, modern and highly effective broadcasting network, the BBC was the initial heart of radio broadcasting for SHAEF, and the planned key conduit for the transmission of American radio reporting from the Second Front as well. As the establishment of ABSIE itself demonstrated, Americans were not content with this dependency on the BBC to carry their news. So the SHAEF radio plan included the development of a direct American Normandy to New York wireless connection three weeks after D-Day. In the meantime, less powerful transmitters would connect both Anglo-Canadian and American armies in Normandy to BBC receivers along the English coast, and from there by landline to the BBC's Broadcasting House in central London. Censors and engineers at Senate House would then cut and redub audio material for release.[85] Recordings for America were then to be sent by BBC transmitter to New York.

The SHAEF media plan also included arrangements to receive and process press copy and photos directly from the beachhead. This included hand delivery of material – including typed copy, and film (both stills and cinema) – through a dedicated bag-drop system which ships, landing craft and aircraft could carry back to the UK. Once the press bags arrived in Britain they were picked up by a courier service and delivered to Senate House for censoring and distribution. Provision was also made to send text by wireless. Three transmission stations (American, British and Canadian) capable of handling some 8,000–10,000 characters per day were to be carried ashore on D-Day. By D+3 two high-speed teletype transmitters capable of 25,000 words per day were to be established, one each in the American and Anglo-Canadian zones. Then, after D+21, the Americans would install a powerful transmitter capable of broadcasting 45,000 words or more per day direct to the USA.[86] For the first four days all press material would be pooled in London. After that period, all American news, photos and film would also be forwarded unedited direct to New York. The PR division reserved the right to pool press stories for coverage of operations considered important.

Film and newsreels presented a particular challenge. Proximity to the front gave the British enormous power and potential influence over the distribution of film. Rough footage received in London on a Monday could be in newsreel distribution in British cinemas by Friday. That same rough footage received on Monday might not reach the US until Friday, and then it would take at least a week to copy, cut into newsreels and distribute across America. The situation was complicated by the screening of British newsreels (also flown across the Atlantic), especially British Pathé, which might be seen in North America a week ahead of the American release of the latest footage. To overcome this delicate problem, the MOI agreed to coordinate newsreel releases so that everyone in the UK and North America saw the same footage at roughly the same time.[87]

The Overlord public-relations plan was issued on 1 May 1944. By then hundreds of reporters were clamouring for a chance to cover the landings. SHAEF was responsible for accreditation and assignment of reporters to American forces. The War Office, Admiralty and Air Ministry looked after reporters for British forces, and the RCAF and Canadian Military Headquarters in London covered the Canadians. The First US Army was assigned forty-six American, six British, three British empire and Commonwealth, and two Allied journalists; the British Second Army was assigned forty-seven British, six American, six empire and Commonwealth, and two Allied journalists.[88] Eighty-six reporters were at sea with naval forces and fifty-five assigned to air operations. Among all these, forty-two Canadian reporters – disproportion-ately more than the scale of Canada's forces warranted – were accredited to SHAEF. A further 169 war correspondents were accredited to Senate House. They would benefit from the daily briefings and communiqués, information available in the media centre in Chancellor's Hall, and the pooled stories from reporters at the front. SHAEF arranged two briefings and two communiqués per day: a 'Background Meeting' at 10.30 a.m. followed by the first communiqué at 11.00, and a second 'Background Conference' at 5.00 p.m. to round up the day's news and the second communiqué (without a briefing) at 11.30 p.m.[89] These were designed to meet newspaper deadlines (morning and evening) in both the UK and North America.

The number of reporters assigned to Operation Overlord was intended to remain constant until FUSAG took the field later in the summer, but the clamour for billets on the far side of the Channel was unrelenting. It started in May 1944 with the American press 'demanding places with the British Army' beyond the six allocated in the PR plan. The British refused. It appears they were miffed that the Americans had limited the number of British reporters with the First US Army to six on the pretext that America was a big country and therefore needed to attach as many American war correspondents as possible. The British were prepared to change the number of Americans covering Anglo-Canadian operations if more British reporters were allowed to cover the Americans (not some-thing that British reporters were clamouring for). Freddie Morgan, now on the SHAEF staff, intervened to increase the number of American reporters with the British Second Army from six to nine.[90] But the British Army went to France in June with many of its press billets empty and they remained so for two weeks.[91] 'The fact that British prestige would be enhanced by satisfaction of American reader interest,' Ernest Dupuy wrote after the war, 'was completely disregarded, despite our protesta-tions.' The rejection of expanded American media coverage for British operations in Normandy proved to be a major self-inflicted wound.

CHAPTER 17

WHAT'S AT STAKE?

Ernie, when we have done this job for you, are we going back on the dole?

British soldier to Labour Minister Ernest Bevin,
Portsmouth, June 1944[1]

Over the winter of 1943–4 the European war stalled. While the press and public on both sides waited anxiously for the Second Front, the British and American governments drifted off into their own world of cares – much of it domestic and postwar. America was absorbed by a struggle for power between the House and the executive branch. With an eye on the 1944 election, Congress was busy slashing taxes and spending to appease isolationist and Republican agendas. Anti-British and anti-Russian sentiment was at an all-time high, and Americans were redeeming their war bonds at an alarming rate. To ordinary Americans the war was 'an evil thing engendered by rivalries and ambitions of other countries – something for which they and their government have no responsibility whatsoever', the Canadian Embassy reported in January. America was fighting to bring the boys home, 'to start making refrigerators and girdles again – to put back 1A players in the major baseball league and return Clark Gable to the movies'.[2]

The European war remained largely inexplicable to Americans. The conference at Tehran had apparently been a great triumph. Plans for the Second Front were settled. FDR spoke glowingly of Stalin as a realist and of the prospects of drawing the Russians into international councils where their rougher edges would be smoothed off. Beyond that, it was all very vague. 'There was little beyond the fact that they intended to win the war,' the *Saturday Evening Post* lamented on 8 January 1944.[3] As Dorothy Thompson reported of Tehran, 'The three agreed to go on agreeing. But what they agreed to no one knows.'[4]

It was Roosevelt's job to 'sell' both the European war and America's new internationalism to Americans. Randall Woods argues that this required the same bold and assertive leadership that sold the New Deal: a President 'who could act decisively and vigorously'.[5] If this was indeed Roosevelt's task he failed miserably, and not simply because of his illness. By late 1943 Roosevelt's administration was under siege, and he had to pick his battles carefully. Republicans still wanted to undo the New Deal, and Southern Democrats were equally unhappy about Roosevelt's 'Economic Bills of Rights' and other 'liberal' trends that threatened to erode white supremacy in the south. In fact, throughout the winter of 1944 Roosevelt's entire legislative agenda was defeated.[6] As the *New Republic* observed in early January, FDR needed a fourth term if only to avoid headlines that read, 'The peace was made and preserved by Chiang Kai-shek, Stalin, Churchill and Dewey.'[7]

And so during the winter of 1944 Roosevelt was careful to tell Americans that the war in Europe was about Hitler and the Nazis, not about Germany. OWI domestic service echoed this view. 'Roosevelt consistently refused to launch a hate campaign against the German nation,' Steven Casey asserts, which might have fired American passion for the war in Europe.[8] Roosevelt seemed to be waiting for the Germans to stain themselves with some – even more – outrageous behaviour. He might have highlighted the systematic extermination of Europe's Jews. His administration had known about this since late 1942 and had suppressed it.[9] So in the winter of 1944 even the Holocaust was too problematic as a way of raising American public interest in the war in Europe.

Lack of leadership on foreign-policy issues occasioned much debate in the American press. At its heart lay the Atlantic Charter, an aspirational document like Wilson's Fourteen Points in 1918, which called for the self-determination of all nations. The Atlantic Charter epitomised the lofty ideals that many Americans stood – and fought – for. But Churchill had already said that the Atlantic Charter did not apply to the British empire, and by early 1944 Roosevelt's plan for eastern Europe made it clear that the Charter did not apply there either. 'At the same time that Roosevelt, Wallace, White and Hull lambasted British imperialism in Asia,' Woods writes, 'American diplomats bent over backwards to accommodate Russian territorial demands in Eastern Europe and the Far East.'[10] Even *Life* lamented the drift in America's war aims, telling its readers on 6 March 1944 that they were about to 'leap into the bloodbath' of the Second Front without any clear idea of what they were fighting for. Something was needed to 'evoke a sense of common cause among the American people'.[11] Most Americans remained convinced that the Germans, too, wanted peace and simply had to find a way to throw off their Nazi bondage. The demand for unconditional surrender was a barrier to ending the war.[12] America's war was with Japan.

While Americans were bored and restless with the war in Europe, Britons had their shoulder to the wheel. Nearly everyone was in the armed forces or working.[13] As a lad of fourteen Leslie Chapman had followed his father underground in the Hemsworth Colliery, Yorkshire, in the spring of 1940, and there he stayed for the duration: forbidden to enlist or change jobs. Six days a week he dropped 2,000 feet to the working level, and then trekked 3 miles to collect his ponies and start moving coal. 'No time for lunch, just "snackers" as you went.' Through the depths of winter he walked to work in darkness, worked in darkness and came home in darkness. The tedium was relieved by a hot shower, money in his pocket, and extra rations collected by his mother: 'No butter. But lots of potatoes and sausages.'[14] 'The RAF motto "per ardua ad astra" ought to be adopted by the entire nation,' *Newsweek* observed of the British on 3 January 1944, 'for the people have won it fairly . . . Everyone works – works harder than you ever thought people could work.'[15]

Americans in the know were deeply impressed by the stoicism, commitment and endurance of the British people. A veteran US war correspondent told Ernest Dupuy in early 1944 that, after just a few days back in the States, 'He became so enraged at the sight of people enjoying themselves, oblivious to the war, that he began quarreling with his best friends!' As Dupuy told his wife, 'I quite agree with him.'[16] The English, Frederick Allen wrote in *Harper's Magazine* in January 1944, were a 'worn and tired people'. But they retained 'a grim and unalterable decision to win at all costs'.[17] Not only was Britain now assembling the most powerful and modern army ever to leave its shores, virtually every man and woman capable of work was in the armed forces or industry. By the winter of 1944 some 23,000 of them were busy building the elements of two vast artificial harbours that would be towed to France to sustain the armies.[18] As Keynes lamented in 1945, Lend-Lease freed the British to exhaust themselves in the effort to win the war.

The primary war aim of the British people was a better postwar life. This vision was embodied in the 'Beveridge Report', the work of Oxford University economics scholar William Beveridge. The report was the blueprint for a welfare state: family allowance, a National Health Service and full employment.[19] In the euphoria of victory at El Alamein and the landings in North Africa, the government published the report as a White Paper and announced its support of the scheme. Within days virtually everyone in the UK had either read the Beveridge Report or heard of it, and the vast majority – some 90 per cent – wanted it adopted.[20]

Churchill's government quickly retreated from its wholesale endorsement of the Beveridge Report: everything depended on the state of the postwar British economy. When the White Paper was debated in Parliament in February 1943, the Tory majority rejected it. But Churchill never said never. So Labour pressed the agenda, and the British people expressed their displeasure at the ballot box. As Todman writes, the opening of the Second Front sometime in early 1944 made dealing with social issues unavoidable.[21] The British people needed confirmation of what they were really fighting for. White Papers on social insurance, education and a National Health Service were all tabled in early 1944. An even more revolutionary White Paper on Employment Policy, based on Keynesian economics, reached the British Cabinet by early May.[22] The Tory response to this pressure was to tie it closely to postwar economic prosperity. Churchill and the Tory Reformers were all determined to avoid another sharp postwar slump in employment and the real destitution that followed.

That said, Churchill was tired and in a petulant mood by the spring of 1944. Like Roosevelt, he was trying to hold his government together and get through the war.[23] When, at the end of March, a Labour MP introduced a slight amendment to the Education Bill proposing equal pay for women teachers, the weary Prime Minister demanded that the amendment be withdrawn and turned the vote into one of confidence in his government. Churchill's anger unmasked the extent to which his government was out of step with the country.[24] Both he and the Chancellor of the Exchequer cautioned that adopting the trappings of a welfare state required financial solvency. In 1944 the only people who could guarantee that were the Americans.

* * *

In the autumn of 1943 five US senators returned from a global fact-finding mission to assess 'the quality and effectiveness of war material under combat conditions'.[25] Their real purpose was to investigate rumours that the British were selling Lend-Lease goods. Apparently, the British were using these goods to win friends, often – it seemed – at the expense of the USA. A review of the Senators' findings by a special Senate committee chaired by Harry S. Truman confirmed the veracity of their claims. Truman's committee concluded that the British would simply have to pay it all back – in cash or in international assets – when the war was over.[26]

The Senate fact-finding mission ignited fierce debate in America in early 1944 over postwar planning, Lend-Lease and the future of the British empire. There were many sources of Anglo-American friction. The British had not yet endorsed Roosevelt's plan for the United Nations. Trade and currency were urgent issues because the Democrats wanted to confirm America's premier place in the world economy prior to the presidential nominating convention in July. The British and Americans had not yet agreed on how postwar civil aviation would work: America had the best planes, Britain controlled the best airfields. America now possessed the world's largest and most modern merchant-shipping fleet, although everyone knew that Britain needed to carry trade by sea to earn hard cash. Then there was oil, especially the vast reserves in the Middle East. The British controlled much of it, but the Americans had a foothold in Saudi Arabia. And finally, there was Lend-

Lease itself. If the value of that programme was converted to a repayable loan, Britain would be lumbered with an unbearable postwar debt.

By 1944 Britain was essentially bankrupt, and it had converted its industry to war production. Her export economy was down to barely 30 per cent of pre-war levels,[27] and consisted of little more than ceramics, bone china, cutlery, woollens, coal and whisky. Britain also remained heavily dependent on food imports, much of that through Lend-Lease. In these circumstances building up a gold and dollar reserve was critical to the postwar convertibility of sterling. But while the USSR was allowed to carry $2 billion in gold and dollar reserves, 'with nary a peep from Washington',[28] the US Treasury Department kept British gold and dollar reserves at or below $1 billion. This effectively robbed Britain of the financial reserves it needed to back the convertibility of sterling – and ensure fiscal solvency (discussed below). The British knew of this double standard and why: as one Treasury Department official explained, Russia was not 'a traditional competitor of ours in international trade'.[29]

What made the short-term economic prospects even more bleak was that Lend-Lease would end the moment Germany capitulated. Britain lacked the wealth to convert its war-wracked industry back to commercial goods, so was unable to export on the scale needed, and would not be able to import enough food to feed its people. By March 1944 John Keynes was already talking about negotiating 'Lend-Lease II' to carry Britain through the final stages of the war against Japan, and 'Lend-Lease III' to cover Britain's transition to a peacetime economy.[30] Only America could bankroll Britain's economic salvation.

Roosevelt's original idea about Lend-Lease, and the one that Churchill clung to, was that it was a form of pooling. In 1941–3 Americans produced, and the British fought – much like 1915–17. The British 'Report on Mutual Aid', published in November 1943, said as much in its opening statement: 'This war is being fought on the significant concepts of mutual aid and of the pooling of resources.' It was up to the President to determine what an ultimate postwar settlement might entail.[31] For the British it was all about simple justice: as Robert Skidelsky wrote, 'the British had made much greater sacrifices for the common cause than had the United States, and . . . this asymmetry should be rectified'.[32] For propaganda purposes, Randall Woods claims, the White

House 'led the British and American people to believe that it [Lend-Lease] was operating on the pooling principle'. As late as August 1943, following the semi-annual review of Lend-Lease, the White House affirmed that 'The Congress in passing and extending the Lend-Lease Act made it plain that the United States want no new war debt to jeopardize the coming peace'.[33]

Nor was Lend-Lease a one-way street. The Mutual Aid agreement of February 1942 counted all 'property, services, information, facilities and other benefits or considerations' provided to the US by the British against the benefits received.[34] The value of this 'Reverse Lend-Lease' never reached the sums of Lend-Lease itself, but it was significant. By the middle of 1943 the US had spent an estimated $12 billion on Lend-Lease, about 80 per cent of which went to the British empire and Commonwealth.[35] In return, Britain spent an estimated $1.4 billion in direct support of US military operations globally.[36] However, figures for Reverse Lend-Lease were notoriously hard to calculate. So much activity in support of the Americans was embedded in existing British infrastructure, like transportation within the UK, shipping, communications, use of bases, etc. And it was hard to put a figure on lost agricultural production as verdant British fields disappeared under American bases and airfields. Nor was it easy to convert the costs from one country to another.[37] As *Business Week* pointed out on 27 May 1944, the estimates of the value of Reverse Lend-Lease were based on 'current rates of exchange' that did not 'reflect the sharp price differences which exist between countries'. If Reverse Lend-Lease was calculated 'at U.S. prices, the real value of reverse Lend-Lease would be at least 100% greater than the dollar figures indicate'.[38]

None of this debate over real or imagined costs had any impact on the American electorate. By the winter of 1944 the idea of Lend-Lease as a pooling arrangement was 'very bad politics' in America.[39] FDR had, in fact, repudiated the 'not a debt' idea as early as September 1943: recipients of Lend-Lease would pay. That had always been the Treasury Department's understanding, and it had consistently administered Lend-Lease as a loan system. Anxious to be seen as a 'businesslike' manager in an election year, and locked in an existential struggle with Congress, Roosevelt also began to describe Lend-Lease as a repayable loan.[40]

This was not what the State Department had in mind. One of the main objectives of Lend-Lease, as outlined in Article VII of the Agreement for Mutual Aid signed in February 1942,[41] was a British obligation to negotiate a 'liberal international trading order' after the war: in short, free trade between the British empire and Commonwealth and the United States. This would be difficult to do with a bankrupt Britain under financial assault by the US Treasury Department. As Skidelsky points out, the Treasury Department's policy of controlling British gold and dollar reserves 'cut across the State Department's aim of getting the British to liberalize their trade ... A country whose "quick assets" were about a tenth the size of its "quick debts", and whose export trade had been reduced to under 30 percent of its pre-war level was an unlikely early candidate for Cordell Hull's free trade world.'[42]

Roosevelt and his Treasury Department wanted to settle the postwar financial arrangements with Britain before the Democratic National Convention slated for July 1944. In February two telegrams, ostensibly from FDR, pressed the British to make some key decisions about economic and industrial planning.[43] Lord Halifax's advice was to simply stay the course and, 'if anything is running rather loose, let it flap and break if necessary and let us see what happens. All this frantic dancing to the American tune is silly.' America was playing domestic politics: 'My recommendation,' Churchill responded, 'is to let it all rip for a bit.'[44] Churchill used the occasion, however, to state his own guiding principles for Britain's postwar economic planning: no return to the gold standard, no abandonment of Imperial Preference unless US trade barriers come down completely, no abandonment of the Wheat Act of 1932 (which subsidised home-grown wheat), and no policy of artificial 'dearness or scarcity of basic food' through tariffs or quotas.[45]

Over the next three months Churchill lost his fight to keep Britain free of America's postwar economic designs. The US Treasury Department position, put forward by Henry Dexter White, proposed a free-trade system backed by an American commitment to support international trade through a limited Stabilization Fund (later the International Monetary Fund) and a World Bank, with currencies ultimately convertible to gold. The White Plan was precisely what Keynes and the British government wanted to avoid: a global system of free trade, a form of gold standard, and the US dollar as the new international currency. 'The British had only one element of leverage at their disposal,' Benn Steil writes, 'and that was the power of disengagement.'[46] The American plan prevailed. In April, White pressed Keynes and the British government to issue a 'Joint Statement of Principles' accepting the White Plan.[47] 'Treasury's aim', Steil writes, was to make the postwar economic plan part of the Democratic Party election platform and use it 'to brand Republicans . . . as isolationists who opposed vital international cooperation'.[48]

Churchill's government was content to let the Joint Statement 'flap a little'. A major report supporting the tentative arrangements presented to the British Cabinet in February by Richard Law, Minister of State in the Foreign Office, failed to move them. The Bank of England dismissed the idea of an international bank as ultimately a failure – soon 'filled up with lenas and dinars'. Worse still, it would be run by foreigners, based in Washington, and would spell the decline of sterling.[49] In any event, Churchill and his coterie of die-hard Tory imperialists were not convinced that Britain's position was as bad as many argued. After all, the Americans had to trade with somebody. They needed a healthy and solvent British empire to ensure their own postwar prosperity. Attempts to get the Cabinet to endorse the Joint Statement in February failed.

By March 1944 Anglo-American relations had reached an impasse on a great many issues. The American solution was to send Edward R. Stettinius, Under-Secretary of State, to the UK on another fact-finding mission. Stettinius had run the Lend-Lease programme from its enactment in March 1941 until his appointment as Under-Secretary of State in September 1943. In January 1944 he published a book on the subject, *Lend-Lease: Weapon of Victory*, in which he extolled its virtues and successes.[50] The origins of Lend-Lease, he argued, lay in America's own self-interest. Roosevelt's homely analogy of lending a hose to a neighbour to put out a fire had morphed into a programme based on the 'principle of sharing, or "pooling"' resources in a common cause. The final reckoning would be left until after the war.

Lend-Lease was directed at a suspicious American public. It included a short chapter on Reverse Lend-Lease – too short for many reviewers – in which Americans were reminded that Lend-Lease was a two-way street. The trade between America and her allies was not balanced in terms of dollar value, Stettinius wrote, but in commitment to winning the war. The British, Russians, Chinese and others had been doing most of the fighting: every Axis soldier they eliminated was one less that Americans would have to fight. And it explained, in a simple graphic, how America's own trade barriers in the 1920s and 1930s had caused European nations to default on their Great War loans.

No one would conclude from Stettinius's book that he was anything but supportive of America's allies. Indeed, some reviewers used the occasion to emphasise how small Lend-Lease aid was as a proportion of America's total effort, and how much America received in Reverse Lend-Lease. However, John MacCormac in the *New York Times Book Review* of 16 January 1944 raised a troubling issue. Stettinius had lumped together America's ammunition production and ship building in a way which implied that it was all going as Lend-Lease. MacCormac was fearful that this was 'better calculated to inspire another "Who won the war?" debate than to become the basis for a correct appraisal of America's contribution to the global conflict'. He might also have noted that any American looking at Stettinius's map, 'Comparison of Supply Lines – United Nations vs. the Axis', could only conclude that no military supplies whatsoever were coming out of Britain or anywhere else: all of the Allies' war material emanated from the USA.[51]

Prior to leaving for Britain, Stettinius was reminded by FDR and Secretary Hull of 'the importance of confronting the British on imperialism' and the imperative of tearing down imperial preference. Roosevelt explained that he hoped to place the colonial possessions of the European powers under the trusteeship of the new international-security organisation, with much of that administered by the US. America would then acquire all the base and access rights it needed in the postwar world.[52]

Stettinius found the British agitated about the postwar world, and Churchill's coalition government in crisis. Not only was the Labour wing now working openly to create a welfare state, but a strong lobby within Cabinet pressed Churchill to issue the Joint Statement of Principles on postwar economic policy that the Americans demanded. Meanwhile his trusted Foreign Secretary, Anthony Eden, threatened to resign unless Britain signed on to plans for the United Nations. Increasingly isolated, Churchill retreated into the company of Lord Beaverbrook and Brendan Bracken. They, too, were not yet ready to surrender the empire.

When Stettinius met with Churchill on 9 April the Prime Minister made Britain's economic plight perfectly clear: Britain was broke and the control of its gold and dollar reserves by the US Treasury Department threatened to seriously impede its postwar recovery. British US dollar reserves had risen sharply since the surge of American troops and air-force squadrons into the UK began in late 1943, but as they did Roosevelt insisted that Britain pay for its supplies in cash. Churchill had refused, but the pressure was still there to shave British US dollar reserves back to $1 billion.[53] The next day Eden pressed Stettinius for US involvement in the European Advisory Commission (EAC) so it could start tackling postwar issues. Stettinius made it clear that the US was not yet ready to engage with the EAC, because assigning 'broad powers' to an international body based in London 'might arouse isolationists at home'.[54]

Stettinius spent 19 April in close discussion with senior officials, including an update on Britain's financial situation by Sir John Anderson, Chancellor of the Exchequer. Stettinius admitted that 'The farmer from Kansas just can't understand why the British are not rich'. Anderson suggested that if he had trouble making this point to Roosevelt or Morgenthau he would be happy to come to Washington to explain it.[55] The afternoon was spent meeting with Churchill and a few others. Eden, Law, Guy Winnant (the American ambassador) and Stettinius all professed themselves in agreement on the proposed international-security organisation; Churchill adamantly was not. Nor was he enamoured of economic conferences. 'I must make it clear to you,' Churchill also told Stettinius plainly, 'as I have to the President, that we aren't going to repay the Lend-Lease debts. That will have to be adjusted someplace else along the lines of utilizing bases, empire preference, tariffs, etc.'[56]

The depths of Churchill's position were revealed the next day during a Cabinet meeting convened to discuss the issuing of the Joint Statement of Principles with the USA. The meeting was stormy. 'Beaverbrook shouted and pounded the table,' Woods wrote, 'nearly upsetting Churchill's brandy.' Beaverbrook's position, and that of the other Tory imperialists, was that the US needed the British empire more than it supposed. 'The Americans are absolutely bound to the rehabilitation of British commerce and industry,' Beaverbrook had written to Churchill that day. 'They must themselves perish if this nation fails to get "Food, Homes and Work". It is imperative that the Americans should be met on this basis and dealt with frankly and firmly.'[57] Beaverbrook's plea for the empire and imperial preference damned the Tories to defeat. Cabinet voted in favour of issuing the Joint Statement of Principles, which went out from the British and American governments the next day. With that, Woods concludes, 'Britain was in the bag'.[58]

Churchill still had cards to play. He told Stettinius that nothing could be decided until the 'all out conference' with the Dominion Prime Ministers, scheduled for May, was complete. There was still a chance that the 'empire' would rally to the old flag.

* * *

For Churchill and other Tory imperialists there was still hope for a unified empire and Commonwealth. By 1944 the Americans had already begun to wear out their welcome in many places, including India and the Caribbean, where America's colour-bar undermined its claims to moral leadership. Meanwhile, Australia's experience with the Americans brought it full circle in its relations with Great Britain in less than two years. In autumn 1942, after the failure of Britain to defend South East Asia, especially Singapore, and British handling of the Australian Imperial Force in the Middle East, Australia had signed on completely to the Statute of Westminster. But the Americans, who came as saviours, proved no more attentive to Australia's concerns than the British, and they tended to operate as if they owned the place. Australians feared that they would be excluded from the final victory over Japan and the making of the postwar peace. The fact that Australian military power was waning quickly by the end of 1943 did not help the mood down under.

By late 1943 the Australian Prime Minister, John Curtin, fully accepted the idea that – in Day's words – 'The "best assurance" of Australia's security was provided by a "scheme of Imperial defence formulated and carried out by members of the British Commonwealth in co-operation".'[59] So, too, did New Zealand's Prime Minister, Peter Fraser. On 24 January 1944 Curtin and Fraser issued an 'Australia-New Zealand Agreement' that contained two critical statements of policy. The first was that there should be no postwar settlement in the South Pacific without participation by the Australian and New Zealand governments. The second was that the US should not be permitted to retain any bases on foreign soil in the South Pacific. The only way to achieve these goals was through unified Commonwealth and empire foreign and defence policies. Even Robert Menzies, who lost his job as PM in 1942 largely due to the failure of Britain to support Australia in its hour of greatest crisis, had become an ardent supporter of a renewed British empire. 'In matters of peace or waging war,' Menzies said on 1 February 1944, 'the British nations must have one broad policy and must stand or fall by it.'[60] If Churchill and his imperial colleagues in London needed encouragement, it would be hard to find a better case than Australia's volte-face by late 1943.

What had also emerged by the end of 1943 was the idea of the British Dominions becoming regional powers. Jan Smuts proposed the idea to the UK Branch of the Empire Parliamentary Association on 25 November 1943. Both South Africa and Australia already had experience with this through League of Nations mandates. South Africa assumed guardianship of German south-west Africa (Namibia), but Smuts's greater vision of South Africa included Bechuanaland, northern and southern Rhodesia, Tanganyika, Uganda and Kenya. Australians latched on to that idea too. An Australian regional Dominion would be created, in David Day's words, from 'the detritus of the European empires that would shield her from future threats and allow for economic development'.[61] They already had a model for this. The south-eastern part of New Guinea was a British colony until 1904, when it was given to Australia to manage. The north-eastern part of New Guinea and the Bismarck archipelago were assigned to Australia under a League of Nations mandate. Since neither the French nor the Dutch had done much to defend the approaches to Australia, the proposed new 'Australian Zone' would also include parts of Dutch Indonesia and French Melanesia. Canada, too, was anxious that the adjacent British colony of Newfoundland should not fall to the

Americans.[62] So Churchill and the imperialists could take comfort from the news that the lure of America was not universal, and that many in both the empire and Commonwealth saw renewed imperial ties as an essential counterweight to America's growing influence.

The preferred Canadian solution to postwar security, however, was multilateralism. The strength of that Canadian sentiment was revealed when Lord Halifax had the temerity to suggest to the Toronto Board of Trade on 24 January 1944 that it was much better 'if on vital issues we can achieve a common foreign policy, expressed not by a single voice but by the unison of many'.[63] Halifax's words, Stacey writes, sent Mackenzie King 'into something like a fit – another temper tantrum'. British officials quickly disavowed Halifax's speech, but Mackenzie King used the opportunity to wrap himself in Canadian nationalism for the opening of Parliament three days later. The rising democratic socialist party, the Co-operative Commonwealth Federation (CCF), lauded Mackenzie King's programme of social-justice reforms in education, health care, unemployment, welfare and family-support benefits, but remained suspicious of his relations with both the British and the Americans. Now, thanks to Halifax, the CCF supported Mackenzie King's nationalist defence and foreign policy as well.[64]

Despite the contretemps ignited by Halifax's speech, Churchill had reason to hope that the kind of imperial unity he needed to maintain Britain's position as a Great Power could be achieved when the Commonwealth Prime Ministers met in London in May 1944. That meeting has been ignored by historians.[65] Even Churchill makes no mention of it in his magnum opus *The Second World War*.[66] Perhaps that was because the meeting was doomed before it started.

The meeting and its portent were no secret. *Newsweek* reported on 10 April that Mackenzie King would play a 'lone hand' and oppose any tightening up of the empire or Commonwealth. That did not rule out – for the moment – the merits of trying. By late April Churchill certainly had the British Parliament on side. For two days it debated the future of the empire and Commonwealth. 'When the Prime Minister appeared,' *Time* magazine reported, 'the House was heady with imperial wine.' Churchill reminded Parliament that so far he had given nothing away: the Atlantic Charter did not trump the interests of the empire, and the Lend-Lease agreement did not surrender Britain's right to maintain imperial preference.[67] It remained to be seen what could be done.

The Prime Ministers' meeting convened in London on 1 May 1944 and lasted two weeks. Mackenzie King arrived early to meet with Viscount Cranborne (the Dominions Secretary) and Churchill. Both were told emphatically that Canada would not commit to any centralisation of the Commonwealth under one unified 'British' foreign and security policy. It is doubtful if the Canadian PM drew any reassurance from Churchill's comment that although the meeting would not 'settle the future of the world . . . great decisions were to be taken' nonetheless. Great decisions were precisely what Mackenzie King came to London to avoid.

The first week was taken up with the war situation and foreign affairs. Week two was spent discussing postwar plans for civil aviation, shipping, the colonial situation, employment and migration. Mackenzie King described the meetings as more of an information session, with Churchill and senior British officials presenting position papers and shaping the discussion. There were always many more British officials in the room than there were Dominion delegates. As early as day two of the conference Mackenzie King lamented 'the helplessness of the situation'.[68] On 4 May, when Eden presented his survey of the proposed British foreign policy, supported by Curtin and Fraser, Mackenzie King objected. He was not opposed to the policy per se, but to the fact that it had been conceived and written in Whitehall without consultation and discussion by the Commonwealth Prime Ministers. Mackenzie King also flatly rejected the idea of permanent Commonwealth representatives in the Foreign Office, where the British would always outnumber the Commonwealth representatives '8–1'.

Throughout the meeting Fraser and Curtin were anxious to find a path to a common and unified Commonwealth defence and foreign policy, and they were willing to defer to the British lead. Britain was about to deploy an enormous portion of her military and naval might to South East Asia and the South Pacific. Keeping some of it there postwar to eliminate reliance on the US was now a major goal for both Australia and New Zealand.[69] But Mackenzie King refused to accept any statement of defence or foreign policy that had not first been discussed and passed by the Dominion Parliaments. He consistently said warm and friendly things about shared heritage, British culture and common values, but Canada was an independent nation and would not be bullied by the British.

Evidence of Mackenzie King's position emerged most strongly during the preparation of the final communiqué on 15–16 May. The draft, written by the British Cabinet Secretary, Sir Edwards Bridges, spoke of 'policy' in the singular form, and assumed that there was a single British Commonwealth plan for the Pacific war, a single British Commonwealth foreign policy, and agreement to centralised Commonwealth defence planning. Mackenzie King torpedoed it all. The revised draft communiqué was tabled on the afternoon of 15 May. Bracken objected immediately that it was too tepid; he wanted something more emphatic. Fraser and Curtin supported him. Mackenzie King would not budge. After much keen debate over the wording, during which Mackenzie King reiterated Canada's position, Clement Attlee – the Deputy Prime Minister who chaired what Churchill knew would be a stormy session – concluded, 'we are all agreed'. Mackenzie King said emphatically, 'No.' Finally, Cranborne 'read a long paper putting forth different suggestions as to policies and so forth . . . and among other things asking for . . . an Imperial Joint Board of Defence'. 'Everything they had been trying for years was jammed in that statement,' Mackenzie King wrote in his diary.[70] He considered Cranborne's attempt to slip that into the final communiqué as underhanded and 'high pressure'.[71] The amended communiqué, reflecting Canada's intransigence, was little more than a statement of basic values and principles.[72]

On the eve of D-Day Churchill rose in Parliament to summarise Britain's effort to date and to explain its foreign policy. Disingenuously he announced that the Dominion Prime Ministers stood 'in firm array' following the recent conference.[73] Those who read the fine print knew better. *Newsweek* reported on 22 May that Mackenzie King's speech to the British Parliament on 11 May was clear: 'Canada would not support any plan of an integrated Empire.' 'The assembled prime ministers turned down flatly the Australian sponsored proposal for a tight intra-empire trade behind high protective tariffs,' *Business Week* reported on

27 May. 'This deprives London of one of its strongest international bargaining threats.' As *Business Week* concluded, the real winner from the Prime Ministers' meeting was the United States.[74]

* * *

The Commonwealth Prime Ministers met in the midst of what one reporter called 'an invasion frenzy'. At the end of April *Time* magazine described the invasion as 'imminent', while the *Nation* agreed that 'The attack will come soon'. On 1 May, Lord Beaverbrook's *Daily Express* reported Swedish belief that the invasion would come either the next day, or on 17 May. The following day it ran a column of snapshots of the recent front pages of dailies from France, Germany, Portugal, Spain and Brazil, all trumpeting the imminent invasion. *Time* carried a Swiss report on 8 May claiming that the foreign press corps in Germany was betting on a landing between 6 May and 7 June, with 10 May – the anniversary of the German attack on the west in 1940 – as a good candidate.[75]

The increased tempo of the air assault on French railways and on coast defences in May was taken as evidence of an imminent landing. These contrasted with the huge figures of tonnage dropped on Germany, which 'have now become too commonplace to attract attention'.[76] By late May the press was able to speculate with increased accuracy. When the initial meeting of the International Air Transport Authority intended for Montreal in early June was postponed, but the international economic summit at Bretton Woods in July remained unaffected, the Toronto *Globe and Mail* observed that the invasion would happen in the first week of June.

Evidence of press guidance by the MOI and OWI in early 1944 is scarce, but it is likely that the press was enlisted in the Overlord deception scheme. A *United States News* story on 5 May observed that the invasion 'won't happen all at once'. There would be more than one landing, leading ultimately to the final assault. Speculation on where the Allies might land also supported the deception operation. The headline of the *Daily Express* on Saturday 29 April was a bold 'ALLIED RAIDS SPARE INVASION HARBOURS', followed by a story date-lined Stockholm which quoted a German admiral saying, 'the Allies are deliberately sparing the Channel harbours in their air attacks because they hope to use them for the invasion'. Harbours were the focus of a

15 May *Time* article titled 'Where?' It reinforced the notion that the Allies needed ports with easy access inland.

The invasion frenzy of late April and May 1944 coincided nicely with the formal commencement of the deception scheme under Operation Fortitude on 24 April 1944. Abwehr remained convinced that the Pas-de-Calais was the main target, and that the Allies had enough divisions to launch several landings. But the Germans knew little that the British did not want them to know, and they had struggled throughout the winter trying to place the First Canadian Army in the order of march. By 20 April, Abwehr had 'worked out' a basic order of battle for the two known Army Groups in England: the 21st AG under Montgomery with the Fifth British and First Canadian armies under command, and FUSAG under Bradley with the First and Ninth US armies.[77] By late April it was time for the Fortitude operators to shuffle the deck, show a few cards and reinforce all of the Germans' anxieties.

What followed was a very carefully choreographed burlesque, with just enough revealed to lead the Germans in the direction they already wanted to go. At the heart of this phase was Operation Quicksilver, a six-part deception scheme designed to confirm the threat to the Pas-de-Calais and the notion that the real landing would commence there forty-five days after a feint in Normandy.[78] Quicksilver I unmasked the threat from FUSAG. The reveal commenced on 24 April with a large-scale wireless deception operation across south-east England.[79] The First Canadian Army, already deployed in Sussex and Kent, was ideally placed for both the wireless (W/T) deception and leading the initial assault. The Third US Army, still forming in Cheshire, sent radio units, supported by the 3103rd Signal Service Battalion, to East Anglia to simulate the American concentration north of the Thames. Quicksilver II outlined the notional FUSAG order of battle, the wireless communications network, and conduct of 'notional combined exercises' by the 2nd Canadian Division in Kent in late April.

Naval and air deceptions were dealt with in Quicksilver III and IV. Some 270 dummy landing craft were deployed in ports from Yarmouth to Folkestone, with appropriate wireless traffic, as part of Quicksilver III. A detailed air deception was conceived under Quicksilver IV, which included moving more squadrons into south-east England, expansion of airfields and – in keeping with the Transportation Plan – increased air activity over northern France.[80]

The heart of Quicksilver was part V, which revealed increased military activity in the Dover area. This was where the headquarters of II Canadian Corps, which was to lead the attack on the Pas-de-Calais, was relocated in May. The Canadians in Kent maintained increased wireless activity until well into June,[81] and in May work commenced on a dummy wireless station outside Dover as part of Quicksilver.[82] II Canadian Corps ran a series of amphibious exercises in the Trent and Medway rivers throughout late May and early June. What made these exercises uniquely interesting is that the tidal and water conditions in the Medway mirrored those of the Scheldt estuary: fast moving, high tides generating muddy water conditions and extensive mudflats at low tide. Then, on 1 June in 'Exercise Rattle', the 2nd Canadian Division began to mimic the radio traffic of the Canadian infantry brigades assigned to Overlord.[83] Finally, Quicksilver VI ensured that all this faux activity was properly reflected in the quantity and quality of night lighting.

Historians typically observe that the key to the success of Fortitude South was General George S. Patton. According to Antony Beevor, Patton was the commander 'the Germans feared the most'.[84] Carlo D'Este asserts that the Germans 'were permitted to learn' that Patton was to command FUSAG, but does not say when and offers no proof.[85] The British official history of strategic deception by Sir Michael Howard makes an equally unsupported claim.[86] They, and scores of other historians, seem to have muddled the timeline. The Germans were told through agents in January 1944 that FUSAG was commanded by Bradley. The Abwehr estimate on 20 April still identifies him in command, and agents confirmed that in early May.[87] At best, the Germans assumed at the end of March that Patton might be in command of the US Third Army. But no confirming information was fed to them as part of the deception operation, and even D'Este observes that 'Patton's appointment as Third Army commander was deliberately kept a secret'.[88]

In fact, Patton was in the news in late April 1944 for all the wrong reasons. When he spoke at the opening of a Welcome Club for American soldiers in Knutsford, he said that the British, Americans and Russians were destined to run the postwar world. Nothing in the short press story from London mentions a role for Russia, so his innocuous state-ment quickly morphed into an assertion that the British and the Americans would run the world. The *Chicago Tribune* headlined the story 'Gen. Patton Says It's U.S.-British Destiny to Rule'.[89] The American press had never forgotten Patton's behaviour in Sicily, and they deeply distrusted him.[90] *Newsweek* lambasted Patton on 8 May as a 'ferocious fumbler', the same day that *Time* said, 'There he goes again'. The *Washington Post*, notorious for its dislike of Patton, ran an editorial that claimed, 'General Patton has progressed from simple assaults on indi-viduals, to collective assault on entire nationalities [i.e. Russians].'[91] Debate reached the floor of Congress, where some demanded his recall. On 29 April, Marshall threw Patton's fate into Eisenhower's lap. Marshall reminded Ike that Patton was the only American Army commander who had experience fighting Rommel, and that he had a particular skill at driving a rapid advance.[92] The next day Eisenhower informed Marshall that he would send Patton home and replace him with Hodges. Then Ike changed his mind. When called on the carpet for his actions on 2 May, Patton was remorseful and was soon 'sobbing'. Eisenhower told him to keep his mouth shut: he would be told when to speak.[93] As Ike informed Marshall the next day, he needed Patton for 'his ability to conduct a ruthless drive'.[94]

The first critical 'reveal' to the Germans about FUSAG and the 'looming' assault on the Pas-de-Calais was made when double agents controlled by MI5 began to feed Abwehr information about the concen-tration of FUSAG in south-east England. The Germans were allowed to believe that FUSAG was entirely US–Canadian, with an American corps in the First Canadian Army, and that many more divisions, including three Canadian, were ready for operations.[95]

The second revelation by agents at the end of April 1944 was the concentration of the First Canadian Army along the Channel coast opposite Calais. In fact, the 'movements' of Canadian units and First Canadian Army formations were among the major cards played as part of Fortitude South in the weeks prior to D-Day. The shift of II Canadian Corps from Sussex to Kent in late April was one of the few actual move-ments of Allied formations undertaken as part of the Overlord decep-tion. The move was not leaked to the Germans: they were allowed to discover it through signal traffic – in accordance with the Quicksilver directive – and then have it confirmed by agent reports. Meanwhile, the notional movement of the First Canadian Army's other real corps, the VIII British, and the movement of some smaller Canadian units, was fed to the Germans through agents. So, too, was the actual movement of a British corps from Yorkshire to the south coast.[96] These movements were supported, in turn, by a very public visit to Dover on 23 May by Montgomery, Crerar, and II Canadian Corps commander Lieutenant-General Guy Simonds, which was captured by British media.[97]

The final reveal was slipped to the Germans on 31 May, when agent BRUTUS reported that Patton had taken over FUSAG – the first hard news Abwehr had of his role. This was done because Bradley would soon turn up in Normandy. The news was, in Hesketh's words, accepted with 'reserve'. The Germans only accepted Patton as FUSAG commander when agent GARBO confirmed it on 12 June.[98]

The comment by Hesketh that the Germans were anxious to know where the Canadians were was not an idle piece of information, and the fact that the First Canadian Army was the designated assault formation of FUSAG was no accident: it had long played a critical role in the campaign for a Second Front.[99] In the spring of 1944 Abwehr estimated that the First Canadian Army was still composed of some thirteen divisions, more than enough to lead the charge.[100] Moreover, since the summer of 1943 the First Canadian Army had been developing plans for a descent on Antwerp, and its amphibious training in the Thames estuary did not go unreported. The Fortitude South cover plan specified the need to keep the Germans fixed 'in *or EAST* of the PAS DE CALAIS area'.[101] The Germans remained anxious about the Belgian coast and, as we shall see, on 6 June fretted about a possible landing near Antwerp. For all these reasons the First Canadian Army, and not George Patton, was the beating heart of Fortitude South.

CHAPTER 18

OK, LET'S GO!

The outstanding feature of public attitudes during May was the concentration of thought and feeling on the coming invasion . . . Late in the month there were a few suggestions that such intense preoccupation with invasion could not be much longer maintained.

War Information Board, Report No. 2, May 1944[1]

By the spring of 1944 Britain and her empire and Commonwealth were engaged in three major land campaigns across the globe. It would have helped Britain's cause in the international community – and especially in American popular opinion – had the scope and scale of its effort been better known and appreciated. This had been a nagging problem for British public relations since 1939, and by 1944 little had changed.

The campaign in South East Asia, which was overwhelmingly British, reached a crisis in the spring of 1944. In March the Japanese Fifteenth Army launched a major offensive across the Chindwin River in central Burma in an attempt to reach Bengal and raise rebellion. It was a desperate gamble. Three regular Japanese divisions, plus most of Subhas Chandra Bose's 40,000-man Independent Indian Army, had no logistics support, just 30,000 oxen, 12,000 horses and mules, and 1,000 elephants for transport.[2] The Fifteenth Army was supposed to subsist on British supplies and local food, and the hope that the Indian Army would defect. Both expectations were badly misplaced.

The Japanese soon enveloped Imphal and by early April had cut the road behind the key pass into India at Kohima. The latter, recently garrisoned by 2,500 British, Indian, Nepalese and Burmese troops, was surrounded by 6 April. A brutal ten-day siege followed. 'Nowhere in World War II – even on the Eastern front,' Alan Millet and Williamson Murray wrote, 'did the combatants fight with more mindless savagery.'[3] The Japanese attack culminated in late April as the Indian Army counterattacked with mechanised forces which the Japanese could not stop. Imphal–Kohima developed into 'the worst defeat in Japanese military history', with over 80,000 Japanese soldiers dead by the end of the summer.[4]

Little sense of this emerged in the contemporary media. Anxious about Indian loyalties, British military censors buried the story. The Canadian War Information Board noted in its May report that 'the war against Japan has been barely mentioned'.[5] American reporters in the region complained that they could get little useful information from New Delhi about the Japanese offensive, or about British and Indian efforts to check it. Preston Grover, a reporter with Associated Press covering Stilwell's campaign in north Burma, published a blistering account of British censorship in mid-April. Even stories by Americans about Americans had to clear Mountbatten's HQ, Indian Army HQ and the Government of India. For Grover the reason for this was clear: 'It is not to Britain's advantage to have too much credit go to the Chinese or Americans.' The *Chicago Tribune* concluded that the British were abusing their censorship powers in order to salvage their empire. The *Tribune* warned that the British did the same in Italy and would likely do it again when France was invaded.[6]

For Americans the war in South East Asia was all about Stilwell's two Chinese divisions, the battalion-sized special force dubbed Merrill's Marauders, American air squadrons in northern Burma and getting aid to China. Stilwell's force, *Newsweek* claimed with more than a little hyperbole, 'may have the greatest influence on the future course of the worldwide struggle'.[7] The Americans feared that the bungling British might leave Stilwell's army trapped. Their anxiety only heightened as the British and Indians continued their 'slow plugging' in the south. Saving India from invasion and rebellion, and defeating the Japanese in the largest land battle of the Asia-Pacific, was, apparently, not all that important.[8] American press coverage of Imphal–Kohima was a portent of what lay ahead over the summer.

So, too, was the coverage of the Allies' major assault in Italy, which began on 11 May. The British invested a great deal in this operation as the best counterpoint to Overlord. Events proved them right.[9] The traditional interpretation of Kesselring's resolve to defend south of Rome attributes it to keeping Allied airpower at bay, guarding against attacks on the Balkans and securing Rome. But it was also necessary to keep the Allies out of the industrial heartland of the Salò Republic – Turin, Milan and Bologna. This area was increasingly integrated into Germany's war industry and provided support to German operations in the region. There was every reason to believe that the Germans would fight south of Rome.

General Alexander's objectives in Operation Diadem were to destroy the right wing of the German Tenth Army holding the Cassino front and push the Germans to the Pisa–Rimini Line. An initial assault by the Eighth British Army in the Cassino area and by the US Fifth Army from the Garigliano beachhead would fix the bulk of the Tenth Army in place. Kesselring would have to reinforce his positions south of Cassino or abandon them. Alexander reckoned that he would not give up without a fight. Once the Germans were fully committed, VI US Corps would burst out of Anzio, forcing the Germans to withdraw to avoid encirclement. The trap would be sprung at Valmontone. In the subsequent advance the US Fifth Army would capture Rome.

Like Overlord, Operation Diadem was supported by a sophisticated deception codenamed 'Nunton', designed to fix German reserves north of Rome. 'In the plot framed by General Alexander's playwrights,' the Canadian official history concluded, 'the leading role was given to the 1st Canadian Corps.'[10] The Canadians, reinforced by the 36th US Division, would land at Civitavecchia, north-west of Rome. Aerial bombing and reconnaissance of the Civitavecchia area was increased, as was amphibious training for the 9th French Division on Corsica slated to capture Elba. Nunton was 'almost perfectly successful'.[11]

Diadem launched at 2300 hours on 11 May. While the Poles captured Monte Cassino, the 8th Indian and 4th British divisions secured a bridgehead over the Rapido River. By 15 May a two-corps assault up the Liri valley was underway: the I Canadian Corps on the left, through Pignaturo, and XIII British Corps along Route 6. Meanwhile, General Alphonse Juin's Corps Expéditionnaire Français (CEF) swept through the southern end of the Hitler Line, the defences guarding the northern exit from the Liri valley, in a lightning strike. By 21 May it had poured through the Arunci mountains and culminated its efforts on the lateral road between the Liri valley and the sea (Route 82) at Pico. Two days later the Canadians had closed up to the Hitler Line between Aquino and Pontecorvo and were preparing a set-piece attack to open Route 6 to Rome. Outflanked and under pressure along the entire front, the German Tenth Army began its retreat on 22 May.[12]

When asked by the press on 12 May 1944 about the purpose of the Allied offensive, Alexander was very clear: 'We are going to destroy the German armies in Italy.' The *New York Times* reported his comment the next day, along with Mark Clark's confirmation that 'We can and will destroy the German Armies'.[13] On 23 May, as the Canadians breached the Hitler Line, Lucian Truscott's VI US Corps – a powerful force of five infantry divisions, the 1st USAD and the Canadian-American 1st Special Service Force (SSF) – thrust eastward across the Pontine marshes towards Valmontone. That day General Lyman Lemnitzer, Alexander's American liaison officer, personally delivered orders to Clark to close the trap at Valmontone. Lemnitzer was shocked to discover that Clark now had other plans. As Clark told Nigel Nicolson in 1970, 'I had been assigned the mission of capturing Rome.'[14] By 25 May, as Truscott was poised to take Valmontone, Clark's Chief of Staff arrived with orders to turn VI Corps north for Rome. According to the US Army official history, Truscott was 'dumbfounded', and his division commanders bitter over the sudden change in orders.[15] Valmontone's capture was just a few hours away, and Truscott wanted to push 'maximum power into the Valmontone gap to ensure destruction of the German army'. In any event, it would be better to launch the drive to Rome up Route 6 than to fight through the Alban Hills – the only part of the final fixed defences in front of Rome that was fully developed.[16] Truscott protested in vain. By the evening he signalled his intent to shift the drive north. That left the 3rd USID and the 1st SSF to continue the thrust towards Valmontone.

It was not enough. The Germans heavily reinforced the Valmontone gap without weakening their forces in the Alban Hills, which says a great deal about what they thought about Valmontone. Nicolson admits that there was merit in securing the Alban Hills, which brooded over the line of march to Rome. Clark's sin was that 'he paid lip service to the Army Group's plan by sending a mere "column" in the required direction, and until the last minute kept to himself an intention of which he knew that Alexander would disapprove'.[17] Clark later claimed that Alexander agreed with his decision, but this is disingenuous. Prodded by Churchill over why it was taking so long to capture Valmontone, Alexander visited Clark on the 27th to find out what was going on. By then VI Corps was 'swarming over the Alban hills' and it was too late to call them back. Alexander acquiesced in a fait accompli.

Clark candidly admitted that he was not interested in helping the laggardly British secure a victory. His contempt for the British Army was barely disguised and was reinforced when Alexander naively insisted that the Americans take Valmontone to unhinge the Germans and allow the Eighth Army to 'conserve losses'.[18] As Martin Blumenson observed, Clark was 'willing to violate Alexander's instructions'. He even tried to cajole Juin into joining him to ensure that the Americans beat the British into Rome: echoes of the race to Sedan in November 1918. Juin politely declined. What most historians miss – or ignore – is that Clark had been given the presumptive date for Operation Overlord (5 June) by George Marshall during his recent visit to the USA. Clark needed to secure the Eternal City before Overlord swept Italy from the front pages. The depth of Clark's ambition and paranoia is revealed in his diary entry for 30 May.

Most of my worries have nothing to do with the immediate battle. They are political in nature.

First, the British have their eyes on Rome, notwithstanding Alexander's constant assurances to me that Rome is in the sector of the Fifth Army. The Eighth Army has done little fighting. It has lacked aggressiveness and failed in its part of this combined Allied effort.[19]

Alexander – notorious for his light hand and lack of 'grip' – was guilty of not reining in his subordinate.[20] His communications with

Churchill revealed nothing adrift, and certainly no hint of reproach for Clark. It was only later, in his memoirs, that Alexander claimed that had Clark stuck to the plan, 'most of the German forces would have been destroyed'. It was the 'immediate lure of Rome for its publicity value that persuaded Mark Clark to switch the direction of his advance'.[21] American historians generally accept Clark's view that escape routes through the hills north of Valmontone obviated any likelihood that closing Route 6 would have trapped many Germans. The British Army official history is generous to Clark as well. In addition to the many escape routes available north of Route 6, the Eighth Army bungled the pursuit from Liri valley.[22] So, in retrospect, there was plenty of guilt to go around for the escape of German forces from Alexander's trap.

The fighting in Italy was followed closely by the international press. Not surprisingly, the more strident American papers like the *Chicago Tribune* ran headlines throughout lauding the successes of the 'Yanks and the French'. During the first two weeks of Diadem the *New York Times* headlines frequently trumpeted 'Allied' success and 'Allied' forces. But after 25 May and commencement of the 'race to Rome' the battle is largely American. Clark's decision to alter the plan and shift his thrust through the Alban Hills is reported as a feint to deceive the Germans.[23] From 2 June to 5 June the headlines report the triumphant American March to Rome, culminating in the final pre-Overlord headline on 5 June, 'Americans in First'.

This was not strictly true. The 1st SSF was at the gates of Rome on 4 June when Lieutenant General Keyes, commander of II US Corps, drove up. When told it would take 'the rest of the day' to occupy the city, Keyes said that would not do: Clark needed to be in Rome for a photo shoot at 1600 hrs. Brigadier General Robert Frederick, commander of the 1st SSF, thought he was joking, but Keyes never cracked a smile. Then Clark arrived. When it was clear that he could not make an easy entry, Clark got a photo posed in front of the 'Roma' city limit sign, then took the sign and left. When Frederick asked what the hurry was, Keyes replied, 'France is going to be invaded from England. We've got to get this [the capture of Rome] in the newspapers before then.'[24]

The 1st SSF captured the heart of Rome,[25] while units of II US Corps reached the Tiber to the north and south. The next day the *Globe*

13. General Mark Clark's moment: on the outskirts of Rome
with Lieutenant General Geoffrey Keyes, commander of II US Corps,
5 June 1944.

and Mail of Toronto ran a banner headline announcing 'Rome Falls: Canadian-American Unit Is First to Enter Capital'. But Clark was not about to share the limelight. The 1st SSF history records that it 'was not permitted to remain in Rome to participate in the orgy of celebration which swept through the city'.[26] Nor were the two British divisions of Clark's army invited to participate.

Clark made a formal entry into Rome on the morning of 5 June 1944. Crowds cheered, he met the Pope, was photographed driving around the Colosseum and had a photo op with his corps commanders.[27] Alexander sent him a warm telegram of congratulations. Clark felt that the Fifth Army had paid a price in blood over the winter of 1944 – and in the drive to Rome – and it deserved the accolades.[28] Alexander stayed well clear of the celebrations. He spent the day driving himself around Rome in a jeep taking in the sights.[29] The delay in launching Overlord gave Clark one day on the front covers of the world's newspapers before the big event swept it all away.

American news magazine coverage of Clark's victory was typically more nuanced than the daily print media. On 5 June *Time* proclaimed that the 'nightmare' in Italy was finally over and gave the credit to Alexander. Five days later the *Nation* raised doubts about the merits of focusing on Rome. 'The symbolic and political value of the Liberation of Rome need hardly be stressed,' it observed, 'but its military significance is not yet clear.' After all, the objective in Italy had been the 'destruction of enemy forces. This end has still to be achieved.' *Time* echoed that point on 12 June: Kesselring's army had escaped.[30]

Ernest Fisher's official American account of Diadem, published fifty years after the event, got the final tone right. 'Rome had been essentially an Allied victory,' Fisher wrote, 'though only Americans savoured the flavour of triumphal entry into the ancient capital.'[31]

* * *

The British Army that gathered in the south-east of England in April and May was the most lavishly equipped, most modern and mechanised army that ever left the shores of Great Britain. This was part of a long and consistent plan on the part of the War Office to ensure that the expeditionary force for the Second Front had everything it might need.[32]

It is one of the mantras of the Normandy literature that the American Army was an expression of that nation's unique motor-vehicle culture, a manifestation of Henry Ford and the industrial might of Detroit. That was all true. But the British Second Army was also the product of a modern, motorised industrial power. It would land more vehicles – including more varied armoured vehicles – on D-Day than the Americans. David Edgerton has argued that the quantity of British mechanised equipment was matched only by its superiority over anything the

Americans landed.[33] Many would disagree. But nothing in the American order of battle matched the 50-ton (plus) Churchill tank. Generally disparaged for its ungainly appearance, slow speed and limited firepower, the Churchill could crush all the beach obstacles except Belgian gates, and it could crash through the hedgerows that would baffle the Americans during the first five weeks ashore. Winston Churchill was dismayed at the scale of vehicles allocated to British assault forces and made an effort to trim them back on the eve of D-Day.[34] That failed. The British Second Army was the most sophisticated and modern army yet fielded by the British Commonwealth, and the most powerful to land on D-Day.

The British also worked hard to ensure that the morale of the men assigned to Operation Overlord was good. In many ways, this was the much harder task: five years of war had taken their toll. Throughout early 1944 army psychiatrists weeded out the war-weary and those likely to falter. Veteran formations like the 50th and 51st divisions and the 7th BAD provided essential experience and leavening, but like the Americans the majority of British assault troops were inexperienced conscripts.[35] Censors reported a high state of morale and readiness in April. That mood began to slip in May as training programmes wound down, as troops moved into holding areas, and as the waiting began. The mood was darkened even further by the paltry pay increases for soldiers announced by Churchill's government in April.[36] The amounts were risible – $3d$ a day for the average Tommy – and in some units prompted talk of rebellion. Ernest Bevin, Minister of Labour, was watching – with tears in his eyes – as soldiers embarked at Portsmouth, when one asked, 'Ernie, when we have done this job for you, are we going back on the dole?'[37]

The British Army censor's report at the end of May therefore came with a warning. The British Second Army was a citizen force 'with absolute faith in the righteousness of its cause, with no love of soldiering, but with a grim determination to see this thing through and the sooner the better'.[38] 'It was "clear",' Jonathan Fennell writes, echoing the censorship report completed just after D-Day, 'that a postponement of the operation might have had serious repercussions. Eisenhower's decision to launch the invasion on 6 June in spite of inclement weather and obvious risks must be understood in this light.'[39] The best that could be said of British morale on the eve of D-Day was that it was high, but fragile.

The contrast with the 3rd CID – indeed all Canadian formations in England – was stark: Canadian morale continued to rise as D-Day drew near. Like the British, the Canadian Army had worked hard to weed out those ill-suited to what lay ahead. And like the British, the training was hard but purposeful, which contributed enormously to their confidence. Canadians, too, looked forward to going home: many had already been away for four years. But the Second Front was what the Canadian Army had been built, equipped and trained for. 'The troops are relaxed and in the highest spirit,' one Canadian Army psychiatrist reported in mid-May. News that I Canadian Corps had breached the Hitler Line in Italy 'had an inspiring effect'. As D-Day approached Canadian morale remained excellent. Canadian troops felt that 'their hour is about to come', the army's mail censor reported. 'They are ready, fighting fit, tough, well trained, confident trps, proud and longing to show their mettle. They say that this is the moment that have lived for, trained for, left their homes for.'[40] It is unlikely that the all-volunteer 3rd CID was matched by any Allied formation in Operation Overlord for its level of training, its commitment to mastering the essential military skills, the quality of its junior leaders or its palpable urge to join the fight.[41] One can only wonder might have happened in Normandy with five eager Canadian divisions ashore by D+14 instead of one.

The other lingering problem that kept British planners awake at night was the shortage of trained men. Virtually all of Britain's remaining manpower was committed. On 30 May 1944 Major P.B Earle, Brooke's Military Assistant, wrote to Freddie de Guingand, Monty's Chief of Staff, advising caution. Given the recent and rapid build-up of German forces in Normandy, Earle predicted – very perceptively – that the Allies would not break out until August. We are, he warned, 'about to embark on this vast project with only THREE WEEKS' RESERVES [of personnel] . . . This is unheard of in the annals of history.'[42]

* * *

The British public-relations objective for Overlord was to present the empire and Commonwealth role as a single unified 'British' effort. Despite the significant Canadian contribution, Mackenzie King was not invited to the final briefing on 15 May, although for some reason Jan Smuts was there. Certainly, Montgomery's view of the Canadians as

'British' had not changed. He refused to allow Mackenzie King to visit the 3rd Canadian Division, and the Prime Minister did not press his case. Mackenzie King also failed to defend Crerar when Montgomery expressed doubts, over lunch on 18 May, about his ability to command, and his wish that Guy Simonds would take over the First Canadian Army. According to Crerar's biographer, Montgomery took Mackenzie King's apparently ambivalent attitude towards Canadian independence and failure to fully back Crerar as a victory for his views: the Canadians were British, just like all the other Dominions.[43]

The Canadians were also all but omitted from the War Office and the MOI documentary *Eve of Battle*. The film was intended for distribution in the week immediately following D-Day, when there would be little hard news. It spoke of British, Czech, Polish, Norwegian and French soldiers, 'and from North America the Americans' who would join in the liberation of Europe. Since there was no mention of Canadians perhaps it did not matter where they were from. These men were backed by the industrial output of Great Britain and America, and basic materials from other places. Apparently, Canada's total industrial and material contribution to Overlord was 'ore'. The RCAF got a passing nod as part of the huge air forces of Great Britain, the British Commonwealth and America that were already smashing the German war machine.[44] *Eve of Battle* also highlighted the experience of Anglo-American forces at El Alamein, Kasserine Pass and Italy, and how they had a score to settle. Nothing was said of the Canadians or of the disaster at Dieppe. In fact, the US War Department had released the German newsreel of the Dieppe landings – conceded by many to be an important precursor to Overlord – for general distribution in early May 1944 as a 'sobering' reminder of what lay ahead.[45]

Eve of Battle was a scandalous slight to Canada. When SHAEF PR screened the rough cuts on 22 May the Americans were stunned by its utter neglect of Canada's major role in Overlord. As Eisenhower's PR staff informed Washington, 'neither the script nor pictures gives adequate coverage or proportional representation to Canadian participation' and 'it is necessary to cut in Canadian film[,] and commentary should mention Canadian contribution wherever generalizations are used as well as specific reference to air, ground and sea services . . . all of which are deeply involved'.[46] The changes to *Eve of Battle* urged by SHAEF never happened, it was just too late. On 5 June Ernest Dupuy informed Washington that Canadian footage would not arrive in time. He asked that one line on the Canadian role in defence of the UK be inserted and a mention that the Canadians 'at Dieppe first probed the Western Front'. Not even those changes were made. Even before Overlord started, the Canadians had been written out of the D-Day story.

Mackenzie King was not prepared to let that happen. SHAEF had asked the Dominion Prime Ministers for their silence and conformity to the D-Day media plan, but Mackenzie King refused to play along. He reminded the British of the Sicilian debacle the previous July when, despite promises to the contrary, Operation Husky was described to the world as an 'Anglo-American' assault. On 19 May, Churchill passed along Eisenhower's hope that (in Mackenzie King's words) 'it would not be necessary for an announcement to be made as to the time of the Canadians going into action. That it was very desirable that the enemy should not find it out.'[47]

Eisenhower had his reasons for making that request. The most char-itable thing that might be said about *Eve of Battle* was that it supported the Canadian role in the Fortitude deception. It is unlikely that Mackenzie King knew of Operation Fortitude, nor could he have possibly known of Operation Nunton, the deception plan in Italy that held German reserves in the north in the early stages of Diadem. Nunton was successful until the moment, on 17 May, when I Canadian Corps was identified in action in the Liri valley. Eisenhower's appeal to say nothing of the Canadian role in Overlord therefore came just two days after the collapse of Nunton revealed what could quickly happen to Operation Fortitude if the Germans found out where the Canadians were.[48] Mackenzie King was undeterred and enlisted the Dominions Secretary to help. Given Canada's major role in Overlord, Viscount Cranborne suggested that if the Canadians could not be identified, then no one should be. Ike had already suggested that only 'general terms should be employed', and so the term 'Anglo-American' was dropped in favour of the more generic 'allied forces'. A SHAEF press directive to that effect was issued on 26 May 1944.[49] Ironically, that descriptor ensured that much of Britain's effort in Normandy would be written out of the American press coverage over the coming months.

* * *

On 15 May 1944 – the day Churchill left John Curtin to make the futile case for a united empire and Commonwealth – the last great briefing for Operation Overlord took place at St Paul's School, London. Chairs across the front of the simple classroom were reserved for King George, Churchill, Smuts and the British Chiefs of Staff. Behind them, on hard benches stretching to the back, were ranks of generals, admirals, air marshals and lesser mortals in descending order. Eisenhower later wrote that Hitler missed his chance that day to kill the entire senior command of the western Alliance with a single bomb.

Everything was now in place for the great assault on France – or so it seemed. Even as the briefing assembled, the final operational orders for D-Day were being issued. The basic plan, the order of battle, the tables of loading, allocation of objectives, call signs, landing schedules – everything needed to get the great machine moving – were now fixed. 'This is probably the largest and most complicated operation ever undertaken,' Admiral Sir Bertram Ramsey, RN, observed in the introduction to naval orders for Operation Neptune, the assault phase of Overlord. The final 'Op Plan No. 2-44' for the Western Task Force, which landed the First US Army, was issued on 21 April: it was an inch thick, double-sided on foolscap paper – all the Canadian vessels in it were identified as British.[50]

Operational orders in the 21st Army Group, with their extensive appendices, tables, traces and schedules, had poured forth in a cascade of paper during April: army to corps, corps to divisions, and by mid-May divisions to brigades and regiments. By the time General Eisenhower called the 15 May briefing to order in St Paul's School, the staff work of modern warfare was largely complete. In that sense the die was cast: it was too late to tinker. Eisenhower now had only three options: launch as planned, postpone the assault (the staff work to do that was ready, too) or cancel it.

Eisenhower spoke first, but much of the attention – especially that of historians – was on Montgomery. There was quiet confidence in his ability. In the early morning hours of 6 June Quentin Reynolds told millions of American radio listeners that they could feel comforted that

Montgomery was in command. The little man in the black beret was a meticulous planner, sparing of the lives of his men, and he 'has a habit of being right'.[51] Monty's comments that day were part information, part inspiration, and he came across as very much in command. 'He looked trim and businesslike,' Nigel Hamilton wrote, and spoke for just ten minutes in a 'tone of quiet emphasis'.[52]

Montgomery warned that Rommel would try to 'Dunkirk' the landings, keeping German armoured reserves close to hit the Allies quickly and hard. The greatest threat to the plan was the ten Panzer or Panzer-Grenadier divisions in France. By May four Panzer divisions were already either in lower Normandy or within easy striking distance. These divisions, and enough mobile infantry divisions, would reach the landing area by D+6 and make a major counterattack possible. The Panzers were supported by a dozen first-rate infantry divisions. Rommel would not wait. He would hurl these at the landings immediately, just as the Germans had done in Sicily and Italy. It was vital to get well established inland as soon as possible to withstand the initial counterattacks. If those failed to dislodge the Allies, Rommel would cordon off the assault while building up reserves for a massive blow later.

Rommel's obsession, Montgomery contended, would be Bayeux, which 'splits our frontal landings in half'. But Monty's ultimate objective was much more ambitious than merely securing Bayeux. 'Once we can get control of the main enemy lateral Grandville-Vire-Argentan-Falaise-Caen, and the area enclosed in it is firmly in our possession,' which Monty hoped to achieve by D+17, 'then we will have the lodgement area we want and can begin to expand.'[53] The capture of Cherbourg, as a key port for further development of the assault on France, remained the initial strategic target – with luck by D+8. This was to be followed by expansion of the lodgement to include ports on the Biscay coast and occupation of the area between the Seine and the Loire valleys west of Paris by D+90.

Others spoke that day as well. Admiral Ramsay explained the naval plan, and Air Chief Marshal Leigh-Mallory outlined the air effort. Bradley, commander of the First US Army and the senior American operational planner, said a few words. He secretly harboured doubts about Montgomery's optimism about the likelihood of driving deep into

Normandy with armoured forces on D-Day. But this was not the time to share them.[54] As Bradley observed in his first memoir, 'Montgomery's incomparable talent for the "set" battle – the meticulously planned offensive – made him invaluable to the OVERLORD assault . . . nothing was left to chance or improvisation in command.'[55] Montgomery's optimism – so essential on the eve of the great undertaking – would soon be recalled by many of his colleagues with bitter resentment.

In April the prospects for Overlord were still good. However, they were changing fast – and for the worse. The month-long delay occasioned by the January expansion of the Overlord plan allowed the Allies to acquire the needed landing craft and support shipping, but it helped the Germans, too. As each day slipped by the Germans added more concrete, more mines, more guns and more wire. Omaha beach, which had been largely undefended in March, was now bristling with strong points. In May alone the strength of mobile divisions in lower Normandy increased by 50 per cent. Delay was not on the Allies' side. In those frantic final weeks of preparation COSSAC's worst fears, and those of other Allied planners, therefore came to pass: the Germans reinforced the Cotentin peninsula with infantry, and concentrated Panzer divisions near Caen. If Rommel had had his way, by the end of May four Panzer divisions would have been echeloned south and west of Caen, poised to attack to the sea at Courseulles-sur-Mer – Juno beach.

Senior Allied officers were clearly aware of the challenge they now faced. The official historian of British intelligence, F.H. Hinsley, suggests that the news on these German forward deployments just prior to D-Day was not 'spelled out with sufficient emphasis when relayed to the Commands'.[56] Perhaps. In late May the British Second Army estimated that, of the roughly 900 German tanks between the Loire and Seine rivers, 550 were concentrated in the Caen–Bayeux area. Worst still for the men of I British Corps, most of these, some 500, were thought to be around Caen. According to intelligence estimates, these included a large number of both Panthers and the heavy Tiger tank with its lethal 88mm gun. I British Corps was warned of this intelligence estimate on 22 May, and of the fact that the 21st Panzer Division – thought to be uniquely well equipped – had moved from Rennes to just west of Caen.[57] The Americans were also warned that the 352nd

German Infantry Division, a small first-rate horse-drawn field division, was now garrisoned at Saint-Lô, and could deploy quickly to Omaha beach.

There is no indication that these revelations changed anything for the Allies. The British had known since April that the 3rd British Infantry Division (BID) lacked the combat power to take Caen on D-Day: reserve forces would have to do that. The open fields north and west of Caen had long been identified as the crucial ground for a major Panzer counterattack – by both the Allies and the Germans. Rommel's redeployment of forces in the spring of 1944 confirms that, as would his reactions to the landings. The Canadians were already trained and equipped to stop that Panzer attack. By May the operational orders had been issued and everything was moving at a frantic pace. The scale and complexity of Overlord precluded any major last-minute adaptation of the plan.

Everything, that is, except the American airborne landings. The original plan was for the 101st Airborne Division to land behind Utah beach, and the 82nd Airborne Division to drop around Saint-Sauveur-le-Vicomte, astride the Cotentin's west coast road north of La Haye-du-Puits. Eisenhower's Deputy Commander, Air Marshal Leigh-Mallory, and others were anxious about the possibility of the 82nd being destroyed before it could be reached. The steady German reinforcement of the Cotentin peninsula in May made this increasingly likely. The tipping point came late in the month when the 91st German Infantry Division was confirmed in the area. At that point it was agreed to shift the 82nd drop zone east, astride the Merderet River north of Sainte-Mère-Église and adjust the landing zones for the 101st accordingly.[58]

This did not ease Leigh-Mallory's anxieties. He remained convinced that the Americans would not even reach the ground safely, and he wanted all the airborne landings on the Cotentin cancelled to avoid a 'futile slaughter'.[59] The issue came to a head at a SHAEF meeting on 27 May, when Leigh-Mallory recommended that the drops be cancelled. Bradley, backed by Montgomery, protested that the risk was acceptable. More alarmingly, Bradley warned that if the airborne assault behind Utah was cancelled, he would cancel the landing as well.[60] This threatened to put the whole scheme for capturing Cherbourg – and it seemed the whole of Operation Overlord – at risk of failure. In the end, Eisenhower backed Bradley and announced that the airborne attack would go ahead. When Leigh-Mallory protested again the next day, Ike told him to put it in writing.[61]

As for the rest, it was much too late to change. It had taken months to wrangle the landing craft already assembled. Nothing could be done to strengthen the assault forces headed for the Anglo-Canadian beaches, where the Panzers were known to be massing. Further delay – until the next moon and tide cycle in early July – would simply allow the Germans to reinforce lower Normandy even more. It may be that Hinsley was right, that the importance of the changed operational situation by late May was not conveyed effectively to lower commands. What could they have done? By the end of May there was nothing to do except launch the assault and hope that it all worked out.

* * *

In the spring of 1944 those on invasion watch – military and civilian alike, Allied and Axis – tracked the weather. During the last weeks of May and the first days of June the English Channel was glorious: bright, sunny and calm. Ideal weather, or so it seemed, for launching the Second Front. Robert McCormick's *Chicago Tribune* ran a regular feature called 'Invasion Weather' that included tide times. The good weather, and Allied operations in Italy, prompted reports from Berlin on 29 May that the invasion was on for as early as the following Tuesday: 6 June 1944.[62] Their cue may well have been the commencement of regular Allied radio broadcasts to western Europe on 20 May warning people to be prepared and listen for instructions.[63]

Had the weather remained good, this German guess of 6 June would have been out by a day: Overlord was scheduled for Monday, 5 June. Forces were already on the move on 3 June when the forecast called for high winds and heavy seas in the Channel for the next two days. At 0430 hours on the morning of 4 June, Eisenhower ordered a twenty-four-hour delay, perhaps more if the weather did not abate. Anything beyond forty-eight hours put the whole operation in jeopardy. At 2130 hours on 4 June SHAEF's weatherman, the dour and humourless Scot Group Captain James M. Stagg, RAF, advised Eisenhower that conditions would moderate slightly beginning Monday afternoon and into

Tuesday, 6 June. Winds would ease to 25–30 knots westerly and the cloud cover lift from 500 feet to perhaps 3,000 feet and clear by about 50 per cent. The air force did not like the forecast, but the navy and Montgomery were prepared to go. So was Eisenhower. 'I'm quite positive we must give the order,' he said quietly to his senior staff when conditions were reviewed at Southwick House outside Portsmouth on the evening of 4 June. 'I don't like it, but there it is . . . I don't see how we can possibly do anything else.'[64] The order was issued at 2145 hours and the whole vast armada was soon on the move – again.

The forecast and the decision to go were reviewed at 0430 hours the next morning, Monday, 5 June. As the anxious staff assembled, Eisenhower looked at the lanky RAF officer and said quietly, 'Go ahead, Stagg.' The weather, it seems, would moderate more than was previously thought on 6 June and then deteriorate again on the 7th, which might trap the assault on the shore without chance of reinforcement or withdrawal. Eisenhower pondered the risk, discussed it with his staff and then said simply, 'OK, let's go!' This time there was no turning back.

If the increase in armoured formations in front of I British Corps bothered Eisenhower he never mentioned it – then or subsequently. Perhaps that was because in the final days before D-Day he, too, was anxious about the American air assault at the base of the Cotentin peninsula. On the eve of D-Day he went to the airfield at Newbury to see off the 101st Airborne Division. Eric Larrabee wrote that there was an uneasy awareness that some of these men were about to die and that Eisenhower was ultimately responsible for their fate (as indeed he was for every man in the assault). British reporter Goronwy Rees observed that during Eisenhower's visit to the paratroopers it was not clear who was reinforcing whom. Ike shook hands with as many as he could, asked names and enquired about hometowns and family. He stayed until the last C-47 lifted off and then turned, with tears in his eyes, and said quietly, 'Well, it's on.'[65]

Book III

OVERLORD

CHAPTER 19

THE SECOND FRONT AT LAST

This was D-Day and the World was waiting.

Colonel Barney Oldfield, USAF[1]

The first Allied troops landed shortly after midnight, when three British gliders hit the ground within yards of the bridge over the Caen canal at Bénouville – famous thereafter as Pegasus Bridge. The second bridge, over the river, fell quickly too. About the same time pathfinders from the British 6th Airborne Division dropped east of the Orne to mark landing zones for the 9th Airborne Brigade, which began to jump at 0050 hours. Poor weather, flak and flooded terrain dispersed the British airborne landing (which included the 1st Canadian Parachute Battalion). However, the key objectives were taken.

American paratroopers landed amid bocage and flooded river valleys, in an area heavily garrisoned by troops expecting an airborne assault. Cloud cover, heavy flak and inexperienced C-47 pilots dispersed the 101st Airborne all over the Contentin peninsula. The 82nd Airborne Division, coming in to secure crossings of the flooded Merderet River, was sufficiently concentrated to secure the high ground behind Utah beach.

By 0350 hours it was clear to the Germans from the scale of the airdrops that a landing between the Orne and the Vire was imminent. Beyond that, confusion reigned. The 200 dummy parachutists dropped near Saint-Lô added to the confusion. Unlike the little rubber men in the film *The Longest Day*, these were nearly man-sized canvas dummies fitted with pyrotechnics to produce a sound and light show. They were supported by two British 'Special Air Service' teams equipped with pyrotechnics, radios and a scheme to simulate a whole division. At 0320 hours half of the 352nd Division – the 915th Grenadier Regiment, the division's Fusilier battalion, and twenty-four assault guns organised as 'Kampfgruppe Meyer' – set off in requisitioned French vehicles and bicycles to destroy the dummy airdrop.[2] It took Meyer's 'mobile' force hours to reach the drop zone. Meanwhile the 21st Panzer Division was released at 0430 hours to crush British airborne forces north-east of Caen.[3] About a third of the division was already deployed north of the city; the rest were garrisoned south-west along the Orne River. Elements north of Caen moved east to recapture the bridges at Bénouville, while a Kampfgruppe moved up west of Caen to replace it. The third Kampfgruppe of the 21st Panzer moved south of Caen to attack the airborne troops east of the Orne River and Caen canal.

Sunrise revealed the sea literally covered with ships. If there was any doubt about the Allies' intent, that was dispelled at 0530 hours when the naval bombardment began, 'with what one eyewitness described as a single ripple of flashes running across the entire horizon'.[4] Waves of bombers then dropped their payloads along the assault beaches – most too far inland to have any effect. As H-hour – the time for the amphibious landings – closed in, destroyers, specialised landing craft equipped with rockets, and LCTs carrying the self-propelled artillery regiments of the assaulting divisions drenched the beaches with fire. Canadians sweeping the approaches to Omaha were barely a mile offshore as the first wave of assault went by. The amphibious assault commenced at Utah beach at 0630 hours, then it rolled like a wave eastward along 80km of coastline with the set of the tide. By 0830 hours tens of thousands of men were locked in desperate struggle along the Calvados coast.

* * *

The landings on Utah missed their beach by a mile, coming ashore in a more weakly held section of the dune. DD tanks of the 70th Battalion arrived on the beach a few minutes later after a 3,000-yard swim.[5] A sudden realisation that they were on the wrong beach occasioned debate about what to do next. Brigadier General Teddy Roosevelt, the 4th

USID's fifty-six-year-old second in command who landed with the assault, sorted that out smartly: 'We'll start the war from here!'[6] As Roosevelt pushed his troops inland the two other regiments of the 4th USID arrived and expanded the beachhead. Twenty-six M7 Priests, self-propelled (SP) 105mm guns, were deployed by the afternoon to provide fire support.[7] Several battalions risked German fire and simply waded across the flooded polder. The 22nd Regiment made it to Saint-Germain-de-Varreville by nightfall, and the 12th Regiment arrived just east of Sainte-Mère-Église by sunset – just in time to have the reserve airborne regiments land among them in gliders. By nightfall the 8th Regiment's 3rd Battalion had linked up with parachutists at Les Forge, the high ground south of Sainte-Mère-Église.

The situation on Omaha beach was starkly different. The landing area was itself a formidable obstacle. The 5km arc of magnificent beach between Vierville and Colleville-sur-Mer is overlooked by steep bluffs – tight to the sea at Vierville but gradually set back behind a dune to the east. By June 1944 Omaha was heavily fortified, with massive bunkers and powerful guns dominating it from either end, and extensive fortifications along the edge of the bluff and in the dune. It had also been reinforced just days before by a battalion of the 352nd German Division, and sixteen guns of that division's field artillery. The Americans had none of the specialised combat-engineer vehicles employed on the Anglo-Canadian beaches, only DD tanks, a few Shermans with dozer blades and a few armoured bulldozers.[8] Much of the obstacle clearance would be done on foot, by USN engineers below the high-water mark, and US Army engineers ashore. The planners of V Corps were confident that they had the firepower to get ashore quickly and safely. 'It was believed,' Adrian Lewis wrote, 'that the German defenders were of poor quality and in a poor state of preparation and readiness, and that American naval and air power would be decisive.'[9]

The sea swallowed much of V Corps' supporting firepower, crippling it for the next week. Anxious about catching crossfire from batteries on the Cherbourg peninsula, the DD tanks supporting the 1st USID were launched 6,000 yards out – in darkness, out of sight of land and into a heavy sea. Most went straight to the bottom – only two made it to the beach.[10] The naval lieutenant in charge of landing the tanks supporting the 29th USID ignored his orders and brought his two companies of DD tanks to the beach. The first three to roll onto Fox Green were immediately destroyed, but most got ashore.[11]

The artillery of V Corps fared worse. The amphibious trucks (DUKWs) carrying the twelve guns of the 111th Field Artillery (FA) launched at 0330 hours 5 miles offshore. Nine sank almost immediately; only one gun got ashore.[12] The M7s scheduled to land dry shod fared little better. But no beach between Vierville and Colleville-sur-Mer was safe for guns that morning, and only few landed in the afternoon. The 7th FA eventually landed six guns; the cannon company of the 16th regimental combat team (RCT) was lost at sea and only one gun of the 116th RCT's cannon company arrived. By 1900 hours on D-Day only twenty-nine American guns were in action on Omaha.[13]

Meanwhile, the two RCTs, the 16th from the 1st USID on the left and the 116th from the 29th USID on the right, landed along the main beach. A Ranger battalion on the extreme right was put ashore by British LCAs, as were the Rangers tasked with capturing the battery position at Pte du Hoc.[14] By 0830 hours the assault on Omaha was a shambles, as men and wrecked landing craft piled up on the beach. While V Corps staff pondered switching their landing to Gold beach, American infantrymen and combat engineers, supported by six armoured bulldozers, took Omaha the hard way: with small arms, satchel charges, whatever heavy weapons got ashore (losses of these at sea were heavy, too), determined leadership and exceptional heroism. Drenching fire from the sea had cut some lanes in the wire, and smoke from burning brushes obscured much of the battlefield, allowing desperate men to get forward. USN destroyers and several small British Hunt-class destroyers pushed well inshore to fire on the defences. The few tanks that landed near Vierville were also effective in suppressing German fire. By late morning small groups of Americans had winkled their way onto the bluff and were clearing the defences.[15] As the American official history observed, without tanks or supporting artillery (or mortars) even 'scattered resistance by small enemy groups constituted in sum a considerable obstacle to American advance'.[16]

By midday the Germans considered the Omaha landing a failure. Another battalion of the 352nd Division, detached from Kampfgruppe

Meyer, was sent to Omaha to help stem the landings, but the Germans launched only small-scale counterattacks on the perilous beachhead. One that included assault guns was 'broken up by the guns of USS *Texas* without the Americans ever becoming aware of its nature'.[17] By the end of the day V Corps had, at a cost of at least 3,000 killed, wounded or missing,[18] gained a slender foothold, little deeper than the old coastal road (now the D514). Mutual exhaustion preserved Omaha overnight. It remained vulnerable. As Gordon Harrison, the American official historian, concluded, 'the artillery that was planned to support the infantry attack particularly in the advance inland did not reach the shore'.[19] Nor did many of the infantry battalions' heavy weapons.[20]

The assault by the 50th BID on Gold beach was powerful and well executed: the best Allied landing of the day. It was supported by the full weight of British specialised armour and two regiments of tanks. And all the assault artillery was self-propelled, including five field regiments all equipped with the new Canadian Sexton 25-pounder SPs and eighty 95mm Centaur SPs of the 1st Royal Marine Assault Squadron.[21] The strong points at Le Hamel and Asnelles, coupled with more and better beach obstacles than anticipated, and the involvement of the 352nd Division, disrupted and delayed the timetable of the 231st Malta Brigade: it took two hours to get off the beach and start moving. The landings of the 69th Brigade to the east, at La Rivière went better. Here the DD tanks and specialised armour and infantry arrived about the same time and, as Simon Trew concluded, 'something resembling the all-arms battle intended in 50th Division's plan actually materialized'.[22] Within two hours 69th Brigade had cleared a route ashore and was moving inland.

British success on Gold beach was sufficient by 0819 hours that General Erich Marcks, the commander of LXXXIV German Corps, ordered his mobile reserve to counterattack. It will be recalled that Kampfgruppe Meyer, a full regiment of the 352th Division, had been sent off to Saint-Lô chasing dummy parachutists. They might have driven the Americans into the sea at Omaha, but the British represented a greater threat. Meyer's force had practised such an attack,[23] but the 50km daylight trek to an assembly area on the Sommervieu–Bazenville ridge was arduous. As the French trucks broke down or were destroyed by air attacks, more men walked. Meyer arrived at the concentration point east of Bayeux at 1550 hours after more than twelve hours of utterly futile effort. His last report was logged at 1600 hours, saying that he was about to attack. The 69th Brigade reported seeing 'forty SPs of the 1352nd Assault Gun Battalion', which were initially mistaken for tanks.[24] Otherwise, 69th Brigade scarcely noticed it. Meyer's attack probably wilted under intense British fire, much of it naval. At 1730 hours Kampfgruppe Meyer reported failure: Meyer was dead and so was his artillery commander. Only ninety men returned: four Sturmgeschütz (StuGs) SP assault guns were lost.[25] The defeat of the strategic reserve of LXXXIV German Corps was one of the unheralded Allied successes of D-Day. By the end of the day the 50th BID was in command of the crucial Sommervieu–Bazenville ridge, with the Seulles River as a moat to the south, and the leading elements of the British 7th Armoured Division were already landing.

East of Gold beach the landing sequence did not follow the set of the tide. The Canadians required a little more water over the offshore reefs for the assault on Juno beach. And so the next landings after Gold took place on Sword beach, near the Orne estuary. Here a gap in the reef opposite a largely undeveloped stretch of beach dictated an assault by brigades in echelon. The leading brigade landed on a two-battalion front, then three more brigades were to pass through in quick succession. Timing was crucial. The beach and its exits had to be cleared quickly, and then movement had to be swift to succour the airborne bridgehead and, if possible, snatch Caen.

The beach was dominated by a series of strong points, and the coastal town of Ouistreham at the mouth of the Orne River was a fortress. If this was not enough, on the high ground 3km south near Colleville-sur-Orne lay elements of Rommel's rapidly developing 'second line' of defensive positions. Strongpoint 'Morris' contained four 100mm guns and behind it strong point 'Hillman' had two 105mm guns. Tucked in safely behind the flat crest of Périers ridge still further south lay two batteries of 155mm artillery from the 21st Panzer Division.

The opening moves went largely according to plan. The pre-landing bombardment was the best on the day, most of the DD tanks arrived well before the infantry and engaged the defences, and the specialised assault and engineer armour did its job. Landings started at 0730 hours and by 0830 hours all of the 8th Brigade was ashore. They were quickly followed by two Special Service Commando brigades to clear the shoreline to the west towards the Canadians, capture Ouistreham and make contact with airborne forces holding bridges at Bénouville. The third force to land, the 185th Brigade, was to set out 'with speed and boldness' to capture Caen. This was now an aspiration, rather than an expectation. The reserve brigade, the 9th, landed last to secure the division's right flank and make contact with the Canadians. If the 185th Brigade failed to take Caen, the 9th Brigade was to attempt its capture from the west. Failing that, the 51st BID and the 4th Armoured Brigade were slated to land on D+1 for the task.

The Commandos reached the airborne bridgehead at Bénouville at 1300 hours, and the bridges over the river and canal were secured. Pressure from the 21st Panzer's Kampfgruppe Luck, however, forced Major-General Tom Rennie to divert some of his strength to Bénouville to help secure the bridges. And the work of the 9th Brigade was disrupted for some time when its headquarters was largely destroyed by a mortar attack. The result of all this confusion and delay was that the 185th Brigade's spearhead down the road to Caen (now the D60) was badly weakened. The 'dash' to Caen had stalled by early afternoon.[26]

Meanwhile, just before 0800 hours the 3rd CID began landing on Juno, astride the Seulles River at Courseulles-sur-Mer and around Bernières further east. The Canadians were supported by a full armoured brigade (roughly 160 Shermans), four artillery regiments equipped with ninety-six M7 Priests (and enough command and OP tanks to form an armoured regiment), 95mm Centaur SPs of the 3rd and 4th Batteries of 2nd Royal Marine Assault Squadron, and the full panoply of the 79th Division and RE armoured vehicles.

Courseulles presented the toughest waterline defences assaulted on D-Day. Five massive concrete gun positions straddled the entrance to the harbour at Courseulles. None of these bunkers were vulnerable to naval gunfire, and all survived the initial bombardments. Two full battalions manned the Courseulles defences. The 441st Ost Battalion, composed largely of Russians, quickly fled, but the German garrison fought well. Nine field guns supported the Courseulles fortress. The coastal defence batteries at Ver-sur-Mer and Mont Fleury, objectives of the 50th Division on D-Day, overlooked the port. Some artillery from the 21st Panzer Division was within range.

Two battalions of the 7th Canadian Brigade captured Courseulles. West of the harbour, where the DD tanks were late, casualties among the Royal Winnipeg Rifles were heavy. Once the DD tanks and armoured assault vehicles arrived the attack quickly moved inland. By 0805 hours the reserve companies were ashore. A few minutes later the Regina Rifles landed east of the Seulles River, in front of the village. Here the DD tanks had been engaging enemy positions from the water for nearly twenty minutes, knocking out guns along the beach. By noon the 7th Brigade was moving inland along the Seulles and the western side of the Sommervieu–Bazenville ridge.

To the east the 8th Canadian Brigade was supposed to land on either side of the Bernières-sur-Mer strong point and take the town from the flanks. But much of the assault touched down in front of Bernières and long before their supporting tanks arrived. The Queen's Own Rifles of Canada took Bernières by direct assault across about 50m of flat, wet sand: A Company left forty dead and wounded below the wrack line. Here, as at Omaha, skill, commitment and daring saved the day. The 8th Brigade's other assault battalion, the North Shore (New Brunswick) Regiment (NSR), landed west of Bernières on either side of gap 'N7' in the little hamlet of La Rive Plage. The NSR's A Company got through the defences west of N7 like a hot knife through butter, their landing immortalised in the only surviving footage of the actual D-Day assault (of which more later). But B Company east of N7 was trapped on the beach, which was soon littered with dead and wounded – and with armoured bulldozers, Royal Engineer armoured vehicles, Royal Marine Centaur SP guns and DD Shermans looking for an exit. Finally, the tank squadron commander simply led his tanks through the minefield in gap N7: three hit mines but a route was opened and soon troops and vehicles poured into the flank and rear of Saint-Aubin-sur-Mer. Just as this was being done the 48th Commando RM arrived in wooden assault boats and was badly mauled by machine-gun fire from the headland.

Saint-Aubin-sur-Mer was a rabbit warren of tunnels, trenches and gun positions stoutly defended by both Germans and Osttruppen (Russian prisoners enlisted in the German army). The Canadians discovered later that they had attacked the western edge of a fully developed coastal-defence system. The radar station at Douvres, the artillery and infantry headquarters in Tailleville, the strong points at Saint-Aubin-sur-Mer and Bernières, as well as the Tailleville forest – just a few kilometres back from the beach – were all connected by tunnels. The radar station itself was a steel-reinforced concrete complex five stories deep, surrounded by huge bunkers, anti-tank guns, wire and minefields. Not surprisingly, the NSR attack eventually stalled at Tailleville.

The Canadian assault through Bernières was also stalled for much of the day. South of the village then – as now – is flat open field from horizon to horizon, rising to a clear crest line on the Tailleville–Bény road about 3km distant. The first three M7s to move south of Bernières were immediately destroyed by a gun firing from more than 2,000m away. Until the gun was silenced no tanks ventured into the open, and without them the infantry would not go either. The chaos and confusion at Bernières only got worse when Major-General Rod Keller landed his reserve brigade there. By 1140 hours, as Will Bird wrote, 'Every lane and road and street and garden was jammed with troops.'[27] Until the guns on the high ground to the south were taken out, no one moved out of Bernières.

The storm surge at high tide around noon also adversely affected landing the anti-tank regiments that were the key to defeating the Panzer counterattack. Spring tides in the Baie de la Seine stand at high water for well over an hour, nearly two hours on a neap tide. The storm surge pushed it higher, virtually eliminating the beach.[28] The surf was so high that it was impossible to land towed anti-tank guns without swamping the Bren carriers pulling them. Eight guns of the 3rd Anti-Tank Regiment (RCA) all M10 SPs got ashore, but most of the 6-pounders had to wait until D+1. The forty-eight 17-pounder guns of the 62nd Anti-Tank Regiment, RA, fared no better. All four batteries arrived off Juno safely and on time, but only eight guns – all M10s – got ashore on D-Day. Their tardy arrival was one of the unknown costs of landing in bad weather.[29] Fortunately, only six of the 3rd CID's M7s Priests were lost on D-Day, leaving it with ninety 105mm guns to fight its first battles.

It was not until 1820 hours, after a fight to clear the Germans off the high ground south of Bernières, that the Canadian advance to Carpiquet began.[30] Terry Copp concluded that 'there is little doubt that the 9th Brigade could reach Carpiquet' before dark (*c.* 2230 hours) on D-Day.[31] But the commander of the British Second Army, General Sir Miles Dempsey, ordered everyone to stop about that time. What Dempsey was worried about was the attack on the 3rd British Division by the 21st Panzer Division.

* * *

The bulk of the 21st Panzer's armour was on the move south of Caen, headed for the 6th Airborne landings, when the priority changed to the destruction of the landing at Sword beach. The most direct route north was through the winding streets of the city. It took five and a half hours to complete.

By early evening the mailed fist of the 21st Panzer, Kampfgruppe Oppeln, with at least 124 tanks, and Kampfgruppe Rauch of two battalions of infantry and division engineers, were concentrated north of Caen. Both Kampfgruppen were liberally equipped with half-tracks, with towed and SP anti-tank artillery in support. General Marcks was at Lébisey to see them off. The ultimate objective was clear. 'Oppeln,' Marcks told his tank commander, 'if you don't succeed in driving the English into the sea, we've lost the war.'[32]

Kampfgruppe Oppeln's attack lapped along the western face of Périers ridge like a long ocean swell rolling down a beach, and like a wave it broke as it went. Panzers on the right were the first to feel the effects of fire from the Staffordshires' tanks and their supporting anti-tank guns. This fire forced the attackers west, across the face of the Staffordshires' A Squadron, which took its own toll on the Germans. Then, as Oppeln's tanks crested the western spur of Périers ridge, Staffordshire tanks and anti-tank guns in defilade shot them to pieces. By the time it was over fourteen German tanks were destroyed and fifty others damaged, with little loss to the British.[33] The attack, Max Hastings observed, had been 'pushed home without determination or subtlety'.[34] The power of the 21st Panzer had not been broken, but it was badly bruised.

Meanwhile Kampfgruppe Rauch reached the sea at Lion-sur-Mer without serious incident. Marcks planned to reinforce this success, but he was undone when 248 gliders and transports of a scheduled reinforcement of the airborne bridgehead darkened the sky. These were followed by fifty C-47s carrying supplies to drop across the Orne. The appearance of Allied aerial might was enough to recall both Kampfgruppen to their start lines north of Caen. This may be the only instance in the war when an armoured division retreated in the face of airborne troops. That ended what Buckingham called 'the strongest and most dangerous threat to emerge anywhere along the Allied invasion front on 6 June'.[35]

Major-General Rennie has since been chided by historians, mostly American and recently the German official history,[36] for lack of aggression and for failing to push onto Caen. This is a patently silly criticism. His division had seen off the largest and most deadly counterattack of the day. Everything Allied intelligence knew about the 21st Panzer indicated that it was a uniquely powerful formation, with Tiger tanks and probably a regiment of Panthers. There was no way that Rennie, or I Corps commander Lieutenant-General John Crocker, could know that the Mk IVs brushed away from the slopes of Périers ridge with such ease were the best that the 21st Panzer possessed. If the intelligence was right, they were just the tip of the spear: more, and bigger and better, were surely en route. In these circumstances consolidation was prudent.

In the event, more Panzers were en route. The two closest divisions, the 12th SS and the Panzer Lehr, belonged to the Panzer reserve controlled by Oberkommando der Wehrmacht (OKW), the German Army HQ. Gerd von Rundstedt, the Commander in Chief West, asked for these divisions at 0445 hours – OKW put them on standby. Shortly thereafter the 12th SS was allocated to LXXXIV Corps and ordered to assemble at Lisieux. Then, for the next five hours, uncertainty reigned. Indecision stemmed largely from not knowing what the Allied landings in lower Normandy meant. They were not a surprise. But throughout much of 6 June, Hitler and his staff debated whether they were just a feint. When Rommel returned to his headquarters at Roch Guyon west of Paris late on 6 June, he focused on defence of the Pas-de-Calais area, where the real attack was expected. It was also believed that the assault in the Fifteenth Army sector would be supported, in the words of the German official history, by 'an imminent attack on Antwerp'.[37] The latter, it will be recalled, had been the planning task of the First Canadian Army since autumn 1943.

Eventually it was decided to release the two Panzer divisions to destroy the landings south of the Seine. By late afternoon the 12th SS, Panzer Lehr, 21st Panzer and 716th divisions were assigned to I SS Corps.[38] By the time the orders were given it was already too late to achieve a decisive result that day. The Panzer Lehr was too far away, and the counterattack by the 21st Panzer was already underway. In any event, the decision to concentrate the 12th SS at Lisieux, ready to operate north or south of the Seine, had wasted precious time. The 12th SS was now ordered to concentrate at Évrecy, south-west of Caen. The 25th Panzer Grenadier Regiment (PGR), which had been garrisoned near Vimoutier and had spent hours moving north to Lisieux, now had to move south to Évrecy. The 12th SS's other units, the 26th PGR and its Panther battalion, had a full 200km to travel and could not be ready until late on the 7th at the earliest.[39] Rommel's plan for a rapid Panzer counterattack conformed to COSSAC estimates made in autumn 1943: the Panzer Lehr and the 12th SS would concentrate west of Caen, roughly along the Caen–Bayeux highway, and attack down either side of the Mue River valley.

The leading elements of the 12th SS began arriving around Évrecy by 2300 hours. Losses on the move were minimal. However, the SS had not budgeted fuel effectively, and the Panther battalion ran out of gas east of the Orne. Rather typically, Kurt Meyer, commander of the 25th PGR and later the division commander, blamed Allied fighter-bombers for the fuel shortage. Major-General Edgar Feuchtinger, commander of the 21st Panzer, commented after the war that there was plenty of fuel available, but the SS were either too arrogant or too stupid to ask for it.[40] So a critical element of the 12th SS missed the opening actions on 7 June.

At midnight on 6 June orders for I SS Panzer Corps attack were passed at the headquarters of the 716th Division, located in a tunnel in a quarry north of Caen.[41] The dying and wounded clogged the passageways. The mood was sombre. And the news was not good: the Allies were ashore in strength. Feuchtinger cautioned the group about the power of their enemy, which he had just witnessed at Périers ridge. Meyer was unimpressed. 'Meyer studied the map,' Feuchtinger recalled, 'turned to me with a confident air and said, "Little fish! We'll throw them back into the sea in the morning".'[42]

* * *

The first news of the Allied landings was carried on the German inter-national radio service in the early hours of 6 June.[43] CBS in New York logged the broadcast at 12.37 a.m. Eastern Standard Time. CBS had been preparing for this moment for months. But German speculation was not hard news, not a clarion call for action. The broadcast spoke of parachute drops and rumours of an imminent landing on the coast around the mouth of the Somme River. CBS reported the rumour in its 1.00 a.m. news, but declined to give it any credibility until the first SHAEF communiqué – issued at 9.30 a.m. London time – arrived at 3.32 a.m.[44] It was one sentence: 'Under the command of General Eisenhower Allied Naval forces, supported by strong air forces, began landing Allied armies this morning on the northern coast of France.'[45] With that, CBS switched to a steady stream of commentary, reflection, pundits and pre-recorded messages.

It was assumed by CBS, based on the German broadcasts, that the landings were north of the Seine – in the Pas-de-Calais. That prompted Quentin Reynolds to broadcast a long reflection on the importance of the Dieppe raid, which he had covered in 1942. 'Dieppe was not a failure,' Reynolds told his listeners, 'it was a glorious success.' Without the hard-won lessons from Dieppe, the Allies could never have launched the Second Front.

Churchill slept until 8.00 a.m., and then wandered down to the map room where the news was far better than he could have hoped.[46] He was soon working on a speech for Parliament. Roosevelt spent a fretful night. At 3.30 a.m. – the time of the first SHAEF communiqué – word arrived from the Pentagon that the assault was underway.[47] Like Churchill he got ready to address the nation. Mackenzie King was completely out of the loop. He understood that the landings would be later in the month, so he slept well on the eve of D-Day. His staff routinely monitored the German broadcasts, but waited for the SHAEF communiqué before waking him.[48] The communiqué simply spoke of Allied forces, as Mackenzie King expected. He was pleasantly surprised when later announcements originating at the 21st AG spoke of 'British, American and Canadian' troops. He learned later that his efforts in May to get the Canadian contribution recognised had failed. Only

Lieutenant-Colonel Richard Malone's last-minute very 'strenuous protest' to the Chief Censor of the 21st AG got the wording changed from 'British, American and Dominion' forces.[49] Another tempest in the imperial teapot had narrowly been averted.

As expected, news from the assault area was scant, and it remained so for days. The scores of reporters sequestered in the conference room at Senate House milled about in bored frustration.[50] The first German communiqué at 7.00 a.m. contained little news, and little real information emerged from the steady stream of broadcasts from Germany during the day.[51] By mid-morning there was not much left to say. 'It is neither good reporting, good faith nor good radio to spin it further,' CBS concluded at that point. At 9.38 a.m. CBS reverted to scheduled programming interspersed with breaking news.[52]

The pattern that followed over the next few days is one familiar to those who track modern news stories: little hard news in a matrix of context and analysis by reporters and specialists. This news gap was, of course, anticipated. Virtually all reporters assigned to Overlord assault forces wrote or recorded backgrounders: what it was like inside the assembly areas, during the final training, flying in a glider, waterproofing vehicles and the like. These were used extensively on D-Day.

The MOI effort to fill the information void in the early days included the documentary *Eve of Battle*, and extensive backgrounders featuring Britain's efforts to make Overlord a success. These backgrounders, the Fighting Packages with their large collection of photographs, began arriving at RAF Northolt for global distribution on 1 June: the last arrived in the early hours of 3 June. The RAF was instructed to get these out around the world immediately. Unfortunately, the Air Ministry did not share the MOI's sense of urgency. None of the Fighting Packages went out on the Saturday, 3 June transatlantic flight, and because the RAF did not fly the Atlantic on Sundays nothing left on the 4th either. Flying was cancelled on Monday 5 June because that was the original date for D-Day, and of course nothing flew the Atlantic on 6 June. When the MOI enquired on 7 June about their packages the Air Ministry replied blithely that they were now expected to be delivered to New York on the 13th. Duplicate sets were immediately despatched to New York via the USAAF, but by the time officials in Washington asked on 9 June why nothing had yet arrived it was already too late. Newspapers, newsreels and radio were already filling up with reports direct from the frontlines.[53] Bitter recrimination between Bracken and Sir Archibald Sinclair, the Secretary of State for Air, over the handling of the Fighting Packages went on all summer.

Fortunately, the British excelled at getting news out of France in the early days, and achieved a PR coup over the Americans on D-Day and the days immediately afterwards that fired American resentment. As noted above, every effort had been made to return either correspondents or their copy to the UK as soon as possible. Special brightly coloured press bags were supposed to be carried by any and all returning vessels. Motorcycle couriers at airfields and ports along the channel coast would carry press material to Senate House in London. At Fareham, near Portsmouth, the BBC established a recording and wireless transmitting unit where radio broadcasters and print press could have their stories recorded and sent to London.[54] BBC studios were also available in London for either recording or live broadcast. The latter were conducted with a censor sitting next to the reporter, primed to cut him off if he deviated from cleared scripts. And of course, the American, British and Canadian press were all equipped with dedicated wireless equipment. As planned, all reporting was 'pooled', and could be used by any agency. On D-Day CBS carried reports and recordings from the National Broadcasting Company (NBC), Mutual, the Blue Network and the BBC.[55] This also allowed reporters stuck in London to build their stories on more than the information provided at the morning briefings.

The relative success or failure of these efforts fuelled Anglo-American rivalry. In theory, getting text to England ought to have been simple: brought by reporters themselves, sent in courier bags, or via short-range wireless. It was assumed that most text, as well as photographs and film, would go by courier. The Americans went ashore with SCR-76 transmitters, while the Anglo-Canadians were to land with the British type 76 wireless set. Within days, each field-army press contingent would also land a larger, vehicle-mounted set, in the Anglo-Canadian case a type 33. With the exception of the Canadian type 33 set these were all hand-operated by key and could handle just a few thousand words per day.[56]

The commander of the Canadian Army press unit, Lieutenant-Colonel Richard Malone, believed it was possible to attach a 'Creed' teletype keyboard to the Canadian-made type 33 set to vastly increase its capacity. He was authorised to get the machine and began to train operators, when on 1 June the War Office declared that it was not possible to attach a teletype machine to a type 33 radio set, and he was not permitted to do so. When Malone threatened to make the issue political, the War Office relented, as much – Malone claims – to keep the Canadians quiet as to prove them wrong. But Malone was right, a teletype keyboard could be attached to the Canadian-built type 33 set. By 8 June, Malone's transmitter was sending back 24,000 words a day. In 1946 he boasted that 'many of the Allied war correspondents can thank the crazy experiment that was made with the Canadian set . . . that their stories cleared at all during the first ten days'.[57]

The flow of media coverage from the Anglo-Canadian beaches was a success from the outset. The first press copy received in London came from Ross Munro of the Canadian press: it arrived at 1130 hours. CBC's Matthew Halton filed his first story at noon.[58] These early returns owed much to one Canadian conducting officer, Captain Jack Wilson, who 'made trip after trip to the beach and waded out to the craft to hand the skipper the canvas press bag'.[59] Correspondents like Matthew Halton and Marshall Yarrow, a Canadian covering the 6th Airborne assault for Reuters, also went back to England to record and broadcast their accounts. Yarrow jumped in the early hours of 6 June and was back in the Fleet Street offices of Reuters later that day, exhausted and still covered in mud.[60] Halton spent the day on Juno beach and came back to England on 7 June to broadcast.

Not all press copy arrived. Charles Lynch, a young Canadian working for Reuters, watched the first thirty-four pigeons released at Courseulles-sur-Mer fly inland – towards Germany. He took the last two to the beach and pointed them towards England before letting go: they, too, turned east. Throwing a fist in the air Lynch denounced the birds as 'Traitors! Damned Traitors!' To his dying days Lynch remained 'bothered' that the makers of *The Longest Day* cast his role as a 'Limey'. 'It was a Canadian cry,' he wrote later, 'and it came from the heart.'[61]

The first film and photos to arrive in England were also from Juno beach. Canadian film footage was especially good and plentiful. It was shot on tripods by cameramen trained at Pinewood Studios in London. Al Calder later lamented that because North American newsreels were compiled in New York, Canadians – or anyone else for that matter – saw very little of their work.[62] That said, one two-minute Canadian D-Day clip became iconic. Among the first batch of film to arrive in England were two (perhaps three) reels from cameras fixed on the landing craft of A Company of North Shore (New Brunswick) Regiment at La Rive Plage. They recorded the LCA's approach to beach, the opening doors, the movement of troops across a smoky obstacle-strewn beach and some small explosions amid the beachfront houses. The footage was screened on D-Day in the War Office to 'gasps and cheering'. No other footage of the actual assault from across all Allied beaches ever made it back to England. According to James O'Regan, this Canadian film became 'the iconic moving picture of D-Day'.[63]

What set British reporting apart from the Americans from the outset was the success of their 'actuality' recording at the front using a small portable recorder dubbed a 'Midget'. The Midget looked and worked very much like a portable record player. A small turntable was driven by a wind-up mechanism, and a needle on the end of an arm cut grooves into acetate discs. The results were often spectacular. Unlike the Germans, who dubbed sound effects in the studio, BBC reporters could describe the scene with the sounds of battle raging around them.[64] 'Actuality reporting' was at the heart of the BBC's enormously popular daily *War Report*, which aired for the first time on 6 June 1944 after the 9.00 p.m. news. As Frank Gillard, one of the BBC's senior war reporters, concluded, actuality reports allowed 'listeners at home by their firesides' to travel 'for a few minutes into the heart of the battle'.[65]

No one used the Midget better than Chester Wilmot, the Australian who joined the BBC War Report Unit in May 1944. Wilmot, his technician Peter Cattle and their Midget began making recordings over the Channel and continued to do so after his glider thundered to a halt in a field east of Ranville at 0321 hours. He recorded the attack on the Merville battery early that morning, the landing of more gliders, the counterattack by the 21st Panzer that nearly reached the British HQ at Ranville later in the day, and much more besides. When a newspaper reporter departed for England on 7 June, Wilmot sent his discs along. His first actuality report aired at 0915 hours on 8 June.[66]

The situation on the American front in the first few days is a study in contrast. 'Nothing seemed to work as planned,' Barney Oldfield, Eisenhower's press aide, lamented years later.[67] The landing craft carrying the Utah beach SCR-76 radio, public-relations officer and censors was disabled on D-Day and simply returned to the UK. Omaha's SCR-76 radio arrived without its antenna. Attempts to jury-rig one failed. 'Reporters that day got their copy out helter-skelter,' Ernest Dupuy wrote, 'by Navy dispatch boat' or any other boat headed to England. Robert Reuben, a Texan working for Reuters who landed with the 101st US Airborne Division, was the first American reporter to get his copy to England: it arrived in Dover around 2130 hours attached to the leg of a carrier pigeon. The first report from Utah itself was not filed until 0300 hours on 7 June.[68] Reporters who got ashore safely on Omaha found that there was no way to get the copy quickly and reliably back to England. The courier-service boats were nowhere to be found. Only late in the day did copy begin to move from Omaha to England on casualty-evacuation craft.[69]

Attempts to make actuality reports from the American front also failed. Thomas Grandin of the Blue Network and his escorting officer Lieutenant Fuller drove their jeep straight into a water-filled shell hole, ruining Grandin's recording equipment. Over the next few days Grandin compiled material while trying to get back to the UK to broadcast. 'Time had just edged over into D plus four [10 June],' Oldfield writes, 'when Fuller deposited Grandin and dropped his pouch of beach-produced copy at the Ministry of Information in London'. By 0300 hours on 10 June, four days after the landings began, Grandin was on the air, talking to New York and recording his experience.[70]

The American audio scoop of the day came from George Hicks, an NBC reporter on the command ship USS *Ancon*. Hicks was just recording his impressions of the day around 1030 hours when the Luftwaffe attacked. He let his recording run, capturing, in Steve Casey's words, 'the uneven throbs of the attacking planes' engines, the howling whistles of descending bombs, and the brutal thuds of massive naval guns throwing up defensive fire'. Amid the excited description of the attack Hicks was able to report the downing of one of the attackers to the sound of cheers from the gunners in the background. His recording got to London and was relayed to New York. It aired at 1130 hours on 6 June on all the major networks.[71]

American airborne war correspondents and film- and photojournalists also had a frustrating day on 6 June. Only ten of the sixty automatic cameras fixed on Overlord's landing craft and vehicles produced results, and none seems to have survived. When Major Chester Hansen, Bradley's aide-de-camp, landed on Omaha beach around 1330 hours it was littered with 'rolls of film'.[72] The *Life* magazine photographer Robert Capa, landing with the thirteenth wave on Omaha beach around 0815 hours, shot some photos that have become legendary. He stayed only a few minutes and then headed back to England to meet his deadline for the 19 June edition (which appeared on American newsstands on 12 June).[73] Bert Brandt, working for Acme newspapers, got the first few photos of the American beaches back by 7 June. Despite some heroic and quite remarkable efforts on the part of reporters, the net result of the American Overlord press effort was an information gap in coverage that lasted for the several days.

Nowhere was the success of the British media in the opening phase of Operation Overlord more apparent than in America. Like everyone else, Americans craved news of the fighting. And they put special stock in what they heard on their radios. 'Radio was a daily companion,' Gerd Horten writes of this period, 'a window to the outside world, a trusted provider of news and information', and Americans listened to it an average of three to four hours a day.[74] On D-Day American radio audiences were 80 per cent larger than normal, and stations '"ruthlessly" scrapped all their commercials' in order to pack in the news.[75] During the first week of Operation Overlord, American reports came largely from studios in London or Fareham via the BBC, while Americans got their sense of the fighting in Normandy from those remarkable British actuality recordings.

The penetration of American airwaves by the BBC during the initial phase of Overlord was unprecedented. On D-Day some 725 of America's 915 radio stations broadcast BBC programmes. Six hundred and twenty-five of these stations were either major networks or affiliates who had their own reporters on the scene.[76] The BBC also made its recordings available to at least 200 independent American radio stations otherwise excluded from the syndicated feeds of the big networks. In New York seven of nine 'worthwhile' independents carried BBC programming. Fred Weber, operator of WDSU in New Orleans, was one of many independent operators who thanked the BBC and praised them for the quality of the coverage. The actuality reporting, Weber claimed, was 'superior to anything released by anybody in connection with the coverage of the invasion'.[77] Some, like WAJE in Morgantown, West Virginia, relied heavily on the BBC. Twenty-two broadcasts on D-Day, sixteen on D+1, and thirteen on D+2 on WAJE came from the BBC before American sources became readily available. The BBC even encouraged WLS-Chicago to set up a shortwave set to monitor them and to keep 'recording and using broadcast after broadcast'. Major networks did the same. The quality and quantity of the BBC programming also allowed independent radio stations to increase their market share in their listening area.[78]

The penetration of the BBC into the homes, workplaces and automobiles of America exceeded their wildest expectations. The interim report from New York compiled in mid-June concluded that 'On June 6th and 7th the vast majority of American radio listeners heard BBC Invasion broadcasts, and with several additional millions they also heard pooled invasion pieces. In this way millions were introduced to the BBC for the first time.' 'The BBC was not only first with a great deal of the news but exemplary in its presentation,' the *New York Times* observed on 11 June, 'and especially fine with its "actuality" broadcasts which were heard chiefly on independent stations.'[79] Henry Stimson felt the same way. On D-Day he sat glued to his radio, immersed in the coverage. Hard news was meagre, he confided to his diary on 6 June, but 'the whole country has been swamped with the greatest volume of reporters' reports and commentators' reports on the radio that we have ever had. Never has any great operation been reported in the detailed way from people right on the ground, so far as they could be, as this one. Never has radio shown up so fully as it has this time.'[80]

Amid the euphoria of the BBC success in America during the first week of Overlord, one dissenting voice offered words of caution. Henry

David, from the Research Department of the BBC's New York office, warned that this success was ephemeral, and not likely to change attitudes towards Britain and its war effort. People subconsciously select what they want to retain, David wrote on 21 June. 'Because of this selective mechanism even the fullest reporting of Britain's invasion role and achievements by radio and press, would [still] result in primary place being assigned to American accomplishments.'[81] It proved to be a prescient observation.

Dupuy claims that American media problems in Normandy were not fully sorted out until 10 June: in reality it took a little longer than that. The problem can be seen in American newspaper coverage. The *New York Times* had already gone to press when news of the landings broke: 150,000 copies of the 6 June 1944 edition had run. Presses were stopped and a 250,000-copy invasion special was printed. The new headline read, 'Allied Armies Land in France in the Havre-Cherbourg Area: Great Invasion is Under Way', with a map showing the Channel coast between the Scheldt estuary and Cherbourg. Sub-headlines told the basics of the story: 'Eisenhower Acts', 'U.S., British, Canadian Troops Backed by Sea, Air Forces', 'Montgomery Leads', 'Nazis Say Their Shock Units Are Battling Our Parachutists', and included mention of Communiqué No. 1. Inside this special edition were some fourteen stories related to Operation Overlord, mostly backgrounders including Washington's wait for confirmation, the lessons of Dieppe (a recurring theme), previous invasions of the Normandy coast, a glossary of 'Invasion Terms', New York's initial reactions, the latest bombing raids on Calais and the like. Coverage on 7 June was more extensive: a little more solid news amid a plethora of background pieces. The first photo of the beaches, an aerial shot from the US Signal Corps, was printed. The next day, 8 June, the *New York Times* carried the first of Bert Brandt's photos from Omaha beach. The first photo prints of the American landings arrived in Washington that day.[82]

Early coverage in American newspapers also reflected the imbalance in stories getting out of France. The first press report from the beaches to appear in the *Chicago Tribune* was Ross Munro's story of Juno beach, which was printed on 7 June. The *Tribune's* editorial that day talked about the importance of Dieppe as a critical formative experience for the Overlord operation. The next day the *Tribune* ran a British Press story about 'The Battle at Caen', in which a German Panzer counter-attack was smashed by Canadians (more about this below). That edition also ran a photo spread featuring several Canadian photographs. The headline on 9 June emphasised the intense armoured battles on the Anglo-Canadian front – 'Tank Battle Raging', the *Tribune* blared, while Rue reported that 'The battle of Normandy has been joined around Bayeux and Caen'.

The *Chicago Tribune*'s early coverage of the Normandy operation was very favourable to the Anglo-Canadians, in part because McCormick – and other American papers – had little else to work with. Americans were not happy about the evident bias in coverage. On 7 June the *Tribune* carried a short story of discontent at SHAEF about the lack of balance in reporting. 'British Press Show Partiality in News of Invasion', the headline read, citing 'an official of' SHAEF expressing disappointment at the heavy British emphasis on British operations. In an editorial two days later McCormick dismissed the charges of British bias. It was a natural thing to do, he claimed, something that Americans and Canadians do as well.

Fortunately for the US Army the solution to the problem of information flow lay at hand. The Overlord media plan called for the landing of low-power radios for press purposes on D-Day, followed on D+3 by two medium-power sets using Creed teletype keyboards operating at 400 Watts. Then, at about D+20, two 3kW transmitters were to be set up, one for the Anglo-Canadians and one for the Americans. These were to be 'super high-speed' commercial-style teletype sets, capable of sending text, voice and wire photos. The American set would be operated by civilians and broadcast direct to the US at a rate of 400 words per minute. Before D-Day SHAEF public relations were informed that the medium-power set designated for the American zone on D+3 was apparently unavailable. Brigadier Neville, the British officer in charge of the press wireless plan, was simply told that the 'Press Wireless' set would be substituted. He apparently assumed this meant another medium-power press wireless, not the super-high-speed Press Wireless set designated for D+20 or later.[83]

If Barry Oldfield is correct, the American medium-power set was not only available, it landed on D+4 and was soon functioning.[84]

According to Dupuy, the decision to send in the super-high-speed transmitter weeks early was taken in light of the US media failures on D-Day. The set landed in France on 12 June, was set up the next day at Vouilly, near First US Army headquarters.[85] When it fired up on 14 June the 3kW transmitter went on the air as 'SWIF' – 'SomeWhere In France' – broadcasting on an unauthorised wavelength that had been assigned to the USN in the Pacific. The signal connected 'crisp and clear' with the station at Baldwin, Long Island.[86] American war correspondents could now get copy to New York in twenty minutes.[87] The battle for Normandy was on.

CHAPTER 20

STOPPING THE PANZERS

On the actual day of battle naked truths may be picked up for the asking: by the following morning they have already begun to get into their uniforms.

General Sir Ian Hamilton, 1906[1]

On 10 June *Business Week* magazine reflected on the meaning and expectations of the Normandy campaign in a lengthy editorial entitled 'The Beginning of the End'. Finally, America's war effort was made manifest. 'Allied equipment is available in almost endless quantities,' and the Allies outnumber the Germans almost two to one. So the strategy, 'from the first, is to apply in reverse the blitz strategy which the Nazis so successfully employed . . . in the spring of 1940'. Germany's only hope was stalemate, 'to make the invasion so costly that the Allies will negotiate a settlement rather than pay the price of victory'. Movement became the essential metric. *Business Week* challenged Americans to 'Read each day's progress with this in mind'. As a rule, they did.

While the Americans expected a blitz, it was the British who really feared stalemate and attrition. As John Buckley writes, they 'simply did not have the manpower and resources to sustain the bloodletting that had accompanied the military effort of the First World War'.[2] On the eve of D-Day Britain's war dead amounted to roughly 298,000, many of them civilians. It was a far cry from the 750,000 killed in the Great

14. Montgomery and his army commanders, Omar Bradley (left) and Miles Dempsey (right), 10 June 1944.

War, but it was enough.[3] And Britain's bloodiest months lay ahead. There was only so much that a nation of 50 million people – even with a vast empire of hundreds of millions – could do. And so, as Buckley observes, the British Army adopted operational and tactical methods and doctrine that 'dovetailed neatly and elegantly with the prevailing political, economic and grand strategic pressures at play' in Britain during the war.[4] The British Army of the Second World War was simply not ready to accept the sacrifice and losses that their fathers and uncles endured a generation earlier.[5] This was a critical difference between the British and American experiences of the Great War.

Montgomery came to epitomise Britain's 'way of war' by 1944: deliberate, and by some standards, agonisingly slow. What Montgomery brought to the army was an artillery-based doctrine similar to that employed in 1917–18: a bite-and-hold operational concept that conquered territory with materiel, and then killed Germans when they – as prescribed by their own doctrine – counterattacked. The British hoped that this form of warfare would be less casualty intensive. Montgomery was also content to wage that kind of attritional warfare because of the British belief that the objective of operations (and tactics) was the destruction of the enemy's combat power. Only then was free movement possible. This had been the basis of his plan at El Alamein, Medenine and Sicily, and even Alexander's plan in Italy in May: destroy the German Army, then advance. Montgomery's plan for Normandy followed this pattern.

Britain's war effort therefore required a delicate balancing act: doing enough to ensure a 'significant influence on the postwar settlement' while not fatally damaging British military, diplomatic and economic power. 'Apart from opposing Nazis aggression,' Dan Crosswell continues, 'the single British war aim revolved around safeguarding the United Kingdom's standing as a global power.'[6] The British Army which Montgomery led onto the beaches of Normandy 'represented Britain's last great throw of the dice'. Crosswell claims that Eisenhower and Bedell Smith (and one might add a great many other Americans) never understood this, nor did Americans accept that Britain's approach to fighting the war was a legitimate expression of national self-interest.[7] For Americans in 1944 Britain was still the heart of a vast and enormously wealthy global empire, and its reluctance to push on regardless of the cost was evidence of the perfidy they had come to associate with the British.

The American conception of Normandy, as *Business Week* suggested, was quite different. Operation Overlord was to be – as Freddie Morgan described it in 1943 – the great conduit through which American military power could be channelled from San Francisco to Berlin. Like most armies born in revolutionary states, the basic doctrine of the American Army – an army of the people – was the attack. The US Civil War provided ample evidence of that, and so, too, did the Meuse–Argonne campaign of 1918. Marshall's enthusiasm for getting something ashore in France in

1942–3 regardless of the cost reflected that doctrine. The US Army was built for a war of movement. The scale of artillery it employed could be limited because the US Army Air Force would provide the mobile firepower it needed for wide sweeping operations. 'Movement was everything in American military planning,' David Kennedy wrote.[8] So far, except for Patton's bloodless drive across Sicily to Palermo, conditions in the European theatre had constrained this mobility. The opening of the Second Front would finally see America's large, mobile army unleashed.

Unfortunately, George Marshall's expeditionary army arrived in France – as Stimson feared it might – with many basic issues unresolved. This has been masked by the tendency of American historians to write uncritical action-based narratives. Americans, then and now, are tight-lipped about their difficulties. In contrast, one does not have to dig very deep into the Normandy-campaign literature to find fault with the British, not least because the British themselves have criticised their own efforts – and Montgomery. American and German historians are only too eager to pile on. The myth that the British, once ashore, did little – and did that poorly – remains remarkably durable in American popular culture. Steven Spielberg even worked it into his 1998 Hollywood blockbuster, *Saving Private Ryan*. When Lieutenant Hamilton (Ted Danson) asks Captain Miller (Tom Hanks) a few days after D-Day how things are going, Miller replies, 'Monty's taking his time moving on Caen. We can't pull out till he's ready.' After a quip about how overrated Monty was, Hamilton says laconically, 'You gotta take Caen before you can take Saint-Lô.' It's hard to know what to say about that one.

* * *

By any measure D-Day was a triumph. By the end of 6 June 1944 some 156,000 troops had landed, about 60 per cent of them British and Canadian. The beachhead was achieved at a cost of roughly 10,400 casualties, including 4,400 dead – the majority of them American, their count skewed by the tragedy on Omaha beach.[9] Churchill (and Mackenzie King for that matter) could relax: it had not been another First Day of the Somme.

In January Montgomery had set out three simultaneous objectives for the initial phase of Overlord: capture Caen, capture Cherbourg and defeat the German counterattack. Unfortunately, the enemy has a say in how all plans unfold, and Normandy proved no exception. The British airborne bridgehead held, but it was under intense pressure from the 21st Panzer Division. The 51st British Division, which General Dempsey hoped to use to seize Caen, was despatched across the Orne to help. Attempts by the 3rd British Division to push into Caen on D+1 were easily swept aside by defenders north of the city. The Canadians (of whom more below) were the first to reach a portion of their D-Day objectives on D+1, when the 7th CIB established their fortress position astride the Caen–Bayeux highway around Bretteville–Putot-en-Bessin–Norrey-en-Bessin in the early afternoon. Meanwhile, by noon the 50th BID had captured Bayeux, which the Germans left undefended in a fit of absentmindedness, had linked up with the Americans south of Port-en-Bessin, had reached the Drôme River in the west, and were driving on Audrieux south-east of Bayeux. For the moment, there was little in their way.

There was little in the way of V US Corps at Omaha either. They faced the shattered remnants of the coastal-defence forces and scattered elements of the 352nd Division. But the losses on D-Day were so severe that V Corps simply could not generate much combat power. A myth soon developed to explain that tragedy: all of the 352nd German Division had been deployed to the coast just before the landing. Eisenhower said precisely that to Marshall in his report on 9 June. Myth or not, V Corps was in no condition to press inland after D-Day. In the days following, artillery, tanks, ammunition and even battalion heavy weapons – mortars and machine guns – remained in short supply. General Leonard Gerow confided to Bradley on 6 June that the 'Brits may have to pull us out on Omaha'.[10] This happened over the course of the day. The situation on Omaha beach was the main Allied concern on D+1. Montgomery and Bradley agreed that the drive on Cherbourg would have to wait.[11]

While V Corps strived to claw its way forward, in the VII Corps sector on Utah, in Rick Atkinson's words, 'confusion remained the order of the day'. The air drops remained scattered, and the bridgehead across the Merderet River was not secure. On D+1 the Utah beachhead was threatened by the only major counterattack on the American beachhead in the immediate aftermath of D-Day.

The attack came from two directions, and at about the same time. The least dangerous was launched by German infantry and some former French tanks across the flooded Merderet River. They had seized control of the west end of what was now a 500-metre-long causeway and bridge leading to La Fière. The attack started around 0800 hours with a fierce bombardment, after which German infantry, led by four Renault tanks, surged onto the causeway. Mines, bazookas and 6-pounder anti-tank guns[12] soon took care of the tanks, while American small-arms fire scythed through the infantry. The Germans withdrew, hammered the Americans again with artillery and mortar fire, and then tried a second time. Eventually a truce was agreed to remove the German dead – estimated at 200 – and wounded.[13] They did not try that a third time.

Meanwhile four battalions of German infantry, supported by ten self-propelled guns, some armoured cars and three artillery battalions, gathered for a strike from the north down what is now the N13 (D974) straight into Sainte Mère Église. Lieutenant Waverly Wray, a hunter from Mississippi in command of a company of paratroopers, sensed trouble and set off on a lone reconnaissance. After ambushing the headquarters of the leading German battalion and wiping it out, Wray – less a portion of his ear – reported that the Germans were coming.[14]

The assault drove in the outer defences of Sainte Mère Église, and for a while, Harrison writes, the situation 'looked gravely threatening'. Then at noon the 8th Infantry Regiment swarmed onto the battlefield, along with about sixty American tanks. The Americans soon counterattacked, using secondary roads to outflank the Germans. Lieutenant James Coyle with E Company of the 505th Parachute Infantry Regiment (PIR) and two tanks eventually found themselves overlooking an entire German battalion deployed along the main road. They opened withering fire at virtually point-blank range. Soldiers of the 8th Infantry arrived to join in, and the German battalion was destroyed.[15] So, too, was the morale of the German attackers, who panicked and retreated.[16]

The high ground around Sainte Mère Église was now secure. The next day Ultra revealed that Germans had consolidated in front of Montebourg and along the Durance River the most direct route from Utah beach to Cherbourg.[17] The only other way to get there now was to drive west, across the base of the Cotentin peninsula – and that meant crossing the bridge and causeway at La Fière. It was going to take longer to get to Cherbourg than planned.

* * *

The third of Montgomery's primary objectives for the opening phase of Overlord was defeat of the German counterattack. Anticipating where the Panzers would go and how to defeat them was a central part of COSSAC planning. The British understood that any landing needed to go deep, and it needed to pack enormous firepower and consolidate for the Teutonic fury that was sure to arrive. Events at Gela, Salerno and Anzio demonstrated that: Normandy would be no different. Montgomery had warned on 15 May that Rommel would attack as soon as he had forces available, and try to 'Dunkirk' the landings. But apart from the attack of the 21st Panzer on D-Day, the Normandy narrative is silent on any Panzer assault in the early stages of Overlord. That does not mean that it did not happen: it just did not hit the British or Americans. The job of stopping the Panzers fell to the 3rd Canadian Division.

Rommel had wanted four Panzer divisions stacked astride the Mue River west of Caen by May 1944. By D+1 he had two in place north and west of the city, and a third expected to arrive the next day. It was enough to hit the Allies before they were fully consolidated. The 21st Panzer Division was to attack north of Caen again, across ground littered with the burning wreckage of its ill-fated attack the day before. On their left, the 12th SS Panzer Division (Hitler Youth) was to attack down either side of the Mue River. The Panzer Lehr was to join in west of the Mue River as it arrived. The attack was scheduled for 1600 hrs on 7 June, with instructions to drive the enemy into the sea and destroy him.

The two Panzer divisions slated to attack astride the Mue River were Germany's most powerful formations. Max Hastings described the 12th SS, composed of Hitler Youth led by veterans from the 1st SS Panzer Division, Leibstandarte Adolf Hitler, as 'the most formidable of all German units now on their way to Normandy'.[18] Its tank regiment (the 12th SS Panzer) operated ninety-eight Mk IVs and sixty-six of the new Mark V Panthers. All told, the division employed some 500 tanks and armoured fighting vehicles. All the infantry units of the 12th SS were overstrength, with rifle companies of 190 officers and men, while the motorised companies (one per battalion) boasted 225 all ranks. On 7 June each of those companies was augmented by pioneer platoons, bringing the average infantry company strength in the 12th SS to over 210, and 250 for the motorised companies. On 6 June, only the division's Jagdpanzer battalion was not fully equipped, and its battery of six 280mm Nebelwerfer rocket launchers had not yet appeared. The 12th SS had an operational strength on 6 June 1944 of roughly 17,000.[19]

The Panzer Lehr was also considered among the best in the German Army. As its name indicates, it was formed from training units. On 6 June the Panzer Lehr was in the midst of a move to the Eastern Front, with its Panther battalion (eighty-nine tanks) already on trains heading east. The rest of the division was available for operations in Normandy. That included ninety-nine Mk IV Panzers and thirty-one Jagdpanzer IVs. The Panzer Lehr's two infantry regiments were carried on 658 half-tracks. Only Lehr's artillery could be rated as ordinary.

On D+1 the 21st Panzer was also thought to operate Panthers and almost certainly Tigers. In fact, it was equipped with about 100 Mk IVs. Its 'special' equipment was a clever blend of German, Czech and Russian guns mounted on former French tank chasses. The most lethal combination of ersatz equipment was the long-barrelled 75mm Pak 40 anti-tank gun mounted on a Hotchkiss chassis, the 'Lorraine Schlepper'. Its shell could stop a Sherman at 2,000 yards.[20] Covered in camouflage, the Lorraine Schlepper looked a lot like a tank – maybe even a Tiger.[21] But if 21 Panzer was not equipped with Tigers, it deployed the Tiger's gun: the Pak 43/41-towed 88mm of Heavy Anti-Tank Battalion 220. It could kill any Allied tank at over 3,000 yards.

The job of organising this early Panzer attack fell to I SS Panzer Corps, commanded by SS General Sepp Dietrich. The result, according to Geyr von Schweppenburg, commander of Panzer Group West (PGW) which was en route to Normandy from Paris, was that no one gripped the battle. 'The first action of the staff of 1st SS Panzer Corps', Schweppenburg lamented after the war, 'should have been to ignore the confusion of contradictory orders, especially since no one in higher headquarters had the slightest conception of tank tactics, except perhaps Rommel and his staff'. Even the Desert Fox was out of his depth. 'Normandy was not Africa,' Schweppenburg said in 1945,[22] and

Rommel was too fearful of airpower. For Schweppenburg, the landscape and weather of northern France permitted careful movement and concentration of forces.

The movement of the Panzer Lehr to the front would seem to support Schweppenburg's point. From its lodgements around Le Mans–Chartres it was some 270km south-east of Caen.[23] When Generalleutnant Fritz Bayerlein, who had been Rommel's Chief of Staff in North Africa, was ordered to start his move towards Caen at 1700 hours, he protested that it would be 'a death sentence'. He was told to get on with it – 'Caen is of the greatest importance to us.'[24] So, late on 6 June, nearly 2,000 tracked and wheeled vehicles set off along five different routes for Normandy. 'Soon, the bombers were loitering over the roads, destroying crossings, villages and cities that were along the advance route and diving on snaking vehicle columns,' Bayerlein recalled. 'At 2300 hrs we passed through the village of Sees. It was lit up like a "Christmas tree" and heavy bombs were already bursting in the small town.' By the time he reached Argentan 'it was as light as day from the fires and explosions'.[25]

Helmut Ritgen, an officer in the Panzer Lehr's tank battalion, was dismissive of the impact of the air assault. The 'first loss reports', he observed, were inflated under the principle 'Always double them!' Postwar historians inflated the losses again. The best estimate in the literature (Buckingham) is that the move cost the Panzer Lehr five tanks, eighty-four half-tracks and ninety wheeled vehicles. However, the figure for half-tracks lost is actually the total from the whole month of June.[26] The Panzer Lehr's history, which described the Chaumont–Villers-Bocage road as 'a scene from hell', declined to give firm numbers.[27] Antony Beevor is a little more emphatic: figures given for the Panzer Lehr's losses on 7–8 June are 'almost certainly a gross exaggeration'.[28]

The greatest blow inflicted on the Panzer Lehr may have been the confusion resulting from the need for radio silence, the dispersion and delay caused by the routes taken and the air attacks, and the loss of perhaps fifty armoured fuel tankers. Bayerlein struggled to locate Dietrich's I SS Corps advanced headquarters near Thury-Harcourt, and only managed to do so late in the afternoon of 7 June. There he was told to mass two battlegroups in front of the Canadians: one at Norrey-en-Bessin and another at Brouay. They were to be ready to attack the next morning (8 June), alongside the 12th SS and 21st Panzer. On his return from this meeting Bayerlein's vehicle was destroyed by air attack and his driver killed: the Panzer Lehr's commander barely escaped with his life.[29]

Dietrich's orders for the Panzer Lehr to assemble in front of the 7th Canadian Brigade led to a disastrous muddle that sapped the power of the Panzer assault on 8 June. On the evening of 6 June LXXXIV Corps assigned the ground west of the Mue River to the 26th PGR of the 12th SS. As a result, when a battalion of the Panzer Lehr infantry arrived to deploy north of Cheux it encountered the 1st Battalion of the 26th PGR preparing for an attack: the Panzer Lehr infantry sought cover and awaited events.[30] To the west, the 2nd Battalion of the 902nd Panzer Lehr Grenadier Regiment pushed on to Brouay, where they got entangled in a nasty fight – presumably with a platoon of Canadians. Bayerlein established his forward divisional headquarters at Le Mesnil-Patry – within rifle shot of the Canadian positions at Putot-en-Bessin – and awaited events.[31]

Despite this confusion, by the morning of D+2 the Germans had accomplished just what COSSAC planners feared in September 1943: three Panzer divisions north and west of Caen, on excellent ground. Fortunately for the Allies, and especially for the Canadians, the result was not a massive armoured thrust to the sea, but the reduction of most of the Panzer Lehr and the 21st Panzer to idleness on 8 June. As Helmut Ritgen observed, the Panzer Lehr 'was unable to strike or to shift its sector' on that crucial day.[32] The Allies could take no credit for this muddle. Schweppenburg lamented after the war that the chaos of 8 June was a self-inflicted wound.

* * *

The massing of Panzers on the Canadian front by 8 June went largely unnoticed at the time and slipped through the Normandy narrative for seventy years. The reasons for this are complex. At the time the story was buried in the welter of steady – but unspecified – reporting of 'tank battles in the Caen area' in the early days, and in the scramble for hard news on the movement of the front. And while news reporting was necessarily vague, so, too, were the 21st AG intelligence summaries and the British Second Army's situation reports. Neither of these critical documents says much about events on the Canadian front in the aftermath of D-Day. It is also clear that even Canadian historians had little idea how 3rd Canadian Division fitted into the Overlord plan. In fact, Canadian official historians were never allowed to see the Overlord planning documents.[33]

What emerges from those chaotic first days ashore is a Normandy narrative that is only vaguely informed by knowledge of German intent, and has little awareness of what was happening on the Canadian front. The key events of the storyline – then and subsequently – were all Anglo-American: the British failure to take Caen, the tragedy of Omaha, the failure of early British efforts to drive deep south of Bayeux, comparatively quick movement of the Americans into the Cotentin peninsula, and ultimately the 'failure' of Montgomery's strategy for Normandy. Defeating the Panzer threat to Overlord, which features so prominently in the planning phases and was one of Montgomery's initial objectives, simply disappears from the narrative. No story more graphically illustrates the way in which accounts of the Normandy campaign were shaped by Anglo-American rivalry than the omission of the early defeat of the Panzer threat.

Nothing in the subsequent planning for Overlord fundamentally altered the scenario for the Panzer counterattack envisaged by COSSAC in September 1943.[34] This was the attack which the 3rd CID was trained and equipped to stop. Its Operational Order of 15 May 1944 was very clear: assume a 'covering position' astride the Caen–Bayeux rail and road links just west of Caen on either side of the Mue River and defeat '*the* counter attack'.[35] Canadian orders called for the establishment of two brigade 'fortresses' along the Caen–Bayeux highway between the villages of Carpiquet and Putot-en-Bessin. Historians have assumed that the Canadian D-Day objective was to cut the road, and have generally thought that their advance beyond these was 'stopped' by fierce German counterattacks. But the 3rd CID had no intention of going deep. Its job was to guard the wide plains on either side of the Mue River that rolled down to the sea, and defeat Rommel's Panzers. The Canadians were allocated an enormous amount of artillery to achieve this task: 144 field guns, ninety-six anti-tank guns, sixteen 4.5" guns, backed by a whole armoured brigade of three regiments. Not all of this got ashore on time, especially the anti-tank guns. But had the same fate befallen Canadian guns on D-Day as those of the Americans on Omaha, the Anglo-Canadian beachhead might have been destroyed.[36]

In the event, the Canadian advance on D+1 pre-empted the attack plans of I SS Panzer Corps. The vanguard of the 9th CIB – a battalion of the North Nova Scotia Highlanders, fifty Sherman tanks of the Sherbrooke Fusiliers, four Vickers machine guns of the Cameron Highlanders of Ottawa,[37] and a troop of M10 tank destroyers – advanced along the east side of the Mue for its D-Day objective of Carpiquet. The twenty-one surviving 105mm SPs of the 14th Field Regiment, RCA, provided immediate support.[38] The vanguard also had a 'Forward Officer, Bombardment' (FOB) from the RN with a radio link to the cruiser *Belfast*'s nine 6" guns just offshore.

The Canadians had to fight their way through Kampfgruppe Rauch, which held a line from Cairon, in the Mue River valley, to Cambes north of Caen.[39] This now included the surviving 88mm guns of Heavy Anti-Tank Battalion 200, a motorised company of Pioneers, about 1,000 men from the 716th Division, and a smattering of SPs and half-tracks. The vanguard, commanded by Lieutenant-Colonel Charles Petch, cut through Kampfgruppe Rauch with comparative ease. The only ominous sign was the steady and effective fire coming from Galmanche and Saint-Contest to the east, in the British sector, and Gruchy to the west near the Mue River. These villages were strongly garrisoned by the 21st Panzer. Around noon, having taken Buron, Petch tried to silence fire from them with artillery, but his Forward Observation Officers (FOOs) were unable to contact the 14th RCA, and the radio link to HMS *Belfast* failed. Undeterred, Petch pushed on.[40] Once Authie was cleared, the Canadians paused. Carpiquet was just 1 kilometre away.[41]

The Canadians had no time to savour the moment. By noon the Canadian vanguard was ringed by about seventy German field guns, and elements of both the 21st and 12th SS Panzer: Petch's force was outnumbered about three or four to one. Enemy tanks were soon seen east and south of Authie, followed a few minutes later by tanks to the west.[42] It was about this time that the whole area around Authie came under intense enemy artillery fire. The Canadians had run into the 12th SS lining up for an attack towards the sea. Kurt Meyer had no choice but to attack and drive the 9th CIB vanguard back. Meyer claims it all happened quickly, but Canadian sources are clear that the German infantry attack was preceded by a two-hour tank battle.[43] The Sherbrook Fusiliers recorded some quick kills before the weight of German artillery, tank and anti-tank fire – some of it from Saint-Contest, which says much about the power of the Pak 43/41 – eventually drove them off.[44]

None of this unsettled the vanguard: reinforcements were on the way.[45] Unfortunately, unchecked German mortar and artillery fire created a traffic jam in Buron, and prevented infantry from getting forward, while the 88mm guns at Saint-Contest swept the open ground south of Buron. The vanguard had been ordered 'to consolidate on high ground between Buron and Authie as a base for further attacks on the objective' if it met serious opposition.[46] As Petch discovered, there was no high ground, just a bullet- and shell-swept stretch of flat farmland. German fire stranded most of two companies in Authie. Things got worse when the FOOs of the 14th RCA, caught under a shower of mortar and artillery fire, withdrew to the anti-tank ditch north of Buron.[47] They could not see the battlefield from there, so Petch and his men continued to fight without artillery support.[48]

At 1530 hours the vanguard was attacked by infantry simultaneously from both flanks. Lieutenant M.J. Fitzpatrick of the Sherbrooke's watched the Hitler Youth and some twenty tanks advance cross 1,000m of flat, open ground south of Authie: 'two waves of infantry and then the tanks moving forward slowly and with determination'.[49] They would never have succeeded had Canadian artillery or the guns of *Belfast* been available. The 14th RCA received no order to fire, while the RN FOB was reduced to tears of frustration over his failure to contact *Belfast*. The Hitler Youth were met nonetheless by ferocious fire. 'Time and again the enemy seemed but yards from the hedge and then they were blown down or hurled back,' Will Bird, the Novas regimental historian, wrote.[50] It took a cordon of tanks and infantry several hours of bloody fighting to capture Authie.[51] Few Canadians escaped. Meanwhile Buron was attacked from the west, from valley of the Mue River, by elements of the 21st Panzer.

Gradually, the remnants of the 9th CIB vanguard pulled back to the anti-tank ditch north of Buron, and prepared to 'fight to the finish'.[52] In the late afternoon Meyer committed a second full battalion to the attack. It moved through Buron and then up the gentle slope towards the anti-tank ditch.[53] What was left of Petch's command was waiting.[54] They held. And then finally – after a long day's wait – at 1900 hours the first rounds of Canadian artillery landed in support.[55] 'The 12th SS tanks vanished at the first sound of artillery,' Bird wrote. What was left of Petch's command counterattacked, the tanks of the Sherbrooke Fusiliers finding 'in some instances the enemy being so numerous they were run over by them'.[56] The vanguard recaptured Buron, 'and the enemy were hounded all the way back to Authie, dying in groups all over the field'.[57]

The recapture of Buron was a signal victory, but it could not be held. The supporting British attack only got as far at Cambes, from which it was driven by Meyer's 1st Battalion.[58] Cambes, Galmanche and Saint-Contest remained in German hands. Buron, on a forward slope overlooked by the enemy, was untenable. The 9th CIB built its brigade fortress on the reverse slope around Les Buissons, which provided broad and open fields of fire against a clear skyline, and little direct observation by the enemy. Meanwhile, the Hitler Youth distracted themselves with a petulant shooting spree of Canadian wounded and POWs. Over the next few days murdered POWs accounted for one in five Canadian deaths.[59]

Historians later lauded the 12th SS for their 'spectacular combat debut',[60] but it was hardly that. The 12th SS was not a very efficient force.[61] Michael Reynolds described German command and control as poor.[62] In the end, the 12th SS never got much beyond their initial gains in the first hour or so. The large number of German casualties in Authie seems to have triggered the murder of POWs that followed.[63] Clearly, the vanguard was not 'thrown back in confusion' as claimed. In fact, once supporting artillery fire arrived, a little more than one reinforced Canadian infantry company drove the Hitler Youth off most of the battlefield.

It is indicative of the gratuitous criticism often directed at the Anglo-Canadians that while the 9th CIB is chastised for moving too quickly, the 7th CIB on the other side of the Mue is criticised for not moving at all. Hubert Meyer, Chief of Staff of the 12th SS and its historian, observed that on 7 June the Anglo-Canadians 'had not taken advantage of the 7km wide gap' in the German lines between the valley of the Mue and the village of Audrieu.[64] He credits both the 12th SS and the Panzer Lehr with spooking the Canadians and forcing them to stop and dig in. Clearly Hubert Meyer had never read the Canadian operation order.

On D+1 there was no organised German resistance west of the Mue, so the 7th CIB got a free pass to its fortress position at Bretteville l'Orgueilleuse and Putot-en-Bessin. The village of Norrey-en-Bessin, on a slight rise south of Bretteville like a bastion along a curtain wall, was immediately added to the fortress. This was the brigade's D-Day objective, and by noon on D+1 they were settling in. About 1,500m behind them the 12th Canadian Field Artillery Group occupied its designated gun area around Bray by 1600 hours. By late afternoon the 7th CIB had anti-tank guns sited, and defensive fire (DF) tasks arranged across its front.[65] It also sat precisely on the start line for I SS Panzer Corps' counterattack to the sea. The immediate German task, pending the arrival of the Panzer Lehr, was to clear the Canadians out of the way.[66] That task also fell to the 12th SS.

Attacks on the 7th CIB fortress started in the early hours of 8 June and lasted for most of four days. Very early on the 8th two companies of Hitler Youth, without tank support, tried to push the Canadians out of Norrey-en-Bessin. They were stopped by artillery fire. As the history of the 12th SS records, 'The positions of the whole Battalion were covered with brisk artillery and mortar fire throughout the day. It slowed any kind of movement.'[67] Norrey-en-Bessin was then shielded by a 'curtain of fire' delivered by the 13th RCA.[68] One of the DF tasks fired on the Hitler Youth at 0500 hours on 8 June was a 'scale 5' from two regiments: 240 shells on a single grid reference in a few short minutes. Two other regimental-sized (24 guns) targets were fired in that area over the next few hours.

Around 0630 hours the 2nd Battalion of the 26th PGR spread the attack westward, which started a nasty six-hour infantry battle with the Royal Winnipeg Rifles for the sprawling village of Putot-en-Bessin. The 248th Battery of the 62nd Anti-Tank Regiment, RA, deployed in depth near La Bergerie farm, engaged German infantry and nine tanks around 0945 hours.[69] By 1300 hours the SS had all but driven the Canadians out. Further west, the 3rd Battalion, 26th PGR, moved north from Brouay to the main Caen–Bayeux highway, driving the leading elements of the 50th BID back. At that point the SS seemed poised to penetrate the seam between the Canadians and the British. This is precisely where the Panzer Lehr was supposed to go, and one battalion had moved up to Brouay already.

However, it was now that the enormous power of Anglo-Canadian artillery proved its worth. Canadian gunners trapped the SS infantry in Putot-en-Bessin with a standing barrage, while the fire of five field regiments (120 guns)[70] walked the brigade's reserve battalion back into Putot-en-Bessin. The Canadians never surrendered Putot-en-Bessin again. While all this was going on British reconnaissance discovered the battalion of the Panzer Lehr in a forested area to the west of Brouay and smothered it with both naval and artillery fire. When the Hitler Youth retreated through Brouay a few hours later the scene was apocalyptic. 'The enemy had virtually cut to pieces units of the Panzer Lehr Division with heavy weapons,' one Hitler Youth recalled. 'SPWs [half-tracks] and equipment had been ripped apart; next to them on the ground and even hanging in the trees were body parts of dead comrades.'[71] This was the fate that might have befallen the attack on Authie the day before had HMS *Belfast* fired. Rather prudently, the SS decided to consolidate along the rail line at Brouay and stay quiet.[72]

It says a great deal about the importance of these clashes astride the Mue River on D+2 that this was the first place in Normandy that Rommel went. He had spent 7 June sorting out the plans to defend the Pas-de-Calais. On 8 June he set off to get a feel for the battle in Normandy and, as always, Rommel went straight to the *Schwerpunkt* – the decisive point. By 1800 hours he was at Le Mesnil-Patry, opposite the Canadians. Amid the sound of crashing artillery and the rattle of musketry, Rommel and Fritz Bayerlein discussed options. 'Bayerlein, all of our positions have been turned aside,' Rommel said. 'The British 50th Division, our familiar friends from Africa, has taken Bayeux.' The abandonment of Bayeux without a fight was a failure of monumental proportions. Bayerlein was ordered to regroup his division, and retake it.[73] He must have been relieved. The operations of the 12th SS were little short of chaotic, and few in the Wehrmacht could have cherished the thought of working closely with them.

The shift of the Panzer Lehr's operations towards Bayeux was not the end of the Panzer Corps attack, it was just delayed pending the arrival of more divisions. On the evening of 8 June what was left of the OKW Panzer reserve was released to Rundstedt's command.[74] Of these, the 1st SS Panzer Division, Leibstandarte Adolf Hitler, and Panzer Regiment Grossdeutschland of the 116th Panzer were assigned to I SS Panzer Corps to join the trust down the Mue River to the sea. Schweppenburg, now ostensibly in command of Panzer formations in Normandy, was unimpressed. The chance for decisive action was now – 8 June. After the war he blamed 'the divergent influence of the high staffs' for the failure of 8 June, probably a euphemism for Rommel. But he was clear about the lost opportunity. 'If one has to pass final judgement on the conduct of this Corps, it should be stated that it missed the psychological moment – and the bus.'[75]

While it waited for the Panzer reinforcements to arrive, the 12th SS was ordered to clear the start line for the I SS Corps attack. So at dusk on 8 June the Hitler Youth struck the Canadians again. This attack, from the east along the Caen–Bayeux highway, consisted of about thirty Panthers, a company of motorcycle infantry and a battery of self-propelled guns. The result was one of the wildest – and least-known – battles of the Normandy campaign. Kurt Meyer led it on a motorcycle. His force was weak in infantry, but he expected support from the 26th PGR dug in around Norrey-en-Bessin. The attack was no surprise. The Canadians spent the day in preparation.

Meyer's attack was reckless, arrogant and a total failure. 'This was the way we fought in the east,' he later wrote. It failed to impress the Canadians. While 'wild rifle fire' from the Regina Rifles stripped away German infantry, 'murderous' and 'violent' Canadian anti-tank fire struck the Panthers.[76] Only a handful of the infantry made it to the village. Three Panthers were destroyed east of Bretteville by Canadian 6-pounders, and half a dozen more hit before the Canadian gunners were overwhelmed. The surviving Panthers withdrew. Two Panthers audacious enough to enter Bretteville around midnight were destroyed by Canadian infantry.

Blocked at the eastern end of Bretteville, one company of Panthers slipped south of Bretteville, where three were immediately struck by anti-tank fire. Meanwhile six Panthers circled around Norrey-en-Bessin to approach Bretteville from the west. They drove through the Regina Rifles' anti-tank gun position south of Norrey-en-Bessin, too close for the 6-pounders to engage – and right over the top of the troop sergeant's slit trench. These and other Panthers took positions in and around the Regina Rifles' D Company position in the Cardonville factory north of the rail line. Captain Gordon Brown, formerly the battalion transport officer, was now acting commander of D Company: fifty survivors of the landing, augmented that day by a platoon of replacements. Brown eventually counted twenty Panthers around his position, firing into Bretteville. Lieutenant-Colonel Foster Matheson, CO of the Reginas, counted twenty-two Panthers around his battalion HQ that night. There may have been some overlap in the counting, but either way there was an enormous concentration of Panthers around a single Canadian battalion on the night of 8–9 June 1944.

Brown later recalled being 'stunned by the attack's tactical stupidity': tanks were not supposed to attack at night without infantry support.[77] When ordered to just lay low, Brown crawled out to the small orchard behind the factory, where the newly arrived men of 16 Platoon were dug in, to find out why no artillery was falling on the Germans. His FOO, Lieutenant R.J. Macdonald, from the 13th RCA, was sitting upright in his Bren carrier, sound asleep. 'For God's sake stay awake,' Brown implored, 'we're being attacked by tanks!' Macdonald got through to his regiment and reported the tanks, but no shells landed among them.

So Brown crawled into the orchard again to find out why his two 6-pounders were not firing at the Panthers. 'What, Sir,' the Sergeant in charge of the gun detachment whispered, 'are we going to do about the six tanks that now surround the orchard?' Brown had not noticed. In a moment he detected the idling of their engines and he soon discerned Panthers at each corner and one on each side of the long, narrow orchard. After concocting a scheme to attack the tanks with sticky bombs Brown scrambled back into the factory compound. The scheme went awry, and the Panthers killed all but two of the Canadians in the orchard.[78]

Now stirred to action, the Panthers snarled and clawed at Captain Brown's walled compound without effect. They were fortunate that the Hitler Youth infantry just across the rail line failed to stir. The Germans later claimed that radio problems prevented coordination of action between the 25th and 26th PGRs that night.[79] It is more likely that the 26th's PGR commander, Wilhelm Mohnke, could not be found because he was busy organising the murder of Canadian POWs.[80]

As the day brightened and the Panthers moved off, the SS compounded their errors by launching an infantry attack. All of Brown's remaining forty-seven officers and men now had machine guns 'of one sort or another (several German), and at least one Vickers'.[81] The attack went on for several hours, with SS dead and dying sprawled around the walls, in windows and doorways. Grenades tumbled into the compound and were hurled back. By the time Brown finally established radio contact with his HQ he figured they could last for about another twenty minutes. Lieutenant-Colonel Freddie Clifford, commander of the 13th Field Regiment, RCA, barked over the radio, 'Tell your men to stay in their trenches, we'll open fire in one minute.'[82] Brown scarcely had time to issue the warning before the first 105mm shells thundered in, catching the Germans in the open. 'It was the best shoot that I ever saw in my nine months of action,' Brown recalled later; 'it was a work of art.'[83] Brown buried fifty German dead later that day, some from the Panzer Lehr.

Fortunately for Brown and the other Canadian infantrymen at the front, Anglo-Canadian artillery had an effective resupply system from the beach, so the guns never stopped firing. The 12th Artillery Group at Bray carried on despite a real danger of being overrun – Meyer's own SP artillery deployed barely 1,500m away over open ground. The 13th RCA fired forty-four rounds of anti-tank ammunition that night, while the 12th RCA detached four M7s and two Shermans to the crest-line south of their position in anticipation of a tank assault.[84] Through it all the 12th Field Group fired on an arc of 180 degrees, supporting the 3rd BID north of Caen and the 50th BID to the west. 'Each time we switched back to the tanks in front of us,' the 12th RCA history recounts, 'the range would be shorter and the appeals of the [Canadian] FOOs more desperate. When we finally stopped them the range was just over 1,600 yards – much too close, especially when we were firing 8,000 yards in the opposite direction!'[85]

The third major attack on the 7th CIB position came at 1300 hours on 9 June, when a company of Panthers, supported by a few infantry, slipped under the rail bridge at La Villeneuve and raced towards Norrey-en-Bessin. Canadian artillery stripped the infantry away, while the Hitler Youth entrenched south of Norrey-en-Bessin once again failed to stir. As the Panthers emerged onto open ground they were shot up in flank by a group of Canadian Shermans which had just arrived on the battlefield. One Firefly commanded by Lieutenant G.K. Henry of the First Hussars destroyed five Panthers with five rounds in a matter of minutes, and was lining up a sixth when his troop sergeant destroyed it.[86] The surviving Panthers fled the carnage, as crews bailed out of stricken tanks into a maelstrom of artillery fire which inflicted heavy casualties.[87] No Canadian casualties were reported. Henry's accomplishment, one of the most remarkable feats of the Normandy campaign, went unheralded. The French awarded him the Croix de Guerre in 1945. The 12th SS continued to attack throughout the 9th and 10th in an attempt to clear the start line for the Panzer Corps assault. These all failed in the face of heavy losses.[88]

The failure of the 12th SS to drive the Canadians off the start line for a major Panzer counter-offensive proved to be decisive. As Hubert Meyer later explained,

[Bretteville and Norrey-en-Bessin] formed a strong barrier, *blocking the attack plans of the Panzerkorps*. For this reason repeated attempts were made to take these positions, through a number of attacks. They failed because of insufficient forces, partly because of rushed planning caused by real or imagined time pressures. Last but not least they failed because of the courage of the defenders which was not any less than that of the attackers. It was effectively supported by well constructed positions, strong artillery, antitank weapons and by tanks.[89]

Michael Reynolds concluded that 'The Canadian defence of Norrey-en-Bessin and Bretteville over the period 8th to 10th June must surely go down as one of the finest small unit actions of the war'.[90] Freddie

Clifford would have agreed. When asked about these battles in 2002 Clifford thought the army's doctrine and training worked superbly. Artillery stripped away the German infantry or kept them in their trenches and left their tanks vulnerable to anti-tank fire. Clifford was unimpressed with the Germans. Although they were brave, they were also arrogant, careless and clumsy. 'The Germans thought we were fucking Russians!' he exclaimed. 'They did stupid things and we killed those bastards in large numbers.'

* * *

By 10 June all of Schweppenburg's dreams of a Panzer Corps thrust down either side of the Mue River were gone – and not just because of the persistent failure to push the Canadians out of the way. That afternoon Rommel visited him at his HQ in an apple orchard near La Caine, 20km south of Caen. The issue was probably Rundstedt's order of 0730 hours that morning. 'As a consequence of certain information,' Roger Hesketh writes in his confidential history of Allied deception, 'CinC West has declared "a state of alarm II" for Fifteenth Army in Belgium and Northern France.'[91] This meant that the armour released by OKW to Rommel barely thirty-six hours earlier (the 1st SS Panzer Division and the Panzer regiment of the 116th Panzer Division) was now diverted to the Pas-de-Calais. The reason for this was a transmission from agent GARBO, the main conduit for the Fortitude South deception, sent just after midnight on 9 June, warning that a major assault on the Pas-de-Calais was imminent.

On 6 June, German leaders, including Hitler and his staff, remained convinced that the landings in lower Normandy were just a feint. Moreover, it was anticipated that the main assault in the Pas-de-Calais sector would be supported, in the words of the German official history, by 'an imminent attack on Antwerp'.[92] The international media was alive with speculation about a second landing in the Pas-de-Calais, and the Allied press monitored German newspapers and broadcasts to glean what they could of enemy reaction and intent. On 9 June the *New York Times* filed a story from London reporting German press accounts that another landing in the Pas-de-Calais was imminent. The speculation that Canadians would lead this attack was confirmed by German radio broadcasts that same day. As it turned out, 2nd Canadian Division had just completed amphibious exercises in the Medway and were now waterproofing and loading their equipment on landing craft in the Thames. 'Combined action is being expected somewhere between Dunkerque and Ostend,' German radio warned. 'For this, special Canadian troops are in readiness as well as several airborne and very strong tank divisions.'[93]

Just before midnight on 9 June, as the wire stories about the imminent landing of 'special' Canadian troops in the Pas-de-Calais were being put to bed in North American press rooms, GARBO's warning was received in Madrid. It was forwarded to Berlin, decoded, verified and forwarded to OKW that evening. GARBO confirmed that the landings in Normandy were a diversion designed to 'draw the maximum of our reserves to the area of operation and to retain them there so as to be able to strike a blow somewhere else with assured success'. The Allies apparently still had some fifty operational divisions available to strike that blow.[94] When asked after the war about the decision on 10 June to redirect the Panzer reinforcements from Normandy to the Pas-de-Calais region, Field Marshal Wilhelm Keitel, Chief of the German armed forces, confirmed that GARBO's message was the reason.[95]

The impact of GARBO's signal was profound. T.L. Cubbage, who tested all of Hesketh's work against the surviving documents in the British archives, claims it changed the course of history. At 0730 hours on 10 June, Rundstedt countermanded the release of the 1st SS Panzer Division and Panzer Regiment Grossdeutschland to the Normandy front and ordered them to Calais.[96] Michael Howard concluded that GARBO's warning on 9 June 'continued to pin down nineteen infantry and two armoured divisions of the Fifteenth Army – units whose intervention in the Normandy battle really might have tipped the scales'.[97] It also ended hopes for the I SS Panzer Corps' attack in Normandy. All the contemporary evidence points to the lingering threat from 'McNaughton's Dagger' as the reason why those critical Panzer forces were diverted on 9 June. Between their role in the deception campaign and the tenacious defence of their positions at Putot-en-Bessin, Norrey-en-Bessin and Bretteville l'Orgueilleuse, the Canadians had defeated the threat of a Panzer counterattack in the opening phase of Overlord. If Cubbage is right, they changed the course of history.

In view of the diversion of Panzer forces to the Pas-de-Calais, Rommel and Schweppenburg agreed that an attack by I SS Panzer Corps was no longer possible. About an hour after Rommel left Schweppenburg's HQ it was swarmed by Allied aircraft. Forty RAF Typhoons rocketed and strafed the orchard, followed by waves of USAAF Mitchells which dropped 436 500-pound bombs. In ten minutes, Craig Luther wrote, 'The entire operations staff was wiped-out.' Thirty-two men were killed, including Schweppenburg's Chief of Staff. Schweppenburg escaped, badly shaken, with minor injuries.[98] Three days later what was left of the command element of Panzer Group West retreated to Paris to rebuild itself.

By 10 June it was increasingly clear to many Germans that it was time to find a way out of the war – preferably less ignominiously than 1918. In the meantime, the immediate threat to the Overlord landings was past. Rommel shifted his efforts to containment. Plain hard fighting remained.

CHAPTER 21

TEMPESTS

Behind that griping story lay . . . the ever present antagonisms and rivalry between British and American press as well as an international struggle for press communications in which the Americans had won out by default.

Colonel Ernest Dupuy, 'Behind the Elephants'[1]

Given American expectations of their highly mechanised army, it was bitterly ironic that it landed in the worst possible place for rapid movement. The bocage of lower Normandy is the legacy of a thousand years of farming a patchwork of small fields in poor soil. Myriad hands created rockpiles around these small fields, where over the centuries trees and dense undergrowth flourished. By 1944 these borders were solid structures, some up to 12 feet high. As a rule, there was only one way in, or out: through the farm entrance. Bocage was – and remains – the prevailing topographical feature south of Omaha beach, west to Avranches and throughout the Cotentin peninsula. There was a very good reason why the Germans garrisoned this area with infantry: it was not the place for an army built for speed and mobility.

There ought to have been no surprise about the Bocage. The *Inter-Service Information Series, Report on France*, vol. 2: *Normandy West of the Seine*, published in January 1943, described it well,[2] and both COSSAC and SHAEF planners concluded that the Germans would not operate

15. The bocage of lower Normandy, in a reconnaissance photo taken by
400 Squadron, RCAF, 12 June 1944.

Panzer divisions in the area. Still, the reality of the hedgerow country,
and the tactical problems of fighting through it, surprised the Americans.
'Damnest country I have ever seen,' Chester Hansen wrote after being
ashore for the first time on 7 June, 'with rows of hedgerows, beautifully
camouflaged'. General J. Lawton Collins, commander of VII Corps, a
veteran from Guadalcanal and New Georgia, confided to Bradley that

the topography of the Cotentin was 'as bad as some of the stuff he hit on Guadal'.[3] Nothing in American training or equipment prepared them for what lay ahead. Americans, it seems, had to learn by doing. They did, but that took time.[4]

The Americans also soon discovered that their logistics system was not up to the task of keeping forces supplied with ammunition. Eisenhower had hoped to subordinate the Services of Supply for Overlord to SHAEF's very able British G-2 (intelligence) and Chief Administrative Officer, Major-General Humphrey Gale. But logistics ran along national lines, and Marshall and the head of the Army Service Force (ASF), General Brehon Somervell, insisted that the ASF in Europe, under General J.C.H. Lee, remain independent of SHAEF. By 1944 the ASF was the largest branch of the US Army, and a law unto itself.[5] It had had two years to sort out the logistics arrangement for Operation Overlord, Steve Waddell argues, and still got it badly wrong.[6]

Within days of landing, Dan Crosswell writes, 'American units already faced critical shortages of artillery and mortar ammunition.'[7] War Department planners allocated Bradley about one-third of the ammunition he wanted,[8] but even that often failed to arrive. Waddell estimates that by D+3 just 31 per cent of the planned supplies had landed on American beaches. 'The identification and disbursement of ammunition,' Waddell writes, 'became a major problem.'[9] This problem is well traced in the US Army administrative histories. But these were published decades after the operational histories appeared, and therefore have had no impact on the Normandy narrative.[10] Waddell's thorough assessment of the American logistics failure in Normandy, including the background to the persistent shortages of ammunition, only alludes to the impact this had on the conduct of the campaign. Moreover, the contrast with the lavish expenditure of ammunition by the Anglo-Canadians is stark. As outlined below, American ammunition shortfalls had a major influence on the conduct of operations in Normandy.

And it seems that the USN was part of the problem. Cargo ships were not combat loaded or loaded by cargo type: ammunition was invariably on the bottom and the last thing ashore. By 9 June, Bradley's staff noticed a distinct reluctance on the part of the navy to bring ships

16. Few shots convey Britain's commitment to Overlord better than this one, of coasters offloading off Utah beach, while LSTs line the shoreline.

inshore to unload for fear of losses. The work of offloading onto DUKWs or Rhino ferries was laborious and slow. The USN also tended to dump the stuff on the beach largely unsorted. As Hansen lamented on the 9th, 'This war will be won or lost on the beaches of Normandy.'[11] Montgomery finally ordered that priority be given to ammunition. 'Soon,' Crosswell writes, 'First Army Depots were awash with ammunition.' Nonetheless, Bradley did not trust Lee's organisation and hoarded ammunition. On 14 June the newly arrived XIX US Corps was limited to twenty-five rounds of 155mm ammunition per gun per day; formal ammunition rationing started the next day. By then Bradley was flying in small-arms ammunition to keep up with the demand.[12]

Perhaps the biggest problem facing America's mobile army was that there was no easy way out of the beachheads it was trapped in. The tragedy on Omaha left V US Corps gutted of its combat power, while the logistics muddle delayed its recovery: V Corps might have broken out through the 'Caumont Gap', a 10-mile-wide stretch in front of the Suisse Normande, which contained virtually no German troops at all.[13]

But the enemy was hard to pinpoint in the bocage and difficult to tackle 'with only light infantry weapons'.[14] By 11 June the 1st and 2nd USIDs were actually out of contact with the enemy in the Caumont Gap, while V Corps stood firm, waiting, despite the 'scanty' evidence, for a Panzer counterattack.[15] Historians would have been less charitable to the British.

In fairness, pushing through the Caumont Gap on 11 June was not an Allied priority. Cherbourg was. But VII Corps was caught between the strong defences of the Montebourg Line on the direct route to Cherbourg, and the flooded valleys of the Merderet and Vire rivers. There was no easy way for VII Corps to cross the Merderet River. Small bands of US paratroopers trapped across the flooded area lacked the power to seize the western side. On 9 June, Lieutenant General Matthew Ridgway, commander of the 82nd Airborne, resolved to push straight across the bridge and causeway at La Fière. The battle for La Fière Bridge revealed how the enormous courage and sacrifice of US infantrymen redeemed the weaknesses of the US Army at this stage of the campaign. When Ridgway called for artillery support for the crossing he was told the guns were out of ammunition. The fortuitous arrival of a battalion of 155mm guns with 180 rounds in caisson, plus whatever mortars and anti-tank guns he could muster, had to do. After an all-too-brief fireplan, Gavin's troops dashed across the 500-yard bridge and causeway. Casualties were heavy, but a bridgehead was established on the other side.[16]

A push to Barneville was now possible, but Bradley's army moved little for the next five days. While VII Corps attempted to crack the strong German positions around Montebourg, the newly arrived 90th Division was sent into the Merderet bridgehead on 10 June to start the push west. The 90th's attack was stopped in a maze of bocage and withering enemy fire. The only major development on the American front during this period was the linking up of the two beach heads at Carentan on the 12th. From there elements of the 82nd Airborne drove west to secure the bridge over the Douve at Baupte, to guard the flank of VII Corps' drive to Barneville. Otherwise the Carentan front, too, stabilised by 14 June.

On 12 June, Hitler ordered his troops in Normandy to stand on the defensive and fight to the death, but they could not stop the Americans blasting their way forward hedgerow by hedgerow. These early efforts were costly in men and explosives. By one estimate, cutting through the bocage required 17 tons of high explosives for every 2,500 yards advanced.[17] By 14 June the Germans had largely given up on hopes of holding Cherbourg and the Cotentin peninsula. They began construction of a solid defensive line across the peninsula south of the Douve River, and the systematic destruction of the port. As Gordon Harrison noted, for VII Corps the way west was gradually opening.

* * *

General Sir Miles Dempsey's problem was how to slip past the growing cordon of steel around Caen. When it became clear that there were few Germans in the Caumont Gap, the idea was hatched to send the 7th BAD through it and in behind I SS Panzer Corps. By the evening of the 12th the leading elements of the 7th BAD were abreast of Caumont, and by 0830 hours the next day the village of Villers-Bocage was in British hands. The road to Caen seemed open.

What no one on the Allied side knew was that a company of Tiger tanks, commanded by Germany's great tank-ace, Lieutenant Michael Wittmann, was waiting just down that road. When he saw the British advanced column stop on the tree-lined road east of Villers-Bocage – nose to tail with little room to turn – Wittmann attacked alone. Surprise, audacity, 55 tons of tank and its 88mm gun quickly laid waste to the British column.[18] Wittmann's Tiger was then knocked out in the town and he escaped on foot. Not much happened for the next four hours, as the British struggled to reorganise. A second attack by Wittmann's four remaining Tigers, and a few MK IVs from the Panzer Lehr, was virtually wiped out.[19] Instead of reinforcing and holding Villers-Bocage, the 7th BAD withdrew to high ground to the west, where they were fiercely counterattacked that night. That evening bombers flattened Villers-Bocage. The Germans held the town for the next two months.[20]

The Germans were mystified by the failure of the 7th BAD to push on. So was Dempsey. In fact, he was furious. After the war he told Chester Wilmot that 'the whole handling of the battle was a disgrace'.[21] The retreat, Wilmot concluded, was the result of a defeat in the 'corps commander's mind'.[22]

The Intelligence Report of the First Canadian Army for 14 June 1944 nicely summed up the situation in Normandy at that stage: 'Throughout the length and breadth of the front, enemy opposition has stiffened and bitter resistance is being offered to our adv[ance].' However, the Germans were not being given the time to concentrate armour and strike on their own terms.[23] Instead, each newly arrived division launched its own, independent counterattacks. It was clear, the Canadian intelligence report went on, that the German army of 1944 was 'Not the well oiled machine of 1940', it was 'rusty . . . in need of repair'. That said, it still functioned. As a result, by mid-June Normandy was 'no longer a battle for the brhead [bridgehead] but the opening stages of the Battle for France'.[24]

Montgomery would have agreed. His plan had been for the British to capture Caen and then strike out across the plain to the south to secure the eastern flank of the lodgement while the Americans made a quick dash to capture Cherbourg and then wheeled into Brittany. Of his three initial objectives, only the defeat of the Panzer counterattack had been achieved. The German response modified his concept of operations. The Germans had committed virtually all their available Panzer forces around Caen, ostensibly in preparation for a counter-attack to destroy the landings.

But two other concerns drew German Panzers to the Anglo-Canadian sector. Hitler's long-awaited wonder weapon, the pilotless V1 rocket plane, was based primarily between Dieppe and Calais. The first four of these 'Buzz Bombs' landed in the UK on 13 June and did little damage. Two nights later, when 144 V1s were launched, damage was extensive in London, Portsmouth and Southampton. For the moment there was no clear way to stop the rockets, and bringing them down soon consumed a large part of the British air effort. The British Second Army could not be allowed to threaten the V1 launch sites. Nor could it be allowed, given the imminent threat of a major landing in the Pas-de-Calais, to threaten the Fifteenth German Army from the rear. It speaks volumes for the skill and dedication of those British officers who conceived and ran Fortitude South – soon dubbed Fortitude South II – that the danger of an Allied descent in the Calais region retained its credibility until well into August. Until then, most German reinforcements sent to

17. General George Marshall, Eisenhower and Admiral Ernie King leaving Omaha beach following their visit to the front, 12 June 1944.

Normandy came from the south and west of France or from Germany itself, not from the Pas-de-Calais.[25]

Despite the disappointment of Villers-Bocage there was a sense in the Allied camp after the first week or so ashore that things were going well enough. On Monday 12 June, George Marshall, Ernie King and Hap Arnold, along with Eisenhower, spent the day in Normandy with Bradley, and toured the front. They were well pleased.[26] So, too, were Alan Brooke, Jan Smuts and Churchill, who visited Normandy the same day. They all joined up at Portsmouth for the train trip back to London. Churchill wrote in his memoirs, 'We dined together in a happy mood.'[27] The happy mood lasted throughout the first day of Combined Chiefs of Staff meetings that followed. Much of the discussions focused on the development of Pacific strategy, and the lingering issue of Anvil. The latter opened old wounds. Eisenhower was increasingly of the opinion that the best use of the divisions intended for Anvil was a landing in western France. The British agreed, but the Anvil debate was pushed back for later resolution.

The meetings nonetheless ended in acrimony on 15 June during a discussion of strategy in Burma. By mid-June the Fifteenth Japanese Army was starving, and facing annihilation.[28] Burma would soon be back in British hands. Meanwhile, the Americans sought to open the road to China to keep it in the war, maintain its status as a Great Power, and as a base for the giant new B-29 Super Fortresses bombing Japan. Debate over Burma grew so heated that Marshall declared in frustration that at least Stilwell was a 'fighter', unlike the soft and useless British generals who surrounded him. Brooke was so enraged that he had to step away.[29]

Marshall's outburst was a portend. That day the US 5th Amphibious Corps, supported by Task Force 58, landed on Saipan in the Marianas group, and the first B-29 raid on Japan was launched from China. Meanwhile, Vice-Admiral Marc Mitscher's TF-58, the most powerful fleet ever assembled up to that point with seven fleet-class and eight light-fleet aircraft carriers and nearly 1,000 aircraft backed by seven battleships, twenty-one cruisers and sixty-nine destroyers, trolled for action off the Marianas. If all went well, the rump of Japan's carrier fleet would be drawn into a decisive battle: Saipan was easily within range of the Japanese home islands for the new B-29s. At issue now was how – and how quickly – US amphibious forces should move on the main Japanese islands. There was little, if anything, that the British could add to this juggernaut.

* * *

Ernest Dupuy lamented in the late winter of 1944, when the Overlord public-relations campaign was being developed, that convincing Americans that Normandy was anything but a US operation was always going to be a tough sell. The generic nature of much of the early press coverage in America did little to dispel that belief. Lord Halifax complained about this as early as 8 June in a telegram to Bracken. 'Amazing and deplorable ignorance prevails among even friendly and usually well-informed Americans,' Halifax wrote, 'about the extent of British participation in the present operations.' He had approached both

Stimson and James Forrestal (the new Secretary of the US Navy) about taking action to correct the distortion. Bracken replied the next day, saying that a quick survey of thirty US papers revealed fairly balanced coverage. However, 'All papers seen carried banner headlines, describing the action as "Allied" and the main agency despatches covering the over-all activity refer to "Allied operations" and mention American, British and Canadian troops.' Nothing more could be done, Bracken lamented, 'until the Generals are willing to release the news of the formations and units involved'.[30] The Joint Staff Mission in Washington piled on three days later, complaining that the MOI was doing nothing to get British human-interest stories into American papers.

In the meantime, acrimony developed between the MOI and the Air Ministry over the handling of the Fighting Parcels prior to D-Day. It will be recalled that these were to be delivered globally by the RAF in the days immediately prior to D-Day to provide British agencies with some-thing to offer local media – including the Americans. The RAF had failed utterly, and they arrived too late to be useful. When Bracken received what he considered a lame apology from the Air Ministry, he fired off a blistering letter blaming the RAF for allowing the Americans to gain a march in the public-relations battle. 'The result of this was that our plans for presenting this operation and particularly the British share in it went badly astray,' Bracken alleged. 'Our Press Attaches had no background on which to work. Consequently, in many countries they are still trying to catch up on a flying start gained by the Americans.'[31]

Although superficially American treatment of the British role seemed slim, to the 'intelligent reader', Aubrey Morgan, Deputy Director of the BIS in New York, told Bracken on 19 June 1944, 'there was an [sic] abundant evidence of the part Britain played'.[32] Weekly summaries in the *New York Times*, and in most American weekly news journals like *Time*, *Newsweek* and *Business Week*, reflected that balance, although they were often vague on details. Even Robert McCormick's stridently anti-British *Chicago Tribune* carried the pooled copy with its accounts of tank battles in the Anglo-Canadian sector.

That said, from the outset newsreel coverage in the USA was much less balanced. 'Judging by the five American newsreels,' the BIS reported on 12 June, 'Normandy was invaded solely by American troops, with a couple of Britishers and Commonwealth troops for effect only.'[33] Since, by one estimate, the vast majority of Americans – 80 million out of a population of 130 million – attended the cinema each week, newsreels were a powerful influence.[34] Other media fuelled the perception that Normandy was an all-American battle. Charles Wertenbaker's feature article in *Life* on 12 June, 'The Invasion Plan', explained that the whole Overlord plan was American, and all the credit for it belonged to Bedell Smith. 'When a definitive history of the operation can be written,' Wertenbaker claimed, 'it will be discovered that General Smith was the man who saw it most clearly, from its inception to the recent fateful Tuesday morning when the actual moment for assault was set.' Not a single Briton is mentioned in Wertenbaker's fanciful account.

Explaining the command structure and the origins of the operation to Americans remained a special challenge. The news magazines, which covered the story in more depth, generally did a good job. Ike was Supreme Commander, but the officers in command of naval, air and land operations were all British. Some media fudged this by pointing out that Eisenhower's policy was to ensure that every British or American staff officer had a deputy or equivalent from the other nation. This paralーlelism was sometimes used to explain that Bradley was Montgomery's equal, and that Admiral A.G. Kirk, USN, in command of the Western Task Force, was the equivalent of Admiral Ramsay. As the BIS newsreel report for 22 June noted laconically, 'The reels are still gagging over Montgomery and Ramsay.' Much was implied as the myth that Overlord was primarily an American operation was being crafted.

Nothing that the MOI or BIS could say to the British Joint Staff Mission in Washington mollified their caustic view of Bracken and the efforts of his ministry. On 19 June, Aubrey Morgan went to Washington to represent the MOI at a regular meeting between the Joint Staff Mission and Lord Halifax. Morgan reported that 'There were some remarks made around the table which clearly indicated that there was a feeling in the room that Britain was not getting her fair share of the news'. When Morgan cornered Air Marshal Welsh, the senior RAF officer in Washington, and told him that the problem started when the RAF failed to deliver the Fighting Parcels, Welsh dismissed him summarily: 'I don't believe a word of it.' Welsh then told Morgan what he really thought: 'At times it seems as if we are winning this war in spite of the B.I.S.'[35] Morgan was deeply insulted by Welsh's outburst and sent a lengthy memo off to Bracken explaining what went on. That further incited Bracken's frustration with Sir Archibald Sinclair and the RAF. Halifax eventually declared the incident closed, but it was not. Bitter exchanges between Bracken and Sinclair lasted for weeks.[36]

The Joint Staff Mission made it clear on 19 June that they were particularly unhappy when the American press – and especially news-reels – talked about 'American and Allied' actions in ways which masked the enormous British role.[37] They had reason to be concerned. A survey of five major American newspapers over the summer of 1944 reveals the persistent use of 'American and Allied', especially by the Associated Press, in ways that imply a dominant American role in the campaign.[38] 'One person asked me,' Morgan told Bracken, 'if we could persuade the Americans to give up the use of the word "Allied" in the headlines. With restraint I replied that I felt it was beyond our powers to change General Eisenhower's communiques.'[39] It will be recalled that the adop-tion of the word 'Allied' as a generic term was the result of Canadian protests that the term 'Anglo-American' did not reflect Canada's impor-tant role in Overlord. It seems that by striving to subsume Canada's very large war effort under their own mantle, the British inadvertently obscured from Americans their own major effort in the opening of the Second Front.

The British were not alone in being sensitive to press coverage. Chester Hansen and his colleagues at Bradley's headquarters found the BBC too partisan. They were particularly offended by a BBC story on 10 June that highlighted the dominant British role in naval operations. Given that roughly 80 per cent of the naval forces – and virtually all the merchant ships – involved were British, including much in the Western Task Force that Americans were reluctant (then and now) to mention, the BBC report was accurate. However, according to Hansen, the broad-cast 'violated Eisenhower's insistence on Allied unity and de-emphasis on nationalities'. Ernie Pyle, and likely many other American corre-spondents in Normandy and at SHAEF HQ, was 'griped on this score'.[40] The mood of the American press was probably not improved by an editorial in the *Daily Telegraph* a few days later, likely in response to

Wertenbaker's *Life* magazine article about the planning for Overlord, that gave all the credit for Overlord planning to British officers.[41]

So it was a rather wounded and frustrated American press corps that finally got access to the fast, high-volume Press Wireless transmitter, which became operational at Vouilly on 14 June. According to Steven Casey, the transmitter was a boon to American correspondents. 'They could therefore bask in the knowledge,' Casey writes – repeating the old American misconception that Montgomery, despite having oversight of all the battles in Normandy as ground force commander, commanded only the British – 'that the outside world was reading about Bradley's exploits, while copy on Montgomery's battles sat in his PR camp waiting to be relayed out.'[42] In fact, the press information flow was now much faster than the movement of information through military channels. SHAEF's sitreps and briefings to correspondents in London were soon found to be up to twelve hours behind the media coverage direct from Normandy.[43]

* * *

The ability to transmit directly to New York, almost instantaneously and on a virtually unlimited scale, fundamentally altered the nature of press coverage. On the same day that the Press Wireless station became operational, VII US Corps began its push west to cut the Cotentin peninsula. The advance to Barneville was an unqualified success. And it made headlines. Late on 18 June, Harold Denny, with the 82nd Airborne Division near the coastal town of Portbail, filed a story from France, 'Americans Slash Germans in Bitter, Close Battles', that appeared the next morning (19 June) in the *New York Times*. It is doubtful if SHAEF had more up-to-date information. In fact, the speed and volume of press accounts of the Normandy campaign now reaching London via New York alerted SHAEF that something had suddenly changed press reporting. The *Chicago Tribune*, noteworthy for its balanced coverage in the early days of the campaign, was all-American after 14 June, as banner headlines trumpeted the advance to Cherbourg (and success in the Pacific). The *New York Times*, more restrained, nonetheless highlighted the success of American arms in both Normandy and the Pacific.[44] In the event, the headlines in Britain, Canada and the US in mid-June spoke increasingly of American battlefield success.

While VII US Corps and much of the Allied press corps turned towards Cherbourg, the expectation of a major British offensive was widespread. This was not unfounded. By mid-June Montgomery estimated that the German situation was ripe for exploitation. Their reserves were largely exhausted, it was difficult to bring in infantry divisions, German command and control was a shambles and the capture of Cherbourg would write off significant forces. Ultra revealed the weakness of German forces now trapped in the north Cotentin peninsula and spurred the Americans to move quickly.[45] By 21 June the First US Army and British Second Army would 'have fresh reserves ready', so it was time to capture both Caen and Cherbourg. The British would organise a major attack east of Caen, to hold German mobile divisions in place and try to encircle the city. The Americans would concentrate on securing Cherbourg.

By the end of 19 June the 9th USID had already closed up on the outer reaches of the Cherbourg fortress in the west. The 79th USID, in the middle, had a slightly harder go but moved well. On 20 June the Germans finally abandoned the Montebourg Line and the 4th USID followed them to the outer ring of the Cherbourg defences. The hard task of breaking through to the harbour now remained. Meanwhile, VIII British Corps was en route to Normandy to form the core of Dempsey's assault on Caen. With half a million men ashore, an average of 25,000 men – the equivalent of a division plus – landing each day, and the Germans under relentless air attack across northern France, there was every reason to believe that a major rupture in the stretched cordon around the Allied beachhead was imminent. The miserable weather that plagued the early days of the campaign abated on 18 June. The 'sun shone on a calm sea', Stephen Roskill wrote, 'and the barometer was steady'. The beach was black with toiling men and machines, while the sea was so alive with ships and small craft that it looked to one British officer 'like Margate on a Bank Holiday'.[46]

Then, early on the morning of 19 June, the wind rose from the northeast to gale force. Waves 6 feet high rolled onto the beaches that day. Had Overlord been delayed two weeks, to the next confluence of moon and tide, this was the weather that would have confronted decision-makers. The storm lasted four days. The British Mulberry harbour at Arromanches, guarded by deep water offshore and a sand bank, weathered the storm. However, Mulberry A off Omaha, upon which the American logistics plan depended,[47] was pounded into a wreck.[48]

Landing craft struggling to bring supplies ashore, one British sailor recalled, were 'crushed by the surf as a dog crushes a bone'. Prior to the storm the Allies were landing an average of 22,570 tons of supplies a day. Between 19 and 22 June the average was 3,400 tons; on 20 June only 999 tons were landed on the American beaches.[49] On 20 June Bradley ordered the beaching of five ammunition-laden British coasters at low tide to create a reserve.[50] The next day 'fourteen LSTs managed to beach in the "Juno" area' in a force-six gale, and 'all got off again successfully'.[51] But little moved across the beaches for four days. By 22 June the beaches from Utah to Sword looked like a junkyard: 800 small craft and vessels driven ashore, piled along the wrack line with wrecked Rhino ferries, pieces of Mulberry, smashed DUKWS, landing craft and trucks.[52] Hansen wrote in his diary on 22 June that the storm did far more damage than the Luftwaffe could ever have.

The Great Storm was an enormous setback for the Allies. 'Our position', Ike told Marshall on 21 June, was not as good as we 'had reason to believe it would be'.[53] Ammunition was again in short supply on the American front, and Bradley resorted to flying it in.[54] The British never wanted for shells, although they did fly in beer – much to Chester Hansen's dismay.[55] By the time the weather abated the build-up was five days, 105,000 tons and 250,000 men behind schedule.[56] It took a month to recover. On the 20th, with most of VIII British Corps still afloat, Dempsey pushed the start date for his major attack back to the 25th, and then again to the 26th. This was a full eight days beyond the date Montgomery had hoped for on 15 June. It was not until 24 June that all of VIII British Corps was safely ashore.[57]

The storm was a double-edged sword: it allowed the Germans to move with impunity. On the Anglo-Canadian front the armour of the 2nd Panzer arrived intact during the storm, as did the HQ of the new LXXXVI Corps east of the Orne, along with much of its medium and heavy artillery. Reinforcements on the American front were particularly noteworthy. The remaining units of the 3rd Para Division deployed north of Saint-Lô into the Caumont Gap, and so did the 353rd Division and a Kampfgruppe and anti-tank artillery of the 266th Division.[58] Even after the storm abated, continued poor flying weather favoured the Germans. The heart of Rundstedt's planned major counter-offensive, II SS Panzer Corps – the 9th and 10th SS Panzer divisions – arrived safely in Paris from Poland on 26 June. The leading elements were soon on their way to Normandy. The poor weather also shielded the V1 sites along the Channel coast from air attack, allowing the rocket campaign against Britain to intensify.

By late June, Eisenhower had every reason to be anxious. The Normandy timetable was slipping. And as if the storm was not enough, Eisenhower was under pressure from Marshall and King to release American ships from Overlord for Anvil, especially fifty LSTs and other assault craft.[59] After the storm Eisenhower's need for LSTs was even greater. On the 21st he warned that he must now use them to make up for the shortfalls occasioned by the storm.

The delay in opening Cherbourg simply added to the logistics problem. The final assault began on 25 June. The city garrison surrendered two days later, but the Germans had wrecked the port and sown the harbour with mines of all types. 'The demolition of the port of Cherbourg,' Colonel Alvin Viney, the US engineer sent in to restore it, concluded, 'is a masterful job, beyond doubt the most complete, intensive and best-planned demolition in history.' It would be months before Cherbourg could handle any major amount of cargo.[60]

Eisenhower's preferred solution to the challenges he now faced was to shift the Anvil landing to Brittany. British Commandos had gone ashore there after D-Day and found the peninsula virtually empty of troops.[61] The capture of Brittany would ease the pressure on the Normandy beachhead, speed up the development of the American logistics plan and the arrival of troops direct from the USA, and concentrate naval and amphibious forces. The British agreed: the US Joint Chiefs of Staff did not. So as the battle for Normandy raged, so too did the struggle over Allied strategy, and with each passing day Britain's influence slipped away.

* * *

It did nothing to help the British cause that the headlines coming out of Normandy between 14 and 26 June were all about the American drive on Cherbourg. Even the British papers, in London and around the country, did not disguise the fact that it was the Americans, not the 'Allies', who were advancing in Normandy.

The British media soon focused their frustrations over the imbalance in press coverage on the Press Wireless station at Vouilly. The sudden arrival in Fleet Street of waves of copy via New York – accompanied by huge charges for 'urgent' transmissions – led to complaints to SHAEF about the balance in coverage emanating from France. While American press copy – 'Buoyed by the thought of beating the British', in Casey's words[62] – flowed freely from the First US Army front, correspondents with the British Second Army were sharply rationed in their wordcount, had difficulty getting copy through to meet deadlines, and were restricted in their movements. An article in the *Daily Express* by Alan Moorehead summarised these frustrations. The Americans helped ease the British problem by setting up a direct teletype link between their press camp at Vouilly and Middle Wallop in the UK, but it remained difficult to get copy from Middle Wallop to the MOI offices in London.[63]

By the time Moorehead's article appeared SHAEF was already moving to rein in the press. Part of the problem was that bored and idle American pressmen at Vouilly had taken to looting French food to supplement their bland army diets, and began to file stories about prosperous and well-fed Normans who had accommodated the German presence, and resented the Allied invasion.[64] Rex North's story in the London *Sunday Pictorial* claimed that six out of ten Frenchmen 'distrusted and detested us', while at least 50 per cent 'seem to be Allies of the Germans'.[65] American news magazines also ran stories of French resentment of American bombing, which seemed unrestrained and grossly inaccurate, and stories of French girls sniping at the Americans who had killed their boyfriends. SHAEF set out to squash these stories, and so began to issue press guidance on 22 June to keep reporters focused on the liberation of Europe. The first directive urged reporters to write about veteran combat divisions and reminded them – somewhat disingenuously – that the Allies judged progress 'by defence positions broken and captured not mileage'.[66]

On 23 June the SHAEF Public Relations Council convened to discuss the particular problems of British media coverage. On 29 June,

Dupuy recommended that a committee be sent to Normandy to investigate. It arrived on 2 July and found the British press camp in the château at Creully humming 'like angry bees'.[67] Meetings with correspondents produced three major gripes. The Public Relations Officer in charge of censorship and despatch of copy for the British Second Army – 'a Guards officer and a charming gentleman' – had no concept of deadlines and saw no reason why an hour or two delay mattered. The second problem was that the methods and speed of despatch of copy had not improved since D-Day. Radio links remained rudimentary, and according to the War Diary of the Canadian Press unit, transmissions were rationed to 900 words per day.[68] This, it turned out, was at peak hours. Key-operated Type 33 sets capable of 5,000 words per day were now practically worthless for press traffic, and the BBC wireless at Creully was so busy that there was no space for text. Perhaps more frustrating still, a teleprinter link between Bayeux and London capable of 10,000 words per day was simply waiting for someone to connect it at the Bayeux end. No one seemed to be in charge. There was a high-speed transmitter at the British Second Army HQ capable of 50,000 words per day, but was averaging just 12,000 'due to lack of copy'. The reason for this, it was claimed, was that many correspondents had left the British Army to cover the siege of Cherbourg.[69] In any event, the British press still relied on air despatch of hard copy, while the requirement for an escorting officer kept many British correspondents idle.

Dupuy's ad hoc committee fixed what they could, replacing the press officer with someone who understood the press, and tried to persuade the British to adopt the American practice of unescorted press travel. The problems of high-speed links back to Britain were, apparently, in hand. But the report then hit the nail on the head: 'It is our considered view that the problems that arose in the British zone were mainly caused through disparity in communications consequent on the installation of the Press Wireless transmitter. Had this not been operating, a fair opportunity would have been given to the P.R. unit to settle down and inevitable initial difficulties would have been ironed out.'[70]

There was, in fact, one more problem which Dupuy's committee was not mandated to investigate: the number of American reporters in the British sector. It will be recalled that prior to D-Day the British rejected appeals to add more American reporters to the British Second Army. About a dozen Americans were assigned (four of which were with the Canadians) for D-Day.[71] By late June it appears that most of these Americans drifted west to cover the Cherbourg campaign. Beaverbrook claimed that by 28 June there were only three US war correspondents left in the British sector.[72] In late June the British were again offered more US reporters and again turned them down. Raymond Daniell, the *New York Times* bureau chief in London, explained why in an article on 25 June: 'the British Newspapers Proprietors Association has requested that no American newspaper correspondents be allowed to go to the British sector until the correspondents of all British papers have been accommodated. This', Daniell observed pointedly, 'makes it difficult for the editors of American newspapers to give the same coverage to the British forces that British editors are giving to the American advance on Cherbourg.'[73] The problem was no secret. 'British officials are frankly, though quietly, concerned,' *Newsweek* reported in its 26 June edition, 'over the failure of the United States press and radio to give more prominence to the part their troops are playing in the invasion beachhead battle.' They understood that each nation should take pride in what they have done, but the imbalance in press coverage 'may create a feeling in either country that its forces alone won the war'.[74] Daniell summed up the Normandy press coverage situation succinctly in a special report to the *New York Times* on 25 June. There 'has been so little in the London papers about British troops in the past fortnight', he wrote, 'that the reader who did not know better might suspect that the liberation of Europe was primarily an American operation. Yet the Canadian and British troops are considerably more numerous.'

Daniell concluded that 'If American troops have stolen the show, it does not mean that they are doing all the fighting'. The British and Canadians were whittling down Germany's combat strength, and many papers acknowledged that. The *New York Times* weekly summary of news for 18 June noted that the front around Caen was moving, but that 'action in this sector was of the toughest kind'. The tactical and technical details of armoured attrition warfare were hard to capture in a newspaper graphic. Lines moving on a series of maps captured public imagination, particularly in America, and these appeared daily in the

press. As Barry Oldfield commented, movement on the Cotentin peninsula drew correspondents to it like bugs to a light.[75] It helped that the
welcoming and very open American Army media policy and access to
the Press Wireless transmitters made covering the Cherbourg campaign
easy. American correspondents were, Casey claims, 'Buoyed by the
thought of beating the British', and found reporting on the Cherbourg
campaign like covering a 'continuously breaking news story at home'.[76]

* * *

The angst about the lack of coverage in the American media had little to
do with hubris: there were big issues at stake by mid-1944, and Britain
needed good press in America. As the storm raged in the Channel, John
Maynard Keynes and the British delegation to the global economic summit
at Bretton Woods, New Hampshire, were en route to America aboard the
Queen Mary. In theory, the key postwar economic decisions had already
been made by Henry Dexter White and the US Treasury Department. But
Keynes was ready to push back on the American plan. White, too, arrived
for the preliminary meetings in Atlantic City, eager to make changes. The
final deal on postwar economic planning was not yet done.[77]

In the meantime, Britain was under attack in America on many
fronts for its imperial and European policies. The disagreement between
Roosevelt and Churchill over the fate of France, and her empire, was a
subject of wide discussion, especially in the news magazines. FDR
wanted the French empire liquidated and anyone but de Gaulle in
Paris. The British, left to salvage Europe on their own, needed a strong
France, and strong anti-Communist governments. On 19 June 1944
Life magazine declared the US liberation of Rome was now a 'hollow
victory' because the British supported a constitutional monarchy as
Italy's new form of government. British policy in Greece was similar.
Cutting deals to keep the Communists at bay was the game plan. Then,
on the day Keynes landed in New York, Roosevelt's Vice President,
Henry Wallace, publicly demanded that Britain and the Netherlands
declare firm dates for liquidation of their Asian empires: a statement
that deeply embarrassed both governments.[78]

The tone of American rhetoric in the last ten days of June 1944 was
bolstered by their stunning success in the central Pacific. On 19–20 June
the USN's Task Force 58, covering the landings on Saipan, inflicted a

staggering defeat on the Imperial Japanese Navy in the Battle of the Philippines Sea. The fine details of what the Americans dubbed the 'Great Marianas Turkey Shoot' did not immediately emerge, but the scope and scale of the victory did. So, too, did the sense that the Pacific war was America's war, and she had it well in hand. 'Some generals expressed surprise at the way any developments in the war with Japan can quickly take precedence in public interest over any developments in the war in Europe,' *US News* observed on 23 June, 'even an invasion'.

On 20 June *The Times* lauded the rise of American power. 'The strength of the American fleet is reaching staggering proportions,' the editor wrote. 'By the end of this year it will have no fewer than 100 carriers.' *The Times* observed that the ability of the USN to concentrate its power in the Pacific – without apparently compromising the Europe First priority at the heart of Anglo-American strategy – owed more than a little to the Royal Navy's success in handling naval operations everywhere else. *The Times* might well have added that having the Canadian Navy cover American operational responsibilities in the North Atlantic helped, too.

As American power grew in 1944 the discourse over the implications of America's rise grew more anxious. Roosevelt was committed to peace and prosperity through a United Nations organisation led and managed by the four Great Powers – Britain, the Soviet Union, China and the USA – and an international monetary and trading system to be hammered out at Bretton Woods. It was less clear what the Republicans would do. As they gathered in Chicago for their nominating convention – which opened on 26 June – the *Saturday Evening Post* speculated that the US was 'drifting towards [an] imperialist solution' to its postwar problems. American planning for air routes simply traced lines through European colonial possessions – and new American military bases – around the globe. Robert McCormick urged the Republicans gathering in his city to just take whatever America wanted. Republican foreign policy ought to be based, McCormick argued, on America's new strength. 'Our aggregation of power at sea and our parallel strength on land and in the air means that America is first among the nations in power and so far in the lead that all others can be regarded almost as auxiliaries of no great importance ... We don't have to ask favors of anybody.'[79]

The shift of American populism (or nativism) from isolation to imperialism was well in keeping with the long arc of US history, but the stakes in 1944 were global for the first time. On the day the RNC convened *The Times* ran a feature article by its principal Washington correspondent which laid out 'The Republican Challenge'. Woodrow Wilson's plan to engage America in world affairs in 1919–20 had been seen as 'an abandonment of their traditions and the subversion of the institutions. What is disturbing', *The Times* correspondent wrote, 'is that the same lack of understanding exists today', in totally different circumstances. Postwar plans still needed to be couched in terms that Americans found comfortable and could easily understand. Put simply, America would not retreat into isolation this time. And they would not just engage the world, they would run it.

* * *

On 27 June Eisenhower's naval aide, Captain Harry Butcher, USN, commented in his diary that the British Second Army had finally started to move, but that its dithering had reduced the likelihood of success. 'He waited so long,' Butcher lamented of Montgomery, 'that at least two additional Panzer divisions face him. In addition, the ten- or twelve-day delay gave the Germans an opportunity to dig in and get set, whereas Bradley kept his fellows moving and the Germans never had much chance to dig in.'[80]

Butcher's spurious characterisation of Montgomery the plodder fit the stereotypical American view of both the general and the British, then and since. Russell Weigley was fond of pointing out in *Eisenhower's Lieutenants* that the British operated on 'the good ground', rolling upland plains, excellent tank country – for both sides.[81] Like Butcher, Weigley's criticism was gratuitous. Montgomery was methodical, to be sure, but there could be no quick rush against Panzer divisions over open ground. While the Americans 'kept their fellows moving' in a bloody brawl through close country that seldom allowed command to span more than a battalion frontage, the open fields in the Anglo-Canadian sector required operations on a much larger scale. Attacks on Panzer Group West developed into 3,000–4,000m tactical bounds across broad fronts won largely by artillery, followed by a dash to defensible ground from which the German counterattacks could be destroyed.

But it meant that Dempsey could not keep 'his fellows moving' to prevent the enemy from digging in. Butcher might have pointed out that VII US Corps kept moving in the Cotentin peninsula because that's where Germans were weak. And, of course, he might have reflected on the impact of the Great Storm: Dempsey could not launch a corps-level attack with troops still at sea.

Finally, Butcher's criticism that Monty's delay allowed two more Panzer divisions to arrive on his front probably refers to the 2nd Panzer and 2nd SS Panzer. But the situation was even worse than that: II SS Panzer Corps was on its way, too. It was part of a wave of German divisions headed to Normandy for Rommel's long-delayed major Panzer counterattack. While II SS Panzer Corps arrived from the east, infantry divisions hustled to Normandy from Bordeaux and Narbonne, the Netherlands and Belgium for frontline duty.[82] Rommel hoped to concentrate eight Panzer divisions for a massive blow west of Caen. Montgomery was soon less interested in taking Caen than forcing Rommel to commit his new Panzer divisions to battle.

The long-awaited British offensive, Operation Epsom, called for a drive by VIII British Corps across the plain west of Caen, through the heavily wooded valley of the Odon River, and then up onto the open farmland around Hill 112. From there Caen and the sweeping countryside along the Orne River towards Falaise are all in view. Once Hill 112 was secure, British armour would surge across the Orne and onto the high ground south of Caen on Bourguébus ridge. Major supporting attacks by the XXX and I British Corps would secure the flanks and help stake out the bridgehead over the Odon. If the British could take and hold Hill 112, Caen would be virtually surrounded. The storm constrained what Dempsey could do. Apart from a limited attack by the 49th British Division, all the supporting attacks had to be cancelled: VIII British Corps was largely on its own. For both the 15th Scottish and the 11th Armoured divisions, Operation Epsom was their initiation into battle. It was the infantry's job, supported by the 31st Armoured Brigade's Churchill tanks, to clear a way across the Odon valley, then 11th Armoured would be turned loose on the open ground around Hill 112.[83]

The preliminaries began on 25 June when the 49th BID – also new to battle – attacked Fontenay and the Rauray spur on the western flank

18. Operation Epsom: the 15th Highland Division, supported by the
Churchills of the 5th Royal Tank Regiment, advance through
chest-high grain, 28 June 1944.

of VIII British Corps. Fontenay fell, but not the spur of raised ground
that gave the Germans oversight into the left flank of Epsom. The next
day – as the Republican National Convention opened in Chicago and
as Cherbourg capitulated – 240 field guns and eighty mediums
commenced the opening barrage, while a further 136 guns fired concentrations on designated targets.[84] The scale of the fireplan was immense.
The War Diary of the 13th Field Regiment, RCA, noted at 0415 hrs:
'We start firing in the biggest barrage of the war. With the assistance of
thirty other regiments we fire a million rounds.'[85] Fighter-bomber
attacks launched from Britain had to be cancelled because of abysmal
weather, but No. 83 Group based in Normandy was able to fly. It was
4 miles to the valley of the Odon: 2 miles beyond there to Hill 112.

It took two days of hard fighting, and both divisions, to simply
establish a bridgehead across the Odon. Clear weather on the 27th
brought the full panoply of Allied air support and allowed reconnaissance to track the movement of German forces. Dempsey committed a
third division – 43rd (Wessex) also new to battle – to the attack. More
German reinforcements arrived, too: tanks from the 2nd Panzer, and

infantry from both the 2nd SS Panzer and the leading elements of the 1st SS Panzer. Meanwhile, the 9th and 10th SS Panzer divisions arrived at their assembly area in the dead ground south of Évrecy. Hard fighting the next day pushed the British to the crest of Hill 112.[86]

The success of Epsom prompted a crisis in the German high command. Rommel and Rundstedt were away in Germany discussing Normandy with Hitler, leaving things to General Friedrich Dollmann, commander of the Seventh Army. Dollmann already carried the responsibility for the loss of Cherbourg, and now he had allowed the British to get across the Odon. In keeping with Rommel's intent, Dollmann ordered II SS Panzer Corps to pinch off the British salient on the Odon.[87] At that point Dollmann died, either from a heart attack or cyanide, and German command and control slipped into chaos. It was resolved when Schweppenburg's Panzer Group West was given command of the front against the Anglo-Canadians, and the Seventh Army took over the American front.

The Allies had good warning of all this through Ultra, which led Montgomery and Dempsey to make a crucial decision. With Anglo-Canadian artillery already in place, on the afternoon of 28 June the British decided to stand on the defensive and let the Germans come to them over open ground. 'Ultimately,' John Buckey writes, 'EPSOM was about to deliver an opportunity to inflict heavy attrition on the remaining fresh frontline forces available to Rommel in the theatre.'[88] The German assault began in earnest the next day, as leading elements of the 9th and 10th SS Panzer divisions joined the fray. Except for the recapture of the crest of Hill 112, their attacks went nowhere. The German effort was largely crushed by the most intense artillery fire yet recorded.[89]

For the next two days II SS Panzer Corps attempted to push the British back. At 0330 hours on 1 July the 10th SS Panzer poured down the north slope of Hill 112 in an effort to annihilate the 11th Armoured Division's bridgehead south of the Odon. The attack was smashed by artillery: British patrols later counted between 300 and 500 dead.[90] Meanwhile, the 9th SS Panzer made five attempts to break through the western flank of the British salient. They were met, according to Brigadier Pemberton, by 'massed artillery fire with devastating effect, and all but one of their attacks were dispersed before reaching our forward infantry positions ... heavy concentrations were brought down on opportunity targets and on several occasions the fire of over 300 guns was concentrated on a single area.'[91] On 2 July, I and II Panzer Corps were ordered to go over to the defence.

The shift of Operation Epsom to a defensive battle went down in history as another British failure. VIII British Corps was supposed to force a German abandonment of Caen. Movement and decisiveness were the key metrics. As recently as 1997 Michael Reynolds wrote, 'there can be no doubt that EPSOM . . . had failed'.[92] Dempsey thought otherwise. 'Second Army task remains the same,' he confided to his diary on 29 June, 'to attract to itself (and to defeat) all the German armour and, when opportunity offers, to take Caen.'[93] The British official history claimed even more: that Epsom 'forestalled and spoiled the last German effort to break the Allied front that could be made while there were still some fresh armoured divisions'.[94] Recent reflection supports that view. 'The German position in Normandy never fully recovered from the mauling it received in EPSOM,' John Buckley writes; 'the initiative was lost for good'. Rundstedt and Schweppenburg were sacked: 'I'm next,' Rommel is reputed to have said. Moreover, German 'tactical methods for assault had been exposed as hugely costly in the face of Allied firepower'.[95] Epsom turned out to be another battle like Third Ypres in 1917: a British 'defeat' from which the Germans never recovered.

The ferocity of the fighting during Epsom could never be effectively captured by the media. People had been reading about 'fierce tank battles around Caen' since D+1. Epsom was more of the same: the lines on the newspaper maps scarcely moved. This was not the new blitzkrieg that Americans expected. SHAEF's press guidance issued for the week of 29 June virtually assured that no excitement would emerge from Epsom. Reporters were urged to 'Build up the coming battle by stressing the German commitment of elite troops, especially armour, against Montgomery's left flank'. And they should try to keep the Germans guessing about Calais. But in the meantime, they were to emphasise successful movement: 'Cherbourg is ours . . . Must continue to build-up Cherbourg. Until the battle around Caen is fully joined we must not expect spectacular developments to follow the fall of Cherbourg.'[96]

CHAPTER 22

STALEMATE

Far behind our original schedule now but that schedule did not take into consideration the great difficulty of fighting in this bocage country.

Major Chester Hansen, Diary, 23 July 1944[1]

On 22 June 1944 the long-awaited Soviet offensive finally began. Operation Bagration was an attack of staggering proportions and stunning speed. The Russians deployed 1.2 million men and 5,000 tanks and assault guns across a 450-mile front east of Minsk. The plan was simple: a sweeping double envelopment that would culminate 200 miles deep into the German positions. The distances were vast, troop concentrations were low and German Army Group Centre was painfully weak. By the time Operation Bagration ended in mid-August, Soviet troops had killed, wounded or captured nearly a million Germans, and smashed a path to the gates of Warsaw.[2]

Bagration contrasted starkly with the plodding Anglo-Saxon armies in the west. Eisenhower was certainly impressed.[3] German propaganda ridiculed Allied progress in Normandy. By early July that tone crept into British and American press reporting, too. Rumours circulated that the Russians had erected a sign west of Minsk saying '1,203 Miles to Caen'. When a delegation of Russian observers arrived at Bradley's HQ on 13 July one American officer quipped, 'My God! Have the Russians broken through at St Lo?'[4]

Those who knew better understood that a comparison of Normandy to the Eastern Front was pointless. Germany's Army Group Centre had barely one armoured vehicle and 148 troops per kilometre of front. German divisions in the east held an average of 25km of the line. In Normandy, German divisions held an average of 6km of front, supported by twenty armoured vehicles per kilometre.[5] It was not hyperbole when the *New York Times* declared in an editorial in early July that the Anglo-Canadians were fighting against 'a German concentration of power declared to have been greater than on any single battlefield in this war or the last war'.[6]

And it was not just the concentration of Panzer divisions around Caen that made Allied progress in Normandy so slow. Fighting in the bocage was brutal for both sides. 'I spoke to a veteran of the Eastern Front today,' a German soldier wrote in July. 'He said that it was hard in the east, but it was never like it is here.'[7] Major General Raymond Barton, commander of the 4th USID, expressed his own frustration with fighting in the bocage. 'We outnumber them 10 to 1 in infantry, 50 to 1 in artillery,' Barton wrote, 'and an infinite number in the air.'[8] And, he might have added, eight to one in armoured vehicles.[9] Still the going was agonisingly slow. Much depended on the willingness of the American soldier to brave concentrated German small-arms fire, typically at very short range, and relentless mortar fire to win the next patch of hedgerow. Either way, whether in the bocage or the open fields around Caen, there was no easy way out.

By early July the glacial pace of the campaign in Normandy brought renewed purpose – and anxiety – to the Anglo-American debate over strategy. Churchill still desperately wanted to win the war in 1944, while Britain retained power and influence over the development of strategy. He set little stock in Roosevelt's plans for a 'World Security Organization' to manage postwar international relations. At best Churchill favoured a 'World Peace Council' composed of the Great Powers, and regional peace councils to tackle local problems.[10] His position was not unique. Walter Lippmann proposed a very similar model for handling postwar international issues in his book *U.S. War Aims*, published in the early summer of 1944.[11] It was evident to the British after Tehran that the new borders of Europe between the Russian and British spheres of influence needed to be set as far east as possible. And Britain would need a powerful ally in Europe, at this stage probably France or if needs be a resuscitated Germany, to check Soviet might. Delay in Normandy frustrated those ambitions.

The flash point in the Anglo-American alliance in late June and early July remained Anvil. The British view was simple: if things were going well in Italy, Anvil was unnecessary, and if things were going badly in Italy then the troops would be needed there.[12] By late June the Fifth US and Eighth British armies were pushing slowly north of Rome, encumbered by the long supply chain stretching back to Naples and Anzio, and by Alexander's caution and Mark Clark's disinterest.[13] Alexander's plan was to reach the Apennine mountains north of Florence and then launch a great offensive to drive the Germans out of the Po River valley and back into the Alpine passes leading to Austria. That would help Eisenhower's armies race across the plains of northern Europe.

George Marshall remained unconvinced. When he visited Alexander's headquarters on 19 June, Marshall still insisted that the Germans would not fight in Italy, and that they had only done so up to now because of a colossal strategic error by Hitler. As Brooke muttered in frustration in his diary on 28 June, 'this is exactly what we kept on telling them would happen!!' The merit in driving hard for the Alps was not simply holding or drawing German forces into Italy. 'British preference for operations along the eastern shores of the [Adriatic] sea,' the US official history *Riviera to the Rhine* stated candidly, 'was motivated in part by post-war political considerations that were not shared by their American Allies.'[14] Put simply, the Americans were fighting to win the war, the British were fighting to win the peace. Even informed elements of the American media understood this. The *New York Times* lamented in early June that Europeans saw the British as their key ally, not the United States, while *Business Week* noted that the British were already planning to feed, clothe and help the liberated people of Europe.[15] America had no plans for anything but fighting. Access gained to the Balkans through the Ljubljana Gap and down the coast of Istria might forestall a Soviet occupation of the whole peninsula. Churchill had already made it clear to Stalin that Greece lay in Britain's sphere of influence. Romania was now trying to get out of the war, Bulgaria would likely follow, and if that happened Turkey might yet join the alliance. Churchill had seen this before, in September 1918, when the Bulgarian defection precipitated the German collapse.[16] He thought this might happen in autumn 1943, and hope for just such a development was renewed in 1944. In any event, it would be good to keep the Russians out of the Balkans. Roosevelt and his Secretary of State, Cordell Hull, loathed this kind of 'power politics', and Roosevelt also feared that an Anglo-Soviet confrontation in the Balkans would unsettle his plans for the United Nations.[17]

Churchill made one final appeal to Roosevelt on 28 June to abandon Anvil and drive the Italian campaign forward at full strength while reinforcing Overlord. Political objectives might be important, FDR admitted, but the western Allies had to stick to the plan: concentrate on the defeat of Germany and conduct Operation Anvil as they promised Stalin. 'It is an interesting document,' Brooke wrote of Roosevelt's telegram, 'as it is not till you get to the last para that you get to the basic reason for the opinions expressed.' Roosevelt's final lines were a candid admission that politics did matter in decisions of strategy, but not the geopolitics of postwar Europe. For 'pure political considerations over here', FDR told Churchill, 'I would never survive even a slight setback in Overlord if it were known that fairly large forces had been diverted to the Balkans'.[18] Brooke noted in his diary that the merits of the case against Anvil or in favour of the Balkans did not matter: 'the Americans now begin to own the major strength on land, in the air and on the sea. They therefore consider that they are entitled to decide how their forces are to be employed.'[19] On 30 June the British acquiesced, and two days later the Combined Chiefs of Staff ordered the launch of Anvil on 15 August. Churchill was heard to mutter that Stalin would be pleased.[20] Since he had control over codenames for the European theatre, Churchill renamed Anvil 'Operation Dragoon' because he had been dragooned into it.[21]

In the end, Churchill's capitulation did not matter: Anvil was going ahead anyway. The American assault divisions were already out of the line in Italy conducting amphibious training. Their orders were cut weeks before any final decision was made by the Combined Chiefs of

Staff. The shift in strategic power was noticed by more than Brooke. On 1 July *Liberty* magazine speculated that FDR and Churchill were no longer making strategy: Marshall and King were.

In any event, by then the rationale for Anvil had changed. Cherbourg was a mess, and unlikely to be serviceable for months. The Americans needed a large and undamaged port to funnel their divisions into Europe: Marseilles now became the target.[22] Eisenhower backed Anvil on this basis alone. He was right. Even a cursory glimpse at the US Army Green Series official histories of logistics reveals the enormous complexity faced by American planners trying to deploy and support sixty or seventy divisions in Europe. The prodigious scale of American logistics support, at roughly two and a half times the British rate per man, meant that once the main force was ashore in France any American role in the Mediterranean would be problematic.[23]

It did little to help the British case against Anvil that the pursuit north of Rome slowed to a crawl.[24] As usual, the Germans fought a successful rearguard action. By late July the Allies were paused along the Arno, waiting for the major ports of Livorno and Ancona to open before tackling the much more formidable Gothic Line along the northern Apennines. Much to Mark Clark's dismay, the American role in all this was small and getting weaker by the day. 'The major obstacle to success in Italy', Blumenson writes, 'was the decreasing strength of [Clark's] Fifth Army.' The British Eighth Army would now have to 'carry the ball,' Clark lamented in his diary. In the late summer the British very generously offered Clark command of a British corps, making the US Fifth Army Anglo-American again.

* * *

In the high summer of 1944 the Anglo-American war against the Axis was still predominantly 'British'.[25] In South East Asia, General Slim's 14th British Army – half a dozen Indian, British and African divisions – dwarfed anything the Americans had yet put in the field. And in early July Anglo-Canadian forces in Normandy outnumbered the Americans by a slim margin: 526,700 compared to 494,000 Americans.[26] Anglo-Canadian and American numbers in Normandy remained roughly even until later that month, when a surge of ASF troops tipped strength on the ground in America's favour. Bomber

Command of the RAF remained – for the moment – roughly equal in size to the American strategic bomber force.

And, of course, everything outside the Pacific depended almost entirely on British seapower. Seaborne resupply of Normandy throughout June and July remained overwhelmingly British: by D+28 fully 2.4 million tons of the 3.4 million GRT of shipping supporting military operations in France was British or British controlled.[27] Much of the resupply was carried in the 200 small coasters pulled from the British carrying trade that could land on the beach at low tide. The escort of small troop ships plying their way back and forth to the beaches was done primarily by British and Canadian ships. Two out of every three convoys destined for the American beaches in June and July were escorted by Canadian corvettes.[28]

Defence of the 300-square-mile invasion zone off the Normandy beaches in the Baie de la Seine remained a predominantly British task. The overwhelming majority of the 255 minesweepers assigned to Overlord were British – an article in the *New York Times* on 2 July extolled their relentless and hazardous work but failed to note that the sweepers were RN.[29] Stephen Roskill claims that the Allies had the mine threat largely in hand by early July.[30]

The same was true of the U-boat threat. Twenty-five were ordered up the Channel in June: seven were sunk, three damaged and five just quit trying. As this wave of U-boats moved up Channel, Anglo-Canadian hunting forces moved with them. The main route to Normandy was guarded by a 'picked force' of two British and two Canadian anti-submarine destroyer groups. The hunters and the hunted played cat and mouse in the Channel for the rest of the summer. U-boat commanders made clever use of tides and a boulder- and wreck-strewn bottom to avoid detection, but they also accomplished little.[31] When Henry Stimson visited Normandy in mid-July he was struck by the orderliness of the movement of men, supplies and equipment from Britain to the continent, and by the fact that it was all done 'practically in absolute safety from submarines'.[32] This was another quiet British success story, one noted by British newspapers in mid-July but not by historians of the Normandy campaign.[33]

Finally, the British kept Fortitude South II going, and in the process held the Fifteenth Army in the Pas-de-Calais. Indeed, as explained in the next chapter, the Fortitude deception was completely revamped during the 'stalemate' period of early July. Operations in Normandy remained closely tied to Fortitude South for the balance of the month.

Still the myth persisted in the summer of 1944 that Overlord was primarily an American operation. John Thompson, the *Chicago Tribune* reporter with Bradley's army, filed a story on 3 July saying as much. According to Thompson, Marshall and Eisenhower had had to overcome British reluctance to launch the operation, which was why they 'supposedly relinquished the major role in the assault to the Americans'. Three days later the *Chicago Tribune*'s editorial supported that view. 'The news from France', McCormick wrote, 'suggests that more than half of the troops so far engaged in Normandy have been American.'[34] On both counts McCormick's newspaper was wrong. As Bradley noted generously in his memoirs, 'England contributed to OVERLORD to the point of exhaustion. In sacrifice, pain and deprivation, the British people paid far more dearly than we did for the final victory.'[35] Even the British home front was engaged. *Time* magazine observed on 24 July that the casualties among Londoners from the V1 campaign were roughly comparable to American losses in the recently completed Saipan campaign. The difference was that the cost for Saipan was now 'paid in full': London was still paying.[36]

Taken all together – Italy, Burma, the air war, Normandy, seapower in the west, stoicism at home in the face of the V1 Blitz – Dan Todman was right: 'the summer of 1944 was the most total moment of Britain's total war'.[37] It also proved to be Britain's bloodiest.

* * *

Chester Hansen recorded that Eisenhower was 'bright and happy over the progress of events' when he arrived in Normandy on 1 July for a five-day visit. Now that the Cherbourg campaign was finished, Ike had come to witness the start of the First US Army's drive south to break out of the bocage and start the war of movement.

It turned out that June and July 1944 were the wettest in Normandy since 1900. The sodden low-lying areas in front of the Americans canalised attacks along predictable routes, and sharply reduced the ability of the USAAF to support them. On some days nothing could fly.[38] If that was not bad enough, ammunition shortages delayed – and then shaped – Bradley's plans. By the time VIII US Corps was ready to attack down the west coast of the Cotentin on 3 July, Bradley writes, 'The Germans had already profited from the ammunition shortages that compelled us to call off Middleton's earlier attack.'[39] More minefields and more Germans were now in place. Small-arms ammunition and grenades could be – and were – flown in from the USA, while 57mm anti-tank and 4.2" mortar rounds remained scarce.[40]

The basic supply problems had not been resolved when Bradley launched his attack on 3 July. Each of his corps now had enough ammunition for about two days of heavy fighting. This, Martin Blumenson wrote, 'was considered adequate to propel the army to the Coutances–Caumont line', and Bradley expected 'no serious interruption in the offensive to the south'.[41] The Americans 'had a marked advantage in numbers and firepower', Wilmot observed: fourteen divisions against six German divisions in the line and one in reserve.[42] The plan was to push all along his line in the expectation that the Germans would break somewhere. The key part was a drive by three divisions of Middleton's VIII US Corps down the west coast of the Cotentin peninsula towards Coutances, 15 miles away. Bradley hoped that this would unhinge the German line and force a withdrawal that would lift the Americans out of the bog they were struck in. He could then use the Saint-Lô–Coutance road as his start line for a breakthrough. What happened over the next fifteen days, in what Weigley dubbed 'the Battle of the Cotentin Plain', was an exercise in frustration and stalemate.

Allied intelligence suggested that the position in front of Middleton's VIII Corps was weakly held by forces with low morale.[43] The Germans were there in strength and morale was good.[44] The 'Mahlmann Line' was a formidable position, anchored on Mont Castré, a 3-mile-long flat-topped, heavily forested feature 300 feet high, from which the Germans were able to see Utah beach. Typically, American literature is silent about the artillery fireplan for this operation. McManus says simply that a dozen battalions (i.e. 144 guns) fired 'hundreds of rounds'.[45] It seems that the plan relied heavily on air support. 'You can get all you want,' Middleton was told on the afternoon of 2 July. He arranged to have it provide direct support to the attacking troops.[46]

Middleton's attack commenced at 0530 hours on 3 July in driving rain and low cloud: no air support that day. It was a portent. The Americans met stiff resistance and made little progress. Good weather on 5 July allowed airpower to have an impact, and some progress was made up the slopes of Mont Castré. But the Germans heavily reinforced the Mahlmann Line, checking the American advance and inflicting heavy casualties. By the end of the day on 7 July VIII US Corps was a spent force. Middleton now slipped the newly arrived 8th USID into the line to renew the effort. It was rated 'as one of the best trained U.S. Divisions in the European theatre'. Like all divisions new to battle – and to the bocage – the 8th stuttered and hesitated, its officers got confused, and decisions and movements were too slow. Four days later Middleton sacked the division commander. VIII US Corps finally reached the high ground above Lessay on 14 July, a week behind schedule.[47]

By then Bradley's attack across the whole American front had also largely stalled. VII US Corps launched its attack south of Carentan on 4 July down a corridor barely a mile and a half wide between flooded lowlands on a one-division front. The first day's objective was Sainteny, just 3km away. After two days the 83rd USID was just halfway there. 'Dry ground suitable for military operations was nonexistent,' Blumenson writes; even without the Germans the 'terrain alone would have been a serious obstacle'.[48] On 7 July XIX US Corps joined Bradley's break-in attack. It was to attack Saint-Lô from the north-west by crossing the Vire River and the Vire-Taut canal, and then swing south. Lieutenant General Charles Corlett, the corps commander, expected a stiff fight against powerful forces. His supporting fireplan involved some 200 field guns, thirty-six 4.2" mortars, and an extensive air assault. By the time the attack was ready most of the Germans in front of him had drifted away to La Haye-du-Puits: just what Bradley hoped would happen.

Rain and fog on the morning of 7 July cancelled air support, but it also covered the 117th Regiment's assault across the Vire. The regiment had been the demonstration unit for assault river crossings at the Infantry School at Fort Benning.[49] Its attack went well. A footbridge was across by 0600 hours and the western end of the Airel bridge was secured by

0830. Two other bridges were soon under construction and by noon armour began to cross. But the 117th Regiment struggled with the bocage as they tried to expand the bridgehead. Their supporting artillery barrage was cancelled because the infantry could not keep up. It was also wasteful. Instead of being laid on the lines of hedgerows and the German defences, the barrage was set on 'lines arbitrarily drawn a hundred yards apart' that only occasionally struck German defenders. Firing barrages that conformed to the enemy defences (and not just to the map grids) required considerable skill: it could not be easily improvised.[50] The division commander, Major General Leland Hobbs, called the advance off, although not before the division's 4.2" mortars had fired 'so much ammunition that expenditures were restricted for the remainder of the month'.[51] That effectively removed the First US Army's most effective weapon for hedgerow fighting from the order of battle. The 4.2" mortar, with its rifled barrel, was extremely accurate, and the bomb had nearly twice the bursting power of a 105mm shell. More ammunition for the 4.2" was known to be either in the holds of ships offshore or lost in depots, but manifests were so poor no one could find it.[52]

At 1330 hours phase two of the XIX US Corps attack began, when the 120th Regiment waded the Vire-Taut canal and headed south to link up with the Vire bridgehead. Things looked good enough by the end of the day that Bradley released the 3rd USAD to give the drive a push. Soon a column of men and vehicles 20 miles long was creeping its way towards the bridge at Airel.[53] Enough of the 3rd USAD got across to attack the next day, but the same problems which plagued German tanks in close country – infantry with anti-tank weapons – soon brought that to a halt. Meanwhile a colossal traffic jam developed at Airel as both the 30th USID and the 3rd USAD tried to cross at the same time.

By 8 July the Americans were attacking everywhere and going nowhere. 'As Corlett's XIX Corps bellied forward through the hedgerows towards Saint-Lô and Collins crawled through the Carentan swamps,' Bradley recalled after the war, 'more and more newsmen began to ask if the Allies had learned anything since climbing out of the trenches in France 26 years before.'[54] The only good news, had they been aware of it, was that the Americans were destroying about a battalion and a half of German troops every day.[55]

The other bit of good news to come out of this frustrating series of battles was that the Americans could handle German tanks. There had been some angst about this, especially after some US armoured officers witnessed the later stages of Epsom.[56] Major General Edward Brooks of the 2nd USAD watched British Fireflies in action and told Eisenhower that he, too, wanted to kill Panthers at 'their own range'.[57] Nothing in the US arsenal could do that. Brooks wanted 17-pounders, preferably on tanks but he would take towed if they could be supplied. Leroy Watson at the 3rd USAD echoed Brook's sentiments.[58] This anxiety was allayed when the Panzer Lehr attacked VII US Corps in the Vire bridge-head on 11 July. Two weak Kampfgruppen supported by about fifty tanks and assault guns, shrouded by fog, penetrated the American lines. Sunshine, resolve and skill soon stopped them cold, as the Panzer Lehr's armour was hunted and killed. When shells from their M10s bounced off the Panther's frontal armour, the hunters circled around and killed them from behind. Ranges were often short, typically 150 yards, and as Beevor comments, 'the tank destroyer crews fought with impressive self-control'.[59] In close country the Panzer Lehr's tanks were also vulnerable to infantry anti-tank weapons.[60] Lehr lost a quarter of its remaining combat strength in less than twelve hours. Collins estimated that his men destroyed thirty German tanks.[61] American anti-tank weapons, when handled with skill and determination, worked fine.[62]

Apart from that milestone, the frustrating week-long effort to clear the swamps and the worst of the bocage 'had to be', in Russell Weigley's words, 'considered a grave disappointment, both in its rate of advance and in the combat showing of most of the American divisions involved'.[63] By 10 July, Bradley had to admit to the senior officers of the 21st AG (at a conference that day) that his efforts to break through the cordon of bocage, swamp and Germans between Saint-Lô and the west coast of the Cotentin had failed. 'Never mind,' Monty said soothingly. And then he suggested gently, 'Probably need to concentrate a little more.'[64] Apparently, Bradley did not need reminding: he had taught cadets at West Point the importance of concentration of effort.[65]

* * *

Meanwhile, fighting on the Anglo-Canadian front in the first two weeks of July seemed equally futile. Dempsey launched a series of operations which have largely escaped notice in the general literature on the campaign – Windsor, Jupiter and Greenline. Even Operation Charnwood, which ultimately captured most of Caen, seemed an empty gesture by this stage: a shattered city with all the bridges across the Orne to the south blown by the Germans. In the event, this Anglo-Canadian stalemate became an important part of the enduring Normandy narrative, and a flashpoint for contemporary and postwar criticism of Montgomery's strategy.

While Bradley launched his campaign to bust out of the bocage, the Anglo-Canadians wrestled with the problem of Caen and Hill 112. 'As long as the Germans held Carpiquet airfield,' Terry Copp writes, 'they could observe and respond to every movement towards Hill 112.'[66] Capturing Carpiquet was part of the original Epsom plan but it was called off when VIII British Corps went over to the defensive on 29 June.[67] In early July, Dempsey revived the attack on Carpiquet, but now as a preliminary move in the final capture of Caen.

Even the Canadian official history dismisses Operation Windsor as a bloody failure.[68] Carpiquet lay 2,500 yards deep into the German position across farmland as flat and bare as a billiard table. It was held by a battalion of the 12th SS and overlooked by the Germans from high ground to the north. The Canadian attack was massively supported: over 500 guns, plus the 16" guns of HMS *Rodney* and the 15" guns of the monitor *Roberts*. Anyone who wants to listen to the opening barrage can simply google Matthew Halton's CBC radio broadcast from that morning. For the attacking infantry, the advance was like something conjured by Dante. As the supporting barrage marched ahead of them, a German counter-barrage marched in step just behind it, trapping the men of the 8th CIB in a maelstrom of dust, shrapnel and burning wheat. By the time the North Shore Regiment reached the western edge of Carpiquet at 0625 hours they had lost 40 per cent of their men. Attempts to take the bunker complex on the south side of the airfield and the control building to the east both failed. By the end of day three, Canadian battalions held a narrow finger-like salient stuck deep in the German lines.[69]

Dempsey expressed his disappointment with Operation Windsor the next morning, and the odour of failure stuck. Even the Canadian army historians accepted this conclusion. Had they but looked at their own narratives prepared in 1944 they would have known that during the night of 4–5 July, Carpiquet was counterattacked five times by the 1st SS Panzer, the operational reserve for the Caen sector. By their own estimate, the 1st SS lost about 115 infantry and twenty tanks in those attacks. These are conservative estimates. By the morning of 5 July, I SS Panzer Corps had to admit that the effort to retake Carpiquet was a failure.[70] The Canadians now had observation into the Germans' reverse-slope positions behind the Abbey d'Ardennes and into Caen itself. 'The Germans concluded that the main attack to take Caen would follow shortly,' Copp writes, 'and could not be won.'[71]

* * *

In the first week of July frustration mounted over the rate of progress in Normandy. The V1 campaign was taking its toll on London and on Churchill's patience. Constant attack by Allied bombers in Operation Crossbow, which Phillips O'Brien described – on the basis of resources committed by both sides – as 'one of the greatest battles of World War II',[72] seemed to have little impact on the rate of launches. Fully half of the RAF's fighter effort was now devoted to stopping them, albeit with increasing success. But the V1s had reduced London's industrial output by 25 per cent, and casualties mounted each day. The only certain way to stop the Doodlebugs seemed to be breaking out of Normandy.

Churchill had to explain it all, and the steps his government was taking to mitigate the V1 campaign, to Parliament on 5 July. By the time Brooke arrived late that evening, Churchill was in a 'maudlin, bad tempered, drunken mood, ready to take offence at anything, suspicious of everyone and in a highly vindictive mood against the Americans'. When Churchill began to 'abuse Monty because his operations were not going faster', a view incited by Eisenhower's comments that Monty was too cautious, Brooke could not restrain himself. 'I flared up,' Brooke recorded in his diary, 'and asked him if he could not trust his generals for 5 minutes instead of continuously abusing and belittling them.' What followed was 'one of the heaviest thunderstorms that we had!' It did not help that Eden sided with Churchill: the campaign in Normandy needed to go faster.[73]

While Churchill consoled himself with booze and Brooke tried to recover his equilibrium, Montgomery's latest offensive was about to launch: the capture of Caen. Operation Charnwood features in the Normandy literature largely because of the use of strategic bombers for the first time in Normandy to help forces move on the ground. Leigh Mallory, Eisenhower's deputy, decided it would be a good idea. The evening before Charnwood was due to start he arranged for 450 Lancasters and Halifaxes to drop 6,000 bombs with delayed-action fuses across the northern edge of Caen. Historians tend to focus on the destruction of Caen that followed. This obscures the fact that on the ground Charnwood was, in Terry Copp's words, 'one of the most difficult battles of the campaign'.[74]

The opening barrage started at 0420 hours on the morning of 8 July, and Anglo-Canadian gunners never stopped firing that day. The 3rd BID advanced with comparative ease through Lébisey against a Luftwaffe division, but the 12th SS holding the rest of the line fought stubbornly. It cost them dearly. On one occasion the 13th Field Regiment, RCA, trapped a concentration of the Hitler Youth with fire and then brought down 'scale 10' fire from the 216 field guns of I British Corps: 2,160 rounds in one concentration. 'The damage to the enemy,' the 13th Regimental history records laconically, 'was colossal.'[75] The Canadians drove the Hitler Youth from Buron and Authie, and pushed to the edge of the city by the end of the day. Fearful that the 12th SS would be annihilated, it was ordered to retreat across the Orne around 2200 hours that evening. The advance into Caen the next day was slowed by rubble, booby traps, mines and scattered rear guards. Bridges across the Orne were blown as Canadian patrols approached.[76]

On 8 July, Montgomery visited Dempsey's HQ to plan the British Second Army's next move. 'He wants me to press strongly with the 8 Corps attack,' Dempsey wrote in his diary, 'so as to help First [US] Army get on.'[77] Keeping German armour fixed around Caen remained a priority. While the newly arrived 2nd CID and the newly established II Canadian Corps began to winkle their way around Caen from the west, and Dempsey made plans for a major attack east of Caen, a new series of attacks was launched to take Hill 112 – a position too important for the Germans to abandon, and therefore an opportunity to hold them in place.

It says a very great deal about what happened on Hill 112 in the summer of 1944 that it is perhaps the only place in Normandy where

19. Caen at last: British troops in the centre of the city near the church of Saint-Pierre, 10 July 1944.

shrapnel could still easily be found seventy years later. In the 1990s and early 2000s it was customary to find coachloads of aged men with broad northern British accents, wearing black berets and the Royal Tank Regiment cap badges, milling about the Churchill tank and monument just off the D8. They told tales of Churchills grinding up the long open slopes, succumbing to fire from guns they seldom saw. Hill 112 has since become a major focus of British commemoration, enough that the French rerouted the D8 to accommodate a garden, a spacious car park and a 25-pounder field gun.

In early July, Operation Jupiter added to the tale of heroism and woe commemorated atop Hill 112: five days of what Antony Beevor called 'pitiless' fighting. The 43rd Wessex Division launched 129th Brigade straight up the hill, while 130th Brigade drove across the face of it towards Etavaux and Maltot to the east. Casualties mounted even before the British reached small-arms range, then the combination of barbed wire and machine guns kept them at bay. All the while British shells ploughed the hill. 'Not a metre of ground escaped,' a German soldier commented later.[78] Amid the maelstrom and confusion the Germans abandoned Hill 112 during the night of 10–11 July, allowing the British to occupy it briefly. The battle continued for most of the week, reducing the crest of Hill 112 to a wasteland of shell holes, splintered trees, bodies and wrecked tanks. At one point, in the face of relentless British shelling, the Germans left a solitary Tiger to 'hold' the hill.[79] The Wessex lost 2,000 men in the first two days, and 5,000 more by 22 July.

Dempsey spread the attack westward, along the ridge towards Évrecy. Operation Greenline was launched by the 15th Scottish Division on 15 July from the valley of the Odon, in an attempt to capture Évrecy, Hill 112 and Esquay. Once again the Scots and their supporting tanks climbed the open slopes of Hill 112, briefly capturing Évrecy and Esquay before counterattacks drove them back. Losses were heavy on both sides: 3,500 British and over 2,000 Germans.[80] On 16 July XXX British Corps joined the attack further down the Caen–Villers-Bocage road. This brutal series of battles, subsequently dubbed the Second Battle of the Odon, succeeded in holding the German armour in the Caen sector and writing off some of it. But Hill 112 remained in German hands, and it brooded over the Caen–Falaise battlefield until 4 August.

The British casualty bill in early July was enormous and ultimately unsustainable, but Montgomery was working to a plan and he was about to throw his armour in. On 12 July he told Eisenhower that 'I am going to launch two very big attacks next week'. On 17 July he planned to send three armoured divisions across the plain east of Caen, up onto Bourguébus ridge and start probing towards Falaise. This was intended 'to draw enemy forces away from First US Army'. The next day – 18 July – the Americans would attack 'with six divisions about 5 miles west of St Lo'. Monty's appeal to Eisenhower was largely meant to soothe

Ike's anxiety about the battle stalemating and to secure support from strategic bombers to help blast a way through the German front.[81]

* * *

By mid-July the Normandy campaign seemed to be stuck. It was true that Caen had finally fallen, but capturing the northern part of that shattered city with no easy access across the Orne was a pyrrhic victory. As Bradley recalled, 'we could sense the growing impatience of the newsmen who looked critically on the deadlock that seemed to have gripped our beach head . . . Those who had awaited Monty's assault on Caen as the signal for an Allied breakthrough trooped back disheartened to their gloomy press camps when the attack went no further.'[82]

The first public utterance of disappointment about the pace of the Normandy campaign may have been Hanson Baldwin's story in the *New York Times* datelined London, 8 July. It ran on page seven. The 'Allied advance in Normandy for the past ten days has been a slow and plodding one', he wrote. 'Undeniably disappointing.' Caen had not yet fallen, and Bradley's new offensive 'that started last Monday morning, and from which much was expected, has developed with discouraging slowness . . . We have made gains, but they are measured in yards and miles, not in scores of or hundreds of miles, as on the Russian front.' Half the summer-fighting weather was gone and the Normandy front had scarcely moved. Brutally wet weather and the restricting nature of the bocage were partly to blame. Rain kept American medium bombers grounded for twelve successive days in June, and French mud, 'famous in World War I, has again been taking its place in history'. The Americans were paying a price for their inexperience, Baldwin admitted, but even veteran British divisions were doing little better. In the final analysis, Allied tactics were too cautious, too focused on punching and too little on pushing through and releasing the armour. 'We must fight a war of manoeuvre, not of position,' Baldwin asserted; 'the time for caution has gone.'[83]

In a matter of days the story of 'delay' in Normandy leapt to the front pages of major British and American dailies. On 14 July the *New York Times* carried a sub-headline, top right above the fold, proclaiming, 'Normandy Situation Said to Discourage Optimism'. The story was filed by Drew Middleton at SHAEF HQ near Portsmouth, so it was perhaps an accurate reflection of the sentiment there. It was true, Middleton wrote, that the British and Canadians were killing German tanks at a prodigious rate – 150 claimed over the last two days – but they were also 'paying the price always expected by savage fighting at short range'. The net result was little movement of the line. In the meantime, Bradley's First US Army was moving 'steadily forward', but it was doing so by systematically smashing its way through its objectives employing 'heavy American shelling'. 'The general picture on the 100-mile front,' Middleton concludes, 'was not optimistic.'[84]

The next day, 15 July, the *Daily Express* – Beaverbrook's newspaper and, with a print run of over 3 million copies a day, the most widely circulated newspaper in the world – put the story on the front page. Their correspondent with the British Second Army, Alan Moorehead, opined that two questions were 'uppermost in the minds of soldiers: 1. Why did the advance not go more quickly?' and second, 'Were we on the right lines with our bombing of the Norman towns?' Moorehead had recently travelled through twenty smashed towns and villages, and yet the bridgehead held by the British Second Army was virtually unchanged since the first week ashore. Monty, sequestered in his 'secret headquarters', had seldom been seen in the past week, 'and his published orders to his troops gave no clue whatever to his intentions'.[85]

Correspondents in France did not require anyone to tell them that the campaign needed to move faster. Nearly a million Allied troops were now crammed into the narrow beachhead, along with a quarter of a million vehicles. Despite the construction of new roads, like the ring road around Bayeux which still serves the city well, Wilmot recalled traffic jams that 'sometimes extended for ten or fifteen miles'.[86] Steven Casey described the American press corps at Vouilly as bored and idle during Bradley's failed attempt to break out between 3 July and the fall of Saint-Lô on 19 July – a sentiment echoed in Bradley's memoirs. This was especially true of the forty correspondents who arrived with Patton in early July, and who had no priority for filing stories until the Third US Army became operational.[87] Their 'long alcohol-fuelled conversations', Casey writes, suggested that 'much darker thoughts were festering just below the surface'. Unhappy with the food, unhappy with the lack of progress in the campaign, and unhappy with the hostility of the local

Normans, this discontent seems to have emerged entirely from the American press camp.[88]

However, British press commentators who disliked Montgomery joined the fray. Among them was J.F.C. Fuller, accepted by many as the father of modern mechanised warfare – and therefore blitzkrieg. The problem in Normandy, Fuller claimed in the *Sunday Pictorial* on 16 July, was that Montgomery kept hitting at strength rather than weakness, conducting Great War-style attritional warfare based on lavish use of artillery. He had done so at Cassino and was now doing at it again at Caen: attacking the hinge that did not need to be attacked. Fuller admitted that there were no evident weaknesses in the German line in Normandy, but even so he was 'shaken' every time he heard of another attack preceded by 'the heaviest artillery barrage that ever was'.[89] Fuller was anxious about Montgomery's strategy for another reason: the prospect of domination of Europe by Communists. He was not alone in that, and the worry had no necessary links to fascism (as Fuller did). While American journalists and officers fretted over the slow pace in Normandy because it extended the length of the war, many Britons were fearful of what the rapid – and seemingly unstoppable – Soviet advance could mean for western Europe. The western Allies needed to get as far east as possible, and quickly.

The notion that Montgomery and his strategy were the real culprits in the apparent stalemate was taken up with enthusiasm by reporters from the *Chicago Tribune* attached to SHAEF. One of these was Wes Gallagher, based at SHAEF HQ in the UK. Dupuy described him disparagingly as a 'clever, unscrupulous police reporter',[90] but he probably reflected a widely shared sentiment. As Baldwin had done a week earlier, Gallagher's story published on 16 July emphasised the lack of movement in the Allied line after forty days. He accepted that bad weather was a factor, but the real problem was Montgomery. British and American attacks had not been properly coordinated. In any event, Bradley would never be able to break out 'as long as the Caen sector remains the same'. Only a break-out by the British Second Army would draw German forces onto the Anglo-Canadians and ease pressure on Bradley's front.[91] The real problem was that Montgomery was simply too slow, too cautious. His plodding in Italy had jeopardised the Salerno landing, and now he was doing it again.[92] Gallagher's senior *Chicago Tribune* partner at SHAEF, Larry Rue, piled on the next day, alleging that the last four to five weeks were evidence of 'part of the elaborate and almost formalized warfare between Montgomery and Field Marshall Rommel'.[93]

American news magazines echoed the frustration. *Time*, generally well balanced in its coverage – and its assessment of Montgomery – nonetheless lamented in its 17 July issue that the pace was too slow. Poor weather, bad terrain and the Germans had a great deal to do with that, but so too did cautious Allied tactics. 'Some Allied military men now thought that a speedier, even a more reckless assault from the north might shorten the battle and save lives in the end . . . the battle at week's end was still being fought at footsoldier's pace.'[94] By 16 July 1944 a rumour was circulating in the SHAEF press camp that Field Marshal Alexander had sent a telegram from Italy to Montgomery saying, 'Hold on. We'll soon be there to help you!'[95]

* * *

Rundstedt, Rommel and Schweppenburg had all wanted to abandon Caen weeks ago, and adopt a more flexible strategy, drawing the Allies beyond the range of supporting naval fire and engaging them in a battle of movement. These ideas were all rejected by Hitler. Between Dollmann's death on 28 June and the sacking of Rundstedt on 3 July, he replaced all the senior German commanders in France – save Rommel – with veterans of the Eastern Front. SS General Paul Hauser took command of the Seventh Army in front of the Americans, while General Hans Eberbach took over Panzer Group West opposite the Anglo-Canadians. Field Marshal Günther von Kluge ('clever Hans') replaced von Rundstedt as Commander in Chief West. Kluge was a Prussian of the old school, known to be cold, self-possessed, ambitious and a little vain. But he was also known for speaking plainly to Hitler.[96]

Kluge arrived in France convinced that the problem in Normandy stemmed from 'mistakes and omissions on the part of commanders and troops'.[97] A quick tour of the front soon convinced him that the local view was correct: the situation was critical. Under relentless attack along the whole Normandy front, he could no more concentrate a counter-attack force than Rundstedt. With new Allied landings looming at Calais and perhaps in southern France, and with the Russians still on the move in the east, there was no great mass of reserves available to break the deadlock in Normandy. On 8 July, Hitler ordered Kluge to dig in and hold.[98] The faint hope was that a stalemated war of attrition in the west, and a victory by the Republicans in the American presidential election in November, would result in a negotiated settlement with the western Allies.

The decision to hold in Normandy set Eberbach to work building defences in depth and reserves in the Caen sector – Hauser's Seventh Army, in front of the Americans, would have to make do with whatever it had. The one place where Eberbach's Eastern Front experience achieved full expression was on the plain east of Caen, where the British had not yet attacked in force. There were no natural obstacles, just scattered stone villages and two rail lines running east of Caen. To the south lay Bourguébus ridge. If the high ground further south around Saint-Aignan-de-Cramesnil and Cintheaux on the N158 could be reached, an even wider, more inviting plain down to Falaise beckoned. So Eberbach created a defensive zone east of Caen 10 miles deep and filled it with Panzer forces and anti-tank guns.[99]

This was the very ground over which Montgomery planned to launch the first of his two-punch break-out plan. He had hoped to launch Goodwood on 17 July, with the American Operation Cobra the next day. When Bradley re-introduced ammunition rationing for his artillery on 14 July, Montgomery pushed back the start by a day. But, as Nigel Hamilton commented, 'Monty dared not delay GOODWOOD' any further.[100] The urgency had nothing to do with disgruntled pressmen.

CHAPTER 23

FANCY SKATING

> Montgomery was spending his reputation in a bitter siege against
> the old university city of Caen . . . had we attempted to exonerate
> Montgomery by explaining how successfully he had hoodwinked
> the German by diverting him towards Caen from the Cotentin, we
> would also have given our strategy away.
>
> General Omar Bradley, *A Soldier's Story*[1]

The metric for the success of the great mechanised armies thrust so
boldly onto the beaches of Normandy was blitzkrieg – lightning
war. The first six weeks were anything but. As Bradley opined seven
years later, 'while we slogged afoot toward the Périeres road, our vastly
superior motorized equipment lay wasted under camouflage nets'.[2] Soldiers, politicians and the press were all frustrated by the lack of progress.
Ernest Dupuy noted the tension in his diary entry of 9 July: 'I wonder
about the politics – Air Ministry, War Office – Anglo-American Relations, the fierce fight between the British and American press. Its fancy
skating on thin ice.'[3]

Much of the angst over the slow pace in Normandy emanated from
SHAEF itself: 100 sea-miles from the action, besieged by idle and frustrated journalists, and much less well informed than it ought to have
been. Eisenhower grumbled to Churchill about Monty's dawdling: he
found a sympathetic ear.[4] The Prime Minister was tired, unhappy and

burdened by the war. By 6 July the V1s had already killed over 2,000 civilians and wounded 18,000 more. Dan Todman claims that the V1 campaign, and looming threat from the V2 – a ballistic missile carrying perhaps a ten-ton warhead which could not be stopped – put Churchill into a panic.[5]

But there was much more on Churchill's mind. He fretted about the campaign in Italy (increasingly a British task) and the fate of Greece, about the Russian stampede across eastern Europe, the costly campaign in South East Asia, about the shortage of manpower to support the British Second Army in France, about Lend-Lease, and the postwar British economy. And he remained bitterly unhappy about Operation Anvil, a diversion which promised to deliver all of southern and eastern Europe into Stalin's clutches. It had all driven him into a funk. He told Brooke on 4 July that he was 'longing for a good row' with Roosevelt to sort it all out. And then there was Monty.

Americans were predisposed to consider Montgomery a plodder, but Monty's sharpest critics were British. Ike's Deputy, Air Marshal Tedder, had been at odds with Montgomery since the North African campaign, and was weary of his high-handedness. Tension over the use of tactical airpower, which Montgomery believed was misdirected by the commander of 2nd TAF – Arthur Coningham, who also vehemently disliked Montgomery – did little to help. Throughout July, Tedder and Coningham waged a steady guerrilla campaign against Monty. Ike also had to listen to the grumblings of Freddie Morgan, now his Deputy Chief of Staff. 'Because of his paternal association with the original plan,' Wilmot wrote in 1950, 'Morgan was regarded at SHAEF as the expert on the operation.' Morgan's admiration for Eisenhower was 'matched only by his antipathy towards Montgomery – a sentiment which, by all accounts, was reciprocated'. In short, Americans disliked and distrusted Montgomery, but many of his countrymen bluntly hated him.

* * *

Montgomery was seemingly unmoved by the criticism. Some believed at the time, and since, that this stoicism masked incompetence.[6] Generations of his detractors have gone to great lengths to demonstrate that Monty had no plan, that he made it up as he went, that the

Germans concentrated their armour at Caen for their own purposes, that he had no role in planning the break-out, and that despite his outrageous postwar claim that everything went according to plan, it did not.[7] The last point is certainly true. Monty's monumental ego led him to make that claim after the war, when his real strength was that he adapted the Overlord plan and made it work. The origins of the Goodwood/Cobra plans, therefore, and the ultimate break-out from Normandy, form one of the key flash points of the Normandy story – then and since.

Part of the confusion arises from Montgomery's practice of controlling Bradley with a light hand. 'During these operations in the lodgement where Montgomery bossed the First US Army as part of his 21st Army Group, he exercised his Allied authority with wisdom, forbearance, and restraint,' Bradley wrote in 1951.

> While coordinating our movements with those of Dempsey's, Monty carefully avoided getting mixed up in U.S. command decisions, but instead granted us the latitude to operate as freely and as independently as we chose. At no time did he probe into First Army with the indulgent manner he sometimes displayed among those subordinates who were also his countrymen. I could not have wanted a more tolerant or judicious commander. Not once did he confront us with an arbitrary directive and not once did he reject any plan we had devised.[8]

It stretches credulity, however, to suggest that the Overlord Ground Commander had no role in the formulation of the strategy and operations of his campaign. According to Carlo D'Este, Bradley was loath to admit that 'Montgomery ever did anything positive to assist him'.[9] The specific details of Operation Cobra were certainly a 'made in America' plan, but the larger context into which they fitted, and which made Cobra successful, belonged to Montgomery.

Dan Crosswell's account of the planning for Goodwood and Cobra is the most balanced and comprehensive yet written. Crosswell accepts that the origins of the break-out lay in plans developed by the 21st Army Group in mid-June.[10] The basic concept was that the First US

Army would breach the front between Saint-Lô and Coutances, push south towards Avranches, and then turn west into the Brittany peninsula and east towards Vire. While the Brittany ports were opened, the Allies would launch a wide envelopment to the Seine. Securing the ports of Brittany and developing ports in Quiberon Bay were the key objectives of the break-out plan.

By early July, Montgomery had concluded that the best way to do this was to draw and hold as much German combat power as possible, especially Panzer divisions, onto the British Second Army, thus clearing the way for Bradley to break out. This strategy was confirmed between Eisenhower and Montgomery in an exchange of telegrams on 6 and 7 July 1944, just prior to Montgomery's meeting with his army commanders on the 10th. Dempsey recalled that at that later meeting he offered to break out, Montgomery said no.[11] Then he laid out the plan for a tightly coordinated double blow designed to set Bradley's army free: the British Second Army east of the Orne on 17 July to pin Rommel's armour, then the First US Army would break through the next day, 18 July. Eisenhower was informed that day – 10 July – of the plan.

The timing of the Goodwood/Cobra operations had nothing to do with the clamouring for movement: it was tightly tied to drawing Panzer divisions into the Caen area and to sustaining the Fortitude South II deception plan. The original purpose of Fortitude South was to hold the Fifteenth German Army in the Pas-de-Calais until the lodgement in Normandy was secure – at best perhaps until 26 June. However, the British operators of Fortitude continued to feed the deception and the Germans continued to 'buy' it. By early July the Germans estimated that the Allies still had fifty-four divisions ready in the UK to land somewhere in France.[12] In anticipation, the strength of the Fifteenth Army had risen from nineteen divisions to twenty-two in the weeks after D-Day.[13] In mid-July four of these, all infantry divisions, were known to be en route to Normandy. Eberbach planned to use them to relieve Panzer divisions from the front to create a powerful reserve. That could not be allowed to happen.

The maintenance of a continuing threat of a landing north of the Seine required the creation of an entirely new storyline. Among the deception problems by mid-July were what to do with FUSAG and

George Patton – who played a key role after 12 June. The solutions were simple but elegant. FUSAG as a fiction would remain, including the presence of both the First Canadian and Third US armies. The disappearance of Canadians – still the FUSAG assault divisions – from the coastal areas of southern England was explained as withdrawal to escape the V1 campaign.[14] A new US army group, designated the 12th AG, under Bradley would be established in France. It would assume command of both the First US Army and, when it became operational, Patton's Third US Army. The 'demotion' of Patton from Army Group (FUSAG) to an army command would be explained away as the result of another hideous indiscretion. His place in command of FUSAG required a known general of considerable stature. Marshall appointed Lieutenant General Lesley McNair, commander of Army Ground Forces, to the post.

By the time the new scheme for Fortitude South II was approved on 18 July, it was already well underway.[15] Some indications of the new spin can be gleaned from reports of German news and press carried in British and American newspapers. On 5 July the *Manchester Guardian* reported the latest German speculation about the second landing. Not only was the Pas-de-Calais threatened, but the Germans suspected that the British would push to have the V weapon sites along the coast between the Seine and Calais eliminated by the second landing.[16] The reason this had not yet happened, the German commentator 'Sertorius' observed on 4 July, was because the slow progress in Normandy forced Eisenhower to commit more troops there than previously planned.[17]

All of this meant closely scripted moves, designed leaks, well-choreographed double agents, and cover stories designed and implemented by the London Controlling Section in conjunction with SHAEF. As Ike told Bradley's staff on 2 July during a discussion of deception, 'British are far ahead of us. [They] Practice things we don't even begin to understand.'[18] Ralph Ingersoll, the stridently anti-British journalist and publisher who served in Normandy, later admitted that the British running of Fortitude 'approached genius'.[19]

Not all Germans believed in the continuing threat to the Pas-de-Calais, but enough of them did. The German Intelligence Summary of 10 July dismissed the divisions remaining in England as of inferior quality: the best were already in Normandy and they represented a direct threat to Paris.[20] Signals from the Japanese ambassador in Berlin, decrypted on 10 July, nonetheless confirmed the German belief that there was a link between an imminent landing in the Pas-de-Calais and the likelihood of major Allied operations in Normandy. The Germans were particularly anxious about the 18–19 July period, when the moon and tide state would be ideal for an amphibious landing in the Pas-de-Calais.[21] Hitler still believed that the threat north of the Seine was real.[22] On 15 July, Foreign Armies West warned that 'the start of an operation on a larger scale across the Orne towards the southeast' was imminent. 'It is noteworthy,' the report continued, 'that this time coincides with the period most favourable for new landing operations.'[23] Since one of the Germans' great fears was a link-up between the British Second Army and FUSAG, this revelation alone helps explain why keeping Goodwood and Cobra on schedule was so important.[24]

So Montgomery played to German fears of an imminent British break-out on the eastern flank. The need to sell that lie increased dramatically when Bradley told Montgomery that he could not attack on the 19th, and probably not until the 21st. The failure to launch the American break-out to coincide with Goodwood is usually attributed to bad weather. The truth, however, is that from the 18th to the 20th the weather was good: the First US Army had not yet overcome its ammunition shortages.[25] The campaign across the Cotentin had consumed more ammunition than the US logistics system could supply, as the rate of firing reached the highest point of the campaign for the First US Army. By mid-July Bradley needed 7,500 tons of ammunition daily but only 3,000 tons was being landed.[26] Steve Waddell confirms that the ammunition crisis peaked in mid-July. There may well have been enough ashore, but the chaotic rationing of ammunitions and poor record keeping meant that much was 'lost in the system'.[27] The destruction of the main ammunition depot on 12 July, along with 5,000 tons of supplies, exacerbated the problem. And so, 'On 16 July,' Thompson and Mayo write, 'Bradley began to restrict the amount of these types that could be fired.'[28] 'Rationing on arty [artillery] ammo is most difficult supply problem in the army,' Chester Hansen noted that day, as Bradley tried to husband ammunition for what Hansen called 'the giant COBRA operation'. In the meantime, gunners were restricted to one-sixth of their daily allocation (a 'unit of fire' in US Army parlance) – twenty-five rounds for the 105mm and about a dozen for the 155mm. 'Everyone grumbles,' Hansen commented, 'although admitting the necessity of it. Commanders like to use arty. It's a good way of saving doughboy's lives.'[29] Indeed.

The next day, 17 July, the Secretary of War, Henry Stimson, visited Bradley's HQ. Montgomery told Brooke two days later that Stimson stayed so long that 'the attack had to be postponed for 24 hours'.[30] Perhaps. But the real reason was still the shortage of ammunition. On 18 July, the day Goodwood launched, Hansen described the ammunition situation as 'Critical'.[31] The best that Bradley could now promise was to launch Cobra on 21 July. Even the details of the air support for Cobra were still not worked out when Goodwood launched.

With the American delay it became necessary to oversell Goodwood and keep the fiction of an Anglo-Canadian break-out alive – initially for a just few days. Some reporters were in on the deception, but Eisenhower had given Monty full reign to control media coverage of Goodwood/ Cobra.[32] Bradley's unique reflection on the links between Montgomery's strategy, the press and public perception is worth quoting:

> The containment mission that had been assigned Monty in the OVERLORD plan was not calculated to burnish British pride in the accomplishments of their troops. For in the minds of most people, success in battle is measured in the rate and length of advance. They found it difficult to realize that the more successful Monty was in stirring up German resistance, the less likely he was to advance . . . In setting the stage for our breakout, the British were forced to endure the barbs of critics who shamed them for failing to push out vigorously as the Americans did.[33]

Dempsey recalled in 1952, that 'Monty felt it was necessary to overstate the aims of the operation'.[34] However, he did make an effort to ensure that key people knew that his intent for Goodwood was quite different from his public utterances. He sent his Military Assistant, Lieutenant-Colonel Christopher Dawnay, with a personal letter to Brooke and the War Office on 14 July explaining that he had no intention of racing eastward and putting at risk his solid front at Caen.

Monty's Chief of Staff, Freddie de Guingand, also briefed Eisenhower on the plan that same day. Goodwood would be sold as a break-out, but its real purpose was to clear the way for Bradley to do so.[35] On 15 July, Montgomery cautioned Lieutenant-General O'Connor, commander of VIII British Corps, that his primary objective was to contain and write down German strength and, ultimately, allow the capture of Brittany by the Americans. As the strength of the German position east of Caen became clearer, Montgomery warned Dempsey on 17 July not to push too hard and become unbalanced. The eastern flank had to remain a threat to the Germans.

Dempsey planned another feint across the Odon, over blood-soaked ground south-west of Caen, followed by a rapid transfer of armoured divisions north of Caen across new bridges over the Orne and the Caen canal, and onto the plain east of the city. The Germans were not fooled. Their own intelligence and POW information indicated where the main British blow would fall, and Luftwaffe photo reconnaissance captured the hasty bridge construction north of the city. Sepp Dietrich, now in command of I SS Panzer Corps, confirmed it all by putting his ear to the ground, which echoed with the sound of 700 tanks on the move.

* * *

Historians have been transfixed by the massed bombing in support of Goodwood, and with good reason.[36] On the morning of 18 July the sight of masses of low-flying four-engine aircraft buoyed Allied troops. The 'whole northern sky was filled with them as far as one could see – wave upon wave,' one awe-struck British soldier later wrote.[37] Over 1,000 Lancasters and Halifaxes dropped the equivalent of a tactical nuclear device on each of five fortified villages.[38] German defenders were driven mad, and Tiger tanks were tossed in the air. The resort to carpet bombing seemed to reflect the depth of desperation into which Montgomery's strategy had sunk by the middle of July.

Despite Dempsey's claims of a shortage of ammunition,[39] the artillery fireplan for Goodwood was enormous. Over 800 field and medium guns, with 297,000 shells allocated for the initial fireplan, plus twenty-one naval guns.[40] Every German position within range to a depth of 4 miles was pummelled. Supporting fire beyond that point would be provided as and when possible.[41] Meanwhile, 318 Mitchells and

Marauders attacked selected targets, and 570 American B-17s and Liberators dropped thousands of 100lb fragmentation bombs on Troarn and the Frénouville–Bourguébus area.[42]

Not everyone was happy with the plan. Major-General 'Pip' Roberts, in command of the 11th BAD, complained that his infantry was assigned to clear villages, while his tanks raced unsupported to capture Bourguébus ridge. As John Buckley writes, 'Major Terry Sergeaunt of the British Army's No. 2 Operational Section attached to 21st Army Group was horrified by the GOODWOOD plan,' which left the tanks also unsupported by artillery.[43] Only two regiments of guns were slated to move forward to assist the charge up Bourguébus ridge.[44] It was not enough. The 2,000–3,000 yards of open ground from the Caen–Vimont railway to the ridge was overlooked by German guns that could easily kill Allied tanks at that range. As Buckley concludes, 'just when the British tanks might well need their artillery the most would be the very moment they were least likely to get it'.[45]

Beneath all the bluster Goodwood was a limited assault of massive proportions. It was, in fact, all a big lie: big enough to convince many at SHAEF HQ and, more importantly, in the press, that this was the great moment. And big enough to deceive the enemy. Masses of tanks racing for open ground against unbroken guns conjures images of the Charge of the Light Brigade. But Balaclava was an error; Goodwood was deliberate. The British had plenty of tanks: Dempsey was prepared to lose 200–300 – in the hope that personnel losses would be light.[46] And there was a chance that it might work. Dempsey prepared for that, too, but kept those plans to himself.

Not surprisingly, the initial advance went well. The 11th BAD reached the Caen–Vimont rail line in just three hours. But when the attack moved south of the rail line, the fears of those who had seen the plan were realised. When C Squadron of the 23rd Hussars came within range of gun on Bourguébus ridge it was annihilated. As their regimental history records, 'With no time for retaliation, no time to do anything but take one quick glance at the situation, almost in one minute, all its tanks were hit, blazing and exploding. Everywhere wounded or burning figures ran or struggled painfully for cover, while a remorseless rain of armour-piercing shot riddled the already helpless

Shermans.'[47] The 11th BAD lost 126 tanks that day. As horrific as the experience had been, Dempsey wrote in his diary on 24 July, 'Casualties in personnel throughout this operation were extremely small.'[48] By the afternoon of 18 July, Goodwood was largely over. Counterattacks struck Goodwood for the remainder of the day: these withered in the face of British anti-tank and artillery fire. The Germans contented themselves with having stopped the British from driving deeper into their lines.[49]

Ernest Dupuy later wrote that the correspondents covering Goodwood had all been 'fully briefed'. But as they began to file their stories on 18 July, Montgomery suddenly imposed a twenty-four-hour embargo on all news from Normandy – except of the aerial bombardment. He then issued a statement, claiming that 'Early this morning British and Canadian troops of the Second Army attacked and broke through into the area east of the Orne and southeast of Caen'. Professing himself 'well satisfied with the progress made in the first day's fighting of this battle', Montgomery then staged a press conference announcing that 'the break out is imminent'.[50] Bradley agreed with the deception, but he could not get all of the American press to support it.[51] He warned Hansen Baldwin, one of the first correspondents to break the stalemate story, not to fall into an 'error in judgement and advised him to stick around for a while' to see how the story unfolded.[52]

After the war Dupuy told West Point cadets that Montgomery's combination of the embargo of reporting on Goodwood and a bare-faced lie about the alleged breakthrough did 'nothing to assuage his audience, for this was Monty at his benign worst'. Wilmot remained incensed at Montgomery's treatment of the press long after 1944. 'This announcement was premature and indiscreet to say the least,' Wilmot wrote in 1951, and could not be justified 'even as a device to fool the enemy, for Montgomery disclaims any such intention . . . In any case, however, it was a grave mistake to use the word "break-through", for that (in conjunction with the news of the colossal air bombardment) naturally led Fleet Street to the conclusion that this was another and greater El Alamein, and the headlines were written according.'[53]

But that, of course, was precisely the idea. SHAEF communiqués, droll as ever, made no grandiose claims, but the press did. On the morning of 19 July *The Times* proclaimed, 'Second Army Breaks

Through', 'Armoured Forces Reach Open Country' and 'British Arms in Full Cry'. Even the American media was swept up in the euphoria – or the deception. Drew Middleton's story in the *New York Times* on 19 July, filed from SHAEF HQ, trumpeted 'British Rip Line Open East of Caen', and described it as 'the most significant act in the Normandy Campaign since the fall of Cherbourg ... Montgomery was on the verge of an impressive triumph'. But there had been no break-out, no slashing armoured columns racing across the rolling plain towards Falaise – no ground captured for airfields. Operation Goodwood, it seemed, was just another failure.

The press – generally – followed the script, but the British press corps in particular remained a profoundly unhappy lot. They were still restricted by the need to be accompanied by a conducting officer, the transmission of copy back to London remained – by all accounts – unsatisfactory, and deadlines were not being met. And now, in the wake of Goodwood, it was clear that Montgomery was manipulating them as part of the deception operation. 'The Br Warcos [war correspondents] held another mass protest meeting,' Lieutenant-Colonel Richard Malone, the commander of No. 3 Canadian Public Relations Group, reported to the 21st AG PR on 25 July. They 'filed a joint letter of complaint to the CinC and their newspaper association protesting treatment they are receiving'.[54] As Freddie de Guingand lamented in his memoirs, he, too, 'was not at all happy' about Montgomery's relations with the press at this stage of the campaign, 'for I realized the danger of a lack of confidence springing up between the press and the Commander-in-Chief'. The crisis was only resolved by the profound change in the nature of the campaign at the end of the month.[55]

The British were able to keep the press unrest in the British Second Army under wraps, but the difference between Montgomery's claims and the reality on the ground ignited a firestorm at SHAEF that could not be so easily contained. The airmen wanted Monty's head. Tedder was on the phone to Ike on the evening of the 19th telling him that the British Chiefs of Staff would back him if he fired Montgomery.[56] Both Ike and Brooke made plans to fly to France on that day, but only Brooke got off the ground. Before he left Brooke was summoned to No. 10 where he found Churchill 'in a holy rage', and literally frothing at the mouth. It had nothing to do with Goodwood. Monty had issued an edict prohibiting visitors, which Churchill thought was directed at him. It probably had more than a little to do with Stimson's disruption of Bradley's planning for Cobra on the 17th. When Brooke arrived at Monty's HQ that afternoon he found the 21st AG Commander 'in grand form and delighted with his success east of Caen'. Monty dictated a letter clarifying his stance on visitors, and Brooke delivered it to Churchill that evening. Nowhere in his diary or his postwar annotation does Brooke mention the 'failure' of Goodwood, or support for sacking Montgomery.

Bradley flew the Channel that day, too. His tentative plans for Cobra were now complete, but he needed to organise air support for the attack now scheduled for 21 July. The airmen and Bradley left the meeting with different assumptions about what had been agreed on the routes of approach for the air strikes. But the bombers were committed. Back in Normandy, Bradley raced to Collins's HQ to tell him that 1,800 heavy bombers, 300 mediums and hundreds of fighter-bombers would support the attack – and none of them would be British. Collins was 'exuberant'. It mattered that the aircraft were all American. As Hansen noted in his diary, Leigh-Mallory 'was a triflevexed [sic] that the RAF had not been brought into the pic, Brad kept it an all American show'.[57] The RAF would later have reason to be pleased that it was excluded from Cobra.

Meanwhile, Ike spent 19 July, goaded by Monty's detractors and frustrated by another apparent failure, in a blind rage. Monty had invited him – but no airmen – to his HQ, but Ike's staff refused to let him fly in dreadful weather. News the next morning confirmed that Goodwood had stalled, so the Supreme Commander was in a foul mood when he finally landed in Normandy on 20 July. He started his day at Bradley's HQ, where he learned that Cobra, intended for the next day, was to be pushed back yet again – now because of weather. The news 'deeply disappointed' Eisenhower. So he was in a very sour mood when he arrived at Monty's HQ. 'The grim look on his face as he entered Montgomery's map caravan,' Crosswell writes, 'told the story.' Eisenhower expected a confrontation, but he found Monty calm and contented. 'Neither man ever revealed what transpired, but when he emerged, Eisenhower flashed his trademark smile.' Crosswell contends that Ike got what he wanted: confirmation that Montgomery's forces would keep attacking, and relief that 'there was no confrontation, and no need for drastic action'.[58]

But now that the American attack was delayed even further, it was necessary to keep the pressure on in the Caen sector. This was exactly what Dempsey planned to do. 'Once it was evident that with the armour we were not going to break out,' Dempsey wrote in 1952, 'the operation became an infantry battle – and it was no part of the "GOODWOOD" plan to get drawn into a costly struggle of that kind.' This was strictly true, and it is a central tenet of this phase of the Normandy narrative that the British were running low on infantry. But somebody's infantry had to maintain the pressure south of Caen, at least until the Americans launched their attack. That task fell to the Canadians.

* * *

'Three miles or so south of Caen,' Charles Stacey wrote in 1960,

> the present-day tourist, driving down the arrow straight road that leads to Falaise, sees immediately to his right a rounded hill crowned by farm buildings. If the traveller be Canadian, he would do well to stay the wheels at this point and cast his mind back to the events of 1944: for this apparently insignificant eminence is the Verrières Ridge. Well may the wheat and the sugar-beet grow green and lush upon its gentle slopes, for in that now half-forgotten summer the best blood of Canada was freely poured upon them.[59]

Apart from the conversion of the N158 into a four-lane divided highway, the battlefield that caused Canada so much grief in July 1944 remains largely unchanged: open, rolling farmland. To Harry Crerar and anyone knowledgeable about Canada's role in the Hundred Days Campaign of 1918, the ground and the situation in July 1944 looked eerily familiar. Twenty-six years earlier the Canadian Corps had driven down an arrow-straight road across an open plain between Arras and Cambrai, broken through the strongest point of enemy defences in the west and inflicted a stunning defeat on the Germans. Now they were poised to do that again. Even the situation on the German home front, where on 20 July plotters wanting to end the war tried to kill Hitler (more below), seemed to echo the end of the earlier war.

The troops whom Dempsey called upon to sustain pressure on the Caen front while Bradley teed up Cobra were commanded by Montgomery's protégé, Guy Simonds. Between 18 and 21 July meetings with Simonds dominated Dempsey's day. On 19 July, as Goodwood stalled, Dempsey spoke to or visited Simonds four times. With Cobra delayed, it was imperative to continue to sell the lie. Simonds was convinced that his Canadians could do that. As Terry Copp observed, 'If British generals fought cautiously with visions of the Somme as part of their active memory, Canadian generals were more likely to think in terms of bold, successful attacks in a war remembered for its victories.' So, Copp concludes, Simonds was 'anxious to prove that he and his corps were worthy successors to Arthur Currie and the Canadians who had captured Vimy Ridge and led the Allied advance in the "Hundred Days"'.[60]

Anglo-American historians lose interest in the action south of Caen at this point, and even Canadian historians dismiss what follows as pointless. The ostensible objective was the high ground around the tiny village of Verrières (Hill 72 to the Germans). This would not only keep the pressure on Panzer Group West, but Verrières ridge was also an excellent start line for the next phase of the drive to Falaise. A push down the Caen–Falaise highway was precisely what the Germans expected and feared. The Daily Report of Army Group B warned on 20 July that an 'imminent large-scale attack from an unusually massive concentration of armour along the Caen–Falaise road' was likely, especially since the ground 'is particularly suitable for the employment of armoured formations'. Dempsey continued to think so, too. He put the 7th BAD under Simonds's command 'at once' and alerted the Guards Armoured to be ready to transfer to the Canadian Corps 'when required'.[61] The Anglo-Canadian threat on Bourguébus–Verrières ridge remained real.

On 20 July II Canadian Corps launched the first of a series of attacks on the high ground around Verrières village and in the Orne valley through Saint-Martin-de-Fontenay towards May-sur-Orne. That morning the 7th BAD attacked toward Verrières, but was driven back by concentrated fire. Canadian infantry renewed the attack at 1500 hours. The South Saskatchewan Regiment was about to consolidate on the

20. Montgomery and his Canadian generals, in this case in February 1945.
Body language says it all. His protégé Guy Simonds is on the left, while
Harry Crerar keeps his distance on the right.

western end of Verrières ridge in a field of chest-high grain when the SS
struck. The prairie men went to ground while their supporting anti-tank
guns were destroyed. Then the heavens opened up with torrential rain –
the start of four days of bad weather that would change almost everything. As SS infantry, supported by tanks, stalked the South Saskatchewans
through the grain, all the Canadians could do was run. The German
attack was finally checked north of Saint-Martin-de-Fontenay on the
crest of Hill 67, and the Panzers retreated to safety behind Verrières ridge.

Attacks in the Orne valley were no more successful. XII British Corps assisted the Canadians by attacking on the west side of the river. On this front the Canadians and British fought in the shadow of Hill 112, which provided oversight into the flank and rear of II Canadian Corps. All these battles are marked by lavish use of artillery. The rate of Canadian artillery firing was the highest of the war for some regiments: the 5th RCA fired 11,644 rounds on 20th July, and on the 21st probably another 15,000.[62] The record was set by the 4th Field Regiment, RCA: 24,000 rounds – and possibly more – on the 21st alone.[63] Canadian gunners fired at these rates for three days. They did so despite the drenching rain that filled the gun pits and the battery command posts and made the ground all but impassable. George Blackburn later recalled standing in thigh-deep water working the plot in his battery command post. Nearby, gunners of 4th Field worked their guns knee deep in water, barrels red hot and steaming in the rain as their guns slowly sank into the mud.[64]

So while the Americans waited for the weather to clear so they could turn the bombers loose for Cobra, the Canadians fought a nightmare battle of attrition with the SS. The Canadian line was often little more than a series of sodden outposts sheltering FOOs: it was the artillery that kept the Germans at bay. Blackburn recalled that the pace was frenetic. 'Targets coming in from FOOs,' Blackburn wrote, 'are over-lapping; "35 rounds gunfire . . . 45 rounds gunfire . . . 50 rounds gunfire . . . fire until you're told to stop!" '[65] Gunners went without sleep for days, and at night their guns glowed like candles. Ammunition trucks often could not reach the gun positions, so the gunners had to hump their ammunition – tons of it – to the gun pits while others kept the 25-pounders fed. They understood the urgency. The merit of continued Canadian pressure was to draw in even more German reserves to stem Monty's break-out from the Caen sector. Intense fighting continued along the Canadian front until late on 22 July – and so did the rain. Canadian casualties on 20–1 July amounted to 1,149, 254 of them dead.[66] There were more to come.

'Even though there was no major attack up to 26 July,' Eberbach said later of these days, 'not one day passed without minor enemy thrusts. The evening attacks, favoured by the Canadians, were particu-larly disagreeable.' The Germans were forced to counterattack to drive out the penetrations in their line, and this could only be done 'with losses which we could not afford'.[67] Attacks by the SS typically consisted of a battalion of infantry supported by a company of Panthers. Infantry and artillery fire stripped the German infantry away, while Canadian Shermans peppered the Panthers with 75mm fire and smoke to obscure their vision. Then the Fireflies hit them. C Squadron of the Sherbrooke Fusiliers alone claimed thirteen Panthers at a cost of five Shermans.[68]

The Canadian effort worked. The regular report on 'Enemy Strength and Intentions' produced by Army Group B on 23 July stated clearly that Montgomery's primary intent was to 'breakthrough' on the British Second Army front and drive to Falaise en route to Paris.[69] Kluge threw what he could in front of the Anglo-Canadians: the 2nd Panzer from the Caumont sector, the 116th Panzer diverted from Saint-Lô, parts of the 9th SS Panzer, and the 271st, 326th and 363rd Infantry divisions en route from the Fifteenth Army. For the moment, the American threat was dismissed as irrelevant. As Wilmot observed, Kluge learned from Goodwood that the Anglo-Canadians could ride a carpet of bombs across the plain south of Caen and there was nothing he could do to stop them. If they got out, the V1 sites and Paris itself were in jeopardy. On 22 July he told Hitler as much. The fiction of an Anglo-Canadian break-out attempt was maintained.

To those watching the campaign it seemed, nonetheless, that the Allies were now well and truly stuck. 'All along the grey, rainswept Norman front it was bitter, close bloody fighting for one small position after another,' *Time* magazine reported on 24 July 1944. 'It took no top flight strategist to conclude that the invasion of Western Europe was falling farther and farther behind schedule.' If the weather and stout defence make a break-out impossible, *Time* concluded, a new landing was needed.

In the Allied camp, disappointment was now palpable.[70]

* * *

Eisenhower returned to his HQ on 20 July, apparently well pleased with what he had seen and heard. But Tedder remained unmoved. News of the attempt to kill Hitler had just emerged, and the western Allies were in no position to exploit a German collapse. From Tedder's perspective, a sharp letter to Montgomery threatening to sack him would provide evidence of fair warning should it become necessary to do so. Eisenhower obliged. Acknowledging that the British Army was a wasting asset, and that soon the campaign in north-west Europe would be predominantly American, Eisenhower told Montgomery that 'while we have equality in size we must go forward shoulder to shoulder with honors and sacrifices equally shared'.[71]

Although the British were more than sharing the burden of fighting in the summer of 1944, Ike's focus was Normandy – and public perception in the US. Negative press, 'especially in an election year,' Crosswell writes, was a grave concern. So, too, was a perception in the United States, according to Crosswell, that in Normandy 'the Americans did all the fighting and dying while the British and Canadians sat idle around Caen'.[72] This was not an entirely accurate reflection of American media coverage, but the fact that this myth was already deeply entrenched in the American collective psyche suggests the impact of the failure to fully engage the American media on the British Second Army's front. It was perfectly natural, Robert McCormick had asserted in June, for the American press to highlight American stories. The Press Wireless station at Vouilly greatly facilitated that, just as ongoing British reluctance to accredit more than a few American reporters to the British Second Army condemned its story to obscurity in America. Freddie de Guingand admitted that the British Army failed its reporters, but put that down primarily to a shortage of communications equipment. As for Monty's handling of the press during the Goodwood/Cobra stalemate contretemps, de Guingand concludes bluntly, 'My Chief was not at his best.'[73] On 25 July *The Times* frankly admitted that the recent 'offensive was too much "boomed" when in its initial stages' and that the criticism of it as a failure had 'little basis in fact'.

'What hardly anyone realized', D'Este writes (quoting Williamson Murray and Alan Millett), 'was that the British had fought "the best formations in the German Army to exhaustion", kept them from even considering a counter-offensive, and had tied down fourteen divisions (six of them first-rate Panzer divisions) – no mean feat'.[74] There were few American correspondents on the ground to witness that, and unquestionably too few to even dent the inherent prejudices of the cohort of American press clustered around Vouilly. One is left to wonder what might have happened to the subsequent Normandy narrative had the bored and idle mass of American newsmen waiting for Patton's army to be activated been turned loose on Dempsey's front.

While II Canadian Corps gripped I SS Panzer Corps in a deadly embrace south of Caen, the First US Army spent the week between 17 and 24 July building strength for Cobra. Eight new divisions had arrived so far in July, four infantry and four armoured, along with many of the support elements of the Third US Army – hospitals, engineers, tank-destroyer units, logistics units, and even the forward echelons of the ASF's 'Com Z', the logistics service that would feed and equip the huge army waiting to descend on Europe. The beachhead grew increasingly crowded. The only thing that seemed to be in short supply, as always, was ammunition.

Bradley's plan for Cobra was to be a breakthrough not a break-out. It was headed for the Brittany peninsula and the Bay of Biscay, to the ports needed for the American build-up. The focal point was the front west of Saint-Lô, where the road to Périers ran straight as a die. The intent was to burst through between Marigny and Saint-Gilles with six divisions of Lieutenant General Lawton Collins's VII US Corps. If all went well, a thrust westward would then trap German forces facing VIII US Corps along the west coast of the Cotentin.[75] Blumenson points out that Bradley gave Collins a large portion of the First US Army's artillery to support the attack: 600 guns. It was an impressive concentration by American standards but the ammunition shortage dogged artillery planning. VII US Corps was allocated 'almost 140,000 rounds of artillery ammunition'. However, that was for a five-day period – a daily average of 28,000 rounds. The contrast with the scale of artillery support on the Anglo-Canadian front is stark: 297,000 rounds were allocated for the first *day* of Goodwood, and as noted on 21 July, the 4th Field Regiment, RCA (twenty-four guns), alone fired at least 24,000.[76] The Americans were doing everything they could to ameliorate the chronic ammunition shortage. When Major Hansen went to the airfield on 22 July to meet General Lesley McNair, he found it swarming with C-47 cargo planes: 300 in just four hours – an aircraft about every fifty seconds – carrying 'ammunition and mines'. The next day, Bradley met the corps commanders on either side of Cobra to

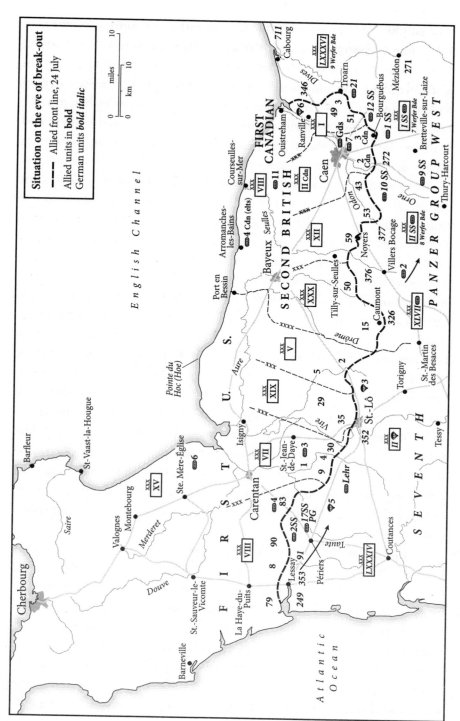

5. The situation on the eve of break-out.

discuss the 'Always disagreeable ... question of ammo allowances'. Gerow and Middleton agreed to help.[77] 'Because ammunition restrictions made all-inclusive pre-arranged fires difficult,' Blumenson writes, VII US Corps 'did not draw up an overall fire plan.' Instead, artillery fire concentrated on known enemy strong points and 'specific targets rather than furnishing general support'. As Russell Weigley concluded, 'The air plan was all the more crucial because it would have to do much of the work ordinarily expected of artillery.'[78]

The air-support plan for Cobra was complex. It required careful and precise choreography, and not all the important details were agreed upon beforehand. Roughly 2,500 aircraft were to strike a target area 7,000 yards long and 2,500 yards wide just south of the Saint-Lô–Périers road. It was agreed, after much discussion, that the attacking troops would withdraw 1,200 yards from the front to allow for errors in bombing. Preliminary attacks along a narrow strip 250 yards deep immediately south of the road would be restricted to fighter-bombers, providing greater precision in targeting and an additional separation between troops and the heavies. The 1,800 B-17s and B-24s of VIII AF would then crush the main line of German defences. When that was completed, a further 350 fighter-bombers would again attack the narrow strip along the road, while the artillery programme commenced and 396 medium bombers attacked the southern portion of the target zone. Bradley had chosen the ground because the Saint-Lô–Périers road provided a clearly visible demarcation between his forces and the Germans, and he asked – and assumed – that the bombing runs would be made parallel to and south of the road to reduce the danger of shorts and 'creep back'.[79]

The forces facing Collins's VII Corps were outnumbered five to one. The area between Marigny and Saint-Gilles held what was left of the Panzer Lehr, perhaps 3,200 combat effectives – including 1,000 men from other shattered units – and forty-five armoured vehicles. Two infantry regiments of the 275th GID were in reserve south of Panzer Lehr. The situation westward, to Lessay, was no better: 'many units', Blumenson writes, 'but relatively few troops'.[80] As it turned out, Kluge was content with the situation; the greater danger lay in the Caen sector, where the threat of an Anglo-Canadian breakthrough was relentless.

To sustain that threat, and ensure a clear run for Cobra, on the evening of 22 July Dempsey ordered the Canadians to capture Verrières ridge, and then turn the armour loose to reach the high ground at Hill 122 and the co-called 'Cramesnil Spur'. The Canadian attack, Operation Spring, was timed for the early hours of 25 July to follow Cobra – now tentatively set for 24 July. Then on 28 July Dempsey would renew his attack west of Hill 112 towards Évrecy, and on 30 July build off the success of Spring with another drive down the Caen–Falaise highway. Only later, at some unspecified date, would the Anglo-Canadians launch a full-blooded armoured thrust to Falaise.[81]

Operation Spring was a ridiculously ambitious scheme, but Simonds understood that it was a holding attack. Division and brigade commanders in II Canadian Corps were not let in on the secret, but they could see the weaknesses of the plan. Brigadier W.J. Megill, commander of the 5th CIB, believed that Simonds's plan was simply impossible, not least because the two Canadian infantry divisions were seriously depleted from heavy fighting since 18 July. Meanwhile, those closest to the front knew that the Germans controlled most of the designated start line, while the artillery plan was 'not great'.[82] Simonds mustered 488 guns to support Spring, but the ammunition allocation was small.[83] A modest programme by 100 medium bombers flew in support.

On 24 July I SS Panzer Corps was, as Charles Stacey called it, 'a most formidable array'.[84] Three powerful Panzer divisions, reinforced by a first-line infantry division, with another Panzer division in reserve, stood in front of II Canadian Corps. II SS Panzer Corps, specifically the 10th SS Panzer Division, overlooked the Canadian positions from Hill 112.[85] It was going to take more than Simonds could deploy to move them, but of course that was not the objective.

* * *

Rain soaked Normandy for three days until Allied weathermen thought they saw a break coming around noon on 24 July. Cobra was on. Air Chief Marshal Sir Trafford Leigh-Mallory, RAF, the commander of the Allied Expeditionary Air Force, gave the go-ahead, and flew to Normandy to watch the attack. USAAF commanders doubted the forecast. When clouds closed in, Leigh-Mallory called off the preliminary air bombardment. Most of the aircraft were either en route or minutes away from bombing. There was no easy way to recall them, no direct radio link with forces on the ground. By noon the sky was 'heavy' with P-47 Thunderbolts.[86] Most bombed effectively. One flight of P-47s bombed the house where Chester Hansen and the American generals were watching. Not far away General McNair, oblivious to the bombs creeping his way, was pushed from his car and hustled to safety.[87] Most aircraft turned back. Only 350 heavies bombed that day, but one squadron dropped short and everyone else in the formation followed. Their bombs landed among the 30th USID, killing twenty-five men and wounding 131.[88]

The partial bombing ignited a chain of events that spiralled throughout the day. Collins wanted to attack anyway. At the very least, he needed to regain the 1,200 yards back from the road given up to the bomb-safety line. The Germans assumed that an attack was actually underway and responded with heavy artillery fire. 'All three assault divisions had a difficult time that afternoon,' Blumenson wrote. Costly fighting was necessary to regain positions along the road.[89] But it was not the short bombing that upset Bradley the most, it was that the heavy bombers had attacked perpendicular to the road. 'I left Stanmore with a clear understanding they would fly parallel to the road,' he told Leigh-Mallory when the airman arrived at Vouilly that afternoon. Leigh-Mallory promised to sort it out. He called Bradley later that night: 'they tell me the course they flew today was not accidental'. When asked to explain why, Leigh-Mallory said it would take too long to funnel the heavy bombers down the narrow axis of the target area, so the airmen had decided to bomb perpendicular to the road. Worse news followed. Bomber crews were about to be briefed for another attempt the next day, the 25th. If Bradley insisted on a parallel approach, the attack would have to be delayed. Bradley relented. 'We've got no choice,' Bradley told Leigh-Mallory, 'the Boche will build up the front if we don't get this thing off soon. But we are still taking an awful chance. Another short will ruin us.'[90]

Meanwhile, on the Anglo-Canadian front Operation Spring, intended to follow Cobra, got underway in the wee hours of 25 July: nine infantry battalions launched against I SS Panzer Corps over open ground. Russian

21. Operation Cobra: a mine-hunting team from the 8th Infantry
Regiment, 4th USID, moves into place north-west of Saint-Lô,
23 July 1944.

liaison officers were stunned by the audacity of the Canadian attack:
they preferred to outnumber the enemy ten to one. It had not even been
possible to clear the start line before the attacking battalions arrived.
Fighting along the Odon valley was confused, bloody and ultimately
futile. Further up, on Verrières ridge itself, the Royal Hamilton Light
Infantry (RHLI) captured Verrières village, and held off repeated attacks
from the 1st SS Panzer Division. Meanwhile, just across the N178, the
North Nova Scotia Highlanders got a toehold in Tilley-la-Campagne
just before sunrise. By 0730 hours on 25 July, Simonds determined it
was time to launch Phase II: the armoured breakthrough, over Verrières
ridge, through Rocqancourt to the high ground beyond.

It was crucial to Phase II to take Fontenay-le-Marmion, tucked
tightly into a sharp reverse-slope position behind Verrières ridge: it
could enfilade any advance south. The Canadian Black Watch was

supposed to do that, but the men were delayed by the confusion of the night battle and by the death of their commanding officer. Command devolved to twenty-six-year-old Major Philip Griffin. Having missed their initial supporting fire at 0530 hours, Griffin led the Black Watch, a toney Montreal regiment officered by the city's social elite, up the open slope towards Fontenay at 0900 hours. They were met by a torrent of fire from a full enemy battalion and a battlegroup from the 2nd Panzer Division. Only fifteen of Griffin's 325 officers and men returned.[91]

By late morning Spring was slipping from bad to worse. When the North Novas' tenuous foothold in Tilley fell apart, the Stormont, Dundas and Glengarry Highlanders were ordered into Tilley to help. Their CO, Lieutenant-Colonel G.H. Christiansen, refused. His briga-dier, D.G. Cunningham, backed him, and so did Petch, the Novas' CO. Cunningham was warned that he would be dismissed if he failed to execute the order: Cunningham stood firm. As Copp concluded, 'There would be no daylight attack on Tilley.'[92] By the evening the revolt against Simonds's orders spread: both the 5th CIB and the 6th CIB were quietly pulling back and consolidating. Simonds admitted to Dempsey that evening that it was pointless to continue. Only Verrières village held out: everywhere else the Germans regained their positions.[93]

James Carafano spoke for generations of historians when he concluded that the Canadian 'attack did nothing to advance the cause of Operation COBRA'.[94] But the facts say otherwise, and recent historians have been more generous. For five arduous days II Canadian Corps, supported by British formations, covered for delays in the launching of Cobra. They did so against 'the most powerful German defence arrangement encoun-tered by any of the Allied armies throughout the Normandy Campaign'.[95] In the process, the Canadians set a new standard for measuring casualty rates. The British Commonwealth system was based on three scales: Quiet, Normal and Intense. The experience of Verrières Ridges added a fourth, 'Double Intense', to that scale.[96] It cost II Canadian Corps 3,000 casualties, of whom roughly 1,000 were killed.[97] Canadians paid dearly for the American ammunition shortage, and by the evening of 25 July they had nothing left to give.

The Germans quickly determined that Spring was not the antici-pated major attack down the Caen–Falaise highway. However, Spring virtually destroyed the 272nd GID and Eberbach was forced to commit the 9th SS Panzer to the line on Verrières ridge, while Kluge ordered PGW to hold its reserves 'ready for an immediate counterattack as an absolute sine qua non'.[98] Canada's second worst day of the war – after Dieppe – helped ensure that no relief was available for the Seventh German Army when Collins and his 120,000 men crashed through the line west of Saint-Lô that afternoon.

CHAPTER 24

BREAK-OUT

The British may have saved us, but we don't need them anymore.
Robert McCormick, *Chicago Tribune*, 25 June 1944[1]

When Drew Middleton returned to London from the Mediterranean in late 1943 he sensed a change in the balance of Allied power. Britain still fielded 'powerful armies, fleets and air forces . . . more numerous, experienced and skilled than those deployed by the United States'. Even British politicians, and especially Churchill, were without equal in America, and London remained 'the capital of the war in the West'. But the writing was on the wall. 'All this tended to obscure the reality of a country that had spent blood and treasure on three continents and was now fighting on material and financial resources increasingly furnished by the American ally.' In the winter of 1943–4 the 'American take over was more real than apparent'.[2] In July 1944 that reality became all too apparent.

In the high summer of 1944 Anglo-American plans and strategy drifted forward on inertia. There was no high-level summit after Tehran and Cairo the previous autumn. Illness, elections and Overlord intervened. The Allies groped their way forward amid increasing victories and portentous developments. 'With the establishment of a firm lodgement on the continent,' Henry Luce wrote in *Life* in June, 'we are now the most powerful nation on the earth.' Roosevelt believed that he and America could now manage global affairs, including drawing Stalin into the new world order.[3] The new United Nations would police the world, and America's central place in the global economy was about to be secured at Bretton Woods. All Roosevelt had to do now was get re-elected as President.

And so in 1944 the relentless American electoral cycle imposed itself across the globe. Even visits to Washington by the leaders of occupied European states – the very countries America was striving to liberate – were very carefully managed. There could be no hint of Roosevelt's abandonment of eastern Europe for fear of 'domestic political repercussions'.[4] Seven million Polish-Americans voted as a bloc in the crucial states of Pennsylvania, New York, New Jersey, Illinois and Michigan.[5] FDR could not afford to alienate them. The future of Poland dominated the annual American-Polish Congress in Buffalo in late May. All the delegates except the Communists agreed that no division of Polish territory was acceptable. These views were passed on to Prime Minister Mikolajczyk in London. Polish-Americans 'were ready to sacrifice everything', the New York Polish newspaper *Nowy Swiat* reported on 6 June, to keep their country unified and free, 'and cannot be deceived by Stalin's promises'.[6] Roosevelt put off Mikolajczyk's visit to Washington for months, despite urging from Churchill.[7] His visit in June did little to ease the concerns of Polish-Americans. *Glos Narodu*, based in Jersey City, NJ, warned that Russia wanted to seize half the country and dominate the rest. Given the circumstances, there was little that Polish-Americans could do but have 'faith in America and Pres. Roosevelt'. In the circumstances, it was a slim reed to grasp.[8]

The Polish problem was not unique. American relations with France in the summer of 1944 were, as one Frenchman described them, a 'hideous mess'.[9] Admiral Daniel Leahy, former US ambassador to Vichy France and by 1943 Chairman of the Joint Chiefs of Staff, complained that the French were obstructionist at best, and they 'embarrassed us at every turn'. They were fighting in Italy 'on their own terms' while their leader sulked in England.[10] The British put up with de Gaulle's petulance and arrogance because they needed France – especially after Tehran. Roosevelt did not: there was no Franco-American voting bloc. FDR wanted nothing to do with de Gaulle.[11]

After D-Day de Gaulle sulked in England, furious over being shut out of Operation Overlord. The Comité français de libération nationale

(CFLN) sent only a few liaison officers to Normandy, where their language skills would have helped the Americans enormously. As Demaree Bess wrote in the *Saturday Evening Post* in late July 1944, the Allies attacked France 'with almost no Frenchmen in evidence among the invading forces'. Worst still, they did so 'even without the whole-hearted support of French émigré officials'. Moreover, 'the manner of our coming' – blasting cities and towns to rubble – shocked and stunned the French. They wanted the Germans out, but were appalled by the price. This played into the hands of Axis propagandists, 'and they made the most of it'.[12] The British, desperately in need of powerful allies in postwar Europe, backed de Gaulle. Speaking to the British-American Dining Club in London on 11 July 1944, Sir James Grigg made it perfectly clear that, in the absence of an American commitment, Britain needed a strong France to guard western Europe from the Russians. 'There is much truth in Grigg's speech,' Ralph Ingersoll wrote in his diary that night, 'much foresight.'[13]

Eisenhower needed de Gaulle, too, and so he granted the CFLN the title of 'Provisional Government of the French Republic' in June. But de Gaulle did little to legitimate the Normandy campaign, to facilitate Allied operations or to ease French acceptance of the cost. His aloofness left George Marshall in a 'white fury' by the end of the month.[14]

When de Gaulle finally arrived in Washington on 6 July, Roosevelt greeted him warmly, but made his plans for France perfectly clear. 'The Roosevelt who revealed himself to de Gaulle,' Eric Larrabee wrote, 'was a very different man from the liberal internationalist we have come to expect. A streak of the World War I imperialist was still alive in him too, and shows itself here in a clear connection with military power at its rawest and most naked form.'[15] De Gaulle won a grudging acceptance of himself and the CFLN as the 'temporary de facto authority for civil administration in France'.[16] It was enough to satisfy de Gaulle. But Roosevelt left the French leader with no illusions about his plans for France – and for Europe. He could afford to be blunt: there was no French bloc in the American electorate. France would be divested of her empire, with some of the key pieces retained by the Americans. The Allies would oversee postwar elections, to ensure that de Gaulle was not left in charge, and Europe's problems would be tackled by the new

United Nations. Not surprisingly, the formal dinner to honour de Gaulle's visit was a sombre affair, with the Frenchman granitic in his silence while the Americans chattered nervously. De Gaulle told Helen Essary of the *Washington Times-Herald* that the French empire would be 'complete again' after the war. This caused a stir in Washington that Americans were fighting for 'white ascendancy forever over parts of Asia'.[17] That did not stop the clamour for asserting American rights to retain bases built and islands conquered in erstwhile European colonies.

It was during de Gaulle's visit that Roosevelt finally decided to run for a fourth term. The announcement was made on 11 July, and two days later FDR headed west to the Democratic National Convention in Chicago. He stopped only long enough to arrange his nomination and then arrived in San Diego on 18 July to visit his son Jimmy, a Marine Corps colonel, and watch training exercises. It was there on 20 July that Roosevelt had a debilitating attack of angina: the first significant manifestation of his critical decline in health. He recovered sufficiently to deliver his nomination acceptance speech on national radio that evening. His mission, FDR told Americans, was to win the war – fast; manage the peace; and build the economy to provide work for all Americans. Newsreel footage and still photos shot at the microphone revealed an emaciated and exhausted man. Many believed he would not live to complete another term as President.

On that same day 7,000 miles away Adolf Hitler also had a brush with death when a bomb exploded at the OKW headquarters in Poland. Hitler was spared the worst of the blast. For a few hours, however, it seemed that the Führer was dead, and the conspirators attempted to take charge in Berlin. Their intent was to seek a negotiated end to the war in a scenario not unlike October 1918, when the Social Democrats took power, the Kaiser fled and an armistice was arranged. The 20 July plotters included a wide range of supporters – even Communists – but they were not the Social Democrats of 1918. The leadership was overwhelmingly conservative, aristocrat and Junker class. It was anti-Nazi only because the war had turned badly for Germany. Their vision of a postwar Germany was grand, and the peace they sought was no capitulation. It is unlikely that the Allies would have presented terms which they would accept.

The plot was quickly crushed, and its perpetrators and fellow travellers ruthlessly hunted and killed. The show trials revealed for all the world the brutality of the regime. But there was no evidence of the coup attempt among troops on the ground. As one officer from the 1st SS Panzer recalled, 'Our lack of understanding and inner rejection of everything we heard from "up there" or "back home", led us to accept only one last "Heimat", one final homeland. That was our unit, our little heap of men . . . We were simply front soldiers and that was a deeply felt self-identification.'[18] Nor, as Ian Kershaw writes, was the Germany of 1944 anything like that of 1918.[19] Ordinary Germans retained faith that somehow Germany would emerge victorious and they remained loyal to Hitler.

American and British responses to the coup attempt were the same: 'chilling', as Klemens von Klemperer described it. The Allies considered the war nearly won and wanted nothing to do with the plotters. Roosevelt ordered a complete veil of silence on the subject, with no intimation that there was effective opposition to Hitler. The British dubbed the plot 'The Revolt of the Generals', a concept which dismissed out of hand any interest in, or sympathy for, the wider anti-Hitler resistance. Hitler's would-be assassins were labelled, as von Klemperer writes, 'no friends of the Allies'. When asked to prepare a brief for the British government on the events of 20 July, John Wheeler-Bennett recommended no action. After all, 'the killing of Germans by Germans will save us from future embarrassment of many kinds'.[20]

* * *

About the time German officers were putting their bomb plot into action, the fate of Britain as the dominant economic power was decided in the sleepy hills of New Hampshire. It will be recalled that in late April a 'Joint Statement of Principles' on postwar economic plans was issued in Washington and London representing a path towards fulfilment of Article VII of the Lend-Lease agreement: liberalised international trade. The British had issued the statement without enthusiasm – or commitment – because it threatened to erode Britain's economic position. Keynes saw little option other than acceptance, but he still hoped to modify the plan, and naively trusted his American counterpart, Harry Dexter White, to help.[21] But White, like Roosevelt, was bent on opening the world for American trade and establishing a global New Deal. The future, Robert

Skidelsky writes of White's motives, lay in an 'American-Soviet condominium not Anglo-American cooperation'. It was later claimed that White was a Soviet agent. If so, he had no difficulty reconciling American liberalism with Communism. 'White's beliefs were not much different from those of Harry Hopkins or Vice President Wallace,' Skidelsky claims, 'who "saw in the march of history a coming together of the Soviet experiment in Russia with the New Deal programmes of the United States" for the greater good of mankind'.[22]

The conference was preceded by a week-long preliminary meeting of seventeen nations in Atlantic City, NJ, between 24 and 30 June. Both the British and American delegations arrived intent on altering agreements already in place. Louis Rasminsky, the Canadian representative who had worked closely with both Keynes and White, deflected those efforts. Here too, Canada's preference for postwar multilateralism worked against the empire and Commonwealth. A member of the Brazilian delegation credited Rasminsky with saving the whole Bretton Woods process. 'He could talk back to Keynes . . . He was bold enough to discuss with him and contradict him, and had a much better view of the American position.'[23] Keynes warned the House of Lords in late May that Britain had no real choice. Only the British – 'and we alone of the United Nations – have burdened ourselves with a weight of deferred indebtedness to other countries beneath which we shall stagger'.[24] Only America could save Britain from catastrophe.

The United Nations Monetary and Financial Conference was a public spectacle confirming America's achievement of global economic dominance. Whatever was decided at Bretton Woods would still have to pass the US Congress and Senate. Shadows of the US rejection of the League of Nations in 1919 loomed. America needed to buy in. Ten members of the American delegation, therefore, were senators and congressmen, a bipartisan group that kept the Treasury Department delegates in a constant state of turmoil. But whatever was decided at Bretton Woods would be accepted by the world. It helped that the Europeans and Latin Americans supported White's plan; after all, the Americans had all the money and the gold.

This was Henry Dexter White's moment of triumph. He was the ringmaster and he had written the script.[25] White chaired the conference, and the critical Commission I, which established the International

Monetary Fund (IMF) to regulate currency-exchange rates, stabilise international trade and provide short-term loans. The IMF was the key to everything that followed. Rasminsky was the reporting delegate for this Commission. Commission II was responsible for the International Bank of Reconstruction and Development (the World Bank), an institution designed to provide long-term credit to tackle the burden of war debt and the cost of reconstruction in a way that would not cripple economic recovery and a viable, global economic system. Commission II, chaired by Keynes, only really began work once the IMF details were finalised. White was well aware of Keynes's failing health and his aim 'was to neutralize him . . . This strategy worked.'[26] Sub-committees were designed, in Skidelsky's words, to keep the delegates uselessly busy. 'The chairmen of the Commissions' various sub-committees were non-Americans,' Skidelsky writes, but 'they had American rapporteurs and secretaries, appointed and briefed by White'.[27] They were instructed not to interfere with their committee discussions. Since there was no voting on motions and all decisions were determined by 'consensus', White's rapporteurs were warned 'that they were not under any circumstances to deviate from the official American position'.[28] Other issues of international trade and finance were pushed down to Commission III, chaired by Mexico. Unresolved problems were to be referred to a special committee chaired by Henry Morgenthau, the Secretary of the US Treasury Department and White's boss.

There was ample opportunity in the three-week programme for delegates to speak, Emanuel Goldenweiser of the US Federal Reserve Bank observed, 'provided he doesn't say anything'.[29] In the event, 'many did not speak or understand' English and without simultaneous translation most of what was said was simply ignored.[30] Only a few of the delegates were financial or economic specialists. As Lionel Robbins wrote on 12 July, 'with the single exception of the Canadians, there are no other delegations who really have sufficient technical knowledge to grapple with these arcana'.[31] White trusted Rasminsky and gave him 'the authority to draft the IMF document'. Rasminsky also chaired the drafting committee for the final 'Articles of Agreement'. Part of that task, Edward Bernstein, Assistant Secretary of the Treasury Department, observed, 'was making sure that any continuing arguments between the United States and the United

Kingdom didn't stop [the conference] from getting the International Monetary Fund created'.[32]

Keynes's six-man British delegation was excellent, but it was in no position to forestall White's plan to make the US dollar the global currency by making it convertible to gold. The Americans slipped that scheme into the proceedings on 6 July without ever clearing it with the British.[33] The British member of that committee, Dennis Robertson, saw the proposal as a book-keeping issue and raised no objections. According to Steil, Robertson had walked into a trap set by White. And since there was no voting, merely a declaration by the chair that there was consensus, the scheme was adopted.[34] It did not help that the British delegation fought amongst themselves publicly, and made headlines in the American press as a result. The Australian delegate was ordered by his government not to cooperate with any agreement that liberalised global trade at the expense of the sterling bloc. Canada, of course, worked equally hard to make sure that the British accepted just such an agreement. The pattern of the May Prime Ministers' meeting therefore repeated itself, this time with Rasminksy taking the lead. The Articles of Agreement were signed at the final plenary session on 22 July.[35]

Bretton Woods accomplished three things of critical importance to Anglo-American relations and to the postwar world. The IMF brought currency stability and promised to eliminate the volatility of global trade evident in the interwar period. It did this, in part, by obliging participating states to deposit a specified amount – determined largely by the Americans – totalling $9.1 billion USD. This would provide short-term loans to cover short-term crises in balance of payments once the war ended. The IMF tied the value of all currencies to the US dollar, which became the only major world currency convertible to gold.[36] The second major accomplishment was the International Bank for Reconstruction and Development, quickly dubbed the World Bank. It drew on the IMF fund to issue long-term loans through which long-term debts and the establishment of viable economies could be managed. The third critical accomplishment of Bretton Woods was the confirmation of America's role as the new global hegemon: America had 'broken out'.

The world signed onto the Bretton Woods agreement, although there was no certainty that it would clear the US Congress. As *Newsweek* noted on 24 July, the plan faced 'Hard Sledding' in the Republican-dominated House.[37] *The Times* greeted the news of the IMF very favourably in its editorial of 24 July, despite the fact that everyone knew what it meant for Britain as a Great Power. British economists, financiers, civil servants and politicians had not expected such a complete capitulation to liberal multilateralism. Goldenweiser described the IMF a few months later as 'an acknowledgement of the fact that London has lost its position as the financial centre of the world'.[38] Henry Clay, an official at the Bank of England, later described Bretton Woods as 'the greatest blow to Britain next to the war'.[39]

* * *

By the summer of 1944 America possessed a crushing superiority over the Japanese in the Pacific. There was little – perhaps nothing – that the Japanese could do to forestall the American advance: logistics and securing key bases, not resistance, were the prime determining factors. Formosa and mainland China had long been the preferred targets for a base of operations against the Japanese home islands. But by July, with the Japanese summer offensive overrunning southern China, options for the next phase were much less clear. America needed a new strategy.

The course of the final thrust on the Japanese home islands was set in Hawaii in late July when Roosevelt met his senior Pacific commanders. The trip, D. Clayton James writes, 'was politically motivated'. FDR needed to be seen as the Commander in Chief, and he needed at least a passive endorsement of that role from Douglas MacArthur, the darling of the Republican Party.[40] 'The blunt fact is that he was running for a fourth term,' William Manchester wrote, 'and being photographed with MacArthur and Nimitz would be more impressive to his constituents than pictures of him politicking at the Democratic National Convention.'[41]

And so on 22 July a frail FDR left San Diego aboard the USS *Baltimore* for a secret rendezvous in Hawaii. Admiral Chester Nimitz and other senior officers hustled aboard the cruiser as soon as the brow was open, but MacArthur was busy taking a bath after his long flight from Australia. FDR, Nimitz and a gaggle of senior officers were just leaving *Baltimore* when MacArthur rolled up in an open car, wearing a flying jacket in the heat, surrounded by a motorcycle escort with sirens blaring. 'Just landed from Australia,' he explained in an outright lie. 'It's pretty cold up there!'[42] So much for the secret visit.

Not to be upstaged, Roosevelt secured a red convertible for a day of touring and glad-handing on 27 July, with MacArthur and Nimitz ornamenting the back seat. Serious discussion of Pacific strategy began that evening. MacArthur made an impassioned appeal for a return to the Philippines. Not only would that guard the left flank of the final advance on Japan, MacArthur believed that the failure to liberate America's primary colonial possession in Asia would mean that 'The reputation of the United States would be sullied with a stain that could never be removed'. FDR thought that liberating the Philippines would be too costly. MacArthur insisted that it would be neither lengthy nor costly. Nimitz conceded that if Formosa was the next target, Japanese bomber bases on Luzon were a threat.

Both of MacArthur's primary biographers note that the whole meeting was overlain by unmentioned political assumptions. The British and the Dutch were not to be allowed to reclaim their colonies in Indonesia and Borneo. Indeed, FDR, Nimitz and MacArthur agreed that the British were not only irrelevant, but 'likely to cause problems'.[43] Meanwhile, America's central Pacific strategy had secured new bases that, because they were small enough not to incur the odour of colonialism, would simply be kept after the war. As for the decision to liberate the Philippines, Nigel Hamilton claims this was entirely altruistic.[44] Perhaps. But Manchester says that MacArthur and FDR did a deal: MacArthur got to return to the Philippines, and Roosevelt got a political boost from MacArthur.[45] The decision to return to the Philippines ensured that the liberation of America's most important colony remained on the front pages of American newspapers throughout the election campaign.[46]

FDR met the press on 29 July to announce that the next phase of the war against Japan had been sorted out. 'We are going to get the Philippines back!' Roosevelt trumpeted, and MacArthur would be in on it.[47] When pushed by reporters to say what the British thought of the new plan, FDR's response was revealing. 'No meeting with Winston Churchill was planned,' the media was told according to Nigel Hamilton, 'since the Pacific War was being conducted under American Supreme Commanders.'[48]

* * *

By the time Roosevelt met the press in Hawaii the American break-out was well underway in Europe, too. The errant bombing in front of VII US Corps on 24 July, and the subsequent intense fighting, convinced Fritz Bayerlein that the anticipated American attack had failed. Kluge went to Caen sector on 25 July. 'The attack, by the Canadian II Corps, which had resumed on 25 July near Caen,' the German official history observed, 'seemed to justify focusing on this area.'[49] 'It was this,' Blumenson writes, 'that made the German surprise even greater when COBRA came.'[50]

At 0938 hours on the morning of 25 July fighter-bomber strikes hit German positions along the Saint-Lô–Périers road again. The 1,500 heavy bombers arrived, flying in again from the north. By 1040 hours bombs were falling as far back as American artillery positions. One hundred and eleven soldiers were killed and nearly five hundred wounded. The second short bombing in two days was a shattering blow to morale.[51] 'Everyone angry,' Hansen noted cryptically in his diary. Ike was livid. 'I don't believe they [heavies] can be used again in support of ground troops,' he told Bradley in Hansen's presence. 'That's a job for artillery . . . this is the last one.'[52] Eisenhower was right on the first conclusion, and wrong on the second.

Despite the errors, the weight of bombs fell on the Germans. An estimated one thousand men were killed outright, and their supporting tanks and vehicles thrown about like toys. 'Huebner,' Hansen wrote, 'who is an old front line campaigner, said it was the most terrifying thing he had ever seen'.[53] Bayerlein described what he saw as 'mondlandschaft' – a moonscape.[54] Perhaps only a dozen of the Panzer Lehr's tanks and tank destroyers survived. Command and control was shattered. As Blumenson wrote, the breakthrough zone was 'inhabited by isolated units, by bewildered individuals, and by departed souls'.

The expectation was that the advance would be largely a mopping-up operation, and then the armour would race to Coutances. It was nothing of the sort. The German 5th Parachute Regiment holding the western shoulder of the attack zone (and outside of the bombed area) refused to budge. Just to the east astride the road to Marigny, the 9th USID struggled against 'increasingly troublesome centers of resistance'.[55] The 4th

USID, attacking in the centre, was also slowed by small groups of well-sited Germans, often supported by a few tanks or anti-tank guns. By the time the 4th USID reached the outskirts of La Chapelle-en-Juger, halfway to the Saint-Lô–Coutances road, they were content to stop for the day.

On the left, the 30th USID – bombed and strafed again by its own air force – got little further than the Saint-Lô–Périers road, where it encountered a German strong point. The garrison of Hébécrevon, on the east shoulder of the Cobra zone, had also survived the bombardment and offered strong resistance. The Americans had to wait until darkness to get into the village: it fell at midnight. The 30th Division commander, Major General Leland Hobbs, lamented at the end of the day that 'There is no indication of bombing in where we have gone so far.'

Most histories of the Normandy campaign suggest that 25 July was the day of the break-out, but the reality was quite different. 'We all thought the Americans were being very slow,' one of Montgomery's staff officers recalled after the war, 'and the fact that they were twice bombed by their own bombers didn't help.'[56] The literature says nothing of American artillery support on that day. It will be recalled that the allocation was only an average of 28,000 rounds per day for the whole corps. Waddell described the First US Army artillery provisions for 25–30 July as a 'block allocation' for a five-day period: artillerymen could fire whatever they wanted, but they would get no more until 31 July.[57] Ammunition restrictions may explain why none of Cobra's objectives were reached on 25 July. Certainly, the Germans were optimistic that they could hold. It was assumed by the Seventh Army that the Panzer Lehr remained a viable formation, and that a new defensive line could be built. Reinforcements were ordered to La Chapelle-en-Juger, and a company of tanks and a company of infantry sent to Marigny.

Lawton Collins was optimistic, too. Resistance had been random, isolated and, with some exceptions, out of touch with higher formations. More importantly, there had been no immediate counterattacks. He concluded that the German defences were shattered, and all that was needed was a little weight to push through them. So late on the afternoon of 25 July he brought his armoured columns forward to attack early the next morning. Collins was right. By the afternoon of

26 July the leading elements of the 2nd USAD reached Saint-Gilles almost unmolested. By the end of the day there was no organised resistance in front of VII US Corps. Meanwhile, to the west VIII US Corps began its own advance to Coutances, and the XIX and V US Corps east of Saint-Lô attacked to keep the Germans from shifting resources.[58] The situation, Blumenson writes, now 'demanded speed rather than caution'.[59] Collins was ordered to keeping attacking through the night.

For the moment there was no panic in the German camp. The troops in front of VIII US Corps began a cautious retreat to a new mainline of resistance, which Hauser hoped to build between La Chappelle-en-Juger and Coutances. On 26 July, Kluge remained in the Caen sector, assessing the aftermath of Operation Spring. Even Chester Hansen had to admit that day that the tentative success of Cobra so far made it look like it was a deception to cover a major attack in the Caen sector.[60]

The revelation of Cobra's success came the next day, the 27th. Patrols from VIII US Corps, advancing cautiously that morning between Cobra and the sea, found an enemy poised to resist. When the attack went in that afternoon the Germans were gone. In fact, they were drifting away across the whole front of the First US Army. The advance was now fast, and by the afternoon the VII Corps units racing west towards Coutances were in action against German artillery firing to the north on VIII US Corps. Hauser ordered his troops to withdraw south of Coutances, an order confirmed by Kluge in the late afternoon of 27 July when he returned from the Caen front.[61]

Kluge now struggled to find reinforcements for the Seventh Army. As the German official history observes, 'because of the attacks by Canadian troops near Caen'[62] he had failed to create any operational reserve in the American sector. By 27 July, Bradley's army had broken into a space devoid of organised resistance. Kluge ordered the 2nd Panzer Division west, and, having convinced Hitler to release the 9th Panzer from the south of France to PGW, later ordered the 116th Panzer Division to the American front as well.[63]

However, Kluge was not yet done. The American breakthrough occasioned the largest movement of Germans formations since the initial landings. Having concluded that there was no longer a threat to the Pas-de-Calais, Kluge asked for two more infantry divisions from the

Fifteenth Army, and two from southern France. To keep the Anglo-Canadians in check PGW was to be upgraded to 'Fifth Panzer Army', and reinforced by 100 anti-tank guns, sixty tanks and some Panzer Grenadier battalions. The next day (28 July) OKW authorised the release of three more infantry divisions from north of the Seine.[64] By the end of the day the 116th Panzer was on the march to the American front from its laager north of Falaise, and Kluge had ordered the 21st Panzer and a battalion of Tigers west as well.[65] Time was of the essence. As Blumenson writes, 'The Americans were running wild.' Bradley expected the Anglo-Canadians to keep the mass of German armour off the back of his army while it ran free. He told his corps commanders on 27 July that 'I'll have to collect a bottle of scotch from Bimbo [Dempsey] for each division he lets come to this front'.

The American success prompted Montgomery to issue a new directive on 27 July. The First Canadian Army, about to assume responsibility east of the Orne, would try to keep Panzer Group West busy, while Dempsey concentrated three corps of the British Second Army in the Caumont area to drive-in the right wing of the Seventh Army. Since mid-June the Germans had fortified and mined the 'Caumont Gap' heavily. Behind it lay the rolling hills of the 'Suisse Normande', with its deep valleys and hedgerows. Dempsey now planned to strike through it, take Vire, and shatter the hinge of the German position, allowing US forces to wheel into Brittany.[66] The date for Operation Bluecoat was 2 August, which suggests the tentative nature of Cobra's success on its third day.

By 28 July the Germans west of Saint-Lô were in full retreat. The concentration of vehicles and troops on the road provided a 'feeding frenzy' for Allied fighter-bombers. 'For six hours,' Rick Atkinson writes, 'Allied planes, eventually joined by artillery, tanks and tank destroyers, lashed the column, until 100 panzers and 250 other vehicles stood wrecked if not burning . . . The Hun had been hazed.'[67] The slaughter and destruction in the 'Roncey Pocket' was a portent of worse to come. On 28 July it looked like the American breakthrough was quickly turning into a break-out.

The rapidly changing situation is well reflected in Dempsey's actions. Early on the morning of 28 July he met with his corps commanders, and the commanding officer of 83 Group, RAF, to work out plans for the British attack from Caumont.[68] Dempsey intimated that Bluecoat might have to start sooner. After lunch he flew to Montgomery's headquarters, and then they drove the short distance to meet with Bradley. By then Monty probably had Eisenhower's message admonishing him to attack at Caumont right away: better three divisions today than six in five days' time. Moreover, Ike claimed – erroneously – that on the Caumont front 'the enemy has only four regiments and an occasional dug-in tank'.[69] Monty may also have received Brooke's note to get moving. Ike told Brooke bluntly on 28 July that the British Second Army needed to be more 'offensive'. The press had apparently learned that American casualties in Normandy were significantly higher than those of the Anglo-Canadians, so it seemed – Brooke warned Montgomery – that the British were 'not taking their share of the fighting'. The 'idleness' of the British Second Army annoyed Ike. Monty needed to get Dempsey moving as soon as possible.[70]

Montgomery was already on it. It was decided at Bradley's HQ on 28 July that Bluecoat would launch on 30 July instead of 2 August. Dempsey had already told Montgomery that 'I want heavy air support for this operation, which will be in difficult country and I will not have very heavy artillery support'.[71] Now he had less than forty hours to mount a two-corps attack at the western extremity of the British line. VIII British Corps had only just begun to move from east of the Orne, and so he would have just two divisions in line by the 30th. The rest would simply follow as they arrived. It was understood that artillery and air support for Bluecoat would be sketchy. Monty made it clear – in a not-so-subtle jab at delays over Cobra – that the British would attack regardless of the weather.[72]

During those same fateful days the best that Kluge could hope for was an attack by two Panzer divisions at Vire that would cause the Americans to pause, allowing the large force which had escaped the Roncey Pocket to restore the front. By 28 July the 2nd Panzer was in place near Tessy-sur-Vire, with the 116th Panzer to the south around Percy–Villebaudon–Beaucoudray by the evening of the 29th.[73] The presence of the Panzer divisions was revealed on the 29th when the 30th USID ran into the 2nd Panzer. The next morning the 116th Panzer attacked. For the next five days XIX US Corps fought the Panzer divisions to a standstill. Dempsey now owed Bradley two bottles of scotch.

But most of the armour Klug sent to stop the Americans never got to them. On 30 July Dempsey launched Operation Bluecoat. Often described as the 'British break-out', it was no such thing. The plan once again was to tie down German forces so the Americans could run free. For the Germans the key ground was Hill 309 on the western edge of the Suisse Normande near Vire. It provided clear sight over a wide area, overlooked the approaches to Vire, and the wooded uplands behind it were good cover for troops, guns and vehicles. If the Germans could hold this 'hinge' they could maintain a threat to the American drive into Brittany. It was poor country for tanks, and the steeply rolling bocage promised to be a nightmare for infantry. Both the VIII and XXX British Corps planned to lead with infantry, but they also had plenty of tanks, including three armoured divisions and two tank brigades. 'The mobility of the British,' Buckley writes, 'was something the Germans simply could not match.' In fact, the scale of Bluecoat came as a shock to Kluge and his senior officers.[74]

Bluecoat launched under heavy cloud in the sweltering heat of high summer. As Wilmot wrote, 'more than a thousand "heavies" and "mediums" made their attacks in defiance of the conditions and hit their targets with remarkable accuracy'.[75] British infantry then moved forward in shirtsleeves alongside their supporting tanks. VIII British Corps attacking towards Vire made excellent progress.[76] There was no need for specialised equipment to get through the bocage. The Churchills simply smashed through or over the hedges. 'One climbed slowly up the face of the bank,' Major Mark Millbank wrote later, 'balanced precariously on the top, warned the occupants to hold tight as one launched forth down the other side. In several tanks, men were knocked senseless by the battering.'[77] Given the terrain there were few anti-tank guns. When the infantry was stopped by small-arms and mortar fire, the tanks simply kept rolling, using 'on call' artillery support as needed.[78] By 1600 hours the 6th Guards Tank Brigade had captured Hill 309, the high ground the Germans thought was critical. The first day on VIII Corps' front was an unqualified success. O'Connor committed the 11th BAD to battle that evening with orders to push the attack through the night.

Things did not go as well for XXX British Corps. The advance was hesitant through thick minefields and close country. 'To be the leading tank of the leading squadron of the leading regiment,' Stuart Hills wrote, 'with an axis of advance along a narrow lane into a village known to be held by enemy armour and infantry, was, to put it mildly, bloody dangerous.' It helped that the RAF supplied a Forward Observer with the lead squadron, with rocket firing Typhoons 'Cab Ranked' over-head.[79] But it was all slow going, and the next day key officers in XXX British Corps and the 7th BAD were sacked. Regardless of the faltering efforts of XXX British Corps, Kluge ordered the 21st Panzer Division to move immediately to the British front south of Caumont. The 43rd BID began to spar with them early the next morning.

The success of Bluecoat was enough to spread panic among the German senior staff. Kluge hoped to send II SS Panzer Corps to attack the Americans, who that day crossed the bridge at Pontaubault: the final barrier to Brittany. But he now faced the collapse of the hinge of the whole German line. On 31 July, as American mechanised forces began to pour into Brittany, Kluge elected to stop the British: the 9th SS and 10th SS Panzer divisions were soon on the move.[80] So, too, was the 8th Werfer Brigade, a heavy anti-tank battalion, a company of Panthers, a grenadier company, a battery of self-propelled artillery and six armoured cars.[81] Bluecoat had done its job. Bradley ought to have sent Dempsey three bottles of scotch.

* * *

The American break-out in late July was a stunning achievement. Freed from the smothering embrace of the bocage, and with a broken enemy before them, Bradley's army was finally loose. This was the kind of campaign that Americans expected in Normandy from the outset. With more than a little hyperbole, John McManus wrote that this success derived in part from the fact that the US Army 'was, by far, the most mechanized force in existence' – a claim that the Anglo-Canadians could make themselves. McManus is on firmer ground with his asser-tion that the barely managed chaos of the American break-out seemed ideally suited to American individualism – rugged or otherwise.[82]

Once through the crust of the German defence, the advancing columns followed the road net. Artillery ammunition remained rationed, but the speeding self-propelled guns of the armoured divisions used their machine guns more than their cannons. What the advancing columns relied upon was the great American innovation of 'Armored Column Cover' by the USAAF. Relays of four P-47s armed with bombs or rockets were controlled by direct VHF communications with a Forward Air Controller embedded with the advancing armoured columns – something the Anglo-Canadian Cab Rank system of aircraft loitering over the battlefield was never able to match. McManus recounts the tale of 'Task Force X', led by Lieutenant Colonel Leander Doan. It was sweeping east of Avranches on 31 July at a steady 25mph with four P-47s hovering overhead when Doan approached a railway crossing and asked his air escort to check it out. Sure enough, there was a German blocking group there with several anti-tank guns. The P-47s strafed the area, killing or scattering the enemy. 'Doan's column rolled right through them,' McManus writes, 'shooting up the enemy guns and kept moving.' When Doan reached the outskirts of Brécy, his P-47s provided an immediate fifteen-minute air strike with bombs and machine guns. Doan's column drove through the town, cutting down Germans lounging in the street. Satisfied that Brécy was clear of the enemy, Task Force X carried on, fighting through the night against random parties of the enemy. By morning it occupied the high ground south of the river.[83] Fair weather helped enormously. Between 25 and 31 July IX Tactical Air Command flew over 9,000 sorties in support of the First US Army.[84] 'The cooperation between advancing columns and the fighters and fighter bombers of the Ninth Tactical Command,' Bradley told Marshall on 31 July, 'has been of a superior nature.'[85]

Once the Americans got into Brittany the pace of the advance quickened even more, the result – some would claim – of the arrival of George Patton on the battlefield. Patton had been in France since early July, chafing at the bit to get in the fight – and trying to bribe Eisenhower by offering him $1,000 for every week he got in early. By late July the eighteen combat divisions of the First US Army were becoming unwieldy for a single army HQ. The Anglo-Canadians, with fifteen divisions in the field, had already split their forces into the British Second and First Canadian armies.[86] However, Bradley was in no hurry to bring Patton into the action. The breakthrough would be all Bradley's.[87]

Patton's moment came on 1 August. On that day Bradley passed command of the First US Army to Courtney Hodges, Patton's Third US Army was activated, and Bradley assumed command of the new '12th Army Group'. Hodges was to secure the flank of the break-out; Patton was to drive into Brittany and capture the ports. This was the original Overlord plan and Eisenhower was anxious to see it completed.

Nothing was said of this American reorganisation to the press. For the time being Montgomery remained the overall ground-force commander as well as commander of the now entirely Anglo-Canadian 21st AG. Only when Eisenhower arrived later to take direct charge of the ground campaign would Monty and Bradley actually be equals. The Germans did not need to know about the new command arrangements. Perhaps just as importantly, neither did anyone in America, where American subordination to Montgomery rankled. And to prevent Patton from hogging all the glory, the announcement of his involvement in the campaign was delayed until mid-August. Patton, Hansen concluded, was primarily interested in fighting for headlines. There was fear in Bradley's camp, Hansen wrote on 6 August 1944, 'that Patton may unjustly crab credit for the breakthrough which was made and sealed before he arrived'. Concern for secrecy over the new command structure, and masking Patton's role, did not prevent the Germans from reporting that Patton was now commanding forces in Normandy, and British newspapers briefly picked up the story.[88]

And so while Hodges and the First US Army – alongside the British Second Army – fought to break the hinge of the German position around Vire, Patton's army raced across Brittany. By 3 August it had reached Rennes, the key road, rail and media hub of Brittany. The Germans slipped away and it fell the next day without a fight. By then the 4th USAD had reached Vannes, a secondary port on the north coast of Quiberon Bay, thus severing the Brittany peninsula. The Germans retreated into the fortresses of Lorient, on the south coast of the peninsula, and Saint-Nazaire on the eastern shore of Quiberon Bay. Hitler ordered that these be held to the last man. They did not capitulate until May 1945.

Progress by the 6th USAD towards Brest was eased by the mobilisation of 'French Forces of the Interior', the FFI. 'It was in Brittany,' according to

Olivier Wieviorka, 'that real cooperation between the Allies and the French underground was first achieved.'[89] 'Everywhere they arrived,' Wieviorka writes of the 6th USAD, 'they found the FFI engaged with the enemy or in command of the area.'[90] But no one controlled the night, when American laagers were continuously attacked. And, according to Waddell, ammunition shortages 'hindered effort of VIII Corps to clear the Brittany Peninsula'.[91] The limited range of American radios exacerbated the problem, because no one at Third Army HQ – much less Bradley – really knew what was going on. By the time the 6th USAD reached Brest on 6 August it was in no state to attack it. Some 280,000 German troops were now locked up in the ports America needed for its build-up.

By early August, Kluge was on the horns of an insoluble dilemma. He could not let the Americans run amok in his rear area or reach Paris, nor could he strip Panzer Group West of more forces without inviting an Anglo-Canadian break-out. At least eight divisions were rushing to shore up the Seventh Army, and new corps headquarters were also en route to command them. OB West concluded that 'This was not enough'. General Hans Eberbach, commander of PGW, recommended a retreat to the Seine. Hans Speidel, Kluge's Chief of Staff, agreed to make the case to Hitler. German forces in Normandy now needed to get out or they would be destroyed.

The next day, 2 August, orders arrived that sealed the fate of German forces in France. Kluge was ordered to concentrate his Panzer divisions to sever the American break-out at Avranches. 'The outcome of the thrust to Avranches,' the War Diary of Army Group D noted on 3 August, 'would decide the Battle of Normandy.' That day General Walter Warlimont, Deputy Chief of the Operations Staff at OKW, visited Kluge's HQ to discuss the situation. Eberbach was adamant that retreat to the Seine was the only option. Warlimont rejected the plea. He knew that Hitler had ordered work on a fall-back position along the Somme–Marne–Saône line north and east of Paris, but was forbidden to tell anyone because Hitler feared that his generals would simply retreat into that new position.[92] Warlimont's message was therefore blunt: Kluge had to fight it out. At the very least, he had to buy time until the new ME 262 fighter jets arrived en masse in late August and broke Allied command of the air. In any event, the morale of the British people, already weakened by the V1, would soon be shattered completely by another wonder weapon, the V2. All the Führer needed was a month. Eberbach pointed out that German forces in Normandy did not have a month. Warlimont was on more solid ground when he observed that if the current forces could not hold a 120km front in Normandy, 'it will certainly not be feasible further back'. It was time, Warlimont pressed, to start moving Panzer divisions into place for the attack towards Avranches.[93]

Hitler wanted Kluge to take his time assembling the Panzer divisions and all the available air support before launching Operation Lüttich. But every hour of delay saw the Americans drive deeper into Brittany and increased the danger that they might push east towards Paris. Kluge spent 4 August at the HQ of the Seventh Army trying to find a solution. Infantry divisions were en route to relieve the Panzer divisions, but air attack, wrecked bridges, smashed rail lines and partisan attacks slowed movement. To help, Kluge shortened his line by withdrawing south of Mont Pinchon, opening the route for XXX British Corps to finally achieve its Bluecoat objectives. Hitler had urged patience and deliberation: Kluge had little of either. Operation Lüttich was set for 6 August. It remained unclear just how many Panzer divisions – and how much of each – could be ready by then.

* * *

'We're winning this war the wrong way,' Major General John S. Wood, commander of the 4th USAD, complained on 1 August; 'we ought to go to Paris.' Brittany was critical to the Overlord plan, but it was tantalising to think that those ports might not be needed if the war ended quickly. Churchill thought that Germany would fall before the end of the year, and Bradley's HQ was swept by victory fever. The decision to swing east and drive for Paris came from Montgomery.[94] As Weigley commented, Montgomery was 'a commander of greater audacity than the Americans sometimes liked to admit'.[95] And so, on 3 August, Bradley told Patton to turn east with half his army – three infantry and two armoured divisions – leaving the other three infantry and two armoured divisions to clean up Brittany. John Wood later described the retention of armoured divisions in Brittany as 'one of the colossally stupid decisions of the war', but for the moment Eisenhower was hedging his bets: the ports might yet be needed.

Kluge's great fear in early August was that by shifting the weight of his Panzer forces west he left the critical area south of Caen open to an attack that would tumble his whole position into chaos. His fear was justified. Montgomery ordered the First Canadian Army to deliver just such an attack no later than 8 August. In the meantime, the Canadians kept I SS Panzer Corps busy with attacks focused around Tilley-la-Campagne beginning on the night of 31 July–1 August. 'We are holding down a very large proportion of armour on our front and this is facilitating the advance of the Americans and British,' Lieutenant-Colonel H.E.T. Doucet, the Public Relations Officer of the First Canadian Army, told the press in late July.[96] The Germans read events this way, too. Their intelligence estimate of 31 July noted that the Anglo-Canadians had some 120–30 artillery batteries (perhaps over 900 guns) in place east of the Orne. It was just a matter of time before they renewed their assault down the Caen–Falaise plain.[97]

As their position in Normandy began to unravel, a mood of panic gripped the German camp. By 6 August, Patton's forces were probing the Loire north of Nantes, and XV US Corps had crossed the Mayenne River, halfway between Rennes and Le Mans. The advance was little more than a road move against scattered resistance. On that day Montgomery issued Directive M-517. It was, as Rick Atkinson described it, 'a simple, handsome thing'.[98] The three armies aligned across what remained of the original Normandy line – First Canadian in the east, Second British in the middle and First American in the west – would hold what was now called the Fifth Panzer Army in place, while Patton's Third US Army swung around behind and enveloped it. The plan was now to trap and destroy the German Army in Normandy.

CHAPTER 25

GET 'EM ALL AND HAVE DINNER IN PARIS

American might has now been unleashed.

Daily Express, 5 August 1944[1]

'Political affairs – international ones I mean – are not going very well,' Sir James Grigg, the Secretary of State for War, warned Montgomery on 25 July 1944. 'I can't get out of my head the idea that the Americans and the Russians are going to frame us in the end and that unless we make up our minds for a generation of hard work and self denial (and no Beveridge) we shall be left in the position of the Dutch after Utrecht in 1713.' In that long-ago war the Dutch, the Holy Roman Empire and the British joined forces to check the ambitions of France. The Allies won, but the long years of conflict destroyed the Netherlands as a Great Power and marked the ascent of Great Britain.

History was now repeating itself. A week later, in another lament to Monty, Grigg linked the plight of Great Britain to press coverage of the Normandy campaign – especially now that Patton was loose in France and the presidential race was on in the USA. 'The Americans at the best of times would do their damnedest to write down our effort and write up their own, to laud others and diminish you.' It did not help, Grigg observed, that senior British airmen and both British and American army officers at SHAEF HQ had joined the press in disparaging Montgomery and his strategy.[2]

In his memoir, *A Soldier's Story*, published in 1951, Bradley gave credit to Montgomery for 'spending his reputation' to make the American break-out possible. But he was disingenuous and misleading in his praise.[3] The British had held the weight of German Panzer forces, Bradley claimed, by adopting a '*passive role* with patience and forbearing'. As a consequence, 'the British were forced to endure the barbs of critics who shamed them for failing to push out vigorously as the Americans did. The intense rivalry that afterward strained relations between the British and American commands might be said to have sunk its psychological roots into that *passive mission* of the British on the beachhead.'[4]

It is unlikely that anyone in the British Second Army would have described their efforts in Normandy as 'passive'. But Bradley's choice of words fits the American narrative that US forces did most of the fighting in Normandy, and that Operation Cobra was a 'made in America' victory that owed little, if anything, to what happened elsewhere. If Hamilton is correct, even SHAEF failed to connect the dots. 'The relationship between Dempsey's offensive and Bradley's thrust,' he writes, 'was ignored by SHAEF and the Allied air commanders.'[5] To have thought otherwise required acceptance that Montgomery's strategy worked, something his detractors were not willing to do. The same could be said of generations of postwar historians, who saw little connection between Anglo-Canadian efforts south of Caen and the ultimate success of the much-delayed American attack on 25 July. The myth of a 'made in America' victory has proven remarkably durable.

The roots of that myth, as James Grigg suspected, may lie in the press coverage of the Normandy campaign, but perhaps more importantly it was embedded in the collective psyche of Americans who fought in Normandy. The campaign had not followed the script. Those who expected otherwise were disappointed – indeed, often angry. Instead of racing across France, America's vaunted mechanised army slogged its way forward, yard by yard, for nearly two months through bocage and swamp. The *Chicago Tribune*, which, along with the *New York Times*, were the only two newspapers allowed to circulate in the US Army, would have confirmed this view. The emotional release from that dreadful purgatory fuelled the sense of accomplishment that followed. Suddenly, American spearheads were dashing across western

France, spurred by Patton's relentless drive. This was precisely the way the American media visualised the campaign from the outset. Chester Hansen confided to his diary in mid-August his belief that it took so long to achieve that mobility because of Montgomery. 'Newspaper correspondents who during the last week of July were criticizing us for a stablemindness which they say dominated our front,' Hansen wrote on 12 August, 'may instead be speaking of the British effort which appears to have logged itself in timidity and secumbed [*sic*] to the legendary Montgomery vice of overcaution.'[6]

Grumbling over the conduct of the Normandy campaign was not limited to those in the UK and France; in Washington in late July and early August it seems to have been widespread. When Beaverbrook arrived in late July he found the American mood towards Britain's efforts in Normandy openly hostile. This hostility, Robert Sherwood wrote, 'was attributable to the sentiment, widely expressed in Washington at the time, that while the American forces in France were dashing ahead at a devil-may-care rate of speed and with thrilling success, the British under Field Marshal Montgomery on the Allied left flank seemed to be "dragging his feet".'[7] For his part, Robert McCormick was under no illusions about what recent events meant. 'The Victory is American,' he said an editorial on 2 August. 'We are winning this war,' he wrote. 'We Americans are winning this war.' Not only had *Americans* broken out of Normandy, they were doing most of the fighting in the Pacific – especially MacArthur's campaign – and the fruits of American industry were the difference between stalemate and victory on the Eastern Front. Those who thought otherwise – which might include readers of the *New York Times*, who learned on 21 July that Australians outnumbered Americans in MacArthur's command six to one[8] – McCormick labelled traitors to the American cause.[9]

American newsreels continued to confirm the view that America was now doing all the fighting. Releases from the big five newsreel companies (Pathé, Paramount, Movietone, Universal and News Day) focused on what Americans were doing – in the war, in industry, in entertainment, in sports and in culture. Little was said about the British (or anyone else's) war effort.[10] The trend in American newspaper coverage as the US Army swept across France simply confirmed what the newsreels said: Normandy was an American campaign with an Anglo-Canadian supporting cast.[11]

Getting the press off Montgomery's back or convincing the Americans that Britain was carrying its weight in Normandy proved to be a Sisyphean task. *US News* summed up the sentiment on 4 August: 'General Montgomery's emphasis upon the number of Germans chewed up in a war of attrition around Caen in France was an alibi for the earlier failure to break out. All U.S. high command plans for operations in France call for a war of high movement, not a war of attrition.'[12] If *US News* magazine was right about the gossip spreading in Washington, then the break-out did not confirm the soundness of Montgomery's strategy, in fact quite the opposite. But for dithering Anglo-Canadians, the Americans would have broken out sooner. It was at this moment, perhaps more than any other, that the failure to allow American correspondents to cover the operations of the British Second Army profoundly affected the developing narrative – and myths.

* * *

As it turned out, the movements of the Third US Army between 31 July and mid-August were poorly covered by the contemporary media. This was partly because the front moved faster than copy could get back to the Press Wireless station at Vouilly. 'Teletype communications with the fast moving Third US Army did not exist,' Lieutenant Colonel John Redding, the SHAEF Public Relations Officer, recalled; it was 'impossible to guarantee transmission of copy to the United Kingdom'. American service radios could not carry the traffic. The MacKay commercial wireless set allocated to Patton's army worked 'admirably' but could not transmit voice.[13]

Poor press coverage of the American dash across France was caused by Bradley's very tight control of information. He instituted strict censorship on what general officers said, and a complete ban on any reporting of comments from George Patton. Since Bradley, who acted as the censor himself, seldom let any quotes from his generals pass, the American press soon gave up on trying to include comments from general officers.[14] That, it seems, suited Bradley's staff just fine.

But Bradley also did not want the Germans to know how fast and how far the Third US Army was moving. And so, he introduced a series of news blackouts and delays which infuriated the press. 'News – the biggest sort of news – was breaking,' Ernest Dupuy wrote in his memoir, 'news to thrill the peoples of the Allied nations. Most of the SHAEF correspondents wanted to cover it as they would a football game. Yardage gained was their shibboleth, but they couldn't get it . . . Without pinpointing advances, none of the details they ached to write could be filled in, no definitive box scores of ground gained could be compiled.'[15] Barney Oldfield, who on 1 August became the PR director for the 12th Army Group, had observed during the advance on Cherbourg that movement attracted correspondents like bugs to a light. For much of early August the scores of correspondents with Patton's army were bugs in a bottle.

The most detailed coverage during this period came from the 'established' Normandy front, between Vire and Caen: from the First US, British Second and First Canadian armies. Much of what appeared beneath British banner headlines about America's break-out was accounts of British and Canadian battles in the ongoing war of attrition with the Fifth Panzer Army.[16] The *New York Times* principal correspondent, E.C. Daniel, filed most of his front-page coverage from SHAEF HQ, and accurately reflected the comparative wealth of in-depth news from the old front lines. But movement made the headlines, and throughout August these were all American. Now, *The Times* announced, things looked 'more like a real "break through" than any manoeuvre since the landings', a tone echoed in other papers. The *New York Times* speculated, based on German claims, that Patton had something to do with this. As the *Daily Express* put it, the Americans were moving so fast they did not even have time to eat. What was happening was anyone's guess.

By early August even Bradley had no clear idea where George Patton or his army were. So he went looking for him on the 2nd. Troy Middleton, commander of VIII Corps driving west into Brittany, had no idea either where Patton was, but he told Bradley that he was uncomfortable with no one to guard his back. On the spot Bradley ordered the 79th USID to turn east and link with the First US Army at Avranches and told Middleton to back it with more forces. 'Dammit,' Bradley told Middleton, 'I am not interested in making news: I want a solid front and then get going.' Bradley eventually found Patton, standing by his jeep 'with brass buttoned battle jacket and trimmings'. 'For Christ's sake, George,' Bradley exclaimed, 'what are you doing about this open flank you have?' Small wonder the news had trouble getting out.[17]

The dearth of hard news from the Third US Army led to speculation. The only source for the claim that Patton was in command was German. The *Daily Express*, which reported on 3 August that American tanks were driving through France trying 'to find the enemy', estimated Patton's positions two days later based on news from the German short-wave service. Other papers did the same. The *Times* editorial of 7 August was largely a speculation on where the Americans might be. German, Swiss, Vichy, Spanish and Vatican reporting were all used to try to pinpoint the spearheads headed for Paris.

Editorials and features in Allied newspapers on Sunday the 6th nonetheless assessed the situation in Normandy with considerable accuracy. 'Scrutator' in the *Sunday Times* concluded that the German high command had two options, defeat or withdrawal. With the Americans surging behind him and capturing his supply depots, Kluge could not afford to stand and fight. But neither could he easily cut and run. His horse-drawn infantry divisions could not outrun the Americans, and he would never get his armour across the Seine. Scrutator concluded that Kluge would stand and fight. Others felt the same. The *Observer* that same day noted with considerable prescience that 'this breakout is now due to change its [the Normandy campaign's] character. It will create a situation of infinite possibilities'.[18]

There was, finally, a subtle but perhaps important difference between British and American reporting of the Normandy campaign in early August 1944. The British press, and especially their commentators, focused largely on defeat of the German Army. There were echoes of this in the American press. Captain Lowell Limpus, writing his Sunday 'War Review of the Week' for the *Washington Times-Herald* on 13 August, noted that Montgomery was not trying to take Paris: he was trying to destroy the German Army. But American headlines were captivated by movement and by the French capital. Henry Gorrell, a United Press reporter whose 9 August 1944 dateline was 'On the Road to Paris', spoke for many in the Third US Army, and the American home front. 'Paris', Gorrell wrote, '– the city of wine, women and song – is the magic word. You see, hear and feel it everywhere along this road.'[19]

* * *

In early August the plan was still for the Allied armies to swing like a door, hinged on Caen, and push the Germans against the Seine. By 6 August, however, Montgomery had a new idea. 'If he continues to hold strongly in the north, as he may well do,' Directive M517 that day said of Kluge's dilemma, 'that is the chance for our right flank to swing round his southern flank and thus cut off his escape.' This was the origin of what became known as the 'short envelopment'. Bradley was thinking even bigger that day: an American envelopment sweeping around Paris and then driving to the sea at Dieppe. 'Don't know why we can't do it,' Bradley commented in a moment of euphoria. 'Gosh, we get 'em all and have dinner in Paris.'[20]

By the time Montgomery's latest directive was decoded in Bradley's HQ in the early hours of 7 August, Kluge's counterattack through Mortain to Avranches was underway: it changed everything. The rolling hills around Mortain forced the attack onto a limited road net in difficult terrain. But west of Bellefontaine in the valley of the Sees River, Michael Reynolds writes, 'the country opened up and the way to the west was relatively unrestricted'.[21] Much depended on speed and surprise, and on powerful support from the Luftwaffe. Kluge was urged to take his time to muster a steamroller, while Hitler arranged for 300 Luftwaffe fighters to be over the battlefield.

Most Panzer divisions simply could not get away from the front: three were barely holding the British in the Suisse Normande, and two were in reserve along the Caen–Falaise highway, where a major attack appeared imminent. That left the 2nd Panzer and 2nd SS Panzer divisions, both now down to 60 per cent strength, and the shattered 116th Panzer – with twenty-five tanks – as the main attack force.[22] It was not enough, and the reinforcements Kluge hoped to assemble to support them failed to materialise. The commander of the 116th Panzer, Lieutenant-General Graf von Schwerin, simply refused to send his tanks to the 2nd Panzer, and then declined to participate in the offensive. The Panther battalion from the 1st SS Panzer – what was left of it – was late, and the reinforcements from the II Parachute Corps failed to show. The 1st SS itself was late arriving, too, and was, in any event, down to a single Kampfgruppe.[23] Kluge launched the attack anyway just after midnight on 6–7 August. Time was against him, and he had little hope of success.

The fate of Operation Lüttich was decided in little more than eighteen hours, in two distinct phases. The first, fought in darkness and heavy morning fog, was a signal American victory. The initial contact came along the Sees valley between the 2nd Panzer Division and the leading elements of the 9th USID preparing to attack the 116th Panzer. The Germans were taken under effective fire at short range, which took a heavy toll of both vehicles and Panzer Grenadiers.[24] About the same time further south, the forward outposts of the 120th Infantry Regiment, holding the area around Hill 314 just east of Mortain, were driven back to the crest by tanks and SS infantry. The tireless work of Lieutenant Robert Weiss from the 230th FA Battalion from the top of that hill remained a thorn in the side of Lüttich for the next four days.

All efforts to surge into the Sees River valley were thwarted by stout defenders. The river crossing at L'Abbaye Blanche just north of Mortain was defended by Lieutenant Tom Springfield with four towed 3" anti-tank guns, one 57mm, some bazookas and a few supporting infantry. Around 0500 hours, a German column crawled up the steep slope on the American side and right into Springfield's position. Burning tanks and half-tracks soon glowed in the fog, as the German infantry were slaughtered by Springfield's men. Michael Reynolds wrote that Springfield's roadblock 'inflicted astonishing casualties on the northern thrust of the 2nd SS Panzer and remained in place undefeated when the Germans finally withdrew four days later'.[25]

A similar action unfolded at a roadblock set up by Lieutenant George Green and four anti-tank guns further north, near Saint Barthélemy. Green ordered his gunners to aim for muzzle flashes in the fog. The first round hit the lead Panther and disabled it. Over the next forty-five minutes the Americans could hear German efforts to drag the Panther away. Then, around 0700 hours – now daylight but still dense fog – the SS advanced again. By the time Green and his men were overrun, as many as fourteen tanks were lost to his guns alone.[26] Efforts by the 2nd Panzer and 1st SS Panzer to slice through Saint Barthélemy, head-quarters of the 1st Battalion of the 117th Infantry Regiment, fared no better. The Americans exacted a heavy toll, and perhaps more importantly they bought time.[27] 'It took the Germans six precious hours to secure Barthélemy,' McManus writes. By mid-morning they were still

16 miles from Avranches, 'their timetable was completely blown, and their strength was ebbing as a result of the staunch resistance from U.S. ground troops'.[28] Then the fog began to clear.

All of the Allies' tactical airpower was committed to helping the Americans. This included six squadrons of British Typhoons equipped with 3" rockets and four 20mm cannons, and three Canadian Typhoon squadrons armed with 20mm cannons and two 500lb bombs. It was claimed by some that the rocket-firing Typhoon packed the firepower of a medium artillery regiment.[29] The rockets were frightening but notoriously inaccurate. However, the steady splash of exploding cannon shells was a nightmare for men and soft-skinned vehicles.

The first Typhoons arrived around 1300 hours and found 'some 50 to 60 tanks and 200 vehicles filling the hedge lined road from St Barthelemy to Cherence via Belle Fontaine'.[30] They attacked the front and tail of the column to trap it on the road, and then rocketed and strafed it. By 1400 hours a 'shuttle service' of Typhoons began, including the Canadian 'Bombphoon' squadrons.[31] The impact of the Typhoon assault was devastating.[32] Werner Josupeit of the 1st SS Panzer Division recalled that the Typhoons 'bore down on us and chased us mercilessly. Their shells fell with a terrible howl.'[33] 'It was like a scene from Dante's Inferno,' according to Flight Lieutenant Derek Stevenson, a Canadian flying with 245 RAF Squadron. The IX USAAF joined in the swarming. By mid-afternoon Lüttich was at a complete halt. The attack on the leading elements was only the most dramatic part of a massive Allied air effort on 7 August. The USAAF also destroyed the Luftwaffe air fleet en route to Mortain. They were helped by American fighters from the UK making sweeps over airfields west of Paris during the day. The closest any German aircraft came to Mortain was Couterne, 40km to the east, in the evening.[34]

By then Kluge had concluded that Lüttich was a failure.[35] Hitler admonished him to keep pushing and ordered more Panzer divisions to join the attack. It was madness. Hauser told Kluge at 1930 hours that he now had three choices: stay and be annihilated; retreat east and allow the looming attack on the Caen–Falaise highway to break through; or fall back towards the Seine and abandon hopes of retaining Paris. Given Hitler's explicit orders, there was only one course open to Kluge: stay and fight. If all went well, the attack might be renewed by 9 August. This was what the Allies hoped for. As Monty told Brooke that evening, 'If only the Germans will go on attacking at Mortain for a few more days, it seems that they might not be able to get away.'[36]

* * *

While the Germans immolated themselves at Mortain, the Canadians finally struck south from Caen. In early August the front was held by I SS Panzer Corps,[37] backed by parts of the III Luftwaffe Flak Corps and the 83rd Werfer Regiment. Wilmot estimated that 100 88mm and 75mm anti-tank guns were deployed, as well at least 100 field howitzers. The 101st SS Heavy Tank Battalion with perhaps eight combat-ready Tigers was in reserve. Simonds came up with a novel solution to the problem of crossing the open ground from Verrières ridge to the plateau near Cintheaux in the face of this opposition: crash through the German forward position in a massive armoured phalanx, then turn two armoured divisions loose for a thrust towards Falaise. It would all be supported by heavy bombers. The Canadians had a little more than a week to meet Montgomery's directive for an attack no later than 8 August.

Twenty-six year earlier, on 8 August 1918, the Canadians had surged through German lines at Amiens in troop-carrying tanks. Crerar and Simonds were determined that the Canadians would do so again. Nearly 100 M7 Priests were available following the 3rd CID's artillery reconversion to towed 25-pounders. By 6 August seventy-six of these had been converted into 'Kangaroo' personnel carriers by removing their gun and plating over the embrasure. Bren carriers, scout cars and half-tracks were pressed into service, and more half-tracks and new 15cwt Canadian armoured trucks were rushed from the UK. More than 1,000 armoured vehicles were assembled.[38] They would carry the 3rd CID and the 51st BID in the attack. The exploitation would be done by the newly arrived and untested 1st Polish Armoured Division (PAD),[39] and the 4th CAD.

Simonds had some trouble securing his fire support. Sir Arthur Harris rejected night bombing. But a trial on the night of 6–7 August was a success, so he was persuaded: Bomber Command would attack targets on the flanks in support of marching infantry attacks. Bombing for

Phase II, the armoured thrust south, would be done by the Americans in daylight, this time flying parallel to the front so there would be no chance of a short bombing.[40] Simonds also mustered 788 guns and 205,000 rounds of ammunition for the day. Counter-flak and counter-battery fire were laid on, as were two batteries firing red and green indicators to guide bombers, and tracer ammunition along the axis of the armoured advance to help guide the attack.[41]

As the preparations for Operation Totalize were underway Panzer divisions began to slip away for Operation Lüttich. This brightened the prospects for Totalize, and Simonds adjusted the plan to move his armoured divisions forward sooner with hopes that they might go deeper than originally planned. The overly optimistic intelligence estimate on 7 August heightened expectations. Crerar and Simonds started thinking about taking Falaise and pushing even further.[42] Crerar told Montgomery as much that evening.[43]

The First Canadian Army was now to assume the mantle of the Canadian Corps of the Great War: driving down an arrow-straight road, across a rolling plain, through the strongest point of the German defences in the west to achieve a victory that might decide the war. It was to be launched on the anniversary of the Amiens battle 'The Black Day of the German Army' and the start of the Hundred Days Campaign that ended the Great War. 'We have reached what very much appears to be the potentially decisive period of this five year war,' Crerar told his senior officers hours before the attack started. 'I have no doubt that we shall make August 8th, 1944, an even blacker day for the German Army than that same date twenty-six years ago.'[44]

What Allied intelligence missed, and what Canadian planners – and many subsequent historians – failed to note was that as the Panzers slipped away, the anti-tank guns arrayed in depth behind the German front south of Caen remained unaltered. Wilmot says 100, Pemberton says ninety, along with perhaps sixty dug-in tanks and SPs.[45] 'These guns possessed such a range and the infantry were disposed in such depth,' Wilmot observed, 'that a rapid breakthrough was not easy to achieve.'[46]

By any measure, the opening phase of Operation Totalize was a stunning success. At 2300 hours on 7 August over 1,000 Lancasters and Halifaxes of Bomber Command began their carefully controlled run.[47]

No casualties among the Canadians were reported. Nor, it seems, did the bombing have much impact on the Germans.[48] At 2330 hours the artillery barrage started and the armoured columns moved in unison across their start line at a stately 5mph. Planners put every conceivable effort into ensuring that the columns of armour reached their objectives in good form. But the advance was more like a tsunami than a bulldozer, as hundreds of armoured vehicles, their drivers blinded and choked by dust and smoke, rolled their way through or around obstacles and Germans. The advance of the 51st BID east of the road went best of all. By 0700 hours they secured Cramesnil Spur, the critical objective. 'Fuck me!' the commander of the 1st Battalion, Black Watch, exclaimed in amazement. 'We've arrived.'[49]

The Canadian advance turned into something of a shambles. The column adjacent to the highway quickly ran into mines and anti-tank fire which slowed it measurably. All the other columns were supposed to pass west of Rocquancourt, but darkness, dust and enemy fire drove them east. The column carrying the Royal Regiment of Canada drove on to Gaumesnil on the high ground beyond Hill 122, but the RHLI and Essex columns crashed directly into Rocquancourt. The RHLI kept moving and consolidated on their objective by 0400 hours. The Essex disembarked in Rocquancourt and got engaged in fighting. At 0845 hours the next morning they regrouped for the advance to their objective. In the meantime, Canadian infantry attacked May-sur-Orne and Fontenay-le-Marmion on the right flank.

Tales of woe from Phase I of Totalize abound, but by early morning the better part of two infantry and two armoured brigades were on their objectives.[50] The most heavily defended German front in the west had been ruptured to a depth of 6,000 yards at a cost – among the infantry in Canadian columns – of seven men killed and forty-six wounded. Supporting armour lost just twenty tanks. The marching infantry on the flanks suffered 250 casualties by the time they took May and Fontenay.[51] Simonds's scheme had worked. By any measure, Phase I of Totalize was, in Doug Delaney's words, 'a tremendous success'.[52]

That said, Brigadier Pemberton's conclusion that 'Mopping up was not so easy' was an understatement.[53] By some estimates perhaps fifty per cent of Germans who were overrun carried on the fight. By noon

local counterattacks, supported by tanks, were coming in from all directions. In the circumstances, both the 4th CAD and 1st PAD struggled
to get forward. In the meantime, Kurt Meyer, now commanding the
12th SS, quickly pulled together a powerful counterattack force of seven
Tigers led by the tank ace Michael Wittmann, and Kampfgruppe
Waldmüller with a company of Jagdpanzer IVs, thirty-nine Mk IVs and
about 200 infantry. They advanced at noon. Kampfgruppe Waldmüller
attacked the British position in Saint-Aignan from the south-east, while
Wittmann led the Tigers straight up the highway towards Caen.

Wittmann's attack across an open and flat plain was audacious. It was
also a total failure. Radley-Walters's C Squadron of the Sherbrooke
Fusiliers was tucked behind the walls of a château on the west side of
the road, with loopholes cut through to give their guns oversight on
the battlefield.[54] The advance of the Tigers was also watched by the
Northamptonshire Yeomanry from the wooded area just south of Saint-
Aignan. At 1240 hours, when the range shorted to 800m, a Yeomanry
Firefly opened fire. Two rounds set the rear Tiger on fire. Seven minutes
later the Yeomanry hit a second Tiger, which immediately blew up. Fire
from the British squadron disabled a third Tiger, which Lieutenant
James then destroyed at 1252 hours. The Yeomanry claimed three Tigers
in twelve minutes.

Meanwhile, Sydney Radley-Walters's squadron held their fire until
the Germans were abreast of them, about 500 yards away. One of the
first tanks hit was the Tiger closest to the road. Soon B Squadron of the
SFR, a little further north, added to the din. By the time the action was
over, the Sherbrookes claimed two Tigers, two Mk IVs and two SPs.[55]
Wittmann's force was all but annihilated, and he died in the maelstrom.
Historians have been arguing over who killed him for decades.[56]

Meanwhile, the assault on the British at Saint-Aignan by
Kampfgruppe Waldmüller went on for hours. It peaked at about 1400
hours when masses of German infantry appeared, so many 'that they
seemed to blacken the standing crops in the field they were advancing
through'. Untold numbers of German infantry were killed or wounded,
and the British eventually claimed fifteen tanks and five SPs at the cost
of twenty Shermans. Brian Reid describes the British defeat of
Kampfgruppe Waldmüller as the key moment in Totalize.[57] It was at its

height when the leading elements of 1st PAD reached their start line at 1335 hours.

The first wave of American bombers arrived from the south-west at 1226 hours, flying parallel to the Canadian front – a lesson learned from Cobra. They bombed Bretteville-sur-Laize and Saint-Sylvain with accuracy. When the second wave arrived at 1335 hours their target area was shrouded in dust and smoke. The bombing was scattered. More critically, one twelve-plane section 'veered off from its run and headed northeast towards Caen and the coast'. Allied troops watching assumed they were simply going home. But then, immediately south of Caen – 8 miles north of their target and 6 miles inside Allied lines – most of the Fortresses dropped their bombs. Then a second group of twelve bombers did the same thing. 'The question kept running through their minds,' Reid writes of the men on the ground, 'how had the Germans managed to capture all those Flying Fortresses?'[58] The bombs devastated 'troop concentrations, unit echelons, gun positions, the headquarters of 3 [Canadian] Division and 2 [Canadian] Armoured Brigade' and destroyed about one-third of the corps ammunition dump. Charles Stacey recorded sixty-five dead and 240 wounded. Several batteries of medium guns needed to fire in depth for Phase II were destroyed, and the exploding ammunition dump affected operations for five hours.[59]

The impact of the errant bombing was revealed when the Polish division tried to push south in the afternoon. It ran into a hail of anti-tank fire that it could not overcome, losing fifty-seven tanks in a few hours. The Poles blamed the difficult ground, but also the weak artillery support – a direct effect of the bombing.[60] As a result, the left wing of Totalize Phase II stalled where Phase I had stopped. Things went better on the Canadian side of the highway. By 1800 hours the vanguard of the 4th Armoured Division was consolidating in Cintheaux, and there it stopped for the day. Simonds had been adamant that the attack should continue throughout the night. But the men on his right flank decided otherwise.[61]

Totalize was effectively over by the evening of 8 August, but there was a bloody denouement. In the early hours of 9 August a battlegroup from the 4th CAD surged deep into the German defences. Disorientated by the dust and darkness, and reduced by chaos and losses, thirty-one

Shermans of the British Columbia Regiment, two companies of the Algonquin Regiment and one lost British FOO ended up on Pt 140, 5km east of their objective, Pt 195. Their presence caused a mild panic in the German camp. Five Tigers, fifteen Panthers, a couple of companies of infantry from the 85th GID and an unknown number from the 12th SS were sent to destroy it. The Canadians tried all day to find this errant band, but it was so far adrift even its FOO had no idea where they were: requests for supporting fire landed miles away all around Pt 195. Typhoons arrived to help, and the Poles got within 300 yards, but no one reported their position. Finally, at 2200 hours, survivors were ordered to get away. The British Columbia Regiment lost forty-four tanks that day.

For many, then and later, the novelty of Totalize outweighed the disappointment of Phase II. But for Crerar, Simonds and postwar Canadian historians the failure was visceral. There was no second 'Black Day of the German Army', no sweeping rush to Falaise and certainly no probing further afield with mechanised columns. A brilliant break-in had been followed by a botched break-out. Disappointment about the pace of the Canadian (and Polish) move down the Caen–Falaise plain in August 1944 lingered long after the war and coloured the way Charles Stacey and Anglo-American historians wrote about the Canadians in Normandy.[62] 'There is little doubt,' Wilmot concluded, 'that, if the armoured divisions had been more experienced and aggressive, the Canadian offensive would have been completely successful.'[63]

What mattered, however, was that Totalize profoundly altered the nature of the Normandy campaign. 'A break through has occurred south of Caen such as we have never seen,' Kluge told Hausser late on 8 August. When Kluge got through to Eberach they stayed on the phone for most of three hours.[64] The enemy had attacked, Eberbach began, 'with a very large number of tanks, about 500'. 'What, 500?' was Kluge's shocked reply. Eberbach was hurriedly building a new 'battle line with anti-tank guns and flak guns', but was not sure it would hold. Kluge had little to offer Eberbach but sympathy. 'I have always anticipated this,' Kluge lamented, 'and have always looked forward to the coming day with a very heavy heart.' When asked what he needed, Eberbach said simply, 'Tanks.' To find them Kluge abandoned plans for a renewed attack at Mortain on 9 August. 'That is a very weighty decision for me,' Kluge confided, 'a major abandonment of an order that has been given to me. I know of no other solution – have no further forces. If it goes like this tomorrow, there will be no more stopping [it] at all.' That decision, and those forced on him over the next few days, cost Kluge his life.

The Canadian attack animated Allied senior officers, too. On 8 August Ike had dinner with Bradley, and they talked with Montgomery on the phone about 'Canadian developments'.[65] With Operation Lüttich going nowhere and the Canadians pressing hard down the road to Falaise, Bradley recommended that the Third US Army be turned northward, towards Alençon and Argentan.[66] Bradley was now convinced that the German Army in France was broken and, in the words of Wing Commander Jim Rose, one of the Ultra boffins helping distribute this very sensitive material, was 'no longer a factor with which we need to reckon'.[67] The next morning Bradley ordered Patton to turn north and drive for Argentan instead of Paris.[68]

XV US Corps, under Lieutenant General Wade Haislip, shifted its axis north to commence the short envelopment. Resistance was minimal and the Americans moved quickly.[69] By the evening of 12 August, Haislip told Patton that his troops were now on the outskirts of Argentan, poised to push through to Falaise and link up with the Canadians. Patton told Haislip to keep going. The next day Haislip's patrols were just 10km south of Falaise.[70] In the meantime, only scattered elements of the 80th USID covered the 25 miles of XV US Corps' left flank. A major Panzer counterattack through that gap, Blumenson writes, 'might well have dealt the U.S. Corps a crippling blow'.[71] Stanley Hirshon claims that Patton was not worried about it. And in any event, the First US Army was beginning to slip eastward to secure Haislip's flank.[72] So far as Patton was concerned, Haislip was cleared to push through to Falaise. Charles Stacey described the situation south of Falaise on 13 August as 'one of the greatest opportunities of the war'.[73]

All the Allied senior officers, including Bradley, knew that the Canadians were poised to launch another major mechanised thrust to capture Falaise — and that there was (apparently) little now between them and Haislip. Dempsey had also been ordered to shift his effort to the east of the Orne and, along with the 2nd CID, drive on Falaise from the north-west.[74] Montgomery believed that the British and Canadians would now have an easier passage southward because the Germans were likely to concentrate their weight to check the Americans. For this reason, Hamilton claims, Bradley concluded on 13 August that the Americans should not go any further north.[75] In fact, Bradley feared that an over-extended XV US Corps would be stampeded by nineteen divisions racing east to escape the trap. And he had little faith that Patton would know what to do: the Third Army was, in Crosswell's words, 'flush with victory but short on battle experience'.[76] And so on 14 August Bradley – on his own and without consultation with Montgomery or Patton – ordered Haislip to consolidate on the inter-Army Group boundary south of Argentan.

Many spurious reasons were advanced at the time and since for Bradley's fateful decision. The threat of unexploded delayed-action bombs littering the ground north of Argentan, apparently dropped by the British, was a complete red herring. The bombs were dropped on 12 August by the IX USAAF with a twelve-hour delay: they were neither British nor a threat by 14 August.[77] Bradley later cited the issue of Army Group boundaries. After the war he claimed that he never asked for permission to go beyond his 12th AG boundary and Montgomery never offered. This was not true. Charles Stacey described that claim – still current in 1956 when the Canadians reviewed the draft of Blumenson's official history volume – as a 'slander which has now been shown to have no foundation'.[78] In fact, the boundary issue was discussed at a meeting on 13 August between Bradley, Dempsey and Montgomery. 'So long as the Northward move of Third Army meets little opposition,' Dempsey recorded in his diary, 'the two leading corps will disregard inter-Army boundaries.'[79]

Bradley also managed to convince himself – in ways historians have never explained – that most of the German forces to the west of Argentan had already escaped anyway.[80] The most generous explanation for Bradley's action on the 14th might simply be that he was overwhelmed. With the 12th AG spread from Brest to Le Mans he was probably more than a little fearful of what might happen to his badly extended forces. In any event, he made two fateful decisions on 14 August without consulting Montgomery. The first was to halt Haislip's advance. 'Better a solid shoulder at Argentan,' was his famous quip, 'than a broken neck at Falaise.'[81] The second error was to direct Haislip's corps east, to rejoin Patton's drive towards Dreux and Chartres. Patton called the stop order 'a great mistake', and blamed Montgomery for it.[82]

Bradley's instinct after the war was to blame Montgomery, too.[83] Rick Atkinson concludes that at this stage of the Normandy campaign no one was in effective control of Allied forces in Normandy. Monty was content to issue directives and leave Bradley to fight his own battles. Bradley was in well over his head, but Montgomery 'evinced his usual sangfroid without imparting either energy or command omniscience'. Meanwhile Eisenhower swanned around Normandy with his attractive English driver Kay Summersby, 'fashionably garbed in suntans with Egyptian suede shoes'.[84] No one gripped the battle.

* * *

The final Canadian drive to Falaise started in the early afternoon of 14 August, against what was supposed to be light opposition. Operation Tractable was a variation on Totalize: two massive armoured columns charging over the open high ground north of the Laison River, and then over the river and across open rolling countryside to the high ground north-east of Falaise. The defenders, primarily the 85th GID, were, in Copp's words, 'as good an infantry division as the Germans possessed at this stage of the war'.[85] Although there was no operational order issued for Tractable – just a verbal briefing to formation officers on 12 August and O Groups for units on the 13th – copies of the phase lines, bombing targets and artillery plans were captured by the Germans on 13 August. This information allowed them to anticipate in ways that slowed the Canadian attack and increased casualties. Simonds claimed it cost him a day getting into Falaise.

On 14 August, amid clouds of dust and smoke fired to provide cover, the massed columns of armoured vehicles set off. The attack drifted a little east and – typically – went slower than the planners hoped. As Charles Stacey observed, 'it was the 88-mm guns that were to give us most of the trouble'.[86] So, too, did the Laison River. Reconnaissance had dismissed it as insignificant. But it was steep-sided and an effective vehicle obstacle.[87] Movement once south of the Laison went well. Although a band of diehard Wehrmacht and SS held out on Hill 159, near the main highway, Simonds's corps was soon on the escarpment south of Olendon overlooking Falaise and the Dives valley. Meanwhile, the 2nd CID and XII British Corps fought towards Falaise through the bocage along the valley of the Orne.

Anyone who has seen the view from Falaise flying club overlooking the Dives River valley will wonder why the Canadians went into Falaise at all: that rolling open farmland along the eastern edge of the Pays d'Auge beckons. Moreover, Falaise was already an impassable pile of rubble. By occupying the high ground north-east of Falaise the route to Lisieux came under effective fire: nothing could now move through Falaise along that route. But Monty maintained Falaise as an objective. And so the First Canadian Army spent considerable effort – and manpower – capturing the rubble. The only major roads that mattered now to the escaping Seventh and Fifth Panzer armies were through Trun and Chambois. The next day – 15 August – 1st PAD was ordered to start the thrust to Trun. The 4th CAD was to follow shortly.

Montgomery met with Bradley and Dempsey on 15 August to discuss their next moves. 'As far as Montgomery was concerned,' Terry Copp wrote, 'closing the gap was not a priority – it was now a race to the Seine.' News of the successful Allied landing in the south of France that day encouraged the expectation that the Germans would bolt from western France or risk being cut off. Military intelligence confirmed that, for the moment, most of the Seventh Army and the Fifth Panzer Army were still west of Argentan. With the Canadians driving towards Trun, Bradley now wanted the Americans to meet them there. Orders were issued the next day.[88] This would close the short envelopment.

With Haislip's corps already marching east, Patton pulled together a provisional corps – the newly arrived 2nd French Armoured Division (FAD), 80th and 90th USIDs – under his Chief of Staff, Major General Hugh Gaffey. 'All units were ready to attack by 1000, 17 August,' according to Blumenson.[89] The 2nd FAD would take Trun and the 90th USID Chambois, while the 80th secured the western flank. The French commander, Major-General Jacques Leclerc, flatly refused the order. If he took Trun, Leclerc explained, his division – which was supposed to liberate Paris – would be ruined. Gaffey was stunned and asked Leclerc if he was refusing to obey an order. Leclerc demurred: the attack was impossible but he would support it.

Before Gaffey could attack, Gerow arrived and announced that he was now in command. While Gaffey and Gerow waited for Bradley to confirm who was to lead, a liaison officer from the First Canadian Army arrived at Patton's HQ to coordinate the link-up. Patton told him to come back with written authorisation from Bradley. 'Wilful obstructionism and an atmosphere of near anarchy pervaded Third Army's activities,' Hamilton wrote of these crucial days, 'so that Bradley soon determined to give the operations to close the Falaise Gap to Hodges' First US Army – which he did on 17 August.'[90] Gerow was confirmed in command and ordered the attack to start on the morning of 18 August.[91]

By the time Gerow was ready the situation in the pocket had changed dramatically. The American advance further east – to Sees, Dreux and Chartres – severed the Seventh Army's supply system. Ammunition, fuel and food were running short, tanks were being abandoned and burned. The Canadians' rupture of the I SS Panzer Corps' front at Falaise meant that Kluge could only hold if reinforcements were shifted away from the Americans. On 14 August, therefore, he recommended a general withdrawal. The situation deteriorated by the hour. The next day, 15 August, Kluge went missing. His car was strafed by Allied aircraft and his radios destroyed, then he was trapped in the chaos of retreating traffic. Kluge finally surfaced at the Fifth Panzer Army HQ at 0450 hours on 16 August. By then the British had penetrated west of Falaise, and the Canadians were fighting their way through the town: Falaise was no longer available as an escape route.[92]

Kluge talked to Jodl at noon, confirming that the situation was hopeless. A few hours later Hitler ordered a withdrawal behind the Dives, holding Falaise as the northern anchor, and ordered Eberbach once again to attack the Americans to widen the zone for the retreat. Falaise fell to the Canadians that night. And so instead of striking at the Americans, Eberbach ordered I SS Panzer Corps to form a new defensive line in front of the Canadians and Poles. Meanwhile, II SS Panzer Corps was ordered to Vimoutiers to form an Army Group reserve. The withdrawal of II SS Panzer Corps on 17 August left the southern side of the pocket east of Argentan, in Eberbach's words, in the hands of 'weak security detachments'.[93]

While Montgomery focused on the Seine and the Americans argued, the Poles drove towards Chambois through the hills skirting the brooding eastern woodland of the Pays d'Auge. These run almost like an escarpment from just east of Jort to Chambois. Above this ridge line lies a rolling plateau of farms and timber-framed buildings famous for its soft and pungent cheese named after the village of Camembert. By late on 16 August the Poles had moved through this verdant but deadly landscape to within 12km of Chambois.

For the moment, they were alone. Major-General George Kitching muddled the 4th CAD's advance into the Dives valley on 16 August, so it was not until the evening of 17 August that the 4th CAD was within a few kilometres of Trun. That evening Montgomery phoned Crerar to admonish him to get going and close the gap. It was, Monty said, 'absolutely essential that both Armoured Divisions of 2 Cdn Corps . . . close the gap . . . at all costs and as quickly as possible'.[94] That same evening – 17 August – for reasons unknown, Monty sent Brooke a telegram saying that the gap was now closed. It was pure wishful thinking. Four days of intense and brutal fighting lay ahead before that claim could be made.

By the time Kluge returned to his headquarters at La Roche-Guyon his replacement, Field Marshal Walter Model, Hitler's 'Fireman', was waiting. Model had a reputation for ruthless efficiency and salvaging something from disasters on the Eastern Front. He took command of Army Group B at 2000 hours on 17 August. Kluge left the next day for Germany, well knowing what fate awaited him. He penned a note to Hitler professing his loyalty and pleading with the Führer to stop the war, and then committed suicide.

By 0900 hours on 18 August, Model was at the Fifth Panzer Army HQ for a conference with Dietrich, Eberbach and senior staff officers. Model wanted a coherent front established to the north to hold Trun and secure the route out to Vimoutier. This much Eberbach had tried. But Model also ordered II SS Panzer Corps, assembling at Vimoutier, to launch a counterattack from the east to help keep the corridor open. This had been Model's trademark in the east. Until now Hausser had conducted a systematic and orderly retreat. By the time Model left the meeting on the morning of 18 August all of that was about to change.

By 18 August the retreating Germans were concentrated in the sprawling Forêt de Gouffern around Argentan, which provided excellent refuge for troops and vehicles. But they had to cross a couple of kilometres of open farmland to the crossing points over the Dives – all of it overlooked from the eastern side. Over the previous days, with Allied tactical airpower focused on the Seine and the Canadians stalled short of Trun, the route through Trun had worked well.[95] But the 4th CAD was now perched on the road to the north of Trun, and the Allied tactical air forces had arrived in force. The Canadians waited until American P-47s had thoroughly beaten up Trun before taking it from the 1st SS Panzer in a fierce battle. That closed the last good route east. Ultra revealed Model's plans to get it back by launching II SS Panzer Corps westward from Vimoutier and by attacking from inside the pocket. Simonds's response was to hold the 4th Canadian Armoured Brigade at Trun, slide the 2nd CID into position between Trun and Falaise, and backstop Trun with the 3rd CID. Meanwhile, the Poles, beating away waves of retreating Germans and dodging Allied air attacks, fought through the hills of the Pays d'Auge, towards Coudehard and ultimately Chambois.

Throughout 18 August fighter-bombers swarmed the massed columns of German troops and equipment streaming towards the remaining crossing points of the Dives at Saint-Lambert-sur-Dives, Moissy and Chambois. In over 3,000 sorties Allied tactical air forces claimed nearly 3,000 vehicles and 224 tanks destroyed or damaged. It was not always easy to distinguish friend from foe: 149 Canadians and Poles were killed, and 400 wounded that day by Allied aircraft. But it was, as Stacey called it, 'A day of supreme disaster for the fleeing enemy'.[96] The air forces wrecked the tidy order of Hausser's withdrawal.

While the Canadians firmed up their position at Trun, all that Kitching had for a push to Chambois on 18 August was his reconnaissance regiment and a few bits and pieces to support it. And so at 1800 hours C Squadron of the South Alberta Regiment (SAR) under Major David Currie – plus a troop of M10s, a reconnaissance troop and a company of the Argyll and Sutherland Highlanders of Canada (the Argylls), about fifty men – moved down the D13. They reached the village of Saint-Lambert-sur-Dives, 3 miles from Chambois, at dusk.

22. Major David Currie, on the left with pistol in hand, in the process of winning a Victoria Cross, Saint-Lambert-sur-Dives, 19 August 1944.

There, where the Dives cuts deeply into the rock and creates a very effective vehicle barrier, a small stone bridge spans the river. It would hold a Tiger. Beyond that was a ford at the hamlet of Moissy. The next crossing point, the bridge at Chambois, was already under fire from the 30th USID.

Currie's small band was desperately short of infantry, but there was never a shortage of ammunition – or targets. The regiment's supply echelon made steady trips from Trun on 19 August, carrying gasoline and ammunition along the D13, dodging groups of fleeing Germans. The day was remembered as 'Target Practice Day'. Everyone and everything fired all day. When Bob Rasmussen pulled his truck alongside Jim Grove's tank to say hello, Grove passed him some binoculars and told him to watch. Grove fired his 75mm gun on a column of horse-drawn carts, sending the animals flying through the air. 'Jesus Jimmy,' Rasmussen exclaimed, 'how do you get a job like this?'[97] Not everyone was impressed. Decades later Trooper Carson Daley recalled that some rear-echelon troops who came down from Trun were given a .50 calibre machine gun and a box of ammunition and allowed to fire away. Some did: they could watch the bullets fly and the men fall. But many gave it up because they had not gone to war to simply kill people. Daley himself remained haunted by his days at Saint-Lambert-sur-Dives: as he recalled, 'We just shot people.'[98] During the day a second company of Argylls arrived and so did an FOO from a Canadian medium regiment, the 15th RCA. Currie's tanks were now a little more secure, and well-directed artillery fire added to the carnage inflicted on the fleeing enemy.

Whether anyone expected much relief from the long-awaited American attack that day is unclear. It had finally launched on the 18th. The French deployed a 'Tactical Group' of eighty Shermans east of Chambois, just 2 miles from the Poles. But, as Denis Whitaker noted, the commander was under 'strict orders from General Leclerc to remain in a passive role and keep his unit free to proceed to Paris'.[99] Gerow was content to sit back and hammer the Germans with artillery.[100] The French, with an eye on Paris, soon retreated from Frénaye. That same day, XII British Corps, just 10km north-west of Trun and facing 'light opposition', stopped to prepare for the advance to the Seine.[101] The British Second Army was now effectively out of the battle. Only the guns of XII Corps, which had a good vantage point over the pocket, and elements of the 59th BID remained active.[102] The Americans broke into Chambois on the afternoon of the 19th, where they encountered a patrol from the Polish division. According to most subsequent accounts, this tenuous contact was the moment the Falaise Gap was closed. Unfortunately, no one told the Canadians or the Poles or the Germans.

CHAPTER 26

PARIS

> Paris freed from the yoke of Nazi brutality would be news in the biggest sense of the word . . . Every newsman in the world wanted to get into Paris.
>
> Ernest Dupuy[1]

While the Canadians and Poles struggled to close the Falaise Gap, the British, the Americans and the French were not prepared to send their troops into the cauldron. Nigel Hamilton suggests that was because the power of the British Army of liberation was dwindling rapidly.[2] According to Stephen Hart, 'the maintenance of Britain's international influence necessitated that British forces assume a prominent role in the prosecution of the vital Northwest Europe campaign'. The only apparent solution to keeping formations in the fight was to cannibalise the army. This was ultimately self-defeating. 'The fewer number of combat experienced divisions that the British emerged with at the end of the war,' Hart concludes, 'the smaller her influence on Europe was likely to be in the face of the growing military might of the two nascent superpowers.' Britain needed victory in 1944.[3]

The British role in Normandy remained under intense scrutiny by the American press throughout August. As Dupuy wrote of this period, 'Some Americans felt – and spread the whisper – that it was intolerable that a Britisher, Montgomery, should continue to control two American armies.' Wes Gallagher finessed a story through the censors on 14 August announcing the changes in command of Allied forces that SHAEF had been anxious to mask. The revelation that Patton was in command of the Third US Army allowed the US media to champion the rehabilitated and dynamic architect of the incredible drive to Paris. That much was a nightmare for Bradley. Worse still for Anglo-American relations was Gallagher's claim that Bradley was finally out from under Montgomery and in command of 'the whole American fighting forces in France'. With that, Dupuy wrote, 'the fat was in the fire. British correspondents and a part of the British press chose to believe that the change was a reflection on Monty, while the American press ran up a chauvinistic Stars and Stripes to three hearty cheers.' Eisenhower was furious. SHAEF issued a clarification on 16 August, announcing that Bradley remained under General Montgomery as overall Allied ground-forces commander. The American press saw this as a capitulation. Hansen Baldwin was soon in the *New York Times* demanding that the Americans be given 'equal status' in Normandy.[4]

The context for another meeting between Montgomery, Dempsey and Grigg on 16 August was therefore complex and fraught. There is, apparently, no record of that meeting. It is certain that they discussed how the British might salvage some geopolitical weight from the Normandy campaign. Hansen's diary speculations suggest the drift of some American thought at Bradley's HQ. He described the decision to halt XV US Corps at Argentan on 14 August as evidence of a British effort to steal prestige for closing the trap. And while the British 'permitted much of the strength in the pocket to escape eastwards towards the Seine', nothing could be said about that because of the 'almost papal immunity' which Montgomery enjoyed.[5] Gallagher was more blunt: Montgomery was the real reason why the American Army had not been moving at speed since June.

By mid-August, the campaign and its media coverage were unfolding in ways not likely to add lustre to British arms. Now the Americans seemed destined to liberate Paris – the biggest prize of the war save for Berlin. Eisenhower intended that the British and Americans would march arm-in-arm through Paris and share the glory. But Patton now stood to win the prize. Paris – like Rome – would be an American triumph. Most historians are content to tell this story as simply an unfolding narrative. But as Stephen Hart reminds us, the politics of the campaign were never very far from the thinking of politicians, senior officers and the press.

By the time Grigg arrived at Monty's HQ on 16 August the only way to close the Falaise Gap would have been to reinforce the First Canadian Army. 'In the final stages Montgomery had British divisions to spare,' Wilmot contended, 'but Simonds was not reinforced.'[6] Montgomery ordered the Americans to help, but they had little combat power in the area and even less enthusiasm for doing so. Leclerc's flat refusal to commit his division to an attack towards Trun is telling. On 19 August, the day Montgomery claimed that the gap was closed, he also ordered Simonds to hold half of his strength for the pursuit to the Seine.

There was no 'failure' to close the Falaise Gap; it was never a serious option.

* * *

On 19 August Eisenhower decided to try to win the war quickly. 'Instead of halting at the Seine to reorganize and build up a supply base west of the Seine,' Blumenson writes, 'The Allied command decided to move immediately into post-OVERLORD operations directed at Germany.'[7] That evening Montgomery justified the decision by telling Brooke that 'all exits from the pocket are completely blocked, and no further enemy will escape'.[8] At that moment the HQs of two German armies, four corps HQs, and the remnants of five Panzer divisions, seven infantry and one parachute division, 'plus a mass of stragglers, service elements and trains', were still west of the Dives.[9]

The Germans planned to attack the gap between Trun and Chambois from two sides and open a corridor to allow this force of 65,000–70,000 men to escape. In the early hours of 20 August what was left of four parachute regiments began slipping across the Dives south of Trun. The night was dark, with a drizzling rain that facilitated the movement of hundreds of paratroopers eastwards. Currie's men at Saint-Lambert-sur-Dives sheltered in their tanks, praying that no Panzerfaust – hand-held anti-tank rockets – burst out of the dark, or in slit trenches, firing at shadows. By late morning perhaps as many as 3,000 Germans had reached the rally point below Hill 262 and began an attack on the Poles.[10]

By then the second and third waves of fleeing Germans began to wash along the Dives. At Chambois, Panzer forces overwhelmed the Poles and the Americans and pushed them back,[11] while the 9th and 2nd SS Panzer divisions struck south of Trun.[12] As the day brightened, Currie's force reported masses of the enemy crossing the river at Saint-Lambert-sur-Dives and Moisy. Waves of infantry and support troops ran across the fields west of the Dives through a gauntlet of Allied fire. The dead piled up in heaps. Lieutenant Jake Summers said it was 'like trying to stop a buffalo stampede'. Captain Theodore Walwicz, perched on Hill 262, recalled that 'They were coming in wave after wave', and that his machine guns fired 'until they exploded'.[13] This was, Stacey wrote, 'the fiercest day of the Gap Battle'.[14] It was made worse when II SS Panzer Corps attacked from Vimoutier to re-open the gap from the east.

The 2nd SS captured the high ground between the Canadians and the Poles, allowing thousands of men to pour through. Further east, they reached Saint-Pierre-la-Rivière and opened an exit through Chambois south of the Polish position.[15] Much of the carnage was inflicted by Allied artillery, including those of XII British Corps, and the American and French guns of Gerow's provisional corps. But smack in the middle were over 250 Canadian and Polish guns concentrated on the high ground north of Trun. Some fired on waves of Germans over open sights,[16] while 12th Field RCA was ordered to 'Prep for tanks!' The guns were packed so tightly, and the enemy so ubiquitous, that regiments fired over each other in opposite directions.[17] Eventually, most regiments simply left some guns pointing north and east, and others south and west.[18] There was no shortage of targets.

By evening on 20 August Simonds's greatest concern was for the Poles, isolated and under unrelenting attack. In the evening he visited 2nd PAD HQ, only to learn that Major-General George Kitching, commander of the 4th CAD, had rejected repeated appeals from the Poles to help. 'To hell with them,' Kitching told Simonds. 'They have run out of food and ammunition because of the inefficiency of their organisation: our people have been fighting just as hard but we have managed to keep up our supply system.'[19] Kitching was ordered to relieve the Poles.

Early on 21 August the final wave of desperate infantry and tanks struck the Canadian front south of Trun. It was over within an hour, after what Stacey called a 'terrible slaughter'.[20] A column of hundreds of Germans marched out of the morning mist into the killing ground in front of the Algonquin regiment. The Algonquin's War Diary described it as a massacre: 'The ditches actually ran with blood.'[21] By noon it was all over. Canadian tanks finally reached the Poles that afternoon, to a reception of 'delirious joy . . . laughter, tears and embraces'.[22] Simonds sacked his friend George Kitching later that day.

The scene left behind was apocalyptic. Most of the estimated 10,000 German soldiers – and perhaps 8,000 horses – killed while trying to escape the Falaise pocket lay in a few square kilometres between Saint-Lambert-sur-Dives, Chambois and Mont-Ormel. By one estimate, 5,000 dead and wounded were sprawled around Currie's position alone.[23] Ross Munro, a hardened veteran Canadian reporter who had covered Dieppe, Sicily and the Italian campaign, had seen nothing like this. 'All afternoon I drove along roads of sudden death, past heaps of stinking dead horses, dead men and dead vehicles and tanks,' Munro wrote in 1945. 'At Saint-Lambert-sur-Dives the carnage eclipsed anything I have ever seen . . . Hundreds and hundreds of Germans had been cut down like wheat . . . The ground was grey-green with Germans in their blood-stained uniforms.' These were the men, Munro reflected, 'who had stormed through Europe and had pillaged and looted and forced endless disorder and grief on the world in their aggression from Warsaw to Athens, from Kiev to Brest. I hate the sight of death, but this afternoon I liked it. I got an insensate pleasure out of this disaster.'[24]

Ernie Pyle, reporting for the Scripps-Howard newspaper chain in the USA, arrived that afternoon, too. He summed up the scene succinctly: 'Everything is dead.'[25] The stench soon became unbearable. Even pilots high over the battlefield put on their oxygen masks. Thousands of bodies were bulldozed into mass graves or burned in huge pyres. The horses took longer to bury or burn – that was not complete until November. Local water was not potable until the 1960s.

There is no reliable estimate of the number of German troops who escaped on 20–1 August: even the Germans did not know. Eberbach estimated that perhaps 20,000 got through.[26] Army Group B believed at the time that 40–50 per cent of those still inside the pocket on that day escaped.[27] That would put the count of escapees as high as 40,000, in line with the US Army official history estimate of 20,000–40,000.[28] Critically important cadres made it out, especially those of the Panzer divisions and command echelons. Montgomery had boasted on the evening of 19 August that 'all exits from the pocket are completely blocked, and no further enemy will escape'.[29] He, and the many historians who ended their accounts of the closing of the gap on that day, could not have been more wrong.[30]

News coverage of the final battle for the Falaise Gap was slim – for reasons explored below. But the aftermath was reported on for days. 'The leaders of Nazis Germany should have been on the road from Trun to Chambois today,' *The Times*'s special correspondent reported on 23 August, 'to see what has happened to the pride of their armies in the west.' Through the midst of it all rode a group of American soldiers on 'sleek German horses', looking like Texas Rangers. As for the Canadians, 'dog-tired from days and nights of fighting', many 'lay asleep in the sun', oblivious to what they had wrought.[31]

* * *

'During the bitterest fighting around Trun, Saint-Lambert-sur-Dives, Chambois and Mount Ormel,' Blumenson wrote of the Falaise Gap controversy, 'the principal Allied commanders ... were already pondering post-Overlord ventures, figuring out how to get to the Rhine River, thinking about overrunning Germany.'[32] Their enthusiasm was inspired by the insistent intelligence estimates that claimed Germany was on the brink of defeat. The Joint Intelligence Committee said as much on 14 August, and it was repeated by the Combined Intelligence Committee again on 27 August: 'we consider that organized resistance is unlikely to continue beyond 1 December 1944, and that it may end even sooner'.[33] The new focus of strategic planning by late August became the 'broad front versus narrow front' controversy that drove Anglo-American animus to new heights (discussed in the next chapter). What transpired in the immediate aftermath of the Falaise Gap became irrelevant.

The urge to win the war in 1944 conflicted directly with the imperative to finish off the German Army in north-western France. Patton's XV Corps was already across the Seine at Mantes on 20 August, the day fighting in the Falaise Gap reached its peak. Patton wanted to drive to

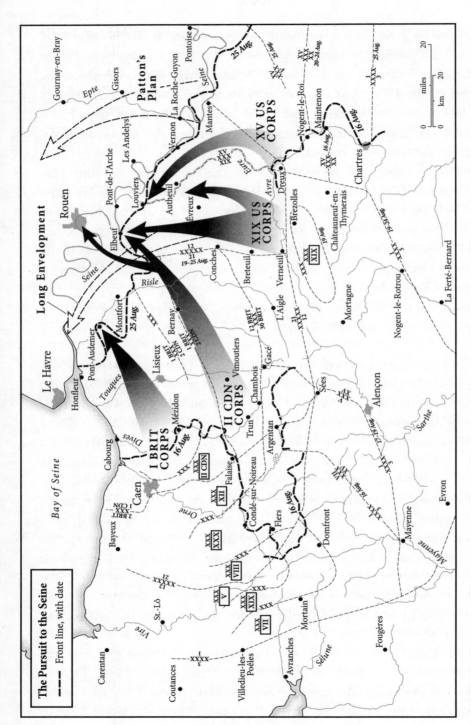

6. The pursuit to the Seine.

the Channel coast, and complete a long envelopment. He was right. Certainly there was nothing that the British could do. The link-up between the Canadians and Americans at Chambois 'pinched out' Dempsey's army. Only the Americans were capable of decisive action. Bradley had toyed with the idea of a sweep around Paris and then a drive north to Dieppe.[34] As he told Hansen on 16 August, the objective was to destroy the German army: then anything was possible. However, instead of turning Patton loose north of the Seine, Bradley now asked if he might try a long envelopment south of the river.[35] His XIX Corps, then concentrated around Mortagne–Brezolles west of Dreux, might even drive to the sea.[36] Monty's directive of 20 August accepted the idea: finishing the enemy in western France was the 'first priority'. As Charles Stacey observed, 'another encirclement was to be attempted'.[37]

The logic of the long envelopment was irrefutable, but it needed to happen quickly. One division of XV US Corps, poised at Mantes, would push along the southern bank of the Seine. Meanwhile, two divisions of XIX US Corps would strike north and west, through the wide triangle of open upland plateau between the Seine and the Risle rivers, towards Louviers. No obstacles barred this route and it was ideally suited for rapid movement.[38] It was agreed that since the bulk of the Fifth Panzer and Seventh armies were headed for Rouen, planning anything beyond Elbeuf–Louviers was problematic, but patrols might be sent forward towards the sea.

And so on 20 August the Americans commenced the 'long envelopment'. To support it, the area between the Seine and the Risle – virtually the whole area ahead of Anglo-Canadians – was allocated to the IX USAAF. While this was happening, Dempsey would send XXX British Corps through the Americans to secure a British crossing over the Seine around Vernon. The plan was a plumber's nightmare, with corps and divisions criss-crossing behind each other in all directions: the kind of movement that got Andy McNaughton fired.

When these decisions were made the Germans were still hoping to hold south of the Seine. Five infantry divisions and one Luftwaffe division were en route from the Pas-de-Calais, two from elsewhere in France.[39] On 20 August a series of defensive lines was promulgated, stepping back towards the Seine. To strengthen this line, four more divisions were soon on their way. Reports by Army Group B between 22 and 23 August indicate that the Panzer divisions west of Paris totalled little more than a weak division. However, the newly arrived infantry divisions were in good shape. Once the line was stabilised and the Allies stopped, a 'harmonised' withdrawal to the north would begin to more prepared positions along the Somme River.[40]

Before the German plan could mature, XIX US Corps, moving across the front of the Anglo-Canadians, reached the outskirts of Le Neubourg, about 20km south of the Seine at Elbeuf.[41] Meanwhile, the 5th USAD – in five days of fighting – ran into a wall of resistance at Elbeuf on 24 August. Bradley had no reserves to strengthen the drive – they were en route to Paris, while XXX British Corps was snarled in traffic confusion as it passed behind XIX US Corps. And Dempsey was still complaining to his diary that day that the Canadians had not yet cleared a path east for XII British Corps.[42] Anglo-American historians say absolutely nothing about this tangle. But it did not bring the long envelopment to a halt: Eisenhower did that.

The collapse of the American drive to the sea had its origins in the resolution of Allied strategy for the final assault on Germany. On 19 August, Montgomery proposed that the Allies drive north-east from Paris in a single, solid, unstoppable phalanx of four armies and forty divisions. The objective was to secure Antwerp as a base, build airfields in Belgium and drive into the Ruhr and end the war. The route had the additional merit of being close to ports. It was precisely what the Germans feared. It was also what the Allies had planned to do. Since May a drive to the north-east from Paris had been the preferred option for operations once across the Seine. Indeed, American logistical planners assumed as late as 22 August that the pursuit would build on Patton's crossing at Mantes for a drive to Antwerp.[43] The alternative route, east of Paris, through Metz to the Saar region, was a poor second choice. As Mark Calhoun writes, it was 'much longer than the northern route: it led to a less economically significant region of Germany: and it passed through much more difficult terrain east of the Rhine'.[44]

A push north to Antwerp, capturing the bridges over the Waal and the Rhine and on into Germany, was the key to ending the war in 1944. Bradley initially bought the idea: Patton later claimed it for himself as his most brilliant strategic concept. But Bradley cooled and Eisenhower retreated. Ike was concerned about the mounting pressure from Washington to get American armies out from under British command – Gallagher's claim and SHAEF's fumbled rebuttal had poured gas on that fire. Lieutenant-General Nye, the Vice Chief of the Imperial General Staff, warned Monty that Ike's concern was politics at home. In fact, as Hamilton points out, the critical issue at that moment was 'the idea that the American armies *must be separated from the British*'.[45] Montgomery's 21st AG was too weak to make the northern drive on its own: he needed a dozen American divisions to screen his right flank. Eisenhower told him bluntly that that was not going to happen in a presidential election year. So Eisenhower split the Allied advance beyond Paris: the 21st AG to the north and the 12th AG east towards the Saar. This was confirmed on 23 August: the orders went out the next day.

Montgomery would later date the failure to end the war in 1944 to 23 August and Eisenhower's fateful decision.[46] 'Eisenhower agreed that the northern thrust should be the main effort,' Mark Calhoun writes, but the politics of the moment made it impossible to keep American troops under Montgomery's command. Nor could he 'sideline an American army group while giving a Commonwealth army group responsibility for the main effort in the final campaign in the war against Hitler'. The American public expected their army to take the lead and reap 'its share of the glory'.[47] American domestic politics trumped strategy. Like Solomon, Eisenhower elected to divide the baby. The true mother wept, but that did not stop the sword from falling: the Americans would push east of Paris, over their Great War battlefields, towards the dragon's teeth of the Siegfried Line and the forests of the Saar.

Bradley, in Hansen's words, was 'anxious to go east into Germany'.[48] Most of the German Army, he surmised, was already across the Seine. He may well have been right. Before the American drive reached Elbeuf and pinched out the main crossing points for enemy personnel between Andé-Les Mesnil and Pont de l'Arche, an estimated 100,000 Germans had crossed safely at that point alone.[49] But by some estimates, 75,000 Germans (some put the estimates much higher) remained trapped south of the Seine when the Canadian advance finally began on 23 August.[50] They were retreating along the best road network in northern

France, fully developed and well maintained by German engineers throughout the Normandy campaign. At Rouen the escape route linked to a spider's web of excellent roads north and east. With the bridges across the Seine destroyed it was reasonable for the Allies to assume that airpower would make alternate forms of crossing the river largely untenable.

The First Canadian Army's drive to the Seine had actually begun on 16 August, when I British Corps attacked towards Lisieux. The Germans along the coast were expected to offer stiff resistance, and Crocker's I British Corps, seriously weakened by fighting, needed to be handled carefully. His two infantry divisions, the 43rd and 51st BIDs, were not considered solid, the 7th BAD was well past its best, and no one expected much from the 6th Airborne after two and a half months in the line. Crocker had the equally lightly equipped Dutch and Belgian brigades, and the 1st and 4th Special Service Brigades, Royal Marines, to help. Their advance was through heavily wooded, broken country: superb for delaying actions. As the 1st Canadian Parachute Battalion was told, 'advance if and when it is certain that the enemy were withdrawing'.[51] Crocker's troops were 'beaters' not cavalry.

By 22 August, Crocker had closed up to Lisieux, where the only real large-scale action during the Anglo-Canadian pursuit to the Seine was fought. Highlanders did much of the fighting, and suffered for it. By the end of the battle the 1st Battalion of the Gordons was down to one subaltern and one composite rifle company composed of 'the Pipe Band, the pioneers and as many drivers and clerks as could be scrapped together'.[52] The 51st BID was then pinched out and went into reserve while the 43rd BID and 7th BAD drove for the Risle crossings.

II Canadian Corps began moving on 23 August, their advance delayed by German wreckage clogging the roads, French civilians who swarmed their vehicles and blown bridges. Even so, on 24 August Canadian reconnaissance units reported contact with Americans headed for the Seine estuary around Le Neubourg. The result, Terry Copp wrote, was a 'monumental traffic jam' as the leading elements of two corps travelling at right angles intersected.[53] Nonetheless, by that evening the 14th Canadian Hussars reached the Seine: the first unit of the 21st Army Group to do so.

It says a great deal about what senior Allied commanders expected would happen along the lower Seine that they marked the area on their maps 'the killing ground'.[54] Presumably, much of this killing would be done by the air force, which would slaughter those waiting to cross. The contemporary press and later histories blame poor weather for this failing to happen. It did rain – heavily – on the 21st, but after that the weather seems to have been generally good. Dempsey's diary records 'Fine' weather for three of the next four days. The War Diary of 3 Canadian Public Relations Group, headquartered near Caen, lists similar conditions.[55] The RAF flew reconnaissance over the lower Seine during this period and kept a 'close watch' on the crossings at night, illuminating them with flares and taking photos. The real reason that airpower failed to interdict the Seine crossings over three critical days, 22–4 August, was the American attempt at the long envelopment.

It will be recalled that the area south of the Seine had been assigned to the USAAF to support the long envelopment. But IX Tactical Air Command was overstretched, lacked advanced airfields in the area and was, in any event, preoccupied by operations in Brittany.[56] Advanced bases around the Le Mans area were only just becoming operational.[57] Only IX Bomber Command, based in England, launched a few attacks on the Seine crossings during these critical days.[58] 'Only a massive, concentrated air assault on the German forces there might have made a difference,' David Spires concluded in his study of the IX USAAF, 'but XIX TAC planners apparently never contemplated this in view of competing priorities, worsening weather and perhaps the command's preoccupation with getting the Le Mans airfields ready.' Spires goes on to quote a postwar US Army Air Force assessment of the missed opportunity: 'Allied air forces, with more night reconnaissance and night air attacks, could have effectively prevented most of [the German equipment] from crossing.'[59] The result was that until 25 August the Germans crossed the Seine – day and night – with impunity. By German estimates, at least 25,000 vehicles and an untold number of men crossed the Seine between 20 and 25 August.[60]

On 25 August, a day that dawned bright and clear, 2nd TAF was finally cleared to attack, and it launched some 730 sorties that day. These concentrated on the Rouen area, but extended down the Seine to the estuary. 'The situation on 25 August,' the RAF narrative observed, 'resembled scenes of destruction around Vimoutiers seven days earlier.' The air force claimed that movement across the river was halted. Allied medium bombers continued the task that night. The success of these attacks supports the USAAF postwar assessment that had a serious effort been made by Allied air forces the Germans might have been stopped at the Seine.

23. The British pinched out again:
Canadian and American troops meet at Elbeuf,
on the Seine, 27 August 1944.

The Canadians got over the Seine east of Elbeuf late on 26 August and were soon pushing north towards Rouen. Meanwhile, the 2nd CID was ordered to take the southern end of the Rouen crossings. The advance would be, according to Harry Crerar, a 'non-tactical move and . . . no or very few enemy would be encountered'.[61] All the leading battalions had to do was walk through the Fôret de la Londe, which spanned the 3-mile base of the peninsula, and it was open country from there to the wide bend in the Seine at Rouen.

The weak and exhausted battalions of the 2nd CID plunged into the thick woodland only to meet an excellent German division, the 331st, backed by elements of four Panzer divisions and some paratroopers. It was suggested by brigadiers and battalion commanders that the attempt be abandoned. The division commander was adamant that they press on.[62] When the South Saskatchewan Regiment headed into the Fôret de la Londe on 26 August its leading company mustered thirty-five men – smaller than a platoon. By 30 August, when the 331st GID withdrew in good order across the Seine, 577 Canadians were dead, wounded or missing – for no apparent reason.[63]

Allied assessments concluded that 90 per cent of vehicles that reached the Seine got across, and so did 85 per cent of tanks that reached the river. Perhaps more critically, 95 per cent of German personnel who reached the Seine – some 225,000 – also got across.[64] As the *Sunday Times* speculated presciently on 20 August, the situation was more like Cassino in the spring than Tunisia in May 1943. The Allies would come to rue the day they failed to close the Falaise Gap or vigorously pursue the long envelopment.

* * *

In the efforts to close the Falaise Gap, the race to the Seine and drama over the liberation of Paris, Britain's army largely disappeared from the public eye. While the Americans and the Canadians copped the headlines, *The Times* evening edition did not feature a British accomplishment as its lead headline for thirty days: not until they trumpeted on 31 August 1944 that 'British Forces Reach Beauvais', 27 miles from the Somme River.[65] *The Times* was not alone. The headlines of Beaverbrook's *Daily Express* in mid-month were all American, except for a laudatory report on Monty's strategy.

And if that were not enough, early reports of the drive to the Seine highlighted the efforts of the Canadian Army, subsuming everyone in it – including Crocker's I British Corps – as 'Canadians'. For the British this was a new and unsettling experience. Phil Ault's story in the *Washington Herald-Tribune* on 18 August claimed that 'the Canadians' had captured Troarn. The next day he wrote that Canadians had taken Deauville and were pressing on to the Touques River. On 23 August, Ault reported that the Canadians were approaching Lisieux. Even *The Times* of London ran articles on 22 and 23 August describing the 'Canadians' Good Work' at Deauville and Dozulé, and having forced a crossing of the Touques at Fervaques. Someone sorted them out, and thereafter the work of Crocker's corps was attributed to the appropriate Dutch, Belgian or British units. But being part of the First Canadian Army meant hereafter that the efforts of its formations were often described as 'Canadian', much to the dismay and frustration of the British troops under Canadian command.

But it was the speed and scope of the American advance in August that captured the imagination of British reporters, the British public and the headlines: it portended an end to their suffering. 'Every man and woman in Britain is today standing on the tip-toe of great expectation,' the *News Chronicle* of London exclaimed on 15 August. The magic of those rapid advances was enhanced by Bradley's media 'blackouts', which apparently guarded the secret that Paris was the objective. When the blackout was lifted on 18 August *The Times* was almost ecstatic about the revelations. Patton's troops were in Chartres and Orléans, and probably Dreux. There was now no escape for the Germans except north, across the Seine. 'The situation was pregnant with possibilities,' *The Times* waxed. 'American success makes victory possible.' The *Daily Telegraph* echoed that enthusiasm, running a story headlined 'Falaise Battle Masked a Big American Sweep'. 'Almost total secrecy of necessity shrouded the movements of the American forces during the past few days,' the *Telegraph* story explained, to hide that movement from the Germans. American speed ensured that the Germans now had no way out.

According to Mollie Panter-Downes, London columnist for the *New Yorker*, the fact that the Americans were making all the news did not matter to the British. Her 19 August 1944 'Letter from London' observed that the British people were optimistic that the war would end in autumn. The thrust of her argument was paraphrased by the British Information Services: 'No one seems to mind much that the British sectors in France haven't as yet provided the most spectacular headlines.'[66] That day, with the British Second Army effectively pinched out west of Argentan, there was no news *at all* of British military efforts in France on page 4 of the evening edition of *The Times*.

American papers naturally highlighted the tremendous success of their armies in August, and the headlines announcing American victories on all fronts (except Italy) were often rapturous. But the overall coverage was not unkind to what the other Allies were doing in Normandy. The *Washington Times-Herald*, run by Robert McCormick's cousin Cissy Patterson, ran a story on 13 August from William Hardcastle, a Reuters reporter at SHAEF HQ, describing Monty's strategy as likely to rival any dashing envelopment on the Eastern Front. The same day the *Washington Times-Herald*'s own military pundit, Captain Lowell Limpus, author of their 'War Review of the Week', described Montgomery's strategy in Normandy as 'a brilliant conception . . . with glory aplenty for Eisenhower, Montgomery, Bradley and Dempsey' if it comes off. Even Robert McCormick's *Chicago Tribune* was remarkably balanced in its handling of the British effort in Normandy. Colonel Conrad H. Lanza, a local pundit, and John Thompson, the *Chicago Tribune*'s own reporter with the First US Army in Normandy, made clear the critical role which the Anglo-Canadians played in making the great American sweep possible. In 'Panzers Tied Up as U.S. Armor Races on', published on 14 August, Lanza pointed out that 'To keep the Panzers from interfering with the American armored troops is a prime objective of the attacks by the British and Canadians. They forced the Germans to keep important numbers of troops opposite them who would otherwise be available to try to head off or, worse yet, encircle the Americans.' The *New York Times* ran a similar explanation of Allied strategy – and the role of the Anglo-Canadians – in its 'War Summary' in the Sunday edition the day before. On the 20th John Thompson explained to *Chicago Tribune* readers how the Anglo-Canadians held the Germans in place so Americans forces could break out in the first place and lay the ground work for the Falaise pocket, and then on the 23rd how the attempt at the long envelopment was made: 'While the British again acted as a containing force, Bradley looped his forces in another wide end run.' If anything, McCormick's fondness for Canada meant that the Canadian role in closing the Falaise Gap and the pursuit to the Seine got very good coverage in the *Chicago Tribune*.

All that said, McCormick never wavered from his belief that the victory in Normandy was all-American. The tone of his editorials was echoed in Cissy Patterson's *Washington Times-Herald* and some American news magazines. Even before the fall of Paris the *United States News* 25 August edition made the case that victory in Normandy was an 'American blitz . . . The success of America's huge mechanized and motorized Army is the big new element in the brilliant victories that are now being won in France.' The Americans did not do this alone, the *United States News* admitted: the British helped to win the *air war* and the *war at sea* (my emphasis) that allowed those victorious American armies to land. But as for the Anglo-Canadian forces ashore in Normandy, they did not contribute much. 'General Montgomery's British and Canadian troops have been confined to a small area near the beaches where the original landing was made.' There 'he fought a stationary war, with infantry and artillery. This has surprised those who know General Montgomery as the master of the war of movement.'[67]

The 'failure' to close the Falaise Gap confirmed for many Americans the glacial slowness of the Anglo-Canadian armies. That view was re-inforced by many Britons who also openly criticised the pace at which Dempsey's army moved. Alan Moorehead, covering the British Second Army for the *Daily Express*, unburdened his frustration with a small front-page piece titled 'The 15 m.p.h mind' on 22 August. British Army transport drivers were apparently restricted by regulation to the stately pace of '15 miles an hour just as though this break-through had never happened'. Speed, he said, 'is something we have got to learn from Patton and the Americans'. In contrast, American trucks went barrelling by at 35–40mph,[68] which British and Canadian trucks were perfectly capable of matching – and eventually did.

Even Bradley could not resist chiding the dawdling British when he met the entire press corps of First US Army at his new advanced HQ in Laval on 21 August. The event was probably an effort to deflect hype from Patton, whom the press increasingly lauded as the architect of the American advance – just as Hansen and his colleagues had feared. As one commentator observed, Patton could now slap a whole regiment if he wanted, and the Senate authorised his promotion to Major General with unrestrained enthusiasm. But Bradley's press conference on 21 August, perhaps more than any other single event, solidified American myths about the Normandy campaign and the narrative that emerged after the war. The press was reminded that the breakthrough plan was 'conceived, planned and executed' by Bradley.[69] In Bradley's summary of events since Cobra there were no decision-makers but himself – except for the order to stop XV US Corps at Argentan, which was Montgomery's. The failure to close the gap was due to the slowness of the Canadians. As a result – in Hansen's words – 'a significant portion of the enemy managed to slip out of the trap while our forces on the south were held on a limited line and did not advance'. American forces eventually reached Chambois 'with difficulty' and the Canadians 'finally pushed south and closed the hinge at that town . . . General [Bradley] repeated again and again,' Hansen's diary records, 'that the primary rule of warfare is to destroy the enemy's forces.' This, apparently, the Anglo-Canadians had consistently failed to do. Bradley told the reporters that he had offered to transport British combat elements north, to the Seine, to launch the long envelopment. When Dempsey declined, he sent the XIX and XV US Corps north and west along the Seine, 'with the plan of taking the river up to the mouth of the Seine, pocketing off the remaining Germans and those supply elements left'. This operation, which on 21 August was just getting underway, would make the ultimate destruction of the 'German 7th Army' (no mention of the Fifth Panzer Army) an American accomplishment, after which he would turn 'the area over to the British as they come in from the west'. The British would then go north, to the 'Rocket Coast', which some Americans dismissed as a sop to British domestic pressure and therefore a 'political' not military decision. Meanwhile, the Americans would get on with winning the war: 'We go into Germany.'[70]

The failed attempt at a long envelopment did not go unnoticed at the time, especially by the British press. Morley Richards's report in the *Daily Express* on 23 August talked about a 'Second Vast Pocket', and

Peter Lawless in the *Daily Telegraph* on the same day described 'The American's new drive North Along the Seine'. The British press, as a rule, were less sanguine about the possibilities of a successful long envelopment. The *Evening Standard* warned on the 23rd that poor weather had favoured the Germans, and 'made air operations almost impossible'. Everything depended on the speed of Bradley's advance to the Seine estuary. If the Americans did not move fast enough, the Germans would 'extract a fair portion of their armies'. By the 26th British pundits admitted that the Germans had escaped. Alex Clifford, reporting in the *Daily Mail* that day, said the enemy 'has been evacuating systematically for a good week . . . it is unlikely that the Germans will be badly caught this time'. The military correspondent for the *Daily Telegraph* concluded on 28 August that General Hausser 'has evidently continued to avoid the complete encirclement which the Allies had designed for him on the lower Seine'. No one was to blame. This suited both the Americans and the British well. Neither of them was able to execute a meaningful attempt to interdict the retreating Germans. In the euphoria of the liberation of Paris, the story of the total collapse of the long envelopment was simply allowed to die.

* * *

No Anglo-American general wanted to enter Paris. Whole divisions – if not corps – would disappear in its warren of streets, and the logistical burden of feeding the population would be enormous. There was also some fear that the Germans might turn it into another Stalingrad. And Eisenhower was worried that wine, women and song would speed his men to perdition. But if the Allies had to liberate Paris, Ike wanted Leclerc's division to lead, supported by token British and American units.[71]

The lure of Paris was irresistible. 'Paris freed from the yoke of Nazi brutality would be news in the biggest sense of the word,' Dupuy wrote in his memoirs. 'Every newsman in the world wanted to get into Paris.'[72] Newspapers in Britain and America speculated on whether the Allies were, in fact, secretly headed to Paris. The *Chicago Tribune* ran maps showing how far the Allied armies had to travel to reach the city. As early as 10 August, as the Mortain offensive sputtered to an end and the Canadians pressed towards Falaise, Dupuy struck a committee to manage the press coverage of the looming liberation of Paris.[73]

Lieutenant-Colonel Dick Malone, the Canadian representative, came up with the plan to use the Hôtel Scribe in the heart of Paris as the Allied press centre. It was owned by Canadian National Railways and had been the home of CN Telecom and the Canadian press's Paris bureau before the war. It was already set up with a broadcast room and had ample working space, and enough hotel rooms to accommodate a large press corps. In fact, the Germans were using the Hôtel Scribe as a press centre. Malone's scheme was adopted.[74]

By the middle of August war correspondents began to concentrate at Chartres in anticipation. 'From the United States, from Fleet Street, service messages began to bang into correspondents from editors,' Dupuy recalled. ' "Be the first man to enter Paris" was the usual theme, and the correspondents were urged to spare no means to get there first.' Some American editors felt that they were being duped, urged to emphasise Paris while Bradley's armies moved in other directions. They may well have been right. But Dupuy pushed back by noting that the daily briefings were comprehensive and clear. Eventually enough American war correspondents were killed, wounded or captured trying to reach Paris that United Press told its reporters to 'take no chances'.[75]

The migration of war reporters to Chartres affected the coverage of the wider campaign. 'Some of the lads who dashed off to the Chartres camp I feel have made a mistake,' Malone wrote on 23 August. 'They are missing a tremendous story on this front [Falaise] . . . Both CBC correspondents have been waiting down there for a week now, leaving the Canadian story, up here, which is now moving quickly, completely uncovered.'[76] Based on the anecdotal information in Malone's reports and memoirs, British reporters were no less affected by the scramble to get into Paris. What they all missed was the effort to close the Falaise Gap.

In the end, the French set the agenda for the liberation of Paris. Paris was convulsed by strikes on 11 August amid calls by the local FFI leadership, which was Communist, to liberate the city before the Allies arrived – not unlike what the Polish Home Army was trying to do at the same time in Warsaw. De Gaulle immediately ordered that there should be no insurrection. The last thing his provisional government wanted was another 'Paris Commune', a reference to the radicals who took over the city in 1870–1 when it was besieged by the Prussians, and refused to recognise the authority of the Third Republic. Only about one-fifth of the estimated 20,000 FFI in Paris were known to be Communists, but they had most of the guns. Things were quiet for several days until 19 August when the Paris gendarmes revolted. They quickly seized the island in the middle of Paris – the 'cité' – where their HQ and Notre Dame are located.

When de Gaulle arrived at Eisenhower's advanced headquarters outside Bayeux on 20 August he demanded that the Allies immediately occupy Paris and pre-empt a Communist victory.[77] That day the German garrison commander in Paris, General Dietrich von Choltitz, agreed to a three-day armistice to allow the Germans to get out. It will be recalled that on this day elements of Leclerc's division were in position east of Chambois and poised to help stem the German break-out. On 21 August – without informing anyone – Leclerc despatched a small force towards Paris. When the commander of V US Corps, Gerow, found out, he ordered the small column to return. Meanwhile, envoys from the Paris FFI arrived at Bradley's HQ to plead for an immediate entry into Paris. When Ike asked Bradley if he could do that, Bradley told him he had enough newspapermen accredited to his HQ who would take Paris 'any time you want'.[78]

Now, in the midst of the pursuit to the Seine and the attempt to close the long envelopment, Bradley was ordered by Eisenhower to liberate Paris. On 22 August, Bradley flew to the HQ of the First US Army to confirm the decision with Hodges. Leclerc was waiting to learn his fate. Bradley brought him the good news and Leclerc announced joyously to his command, 'Mouvement immédiat sur Paris!' No serious resistance was expected. 'Go quickly,' de Gaulle admonished Leclerc, 'we cannot afford another Commune.'[79]

That day the London-based commander of the FFI, General Phillip Koenig, announced that the 'cité' had been liberated. Anglophones assumed that meant Paris itself. The news prompted Charles Collingwood of CBS to pre-record an entirely fictitious 'description' of Leclerc's tanks entering the city – the scoop every newsman wanted. MOI London released both Koenig's announcement and Collingwood's 'news' report on 22 August, which ignited a storm of anger among the press who had been excluded from the breaking news, and speculation about whether, in fact, Paris had fallen. While Dupuy worked to tamp down the blaze, the bells of St Paul's pealed in celebration and King George sent his public congratulations to de Gaulle.[80]

Leclerc's advance on Paris drew in 'hundreds of resistance fighters . . . including a circus truck of sharpshooters'. Scattered among the French columns, in Rick Atkinson's words, were 'scores of frisky "Warcos"' who 'buzzed about swapping rumours'. Among this entourage was America's most famous contemporary writer, Ernest Hemingway, guarded by seventy 'French cut throats' whom he had supplied – somehow – with vehicles and weapons.[81] Leclerc disobeyed orders once again and sought his own way in. He was stopped 5 miles west of Porte d'Orléans after losing 300 men, 35 Shermans and some 117 vehicles. When Leclerc stalled, Bradley turned Gerow loose. 'To hell with prestige,' Bradley barked, 'tell the Fourth [ID] to slam on in and take the liberation,' Mike Neiberg writes, 'with a copy to Leclerc, stating that "precedence in favor of the French no longer applied".'[82] That night Leclerc reached the Hôtel de Ville. German resistance – if not presence – melted away. The next day the rest of the 2nd FAD and the 4th USID reached the heart of the city.[83]

The situation was still very fluid as the press poured in. The Canadian press party got in by simply calling the Hôtel Scribe to ask if it was safe, and then called the FFI headquarters to arrange a guide. By the time they arrived at the hotel the advance party of SHAEF public relations was already there.[84] A boisterous party erupted in the cocktail lounge, fuelled by champagne that the manager, Monsieur Louis Regamey, had hidden from the Germans. Eventually bottles of Canadian rye whisky emerged from the basement as well. Remagey also had 7 million francs to remit to the Canadian government, rent collected from the Germans since 1940.[85] Malone requisitioned the hotel on behalf of SHAEF, and transferred it to Lieutenant Colonel Redding when he arrived that evening. The Hôtel Scribe became the press centre for SHAEF for the balance of the war. Dupuy had estimated that his Paris staff would have to wrangle roughly 100 war correspondents: the number soon swelled to 500. Dupuy recalled that every reporter in France 'went AWOL to get there'.[86]

With the liberation of Paris whatever plans or policies that had guided SHAEF PR up to that point dissolved. The Canadians – once again – had their own effective transmission service, and the Americans soon opened more commercial channels for direct broadcast back to the USA. Malone recalled that the British press corps remained a particularly demanding and unhappy lot. There may have been a good reason for that. It took time for a teletype link to be established between Paris and London, and the less powerful British press-radio system designed to reach London was constantly jammed by military traffic.[87]

While all this was going on de Gaulle arrived on the afternoon of the 25th and spoke from the balcony of the Hôtel de Ville. Paris, he said, was 'Liberated by herself, liberated by her people, with the help of the whole of France'. As Rick Atkinson observed, he said little about 'the Americans, British, Canadians or Poles who together since June 6 sacrificed more than fifty thousand lives for this moment'.[88] De Gaulle ordered Leclerc to organise a parade for the next day, which once again forced Leclerc to disobey orders from Gerow to secure the city. Gerow did not press his case. The Americans accepted that Leclerc's division had 'gone to pieces' amid the 'wild ovation of Paris'.[89]

It was estimated that a million people lined the route for de Gaulle's parade. Ralph Allen, reporting for the Toronto *Globe and Mail*, caught the rapture: 'Paris is Betty Grable on a bicycle and Billy the Kid on Bender.'[90] When the parade reached the Place de la Concord it drew gun fire from the buildings around, and the crowd went to ground like a wheatfield in a gust of wind. De Gaulle marched stoically on towards Notre Dame. The next day it was the turn of Eisenhower, Bradley and Gerow to make their own grand procession down the Champs Élysées. Montgomery was invited, but he declined.[91] He was in no mood to celebrate the liberation of Paris. He was not alone. The British felt no exuberance about the liberation of Paris. Perhaps because it was just another American PR triumph. But Paris had also survived four years of war virtually unscathed while large parts of London lay smouldering. The V1s were still falling on London and the V2s were next: there was still a war to be won.[92]

On Monday the 28th USID marched triumphantly down the Champs Élysées on its way to the front. The British had been invited to send troops to join the parade, but declined this invitation, too.[93] In bright morning sunshine, and led by the division band, it was a 'sight

24. 'Paris is Betty Grable on a bicycle and Billy the Kid on Bender':
members of Britain's 5th Army Film and Photograph Unit share the
enthusiasm of liberation, 26 August 1944.

so grand that its image soon appeared on a three cent postage stamp,'
Atkinson writes. The metaphor was not lost on Simone de Beauvoir;
the Americans were 'freedom incarnate'. The Americans, Neiberg
observed astutely, 'brought with them an optimism about the future
that Parisians themselves had long since lost'.[94] He might well have
been speaking of all of Europe. In the final analysis, what America
offered Europe was hope, and nowhere was that hope more manifest in
1944 than in the liberation of Paris.

* * *

Press reaction to the liberation of Paris varied significantly. In many ways the euphoria was dissipated by the false reports based on Collingwood's premature piece. So the liberation of Paris turned from a long-anticipated event into a process played out over several days. The *Chicago Tribune* ran Paris headlines on the 25th and 26th, sandwiched in between the defection of Romania from the German cause on the 24th and the Bulgarian capitulation on the 27th – clear evidence, for anyone who remembered 1918, that the Germans would soon capitulate.

As a rule, the headlines marched on with the war. The *Chicago Tribune* was particularly animated by Patton's drive through the famous American battlefields of World War I: the Marne (28th), Château-Thierry (29th) and Belleau-Wood and Soissons (30th). The *New York Times* headlines recorded the same milestones, then on the 31st it announced boldly that the British – now back in the news – were approaching the Somme. British and Canadian headlines also marched with the war. Both *Time* and *Life* ran extensive coverage of the liberation in their 4 September editions. But the caption under a photo of GIs marching through Paris in the 18 September edition of *Life* pointed out that 'This was not a triumphal parade . . . The official parade would, of course, include all the Allies, possibly headed by the British, who had fought longer than anyone else in the long war to liberate Paris'.[95]

If there was controversy in the press coverage of events in France during the last days of August 1944 it had nothing to do with Paris. A.J. Cummings commented in the *News Chronicle* on 29 August that people in America and Australia – where press coverage of Normandy in August tended to focus on the Canadians[96] – had been asking, 'Where are the British?' As it turned out, Anglo-Canadian soldiers themselves were 'angered and depressed by the seeming failure to give them their due'. Cummings supported the proposition advanced in the *Observer* two days earlier that Anglo-Canadians had won 'The Decisive Battle of the Seine'. This was a forty-day battle of attrition to tie down German forces in Normandy so that the Americans could drive through France. In the process, the British and Canadians had effectively destroyed the main German Army in the west. Cummings was ready to applaud the Americans' successful exploitation of this enormous sacrifice, but it was high time that the British government 'make full and generous acknowledgement of this vital fact'.

The *Observer*'s claims for the 'Battle of the Seine' were like waving a red flag for many Americans. The *Chicago Tribune*'s chief European reporter, Larry Rue, who had spent the whole campaign in London, had little time for British claims. The next day – 30 August – Rue reported on the *Observer* article and Cummings's support of it. The news prompted an editorial by McCormick refuting the very premise that the British contribution to the Normandy campaign – and indeed the war itself – was decisive. McCormick accepted that the Germans had concentrated their armour against the Anglo-Canadians, but the break-out was an American accomplishment. It had only been achieved when Eisenhower interceded and allowed Bradley to develop his own strategy: 'Bradley not only took more ground; he also took many more prisoners.' Americans did all the important fighting in Normandy. The British claims had 'the studied purpose of building up the reputations of powers that but for our protection would have ceased [to exist] by now' and to ensure that 'American influence may be minimized in writing the peace'.[97]

At the end of August, Eisenhower attempted to rescue Britain's reputation by directly addressing the Anglo-Canadian role in Normandy. 'Of the German stand in the Caen area,' *The Times* reported, 'General Eisenhower said that every foot of ground the Germans lost at Caen was like losing 10 miles anywhere else.' He chastised British reporters for their tendency 'to apologize for slow progress in that area' when 'they ought to be bragging'.[98] It is doubtful if Eisenhower's efforts had much impact. Larry Rue reported Eisenhower's claims to Robert McCormick in mid-September and dismissed them summarily. Had it not been for the dithering British, Rue wrote, the US Army would already be in Tokyo.[99]

CHAPTER 27

AMERICAN VICTORY

[I]t is unfortunate that the coverage has been so lopsided: it may lead to another 'we won the war' attitude and already it has led, in my hearing, to muttered remarks about the British not doing very much.

Charles D. Bolte, *Nation*, 23 September 1944[1]

On Wednesday, 23 August, the Head of the British Treasury Delegation in Washington, Robert H. Brand, wrote to his boss in London. 'I am writing you a line on what you may think is somewhat outside the sphere of the work of the Treasury Delegation,' Brand told Sir John Anderson, Chancellor of the Exchequer, 'but which I assure you is not really so at all. When we come to negotiate some large settlement of our financial problems with the United States our path will be made either more difficult or easier, according to the estimate which the American nation have of our accomplishments in the war.' Brand was alarmed that after five years of war, nearly three of them in a common cause with the United States, Americans knew next to nothing about Britain's war effort. With the exception of the Eighth Army in the desert, he told Anderson, Americans believed that 'British armies have done surprisingly little in the war compared to American armies . . . In the last few weeks one might have thought that there were very few British in France, and that they had done very little.'[2]

If anyone had the measure of America's knowledge of Britain and her war effort it would be Brand. He had served on the Imperial Munitions Board in the US during the Great War; and as a director of Lazard Brothers, the world's largest investment bank, Brand was well known as an international finance expert. His wife, Phyllis (who died in 1937), was one of the five 'glamorous' Langford girls from Virginia, and a sister to Lady Astor, the first woman elected to the British Parliament. Brand served as head of the British Food Mission in Washington from 1941, and in May 1944 he was appointed head of the Treasury Delegation. All of Brand's children grew up in England and by July 1944 his only son James was in Normandy with the Coldstream Guards.

Brand was at the heart of negotiations to secure American support for Britain's postwar recovery.[3] His particular task was to prevail upon America's sense of moral obligation to Britain for its selfless war effort, and obtain some recognition of the enormous British wealth that underwrote much of America's celebrated wartime industrial boom. The British now wanted a retroactive 'Lend-Lease 0' to cover expenditures in the United States prior to March 1941, 'Lend-Lease II' to cover the war against Japan after the German collapse, and 'Lend-Lease III' to assist Britain's economic transition to peacetime conditions. It was a tall ask.

Many Americans, among them the former isolationists who had emerged as the new 'imperialists', were strongly opposed to any effort to 'bail out' the British empire. The US National Association of Manufactures came out publicly against Lend-Lease II and especially III. Congress was opposed as well. It grew increasingly anti-British over the course of 1944, and in any event wanted nothing to do with extending Roosevelt's New Deal to the wider world. As for Roosevelt and his administration, they were not inclined to make any commitments in an election year. The White House was concerned, Woods writes, 'that 1944 was not an opportune time to do domestic battle over a large loan to Great Britain'. Any such discussion would shift 'inevitably back to Lend-Lease', and FDR's department heads and Congress were in a constant battle over who would control that. The discomfort the British were experiencing over their future also suited Roosevelt's long-term goal of eliminating the British empire. When on 19 August, Henry Morgenthau, the Treasury Secretary, briefed FDR on his meeting with Anderson and the state of Britain's economic plight – 'Britain is broke,' he told the President – Roosevelt feigned surprise. If Britain could not maintain her empire, FDR quipped, then perhaps the United States should take it over.[4]

The battle over the empire was now fairly joined. Beaverbrook had tentatively concluded an agreement on Middle East oil, over which the British had enjoyed a near monopoly, which opened up the Persian Gulf fields to American companies. Negotiations were underway over international air travel. Long-distance routes across the globe depended on air bases often constructed at American expense on foreign soil. In August 1944 the Canadian government bought back fifteen American airfields controlling the routes through Canada to Alaska and across the North Atlantic, much to the consternation of American imperialists.[5] But Britain, the Netherlands and France were in no position to do that. The American 'imperialist' press clamoured for the United States to simply seize what it needed to create global American air routes. Bases would also be needed to ensure postwar American power projection. By 1944 the Americans were nibbling on Europe's empires even before they were dead.

August 1944 also brought the collapse of Churchill's aspirations to shape and control the peace. Two days before Brand wrote to Sir John Anderson, a conference of three Great Powers opened at Dumbarton Oaks estate outside Washington to settle the format for the United Nations. The UN was very much Roosevelt's vision, a new and improved League of Nations run by the most powerful nations who would act as the world's policemen. He needed to get the Russians on side. Churchill was uninterested. He accepted that the Great Powers ought to run the world, but he preferred regional power blocks, like the European Advisory Council (which the Americans disliked). As for the smaller states, Churchill was content to let them participate in some meaningless general council so long as it did not impede what the Great Powers had to do.[6]

In the summer of 1944 all of this and Britain's fate was tied up in the tyranny of America's endless election cycle, and in the infotainment nature of its popular media. Congress was important, but Brand warned Anderson that it was 'not the grand assize of the nation as Parliament is'. Policy and law were made in 'at least 100 committees', whose great moments of drama – 'Everything in this country requires to be a drama' – were reported in the press. The key members of Roosevelt's government did not have to appear before Congress and explain their actions, 'but have to go and be cross-examined possibly in private, possibly in public before endless committees and are, in consequence, terrified'. In these circumstances, Brand claimed, it was impossible to have the members of Roosevelt's administration explain the British contribution to the war effort to the American people. 'It is a matter of daily occurrence almost for departmental officials to tell us how embarrassed they will be before some such committee if we insist on pressing some point or other . . . The moral I wish to press on you,' Brand implored Anderson, 'is that it is the press that forms public opinion in this country more than any other agency.' What Americans knew about the war they learned from American correspondents, especially a handful who were widely syndicated to 600 to 800 newspapers. American overseas reporters were good, Brand admitted, but they reported largely on American activities.

Then Brand hit upon the critical failing in the coverage of the Anglo-Canadian campaign in Normandy. 'If we had wished to make any dent at all upon American public opinion as to the doings of the British or Canadian armies, we should have had to make special care that American correspondents were attached to these armies.' Given their penchant for 'drama', American accounts of the Anglo-Canadians in American papers would have helped to 'establish a full understanding of their importance'. Brand suggested that probably Brendan Bracken had thought of all this and made every effort to get it right. In this Brand was very wide of the mark. By July 1944 Lord Halifax and the British members of the Combined Chiefs of Staff in Washington believed that the MOI had failed in its duties. Brand nonetheless believed that it was not too late. The Americans were a generous people, 'but their willingness to aid will certainly be less or more according to whether they are ignorant or not of the true part played by the British fighting men all over the world'. The time to act was now.

Brand may well have got his inspiration from James Langsdale Hodson's article in the July edition of *Atlantic Monthly*, 'No Hard Feelings'. Hodson was a novelist, journalist and script writer who had served in the Great War, and in the early years of the Second World War as a correspondent. The script for the Oscar award-winning documentary *Desert Victory* was his. He arrived in New York in late December 1943 for a five-month tour to assess what Americans thought about Britain's war effort. What he found was not simply profound ignorance, but an implacable antipathy towards Britain itself. All of that was fuelled by myth and legend, and not just from the revolutionary war era. Americans considered the British arrogant and undemocratic (because they still had a king), and deeply resented them for reneging on their Great War loans.

Hodson wrote for both a British and American audience. The essence of his lengthy piece was that it was time to stop pandering to Americans and tell them what the British had been doing to win the war while they dithered. He reminded Americans that they would accept only US dollars for the Great War debt settlement at a time when Britain was owed much more by other nations who refused to pay her. His rhetorical question, 'would you, anyhow, pit your lost dollars against our English dead?' mattered little. America's list of grievances was long and deeply rooted. Britain had suckered America into the war against the Kaiser, and had done it again against Nazi Germany. Americans resented British meddling in their elections – something the British studiously avoided doing – and they resented the empire, and the Dominions, and British rule in India: the list went on.

None of this had been mitigated by the scope and scale of Britain's contribution to the Allied war effort since 1939. Hodson described his travels and elaborated on his discoveries in a small book published in 1945.[7] Not one in a hundred Americans, he discovered, knew that British casualties in Tunisia were twice those of the Americans, or that Salerno was largely a British landing, or that Mark Clark's US Fifth Army was predominantly British in 1943. When Hodson met Political Science students at William and Mary College in March 1944 most believed that the United States was fighting all by itself in Italy, Burma and New Guinea. The reasons for this striking ignorance of Britain's efforts emerged steadily during Hodson's travels. Particularly strong anti-British sentiment in Boston, Chicago and southern California, and especially among the Hearst newspapers, precluded fair coverage of the British effort. That sentiment was fuelled by an almost unbridled and very effective German propaganda campaign that played to American prejudices. In any event, American newspaper editors tended to bias their accounts of Britain's war towards Dominion and colonial troops – confirming the myth that Britain always fought her wars with her underlings. When Hodson held a press conference in San Francisco in February to talk about Britain, no stories appeared in the local papers. No one wanted to hear his message. His visit to Hollywood confirmed what he had already been told about the distribution of British feature and documentary films: as a rule, they did not circulate. British documentaries were deemed too stodgy, and few of the features warranted cinematic release. The exclusion of British film from American cinemas contrasted, Hodson noted, with the domination of American films in Britain. And if all that were not enough, the legacy of the 1941 act limiting the work of foreign agents meant that anyone who wanted to speak on behalf of Britain – America's most important ally – had to register as an agent of a foreign government.[8] In short, Hodson found America hermetically sealed against any serious and systematic penetration by British information.

'The English,' Hodson urged in his *Atlantic* article, 'should hit back and hit hard – fairly, but hard. When we do not, you [Americans] are encouraged to believe we have no answers, that our conscience is bad and our case is bad. Neither is the fact . . . If you attack us on India, I can see no reason why we should not remind you of your Negro problem.' Hodson wanted to trade punches, open a frank discourse and make Britain's case in what was clearly a hostile environment. It was, perhaps, typical of the British problem in America that Hodson's appeal to strike back against American ignorance appeared in the *Atlantic Monthly*, an elite monthly publication with a limited circulation. That said, events over the course of the next year suggest that it may have been well placed.

* * *

For those who tracked the story, there was ample evidence of the empire in retreat by September 1944. The summer had been bookended by the American liberation of Rome and Paris: militarily meaningless but highly symbolic accomplishments. The astonishingly rapid movement of Dempsey's army once across the Seine – 250 miles in a week – and the liberation of Brussels on 4 September seemed poor compensation. The British Chiefs of Staff got a measure of the impact of their military efforts on America when they boarded the *Queen Mary* in New York in late September following the second Quebec conference. 'In Europe as a whole we had as many fighting men employed against the enemy as the Americans,' John Colville lamented as they steamed away. 'From the Americans papers one would scarcely suppose any British troops were fighting.'[9] Charles Bolte's piece in the 26 September edition of the *Nation* would have warmed their hearts. Britain had never stopped fighting, Bolte argued, and fighting hard. The British effort in north-west Europe had been critical to the outcome of the campaign. 'Actually it is now clear,' Bolte wrote, 'that the battle of Germany was decided at Caen and Falaise, where British and Canadian troops tied up the bulk of the German divisions on the beachhead front and formed the all-important pivot of manoeuvre around which the Americans wheeled.' Bolte proved to be a lonely advocate for that view.

The 'Octagon' conference convened at Quebec on 12 September in a spirit of great optimism – and angst. It was generally agreed that Germany would fall before Christmas, perhaps as early as November. The Americans were in a generous mood. For the first time the British arrived in some disarray, burdened by the seemingly intractable problems of what Sherwood later called 'the cataclysm of sudden total victory'.[10] Churchill desperately needed American help sorting out Europe, and he needed to secure Lend-Lease II to cover the gap between the end of the German war and the defeat of Japan. If Lend-Lease II could not be secured, Britain's economy would probably collapse before it could transition to peacetime exports. The potential costs of securing the peace in Europe and sorting out the empire were well beyond Britain's projected income. Keynes estimated that Britain would have to earn 50 per cent more from exports than it had in 1939 to meet those costs.[11] Given that current earnings from exports were running at 30 per cent of the 1939 level, this was a tall order.

American support for a thrust east from Italy, into Istria, played well with Churchill, but the British Chiefs of Staff had largely given up on Italy. As for the Pacific campaign, Ernie King was nearly apoplectic with rage when he discovered that Roosevelt had accepted Churchill's offer of help.[12] The Americans did not need the British in the Pacific. The RN lacked the fleet train required to sustain operations there and King had no interest allowing the British to use his. It was agreed that the 'British Pacific Fleet' would be welcome if it could look after itself. How the RAF, with its short-range bombers, and the Commonwealth armies would fit in remained to be determined.

It was important, nonetheless, for the British to demonstrate their commitment to the war against Japan, not least because they needed Lend-Lease II: the cloud that hung over everything at Quebec. It helped that Henry Morgenthau, an anglophile, found a sympathetic ear in Churchill for his plans to pastoralise Germany and in the process give Britain a virtual monopoly on the production of steel in Europe. It was Morgenthau who pressed FDR to make a decision on Lend-Lease II. On the last day of the conference, as Roosevelt was to sign the memorandum of understanding on Lend-Lease II, he hesitated. When Churchill could take the dithering no longer he burst out, 'What do you want me to do, stand up and beg like Fala?'[13] Roosevelt signed. Two months of difficult negotiations followed, and the begging had only just started.

Peter Clarke concludes that the British had every reason to be pleased with the outcome of the Octagon Conference, and there was hope yet for an early end to the war. While Bradley's 12th AG pushed the remnants of the Seventh German Army east, and the First Canadian Army drove the Fifteenth German Army and remnants of the Fifth Panzer Army north along the Channel coast, Dempsey's army shot through the middle. The British Army captured the great port of Antwerp, which fell complete and without a fight on 3 September, and then entered Brussels the next day: the road to Germany was wide open. The British still had fuel for another 100 miles, sufficient to carry them over the major bridges at Nijmegen and Arnhem to the east side of the Rhine. Instead, the British Second Army paused for three days: Brian Horrocks, commander of XXX British Corps, reckoned that the pause settled the course of the war.[14] By the time the British moved again, the Germans had closed the gap.

But that was not all. The capture of Antwerp, a port large enough to sustain all of Eisenhower's armies, was not followed immediately by an advance across the Albert canal to secure the northern side of the Scheldt estuary, the key approach to Antwerp and the escape route for the Fifteenth Army. In the weeks after the fall of Antwerp 60,000 men crossed the Scheldt to Walcheren and made their way east along the Beveland peninsula. Indeed, all across the front from the Ardennes to Walcheren, the men who escaped death or capture in Normandy rallied alongside reinforcements sent west to stem the tide. The Allies were about to pay the price for failing to complete their victory in Normandy.

In early September, as the great gap in German defences along the arc of the Rhine and Waal rivers beckoned, no one gripped Allied strategy. Eisenhower assumed command of the ground campaign on 1 September, and immediately moved to his advanced headquarters at Granville in Brittany. Communications from this new HQ were so poor that Eisenhower virtually disappeared for ten days. Meanwhile his armies spiralled off in all directions – against the protests of his logisticians and 'Beetle' Smith, who knew that supplies could not keep up. In the absence of any effective control, Montgomery clamoured for his reinstatement as ground-force commander and for a thrust north-east, through Belgium and into Germany. By the time Ike finally surfaced for a meeting with senior officers in Brussels on 10 September, Montgomery was unable to control his frustration. After an outburst in which he described Eisenhower's latest directives as 'balls, sheer balls, rubbish', Ike issued a caution: 'Steady Monty!' he said. 'You can't speak to me like that. I'm your boss.'[15] Normandy, and especially the handling of strategy after the fall of Paris, opened a chasm between senior British and American officers that never closed. 'The change in attitude of American officers is startling,' Ralph Ingersoll recorded in his diary on 16 September. 'While there used to be a very favourable attitude towards the British, it has recently swung through the unfavourable to the bitter . . . The speed and completeness of the change in attitude are truly remarkable – all the good work of Anglo-American relations for a period of two years has been toppled in two months.'[16]

But Ike backed Monty's scheme for a drive to the north, across the bridges to the far side of the Rhine, and gave him the First Allied Airborne Army to make the leap. He also instructed Bradley to support the attack by concentrating his logistics on the First US Army and halting Patton's advance towards Lorraine and Alsace. While Montgomery set off to prepare his attack for 17 September, Eisenhower issued another directive on the 13th which served only to give Bradley licence to continue his drive towards Germany.[17]

Operation Market-Garden was one of the most dramatic moments of the Second World War. The heroism, pathos and tragedy of the battle achieved lasting fame in Cornelius Ryan's famous book, later a block-buster Hollywood feature with a star-studded cast, *A Bridge Too Far*. Operation Market laid down a carpet of three airborne divisions along a 100km corridor over eight water courses between the Meuse–Escaut canal and the Neder Rhine bridge at Arnhem. They were supposed to be connected by a rapid thrust by XXX British Corps, Operation Garden, which would carry the Allies onto the north German plain. It was a daring and ambitious plan.

While the strategic concept was bold, the tactical execution, espe-cially at the final bridge, was cautious. The 1st British Airborne Division was tasked with capturing the crossing over the Neder Rhine at Arnhem and holding it for three days until Brian Horrocks's corps arrived. But good landing zones on or near the bridge did not exist. The northern end was urbanised and the ground on the south side too wet for gliders. So landing zones 10km west were chosen, and armoured jeeps were loaded in gliders for a mad dash to the bridge. The presence of II SS Panzer Corps in the area, recuperating from its Normandy ordeal, was known, but it was also known to be weak and dispersed in garrison across a wide area. The risk was acceptable. More problematic was the inability to lift all of the airborne forces assigned to Arnhem in the first day: it would take three 'lifts' over two days to complete that job, weather permitting.

The airborne assault went much as planned on 17 September. The loss of most of the gliders carrying the 1st British Airborne's armoured jeeps, however, turned the dash to the Arnhem bridge into a forced march. Lieutenant-Colonel John Frost arrived with enough men to hold the northern end, but not enough to seize the southern end. He was also soon cut off from the main body of the division. The airborne landings along the Market corridor by the 82nd and 101st US Airborne divisions went well, although some of the bridges were blown before they could be captured. XXX British Corps launched its advance at 1435 hours that afternoon: it was given three days to reach the Arnhem bridge.

It could not be done. II SS Panzer Corps soon had Frost's position at Arnhem surrounded. Savage German counterattacks struck the advancing column of British and American troops, and weather prevented a glider regiment from landing and securing the Nijmegen bridge on time. That same weather prevented the Polish airborne brigade from dropping south of the Arnhem bridge to secure it. By the time XXX Corps was across the river at Nijmegen on 21 September the Poles had dropped at Driele, on the south side of the Neder Rhine, but II SS Panzer Corps had secured the Arnhem bridge and was building defences at Elst, halfway to Nijmegen. When it became clear that the beachhead north of the Neder Rhine could not be expanded, much less held, it was abandoned. By the narrowest of margins the Allies were denied the crucial Rhine crossing that many claimed at the time, and since, might have ended the war in 1944.

The press lauded another epic British battle, backs to the wall against hopeless odds, as *Newsweek* described it a week later. The *Newsweek* article touched on the critical importance of Market-Garden when it observed – with telling accuracy – that 'now the world spotlight *for almost the first time since D-Day* focused on the Tommies'.[18] And so it had. Of the 10,000 British paratroopers landed north of the Neder Rhine, 1,130 were killed in action and some 6,000 – half of them wounded who could not be moved – were captured. It was a tragedy of epic proportions, and the failure was apparently uniquely British. In early October *Newsweek* offered two cautions to every American family. The closing of the Dumbarton Oaks conference without 'full agreement' about the UN from Russia cast a shadow over planning for the postwar world. But it was the *British* defeat at Arnhem that 'set back for weeks or months the day of victory in Europe'.[19] As Clark observed, Monty had 'once again failed to deliver the goods'.[20]

At a meeting in Versailles convened by Eisenhower on 24 September it was agreed to keep the 21st AG pushing to the north, supported by the First US Army. Operations by the Third and Nineth US armies were to be reduced to holding actions. This was precisely what Montgomery wanted a month earlier. It was now too late. He declined to attend the meeting, according to Wilmot, because he could not trust himself not to come unstuck.[21] Freddie de Guingand went instead. In theory, Monty got what he wanted: full support for a continued northern thrust. In practice, Eisenhower's light hand and Bradley's duplicity meant that the Allies continued to attack all along the line.

The failure to capture the bridge at Arnhem signalled the end of hope for many, not least many Britons, that the war would end in 1944. Peter Clarke marks it as a watershed. The war would drag on into 1945, Britain's economic, political and military power would continue to ebb, and the victory, when it came, would be American.

* * *

It was now that the cost of the frenetic thrust for quick victory after Normandy revealed itself. The Germans were recovering quickly, and the tangled skein of Allied logistics strangled their efforts to advance. By the end of September the 12th AG – stalled in the Eifel, Lorraine and Alsace having parried German counterattacks – was drowning in gasoline but short of ammunition. The ammunition shortage plagued American operations throughout October, as the 'Advanced Section' (ADSEC) of Army Service Force's 'Com Z' laboured to bring it forward and to build infrastructure to support operations.[22] There was a tendency among ill-informed Americans to blame the priority given to Montgomery for their problems. But Americans in the know blamed the Com Z commander, J.C.H. Lee – know by many as 'Jesus Christ Himself' Lee. Beetle Smith certainly felt that way. So did Ralph Ingersoll. Responding in 1946 to a complaint from George Hotaling, who had served in the ETO Office of the Chief of Transport, about British meddling with logistics, Ingersoll pointed the finger squarely at Lee: 'ADSEC was an abortion . . . I wonder if 50% of the supplies that left the beaches and the base dumps for the fighting armies reached their destinations.'[23] What the Americans really needed by late September was access to Antwerp, Europe's greatest harbour. In 1939 alone it cleared 57.8 million tons of cargo, more than enough to keep Eisenhower's armies fighting, and it was much closer to the First and Third US armies than their bases in Normandy.[24]

The job of clearing the approaches to Antwerp was given to the First Canadian Army. What Copp dubbed 'The Cinderella Army' was habitu-ated to doing much with little and getting even less credit for its efforts. And so it would be in the Scheldt. In theory Crerar had two corps, but I British was rebuilding. Throughout September II Canadian Corps, with three weakened divisions, was spread along the coast from Dieppe to Bruges. It was not able shift its focus to the Scheldt until 1 October. Clearing the estuary was expected to take two weeks: it took six. Fighting was brutal and intense, much of it below sea level in flooded polder. While the Canadians struggled through the mud and mortars, Montgomery's eye was firmly fixed on regaining command of the ground campaign. When he pressed his case with Eisenhower again on 14 October Ike simply demanded that he obey orders and get on with the war – including reinforcing the Canadians so they could get Antwerp open. Montgomery finally ordered the 52nd Lowland Division, a highly polished formation trained in mountain warfare, to help. The Scotsmen found the Scheldt and the mud-caked Canadians a squalid introduction to war.

Crosswell blames Canada's tiny population for the Canadians' inability to clear the Scheldt estuary quickly. But the slow progress owed more than a little to decisions taken to get rid of Andy McNaughton by sending half of his army to Italy. This created a personnel pipeline to the Mediterranean that absorbed a large number of infantry replace-ments in long transit times. Wedged in between heavy losses to II Canadian Corps troops in Normandy and the Scheldt in the summer and autumn of 1944 were very high Canadian casualties at the Gothic Line in Italy during September. By October both corps were desper-ately short of infantry, and another dreaded conscription crisis was brewing in Canada. Colonel Ralston, who had engineered McNaughton's removal and the despatch of I Canadian Corps to Italy, resigned as

Minister of Defence over his government's refusal to send conscripts overseas. Mackenzie King appointed McNaughton to his Cabinet in a futile effort to avoid a crisis. When McNaughton's attempts to persuade conscripts for home service to volunteer for overseas duty failed, Mackenzie King's government ordered 16,000 of them abroad. Riots and mutinies followed, but given the threat of further conscription more men came forward than were actually needed. The operational tempo dropped sharply in late 1944 in any event, and so by the time the conscripts arrived the casualty crisis had resolved itself. Mackenzie King himself proved to be the architect of his own conscription crisis.[25] For the Allies the Canadian reinforcement crisis meant delay in opening Antwerp.

By 31 October, the First Canadian Army had cleared the South Beveland peninsula to the road and rail causeway to Walcheren Island. All attempts to attack across the causeway ended in bloody failure. Meanwhile, the Canadians launched an amphibious assault on the 'Breskens Pocket' on the south side of the Scheldt, followed within a few days by British amphibious attacks on the Island of Walcheren. The German garrison capitulated on 8 November. The cost of opening the Scheldt was prodigious: 12,873 casualties, about half of them Canadian. The first ship to enter the port, the Canadian-built SS *Fort Cataraqui*, was received with fanfare by representatives from 'almost every' Allied headquarters. No Canadians were invited.[26]

* * *

By the autumn of 1944 the optimism of the spring that a new kind of world would emerge from the war based on American idealism and a new liberal order was fast slipping away. Roosevelt knew that Churchill was not going to give up the empire. In September both the Dutch and the French also professed ambitions to re-establish their empires. In fact, in the liberated parts of the Netherlands the Dutch introduced conscription to build forces to reclaim their colonies.[27] Soviet Russia, which Roosevelt had hoped to restrain through his new United Nations, was busy laying claim to its old empire in eastern Europe, while adding new conquests in the Balkans – as Churchill had feared. For their part, the British announced a return to balance of power politics in Europe through a plan to establish a coalition of western states, the 'Atlantic

Community', to offset Russian power in the east. And America, too, revealed itself as an imperial power. *Collier's* magazine urged in mid-September that America should forgo the Four Freedoms and claims of unbiased internationalism and simply seize what it wanted in the Pacific while it had the power to do so.[28] So much for the Atlantic Charter.

Churchill, Eden and Brooke spent much of the autumn of 1944 trying to salvage something from eastern Europe, while fighting the case for Lend-Lease II. Bereft of American support in the aftermath of Tehran, Churchill led a British delegation to Moscow in early October to settle spheres of influence in postwar Europe. Containment was a major theme. The fate of Poland, now that the Lublin Poles were ensconced in Warsaw, was already decided. Russia would be allowed domination of Romania and Bulgaria, and share influence over Yugoslavia. Churchill guarded both Italy and Greece against Communist influence, in part by working closely with local conservatives and monarchists. This infuriated the Americans, leading to an uncharacteristically sharp telegram from Stettinius to Churchill which emerged as a public rebuke of British policy in the Balkans.[29]

It seems that Churchill could not have cared less about what the Americans thought of the British return to balance-of-power politics in Europe. The new world order under Roosevelt's United Nations was still a dream: events were unfolding quickly and needed to be addressed. That said, two hurdles had to be cleared in the late autumn before the British could intervene decisively in either Greece or Italy. One was the US election, which preoccupied Roosevelt and the American body politic until 7 November. Roosevelt won in a landslide. The Democrats were returned with a strengthened majority in Congress and held on to their majority in the Senate. FDR had won a clear mandate to finish the war. The news was welcome in Britain, where Roosevelt remained a popular figure and was admired for what many believed his 'pro-British' sentiments.[30]

Among the other tasks delayed during the autumn was a final settlement of the agreement on Lend-Lease II. Nothing could be announced prior to the election, but Roosevelt, and many more Americans, were also reluctant to extend aid to Britain for fear that that would give them a leg-up in postwar exports. And Roosevelt was unhappy about the direction of British foreign policy and Churchill's determination to restore the empire. Roosevelt's report to Congress on Lend-Lease on 25 November, which according to Clark was not widely circulated, was nonetheless very favourable to the British: a portent of the drift of American thought about the merits of the British claims to 'justice' in the settling of wartime accounts.[31]

During the lengthy and often bitter negotiations that went on in Washington over Lend-Lease II in October and November, the British made it abundantly clear that they were headed for an 'economic Dunkirk'. Britain had ruined itself to win the war, and only the Americans were in position to mitigate the worst of that. Four key points were driven home. The first was that Lend-Lease had allowed Britain to release manpower from industry to the armed forces. As Charles Kindleberger observed, it made as much sense for the Americans to pay Britain to crew an American tank as it did to charge Britain for the tank itself.[32] The second point was that the British public was entitled to some 'easement of living conditions' after over five years of war. They had been impoverished and dehoused by the war – both by enemy action and the use of Britain as a vast military base – and British infrastructure, roads, railways, dockyards, industry and much more were ruined by enemy action, overuse and neglect. Thirdly, Britain had neither the money nor the manpower to rebuild. Britain needed to start exporting, and needed the export restrictions imposed through the Lend-Lease agreement removed as soon as possible. This much had been discussed at Quebec and generally agreed upon. And finally, British reserves of gold and US dollars needed to grow. This request was new and occasioned much debate over the future of sterling.[33]

Negotiations over Lend-Lease II were helped, it seems, by the publication of a booklet in November outlining Britain's war effort. *Statistics Relating to the War Effort of the United Kingdom* was a compendium of information on manpower, home war production, shipping and foreign trade, civilian consumption, and finance. What it revealed was a nation at full stretch, indeed overcommitted in an effort to win the war. Churchill presented the findings to Parliament when the booklet was released. Harry Hopkins acquired a copy for the White House at the end of the month.[34] The booklet later formed the basis for the MOI publication *What the British Empire Has Done*, published for wider distribution shortly after the war.

As the negotiations drew to a close Roosevelt could not resist trying to squeeze the British in their hour of weakness. In late November he intimated that he would not sign off on the Lend-Lease II agreement unless the outcome of talks on postwar aviation, air routes and base use was favourable. These talks were deadlocked in Chicago and, to the Americans who were about to give the British access to billions of dollars in aid, the request seemed reasonable. Colville called it 'pure blackmail'. Guy Winnant, the American ambassador to Britain, was embarrassed. Churchill consoled him at Chequers by saying that 'even a declaration of war should not prevent them having a good lunch'. Protests to Roosevelt followed, and he signed the Lend-Lease II agreement on 30 November. The British would receive $5.6 billion to carry them through to the end of the war with Japan.[35] In order to forestall American domestic protest, the right to renew an export economy would commence officially when the war with Germany ended. Unofficially, Britain was at liberty to start rebuilding its export economy on 1 January 1945.[36]

As frustrating and acrimonious as the negotiations for Lend-Lease II had been, they would – in the end – form the basis of a postwar 'concordate' with the US that would eliminate virtually all of Britain's debt to America. The American public had not been persuaded of the virtue of Britain's sacrifice and the need for redress, as Brand, Hodson and others fervently hoped, but Roosevelt's administration had.

* * *

Over the winter of 1944–5 Anglo-American relations sank to an all-time low. While diplomats, politicians and bureaucrats argued,[37] the generals fought each other, too. It was clear by autumn 1944 that the war would not end soon: the Third Reich, unlike the Second, would go down fighting. In the meantime, Eisenhower could not bring America's power to bear. The same lack of ports and transportation that stalled the Allies at the border of Germany also crippled the rapid build-up of Marshall's great army. The number of American combat divisions in north-west Europe doubled between the end of the Normandy campaign and the end of the year, but many of the new divisions were idle because their equipment was incomplete or they could not be supported at the front.[38] In early December, Eisenhower announced his plan to wait until May 1945 to cross the Rhine. Brooke was nearly apoplectic with frustration over Eisenhower's strategy, and the never fully dormant campaign to get Montgomery – or by early 1945 perhaps Alexander – appointed as ground-force commander continued to fester.

The British needed to end the war. By mid-December, Montgomery's plan was to secure the west bank of the Rhine, and then cross at Wesel. The initial move would be made by the First Canadian Army, with most of Montgomery's divisions under command, with a drive over frozen ground through the Reichswald and Hochwald forests to Xanten, where it would be met by the Ninth US Army (operating as part of the 21st AG) driving up from the south. Dempsey's British Second Army would then cross the Rhine, where it was 1 kilometre wide, in a major amphibious and airborne assault. A meeting with Eisenhower on 7 December confirmed the plan, to be executed as soon as possible after 1 January.[39] The Americans might be waiting for the spring, but the British were not.

Then the Germans changed the timetable. At 0530 hours on 16 December 500,000 men in thirty divisions employing all the tanks Germany could muster attacked through the Ardennes forests and headed for Antwerp. The assault was a complete surprise. Bradley held that 130km stretch of the front with just five divisions. It was a calculated risk. In many ways what transpired was a replay of the great German offensive of March 1918: a last gasp to split the Allies – both physically by driving to the 'sea', in this case Antwerp, and by causing a rupture in the Allied camp which might lead to a British withdrawal and a negotiated peace. It was a mad gamble, and like the British in 1918 the Americans buckled but they did not break. In the cold of a cloudy northern European winter, Bradley's forces rallied on the flanks and contained the German assault, deflecting it away from Antwerp towards the Meuse River. America's retention of the road hub at Bastogne disrupted German logistics and drew reserve forces into a fruitless siege. Eisenhower got a grip on the battle by the 19th, when he assigned the northern flank to Montgomery and shifted American forces to contain the southern flank.

By the end of December, Eisenhower's senior generals were sparring with each other over who was doing the most to contain the German offensive, and the British press was bleating over Monty's role.[40] On 30 December a front-page editorial in *The Economist* threw gas on that fire. *The Economist* was considered 'liberal, fair minded, and, on the whole, pro-American',[41] and was well read in Washington circles, including by Roosevelt. The editorial responded to recent American criticism of British policy in Italy and Greece, old complaints about British abuse of Lend-Lease, the likelihood of the British reneging on their promise to fight in the Pacific, a slackening British war effort, and even a spurious American complaint that 'Rundstedt did not select the British held front for his breakthrough'. The *Economist* editorial was, in many ways, in keeping with Hodson's appeal to stop pandering to the Americans. All of this criticism, the editor observed, would be 'insufferable enough to a people struggling through their sixth winter of blackout and blockade and bombs – but when the criticism comes from a nation that was practising cash-and-carry during the Battle of Britain, whose consumption has risen through the war years, which is still without a national service act – then it is not to be borne'. *The Economist* called out the hypocrisy of American foreign policy, which condemned British efforts in eastern Europe while lauding American promises of a Jewish homeland in Palestine at the expense of the Arabs, and complaints about Lend-Lease whose declared purpose was 'the defense of the United States'.[42] It labelled America a meddling, feckless ally, and urged Britain not to trust in either its rhetoric or apparent good will.[43]

Isaiah Berlin reported from Washington that the *Economist* editorial 'let the cat out of the bag and the genie out of the bottle'. 'For this was not rhetorical vituperation,' Clark writes, 'but a pointed political critique of a relationship of dependence, fostered and concealed by bonhomie and dissimulation: one that traded in a specie of fine promises rather than cash-down delivery.' By the end of 1944 'The question was: "Just how much British safety can be gambled on American good will?"' Raymond Daniell, reporting from London for the *New York Times*, drew the distinction between the sacrifices of the British war effort and the struggle to maintain their empire and therefore their position in the world: 'The Empire is all they have left and they must preserve it to remain a peer among the nations associated with them.' The tragedy for Britain, as Clark observes, was that the destruction of empires – including Britain's – was why the Americans were fighting.[44]

On 23 December the weather cleared, allowing Allied air strikes to cripple the German spearheads. On Christmas Eve the German attack culminated 95km deep into Belgium. Bastogne held out, defying demands for surrender in one word, 'Nuts'. American counterattacks began in earnest on 3 January, impeded by deep snow. Montgomery's press conference on 7 January, in which he lauded the fighting skill and dedication of the American soldiers under his command, got good press coverage. But his body language, his penchant for claiming a personal role stopping the German offensive, and his condescending tone drove the Allied rift deeper into crisis. Among American generals, especially Bradley and Patton, the notion that Montgomery should garner any credit for defeating the German offensive caused bitter resentment. The mood was salvaged by Churchill's magnanimous speech to Parliament on 18 January, in which he made it perfectly clear that the Americans had done the fighting and that the hard-won victory in the Battle of the Bulge was an epic American one.[45] The front was re-established by the third week of January.

* * *

In the aftermath of the German offensive Eisenhower continued to support Montgomery's plan to have the 21st AG lead the charge across the Rhine in a combined Anglo-American-Canadian attack.[46] This was supposed to begin on frozen ground in January, as the Russian winter offensive did on 12 January. Solid footing allowed the Russians to drive from the Vistula to the Oder River in two weeks, a distance of 480km, where they stopped for the rest of the winter. By the time Montgomery's 21st AG was ready to move on 8 February the ground had begun to thaw, and the Germans had flooded vast areas of the Rhine valley. There would be no quick advance. Operation Veritable, with much of 21 AG under Canadian command, led to weeks of hard fighting through cloying mud, dense forest, flooded polder and fortified villages before the Rhine crossing point at Wesel was secure.

In the meantime, Roosevelt, Churchill and Stalin met at Yalta, in the Crimea, to sort out the way ahead. It was, in many ways, a meeting of the 'Big Two', FDR and Stalin. A preliminary meeting between the

British and Americans at Malta produced no joint plan. It was, Clark writes, 'a warning that the British were no longer taken quite so seriously' and that Churchill had become 'a vaudeville act with which he [FDR] was becoming bored'.[47] Things went the American way (and Stalin's) at Yalta because they had the whip hands. The western Allies would concentrate on north-west Europe, finally sending I Canadian Corps back to its parent army and reducing the Italian campaign to a holding action. The British were firmly defeated in their campaign for the appointment of a Briton as SHAEF ground-force commander.

The Americans also won the Russians over to the UN by agreeing that the Great Powers would have a veto in the security council. The mechanics of all this would be settled in San Francisco in the spring. The advent of a new League of Nations raised the thorny issue of 'mandates' for former colonial possessions, which caused alarm in the British camp. They were soothed by assurances that these would be former enemy colonies. Roosevelt blithely accepted that the Soviet Union was not an imperial power, nor – by its own definition – was the United States. That left only the British empire among the Big Three as the target of ongoing anti-imperial rhetoric.[48]

Britain's position at Yalta was weak to begin with, and, as at Tehran, Roosevelt dealt directly with Stalin. He accepted that the fate of Poland was sealed, but the Russians promised that Poland would be open to a democratic process. The Russians would be allowed to re-establish their dominance of the Baltic states and include much of the Balkans in their new sphere of influence. Zones of occupation – regardless of where the armies reached – were agreed, and Stalin accepted that a French zone could be carved out of the Anglo-American portion. To draw Russia into the war against Japan, Roosevelt was also willing to sell out China. American anxiety to secure Russian help against Japan may well have stemmed from the campaign of attrition then unfolding in the Philippines. MacArthur had promised a quick campaign with minimal casualties: it was anything but. The liberation of the American colony had begun in October. By mid-February it was bogged down in house-to-house fighting in Manila. By the time it fell on 3 March, 1,000 Americans, 16,000 Japanese and perhaps 100,000 Filipinos lay dead in the ruins. The overall cost of recapturing the Philippines was 46,930

Americans killed, wounded or missing.[49] Beating the Japanese would need Russian manpower. Allowing Stalin to use northern China as he wished was well worth getting that commitment. Having achieved his objectives, Roosevelt left early to meet the kings of the Middle East, to smooth the way for a Jewish state in Palestine. Churchill saw him briefly in Alexandria on 15 February, the last time the two would ever meet.

Americans viewed Yalta as a great success. Plans had been made for postwar Europe and the Soviet Union had been brought into the community of nations. All the British pursued at Yalta, according to the American press, was their own self-interest: Roosevelt had to bully Churchill into doing the right things. In fact, as Clark concludes, FDR had kept Churchill at arms' length in order to secure his global New Deal. The 'dilapidated British Empire', Clark concludes, was 'an anachronism in the phase of world history that dawned at Yalta'.

* * *

Anglo-American plans for a final assault across the Rhine in March simply heightened the rivalry. Eisenhower promised Montgomery that the thrust by the 21st AG would be supported by no less than thirty-five Allied divisions, most of them American. Bradley and Patton understood that Monty was trying to make the Rhine crossing a British victory so they worked to sabotage Eisenhower's scheme. They reasoned that if they achieved success along the Rhine in the American sector, and overcommitted their forces, Ike would have fewer American troops to give Montgomery. The plan worked. The First US Army captured an intact railway bridge at Remagen on 7 March and, although the ground east of the river was unsuitable for rapid exploitation, Patton's advance went faster than expected. A few days later he asked Bradley to release the news: 'I want the world to know Third Army made it before Monty starts across.'[50] By the time Operation Plunder launched across the Rhine near Wesel on 24 March, the First and Third US armies were on the march in the south. Eisenhower decided not to heavily reinforce Montgomery.

The assault by the 21st AG was a superb piece of planning and execution, supported by a paratroop drop by British and American divisions, and extensive bombing and artillery support. Within a day Montgomery had a bridgehead 35 miles wide and 20 miles deep, and both the British Second and Nineth US armies had a clear run to the Elbe River. The First Canadian Army also slipped across the Rhine at Wesel, but drove north into the Netherlands. The 'Hunger Winter' had driven the Dutch to starvation, and relief of the civilian population was a major priority. That left the 'British' drive into northern Germany in the hands of Dempsey's army – less than a dozen divisions.

The final campaign to conquer Germany therefore fell largely to the Americans. Just as their armies had swept through France, now American forces swarmed across central and southern Germany. By March, Eisenhower had fifty-six American divisions in combat (the size of the BEF in 1918), plus eleven French divisions under command. More were waiting. When the Ninth US Army was returned to Bradley, the Americans controlled two Army Groups spanning Germany from Wesel to Switzerland: the 12th in the north under Bradley and the 6th in the south under Devers. Eisenhower set the thrust line of the final push towards Leipzig. The unmasking of Russian intent in eastern Europe made it clear to many that Russian good will at Yalta was a scam. British appeals that the new borders of Europe should stand where the armies met – and that the western Allies needed to get forward quickly – made no impression on the Americans. After returning from Yalta, Roosevelt retreated to Warm Springs to convalesce, and never responded to Churchill's appeals. 'For Churchill the slight was as great as for Montgomery,' Clark writes. 'No Berlin, no British glory, no support from Washington.'[51]

In this final campaign the British were given a supporting role, guarding the northern flank of the American drive. So the British Second Army raced for the Baltic to forestall Russian access to Denmark. The 1st Canadian Parachute Battalion beat the Russians to Wismar on the Baltic coast on the morning of 2 May by a matter of minutes. The Russian commander explained that his objective was Lübeck and demanded that the Canadians withdraw. The Canadians refused and prepared to resist any attempt by the Russians to push through. The Russians relented: Denmark was safe. Meanwhile, the First Canadian Army – fully restored by late April with the arrival of I Canadian Corps from Italy – liberated much of the Netherlands and drove on towards Hamburg. The Russians fought their way into Berlin, in a final

Wagnerian Götterdämmerung well suited to Hitler's intent to bring Germany down around him in defeat. He hoped that Roosevelt's death on 12 April would produce a miracle of deliverance. But it was not to be. Hitler committed suicide on 30 April as the Russians closed in. American spearheads met the Russians on the Elbe River, and were into both Czechoslovakia and Austria when the war ended. Germany, much of it now in ruins, capitulated on 8 May 1945. Marshall's great army – sixty divisions strong by May 1945 – had seized the victory.

CONCLUSIONS

For many, the 'bomb', which ended the Pacific war suddenly in late August, epitomised the triumph of American military power, science and technology – although it was not a uniquely American innovation. Even so, by then America was a military colossus, with over 12 million men and women in uniform, a fleet of more than 4,000 major warships and over 43,000 operational aircraft.[1] America had done it all while sustaining a consumer economy. As Maury Klein concluded, 'The future turned out to be far kinder than expected.' There was no postwar depression. Wartime savings soon 'unleashed a torrent of consumer spending'.[2]

Across the Atlantic the prospects were bleak. The great relief displayed by Britain during celebrations on VE-Day masked a victory that had come at an unimaginable cost. True, the loss of life was mercifully less than that of the Great War. But as Britons pondered their meagre rations amid the ruins of their cities, bureaucrats in the Treasury tallied the sums. The amounts were staggering. As a benchmark, the first wartime budget in 1939–40 was $7.65 billion (figures given in USD).[3] By 1945 Britain owed some $103 billion to its creditors. British national wealth had plummeted 28 per cent since 1939.[4] There was nothing left in the vault. Britain was, according to Pater Clark, 'the greatest debtor in the history of the world'.[5]

The Americans cut off Lend-Lease on the day the Japanese capitulated, 2 September 1945. There was no Lend-Lease III. Negotiations

650

over Britain's financial needs began in Washington nine days later, complicated by American fears that the British would use any money they received to pay down their huge debt to the sterling bloc and shore up the empire. Nonetheless, the Americans offered a loan of $5 billion. The British, hoping to wipe the debt slate clean completely, declined. As Britain struggled to meet its needs, a further offer of $3.75 billion was made by the Americans in late autumn, contingent upon the final approval of the Bretton Woods agreement. Both were accepted in December, as was a Canadian loan of $1.25 billion.[6]

Confirmation of the American loan dragged on in the House of Representatives and Senate into 1946, with the British threatening to abandon their military presence in the Far East, the Middle East and the Mediterranean unless the loan was approved.[7] In the spring of 1946 an Anglo-American financial concordat settled accounts. The Americans wrote off most of the outstanding $22 billion Lend-Lease debt, leaving just $650 million written over fifty years at 2 per cent interest. The same payment terms were agreed for the Canadian loan: the last payments were made in 2006.[8]

The settlement of the spring of 1946 was not a demonstration of American altruism. Rather it reflected the culmination of a decades-old American ambition to lead the global economy, an aspiration reinforced and accelerated by the depletion of Britain's national wealth during the First World War. The residual Great War debt to America, and Britain's inability to pay it off, had added an emotive element to what was, at heart, American economic interest. So the 1946 settlement was about confirming British alignment with the American vision of the postwar global economy. It obliged Britain to make sterling convertible to dollars within a year, negotiate a reduction of its sterling debt to other countries and parts of the empire, and end all discrimination against US exports by 1956. Australia and New Zealand wrote off what Britain owed them. But the British government's reluctance to go cap in hand to India, Egypt, Sudan, Iran and others to ask for a reduction in the enormous debt owed to these countries, and the failure of the convertibility scheme, drove Britain deep into financial crisis by 1947. When the Americans were told that Britain could no longer finance western Europe's efforts to resist Communism and the Russian menace they stepped in with the Truman Doctrine, followed by the Marshall Plan to save western Europe and revive its economy.[9] This confirmed what had become apparent during those climactic days in the high summer of 1944: the United States had surpassed Britain to become the dominant economic and military power in the world.

Americans had also chafed at Britain's imperial sway. Although Roosevelt was consistent in his desire to see the dismantling of the empire, deliberate action on the part of the United States was not required. Britain's postwar financial crisis made it all but impossible to hold the empire together. However, it was not just lack of money that led to the precipitous collapse of Britain's empire, but the centrifugal forces spinning within it – already manifest well before 1939. The Jewel in the Crown, India, had been promised independence after the war: there was no stopping that process. The best the British could hope for was that an independent India would remain an active member of the Commonwealth. The British supported partition between Muslims and Hindus in 1947 when independence was finally granted. The result was an orgy of sectarian violence that many long feared, as Muslims gravitated – or were pushed – into west and east Pakistan. Since India was the linchpin of the empire in Asia, once it gained independence the principal rationale for the British military presence east of Suez vanished almost overnight. This also undercut the British will to hold on to Palestine, which was now a catastrophic liability as the Americans intrigued to establish a Jewish state. Meanwhile, Egypt, frustrated by British abuse of their 1936 treaty, ordered them out. British oil continued to flow from Iraq and the Gulf, where the visible and unwelcome empire was replaced by an invisible one that eventually operated under the radar. For the moment, Great Britain still functioned as a Great Power, and the dominoes had not yet started to tumble in Africa.

Nor could Britain any longer count Canada and South Africa under its influence. By 1945 Canada possessed the fifth-largest navy and the fifth-largest air force in the world, and a small but powerful field army. Moreover, Canada's industrial production had been prodigious: fourth largest of the Allied powers by a wide margin. Outside of the Great Powers, Canada possessed the largest economy in the world. None of this potential was 'inaccessible' to Britain should it face imminent peril, but Mackenzie King's government continued to chart its own multilateral course through the Commonwealth, the UN and, by 1949, the North Atlantic Treaty Organization.

* * *

The long and often bitter struggle between Great Britain and the United States for global hegemony provides the context for understanding how the Second World War unfolded, and how the Normandy campaign in particular has been portrayed in literature and the popular media. The enduring memory in much of western Europe is the arrival of American liberators. Even modern D-Day commemorations in Normandy rely heavily on American iconography. America's wealth and its military power not only freed Europe but were also critical to preserving it from the maw of the Soviet Union. As the liberation of Paris revealed, America offered Europeans something which Britain could not: hope. The Marshall Plan, which brought relief to a continent struggling to get back on its feet, was proof that that hope was not misplaced. How that all happened shaped and defined the narrative of the war. Unlike 1918, when Britain and her empire won decisive victories in the final stages of the war, American ownership of victory in 1945 was an easy claim to make. Furthermore, it provided Americans with a sense of moral superiority that substantiated their 'right' to lead.

However, as this work has argued, the tendency to slip into descriptive narratives of American operations after Pearl Harbor masks the fact that once again the Americans came late to the war. Apart from the central Pacific, where the USN concentrated – thanks to the efforts of the British and Canadian navies in the western hemisphere – American military power did not peak until after the Normandy campaign. North Africa and Italy were predominantly British campaigns. The campaign in Burma was overwhelmingly British, and until the landings in the Philippines in the fall of 1944, MacArthur's campaign in the southwest Pacific relied heavily on Australian troops. As the editorial in *Life* magazine on 3 January 1944 observed, at that point Romania had more divisions in the field than the US. Even the Normandy campaign itself was a balanced Anglo-Canadian and American combat effort until the very end. Had the Third Reich collapsed in the fall of 1944, as everyone fervently hoped, the debate over who won the war would be quite different.

The notion that the British were incompetent slackers who manipulated the naive Americans, drew them into imperial conflicts, and needed America to save them was deeply embedded in the American national consciousness before 1939. The impassioned debates of the 1920s over who actually 'won' the Great War, how it was remembered, the lingering debt issue, the revolution in the media landscape, and the bald admission by the British that they had manipulated the American press in 1917 all laid the groundwork for a deeply troubled Anglo-American relationship during the Second World War. This was indeed a 'special relationship', but not in the positive way Churchill later suggested. Roosevelt's treatment of Churchill in the last eighteen months of the war was deplorable, and it is telling that Churchill did not make the effort to attend FDR's funeral.

America constituted a Second Front all on its own, one that the British hoped but failed to win. In the circumstances, the death of Lord Lothian in December 1940 was a devastating blow for Britain. Americans did not warm to Lord Halifax. His efforts to have the MOI expand its operations across the continental USA in 1942 might have worked had Bracken not killed the idea. So while America remained open to Axis propaganda throughout the war, the British message was thwarted by a combination of American legislation, a suspicious Congress, openly hostile media, and the intransigence of the British military itself to effective press coverage – even by its own nationals.

In fairness, the British task may well have been insurmountable. The very nature of the American infotainment media, the relentless nature of America's election cycle, and the public nature of American government mitigated against Americans 'hearing' information outside of their own social and political discourse. As senior British officials discovered, American politicians and bureaucrats dared not say anything positive about Britain in public. The evil, unaltered bogeyman of the American revolution was a critical part of America's visceral anti-British sentiment. It was no accident that the Lend-Lease legislation was Bill HR-1776, or that the delegates to Bretton Woods conference were reminded on the opening day – 3 July 1944 – to reflect on the spirit of

1776. As Eden lamented in November 1944, 'George III had a lot to answer for.' Except for a brief period in the autumn of 1941, before Congress initiated renewal of the Foreign Agents Registration Act, the British were extremely cautious about what they said and did in the American media. After that they were again tightly constrained. In contrast, Nazi propaganda – so embedded in the American right, as the Canadian Embassy reported and as Rachel Maddow has recently demonstrated – operated virtually without hindrance throughout the war. The appeals by Hodson and Brand in the summer of 1944 to push back came on the heels of the apparent total failure of the British to highlight for Americans their critical role in the war, especially in the Normandy campaign.

Dan Todman has argued that the six-month period in the middle of 1944 was 'the most total moment of Britain's total war'.[10] Operation Overlord certainly reflected that total British commitment. This work has attempted to demonstrate that fact by widening the lens through which Overlord is viewed, to include shaping operations, naval, air and merchant shipping efforts, as well as by the powerful British military effort in Normandy. Robert Brand certainly expected Britain to make a case in the US about the scale of this commitment, and some in the MOI claim that they did. But, as argued here, the Americans had long since convinced themselves that they were carrying the burden. The myth of Normandy as primarily an American operation probably began in December 1943, when Senator Johnson revealed that the coming 'invasion' of Europe would be '75% American'. Stimson confirmed that on the first anniversary of D-Day when he claimed that the US provided 75 per cent of forces 'employed in the invasion of Europe', while the British welched on their promise to contribute 27 per cent of the invasion army.[11] Stimson's accounting was disingenuous. His figures reflected the state of things by May 1945, not the summer of 1944.

If the press is the first draft of history, then the problematic and often fraught American press handling of Britain's role in Operation Overlord was critical in shaping the narrative, not least because American popular history has such a powerful global impact. At the root of this was the enduring reticence of the British military to allow extensive media coverage of its operations. Early in the war, this left the news-hungry American media open to Axis propaganda. In fact, international wire services and shortwave radios allowed the Axis to develop a feedback loop to America, tracking what was said and re-inforcing – or countering – it. Axis propagandists were able to foster anti-British sentiment and Anglo-American antagonism. It did not help the British cause that after Dunkirk, while the bulk of what was left of the British metropolitan army secured the United Kingdom from invasion, the fighting in Africa, the Middle East and South East Asia was done primarily by Commonwealth and imperial troops. For many Americans, this fit the stereotype perfectly: Britain always fought its wars with someone else's soldiers.

The British usurpation of Canada's contribution, in particular, which grew out of this quest to maintain the semblance of British power, also skewed both the narrative of the war and, especially, that of Overlord. When the RCAF took public relations matters into its own hands in early 1943 – much to the dismay of the Air Ministry – people were genuinely surprised at the scope and scale of Canada's involvement in the air war. The same might have been true had Churchill acknowl-edged Canada's major role in the Battle of the Atlantic in his 'victory' speech in June 1943, or that Montgomery's victory in North Africa was – in McNaughton's words – 'trucked and gunned by Canada'.[12] The Academy Award-winning documentary *Desert Victory* highlighted British and American industry, but not Canadian – or Indian. If McNaughton was right, by mid-1943 the British set out to 'put Canada in its place'.

While Mackenzie King was busy torpedoing Churchill's hopes for a unified Commonwealth and empire in May 1944, the British were busy scrubbing Canada from the Operation Overlord story. Even the Americans were appalled by the omission of Canada from the docu-mentary *Eve of Battle*, prepared by the MOI for release the week of the landings in Normandy. This may well have eased Eisenhower's decision to use the word 'Allied' as the generic descriptor for Overlord forces rather than the usual term 'Anglo-American'. The American press were only too happy with that word, and typically modified it to 'American and Allied' during the summer of 1944. As explained, it did not take long for British senior staff in Washington to complain bitterly that the term 'American and Allied' masked the British effort from American readers. They were right.

The British-orchestrated failure to include Canada's significant role in the whole Overlord story is, perhaps, the single most important omission from the Normandy narrative. Leaving the Canadians out affects everything from developing and sustaining the threat of a Second Front from 1941 onwards, to the shaping of the final Overlord plan, to plans to defeat the counterattacks, the success of Operation Fortitude, and the final defeat of the German armies in Normandy. Canada's role was not large, but for reasons explained here it was critical. The British continued to ignore or downplay Canada's contribution to both the war and Overlord long after 1945.[13] Even Ellis's official British history of the campaign, published in 1962, does not list Canada among the nations which fought in Normandy.[14] If David Edgerton is right and the British view of the war became strongly nationalist throughout the 1960s and 1970s, the chances of Canada getting much of a nod for its role until recently were slim indeed.[15]

Nor were historians likely to find much evidence of Canada's key role in Operation Overlord in Canadian publications. Andy McNaughton told Colonel Ralston in late 1943 that Canada needed a united First Canadian Army in the field if it wanted a seat at the table. He was right. But the dismantling of McNaughton's army also affected the writing of Canada's military history of the war. McNaughton's removal and the impact on the army was an embarrassment and could not be dealt with by Canadian official historians while those who removed him were still in senior positions in the army. Canadian official historians were also denied access to critical documents, like the Overlord plans and Operation Fortitude. As a result, 'McNaughton's Dagger' is typically a term of derision, and it does not appear in the wartime narrative crafted by Anglo-American historians. As Charles Stacey lamented in his 1949 review of Hopkins's and Eisenhower's memoirs, 'It is a pity to spend one's life reminding the world of one's existence, but that seems to be what we Canadians are up against.'[16] It turns out, however, that the Germans had been watching and listening. They knew the Canadians well from the Great War and expected them to be where the fighting was decisive. One is left to wonder what five eager Canadian divisions and two armoured brigades ashore in Normandy by D+14 might have accomplished – and done to the storyline.

Unquestionably the greater British failure in the crafting of the Normandy narrative was their rejection of large-scale American press coverage of British Second Army operations – twice. We will never know how popular perceptions of Normandy would have evolved had scores of Americans reported on Epsom, or Goodwood, or Jupiter, or Greenline, or Bluecoat. Certainly, Robert Brand thought in August 1944 that more coverage of British operations by American reporters was critical to Britain's ultimate fate. We do know that by the time of Epsom (late June) most of the American reporters accredited to the British Army had drifted away to the Cherbourg front, and that during much of July scores of reporters attached to the Third US Army sat idle and bored at Vouilly. Allowing the Americans into the British sector en masse would have required a cultural shift in British public relations – unescorted visits and unlimited access to teletype machines – and it almost certainly would have made Montgomery's manipulation of the press as part of his master plan all that much harder. But it seems likely that with large-scale American press coverage of the British Second Army there would have been no nonsense about British 'passivity'. No one who has been to Hill 112 and read about what happened there could ever claim that the British failed to fight in Normandy.

Quite understandably, the Americans worked hard to sell their own campaign at home. Marshall had chafed under the reporting system from the Mediterranean, where the news was funnelled through an Anglo-American filter before getting to the USA. Normandy would be different. Getting America's army ashore in France so it could win the war had been the plan since 1941. Moreover, Roosevelt needed a victorious American army ashore in France to secure a fourth term as President. Americans would report direct to Americans about what Americans were doing. The establishment of the Press Wireless station at Vouilly, with enough power to blast signals to New York in minutes – in contravention of the SHAEF press plan – was proof of that. For all these reasons, Normandy had to be an American show – and an American victory. It was a presidential election year, after all.

Finally, it did not help Britain's profile that the British Second Army slipped noticeably from the public eye at the moment of Allied victory in Normandy. In August, Dempsey's army was pinched out of the line twice, once at the Falaise Gap and again at Elbeuf. Britain's army in France only made the top headlines in *The Times* twice in August: once on the 1st and again on the 31st. In the last weeks of August, Canadian and American armies were on the move, and they copped the headlines. Ironically, the major British share in that effort, I British Corps operating as part of the First Canadian Army, was even briefly described in London papers as 'Canadian' (not the last time that would happen).

It seems, in the end, the carefully scripted Office of War Information scenario laid out in 1942 had played out: 1942–3 was about the mobilisation of men and machines, then in 1944 America arrived to crush its enemies and win the war. That summer America also took control of the global economy, laid out the future of international conflict management with the UN plan, and was busy determining which of the possessions it had conquered would be kept for postwar bases and whose oil it wanted. Even the isolationists had switched their tune: they were now openly imperialist. If America was going to get stuck in, it might as well run the whole show.

James Grigg warned Montgomery in July 1944 that the British – like the Dutch in 1713 – would be ruined by victory. Keynes understood this very well. Whether a concerted (and by some measure successful) campaign to sell Britain's war effort to the Americans would have changed that is a moot point. Arguably, the Anglo-American financial concordat of early 1946 was proof that official Washington noticed. What is clearer now is that the long struggle between Britain and America over global hegemony – that 'Second Front' that loomed over Britain throughout the war – profoundly shaped our understanding of the Second World War and of Operation Overlord in ways that we are only beginning to understand.

NOTES

CHAPTER 1: HALF-FORGOTTEN THINGS

1. *The Penguin Book of First World War Poetry*, ed. Jon Silkin (London: Penguin Books, 1996), pp. 124–7.
2. C.R.M.F. Cruttwell, *A History of the Great War 1914–1918* (Chicago, IL: Academy Publishers, 1991), p. 442.
3. John Terraine, *To Win a War: 1918 the Year of Victory* (London: Papermac, 1978), p. 60.
4. Terraine, *To Win a War*, p. 65.
5. *Pershing's Lieutenants: American Military Leadership in World War I*, ed. David Zabecki and Douglas V. Mastriano (Oxford: Osprey, 2020), pp. 31–2.
6. Donald Smythe, *Pershing: General of the Armies* (Bloomington, IN: Indiana UP, 1986), pp. 72–3.
7. David F. Trask, *The AEF and Coalition War Making* (Lawrence, KS: University Press of Kansas, 1993), p. 55.
8. Paul F. Braim, *The Test of Battle: The American Expeditionary Forces in the Meuse–Argonne Campaign* (Newark: University of Delaware Press, 1987), p. 66.
9. Robert A. Doughty, *Pyrrhic Victory: French Strategy and Operations in the Great War* (Cambridge, MA: Harvard UP, 2005), p. 448.
10. Otto H. Kahn, 'When the Tide Turned: The American Attack at Chateau Thierry and Belleau Wood in the First Week of June 1918', Address at the United War Campaign Meeting of the Boston Athletic Association, 12 November 1918.
11. Mark Ethan Grotelueschen, *The AEF Way of War: The American Army and Combat in World War I* (New York: Cambridge UP, 2007), pp. 80–1.
12. As quoted in Adam Hochshild, *To End All Wars: A Story of Loyalty and Rebellion, 1914–1918* (Boston, MA: Houghton Mifflin, 2012), p. 330.
13. Tim Cook, *Shock Troops: Canadians Fighting the Great War 1917–1918* (Toronto, ON: Viking, 2008), pp. 410–11.
14. Shane Schreiber, *Shock Army of the British Empire: The Canadian Corps in the Last 100 Days of the Great War* (St Catharines, ON: Vanwell Publishing, 2004), p. 21.
15. See S.F. Wise, 'The Gardeners of Vimy', in *Canadian Military History*, vol. 8, no. 3, Summer 1999.

16. See A.J.P. Taylor, *Beaverbrook* (London: Hamish Hamilton, 1972), Chapters 5–7.
17. Col. G.W.L. Nicholson, *The Canadian Expeditionary Force 1914–1919* (Ottawa, ON: Queen's Printer, 1962), p. 350.
18. Richard Norton Smith, *The Colonel: The Life and Legend of Robert R. McCormick, Indomitable Editor of the 'Chicago Tribune'* (Boston, MA: Houghton Mifflin, 1997), p. 207.
19. Nicholson, *Canadian Expeditionary Force*, p. 394.
20. Cook, *Shock Troops*, p. 411.
21. Gary Sheffield, *Forgotten Victory: The First World War – Myths and Realities* (London: Headline, 2001), p. 201.
22. Sheffield, p. 201
23. Edward B. Parsons, 'Why the British Reduced the Flow of American Troops to Europe in August–October 1918', *Canadian Journal of History*, vol. 12, no. 2, December 1977, p. 177.
24. Parsons, p. 179.
25. Parsons, pp. 176–9.
26. Parsons, p. 177.
27. Terraine, *To Win a War*, pp. 128–9.
28. Schreiber, p. 71.
29. John Nelson Rickard, *The Politics of Command: Lieutenant-General A.G.L. McNaughton and the Canadian Army 1939–1945* (Toronto, ON: University of Toronto Press, 2010), p. 17.
30. David Fraser, *Alanbrooke* (New York: Atheneum, 1982), p. 76.
31. John Swettenham, *McNaughton: Volume I, 1887–1939* (Toronto, ON: Ryerson Press, 1968), pp. 131–2. See also, Brendan Hogan, 'Broken Friendship: The Relationship between General Sir Alan Brooke and Lieutenant-General Andrew McNaughton, 1917–1943', *War and Society*, vol. 39, no. 4, October 2020, pp. 256–72.
32. Sheffield, p. 206.
33. Schreiber, Chapter 4.
34. Grotelueschen, p. 108.
35. Grotelueschen, pp. 112–13.
36. Grotelueschen, pp. 120–1.
37. Grotelueschen, p. 55.
38. Doughty, pp. 487–9.
39. Forrest Pogue, *George Marshall*, vol. 1: *Education of a General, 1880–1939* (New York: Viking, 1963), p. 177.
40. Zabecki and Mastriano, p. 48.
41. John J. Pershing, *My Experiences in the World War*, vol. 2 (New York: Frederick A. Stokes, 1931), p. 293.
42. Grotelueschen, p. 127
43. Smythe, *Pershing*, p. 193.
44. Braim, p. 89.
45. Christopher Evan Heenan, 'Triumph, Frustration, and the Question of Structured Warfare: A preliminary Analysis of Canadian Fire-Support During the Battle of the Canal du Nord, September 27th to October 1st, 1918', unpublished MA thesis, University of New Brunswick, 2011, Chapter 3.
46. Schreiber, pp. 95–114.
47. Grotelueschen, p. 129.

48. Smythe, p. 195.
49. Smythe, p. 196.
50. Carlo D'Este, *Patton: A Genius for War* (New York: Harper Collins, 1995), see Chapter 18.
51. Smythe, p. 197.
52. Doughty, p. 488.
53. Schreiber, Chapter 6.
54. Nick Lloyd, *Hundred Days: The End of the Great War* (London: Viking, 2013), p. 177.
55. Robin Prior and Trevor Wilson, *The First World War* (London: Cassell & Co., 2001), p. 194.
56. Lloyd, p. 181.
57. Prior and Wilson, p. 199.
58. Lloyd, p. 187.
59. Sheffield, p. 215.
60. Trask, p. 127.
61. Braim, p. 146.
62. Thomas E. Johnson, *Without Censor: New Light on our Greatest World War Battle* (Indianapolis, IN: Bobbs-Merrill, 1928), see Chapter 12, 'The Propaganda Front'.
63. Trask, p. 128.
64. Terraine, *To Win a War*, pp. 47n, 232.
65. Doughty, p. 491.
66. Holger H. Herwig, *The First World War: Germany and Austria-Hungary, 1914–1918* (London: Arnold, 1997), p. 426.
67. Herwig, p. 437.
68. Groteleuschen, p. 268.
69. Grotelueschen, p. 268.
70. Trask, pp. 174 and 176.
71. Smythe, pp. 227–8.
72. Zabecki and Mastriano, p. 52.
73. Smythe, p. 228.
74. Pogue, *Marshall: Education of a General*, pp. 187–8. Casualty figures from Zabecki and Mastriano: they list 80 killed, 503 wounded, p. 52.
75. Smythe, p. 228; Zabecki and Mastriano, p. 52.
76. Terraine, *To Win a War*, p. 14.
77. As quoted in J.L. Granatstein, *The Greatest Victory: Canada's One Hundred Days, 1918* (Toronto, ON: Oxford UP, 2014), p. 175.

CHAPTER 2: THE SHADOW OF 1918

1. Robert Self, *Britain, America and the War Debt Controversy: The Economic Diplomacy of an Unspecial Relationship, 1917–1941* (London: Routledge, 2006), p. 7.
2. Adam Tooze, *The Deluge: The Great War, America and the Remaking of the Global Order, 1916–1931* (New York: Penguin, 2015), p. 16.
3. What follows is derived from Margaret MacMillan's superb book *Paris 1919: Six Months That Changed the World* (New York: Random House, 2001). See especially Part II: 'A New World Order'.

4. MacMillan, p. 89.

5. MacMillan, p. 461.

6. See Table 7 in Tooze, *The Deluge*, p. 249.

7. Tooze, *The Deluge*, pp. 8–9.

8. Tooze, *The Deluge*, p. 62.

9. Robert Cowley, ed., *What If? The World's Foremost Military Historians Imagine What Might Have Been* (New York: Berkley Books, 2000), p. 166.

10. Leonard V. Smith, Stephane Audoin-Rouzeau and Annette Becker, *France and the Great War 1914–1918* (Cambridge: Cambridge UP, 2003), pp. 69, 71.

11. Paul Fussell, *The Great War and Modern Memory* (London: Oxford UP, 1975), p. 36.

12. Smith, Audoin-Rouzeau and Becker, p. 43.

13. Isabelle V. Hull, *Absolute Destruction: Military Culture and the Practices of War in Imperial Germany* (Ithaca, NY/London: Cornell UP, 2005), pp. 315–19.

14. MacMillan, p. 186.

15. Self, pp. 22–3.

16. Self, p. 31.

17. John Darwin, *The Empire Project: The Rise and Fall of the British World System, 1830–1970* (Cambridge: Cambridge UP, 2009), p. 370.

18. See Joseph Zeller, 'Control of Coal: The Key to Power in the Age of Steam', unpublished PhD thesis, University of New Brunswick, 2016.

19. Correlli Barnett, *The Audit of War: The Illusion and Reality of Britain as a Great Power* (London: Papermac, 1986). See Part II.

20. Self, p. 18.

21. Self, p. 199.

22. Self, p. 19.

23. Self, p. 15.

24. Self, p. 200.

25. Benjamin D. Rhodes, 'The Image of Britain in the United States, 1919–1929', in B.J.C. McKercher, ed., *Anglo-American Relations in the 1920s* (Edmonton, AB: University of Alberta Press, 1991), p. 194.

26. Library of Congress, Eugene Meyer Papers, 'General Correspondence, Brand, Robert H., 1922–1930', journal off-print *c.* 1927, 'Inter-Allied Debt'.

27. Self, pp. 16, 199.

28. Darwin, p. 351.

29. Charles Stacey, *Canada and the Age of Conflict*, vol. 1: *1867–1921* (Toronto, ON: Macmillan, 1977), p. 297.

30. Darwin, p. 395.

31. Charles Stacey, *Canada and the Age of Conflict*, vol. 2: *1921–1948, The Mackenzie King Era* (Toronto, ON: University of Toronto Press, 1981), p. 85.

32. Norman Hillmer, *O.D. Skelton: A Portrait of Canadian Ambition* (Toronto, ON: University of Toronto Press, 2015), p. 155.

33. Stacey, *Canada and the Age of Conflict*, vol. 2, p. 86.

34. Stacey, *Canada and the Age of Conflict*, vol. 2, pp. 89–90.

35. Brian J. McKercher, *Esme Howard: A Diplomatic Biography* (Cambridge: Cambridge UP, 1989), pp. 327, 328.

36. Hillmer, p. 172.

37. Swettenham, vol. 1, pp. 233-4.

38. Darwin, p. 401.

39. Swettenham, vol. 1, p. 252.
40. Mark Derez, 'A Belgian Salient for Reconstruction: People and Patrie, Landscape and Memory', in Peter Liddle, ed., *Passchendaele in Perspective: The Third Battle of Ypres* (London: Leo Cooper, 1997), pp. 450–1.
41. As quoted in Richard Overy, *The Morbid Age: Britain Between the Wars* (London: Allen Lane, 2009), p. 220.
42. Derez, p. 450.
43. Michelin produced a series of guides in July 1920. I have the 1920 edition of *Ypres and the Battles for Ypres 1914–1918: An Illustrated History and Guide* (Clermont-Ferrand), given to my grandmother by friends who visited her brother's grave in 1924.
44. David W. Lloyd, *Battlefield Tourism: Pilgrimage and the Commemoration of the Great War in Britain, Australia and Canada* (Oxford: Berg Publishers, 1998), vol. 10, pp. 28–9.
45. Adam Hochschild, *American Midnight: The Great War, A Violent Peace and Democracy's Forgotten Crisis* (New York: Mariner Books, 2022), p. 94.
46. See also David M. Kennedy, *Over Here: The First World War and American Society* (New York: Oxford UP, 2004).
47. Rachel Maddow, *Prequel: An American Fight Against Fascism* (New York: Crown, 2023), p. 140.
48. Steven Trout, *On the Battlefield of Memory: The First World War and American Remembrance, 1919–1941* (Tuscaloosa, AL: University of Alabama Press, 2010), pp. 26–35.
49. Trout p. 28.
50. Malcolm Cowley, *Exile's Return: A Literary Odyssey of the 1920s* (New York: Penguin Books, 1994 edition), p. 46.
51. Trout, pp. 2–3.
52. Trout quotes Kennedy's *Over Here*, p. 202, which states uncharitably that Pershing's tactics worked best 'when directed at the receding backs of a retreating foe'.
53. Johnson, p. 289.
54. Johnson, p. 281.
55. Lisa M. Budreau, *Bodies of War: World War I and the Politics of Commemoration in America, 1919–1933* (New York: New York UP, 2010), p. 109.
56. Trout, p. xxiii.
57. Budreau, p. 101.
58. Budreau, p. 7.
59. See the account in Mark Zwonitzer, *The Statesman and the Storyteller: John Hay, Mark Twain and the Rise of American Imperialism* (Chapel Hill, NC: Algonquin Books, 2016), Chapters 24–6.
60. Jonathan F. Vance, *Death So Noble: Memory, Meaning and the First World War* (Vancouver, BC: University of British Columbia Press, 1997), pp. 176–80.
61. J.F.B. Livesay, *Canada and the Hundred Days: With the Canadian Corps from Amiens to Mons, Aug. 8–Nov. 11, 1918* (Toronto, ON: T. Allen, 1919), pp. 400–3, quote on p. 402.
62. See Dan Dancocks, *Welcome to Flanders: The First Canadian Battle of the Great War: Ypres, 1915* (Toronto, ON: McClelland & Stewart, 1988).
63. As quoted in Tim Cook, *Clio's Warriors: Canadian Historians and the Writing of the World Wars* (Vancouver, BC: University of British Columbia Press, 2006), p. 50.

64. See Edmonds' lengthy letter of December 1926 published in Tim Travers, 'Currie and 1st Canadian Division at Second Ypres, April 1915: Controversy, Criticism and Official History', *Canadian Military History*, vol. 5, no. 2, Autumn 1996, pp. 7–15. Travers concludes that Edmonds was biased. An earlier article by Travers, 'Allies in Conflict: The British and Canadian Official Historians and the Real Story of Second Ypres', *Journal of Contemporary History*, vol. 24, no. 2, 'Studies on War', April 1989, pp. 301–25, discusses the Australian debate *en passant*.
65. Cook, *Clio's Warriors*, p. 54.
66. I am grateful to (then) Capt. Chris Lardner, Royal Canadian Artillery, for sharing his April 2016 graduate seminar essay, 'I Wonder What History Will Have to Say About All This?', examining the historical debate about 'Who Won the War'.
67. Vance, *Death So Noble*, p. 178.
68. George Drew, 'The Truth About the War', *Maclean's Magazine*, 1 July 1928, p. 1.
69. Budreau, p. 189. A similar phenomenon often greets British Commonwealth veterans and visitors in Normandy, where the iconography of liberation typically features US soldiers. This was especially jarring in the Caen area, liberated by the British and Canadians, during the commemorations of June 2014.
70. American Battle Monuments Commission, *A Guide to the American Battle Fields in Europe* (Washington, DC: US Government Printing Office, 1927), pp. 129–30.
71. Self, p. 200.
72. Budreau, pp. 180–1.
73. Winston S. Churchill, *The World Crisis 1911–1918* (New York: Charles Scribner's Sons, 1923–7).
74. Churchill, *The World Crisis 1911–1918*, pp. 1383–4.
75. Basil H. Liddell Hart, *Reputations: Ten Years After* (Boston, MA; Little, Brown and Co., 1928), p. 310.
76. Basil H. Liddell Hart, *The Real War 1914–1918* (London: Faber & Faber, 1930), pp. 493, 500.
77. Liddell Hart, *The Real War*, p. 491.
78. See 'Pershing and the World War', *NYT*, 26 April 1931, Book Review section; letter to the Editor from Wendell Westover, *NYT*, 10 May 1931, Book Review Section.
79. Lt Gen. Maurice A. Pope, *Soldiers and Politicians: The Memoirs of Lt.-Gen. Maurice A Pope, CB, MC* (Toronto, ON: University of Toronto Press, 1962), pp. 62, 238–9.
80. Self, p. 7.
81. Robert Craigie was the head of the Foreign Office's American Department. As quoted in Self, p. 7.

CHAPTER 3: THE DISSOLUTION OF HOPE

1. Paul Jankowski, *All Against All: The Long Winter of 1933 and the Origins of the Second World War* (New York: HarperCollins, 2020), p. 347.
2. See David M. Kennedy, *Freedom from Fear: The American People in Depression and War, 1929–1945* (New York: Oxford UP, 2005), Chapter 2.
3. As quoted in Kennedy, *Freedom from Fear*, p. 50.
4. Tooze, *The Deluge*, p. 489.
5. Tooze, *The Deluge*, p. 494.
6. Tooze, *The Deluge*, p. 494.

7. Darwin, p. 433.
8. Tooze, *The Deluge*, p. 504.
9. Darwin, p. 434.
10. Stacey, *Canada and the Age of Conflict*, vol. 2, p. 229.
11. Gordon T. Stewart, 'An Objective of US Foreign Policy since the Founding of the Republic', in Phillip Buckner, ed., *Canada and the End of the Empire* (Vancouver, BC: University of British Columbia Press, 2005), pp. 94–116, p. 99.
12. Both quotes from Stewart, p. 98.
13. Jankowski, p. 347.
14. G.D.H. Cole and R.S. Postgate, *War Debts and Reparations: What They Are: Why They Must Be Cancelled* (London: The New Statesman and Nation, [1932]), p. 5.
15. Frank H. Simonds, *America Must Cancel: An American Reviews War-Debts* (London: Hamish Hamilton, 1933), pp. 11, 25.
16. B.J. McKercher, *Transition of Power: Britain's Loss of Global Pre-eminence to the United States 1930–1945* (Cambridge: Cambridge UP, 1999), p. 136.
17. Jankowski, p. 209.
18. McKercher, *Transition*, p. 142.
19. Jankowski, p. 201.
20. As quoted in Jankowski, pp. 204, 205.
21. Tooze, *The Deluge*, p. 507.
22. Jankowski, pp. 213–42.
23. Kennedy, *Freedom from Fear*, p. 121.
24. See Terry Golway, *Together We Cannot Fail: FDR and the American Presidency in Years of Crisis* (Naperville, IL: Sourcebooks MediaFusion, 2009), Chapter 2, and the enclosed CD for a recording of this and other Fireside Chats.
25. Kennedy, *Freedom from Fear*, p. 153.
26. Kennedy, *Freedom from Fear*, p. 155.
27. Adam Tooze, *The Wages of Destruction: The Making and Breaking of the Nazi Economy* (London: Penguin, 2007), see especially pp. 27–9.
28. Kennedy, *Freedom from Fear*, pp. 390–1.
29. *The Story of the Canadian Corps 1914–1934: A Record of the Canadian Corps Reunion August 4, 5, 6, 1934, Toronto, Canada* (Toronto, ON: Canadian Veterans Association, 1934), p. 36.
30. Richard Overy, *The Morbid Age*, was published in the United States as *The Twilight Years: The Paradox of Britain Between the Wars* (New York: Viking, 2009).
31. As quoted in Philip Blom, *Fracture: Life and Culture in the West, 1918–1938* (Toronto, ON: Signal, 2015), p. 47.
32. See Arthur Haberman, *1930: Europe in the Shadow of the Beast* (Waterloo, ON: Wilfrid Laurier UP, 2018).
33. Aldous Huxley, *Brave New World* (London: Arcturus, 2014 edition).
34. See Abram C. Van Engen, *City on a Hill: A History of American Exceptionalism* (New Haven, CT and London: Yale UP, 2020).
35. John M. Muresianu, *War of Ideas: American Intellectuals and the World Crisis, 1938–1945* (New York: Garland Publishing, 1988), see Chapter 1.
36. Kennedy, *Freedom from Fear*, p. 396.
37. Kennedy, *Freedom from Fear*, p. 393.
38. Kennedy, *Freedom from Fear*, pp. 400–1.
39. Kennedy, *Freedom from Fear*, pp. 392–3.

40. David Edgerton, *Britain's War Machine: Weapons, Resources and Experts in the Second World War* (London: Allen Lane, 2011), p. 3.
41. Edgerton, *Britain's War Machine*, p. 7.
42. See Reginald G. Trotter, Albert B. Corey and Walter W. McLaren, eds, *Conference on Canadian–American Affairs* (New York: Ginn and Company on behalf of the Carnegie Endowment for International Peace, 1937), especially the 'Foreign Policy' section for a brief discussion of a possible Canadian role in the organisation.
43. Stacey, *Canada and the Age of Conflict*, vol. 2, p. 226.
44. Nicholas John Cull, *Selling War: The British Propaganda Campaign Against American 'Neutrality' in World War II* (Oxford: Oxford UP, 1996), p. 9.
45. Lord Beaverbrook, *Politicians and the War, 1914–1916* (London: Oldbourne Book Co., 1960), p. 93.
46. Taylor, pp. 138–40.
47. Barnes, p. 646.
48. These elements were identified in the foreword to the 1969 edition of Grattan's book, written by Keith Nelson. See C. Harley Grattan, *Why We Fought* (Indianapolis, IN: Bobbs-Merrill, 1969), pp. xv–xx.
49. Grattan, p. 41.
50. Grattan, pp. 46–7.
51. Robert Calder, *Beware the British Serpent: The Role of Writer in British Propaganda in the United States, 1939–1945* (Montreal/Kingston: McGill–Queens UP, 2004), p. 7.
52. Cull, p. 9.
53. As quoted in Squires, *British Propaganda at Home and in the United States from 1914 to 1917* (Cambridge, MA: Harvard UP, 1935), p. 54.
54. Squires, p. 77.
55. H.C. Peterson, *Propaganda for War: The Campaign Against American Neutrality 1914–1917* (Norman, OK: University of Oklahoma Press, 1939), p. 326.
56. As quoted in Calder, *Beware the British Serpent*, p. 41.
57. Calder, *Beware the British Serpent*, p. 41.
58. Michael Stenton, *Radio London and Resistance in Occupied Europe: British Political Warfare, 1939–1943* (Oxford: Oxford UP, 2000), pp. 9–10.
59. Calder, *Beware the British Serpent*, p. 42.
60. For a recent account of America's fascist movements and the Dies Commission see Rachel Maddow, *Prequel: An American Fight Against Fascism* (New York: Crown, 2023).
61. Overy, *The Morbid Age*, p. 282.

CHAPTER 4: DIFFERENT TRAJECTORIES

1. Evelyn Waugh, *Men at Arms* (London: Penguin Books, 1980 edition), p. 12.
2. Daniel Immerwahr, *How to Hide an Empire: A History of the Greater United States* (New York: Farrar, Straus and Giroux, 2019), p. 6. On the larger issue of the American empire see A.G. Hopkins, *American Empire: A Global History* (Princeton, NJ: Princeton UP, 2018).
3. Immerwahr, p. 13.
4. George Baer, *One Hundred Years of Seapower: The U.S. Navy, 1890–1990* (Stanford, CA: Stanford UP, 1993), p. 130.

5. Baer, pp. 134–5. For the Quarantine Speech see Kennedy, *Freedom from Fear*, pp. 404–5.
6. Jon Klug, 'Building a Global Navy: U.S. Naval Logistics, 1776–1941', unpublished PhD dissertation, University of New Brunswick, 2023.
7. Edward M. Coffman's *The Regulars: The American Army 1898–1941* (Cambridge, MA: The Belknap Press, 2004).
8. Coffman, p. 370.
9. William O. Odom, *After the Trenches: The Transformation of the U.S. Army, 1918–1939* (College Station, TX: Texas A&M UP, 1999), see Chapter 9.
10. Odom, p. 156.
11. Coffman, p. 233.
12. Conrad C. Crane, *Bombs, Cities and Civilians: American Airpower Strategy in World War II* (Manhattan, KS: University Press of Kansas, 1993), see especially Chapter 1, 'Developing Doctrine'.
13. Odom, p. 155.
14. Raymond Swing, *'Good Evening!' A Professional Memoir* (New York: Harcourt Brace, 1964), p. 216.
15. Robert Dallek, *Franklin D. Roosevelt: A Political Life* (New York: Viking, 2017), p. 367; Robert Sherwood, *Roosevelt and Hopkins*, vol. 2: *From Pearl Harbor to Victory* (New York: Bantam, 1950), pp. 164–5.
16. Sherwood, pp. 166–7.
17. Lynne Olson, *Those Angry Days: Roosevelt, Lindbergh and America's Fight Over World War II, 1939–1941* (New York: Random House, 2013), p. 302.
18. Olson, *Those Angry Days*, pp. 113–14.
19. Klug, 'Building a Global Navy: U.S. Naval Logistics, 1776–1941'.
20. Kennedy, *Freedom from Fear*, p. 405.
21. Paul Starr, *The Creation of the Media: Political Origins of Modern Communications* (New York: Basic Books, 2004), see especially pp. 14–18.
22. David Halberstam's *The Powers That Be* (New York: Alfred A. Knopf, 1979), p. 178.
23. What follows is derived from Halberstam's 'Prelude'.
24. Starr, pp. 212–22.
25. Starr, p. 340.
26. Starr, p. 353.
27. John Perkins, ' "Germany Calling": Nazi Short-Wave Broadcasting to Australia in the 1930s', *Journal of Australian Studies*, vol. 18, no. 42, 1994, pp. 43–50.
28. Perkins, pp. 43–50.
29. See Gwenyth Jackway's 'Media at War: Radio's Challenge to Newspapers, 1924–1939', unpublished dissertation, University of Pennsylvania, 1992.
30. History of Canadian Broadcasting, 'Moose River Mine Disaster', accessed online 27 April 2018.
31. Starr, p. 378.
32. Walter Lippmann, *Public Opinion* (New York: Macmillan, 1922), p. 248.
33. French, p. 185.
34. Brian Bond, *Liddell Hart: A Study of His Military Thought* (London: Cassell, 1976), see especially Chapters 3 and 4; see also Williamson Murray, 'Armored Warfare: The British, French and German Experiences', in Williamson Murray and Allan R. Millett, eds, *Military Innovation in the Interwar Period* (Cambridge: Cambridge UP, 1996), pp. 6–49.

35. Shelford Bidwell and Dominick Graham, *Fire-Power: British Army Weapons and Theories of War 1904–1945* (London: George Allen & Unwin, 1982), pp. 134–40.

36. J.F.C. Fuller, *A Military History of the Western World*, vol. 3: *From the American Civil War to the End of World War II* (London: Minerva Press, 1956), p. 380.

37. Bond, pp. 145–6.

38. David French, *The British Way of War, 1688–2000* (London: Unwin Hyman,1990), pp. 14–15.

39. Edgerton, *Britain's War Machine*, pp. 2–3.

40. Dan Todman, *Britain's War: Into Battle, 1937–1941* (Oxford: Oxford UP, 2016), see especially Chapter 9, 'More Suffering to Come'.

41. Bond, pp. 190–1.

42. Bidwell and Graham, *Fire-Power*, p. 191.

43. Bidwell and Graham, *Fire-Power*, p. 191.

44. As quoted in Andrew Stewart's ' "Necessarily of an Experimental Character": The Interwar Period and the Imperial Defence College', in Douglas E. Delaney, Robert C. Engen and Meghan Fitzpatrick, eds, *Military Education and Empire: Professional Education and the Military, Naval and Air Forces of the British Empire and Commonwealth, 1815–1949* (Vancouver, BC: University of British Columbia Press, 2018), p. 197.

45. Douglas Delaney, *The Imperial Army Project: Britain and the Land Forces of the Dominions and India, 1902–1945* (Oxford: Oxford UP, 2017).

46. J.L. Granatstein, *Canada's Army: Waging War and Keeping the Peace* (Toronto, ON: University of Toronto Press, 2002), pp. 158–9.

47. Stephen J. Harris, *Canadian Brass: The Making of a Professional Army 1860–1939* (Toronto, ON: University of Toronto Press, 1988), p. 180.

48. Tim Cook, *Vimy: The Battle and the Legend* (Toronto, ON: Allen Lane, 2017), pp. 274–5.

49. C.P. Stacey, *Arms, Men and Governments: The War Policies of Canada 1939–1945* (Ottawa, ON: Minister of National Defence, 1970), p. 2.

50. W.A.B. Douglas, *The Creation of a National Air Force: The Official History of the Royal Canadian Air Force*, vol. 2 (Toronto, ON: University of Toronto Press, 1986), p. 144.

51. Marc Milner, *Canada's Navy: The First Century* (Toronto, ON: University of Toronto Press, 1999), pp. 80–1.

52. Stacey, *Canada and the Age of Conflict*, vol. 2, p. 201.

53. Hillmer, p. 268.

54. Stacey, *Canada and the Age of Conflict*, vol. 2, pp. 203–6.

55. Stacey, *Canada and the Age of Conflict*, vol. 2, p. 205.

56. Correlli Barnett, *The Collapse of British Power* (New York: Morrow, 1972), p. 227.

57. Stacey, *Canada and the Age of Conflict*, vol. 2, p. 211.

58. Robert B. Bryce, *Canada and the Cost of World War II: The International Operations of Canada's Department of Finance, 1939–1947* (Montreal/Kingston: McGill–Queen's UP, 2005), pp. 16–17.

59. DHH 91/169, 'Sorel Industries Limited', copy supplied by Doug Knight.

60. Stacey, *Canada and the Age of Conflict*, vol. 2, pp. 223–4.

61. Norman H. Gibbs, *Grand Strategy*, vol. 1: *Rearmament Policy* (London: HMSO, 1976), pp. 693–707.

62. French, *The British Way of War*, p. 194.
63. Darwin, pp. 494–5.
64. TNA, INF 2/5, 'Fifty Facts About India' (*c.* 1944).
65. Darwin, p. 498.

CHAPTER 5: IN GOD'S GOOD TIME

1. Self, p. 213.
2. Lloyd Clark, *Blitzkrieg: Myth, Reality and Hitler's Lightning War – France 1940* (London: Atlantic Books, 2016), pp. 45–6.
3. L.F. Ellis, *War in France and Flanders 1939–1940* (London: HMSO, 1954), quote p. 7, details of deployments pp. 16–17.
4. Ellis, *War in France and Flanders,* pp. 19–20.
5. J.R.M. Butler, *Grand Strategy*, vol. 2: *September 1939–June 1941* (London: HMSO, 1957), p. 44.
6. C.P. Stacey, *Six Years of War: The Army in Canada, Britain and the Pacific* (Ottawa, ON: Queen's Printer, 1957), pp. 53–60.
7. Stacey, *Six Years of War*, p. 63.
8. Swettenham, vol. 2, pp. 4–6.
9. As quoted in Swettenham, vol. 2, p. 20.
10. Stacey, *Arms, Men and Governments*, p. 213.
11. For a brief summary see Stacey, *Canada and the Age of Conflict*, vol. 2, pp. 291–6. See also F.J. Hatch, *The Aerodrome of Democracy: Canada and the British Commonwealth Air Training Plan, 1939–1945* (Ottawa, ON: Directorate of History, Dept of National Defence, 1983).
12. Butler, *Grand Strategy,* vol. 2, p. 42.
13. See Milner, *Canada's Navy*, Chapter 5.
14. Stacey, *Arms, Men and Governments*, p. 15.
15. Field Marshal Lord Alanbrooke, *War Diaries 1939–1945*, ed. Alex Danchev and Daniel Todman (London: Weidenfeld & Nicolson, 2001), 9 and 10 May 1940, p. 59.
16. Clark, *Blitzkrieg*, p. 193.
17. William Manchester and Paul Reid, *The Last Lion: Winston Spencer Churchill, Defender of the Realm, 1940–1965* (Boston, MA: Little, Brown and Co., 2012), pp. 65–6
18. Manchester, pp. 66–7.
19. Clark, *Blitzkrieg*, p. 215.
20. Ellis, *The War in France and Flanders*, Chapter 4.
21. See Swettenham, vol. 2, Chapter 5.
22. Alanbrooke, *War Diaries*, postwar note inserted referring to 13 June 1940.
23. Stacey, *Six Years of War*, p. 276.
24. LAC, MG 30, E133, vol. 197, McNaughton Papers, Eden to McNaughton, 9 June 1940, telegram from Dill, 11 June 1940.
25. Stacey, *Six Years of War*, p. 278. See also LAC, MG 31, E42, vol. 3, Swettenham Papers, McNaughton's interview of 1965.
26. Alanbrooke, *War Diaries*, entry and notation for 14 June, p. 80.
27. Clark, *Blitzkrieg*, pp. 366–7.
28. Stacey, *Six Years of War*, p. 282.
29. Alanbrooke, *War Diaries*, 15 June 1940.

30. LAC, MG 30, E133, vol. 197, McNaughton Papers, Dill to McNaughton, 21 June 1940.
31. LAC, MG 30, E133, vol. 197, McNaughton Papers, McNaughton to Dill 29 June 1940,
32. LAC, MG 31, E42, vol. 3, Swettenham Papers.
33. LAC, MG 31, E42, vol. 3, Swettenham Papers.
34. Alistair Horne, *To Lose a Battle* (London: Penguin, 1969), pp. 641–2.
35. David Reynolds, *In Command of History: Churchill Fighting and Writing the Second World War* (London: Allen Lane, 2004), p. 176.
36. TNA, INF 1/102, Ministry of Information 'Special Report No. 6: British Public Opinion and the United States', 23 February 1942.
37. Self, p. 212.
38. Self, p. 212.
39. Self, p. 213.
40. Harold Nicolson, *Why Britain Is at War* (London: Penguin, 1939; 2010 reprint), p. 39.
41. Reynolds, *In Command*, see especially Chapters 11 and 12.
42. Todman, *Britain's War: Into Battle*, p. 416.
43. Sherwood, *Roosevelt and Hopkins*, vol. 1, p. 160.
44. As quoted in Sherwood, p. 160.
45. Kennedy, *Freedom from Fear*, p. 464.
46. TNA, FO 898/106, 'Anglo-American Relations and British Representation in the United States', Memorandum of 26 August 1942 by Alan Dudley, British Mission to Washington, Reports 1941–2.
47. TNA, PREM 4/25/7, Prime Minister to MOI, 26 June 1940; MOI to Prime Minister, 3 July 1940.
48. Cull, p. 10.
49. Cull, p. 11.
50. Cull, pp. 11–12.
51. See Michael Balfour, *Propaganda in War 1939–1945: Organizations, Policies and Publics in Britain and Germany* (London: Faber & Faber, 1988), Chapter 2, 'The Propaganda Ministry in Peacetime'.
52. Cull, pp. 35–6.
53. Cull, p. 24.
54. Cull, p. 15.
55. *British Security Coordination: The Secret History of British Intelligence in the Americas, 1940–1945* (New York: Fromm International, 1999), p. ix.
56. H. Montgomery Hyde, *The Quiet Canadian: The Secret Service Story of Sir William Stephenson* (London: Hamish Hamilton, 1962), p. 11.
57. Hyde, 'Prelude'.
58. *British Security Coordination*, p. xxv.
59. *British Security Coordination*, p. xxvii.
60. TNA, PREM 4/25/7, 'British Propaganda in North and South America', by Emery Reves, n.d. but attached covering letter from Cooper is dated 13 July 1940.
61. TNA, PREM 4/25/7, 'Propaganda in Latin America', by Frank Pick, 20 August 1940.
62. J.R.M. Butler, *Lord Lothian (Philip Kerr) 1882–1940* (London: Macmillan, 1960), p. 250.

63. Olson, *Those Angry Days*, p. 152.
64. Kennedy, *Freedom from Fear*, p. 427.
65. Dallek, *Roosevelt: A Political Life*, p. 365.
66. Kennedy, *Freedom from Fear*, p. 423.
67. Kennedy, *Freedom from Fear*, pp. 429–30.
68. Kennedy, *Freedom from Fear*, pp. 433–4.
69. Kennedy, *Freedom from Fear*, p. 446.
70. Kennedy, *Freedom from Fear*, p. 404.
71. Kennedy, *Freedom from Fear*, p. 446.
72. National Army Museum, 'Defeat in the West 1940', accessed online 15 May 2023.
73. Stacey, *Canada and the Age of Conflict*, vol. 2, p. 299.
74. Brereton Greenhous, Stephen J. Harris, William C. Johnston and William G.P. Rawling, *The Crucible of War 1939–1945: The Royal Canadian Air Force Official History*, vol. 3 (Toronto, ON: University of Toronto Press, 1994), p. 164.
75. Todman, *Britain's War: Into Battle*, p. 419.
76. Clive Law, *Drive to Victory: Catalogue of Canadian Military Vehicles* (Ottawa, ON: Service Publications, 2016), p. 27.
77. Law, pp. 29–32.
78. H. Duncan Hall, *North American Supply* (London: HMSO and Longman, Green and Co., 1955), p. 9.
79. DHH 91/169, 'Sorel Industries Limited'.
80. J. De N. Kennedy, *History of the Department of Munitions and Supply: Canada in the Second World War* (Ottawa, ON: King's Printer, 1950), see especially Chapter 11, 'Gun Production Branch'.
81. Darwin, p. 504.

CHAPTER 6: VERY WELL THEN, ALONE!

1. Evelyn Waugh, *Officers and Gentlemen* (London: Penguin Books, 1955), p. 111.
2. Todman, *Britain's War: Into Battle*, pp. 467–9.
3. Edgerton, *Britain's War Machine*, p. 56.
4. Edgerton, *Britain's War Machine*, p. 65.
5. Sherwood, p. 182.
6. Lee Windsor, Roger Sarty and Marc Milner, *Loyal Gunners: 3rd Field Regiment (The Loyal Company) and the History of New Brunswick Artillery, 1893–2012* (Waterloo, ON: Wilfrid Laurier UP, 2016), p. 247.
7. Dallek, *Roosevelt: A Political Life*, p. 391.
8. Olson, *Those Angry Days*, p. 264.
9. Hall, pp. 43–4.
10. Dallek, *Roosevelt: A Political Life*, p. 392.
11. Arnold Hague, *The Towns: A History of the Fifty Destroyers Transferred from the United States to Great Britain in 1940* (Kendal, England: The World Ship Society, 1988).
12. Captain S.W. Roskill, *The War at Sea*, vol. 1 (London: HMSO, 1954), p. 348.
13. Tooze, *The Wages of Destruction*, p. 89.
14. Sherwood, pp. 230–1.

15. Stacey, *Canada and the Age of Conflict*, vol. 2, pp. 311–12.
16. See the correspondence in Colonel Robert R. McCormick Research Center (hereafter MRC), McCormick Papers, I-60, 'OPC-Canadian Government, 1940–1948'. Stacey, *Canada and the Age of Conflict*, vol. 2, makes the same claim, p. 312.
17. Stacey, *Canada and the Age of Conflict*, vol. 2, p. 312.
18. Kennedy, *Freedom from Fear*, p. 459.
19. Todman, *Britain's War: Into Battle*, pp. 418–19.
20. Hall, p. 39.
21. Reynolds, *In Command of History*, p. 200.
22. Hall, p. 124.
23. David Zimmerman, *Top Secret Exchange: The Tizard Mission and the Scientific War* (Montreal/Kingston: McGill–Queens UP, 1996).
24. Winston S. Churchill, *Their Finest Hour* (Boston, MA: Houghton Mifflin, 1949), pp. 553–4.
25. David Reynolds, 'Lord Lothian and Anglo-American Relations, 1939–1940', *Transactions of the American Philosophical Society*, vol. 72, Part II, 1983, p. 42.
26. Martin Gilbert, *Churchill and America* (Toronto, ON: McClelland & Stewart, 2005), pp. 204–5.
27. Juliet Gardiner, *Wartime: Britain 1939–1945* (London: Headline, 2004), pp. 350–4.
28. Gardiner, p. 354.
29. Lynne Olson, *Citizens of London: How Britain Was Rescued in Its Darkest, Finest Hour* (Toronto: Anchor Canada, 2010), p. 50.
30. Olson, *Citizens of London*, p. 49.
31. Anthony Aldgate and Jeffrey Richard, *Britain Can Take It: British Cinema in the Second World War* (London: I.B. Tauris, 2007), pp. 120–2.
32. Angus Calder, *The Myth of the Blitz* (London: Pimlico, 1991).
33. Martin Doughty, *Merchant Shipping and War* (London: Royal Historical Society, 1982). See also Roosevelt Presidential Library, Hopkins Papers, Box 154G, 'Transportation in War', the text of a speech given by the Director General of the Minister of War Transport in June 1945.
34. 'The Preliminary Planning for Operation "OVERLORD": Some Aspects of the Canadian Preparations for an Allied Re-Entry to North-West Europe, 1940–1', Historical Section (G.S.), Army Headquarters, Report No. 42, 5 March 1952, p. 8 (hereafter AHQ Report No. 42).
35. Reynolds, *Lord Lothian*, pp. 52, 56.
36. Roosevelt Presidential Library, Hopkins Papers, Box 154G, 'Shipping Losses and Replacement', as passed to Harry Hopkins on 8 December 1940.
37. Reynolds, *In Command of History*, p. 202; Olson, *Those Angry Days*, p. 269. Reynolds, *Lord Lothian*, disputes the claim that Lothian ever uttered the words 'It's your money we want' or that Wheeler-Bennett was at the airport to hear them, see p. 48.
38. Churchill, *Their Finest Hour*, p. 559.
39. Olson, *Those Angry Days*, p. 271.
40. Olson, *Those Angry Days*, pp. 272–3.
41. Reynolds, *Lord Lothian*, p. 58.
42. Andrew Roberts, '*The Holy Fox*': *The Life of Lord Halifax* (London: Phoenix, 1997), pp. 272–3.

43. TNA, PREM 4/25/7 No. 133. Halifax's first telegrams concerning propaganda went out in early January, see his 24 April 1941 despatch, which refers to those telegrams.
44. Warren Kimball, *The Most Unsordid Act: Lend-Lease 1939–1941* (Baltimore, MD: Johns Hopkins UP, 1969), p. 143.
45. Darwin, p. 511.
46. Todman, *Britain's War: Into Battle*, p. 531.
47. TNA, PREM 4/25/7, Cooper to the Prime Minister, 29 November 1940, and Reves to Churchill, 20 December 1940.
48. Golway, pp. 158–9
49. Manchester and Reid, p. 221.
50. Dallek, *Roosevelt: A Political Life*, p. 405, emphasis added.
51. TNA, FO 953/7, 'History of British Information in the U.S.A.', by John Wheeler-Bennett and Aubrey Morgan, 1947, quotes p. 70.
52. Benn Steil, *The Battle of Breton Woods: John Maynard Keynes, Harry Dexter White and the Making of a New World Order* (Princeton, NJ: Princeton UP, 2013), p. 105.
53. Harold L. Ickes, *The Secret Diary of Harold L. Ickes* (New York: Simon & Schuster, 1954), vol. 3: *The Lowering Clouds, 1939–1941*, entry for 19 January 1941, p. 411.
54. Sherwood, p. 290.
55. Sherwood, p. 320.
56. Dallek, *Roosevelt: A Political Life*, p. 413.
57. MRC, McCormick Papers, 'Great Britain – General 1941–1945'. See for example a lengthy letter from 'Mrs McAdoo' in the spring of 1941, talking about the millions of American boys who would have to die to save the British Empire.
58. Kimball, p. 148.
59. Mira Wilkins, *The History of Foreign Investment in America, 1914–1945* (Cambridge, MA: Harvard University Press, 2004), p. 492.
60. Ickes, *Secret Diary*, vol. 3, puts the total of investment in new and expanded plants at $550 million. See p. 409.
61. Wilkins, p. 492.
62. Kimble, p. 147.
63. Kennedy, *Freedom from Fear*, p. 473.
64. Reynolds, *Lord Lothian*, p. 53.
65. Wilkins, p. 494.
66. Darwin, p. 512.
67. Steil, p. 108.
68. LAC, MG 26, N1, vol. 4, Grant Dexter Papers, Dexter Correspondence, Pearson to Dexter, 10 January 1941.
69. Sherwood, p. 272.
70. Ickes, *Secret Diary*, vol. 3, 2 February 1914.
71. Alanbrooke, *War Diaries*, 31 January 1941, postwar annotation.
72. David Day, *The Great Betrayal: Britain, Australia and the Onset of the Pacific War 1939–1942* (London: Angus & Robertson, 1988), p. 30.
73. David Day, *Menzies and Churchill at War* (London: Angus & Robertson, 1986), pp. 54–5.
74. Jeffrey Grey, *A Military History of Australia* (Cambridge: Cambridge UP, 2008), p. 160.

75. Day, *Menzies and Churchill at War*, p. 57.
76. Maurice Matloff and Edwin M. Snell, *Strategy for Coalition Warfare 1941–1942* (Washington, DC: Office of the Chief of Military History, 1953), p. 40.
77. Todman, *Britain's War: Into Battle*, p. 553.
78. Day, *Menzies and Churchill at War*, p. 129.
79. Todman, *Britain's War: Into Battle*, p. 565.
80. See also David Day, 'Anzacs on the Run: The View from Whitehall, 1941–2', *The Journal of Imperial and Commonwealth History*, vol. 14, no. 3, 1986, pp. 187–202.
81. John Colville, *The Fringes of Power: 10 Downing Street Diaries, 1939–1955* (New York: W.W. Norton & Co., 1985), entry for 28 April 1941, p. 378.
82. Andrew Roberts, *Masters and Commanders: How Roosevelt, Churchill, Marshall and Alanbrooke Won the War in the West* (London: Allen Lane, 2008), pp. 48–9.
83. Winston Churchill, *The Grand Alliance* (Boston, MA: Houghton Mifflin, 1951), p. 420–3: David French, *Raising Churchill's Army: The British Army and the War Against Germany 1919–1945* (Oxford: Oxford UP, 2000), pp. 185–7.
84. TNA, PREM 4/25/7, Washington to Foreign Office, 25 April 1941, No. 131, EMPAX.
85. For a description of these officers see *The London Journal of General Raymond E. Lee, 1940–41* (Boston, MA: Little, Brown and Co., 1971), entry for 8 January 1941.
86. Mark A. Stoler, *Allies and Adversaries: The Joint Chiefs of Staff, The Grand Alliance and U.S. Strategy in World War II* (Chapel Hill, NC: University of North Carolina Press, 2000). For FDR's position on an expeditionary force see p. 36; quote p. 32.
87. Stoler, p. 37.
88. Matloff and Snell, pp. 37, 41.
89. Matloff and Snell, p. 45.
90. Todman, *Britain's War: Into Battle*, p. 551.
91. Pope, pp. 165–6.
92. Stacey, *Canada and the Age of Conflict*, vol. 2, p. 159.
93. Matloff and Snell, p. 29.
94. Ickes, *Secret Diary*, vol. 3, entry for 8 March 1941.
95. Roskill, *The War at Sea*, vol. 1. See Appendix R: 'British, Allied and Neutral Merchant Ship Losses and Causes', pp. 615–16. Losses in both 1940 and 1941 were 2.7 million Gross Registered Tons (GRT).
96. Samuel E. Morison, *The Battle of the Atlantic, September 1939–May 1943* (Boston, MA: Little, Brown and Co., 1954), p. 54.
97. Morison, *The Battle of the Atlantic, September 1939–May 1943*, p. 57.
98. *The Mackenzie King Record* (Toronto, ON: University of Toronto Press, 1960), vol. 1, pp. 195–6.
99. TNA, PREM 4/25/7, undated memo from George Archibald forwarded to Churchill on 29 September 1941.
100. TNA, PREM, 4/25/7, Ronald Tree to Churchill, 3 June 1941.
101. Kennedy, *Freedom from Fear*, p. 491.
102. As quoted in Dallek, *Roosevelt: A Political Life*, p. 418.
103. Dallek, *Roosevelt: A Political Life*, pp. 418–19.
104. *New York Times*, 28 May 1941.
105. Todman, *Britain's War: Into Battle*, p. 578; Milner, *Battle of the Atlantic* (Stroud: Tempus, 2003), p. 54.

106. Dallek, *Roosevelt: A Political Life*, p. 421.
107. W.A.B. Douglas, Roger Sarty and Michael Whitby, *No Higher Purpose: The Official Operational History of the Royal Canadian Navy in the Second World War, 1939–1943*, vol. 2, Part I (St Catharines, ON: Vanwell Publishing, 2002), p. 183.
108. Data compiled from Ken Macpherson and Marc Milner, *Corvettes of the Royal Canadian Navy, 1939–1945* (St Catharines, ON: Vanwell Publishing, 1993).
109. Joseph Schull, *The Far Distant Ships* (Ottawa, ON: King's Printer, 1950), p. 122.
110. Interview with Captain E.S. Brand, RCN, Kanata, Ontario, 10 August 1981.
111. Marc Milner, *Canadian Naval Force Requirements in the Second World War* (Ottawa, ON: DND Operational Research and Analysis Establishment Extramural Paper No. 20, December 1981), p. 56.
112. Douglas, Sarty and Whitby, *No Higher Purpose*, p. 216.
113. Churchill College Archives, CLVL 1/6, Colville Diary, 4 June 1941, p. 394.
114. Churchill College Archives, CLVL 1/6, Colville Diary, 22 May 1941.
115. See Wikipedia, 'Soldatensender Calais', accessed online 7 November 2023, and Balfour, *Propaganda in War 1939–1945*, pp. 98–9.
116. Forsyth Hardy, *John Grierson: A Documentary Biography* (London: Faber & Faber, 1979), p. 95.
117. Jack C. Ellis, *John Grierson: Life, Contribution, Influence* (Carbondale and Edwardsville, IL: South Illinois UP, 2000), pp. 153–4.
118. Cull, p. 141.
119. Cull, p. 141.
120. Mike Bechtholdt, *Flying to Victory: Raymond Collishaw and the Western Desert Campaign 1940–1941* (Norman, OK: University of Oklahoma Press, 2017), pp. 164–5.
121. Correlli Barnett, *The Desert Generals* (Bloomington, IN: Indiana UP, 1982, revised edition), 'The Blunt Battleaxe'.
122. Manchester and Reid, p. 378.

CHAPTER 7: THANK THE JAPANESE

1. Waugh, *Officers and Gentlemen*, p. 117.
2. Anne Chisholm and Michael Davie, *Beaverbrook: A Life* (London: Hutchinson, 1992), p. 403.
3. Rene Kraus, *The Men Around Churchill* (Philadelphia: J.B. Lippincott, 1941), pp. 259–63.
4. Chisholm and Davie, p. 401.
5. Manchester and Reid, p. 382.
6. Chisholm and Davie, p. 402.
7. Peter Clarke, *The Cripps Version: The Life of Sir Stafford Cripps, 1889–1952* (London: Allen Lane, 2002), p. 222.
8. Manchester and Reid, p. 380.
9. Kennedy, *Freedom from Fear*, p. 480.
10. Sherwood, p. 375.
11. Kennedy, *Freedom from Fear*, p. 495.
12. Michael G. Carew, *Becoming the Arsenal: The American Industrial Mobilization for World War II, 1938–1942* (Lanham, MD: University Press of America, 2010), p. 187.

13. Kent Robert Greenfield, Robert R. Palmer and Bell I. Wiley, *The Organization of Ground Combat Troops* (Washington, DC: Center of Military History, 1987), p. 51.
14. Greenfield, Palmer and Wiley, pp. 36–46.
15. Roman Johan Jaromowycz, *Tank Tactics: From Normandy to Lorraine* (Boulder, CO: Lynne Rienner Publishers, 2001), p. 28.
16. Mark Calhoun, *General Lesley J. McNair* (Lawrence, KS: University Press of Kansas, 2015), p. 227.
17. Greenfield, Palmer and Wiley, pp. 60–83.
18. Major General J.B.A Bailey, *Fire Artillery and Firepower* (Annapolis, MD: USNI Press, 2004), p. 316.
19. See the discussion in Bailey, *Fire Artillery and Firepower*, Chapter 17, and the opening sections of Chapter 18.
20. Mark Stoler, *George C. Marshall: Soldier, Statesman of the American Century* (Boston, MA: Twayne Publishing, 1989), p. 82.
21. Sherwood, p. 376.
22. As quoted in Lynne Olson, *Those Angry Days*, p. 349.
23. J.L. Granatstein and R.D. Cuff, 'The Hyde Park Declaration 1941: Origins and Significance', in J.L. Granatstein, *Canada at War: Conscription, Diplomacy, and Politics* (Toronto, ON: University of Toronto Press, 2020), Chapter 9.
24. LAC, MG 26, N1, vol. 72, Lester B. Pearson Papers, 'Fifth Column Propaganda of the Axis in the United States, Volume Four covering February 15/42 to March 1/42', see Propaganda Targets, p. 3.
25. Kennedy, *History of Department of Munitions and Supply*, vol. 1, pp. 92–4; Law, chart on p. 27.
26. Chris Henry, *The 25-pounder Field Gun 1939–72* (Oxford: Osprey, 2002), p. 20.
27. Kennedy, *History of the Department of Munitions and Supply*, vol. 1, ammunition table p. 51, guns and small arms p. 205.
28. Kennedy, *History of the Department of Munitions and Supply*, p. 98. See also Doug Knight, *The 25-pounder in Canadian Service* (Ottawa, ON: Service Publications, 2005).
29. Sherwood, pp. 376–85.
30. Dallek, *Roosevelt: A Political Life*, p. 426.
31. See Roosevelt Presidential Library, Hopkins Papers, Box 156G, for correspondence related to the assembly of the ships.
32. Hague, p. 188.
33. Manchester and Reid, p. 395.
34. Manchester and Reid, p. 397.
35. Manchester and Reid, p. 397.
36. AHQ Report No. 42, p. 12.
37. Sherwood, as quoted in AHQ Report No. 42, p. 12.
38. Matloff and Snell, p. 61.
39. Manchester and Reid, p. 391.
40. Taylor, p. 481.
41. His Naval Minister, Angus L. MacDonald, informed him on 7 July 1941, *The Mackenzie King Record*, vol. 1, p. 226.
42. *The Mackenzie King Record*, vol. 1, p. 235.
43. *The Mackenzie King Record*, vol. 1, p. 249.

44. LAC, MG 27, J4, Mackenzie King Papers, reel no. H1519, text of speech to the Canadian Club of Montreal, John Grierson, 17 February 1941.

45. Cull, p. 147.

46. TNA, FO 953/7, 'History of British Information', p. 20.

47. TNA, FO 953/7, 'History of British Information', p. 27.

48. Ian McLaine, *The Ministry of Morale: Home Front Morale and the Ministry of Information in World War II* (London: George Allen & Unwin, 1979), pp. 217, 235.

49. Mariel Grant, 'Towards a Central Office of Information: Continuity and Change in British Government Information Policy, 1939–51', *Journal of Contemporary History*, vol. 34, no. 1, January 1999, p. 51.

50. Andrew Boyle, *Poor, Dear Brendan: The Quest for Brendan Bracken* (London: Hutchinson, 1974), p. 268.

51. Evelyn Waugh, *Put Out More Flags* (London: Chapman and Hill, 1942).

52. Boyle, *Poor, Dear Brendan*, p. 266.

53. McLaine, pp. 240–1.

54. TNA, FO 953/7, 'History of British Information', p. 36.

55. Cull, pp. 147–9.

56. *British Security Coordination: The Secret History of British Intelligence in the Americas*, pp. 69–78.

57. LAC, MG 26, N1, vol. 72, Pearson Papers, *Washington Star*, 24 September 1941, clipping.

58. Olson, *Those Angry Days*, pp. 337–9.

59. Sydney Weinberg, 'What to Tell America: The Writers' Quarrel in the Office of War Information', *Journal of American History*, vol. 55, no. 1, June 1968, p. 75.

60. Justin Hart, *Empire of Ideas: The Origins of Public Diplomacy and the Transformation of U.S. Foreign Policy* (Oxford: Oxford UP, 2013), pp. 76, 78. See especially his Chapter 3.

61. TNA, FO 953/7, 'History of British Information', p. 67.

62. Weinberg, p. 76.

63. Hart, p. 76.

64. Hart, p. 78.

65. Hart, p. 78.

66. Patrick Abbazia, *Mr Roosevelt's Navy: The Private War of the U.S. Atlantic Fleet, 1939–1942* (Annapolis, MD: USNI Press, 1975), pp. 249–50.

67. Tooze, *The Wages of Destruction*, makes frequent mention of German anxiety over the potential of Allied airpower, see for example pp. 409–10.

68. Charles Messenger, *Bomber Harris and the Strategic Bombing Offensive, 1939–1945* (London: Arms and Armour Press, 1984), pp. 49–51.

69. Messenger, pp. 50–1.

70. Taylor, p. 487.

71. Todman, *Britain's War: Into Battle*, pp. 690–3.

72. Sherwood, p. 470.

73. Charles Ritchie, *The Siren Years: A Canadian Diplomat Abroad, 1937–1945* (Markham, ON: Fitzhenry & Whiteside, 1974), p. 185.

74. Kenneth Young, *Churchill and Beaverbrook: A Study in Friendship and Politics* (London: Eyre & Spottiswoode, 1966), pp. 214–15.

75. Young, p. 214.

76. Swettenham, vol. 2, p. 164.

77. Quotes from Stacey, *Six Years of War*, p. 297; Swettenham, vol. 2, on p. 184 notes Brooke's agreement.
78. Churchill, *The Grand Alliance*, p. 540.
79. Bidwell and Graham, *Fire-Power*, Chapter 13.
80. Barnett, *The Desert Generals*, p. 88.
81. Barnett, *The Desert Generals*, p. 149.
82. Library of Congress, Eugene Meyer Papers, 'Address on Trip to England to Post Staff', 27 October 1941.
83. Kennedy, *Freedom from Fear*, p. 506.
84. Paul Dickson, *A Thoroughly Canadian General: A Biography of General H.D.G. Crerar* (Toronto, ON: University of Toronto Press, 2007), pp. 164–8.
85. Stacey, *Six Years of War*, pp. 440–1.
86. Franco David Macri, 'C Force to Hong Kong: The Price of Collective Security in China, 1941', *Journal of Military History*, vol. 77, no. 1, January 2013, p. 152.
87. Howe to Ralston, 15 November 1941, as quoted in Macri, p. 153.
88. Stacey, *Six Years of War*, pp. 443–4.
89. Roskill, *The War at Sea*, vol. 1, pp. 554–8.
90. Reynolds, *In Command of History*, p. 263.
91. TNA, PREM 4/27/9, Lord Halifax to Churchill, 11 October 1941.
92. Taylor, p. 502.
93. Ira Katznelson, *Fear Itself: The New Deal and the Origins of Our Time* (New York: Liveright, 2013), pp. 152–5, 315–16.
94. TNA, PREM 4/27/9, Halifax to Churchill, 11 October 1941.
95. Maddow, p. 213.
96. Cull, p. 175.
97. TNA, FO 953/7, 'History of British Information', pp. 43–5.
98. Manchester and Reid, p. 422.
99. Kennedy, *Freedom from Fear*, p. 524.

CHAPTER 8: GYMNAST TO RUTTER

1. *The Papers of Dwight David Eisenhower: The War Years* (Baltimore, MD: Johns Hopkins UP, 1970) (hereafter *Eisenhower Papers*), vol. 1, p. 207, emphasis in the original.
2. Alanbrooke, *War Diaries*, 20 December 1941.
3. Tony Heathcote, *The British Field Marshals, 1736–1997* (Barnsley: Pen and Sword, 1999), p. 104.
4. Alanbrooke, *War Diaries*, 11 December 1941.
5. Edgerton, *Britain's War Machine*, Chapter 3 *passim*.
6. TNA, FO 953/7, 'History of British Information', pp. 39–40.
7. Carew, p. 210.
8. For extensive extracts from the Joint Board Estimates of September 1941 see Sherwood, pp. 495–505.
9. Roosevelt Presidential Library, Hopkins Papers, 'Biennial Report of the Chief of Staff of the United States Army, July 1, 1941 to June 30, 1943', p. 12.
10. Matloff and Snell, p. 108.
11. Ashley Jackson, *Persian Gulf Command: A History of the Second World War in Iran and Iraq* (New Haven, CT and London: Yale UP, 2018).

12. Trumbull Higgins, *Churchill and the Second Front, 1940–1943* (New York: Oxford UP, 1957), p. 85.
13. John Shy, 'Jomini', in Peter Paret, ed., *Makers of Modern Strategy* (Princeton, NJ: Princeton UP, 1986), pp. 143–85.
14. *Eisenhower Papers*, vol. 1, p. 66.
15. See Ronald Schaffer, 'General Stanley D. Embick: Military Dissenter', *Military Affairs*, vol. 37, no. 3 (October 1973), pp. 89–95.
16. Mark A. Stoler, *Allies and Adversaries* (Chapel Hill, NC: University of North Carolina Press, 2000), p. 71.
17. TNA, PREM 4/27/9, Halifax to Churchill, 11 October 1941.
18. Matloff and Snell, p. 112.
19. Matloff and Snell, p. 101.
20. AHQ Report No. 42, p. 21.
21. Chisholm and Davie, p. 425.
22. Taylor, p. 503.
23. Jim Lacey, *Keep from All Thoughtful Men: How U.S. Economists Won World War II* (Annapolis, MD: USNI Press, 2011), pp. 88–9. Chapter 7, 'War and Feasibility', is an essential study of the links between what the US Staff wanted and what American industry was capable of.
24. Parliamentary Archives, Beaverbrook Papers, BBK/D/182, 'Notes on Trip to Washington at the End of 1941'. See also Lacey, p. 83.
25. *Industrial Mobilization for War: History of the War Production Board and Predecessor Agencies, 1940–1945*, Government of the United States, vol. 1, p. 277; Chisholm and Davie, p. 425.
26. Alanbrooke, *War Diaries*, annotation for entry of 29 December 1941.
27. Higgins, p. 87.
28. Manchester and Reid, pp. 491–2.
29. Roskill, *The War at Sea*, vol. 2, pp. 149–60, quote from pp. 159–60.
30. *The Oxford Companion to the Second World War*, ed. I.C.B. Dear and M.R.D. Foot (Oxford: Oxford UP, 1995), 'Singapore', pp. 1009–10.
31. Manchester and Reid, p. 487.
32. Manchester and Reid, p. 489.
33. Chisholm and Davie, pp. 430–2.
34. Roosevelt Presidential Library, Hopkins Papers, Box 134, *The Round Table*, December 1941.
35. Roosevelt Presidential Library, Early Papers, Box 24, Bill Donovan, Director of COI, to FDR, 18 February 1942.
36. LAC, MG 26, N1, vol. 72, Pearson Papers, 'Fifth Column Propaganda of the Axis in the United States', vol. 4, 15 February–1 March 1942.
37. LAC, MG 26, N1, vol. 72, Pearson Papers, 'Fifth Column Propaganda of the Axis in the United States', vol. 6, 8–22 March 1942.
38. LAC, MG 26, N1, vol. 72, Pearson Papers, 'Fifth Column Propaganda of the Axis in the United States', vol. 5, 1–8 March 1942.
39. Maddow, p. 155.
40. MRC, McCormick Papers, 'Great Britain – General 1941–1946', I-60, George E. Mann to Robert McCormick, February 1942.
41. John Charmley, *Churchill's Grand Alliance: The Anglo-American Special Relationship 1940–1957* (New York: Harcourt Brace, 1995), pp. 50–6.

42. Charmley, p. 55.
43. Charmley, p. 53.
44. *Fortune* magazine, vol. 25, no. 4, April 1942.
45. *Fortune* magazine, vol. 25, no. 4, April 1942.
46. Charmley, pp. 51–5.
47. The Halifax Papers are at the Borthwick Institute for Historical Research, University of York (BIHR). See entry for 8 March 1942.
48. Cull, pp. 191–3.
49. NARA, RG 208, Entry 362, Box 817, 'FIS Directive, England I, March 16–23', Directive No. 7, approved on 11 March 1942.
50. LAC, MG 26, N1, vol. 72, Pearson Papers, unsigned memo of 6 March 1942.
51. Swettenham, vol. 2, pp. 190–6.
52. *The Eisenhower Diaries*, ed. Robert Ferrell (New York: Norton, 1981), 9 March 1942.
53. Stoler, *Allies and Adversaries*, p. 76.
54. Sherwood, vol. 2, pp. 515, 523, as quoted in AHQ Report No. 42, p. 23.
55. AHQ Report No. 42, pp. 23–6.
56. Churchill, *The Second World War*, vol. 4, p. 323.
57. Lacey, *Keep from All Thoughtful Men*, Chapter 8.
58. Higgins, p. 69.
59. Pope, pp. 187–8.
60. Pope, p. 197.
61. Alanbrooke, *War Diaries*, 9–13 April 1942.
62. Chisholm and Davie, pp. 430–5.
63. Taylor, p. 525.
64. Chisholm and Davie, p. 434.
65. Parliamentary Archives, Beaverbrook Papers, BBK/D/451, 'Draft Second Front History', p. 38.
66. Chisholm and Davie, pp. 434–5.
67. Parliamentary Archives, Beaverbrook Papers, BBK/D/451, 'Draft Second Front History', p. 39.
68. Taylor, p. 529.
69. Roskill, *The War at Sea*, vol. 2, pp. 185–90.
70. Stacey, *Six Years of War*, p. 329.
71. *Daily Express*, 20 June 1942.
72. *Daily Express*, 16 June 1942.
73. *Daily Express*, 24 June 1942, emphasis added.
74. Mark Zuehlke, *Tragedy at Dieppe: Operation Jubilee, August 19, 1942* (Toronto, ON: Douglas and McIntyre, 2012), p. 104.
75. Zuehlke, *Tragedy at Dieppe*, p. 108.
76. As quoted in Taylor, p. 536.
77. Zuehlke, *Tragedy at Dieppe*, p. 114.
78. Stacey, *Six Years of War*, p. 337. See also LAC, MG 30, E463, 165–6, Hughes-Hallett's unpublished memoir.
79. Stacey, *Six Years of War*, p. 338.
80. Stacey, *Six Years of War*, p. 338.
81. Dixon, pp. 203–4.

CHAPTER 9: JUBILEE TO TORCH

1. BIHR, Lord Halifax Papers, A7.8.19, Secret Diary, entry for 15 July 1942.
2. Henry L. Stimson and McGeorge Bundy, *On Active Service in Peace and War* (New York: Hutchinson, n.d.), pp. 219–22.
3. Forrest Pogue, *George C. Marshall*, vol. 2: *Ordeal and Hope, 1939–1942* (New York: Viking, 1987), p. 341.
4. James J. Kimble, *Mobilizing the Home Front: War Bonds and Domestic Propaganda* (College Station, TX: Texas A&M UP, 2006), p. 45.
5. Roosevelt Papers, Hyde Park, see 'FDR Office File, Second Front'.
6. Nancy Beck Young, *Why We Fight: Congress and the Politics of World War II* (Manhattan, KS: University Press of Kansas, 2013), p. 75.
7. Alanbrooke, *War Diaries*, 18 July 1942.
8. Lucian Truscott, *Command Mission* (New York: Arno Press, 1954), p. 49.
9. Pogue, *Marshall: Ordeal and Hope*, p. 344.
10. Lacey, *Keep from All Thoughtful Men*, p. 125.
11. Truscott, p. 37.
12. Lacey, *Keep From All Thoughtful Men*, p. 120.
13. Compiled from Shelby L. Stanton, *World War II Order of Battle* (New York: Galahad Books, 1984).
14. Kevin Smith, *Conflict Over Convoys: Anglo-American Logistics Diplomacy in the Second World War* (Cambridge: Cambridge UP, 1996), p. 68. See also C.B.A. Behrens, *Merchant Shipping and the Demands of War* (London: HMSO and Longmans, Green and Co., 1955), p. 291.
15. Frederic C. Lane, *Ships for Victory: A History of Shipbuilding Under the U.S. Maritime Commission in World War II* (Baltimore, MD: Johns Hopkins UP, 1951), p. 43.
16. Lane, pp. 27–32.
17. Hall, p. 397.
18. Smith, p. 76.
19. Smith, pp. 74–5.
20. Smith, pp. 81–2.
21. Smith, p. 74.
22. Milner, *Canadian Naval Force Requirements in the Second World War*.
23. See Roskill, *The War at Sea*, vol. 1, Appendix R, and vol. 2, Appendix O.
24. Milner, *Battle of the Atlantic*, see Chapter 4.
25. NARA, RG 208, Entry 363, Box 817, FIS and OWI Directives, OWI Directives 1942–43.
26. See Allan M. Winkler, *The Politics of Propaganda: The Office of War Information, 1942–1945* (New Haven, CT and London: Yale UP, 1978), pp. 49–51.
27. Morison, *The Battle of the Atlantic, September 1939–May 1943*, p. 199.
28. Kennedy, *Freedom from Fear*, p. 569.
29. Rob Fisher, 'We'll Get Our Own: Canada and the Oil Shipping Crisis of 1942', *The Northern Mariner*, vol. 3, no. 2, April 1993, pp. 33–9.
30. Kennedy, *Freedom from Fear*, p. 569.
31. Montgomery Meigs, *Slide Rules and Submarines* (Washington, DC: National Defense UP, 1990), pp. 93–4.
32. Phillips Payson O'Brien, *How the War Was Won: Air-Sea Power and Allied Victory in World War II* (Cambridge: Cambridge UP, 2015), pp. 51–8.

33. Figures compiled from Jürgen Rohwer, *Axis Submarine Successes 1939–1945* (Annapolis, MD: USNI Press, 1983).
34. Alanbrooke, *War Diaries*, 20 July 1942.
35. John Campbell, *Dieppe Revisited: A Documentary Investigation* (London: Frank Cass, 1993), p. 81. The British had only 521 landing craft of all types in service by the end of 1942. See Table 12 in Hall, *North American Supply*, p. 401.
36. Captain Harry C. Butcher, USNR, *My Three Years with Eisenhower* (New York: Simon & Schuster, 1946), p. 28.
37. Butcher, p. 29.
38. Jim Lacey, *The Washington War: FDR's Inner Circle and the Politics of Power that Won World War II* (New York: Bantam Books, 2019), p. 275.
39. Lacey, *The Washington War*, p. 276.
40. *Time* magazine, 10 August 1942, pp. 30–1. Copy in LAC, MG 33, E133, vol. 145, PR.
41. Campbell, pp. 80–1.
42. Campbell, p. 66.
43. Truscott, p. 55.
44. Brian Loring Villa, *Unauthorized Action: Mountbatten and the Dieppe Raid* (Toronto, ON: Oxford UP, 1990), p. 87.
45. *The Memoirs of Field Marshal the Viscount Montgomery of Alamein, K.G.* (London: Collins, 1958), p. 76.
46. Tim Balzar, *The Information Front* (Vancouver, BC: University of British Columbia Press, 2011), pp. 92–4.
47. Villa, p. 94.
48. Balfour, *Propaganda in War 1939–1945*, p. 280.
49. Robert Bruce Lockhart, *Comes the Reckoning* (London: Putnam, 1947), pp. 190–1.
50. *Eisenhower Papers*, vol. 1, cable to General A.L. Surles, 20 August 1942, p. 484.
51. Balzar, p. 101.
52. *Washington Despatches 1941–1945: Weekly Political Reports from the British Embassy*, ed. H.G. Nicholas (Chicago, IL: University of Chicago Press, 1981).
53. See the introduction to David Garnett's *The Secret History of PWE: The Political Warfare Executive 1939–1945* (London: St Ermin's Press, 2002).
54. Winkler, p. 50.
55. Clayton D. Laurie, *The Propaganda Warriors: America's Crusade Against Nazi Germany* (Lawrence, KS: University Press of Kansas, 1996), p. 110.
56. Laurie, pp. 88–96.
57. NARA, RG 208, Box 3, E6H, Warburg's Chapter 11, 'Information, Propaganda and Political Warfare'.
58. NARA, RG 208, Box 3, E6H, Records of the Historian of OWI, Chapter 7, 'Outposts'.
59. *Washington Despatches* report of 14 May 1942, p. 38.
60. NARA, RG 208, Box 3, E6H, Records of the Historian, Chapter 7, 'Outposts', p. 7,
61. NARA, RG 208, Box 817, E363, General Directive for India, 3/08/42, and India Directive 10/10/42, in Records of the OWI, Miscellaneous Directives, August 1942–June 1943.
62. John B. Hench, *Books as Weapons: Propaganda, Publishing, and the Battle for Global Markets in the Era of World War II* (Ithaca, NY and London: Cornell UP, 2010), p. 56.

63. Hench, p. 27.
64. Calder, *The People's War*, p. 511.
65. Calder, *The People's War*, p. 513.
66. Hench, p. 220.
67. Hench, p. 71.
68. TNA, FO 953/7, 'History of British Information', pp. 51–64.
69. TNA, FO 953/7, 'History of British Information', p. 70.
70. Jackson, *Persian Gulf Command*, p. 327.
71. LAC, RG 36/31, CIPO, August 1942–September 1943, 'An Analysis of American Public Opinion Regarding the War: A Confidential Report by George Gallup', 10 September 1942.
72. *Daily Express*, 'How Good Is Our Army?', 2 July 1942.
73. Major General I.S.O. Playfair, *The Mediterranean and Middle East*, vol. 3: *September 1941–September 1942): British Fortunes Reach Their Lowest Ebb* (London: HMSO, 1960), p. 371. Kennedy, *History of the Department of Munitions and Supply*, notes that in 1942 Canada shipped 140,000 vehicles. See vol. 1, pp. 94–5.
74. Quotes from Robert R. Palmer, 'Reorganization of Ground Forces for Combat', in Greenfield, Palmer and Wiley, *The Organization of Ground Combat Troops* (Washington, DC: CMH, 2004 edition), p. 273.
75. Calhoun, p. 224.
76. Greenfield, Palmer and Wiley, pp. 286–7.
77. Greenfield, Palmer and Wiley, p. 281.
78. Greenfield, Palmer and Wiley, p. 52.
79. Greenfield, Palmer and Wiley, p. 281.
80. Richard M. Leighton and Robert W. Coakley, *Global Logistics and Strategy: 1940–1943* (Washington, DC: CMH, 1995), p. 360.
81. Leighton and Coakley, p. 377. Matloff and Snell claim a figure of 2,500, most of which were larger vessels and tank carriers, as a minimum, see p. 192.
82. Matloff and Snell, pp. 192–3; see also Leighton and Coakley, p. 379.
83. Leighton and Coakley, p. 380.
84. Leighton and Coakley, vol. 1, p. 417.
85. Paul M. Atkins, 'Dakar and the Strategy of West Africa', *Foreign Affairs*, vol. 20, no. 2, Jan. 1942, pp. 359–66.
86. Butcher, diary entry for 15 June 1944, p. 582.
87. Rick Atkinson, *An Army at Dawn: The War in North Africa, 1942–1943* (New York: Owl Books, 2002), p. 29.
88. Robert Bruce Lockhart, *The Diaries of Robert B. Lockhart*, vol. 2: *1939–1945* (London: MacMillan, 1980), 28 September 1942.
89. Calder, *The People's War*, pp. 498–509.
90. Steil, p. 5.
91. Steil, pp. 126–9.
92. For a summary of the two plans, see Steil, pp. 151–3; quotes from pp. 152, 153.
93. Playfair, *The Mediterranean and Middle East*, vol. 3, p. 371.
94. *New York Times*, 'Axis Line Dented', 25 October 1942.
95. *New York Times*, 'War News Summarized', 1 November 1942.
96. *New York Times*, 6 and 7 November 1942.

CHAPTER 10: TORCH TO SPARTAN

1. Sherwood, vol. 2, p. 254.
2. Stanley Weintraub, *Final Victory: FDR's Extraordinary World War II Presidential Campaign* (New York: Da Capo Press, 2012), p. 75.
3. *Washington Despatches*, special election survey, 21 November 1942.
4. Vincent P. O'Hara, *TORCH: North Africa and the Allied Path to Victory* (Annapolis, MD: USNI Press, 2015), p. 107.
5. Rohwer, *Axis Submarine Successes*, see Mediterranean entries for 8–12 November 1942.
6. O'Hara, p. 109.
7. Walter Scott Dunn, Jr., *Second Front Now 1943* (Tuscaloosa, AL: University of Alabama Press, 1980), p. 71.
8. O'Hara, pp. 119–23.
9. Atkinson, *An Army at Dawn*, p. 103.
10. O'Hara, pp. 144–69.
11. See O'Hara, Chapter 12, for an excellent account of the Battle of Casablanca.
12. Sherwood, vol. 2, p. 253.
13. Atkinson, *An Army at Dawn*, p. 150.
14. O'Hara, p. 263.
15. Playfair, vol. 4, pp. 165–73.
16. John P. Downing, *At War with the British* (privately published, 1980), p. 138.
17. Playfair, vol. 4, p. 105.
18. For a succinct discussion of the role of intelligence in this phase of the North African campaign see F.H. Hinsley, *British Intelligence in the Second World War* (abridged edition) (Cambridge: Cambridge UP, 1993), Chapter 14.
19. NARA, RG 208, E363 Box 817, OWI 'German Directive', 8 November 1942.
20. NARA, RG 208, E363 Box 817, OWI Directive on Germany, week of 15 November.
21. NARA, RG 208, E363 Box 817, OWI Central Directive 'A', 7 November 1942.
22. Sherwood, vol. 2, p. 254; No. 6 Commando, Royal Marines, wore US Army uniforms for the landings, see Mike Chappell, *Army Commandos 1940–1945* (Oxford: Osprey, 1996), p. 59.
23. Churchill College Archives, AVHL I 2-16, Professor A.V. Hill Papers, 'Appendix I. Shipping Statistics', spring of 1943, for the most comprehensive accounting of the shipping situation.
24. Christopher Bell, *Churchill and Seapower* (Oxford: Oxford UP, 2013), p. 266.
25. Figures from Bell, pp. 269–70; quote from p. 270.
26. See Behrens, Chapter 14, and R.M. Leighton, 'US Merchant Shipping and the British Import Crisis', pp. 199–223.
27. Marc Milner, *North Atlantic Run: The Royal Canadian Navy and the Battle for the Convoys* (Toronto, ON: University of Toronto Press, 1985), p. 195.
28. Bell, Chapter 9.
29. LAC, RG 24, vol. 6796, NS 8375-4, Roosevelt to Churchill, 18 December 1942; the Pray memo is in TNA, MT 63/70.
30. Bell, Chapter 9.
31. DHH, *Admiralty Monthly Anti-Submarine Report*, January 1943. Some 80 per cent of mid-Atlantic losses from July to December 1942 occurred to Canadian escorted slow convoys.

32. Milner, *Canadian Naval Forces Requirements in the Second World War*, pp. 56–60.
33. Milner, *North Atlantic Run*, Chapter 7.
34. Milner, *North Atlantic Run*, p. 197.
35. Douglas, Sarty and Whitby, *No Higher Purpose*, p. 581.
36. Marc Milner, 'The Royal Canadian Navy's Participation in the Battle of the Atlantic Crisis of 1943', *The RCN in Retrospect, 1910–1968* (Vancouver, BC: University of British Columbia Press, 1982), pp. 158–74.
37. Public Archives of Nova Scotia, Angus L. Macdonald Papers, Diary entry 24 December 1942.
38. *The Memoirs of General the Lord Ismay* (London: Heinemann, 1960), p. 298.
39. BIHR, Lord Halifax Papers, A7.8.19, Secret Diary, 15 December 1942.
40. LAC, MG 30, E133, vol. 249, McNaughton Diary, notes on meeting with Lt General Paget, 10 February 1943.
41. [George Catlett Marshall], *The Papers of George Catlett Marshall*, vol. 3, ed. Larry I. Bland and Sharon Ritenour Stevens (Baltimore, MD: Johns Hopkins UP, 1991), editors' annotation, p. 514.
42. [Marshall], *The Papers of George Catlett Marshall*, vol. 3, pp. 514–15.
43. Ismay, pp. 285–6.
44. Alex Danchev, *Very Special Relationship: Field Marshal Sir John Dill and the Anglo-American Alliance 1941–44* (London: Brassey's, 1986), p. 114. Chapter 6 is titled 'Broker'.
45. Albert C. Wedemeyer, *Wedemeyer Reports!* (New York: Henry Holt & Co., 1958), p. 192.
46. Alanbrooke, *War Diaries*, annotation following entry for 20 January 1943.
47. Wedemeyer, pp. 212–13.
48. LAC, MG 30, E133, vol. 249, McNaughton Papers, 'Memorandum on Strength Estimate of First Canadian Army by 31 August 1943', First Canadian Army Staff meeting, 16 Februrary 1943, Appendix R to February Diary.
49. Major L.F. Ellis, *Victory in the West*, vol. 1: *The Battle of Normandy* (London: HMSO, 1962), p. 302.
50. LAC, MG 31, E42, vol. 3, Swettenham's notes, 15 December 1965, contain the following, 'Did combined trg with Americans (Bradley) but British squeezed us out of that!'
51. Lt Col. G.W.L. Nicholson, *The Canadians in Italy 1943–1945* (Ottawa, ON: Queen's Printer, 1967), p. 24.
52. LAC, MG 30, E133, vol. 249, McNaughton Diary, January 1943, Appendix F, 'Memorandum of Conversation with Brig. Simpson D.D.M.O.(O) WO, 11:30 hrs, 6 Jan 43'.
53. LAC, MG 30, E133, vol. 249, McNaughton Diary, January 1943, Appendix F, 'Memorandum of Conversation with Brig. Simpson D.D.M.O.(O) WO, 11:30 hrs, 6 Jan 43', and 'Minutes of Meeting with Alan Brooke', 6 January 1943.
54. *The Mackenzie King Record*, 'Lt General Stuart Report to the Canadian War Committee of Cabinet, 4 March 1943', p. 494.
55. DHH 010.013 (D5), 'The Invasion of Normandy: Planning Phase', Cabinet Office Narrative by Lt Col. H.A. Pollock, DSC, n.d., p. 21.
56. LAC, MG 30, E133, vol. 249, McNaughton Diary, Appendix I, 'Memorandum of discussion General McNaughton – General Paget', 10 February 1943.
57. Maj. Gen. Sir Charles Loewen, *Memoirs*, vol. 1 (Toronto, ON: privately published, 1985), p. 241. I am grateful to Robin Brass for the loan of his copy.

58. Pollock Narrative, p. 25.
59. John N. Rickard, 'The Test of Command: McNaughton and Exercise "Spartan", 4–12 March 1943', *Canadian Military History*, vol 8, issue 3, Summer 1999, p. 7.
60. Dickson, pp. 213–18.
61. Rickard, 'The Test of Command', p. 7.
62. As quoted in Rickard, 'The Test of Command', p. 7
63. DHH 545.033(D1), 'G.H.Q. Exercise "Spartan"; Comments by Commander-in-Chief Home Forces', March 1943.
64. 'The Strategic Role of First Canadian Army, 1942–1944', CMHQ Report No. 182, 23 May 1949, pp. 51–2.
65. Stacey, *Canada and the Age of Conflict*, vol. 2, pp. 330–2.
66. Stacey, *Arms, Men and Government*, pp. 277–82.
67. Greenhous et al., p. 52.
68. Chubby Power, *A Party Politician: The Memoirs of Chubby Power* (Toronto, ON: Macmillan, 1966), pp. 227–8.
69. Power, *A Party Politician*, p. 226.
70. Stacey, *Arms, Men and Government*, p. 267.
71. Stacey, *Arms, Men and Government*, p. 284.
72. Greenhous et al., pp. 58–9.
73. University of Toronto Archives, Massey Papers, Vincent Massey Diary, 28 January 1943.
74. University of Toronto Archives, Massey Papers, Massey Diary, 28 January 1943.
75. Stacey, *Arms, Men and Government*, see Appendix K for the full text of the letter.
76. There is nothing in Brooke's diary about the battle over Canadianisation, just the more general statement of frustration over the Canadians in the 21 July 1943 entry.
77. Douglas, Sarty and Whitby, *No Higher Purpose*, pp. 594–5.
78. Douglas, Sarty and Whitby, *No Higher Purpose*, p. 623.
79. See W.A.B. Douglas and Jürgen Rohwer, '"The Most Thankless Task Revisited": Convoys, Escorts and Radio Intelligence in the Western Atlantic, 1941–43', in J.A. Boutilier, ed., *The RCN in Retrospect, 1910–1968* (Vancouver, BC: University of British Columbia Press, 1982), pp. 187–234.
80. TNA, FO 371/36603, 'The Post-War Position of the British Commonwealth of Nations', 23 February 1943.
81. LAC, MG 31, E42, vol. 3, Swettenham Papers, pencilled notes.
82. LAC, MG 30, E133, vol. 249, McNaughton Diary, entries for 16 and 26 February 1943.

CHAPTER 11: COSSAC

1. *Eisenhower Papers*, vol. 2, Eisenhower to Marshall, 5 April 1943.
2. LAC, MG 26, J4, vol. 406, Mackenzie King Papers, 'War Strategy Pt 1', microfilm pp. C287422–C287423, text of intercept on 30 January 1943 by British intelligence.
3. Christopher Rein, 'Fredendall's Failure: A Reexamination of the II Corps at the Battle of Kasserine Pass', *Army History*, Summer 2018, p. 11.
4. Carlo D'Este, *Eisenhower: A Soldier's Life* (New York: Henry Holt & Co., 2002), p. 393.
5. Hinsley, *British Intelligence* (abridged edition), pp. 273–6; Atkinson, *An Army at Dawn*, pp. 319–20.

6. D'Este, *Eisenhower*, p. 393.
7. Omar Bradley, *A Soldier's Story* (New York: Popular Library, 1951), p. 52.
8. As quoted in D'Este, *Eisenhower*, p. 394.
9. D'Este, *Eisenhower*, p. 394.
10. Nigel Hamilton, *Master of the Battlefield: Monty's War Years 1942–1944* (New York: McGraw Hill, 1983), see Chapter 3, quote from p. 170.
11. Atkinson, *An Army at Dawn*, pp. 159–60.
12. D'Este, *Eisenhower*, p. 394.
13. D'Este, *Eisenhower*, p. 395.
14. Bradley, *A General's Life*, p. 159.
15. TNA, FO 371/35920, Lord Halifax, telegram no. 54, 22 February 1943.
16. LAC, MG 26, J4, vol. 406, Mackenzie King Papers, 'WSC Pt 2: Post-War Planning', microfilm pp. C164307 to C164319, 'Sequels to Mr. Churchill's Broadcast of March 21'.
17. *New York Times*, 'US–British Talks on India Progress', 22 February 1943.
18. LAC, MG 30, E133, vol. 146, Canadian Press Summaries, no. 7, 16/17 February 1943.
19. MRC, McCormick Papers, Box 36, 'Great Britain-General 1941–1946', see correspondence from January 1944.
20. LAC, MG 30, E133, vol. 146, Canadian Press Summaries, no. 11, 9 March 1943.
21. Lockhart, *Diaries*, vol. 2: *1939–1945*, 19–20 June 1943, p. 242.
22. Manchester and Reid, p. 652.
23. Manchester and Reid, p. 657.
24. Manchester and Reid, quotes p. 652 and p. 657.
25. LAC, MG 26, J4, vol. 406, Mackenzie King Papers, 'War Strategy Pt 1', 'Employment of Canadian Army', memo to Under-Secretary of External Affairs from A.H. Heeney, 28 January 1943, microfilm pp. 287412-14. The quote was a corruption of Henry's words crafted by Voltaire to make it more succinct.
26. Lacey, *Keep from All Thoughtful Men*, see especially Chapter 10, 'Why Marshall Changed His Mind'.
27. NARA, RG 208, E363, Box 817, Central Directives January to March 1943, especially 26 March–2 April 1943, 'Sea War'.
28. Churchill College Archives, AVHL I/216, Professor A.V. Hill Papers, 'Notes on Shipping and the U-Boat Campaign', n.d.
29. Leighton and Coakley, pp. 681–2.
30. Leighton and Coakley, pp. 698–71.
31. Leighton and Coakley, p. 694.
32. Figures compiled from Behrens, Appendix LXVII, 'British and American net gains (+) or losses (-)', p. 293.
33. Leighton and Coakley, p. 680.
34. Smith, *Conflict over Convoys*, p. 174.
35. Douglas et al, *The Creation of a National Air Force*, pp. 538–51.
36. LAC, MG 30, E133, vol. 249, McNaughton Diary, March 1943, Appendix R, 26 'Memo of Meeting with Lt Gen. Sir Archibald Nye, VCIGS, 16 March'.
37. LAC, Diaries of William Lyon Mackenzie King (hereafter Mackenzie King Diary), 4 and 7 April 1943, accessed online.
38. University of Toronto Archives, Massey Papers, Massey Diary, 19 April 1943.
39. See Hector MacKenzie, '"Little Lend-Lease": The American Impact on Canada's Mutual Aid Program', in Paul D. Dickson, ed., *1943: The Beginning of the End*

(Waterloo, ON: Canadian Committee for the History of the Second World War/ Laurier Centre for Military, Strategic and Disarmament Studies, 1995), pp. 83–106.

40. LAC, MG 30, E133, vol. 249, McNaughton Diary, April 1943, see Appendix PP.

41. Atkinson, *An Army at Dawn*, p. 477.

42. Marshall admonished General Alexander Surles, Director of the Bureau of Public Relations, to issue more favourable press releases. See [Marshall], *The Papers of George Catlett Marshall*, vol. 3, Marshall to Surles, 1 April 1943.

43. Atkinson, *An Army at Dawn*, p. 478.

44. [Marshall], *The Papers of George Catlett Marshall*, vol. 3, p. 642, note 3.

45. NARA, RG 208, E363, Box 817, OWI Directive 23–30 April 1943.

46. Dwight D. Eisenhower, *Crusade in Europe* (New York: Doubleday, 1948), p. 152.

47. Atkinson, *An Army at Dawn*, pp. 531–2.

48. D'Este's words, *Patton*, p. 497.

49. 22 May 1943, as quoted in D'Este, *Patton*, p. 495.

50. Parliamentary Archives, Beaverbrook Papers, BBK/A/28, see 'Notes on Conversations'.

51. [Marshall], *The Papers of George Catlett Marshall*, vol. 3, p. 635, note 2, emphasis in the original.

52. AHQ Report No. 42, p. 113.

53. War Cabinet, Chiefs of Staff Committee, '"TRIDENT" (Part II): Records of Plenary Meeting held at the White House, Washington, between 12th and 25th May, 1943', p. 3, as quoted in AHQ Report No. 42, p. 114.

54. LAC, MG 26, J5, vol. 73, Mackenzie King Speeches.

55. LAC, Mackenzie King Diary, 'Memorandum of Proceedings at Meeting of the Joint Chiefs of Staffs, White House, Washington, Thursday, May 20, 1943', accessed online.

56. LAC, Mackenzie King Diary, 'Memorandum of Conversation Mr. Mackenzie King Had with Prime Minister Winston Churchill, White House', Washington, DC, May 21, 1943, accessed online.

57. LAC, Mackenzie King Diary, 26 May 1943, accessed online.

58. LAC, MG 30, E133, vol. 249, McNaughton Diary, *c.* February 1943.

59. LAC, Mackenzie King Diary, 'Memorandum of Conversation Mr. Mackenzie King Had with Lord Cherwell, at the White House', Washington, DC, May 19, 1943, 11.00 a.m, accessed online.

60. *New York Times*, 'June Losses to U-Boat Lowest Since We Entered the Conflict', 10 July 1943.

61. See *The Mackenzie King Record*, pp. 520–6.

62. LAC, MG 30, E133, vol. 249, McNaughton Diary, 'Notes on Meeting with General Paget', 10 February 1943.

63. LAC, MG 30, E133, vol. 249, McNaughton Diary, 'Memorandum of Conference held at H.Q. First Canadian Army, 1730 hours, 13 April 1943'.

64. F.E. Morgan, *Overture to Overlord* (London: Hodder & Stoughton, 1950), p. 60.

65. LAC, MG 30, E133, vol. 249, McNaughton Diary, 'COSSAC Memo No. 1', 19 April 1943, and 'COSSAC Memo No. 2', 22 April 1943, both Appendices for April 1943.

66. LAC, MG 30, E133, vol. 250, McNaughton Diary, February 1943, Appendix II 'Memorandum of Conversation General McNaughton – General Sir Bernard Montgomery, K.C.B., D.S.C. G.O.C.-in C, Eight Army, at the War Office, 1430 hrs, 19 May 43'.

67. LAC, MG 30, E133, vol. 250, McNaughton Diary, May 1943, Appendix JJ, 'Memorandum of Conversation General McNaughton – General Paget (C-in-C. Home Forces) at G.H.Q. Home Forces at 1600 hrs, 19 May 43, Appendix JJ.43'.

68. LAC, MG 30, E133, vol. 250, McNaughton Diary, June 1943, Appendix K, 'COSSAC No. 14, 9 June 1943'.

69. AHQ Report No. 42, 'Combined Chiefs of Staff: Implementation of Decision Reached at "Trident" Conference', Chiefs of Staff (43) 286 (O), 7 June 1943.

70. LAC, MG 30, E133, vol. 250, McNaughton Diary, June 1943, Appendix R 'Memorandum of Conversation Gen. McNaughton – Lt. Gen. Sir Archibald Nye, VCIGS, 1500 hrs, 12 June 43'.

71. LAC, MG 30, E133, vol. 250, McNaughton Diary, June 1943, Appendix V, 'Memorandum of Conversation Gen. McNaughton – Gen. Paget, 1130 hrs, 17 June 1943'.

72. LAC, MG 30, E133, vol. 250, McNaughton Diary, June 1943, Appendix R, 'Memorandum of Conversation Gen. McNaughton – Lt. Gen. Nye, VCIGS at the War Office, 1500 hrs, 19 June 1943'.

73. Hamilton, *Master of the Battlefield*, p. 332.

74. Hamilton, *Master of the Battlefield*, p. 332.

75. Butcher, pp. 367–8.

76. Butcher, p. 368.

77. LAC, MG 30, E133, vol. 250, McNaughton Diary, July 1943, Appendix M, 'Memorandum of Conversation with General Sir Alan Brooke at the War Office', Wednesday, 21 July 1943'.

78. *The Times*, 'Canadians Part in Sicily', 21 July 1943, p. 4.

79. University of Toronto Archives, Massey Papers, Massey Diary, 14 July 1943.

80. LAC, MG 30, E133, vol. 250, McNaughton Diary, April 1943, Appendix FF, 'Memorandum No. 1, COSSAC', April 1943'.

CHAPTER 12: UNCERTAIN TRUMPET

1. LAC, MG 26, J4, vol. 406, Mackenzie King Papers, 'War Strategy Pt 1', microfilm p. C287455.

2. D'Este, *Patton*, p. 500.

3. Rick Atkinson, *The Day of Battle: The War in Sicily and Italy, 1943–1944* (New York: Henry Holt & Co., 2007), p. 173.

4. Hamilton, *Master of the Battlefield*, p. 301.

5. Lee Windsor, '"The Eyes of All Fixed on Sicily": Canada's Unexpected Victory, 1943', *Canadian Military History*, vol. 22, issue 3, Summer 2013, p. 11.

6. Carlo D'Este, *Bitter Victory: The Battle for Sicily, 1943* (New York: Dutton, 1988), p. 372.

7. Lt Col. Albert N. Garland and Howard McGraw Smyth, *Sicily and the Surrender of Italy: The Mediterranean Theatre of Operations, United States Army in World War II* (Washington, DC: CMH, 1993), pp. 235–6.

8. Garland and Smyth, p. 236.

9. D'Este, *Patton*, p. 518.

10. As quoted in Windsor, p. 27.

11. D'Este, *Patton*, p. 525; Nicholson, *The Canadians in Italy*, p. 103.

12. Garland and Smyth, p. 304.

13. Carlo D'Este visited the University of New Brunswick while I was a graduate student. I recollect complimenting him shortly after *Bitter Victory* was published on what I thought was a remarkably balanced handling of Montgomery and Anglo-American tension. His response was a quick smile and a quip that, 'Yeah, I'm taking a lot of heat over that in the States!'
14. All quotes in the above two paragraphs from D'Este, *Patton*, p. 523.
15. D'Este, *Patton*, p. 525.
16. LAC, MG 30, E133, vol. 249, McNaughton Diary, July 1944, Appendix K, 'Memorandum No. 19, COSSAC', 9 July 1943.
17. Hinsley, *British Intelligence* (abridged edition), p. 349.
18. Windsor, p. 29.
19. D'Este, *Patton*, p. 524.
20. D'Este, *Patton*, p. 526.
21. Windsor, p. 29.
22. Garland and Smyth, p. 325.
23. Nicholson, *The Canadians in Italy*, pp. 146–57.
24. Garland and Smyth, pp. 352–3.
25. D'Este, *Patton*, p. 525.
26. Garland and Smyth, p. 390.
27. D'Este, *Patton*, p. 527.
28. D'Este, *Patton*, p. 529.
29. *New York Times*, 'Americans First to Enter Messina', 18 August 1943.
30. D'Este, *Patton*, p. 536.
31. Edward R. Stettinius, *The Diaries of Edward R. Stettinius, Jr., 1943–1946*, ed. Thomas M. Campbell and George Herring (New York: New Viewpoints, 1975). Stettinius published a number of articles extolling the virtues of Lend-Lease and the value of Reverse Lend-Lease, which secured support for Lend-Lease. But he 'never overcame the deeply entrenched suspicion of foreign aid'. See p. xxii.
32. Morgan, as quoted in AHQ Report No. 42, p. 126.
33. Reynolds, *In Command of History*, p. 375.
34. AHEC, Nevins Papers, Box 9, folder 3, 'The COSSAC Plan'. They are also accessible online at: https://www.jcs.mil/Portals/36/Documents/History/WWII/Quadrant3.pdf.
35. Balfour, *Propaganda in War 1939–1945*, p. 345.
36. Max Hastings, *Bomber Command* (London: Pan Books, 1981), p. 246.
37. Balfour, *Propaganda in War 1939–1945*, p. 346.
38. NARA, RG 208, E363, Box 818, OWI Central Directive, week of 2–9 July 1943.
39. Figures from Manchester and Reid, pp. 705–6.
40. NARA, RG 208, E363, Box 818, OWI Central Directive, week of 23–30 July 1943.
41. Balfour, *Propaganda in War 1939–1945*, p. 357.
42. LAC, MG 30, E133, vol. 250, McNaughton Diary, October 1943, Appendix R, 'Memorandum No. 35, COSSAC', 22 October 1944.
43. Manchester and Reid, p. 697.
44. Quotes from Stimson's memo to FDR of 4 August 1943, Stimson and Bundy, pp. 223–7.
45. Chisholm and Davie, p. 445.
46. Hopkins, pp. 347–50.
47. Hopkins, p. 350.

48. LAC, Mackenzie King Diary, 18 July 1943, accessed online.
49. The explanation is repeated in Churchill's memoir, *The Second World War*, vol. 5: *Closing the Ring* (Boston, MA; Houghton Mifflin, 1951), p. 66.
50. LAC, RG 26/31, vol. 10, 'Minutes of the Publicity Coordinating Committee, 20 July 1943'.
51. LAC, MG 27, III, F4, Pope Diary, see entries for 1–30 July 1943.
52. Hinsley, *British Intelligence* (abridged edition), p. 349.
53. LAC, MG 27, III, F4, report of Pope's visit to London.
54. Parliamentary Archives, Beaverbrook Papers, BBK/A/281, C.D. Howe to Beaverbrook, 10 August 1943.
55. LAC, MG 27, III, F4, Pope Diary, 10 August 1943.
56. LAC, MG 30, E133, vol. 250, McNaughton Papers. Figures compiled from the weekly COSSAC Report intelligence summaries for July–September 1943.
57. Manchester and Reid, p. 713.
58. Alanbrooke, *War Diaries*, 13 August 1943.
59. Alanbrooke, *War Diaries*, 15 August 1943.
60. Manchester and Reid, pp. 715–17.
61. Minutes of the Quadrant Conference, CCS 329/2, 'Implementation of Assumed Basic Undertakings and Specific Operations for the Conduct of the war, 1943–1944', 26 August 1944, Appendix I, p. 330.
62. Liddell Hart Centre for Military Archives, King's College London (hereafter LHC), 6/2/2, Alanbrooke Papers, Dill to Alan Brooke, 29 June 1943.
63. LAC, MG 27, III, F4, Pope Diary, 10 August 1943.
64. LAC, MG 27, III, F4, Pope Diary, 20 August 1943.
65. Anthony Eden, *Full Circle: The Memoirs of Anthony Eden* (Boston, MA: Houghton Mifflin, 1960), p. 401.
66. *The Mackenzie King Record*, p. 553.
67. Stetson Conn, Rose C. Engelman and Brian Fairchild, *Guarding the United States and Its Outposts, US Army in World War II* (Washington, DC: CMH, 2000), p. 296.
68. Stacey, *Six Years of War*, pp. 500–5.
69. LAC, MG 27, III, F4, Pope Diary, 21 August 1943.
70. *The Mackenzie King Record*, p. 558.
71. Butcher, p. 398.
72. Butcher, p. 404.

CHAPTER 13: DOMINOES

1. Reynolds, *In Command of History*, p. 388.
2. Dominick Graham and Shelford Bidwell, *Tug of War: The Battle for Italy, 1943–1945* (New York: St Martin's Press, 1986), p. 39.
3. See the graph in *The Oxford Companion to the Second World War*, 'Italy', p. 592.
4. Daniel Todman, *Britain's War: A New World, 1942–1947* (New York: Oxford UP, 2020), p. 369.
5. LAC, MG 30, E133, vol. 250, McNaughton Papers. Figures compiled from intelligence summaries in the weekly COSSAC Reports to the First Canadian Army,
6. Heinz Magenheimer, *Hitler's War: Germany's Key Strategic Decisions 1940–1945* (London: Cassell, 1999), p. 200.
7. LAC, MG 27, III, F4, Pope Diary, 3 September 1943.

8. Graham and Bidwell, *Tug of War*, p. 51.
9. Graham and Bidwell, *Tug of War*, p. 54.
10. Roskill, vol. 3, Part I, p. 159.
11. Roskill, vol. 3, Part I, p. 179
12. Graham and Bidwell, *Tug of War*, p. 92.
13. Graham and Bidwell, *Tug of War*, p. 92.
14. Eden, *Memoirs*, p. 405.
15. Sherwood, vol. 2, p. 349.
16. Lockhart, *Diaries*, vol. 2: *1939–1945*, 13 September 1943.
17. Hinsley, *British Intelligence* (abridged edition), p. 360.
18. Hinsley, *British Intelligence* (abridged edition), p. 360.
19. Taylor, pp. 545–6.
20. Lockhart, *Diaries*, vol. 2: *1939–1945*, 27 September 1943.
21. LHC, 6/2/2, Alanbrooke Papers, Dill to Brooke, 16 October 1943.
22. Maj. Gen. Sir John Kennedy, *The Business of War* (London: Hutchinson, 1957), pp. 315–18.
23. [Marshall], *The Papers of George Catlett Marshall*, vol. 4, ed. Larry I. Bland (Baltimore, MD: Johns Hopkins UP, 1996), note 1, Churchill to Roosevelt, 7 October 1943.
24. Reynolds, *In Command of History*, p. 381.
25. LHC, 6/2/2, Alanbrooke Papers, Dill to Brooke, 16 October 1943.
26. Alanbrooke, *War Diaries*, annotation following entry for 18 November 1943, p. 473.
27. Kennedy, *The Business of War*, p. 313. Kennedy was Director of Military Operations at the time and recorded Brooke's view in his diary entry for 17 November 1943.
28. Magenheimer, p. 216.
29. Reynolds, *In Command of History*, p. 381.
30. NARA, RG 208, E6H, Box 3, 'A Brief History of the Activities of the European Theatre of Operations Division, United States Office of War Information', p. 14.
31. NARA, RG 208, E6H, Box 3, 'A Brief History of the Activities of the European Theatre of Operations Division, United States Office of War Information', pp. 22–3.
32. NARA, RG 208, E6H, Box 3, 'A Brief History of the Activities of the European Theatre of Operations Division, United States Office of War Information', pp. 30–41.
33. NARA, RG 208, E6H, Box 3, 'A Brief History of the Office of War Information', Chapter 8, 'Outposts', pp. 35–6.
34. Parliamentary Archives, Beaverbrook Papers, BBK/A/281, C.D. Howe to Beaverbrook, 28 September 1943.
35. Bodleian Library, Brand Papers, Box 196, 'Address' by Robert S. Brand to the War Committee of the American Bankers Association, New York, 15 September 1943.
36. Bodleian Library, Brand Papers, Box 196, Brand to Lord Woolton, 13 November 1943.
37. For a discussion of the complex negotiations of 1943 see Steil, Chapter 7 *passim*.
38. TNA, INF 1/102, see 'MOI US Organization, 1942–46'.
39. TNA, FO 953/7, 'History of British Information', p. 70.
40. TNA, FO 953/7, 'History of British Information', pp. 71–2.

41. Roland G. Ruppenthal, *Logistical Support of the Armies*, vol. 1: *May 1941–September 1944* (Washington, DC: CMH, 1995), p. 118.
42. O'Brien, p. 52.
43. Morison, *The Battle of the Atlantic, September 1939–May 1943*, p. 157.
44. Morison, *The Battle of the Atlantic, September 1939–May 1943*, p. 308.
45. Ruppenthal, p. 130.
46. Ruppenthal, pp. 120, 130.
47. Matloff, *Strategic Planning for Coalition Warfare 1943–1944*, p. 389.
48. For a definition of Troop Basis see Greenfield, Palmer and Wiley, *The Organization of Ground Combat Troops*, p. 164.
49. Matloff, *Strategic Planning for Coalition Warfare 1943–1944*, p. 389.
50. AHEC, Nevins Papers, Box 9, COSSAC Planning, memorandum to HQ ETO, G5 Section, 'Second Phase Troop Basis', 15 July 1943.
51. Ruppenthal, p. 138.
52. Ruppenthal, pp. 147–8.
53. Lockhart, *Diaries*, vol. 2: *1939–1945*, 13 February 1943.
54. Greenfield, Palmer and Wiley, see Table No. 3, 'Growth of the Army by Branch', and annex to Table 3, Chart A, pp. 203–4.
55. Issued on 25 November 1942, Greenfield, Palmer and Wiley, p. 217.
56. Greenfield, Palmer and Wiley, see Table No. 3, 'Growth of the Army by Branch', p. 203.
57. Compiled from Stanton, *World War II Order of Battle*. See also Matloff, *Strategic Planning for Coalition Warfare 1943–1944*, Appendix D: 'Shipment of Divisions Overseas – January 1942–30 September 1944'.
58. Matloff, *Strategic Planning for Coalition Warfare 1943–1944*, p. 408.
59. Alanbrooke, *War Diaries*, 15 September 1943.
60. Stacey, *Arms, Men and Government*, p. 235.
61. AHQ Report No. 42, p. 134. See also LAC, RG 24, vol. 10540, '"OVERLORD ONE", Notes for Meeting of Branches', prepared by G (Ops), HQ, 21 AG, 5 August 1943.
62. Stacey, *Arms, Men and Government*, p. 237.
63. LAC, MG 27, III, BII, vol. 45, McNaughton Papers, 'Employment of Cdn Troops', Stuart to McNaughton, 31 August 1943.
64. LAC, MG 27, III, BII, vol. 45, McNaughton Papers, 'Employment of Cdn Troops', Churchill to D/PM and BCOS, 31 August 1943.
65. LAC, MG 27, III, BII, vol. 45, McNaughton Papers, 'Employment of Cdn Troops', McNaughton to Stuart, 11 September 1943.
66. LAC, MG 27, III, BII, vol. 45, McNaughton Papers, 'Employment of Cdn Troops'. See a series of telegrams between these men.
67. 'The Strategic Role of First Canadian Army, 1942–1944', CMHQ Report No. 182, p. 70.
68. See Sherwood, pp. 375–86 for the best discussion of the proposal to make Marshall supreme Allied commander. Quotes from pp. 383–4.
69. LHC, 6/2/2, Alanbrooke Papers, telegram to War Cabinet Office from Dill, 19 October 1943.
70. The article in *Collier's*, 'Marshall – Democratic-General', appeared on 18 December 1943. See [Marshall], *The Papers of George Catlett Marshall*, vol. 4, pp. 172–3, note 3.
71. Kennedy, *The Business of War*, p. 312.

72. *History of COSSAC (Chief of Staff to Supreme Allied Commander), Historical Sub-Section, Office of Secretary, General Staff, Supreme Headquarters, Allied Expeditionary Force* [May 1944] (Bennington, VT: Merriam, 2000), p. 14.

73. Gordon A. Harrison, *Cross-Channel Attack* (Washington, DC: Office of the Chief of Military History United States Army, 1951), p. 114.

74. TNA, WO 219/527, Establishment of FUSAG.

75. *V Corps Operations in the ETO, 6 Jan 1942–9 May 1945* (n.p, n.d.), pp. 16–21.

76. Harrison, p. 108.

77. AHEC, Nevins Papers, COSSAC Planning, Box 14, 'Considerations Governing the System of Command and Control for Operation Overlord', no author or date on the document, but later annexes are described as attributed to Devers, forwarded to DCOSSAC on 24 September 1943.

78. Morgan, *Overture to Overlord*, p. 198.

79. Morgan, *Overture to Overlord*, p. 201.

80. AHQ Report No. 42, p. 195. See also the organisation chart in Forrest Pogue, *The Supreme Command* (Washington, DC: Office of the Chief of Military History, 1954), p. 67.

81. LHC, 6/2/2, Alanbrooke Papers, Dill to Chiefs of Staff, 19 October 1943.

82. Stacey, *Arms, Men and Government*, pp. 231–5, and the correspondence in LAC, MG 30, E133, vol. 250, McNaughton Diary.

83. Eisenhower to the Combined Chiefs of Staff, the Joint Chiefs of Staff and the British Chiefs of Staff, 19 October 1943, as quoted in Nicholson, *The Canadians in Italy*, p. 348.

84. Stacey, *Arms, Men and Government*, pp. 231–5, and the correspondence in LAC, MG 30, E133, vol. 250, McNaughton Diary, October 1943.

85. LAC, MG 31, E42, vol. 3, Swettenham Papers, 'Notes on McNaughton interview', 16 March 1966.

86. 'The Strategic Role of First Canadian Army, 1942–1944', CMHQ Report No. 182, pp. 89–90.

87. Stacey, *Arms, Men and Government*, p. 237.

88. LAC, MG 30, E133, vol. 250, McNaughton Diary, November 1944, 'Memorandum of Discussion with Colonel Ralston (Minister of National Defence) and Lt-Gen K. Stuart C.G.S. 5 November 1943'.

89. Stacey, *Arms, Men and Government*, pp. 238–9.

90. Alanbrooke, *War Diaries*, 12 November 1943.

91. LAC, MG 30, E133, vol. 250, McNaughton Diary, November 1944, Appendix L, 'Meeting with General Paget, CinC 21st Army GP, Col. Ralston, Minister of National defence, and Lt-Gen Stuart, CGS Canada', 13 November 1943.

92. Alanbrooke, *War Diaries*, 29 March 1944.

CHAPTER 14: THE AMERICANS ARE COMING

1. Kennedy, *Freedom from Fear*, pp. 679–80.

2. Hamilton, *Commander in Chief: FDR's Battle with Churchill, 1943* (London: Biteback Publishing, 2016), p. 164.

3. Nigel Hamilton, *War and Peace: FDR's Final Odyssey, D-Day to Yalta, 1943–1945* (Boston, MA: Houghton Mifflin, 2019), p. 54.

4. Hamilton, *War and Peace*, p. 60.

5. Eisenhower, *Crusade in Europe*, p. 195.

6. Hamilton, *War and Peace*, p. 84.
7. Todman, *Britain's War: A New World*, p. 488.
8. Hamilton, *War and Peace*, p. 61; Todman, *Britain's War: A New World*, p. 488.
9. Manchester and Reid, p. 750.
10. As quoted by Dallek, *Roosevelt: A Political Life*, p. 536.
11. Dallek, *Roosevelt: A Political Life*, pp. 536, 537.
12. Todman, *Britain's War: A New World*, pp. 492–3.
13. Dallek, *Roosevelt: A Political Life*, p. 537.
14. Hastings Ismay, *The Memoirs of Lord Ismay* (New York: Viking, 1960), p. 339.
15. Ismay, p. 338.
16. Manchester and Reid, p. 764.
17. Todman, *Britain's War: A New World*, p. 490.
18. As quoted in Todman, *Britain's War: A New World*, p. 492.
19. Manchester and Reid, pp. 771–2.
20. Hamilton, *War and Peace*, p. 172.
21. Manchester and Reid, p. 770.
22. Dallek, *Roosevelt: A Political Life*, p. 540.
23. Manchester and Reid, p. 768.
24. Todman, *Britain's War: A New World*, p. 493.
25. Charles E. Bohlen, *Witness to History 1929–1969* (New York: W.W. Norton & Co., 1973), pp. 146–53.
26. Kennedy, *Freedom from Fear*, p. 679.
27. Dallek, *Roosevelt: A Political Life*, p. 775.
28. Matloff and Snell, p. 378.
29. Matloff and Snell, p. 372.
30. Matloff and Snell, p. 381.
31. Harrison, p. 116,
32. TNA, WO 205/643, Operation Overlord: General Plans.
33. Greenhous et al., pp. 270–4.
34. Swettenham, vol. 2, pp. 345–8.
35. LAC, MG 30, E131, vol. 133, McNaughton Diary, December 1944, Appendix D, 'Memorandum of a discussion with Lt-Gen FE Morgan, at Largiebeg, Sunday, 12 December 1943'.
36. Stacey, *Arms, Men and Government*, p. 245.
37. Hamilton, *Montgomery: Master of the Battlefield*, p. 530.
38. LAC, MG 27, BII, vol. 52, Ralston Papers, Broadcast monitored in Ottawa 15.30 GMT, 29 December 1943.
39. LAC, MG 30, E133, vol. 148, 'Public Relations: Change of Command in First Canadian Army', press accounts.
40. LAC, MG 30, E131, vol. 133, McNaughton Diary, December 1944, Appendix D, 'Memorandum of a discussion with Lt-Gen FE Morgan, at Largiebeg, Sunday, 12 December 1943'.
41. LAC, MG 27, III, BII, vol. 45, 'Employment of Canadian Troops', correspondence 18–21 February 1944.
42. Alanbrooke, *War Diaries*, 7 December 1943.
43. Arthur Travers Harris and Sebastian Cox, *Despatch on War Operations, 23 February 1942 to 8 May 1945* (London: Routledge, 1995), p. 196.
44. The remarks were made by Dr Robert Ley, Minister of Labour. Balfour, *Propaganda and War*, p. 345.

45. W.G. Sebald, *On the Natural History of Destruction* (New York: Modern Library, 2004), p. 27.
46. Hastings, *Bomber Command*, p. 246.
47. Hastings, *Bomber Command*, p. 246.
48. Sebald, p. 29.
49. Sebald, p. 35.
50. Figures from Wesley Frank Craven and James Lea Cate, *Europe: Argument to V-E Day, January 1944 to May 1945* (Chicago, IL: University of Chicago Press, 1948).
51. Williamson Murray, *Strategy for Defeat: The Luftwaffe 1939–1945* (Secaucus, NJ: Chartwell Books, 1986), p. 158.
52. Ronald Schaffer, *Wings of Judgment: American Bombing in World War II* (New York: Oxford UP, 1985), p. 66.
53. Tooze, *The Wages of Destruction*, pp. 404–5.
54. Murray, pp. 130–1.
55. Hinsley, *British Intelligence* (abridged edition), p. 403.
56. Levine, p. 105.
57. Hinsley, *British Intelligence* (abridged edition), p. 404.
58. Levine, pp. 111–14.
59. Charles Messenger, *'Bomber' Harris and the Strategic Bombing Offensive, 1939–1945* (London: Arms and Armour Press, 1984), p. 142.
60. Conversation with Professor Gerhard Weinberg, *c.* 2005.
61. Götz Aly, *Hitler's Beneficiaries: Plunder, Racial War and the Nazi Welfare State* (Verso: London, 2006), p. 27.
62. Aly, p. 40.
63. Aly, p. 132.
64. Aly, p. 148.
65. See Wolfram Wette, *The Wehrmacht: History, Myth, Reality* (Cambridge, MA: Harvard UP, 2006).
66. Nicholas Stargardt, *The German War: A Nation under Arms, 1939–1945* (London: Vintage, 2015).
67. Wette, p. 159.
68. University of Wisconsin-Madison Library (hereafter UWML), Papers of Colonel Ernest R. Dupuy, reel 2. Dupuy chose this phrase as the title for Chapter 2 of his unpublished memoir, 'Behind the Elephants: SHAEF Public Relations from the Pentagon to Berlin'.
69. TNA, FO 371/38571, BIS Report No. 114, 21 December 1943, as quoted in 'Survey of Magazine Digest'.
70. LAC, MG 26, J4, vol. 406, Mackenzie King Papers, 'US Situation 1944', Report of Political Developments for the month of December 1943 from the Canadian Embassy, Washington, DC, 19 January 1944, microfilm p. C23758.
71. *Time*, 'Total War, 73%', 10 January 1944; NARA, RG 208, E359, Box 114, OWI Director of Overseas Operations, Policy Subject Files 1942–1946, 'Invasion of Europe, Report on German and Neutral Press in early 1944'.
72. LAC, MG 26, J4, vol. 406, Mackenzie King Papers, 'US Situation 1944', 'Report of Political Developments for the month of December 1943 from the Canadian Embassy, Washington, DC, 19 January 1944', microfilm p. C237580.
73. See for example *Foreign Affairs*, January 1944, 'America at War: The End of the Second Year'.
74. Balfour, *Propaganda in War 1939–1945*, p. 371.

75. Ralf Georg Reuth, *Rommel: The End of a Legend* (London: Haus Books, 2008), pp. 141–2.
76. Horst Boog, Gerhard Krebs and Detlef Vogel, *The Strategic Air War in Europe and the War in the West and East Asia, 1939–1944/5* (Oxford: Oxford UP, 2006), p. 581.
77. Marlis G. Steinart, *Hitler's War and the Germans: Public Mood and Attitude During the Second World War* (Athens, OH: Ohio UP, 1977), p. 258.
78. Reuth, p. 69.
79. Hamilton, *Montgomery: Master of the Battlefield*, p. 520.
80. D.K.R. Crosswell, *Beetle: The Life of General Walter Bedell Smith* (Lexington, KY: University of Kentucky Press, 2010), p. 588.
81. See the Situation Maps as submitted in the COSSAC plan to the COS at Quebec, August 1944.
82. TNA, WO 205/661 FUSAG Planning, maps in 'Annex 1 to Joint Operations Plan U.S. Forces'.
83. Kennedy, *The Business of War*, p. 319.

CHAPTER 15: NO QUITTING

1. D'Este, *Eisenhower*, p. 499.
2. Kennedy, *The Business of War*, p. 320.
3. Maj. Gen. Sir Francis De Guingand, *Operation Victory* (London: Hodder & Stoughton, 1947), p. 344.
4. Kennedy, *The Business of War*, p. 320.
5. Roskill, vol. 2, Part II, p. 10.
6. Roskill, vol. 2, Part II, p. 10.
7. TNA, WO 205/643 Operation Overlord General Part I, Jul. 43–Feb. 44, 'Comparison of Methods of Employment of Additional Resources', SHAEF/ 17100/Ops, 23 January 1943.
8. TNA, WO 219/1837 'COSSAC Int. Estimate of 31 January 1944'.
9. Alanbrooke, *War Diaries*, 24 January 1944.
10. Bradley, *A Soldier's Story*, p. 219.
11. Bradley, *A Soldier's Story*, p. 220.
12. De Guingand, p. 348.
13. Information from Bill Johnson, at DHH, who did the research on 83 Group, courtesy Dr Steven Harris, Director, Directorate of History and Heritage, NDHQ, Ottawa, 30 October 2020.
14. Greenhous et al., p. 272. See p. 269 for an organisation chart and order of battle for 83 Group in June 1944.
15. The featuring of Free French Spitfires in the Hollywood adaptation of Cornelius Ryan's *The Longest Day* drew a chorus of discontent from the audience at the Toronto premiere of the film – as indeed did the whole neglect of the Canadian contribution.
16. Ethan Rawls Williams, LCDR, USN, '50 Div. in Normandy: A Critical Analysis of the British 50th (Northumbrian) Division on D-Day and in the Battle of Normandy', unpublished MA thesis, U.S. Army Command and General Staff College, Fort Leavenworth, 2007, p. 40.
17. Information courtesy John C. McManus, email 15 November 2020.
18. Harrison, p. 162.
19. [Marshall], *The Papers of George Catlett Marshall*, vol. 4, p. 269.

20. [Marshall], *The Papers of George Catlett Marshall*, vol. 4, Marshall to Eisenhower, 7 February 1944.
21. Leighton and Coakley, vol. 2, p. 328.
22. Leighton and Coakley, vol. 2, p. 326.
23. Bradley, *A Soldier's Story*, p. 225.
24. Samuel E. Morison, *The Invasion of France and Germany, 1944–1945* (Boston: Little, Brown and Co., 1955), pp. 56–7.
25. Morison, *The Invasion of France and Germany, 1944–1945*, p. 56.
26. [Marshall], *The Papers of George Catlett Marshall*, vol. 4, Marshall to Eisenhower, 7 February 1944.
27. See Hinsley, *British Intelligence* (abridged edition), pp. 369–75.
28. Lockhart, *Diaries*, vol. 2: *1939–1945*, 22 June 1944.
29. [Marshall], *The Papers of George Catlett Marshall*, vol. 4, Report of MGen Hull, 14 March 1944; Marshall to Eisenhower, 16 March 1944; Eisenhower to Marshall, 18 March 1944.
30. Morison, *The Invasion of France and Germany, 1944–1945*, p. 55.
31. Behrens, pp. 397, 405.
32. D'Este, *Eisenhower*, p. 496.
33. Murray, *Strategy for Defeat*, p. 187.
34. Martin Middlebrook and Chris Everitt, eds, *Bomber Command War Diary: An Operational Reference Book: 1939–1945* (London: Penguin, 1985), p. 448.
35. Middlebrook and Everitt, eds, *Bomber Command War Diary*, editors' note for the Battle of Berlin, pp. 446–8.
36. Middlebrook and Everitt, eds, *Bomber Command War Diary*, p. 448.
37. See Murray Peden, *A Thousand Shall Fall* (Stittsville, ON: Canada's Wings, 1979), for an excellent account of 100 Group.
38. Levine, p. 122.
39. Murray, *Strategy for Defeat*, p. 188.
40. Roger A. Freeman, *The Mighty Eighth War Diary* (Osceola, WI: Motorbooks International, 1990), entry for 14 January 1944.
41. Craven and Cate, pp. 13–14.
42. Craven and Cate, p. 20.
43. Craven and Cate, p. 17.
44. Freeman, *The Mighty Eighth War Diary*, entries for 13, 16 and 20 December 1943.
45. Freeman, *The Mighty Eighth War Diary*.
46. Craven and Cate, pp. 22–4.
47. Schaefer, *Wings of Judgment: American Bombing in World War II* (New York: Oxford UP, 1985) Chapter 5.
48. Craven and Cate, p. 27.
49. Messenger, p. 147.
50. Craven and Cate, p. 27, emphasis added.
51. Pogue, *The Supreme Command*, p. 128.
52. Hastings, *Bomber Command*, p. 327.
53. D'Este, *Eisenhower*, p. 498
54. Levine, p. 121.
55. Levine, p. 122.
56. Richard Overy, *The Air War, 1939–1945* (New York: Stein and Day, 1981), p. 98.
57. Kennedy, *Freedom from Fear*, p. 704.

58. Middlebrook and Everitt, eds, *Bomber Command War Diary*, pp. 448, 472.
59. Greenhous et al., p. 791.
60. Middlebrook and Everitt, eds, *Bomber Command War Diary*, p. 479.
61. The best account of these experimental raids is in Greenhous et al., pp. 791–5.
62. Greenhous et al., p. 794.
63. D'Este, *Eisenhower*, p. 499.
64. Levine, p. 121.
65. D'Este, *Eisenhower*, p. 498.
66. Pogue, *The Supreme Command*, pp. 133–4.
67. TNA, CAB 154/101, 'Historical Record of Deception in the War Against Germany and Italy', p. 199. For the JAEL plan see TNA, Air 37/882 Operation Overlord Cover Plan.
68. TNA, CAB 154/101, 'Historical Record of Deception in the War Against Germany and Italy', pp. 209–18.
69. NARA, RG 208, E359, Box 114, Invasion of Europe, Director of Overseas Operations, Policy Subject Files 1942–1946, 'Report on German and Neutral Press in early 1944'.
70. TNA, CAB 154/101, 'Historical Record of Deception in the War Against Germany and Italy', p. 232.
71. Howard Gotlieb Archival Research Center, Boston University, Ingersoll Papers, 824n unedited copy, see drafts of 'Time out for a War', typescript, retype 3/4, Chapters 1–8, Box 17, file 7.
72. Roger Fleetwood Hesketh, *Fortitude: The D-Day Deception Campaign* (Woodstock, NY: Overlook Press, 2000), p. 39.
73. Hesketh, p. 32.
74. See J.C. Masterman, *The Double-Cross System in the War of 1939–1945* (New Haven, CT and London: Yale UP, 1972).
75. Hesketh, pp. 83–4.
76. Hesketh, pp. 32–7.
77. TNA, CAB 154/101, 'Historical Record of Deception in the War Against Germany and Italy', pp. 235–8.
78. Parliamentary Archives, Beaverbrook Papers, C/159, correspondence with B.H. Liddell Hart, January 1944.
79. TNA, PREM 3/345/2 holds the correspondence of the C.D. Howe incident.
80. TNA, PREM 3/345/4, Ismay to Churchill, 14 January 1944, p. 290.
81. *Time*, 'A Letter from the Publisher', 24 January 1944, vol. 44, issue 4, p. 9.
82. *Time*, 'The Army's Doctrine', 24 January 1944, vol. 44, issue 4, p. 9.
83. TNA, CAB 154/101, 'Historical Record of Deception in the War Against Germany and Italy', p. 248.
84. TNA, CAB 154/101, 'Historical Record of Deception in the War Against Germany and Italy', p. 251.
85. AHQ Report No. 42, p. 208.
86. Hesketh, p. 91.
87. Dickson, pp. 235–43.
88. Hesketh, p. 181. See also organisation chart of FUSAG on p. 90.
89. Hesketh, p. 91.
90. Michael Howard, *British Intelligence in the Second World War*, vol. 5: *Strategic Intelligence* (Cambridge: Cambridge UP, 1990), p. 115.
91. Hesketh, p. 91.

92. Harrison, p. 162.
93. Stimson and Bundy, p. 234.
94. [Marshall], *The Papers of George Catlett Marshall*, vol. 4, pp. 290–1, Marshall to Lieutenant-General Jacob L. Devers, 10 February 1944, reporting on a story by the *New York Times* reporter Cyrus Sulzberger which slipped through the censors before it was finally killed.
95. Marshall Center, Virginia Military Institute, Marshall Papers, file 67/2, Eisenhower to Marshall, 9 February 1944.
96. [Marshall], *The Papers of George Catlett Marshall*, vol. 4, Stimson as recorded by Marshall, 10 May 1944, p. 450, note 1.
97. Steven J. Zaloga, *US Anti-Tank Artillery 1941–45* (Oxford: Osprey, 2005), p. 20.
98. Zaloga, *US Anti-Tank Artillery 1941–45*, p. 19.
99. TNA, FO 371/38572, BIS Report No. 27, 3 April 1944, *Free World*, April 1944.
100. Steven J. Zaloga, 'Debunking an OMAHA Beach Legend: The Use of "Armored Funnies" on D-Day', *Journal of Military History*, vol. 85, no. 1, January 2021, pp. 134–62.

CHAPTER 16: SHAPING OPERATIONS

1. As quoted in TNA, FO 371/38571, BIS Report No. 3, week ending 8 January 1944.
2. Dupuy, 'Behind the Elephants', see p. 52 for McClure's initial estimate and p. 89 for the breakdown on D-Day.
3. DHH 75/315, Abel Correspondence, Colonel Abel to J.W.G. Clark, Deputy Director of PR for the Canadian armed forces in Ottawa, 17 January 1944.
4. Charles Cruickshank, *The Fourth Arm: Psychological Warfare 1938–1945* (London: Davis-Poynter, 1977), p. 39.
5. Dallek, *Roosevelt: A Political Life*, p. 521.
6. Kennedy, *Freedom from Fear*, p. 707.
7. Garnett, p. 327.
8. As quoted in Cruickshank, p. 41.
9. Garnett, pp. 348–52.
10. Lockhart, *Diaries*, vol. 2: *1939–1945*, 6 December 1944.
11. Garnett, p. 350.
12. Garnett, pp. 356–7.
13. Lockhart, *Diaries*, vol. 2: *1939–1945*, see editor's notes pp. 275–6.
14. Garnett, p. 358.
15. Kennedy, *Freedom from Fear*, p. 783.
16. The various histories of OWI, including 'The Brief Account of the Activities of the European Theatre of Operations Division, United States Office of War Information', NARA, RG 208, E6H, Box 3, 'Draft Historical Reports, 1941–48', say nothing of this shake-up.
17. See the OWI directives in NARA, RG 208, E363, Box 818.
18. Gerd Horten, *Radio Goes to War: The Culture Politics of Propaganda during World War II* (Berkeley, CA: University of California Press, 2002), p. 7.
19. Asa Briggs, *The History of Broadcasting in the United Kingdom*, vol. 3: *The War of Words, 1939–1945* (Oxford: Oxford UP, 1970), p. 416.
20. Garnett, pp. 362–3.

21. See correspondence in TNA, FO 898/286, Central Directives 1942–1945, especially Ritchie Calder to MGen Brooks, 25 May 1944.

22. BBC Archives, R28/175 News: News Correspondents Radio Newsreel 1944–1945, memo from H. Rooney Pelletier on 'Criticism from Australia', 18 April 1944.

23. Cruickshank, p. 149.

24. Dupuy, 'Behind the Elephants', pp. 50–1.

25. Dupuy, 'Behind the Elephants', p. 19.

26. Dupuy, 'Behind the Elephants', p. 28 (on Payne); UWML, Dupuy Diary, entry on 7 March 1944 (on Pawley).

27. Dupuy, 'Behind the Elephants', pp. 9–10.

28. Dupuy, 'Behind the Elephants', p. 26.

29. Dupuy, 'Behind the Elephants', p. 60.

30. Dupuy, 'Behind the Elephants', p. 81.

31. Dupuy, 'Behind the Elephants', pp. 60–2.

32. Lockhart, *Diaries*, vol. 2: *1939–1945*, 28 March 1944.

33. Lockhart, *Diaries*, vol. 2: *1939–1945*, 30 March 1944.

34. Roskill, *The War at Sea*, vol. 2, Part I handles inshore operations in early 1944, and vol. 2, Part II focuses on Neptune/Overlord.

35. What follows is derived from J. Rohwer and G. Hümmelchen, *Chronology of the War at Sea 1939–1945: The Naval History of World War Two* (Annapolis, MD: US Naval Institute Press, 1992) and W.A.B. Douglas, Roger Sarty, Michael Whitby et al., *A Blue Water Navy: The Official Operational History of the Royal Canadian Navy in the Second World War, 1939–1943*, vol. 2, Part II (St Catharines, ON: Vanwell Publishing, 2007), pp. 243–4.

36. F.H. Hinsley, *British Intelligence in the Second World War*, vol. 3, Part I (London: HMSO, 1984), pp. 241–3.

37. Churchill College Archives, Fawcett Papers, 'Overinsuring versus Underinsuring Overlord from the U-Boat and W-Boat Threat', 30 March 1944; 'Notes on A/S Aspects of Overlord', by L. Solomon, 23 March 1944; and 'The Case for Increasing the Number of A/S Escorts Employed in Overlord', 30 April 1944.

38. See Marc Milner, *The U-Boat Hunters: The Royal Canadian Navy and the Offensive against Germany's Submarines* (Toronto, ON: University of Toronto Press, 1994), Chapter 4.

39. Roskill, vol. 3, Part I, p. 294.

40. Roskill, vol. 3, Part I, p. 289 claims ninety-four; Rohwer and Hümmelchen claim 'About 100', p. 272.

41. Harrison, p. 270.

42. Harrison, see discussion on pp. 261–3.

43. Douglas, Sarty and Whitby, *A Blue Water Navy*, p. 231.

44. Middlebrook and Everitt, eds, *Bomber Command War Diary*, p. 489.

45. Craven and Cate, p. 151.

46. Figures compiled from Middlebrook and Everitt, eds, *Bomber Command War Diary* for April and May 1944; they do not include 'nuisance' raids by Mosquito bombers over Germany; target figure from Levine, p. 131.

47. Craven and Cate, p. 155.

48. Craven and Cate, p. 153.

49. Craven and Cate, p. 154.

50. Figures compiled from Freeman, *The Mighty Eighth War Diary*.

51. Craven and Cate, p. 154.

52. Craven and Cate, p. 159.

53. Stephen Alan Bourque, *Beyond the Beach: The Allied War Against France* (Annapolis, MD: USNI Press, 2018), p. 191. Figures on the number of aircraft involved are derived from Bourque's narrative.

54. Middlebrook and Everitt, eds, *Bomber Command War Diary*, see entry for 20–21 April 1944, raid on La Chapelle.

55. Middlebrook and Everitt, eds, *Bomber Command War Diary*, p. 505.

56. Greenhous et al., p. 806, see note 27 for details.

57. Greenhous et al., p. 284.

58. Bourque, p. 139.

59. Hesketh, p. 188.

60. Dwight David Eisenhower Presidential Library (hereafter DDEPL) download, Eisenhower to Marshall, 21 March 1944.

61. DDEPL download, 'Minutes of Meeting Held in Conference Room, Widewing 1430 hours, 27 March 1944'.

62. *The Oxford Companion to the Second World War*, 'Pacific War', pp. 855–63.

63. DDEPL download, 'Minutes of Meeting Held in Conference Room, Widewing 1430 hours, 27 March 1944'.

64. Nigel Nicolson, *Alex: The Life of Field Marshal Earl Alexander of Tunis* (London: Weidenfeld & Nicolson, 1973), p. 248.

65. Graham and Bidwell, *Tug of War*, p. 145.

66. Martin Blumenson, *Mark Clark* (London: Jonathan Cape, 1985), p. 195.

67. TNA, FO 371/38571, BIS Report No. 3, week ending 8 January 1944, and BIS Report No. 114, week ending 1 January 1944,

68. Blumenson, *Clark*, p. 195.

69. W.G.F. Jackson, *The Battle for Italy* (New York: Harper and Row, 1967), p. 221.

70. John Ehrman, *Grand Strategy*, vol. 4: *August 1943–September 1944* (London: HMSO, 1956), pp. 257–9, emphasis added.

71. TNA, PREM 4/27/9, Eden to Halifax, 28 January 1944, and Halifax to Eden, 11 February 1944.

72. James Lansdale Hodson, *And Yet I Like America* (London: Victor Gollancz, 1945), p. 250.

73. LHC, 6/2/2, Alanbrooke Papers, telegram from Joint Staff Mission, Washington to War Cabinet Office, personal Dill to PM, 22 February 1944.

74. TNA, INF 2/5, 'Publications to Explain What Britain Has Done',

75. The sad tale of the Fighting Packages is laid out in TNA, INF 1/975, 'Invasion of Europe'.

76. TNA, FO 953/7, 'History of British Information', pp. 73–4.

77. TNA, FO 953/7, 'History of British Information', p. 74.

78. After checking the Bracken Papers at Churchill College, Cambridge, I spent 18–19 May 2011 in the National Archives at Kew trying to find relevant files: INF in the case of the MOI, and FO for the Foreign Office. None were found.

79. See Boyle, *Poor, Dear Brendan*; Roberts, '*The Holy Fox*'; Charles Edward Lysaught, *Brendan Bracken* (London: Allen Lane, 1979).

80. TNA, WO 219/4631, SHAEF PR Plan, 1 May 1944.

81. For brief biographies of McClure and Davis see Pogue, *The Supreme Command*, pp. 5, 14.

82. BBC Archives, R34/883/1 Policy: SHAEF: Summaries, Instructions and Miscellaneous Papers, 1944–1945, file 1A, 'Notes for War Correspondents Accredited to SHAEF', n.d.
83. Briggs, pp. 416–17.
84. Briggs, p. 444.
85. BBC Archives, R28/280/5 News: War Reporting Unit, file 3 Jan.–Jul. 1944, W.A. Frost, Deputy Director of War Reporting, memo of 16 May 1955.
86. TNA, WO 229/56, see the report by Col. R. Ernest Dupuy, Acting Director, Public Relations Division, SHAEF, 5 July 1944,
87. TNA, WO 219/402, Operation Overlord: Film and Photo, telegram to AGWAR from Ingles, E-26876, 9 May 194.
88. TNA, WO 219/4631, Supreme Headquarters, Allied Expeditionary Force, Public Relations Division 'Public Relations Plan Overlord'.
89. BBC Archives, R34/883/1 Policy: SHAEF: Summaries, Instructions and Miscellaneous Papers, 1944–1945, file 1A, 'Notes for War Correspondents Accredited to SHAEF', n.d.
90. TNA, INF 1/974 Invasion of Europe: Representative Press Working Committee, Minutes and Papers, April–July 1944, Minutes of the 'Representative Press Committee' meeting, PRD HQ, 23 May 1944.
91. Dupuy, 'Behind the Elephants', pp. 87–8.

CHAPTER 17: WHAT'S AT STAKE?

1. Calder, *The People's War*, p. 570.
2. LAC, MG 26, J4, vol. 406, Mackenzie King Papers, 'US Situation 1944', 'Report of Political Developments for the Month of December, 1943, from the Canadian Embassy in Washington', 12 January 1944, microfilm p. C237580; see also Weintraub, *Final Victory*, pp. ix–xi.
3. TNA, FO 371/38571, BIS Report No. 3, week ending 8 January 1944.
4. Steven Casey, *Cautious Crusade: Franklin D. Roosevelt, American Public Opinion, and the War Against Nazi Germany* (Oxford: Oxford UP, 2001), p. 146.
5. Randall Bennett Woods, *A Changing of the Guard: Anglo-American Relations, 1941–1946* (Chapel Hill, NC: University of North Carolina Press, 1990), p. 122.
6. Dallek, *Roosevelt: A Political Life*, p. 547.
7. TNA, FO 371/38571, BIS Report No. 3, week ending 8 January 1944; *New Republic*, 'FDR and the Post-War World', 3 January 1944.
8. Casey, *Cautious Crusade*, p. 146.
9. Winik, p. 329.
10. Woods, p. 114.
11. TNA, FO 371/38572, BIS Report No. 19, week ending 4 March 1944; *Life*, 'Last Call for War Aims', 6 March 1944.
12. *Chicago Tribune*, 'Tell Peace Terms before Invasion, Wheeler Asks U.S.', 23 April 1944.
13. LAC, MG 26, J4, vol. 406, Mackenzie King Papers, 'Massey 1943', 'Report on UK Domestic Situation', 1 November 1943, microfilm p. C298957.
14. Interview with Leslie Chapman, 3 December 2020, on his 94th birthday. Chapman emigrated to Canada in 1947– 'Still no butter!' – married and raised a family. The author married his daughter. Like all those in essential war work, Chapman had no 'veteran' status and received no pension for his years below ground.

15. TNA, FO 371/38571, BIS Report No. 1, week ending 1 January 1944; *Newsweek*, 'War: A Sliding Scale of Values', 3 January 1944.

16. UWML, Dupuy Papers, Dupuy to his wife, 16 March 1944.

17. TNA, FO 371/38571, BIS Report No. 1, week ending 1 January 1944; *Harper's Magazine*, Report on visit to UK by Frederick Lewis Allen, January 1944.

18. Nick Hewitt, *Normandy: The Sailors' Story* (New Haven, CT and London: Yale UP, 2024), p. 56.

19. Calder, *The People's War*, p. 528.

20. Calder, *The People's War*, p. 527.

21. Todman, *Britain's War: A New World*, p. 558.

22. Paul Addison, *The Road to 1945: British Politics and the Second World War* (London: Cape, 1975), pp. 236–45.

23. Colville's diary, as quoted in Manchester and Reid, p. 814; TNA, FO 371/38573, BIS Report No. 29, week ending 8 April 1944; *Time*, 'Great Britain – Changes, Pride and Petulance', 10 April 1944.

24. Manchester and Reid, pp. 814–15.

25. US Senate website, Historical Highlights, 1941–1963, 'Combat Tour for Senators', accessed online 7 April 2021.

26. Woods, p. 90.

27. Robert Skidelsky, *John Maynard Keynes*, vol. 3: *Fighting for Freedom, 1936–1946* (New York: Viking, 2001), p. 337.

28. Woods, p. 114.

29. Skidelsky, *Keynes, 1936–1946*, p. 523.

30. Skidelsky, *Keynes, 1936–1946*, p. 340.

31. TNA, PREM 4/18/6, 'Mutual Aid', 'Report on Mutual Aid', Cmd. 6483, November 1943.

32. Skidelsky, *Keynes, 1936–1946*, p. 338.

33. Woods, p. 92.

34. TNA, PREM 4/18/6. See Articles 2 and 6 of 'Principles applying to Mutual Aid', 23 February 1942, agreement between the UK and USA, Washington, DC, 23 February 1942, Treaty Series No. 7 (1942), Cmd. 6391.

35. Edward R. Stettinius, *Lend-Lease: Weapon for Victory* (New York: Macmillan, 1943), p. 312.

36. Parliamentary Archives, Beaverbrook Papers, BBK/D/182, 'Report to Congress on Lend-Lease for the period Ended April 30, 1943'.

37. TNA, PREM 4/18/6, Mutual Aid, 'Report on Mutual Aid', Cmd. 6483, November 1943, paragraph 30.

38. TNA, FO 371/38573, BIS Report No. 4, week ending 3 June 1944; *Business Week*, 'Business Abroad – Lend-Lease – 14%', 27 May 1944.

39. Woods, pp. 92–3.

40. The Wadsworth Amendment. See the British Embassy despatch of 26 April 1944, *Washington Despatches*, p. 351.

41. TNA, PREM 4/18/16, 'Principles applying to Mutual Aid', Cmd. 6391.

42. Skidelsky, *Keynes, 1936–1946*, p. 337.

43. TNA, FO 371/38573, BIS Report No. 40, week ending 20 May 1944; *US News*, 'Hurdles for Postwar Trade: Where the Aims of the Allies Clash', 19 May 1944.

44. TNA, PREM 4/17/11, Postwar Economic Planning.

45. TNA, PREM 4/17/11, Churchill, 'Four Principles for dealing with Post War Planning', published 2 March 1944.

46. Steil, p. 153.
47. Skidelsky, *Keynes, 1936–1946*, p. 320.
48. Steil, p. 176.
49. Woods, p. 119.
50. Stettinius, *Lend-Lease*.
51. TNA, FO 371/38571, BIS Report No. 7, week ending 22 January 1944. Review of 24 January 1944.
52. Roosevelt Presidential Library, Stettinius Papers, Stettinius Diary, 17 March 1944.
53. Roosevelt Presidential Library, Stettinius Diary, p. 44–5.
54. Roosevelt Presidential Library, Stettinius Diary, p. 52–4.
55. Roosevelt Presidential Library, Stettinius Diary, p. 58.
56. Roosevelt Presidential Library, Stettinius Diary, WSC to Stettinius, 19 April 1944, p. 61.
57. TNA, PREM 4/17/11, Beaverbrook to WSC, 20 April 1944.
58. Woods, p. 129.
59. David Day, *Reluctant Nation: Australia and the Allied Defeat of Japan 1942–1945* (Melbourne: Oxford UP, 1992), p. 184.
60. Day, *Reluctant Nation*, p. 181.
61. Day, *Reluctant Nation*, p. 174.
62. Stacey, *Canada and the Age of Conflict*, vol. 2, p. 361.
63. Stacey, *Canada and the Age of Conflict*, vol. 2, p. 364.
64. *The Mackenzie King Record*, p. 648.
65. John Darwin's *The Empire Project* deals with the meeting *en passant*, see p. 523.
66. Churchill, *The Second World War*, vol. 5: *Closing the Ring*, covers this period. See also Reynolds, *In Command of History*, Part V, Chapters 23–7.
67. *Time*, 'Mother England', 1 May 1944.
68. *The Mackenzie King Record*, p. 668.
69. Day, *Reluctant Nation*, see especially Chapter 15, 'A Question of Manpower'.
70. *The Mackenzie King Record*, p. 686.
71. *The Mackenzie King Record*, p. 687.
72. The document was published in full in British newspapers in the days that followed. See for example the *Daily Express* and *The Times* on 18 May 1944.
73. *Time*, 'Plain Talk', 5 June 1944.
74. TNA, FO 371/38573, BIS Report No. 44, week ending 3 June 1944; *Business Week*, 'The War and Business Abroad', 27 May 1944.
75. TNA, FO 371/38573, BIS Reports Nos. 29, 33, 26 April 1944, and BIS Report No. 35, 2 May 1944; *Daily Express*, 1 and 2 May 1944.
76. LAC, RG 36/31, vol. 27, Field Reports 1944, Field Report No. 1, April 1944, War Information Board, Ottawa.
77. Hesketh, pp. 168–72.
78. Hesketh, p. 175.
79. TNA, WO 219/2207, 'Implementation of Wireless Deception', Maj. Gen. l H.R. Bull to SHAEF COS, 15 March 1944, lists the anticipated periods of wireless silence in April and May 1944.
80. Hesketh, Appendix IV, pp. 383–90.
81. LAC, RG 25, 10838, see the radio traffic; TNA, WO 106/4309, Fortitude South II Plans.

82. TNA, WO 106/4309, Fortitude South Plans, 'Plan Fortitude', Maj. Gen. H.R. Bull, SHAEF G3, 23 February 1944.
83. LAC, microfilm reel no. T-1866, 2nd Canadian Corps War Diary, May–June 1944.
84. See Antony Beevor, *D-Day: The Battle for Normandy* (New York: Viking, 2009), p. 3.
85. D'Este, *Patton*, p. 593.
86. Howard, p. 120
87. Hesketh, p. 172.
88. D'Este, *Patton*, p. 593.
89. *Chicago Tribune*, 26 April 1944.
90. Dupuy, 'Behind the Elephants', Chapter 1, frame 787.
91. D'Este, *Patton*, p. 586.
92. [Marshall], *The Papers of George Catlett Marshall*, vol. 4, Marshall to Eisenhower, 29 April 1944.
93. Crosswell, p. 605.
94. [Marshall], *The Papers of George Catlett Marshall*, vol. 4, Eisenhower to Marshall, 30 April 1944, and note 4, which refers to Eisenhower's 3 May telegram,
95. Hesketh, pp. 128, 172.
96. Hesketh, pp. 97–8.
97. C.P. Stacey, *The Victory Campaign: The Operations in North-West Europe, 1945–1955* (Ottawa, ON: Queen's Printer, 1960), p. 46.
98. Hesketh, p. 181.
99. Hesketh, p. 172.
100. Hesketh, p. 180.
101. TNA, WO 219/308, 'Operation Fortitude Deception Plan', vol. 2, p. 1155. The quote is from a plan dated 5 November 1943, emphasis added. See also AHQ Narrative No. 42, p. 131; Boog, Krebs and Vogel, p. 595.

CHAPTER 18: OK, LET'S GO!

1. LAC, RG 36/31, vol. 27, Field Reports, 1944, Report No. 2, May 1944.
2. Christopher Bayly and Tim Harper, *Forgotten Armies: Britain's Asian Empire and the War with Japan* (London: Penguin, 2005), p. 382.
3. Alan Millet and Williamson Murray, *A War to Be Won* (Cambridge, MA: Harvard UP, 2000), p. 350.
4. Bayly and Harper, p. 390.
5. LAC, RG 36/31, vol. 27, Field Reports, 1944, Report No. 2, May 1944.
6. '*Chicago Tribune*, Censorship in India and Elsewhere', 21 April 1944.
7. TNA, FO 371/38572, BIS Report No. 23, week ending 18 March 1944; *Newsweek*, 'Stilwell in Burma points up Divergence in Asiatic Strategy', 20 March 1944; BIS Report No. 27, week ending 1 April 1944; and *Time*, 'Battle of Asia: The Admiral Could Not Laugh', 3 April 1944.
8. Roosevelt Presidential Library, Stimson Papers, Reel 9, Diary of Henry L. Stimson, 18–19 May 1944.
9. Hinsley, *British Intelligence* (abridged edition), p. 376.
10. Nicholson, *The Canadians in Italy*, p. 391.
11. TNA, CAB 154/101, 'History of Deception', vol. 2, p. 307.
12. Blumenson, *Clark*, p. 208.
13. *New York Times*, 'Alexander, Clark Promise Enemy will be Destroyed', 13 May 1944, p. 1.

14. Nicolson, *Alex*, p. 252.

15. Ernest F. Fisher, Jr., *Cassino to the Alps* (Washington, DC: CMH, 1993), p. 165.

16. Jackson, *The Battle for Italy*, p. 243.

17. Nicolson, *Alex*, p. 253.

18. Blumenson, *Clark*, p. 206.

19. Blumenson, *Clark*, p. 210.

20. Graham and Bidwell, *Tug of War*, p. 340.

21. As quoted in Nicolson, *Alex*, p. 253.

22. See the discussion in Brig. C.J. Molony, *The Mediterranean and Middle East*, vol. 6: *Victory in the Mediterranean, Part I: 1st April to 4th June 1944* (London: HMSO, 1984), pp. 289–92.

23. *New York Times*, 'Corps Fouls Nazis', 2 June 1944.

24. Blumenson, *Clark*, p. 214.

25. Robert H. Adleman and Col. George Walton, *The Devil's Brigade* (New York: Chilton Books, 1966), pp. 209–20.

26. Adleman and Walton, p. 218.

27. Blumenson, *Clark*, pp. 216–17.

28. Fisher, pp. 222–3.

29. Nicolson, *Alex*, p. 254.

30. TNA, FO 371/38573, BIS Report No. 47, week ending 10 June 1944.

31. Fisher, p. 222.

32. P.J. Grigg, *Prejudice and Judgment* (London: Cape, 1948), pp. 363–4.

33. David Edgerton, in *Britain's War Machine* (see pp. 219–27), makes the case for the superior quality of British equipment – including tanks.

34. Churchill College Archives, microfilm collection, PREM 3/342/11, 'Operation Overlord (Plans) 1943–44', see letters between Churchill, Ismay and Montgomery, 16–20 May 1944.

35. Jonathan Fennell, *Fighting the People's War: The British and Commonwealth Armies and the Second World War* (Cambridge: Cambridge UP, 2019), p. 473.

36. Fennell, p. 481.

37. Calder, *The People's War*, p. 570.

38. As quoted in Fennell, p. 484.

39. Fennell, p. 485.

40. Canadian Mail Censorship Report, 1–15 June 1944, as quoted in Fennell, p. 486.

41. For an assessment of the motivation and combat effectiveness in the Canadian Army at this stage see Robert Engen, *Strangers in Arms: Combat Motivation in the Canadian Army, 1943–1945* (Montreal/Kingston: McGill–Queens UP, 2016).

42. Imperial War Museum, Montgomery Ancillary Collection, De Guingand Correspondence, Maj. P.B. Earle to De Guingand, 30 May 1944, emphasis in the original.

43. Dickson, pp. 247–53.

44. At the time of writing, the American release, authorised by the US War Department, was available on YouTube.

45. TNA, FO 371/38573, BIS Report No. 37, week ending 6 May 1944; *Life*, 8 May 1944, 'Dieppe Newsreel Teaches Invasion lessons'.

46. TNA, WO 219/402, p. 90, SHAEF memo 2 June 1944.

47. *The Mackenzie King Record*, p. 695; TNA, WO 229/56 COS SHAEF Part II, Eisenhower's memo of 19 May 1944.

48. TNA, CAB 154/101, 'History of Deception', vol. 2, p. 307.

49. TNA, WO 229/56 COS SHAEF Part II. See correspondence in late May 1944.
50. US National WWII Museum Archives, Richard Kennedy Papers, file 2002-510.
51. Roosevelt Presidential Library, Hopkins Papers, Sherwood Collection, Box 334, 'CBS on D-Day', p. 71.
52. Hamilton, *Master of the Battlefield*, p. 582.
53. Hamilton, *Master of the Battlefield*, p. 583.
54. Bradley, *A Soldier's Story*, p. 246.
55. Bradley, *A Soldier's Story*, p. 213.
56. Hinsley, *British Intelligence* (abridged edition), p. 460.
57. According to Hinsley, I British Corps appeared to take no notice of this warning and operated on the assumption that the 21st Panzer was 20–30 miles inland and would not be a factor on D-Day. See vol. 3, Part II, Appendix 14 of the unabridged version of *British Intelligence*. Surviving documents in The National Archives in Britain (checked against Hinsley's claims) support his contention: the presence of the 21st Panzer in the Caen area is very clear in the intelligence summaries of all formations prior to D-Day.
58. Harrison, p. 186.
59. D'Este, *Eisenhower*, p. 516.
60. D'Este, *Eisenhower*, p. 516.
61. Butcher, 30 May 1944, pp. 551–2.
62. *Chicago Tribune*, 'Anti-Invasion Command to Go in Action: Berlin', 29 May 1944.
63. Roosevelt Presidential Library, Hopkins Papers, Sherwood Collection, Box 334, 'CBS on D-Day', p. 84.
64. William F. Buckingham, *D-Day: The First 72 Hours* (Stroud: Tempus, 2004), p. 115.
65. Eric Larrabee, *Commander in Chief: Franklin Delano Roosevelt, His Lieutenants, and Their War* (Annapolis, MD: USNI Press, 1987), p. 455.

CHAPTER 19: THE SECOND FRONT AT LAST

1. Col. Barney Oldfield, USAF (Retd), *Never a Shot in Anger* (Santa Barbara, CA: Capra, 1956), p. 82.
2. 'Extract from the Telephone Diary of the 352nd Infantry Division (Coast Defense Section Bayeux)', in David Isby, ed., *Fighting the Invasion: The German Army at D-Day* (London: Greenhill Books, 2000), p. 207.
3. Buckingham, p. 154.
4. Buckingham, p. 157.
5. Harrison, p. 304.
6. John C. McManus, *The Americans on D-Day: The American Experience at the Normandy Invasion* (New York: Forge, 2004), p. 274.
7. Information courtesy John C. McManus, email 11 February 2021.
8. Zaloga, 'Debunking an OMAHA Beach Legend', p. 159.
9. For the most comprehensive and informed discussion of the American fireplan for Omaha beach see Adrian Lewis, *OMAHA Beach: A Flawed Victory* (Chapel Hill, NC: University of North Carolina Press, 2001), Chapter 8, 'The Joint Fire Plan', quote p. 370.
10. McManus, *The Americans on D-Day*, p. 336.
11. McManus, *The Americans on D-Day*, p. 337.

12. A full account of the 111th FA's odyssey, compiled by S.L.A. Marshall, is reprinted in Joseph H. Ewing, *29 Let's Go! A History of the 29th Infantry Division in World War II* (Washington, DC: Infantry Journal Press, n.d.), pp. 51–2.

13. *V Corps Operations in the ETO*, p. 63.

14. American sources make no mention of the role of the Royal Navy in landing the Rangers. The assault on Pte du Hoc was launched from the British Landing Ship *Ben-My-Chree*. The literature does not record British casualties; nor is there any commemoration of their effort at Pte du Hoc.

15. First US Division Museum, Cantigny, IL, *Selected Intelligence Report No. 1, June 1944–November 1944*, Office of the AC of G-2, First United States Infantry Division, Germany 6 December 1944, p. 9.

16. Harrison, p. 326.

17. Stephen Badsey and Tim Bean, *Omaha Beach* (Stroud: Sutton Publishing, 2004), p. 82.

18. The usual figure for Omaha is 2,000 dead. Badsey and Bean (2004) put it at 3,000; other figures are higher.

19. Harrison, p. 313.

20. Joseph Balkoski, *Beyond the Beachhead: The 29th Infantry Division in Normandy* (Mechanicsburg, PA: Stackpole Books, 2005), p. 176.

21. Ellis, *Victory in the West*, vol. 1, p. 177.

22. Simon Trew, *GOLD Beach* (Stroud: Sutton Publishing, 2004), p. 60.

23. Williams, '50 Div in Normandy', p. 60.

24. Williams, '50 Div in Normandy', p. 61.

25. 'Extract from the Telephone Diary of the 352nd Infantry Division', in Isby, ed., *Fighting the Invasion*, pp. 204–20.

26. For the most comprehensive and succinct account of Sword see Ken Ford, *Sword Beach* (Stroud: Sutton Publishing, 2004).

27. Will Bird, *No Retreating Footsteps: The History of the North Novas* (Amherst, NS: Furlong's, n.d.), p. 63.

28. US National WWII Museum Archives, Kennedy Papers, file SS 2002-510, *ISIS Report on France*, vol. 2: *Normandy West of the Seine*, Part V(B), 'Ports'.

29. Windsor, Sarty and Milner, *Loyal Gunners*, pp. 337–40.

30. Terry Copp, *Fields of Fire: The Canadians in Normandy* (Toronto, ON: University of Toronto Press, 2003), p. 53.

31. Copp, *Fields of Fire*, p. 55.

32. Buckingham, p. 223

33. Ford, *Sword Beach*, p. 80.

34. Max Hastings, *Overlord: D-Day and the Battle for Normandy* (New York: Touchstone Books, 1984), p. 117.

35. Buckingham, p. 228.

36. Boog, Krebs and Vogel, p. 595.

37. Boog, Krebs and Vogel, p. 594.

38. Reynolds, pp. 54–5.

39. Buckingham, p. 233.

40. Michael Reynolds, *Steel Inferno: I SS Panzer Corps in Normandy* (New York: Sarpedon, 1997), p. 60.

41. The tunnel is now part of the museum and commemorative site 'Le Mémorial' in Caen.

42. Reynolds, *Steel Inferno*, p. 60.

43. Michael Balfour says 0450 hours, presumably British time, *Propaganda in War 1939–1945*, p. 374. The log of No. 3 Canadian Public Relations Group records the first German broadcast at 0600 hours British time, LAC, RG 24, vol. 16642. A collection of early international radio notices of the landings can be found in LAC, RG 24, vol. 10420, SHAEF Press Releases.

44. Roosevelt Presidential Library, Hopkins Papers, Sherwood Collection, Box 334, 'CBS on D-Day', p. 13.

45. Brigham Young University, Digital Collections, 'SHAEF Communiqués', 6 June 1944.

46. Manchester and Reid, pp. 838, 843.

47. Larrabee, *Commander in Chief*, p. 457.

48. LAC, Mackenzie King Diary, 6 June 1944, accessed online.

49. LAC, RG 24, vol. 16642, 3 Canadian Press Relations Group (CPRG), WD 6 June 1944.

50. Steven Casey, *The War Beat, Europe: The American Media at War Against Nazi Germany* (Oxford: Oxford UP, 2017), p. 230.

51. LAC, RG 24, vol. 10420, Correspondents – WAR SHAEF Press Releases.

52. Roosevelt Presidential Library, Hopkins Papers, Sherwood Collection, Box 334, 'CBS on D-Day', pp. 39–40.

53. TNA, INF 1/975, 'Invasion of Europe'.

54. *War Report: From D-Day to Berlin as It Happened*, ed. Desmond Hawkins (London: BBC Books, 2019), p. 42.

55. The Blue Network, owned by NBC, was later sold to become the American Broadcasting Network, ABC. See Roosevelt Presidential Library, Hopkins Papers, Sherwood Collection, Box 334, 'CBS on D-Day'.

56. Malone says 2,000, others claim 4,000. Either way, it was not much. See Richard Malone, *Missing from the Record* (Toronto, ON: Collins, 1946), p. 169.

57. Malone, see Chapter 15, 'Press Problems', quote p. 173. See also LAC, RG 24, vol. 16642, 3 CPRG WD, 6–12 June 1944.

58. LAC, RG 24, vol. 16642, 3 CPRG WD, 7 June 1944.

59. Ross Munro, *Gauntlet to Overlord: The Story of the Canadian Army* (Toronto, ON: Macmillan, 1945), p. 70.

60. The accounts of Munro and Yarrow from Dupuy, 'Behind the Elephants', pp. 112–13.

61. Charles Lynch, *You Can't Print That! Memoirs of a Political Voyeur* (Edmonton, AB: Hurtig Publishers, 1983), pp. 56–7.

62. 'Shooters': *The Canadian Army Film and Photo Unit, 1941–1946*, a film by James O'Regan, CD Department of National Defence, 2004. Tragically, much of Canada's wartime film footage was destroyed in a warehouse fire in 1967.

63. LAC, RG 24, vol. 16642.3, CPRG WD, 6 June 1944. The WD of No. 5 Army Film and Photo Section is cryptic, TNA, WO 171/3799. Dr Fred McGlade's *The History of the British Army Film and Photographic Unit in the Second World War* (Solihull: Helion, 2010) contains first-person accounts of the landing.

64. Neil McDonald with Peter Brune, *Valiant for Truth: The Life of Chester Wilmot, War Correspondent* (Sydney: NewSouth Press, 2016), p. 322. For a technical description of the Midget see 'Report No. C.046, the Design of the BBC Midget Portable Disc Recorder', 10 November 1944, downloadable at

http://downloads.bbc.co.uk/rd/pubs/reports/1944-13.pdf. This description includes discussion of battery power, which by all accounts was unavailable on D-Day.

65. McDonald and Brune, p. 321.
66. BBC Text Archives, R29/684/1, programming listed in 'The War Report: "The Story of D-Day"', Selected Scripts, 1944.
67. Oldfield, p. 82.
68. Dupuy, 'Behind the Elephants', p. 112; Oldfield, p. 84.
69. Oldfield, p. 82; Dupuy, 'Behind the Elephants', pp. 110–11.
70. Oldfield, pp. 80–5.
71. Casey, *The War Beat, Europe*, pp. 227–34.
72. AHEC, Papers of Chester Hansen, Hansen Diary, 6 June 1944.
73. Casey, *The War Beat*, pp. 238–9. See also, A.D. Coleman, 'Alternate History: Robert Capa on D-Day', address to the 55th Annual Conference of the Society for Photographic Education, Philadelphia, PA, 2 March 2018, as published online in *Exposure Magazine*.
74. Horten, p. 2.
75. Casey, *The War Beat, Europe*, p. 232.
76. BBC Text Archives, R47/201/1 D-Day Relays, 'Broadcast Report: Subject: BBC's Invasion Service (Final Report)', BBC New York.
77. BBC Text Archives, R47/201/1 D-Day Relays, 'Broadcast Report: Subject: BBC's Invasion Service (Final Report)', BBC New York.
78. BBC Text Archives, R47/201/1 D-Day Relays, 'BBC North American Service Intelligence Memorandum', 19 June 1944.
79. BBC Text Archives, R47/201/1, D-Day Relays, 'BBC North American Service Intelligence Memorandum', 19 June 1944.
80. Roosevelt Presidential Library, Stimson Diary, 6 June 1944.
81. BBC Text Archives, R47/201/1 D-Day Relays, Henry David, Research Department to Warren McAlpine, 21 June 1944.
82. *Chicago Tribune*, 9 June 1944, editorial note on p. 1.
83. TNA, WO 299/56, 'Investigation of the System of Press Coverage and Communications at present in operation in Normandy', Col. R. Ernest Dupuy, Air Cdre Lionel F. Heald and Walton A. Cole, 5 July 1944.
84. Oldfield, p. 86.
85. Dupuy, 'Behind the Elephants', p. 125.
86. See UWML, Dupuy Papers, reel 2, 'History of Public Relations Office', HQ 12th Army Group [spring 1945], p. 7.
87. Oldfield, pp. 88–9.

CHAPTER 20: STOPPING THE PANZERS

1. As quoted in Donald E. Graves, ' "Naked Truths for the Asking": Twentieth-Century Military Historians and the Battlefield Narrative', in David Charters, Marc Milner and J. Brent Wilson, eds, *Military History and the Military Profession* (Westport, CT: Praeger, 1992), pp. 45–55.
2. John Buckley, *Monty's Men: The British Army and the Liberation of Europe* (New Haven, CT and London: Yale UP, 2013), pp. 22–3.
3. *New York Times*, 'British Casualties in War Total 667,159', 28 June 1944.
4. Buckley, *Monty's Men*, pp. 24–5.
5. Buckley, *Monty's Men*, pp. 24–5.

6. Crosswell, p. 634.
7. Crosswell, p. 638.
8. Kennedy, *Freedom from Fear*, p. 715.
9. Figures for D-Day are not entirely agreed upon. See Beevor, p. 151, for a discussion.
10. AHEC, Hansen Diary, 7 June 1944.
11. Hamilton, *Master of the Battlefield*, p. 626.
12. The US Airborne were equipped with the British 6-pounder anti-tank gun because it fit into their gliders.
13. John C. McManus, *The Americans at Normandy: The Summer of 1944 – The American War from the Normandy Beaches to Falaise* (New York: Tom Doherty and Associates, 2004), pp. 76–7.
14. McManus, *The Americans at Normandy*, p. 62.
15. McManus, *The Americans at Normandy*, pp. 67–8.
16. Harrison, p. 344.
17. Harrison, p. 350.
18. Hastings, *Overlord*, p. 118.
19. I am grateful to Chris Kretzschmar for tracking down this information. The size of the companies of 12th SS is confirmed in the notes made in autumn 1944 by the late Walter Keith, then a subaltern in the Regina Rifles, which were provided to the author.
20. Ian V. Hogg, *German Artillery of World War II* (London: Greenhill Books, 1997), pp. 197–200, 214–17.
21. Buckingham, p. 259.
22. David Isby, ed., ed. *Fighting in Normandy: The German Army from D-Day to Villers-Bocage* (London: Greenhill Books, 2001), p. 47.
23. Franz Kurowski, *Elite Panzer Strike Force: Germany's Panzer Lehr Division in World War II* (Mechanicsburg, PA: Stackpole Books, 2011), p. 22.
24. Kurowski, p. 26.
25. Kurowski, p. 27.
26. Beevor, p. 176.
27. Figures from Buckingham, p. 233.
28. Beevor, p. 176.
29. Kurowski, p. 32.
30. Helmut Ritgen, *The Western Front: Memoirs of a Panzer Lehr Officer* (Winnipeg, MB: J.J. Fedorowicz Publishing, 1995), p. 40.
31. Ritgen says 'near Cheux', p. 39, while Kurowski says Le Mesnil-Patry, p. 35.
32. Ritgen, p. 40.
33. See the introduction to Marc Milner, *Stopping the Panzers: The Untold Story of D-Day* (Lawrence, KS: University Press of Kansas, 2014). Confirmation of Charles Stacey's exclusion from the Overlord documents courtesy Roger Sarty.
34. For a detailed discussion of COSSAC planning to meet a Panzer attack see Milner, *Stopping the Panzers*, pp. 40–6.
35. LAC, RG 24, microfilm reel no. T-15455, Overlord Operational Order, HQ RCA, 3rd Canadian Division, 15 May 1944, p. 133.
36. Harrison, pp. 309–13. See also Balkoski, pp. 140–1.
37. Lt Col. Richard M. Ross, OBE, *The History of the 1st Battalion Cameron Highlanders of Ottawa* (MG) (privately published, n.d.), p. 42.

38. LAC, RG 24, microfilm reel no. T-15455, Overlord Operational Order, HQ RCA, 3rd Canadian Division, 15 May 1944, p. 133.

39. Details of action from Jean-Claude Perrigault, *21. Panzer Division*, Bayeuax: Heimdal, 2002, pp. 505–7. See also P. Whitney Lackenbauer and Chris Madsen, eds, *Kurt Meyer on Trial [A Documentary Record]* (Kingston, ON: Canadian Defence Academy Press, 2007), p. 485.

40. DHH, 145.2N2011 (D3), interviews of Capt. J.A. Wilson and Capt. E.S. Gray, both North Novas, late June 1944.

41. Lt Col. H.M. Jackson, MBE, ED, *The Sherbrooke Regiment (12th Armoured Regiment)* (privately published, 1958), p. 124.

42. Jackson, *The Sherbrooke Regiment*, p. 124.

43. Testimony of Major Don Learment, in Lackenbauer and Madsen, eds, *Kurt Meyer on Trial*, p. 161.

44. Copp, *Fields of Fire*, p. 66.

45. DHH 145.2 N2011 (D3), interview with Capt. Gray.

46. Stacey, *The Victory Campaign*, p. 79.

47. LAC, RG 24, vol. 14,471, WD 14th RCA, 7 June 1944; Ellis, *Victory in the West*, vol. 1, p. 229.

48. Malcolm Langille, the Nova's Intelligence Sergeant at the time, recalled in 2003 that he tried repeatedly to raise 14th RCA through various networks and failed. Interview of Langille provided by Doug Hope.

49. LAC, microfilm reel no. T-12758, WD, Sherbrooke Fusiliers, 7 June 1944.

50. Bird, *No Retreating Footsteps*, p. 89.

51. Bird, *No Retreating Footsteps*, p. 95; Lackenbauer and Madsen, eds, *Kurt Meyer on Trial*, p. 162.

52. Bird, *No Retreating Footsteps*, p. 87.

53. Bird, *No Retreating Footsteps*, p. 98; Lackenbauer and Madsen, eds, *Kurt Meyer on Trial*, p. 162.

54. Bird, *No Retreating Footsteps*, p. 98.

55. Bird, *No Retreating Footsteps*, p. 100; LAC, RG 24, vol. 14,471, 14th RCA War Diary says that the first shells were fired at 1800 hours, probably at more distant targets.

56. The North Nova's Diary in Terry Copp and Robert Vogel, *Maple Leaf Route: Caen* (Alma, ON: Maple Leaf Route, 1983), p. 71.

57. Bird, *No Retreating Footsteps*, pp. 100–1.

58. Buckingham, p. 258.

59. See Howard Margolian, *Conduct Unbecoming: The Story of the Murder of Canadian Prisoners of War in Normandy* (Toronto, ON: University of Toronto Press, 1998).

60. Buckingham, p. 259.

61. Bird, *No Retreating Footsteps*, p. 97.

62. Reynolds, *Steel Inferno*, p. 69.

63. Bird, *No Retreating Footsteps*, p. 97.

64. Hubert Meyer, *The 12th SS: The History of the Hitler Youth Panzer Division*, vol. 1 (Mechanicsburg, PA: Stackpole Books, 2005), p. 159.

65. See M. Milner, 'The Guns of Bretteville: 13th Field Regiment, RCA, and the defence of Bretteville-l'Orgueilleuse, 7–10 June 1944', *Canadian Military History*, vol. 16, no. 4, Autumn 2007, pp. 5–24.

66. Meyer, *The 12th SS*, p. 162.

67. Meyer, *The 12th SS*, p. 50.

68. Lt W.W. Barrett, *The History of 13 Canadian Field Regiment, Royal Canadian Artillery, 1940–1945* (privately published, 1945), p. 37. When asked about this Lt Col. Clifford dismissed the idea of a curtain of fire as 'bullshit!' The perimeter was maintained by a series of DF shoots and Mike targets. Interview, 25 April 2002.

69. Meyer, *The 12th SS*, p. 166; Reynolds, *Steel Inferno*, p. 74. Tony Foulds, who participated in the battle, is quite emphatic. See 'In Support of the Canadians: A British Anti-Tank Regiment's First Five Weeks in Normandy', *Canadian Military History*, no. 7, vol. 2, Spring 1998, pp. 71–8.

70. TNA, WO 179/2879, Battle Log of 7th Brigade.

71. Reynolds, *Steel Inferno*, p. 75.

72. Copp, *Fields of Fire*, pp. 68–9.

73. Kurowski, p. 36.

74. Hesketh, p. 202.

75. Isby, ed., *Fighting in Normandy*, p. 48.

76. Reynolds, *Steel Inferno*, p. 79.

77. Mark Zuehlke, *Holding Juno: Canada's Heroic Defence of the D-Day Beaches, June 7–12, 1944* (Toronto, ON: Douglas and McIntyre, 2005), p. 207.

78. Zuehlke, *Holding Juno*, p. 205.

79. Zuehlke, *Holding Juno*, p. 196.

80. Mohnke was south of Brouay arranging for the massacre of men from the Royal Winnipeg Rifles. See Margolin, p. 91.

81. Gordon Brown and Terry Copp, *Look to Your Front . . . Regina Rifles: A Regiment at War, 1944–45* (Waterloo, ON: Laurier Centre for Military Strategic and Disarmament Studies, 2001), pp. 79–84.

82. *Historica: Les Canadiens Face à la Hiterjugend* (Editions Heimdal, no. 23, June 1991), p. 53.

83. Brown and Copp, *Look to Your Front*, p. 84.

84. Barrett, *The History of 13 Canadian Field Regiment*, p. 39.

85. *Into Action with the 12th Field, 1940–1945* (privately published, 1945), pp. 48–9.

86. Michael R. McNorgan, *The Gallant Hussars: A History of the 1st Hussar Regiment, 1856–2004* (Aylmer, ON: The 1st Hussars Cavalry Fund, 2004), pp. 127–9.

87. Meyer, *The 12th SS*, p. 191.

88. Meyer, *The 12th SS*, pp. 194–7.

89. As quoted in Copp, *Fields of Fire*, p. 74, emphasis added.

90. Reynolds, *Steel Inferno*, p. 85.

91. Hesketh, p. 202.

92. Boog, Krebs and Vogel, p. 594.

93. The *New York Times* story was carried in the *Globe and Mail*, 10 June 1944, 'Canadian-British Force Ready for Second Assault, Say Nazis', while the verbatim account of the radio broadcast appears in the *Chicago Tribune*, 10 June 1944, 'NAZIS PREDICT BELGIUM TO BE INVADED SOON'.

94. Hesketh, p. 209.

95. Hesketh, p. 210.

96. Hesketh, p. 210; T.L. Cubbage, 'The Success of Operation Fortitude: Hesketh's History of Strategic Deception', in Michael I. Handel, ed., *Strategic and Operational Deception in the Second World War* (London: Frank Cass, 1987), pp. 327–46.

97. Howard, p. 189.

98. Craig W.H. Luther, *Blood and Honor: The History of the 12th SS Panzer Division 'Hitler Youth', 1943–1945* (San Jose, CA: James Bender, 1987), p. 180.

CHAPTER 21: TEMPESTS

1. Dupuy, 'Behind the Elephants', p. 122.
2. US National WWII Museum Archives, Kennedy Papers, file 2002-510, *Inter-Service Information Series, Report on France*, vol. 2: *Normandy West of the Seine*, January 1943.
3. AHEC, Hansen Diary, 7 and 9 June 1944.
4. Michael Doubler, *Closing with the Enemy: How GIs Fought the War in Europe, 1944–45* (Lawrence, KS: University Press of Kansas, 1994), see especially pp. 48–51.
5. Dominick Graham and Shelford Bidwell, *Coalitions, Politicians and Generals: Some Aspects of Command in Two World Wars* (London: Brassey's, 1993), pp. 200–1.
6. Steve R. Waddell, *United States Army Logistics: The Normandy Campaign, 1944* (Westport, CT: Greenwood Press, 1994), p. 163.
7. Crosswell, p. 641.
8. Crosswell, p. 641.
9. Waddell, p. 59.
10. William Ross and Charles F. Romans, *The Quartermaster Corps: Operations in the War Against Germany*, 1991; Lida Mayo, *The Ordnance Department: On Beachhead and Battlefront*, 1991; Richard M. Leighton and Robert W. Coakley, *Global Logistics and Strategy 1940–1943*, 1995; and Roland G. Ruppenthal, *Logistical Support of the Armies*, 1995. All published in Washington, DC, by CMH.
11. AHEC, Hansen Diary, 9 June 1944.
12. Ruppenthal, vol. 1, p. 446; AHEC, Hansen Diary, 14 June 1944.
13. Harrison, p. 351.
14. Harrison, pp. 368–9.
15. Harrison, p. 372; see also *A History of the Second United States Armored Division, 1940–1946* (Nashville, TN: The Battery Press, 1946), Chapter 5.
16. Keith Nightingale, 'The Taking of La Fière Bridge', *Small Wars Journal*, 28 May 2012, accessed online 2 December 2021.
17. Rick Atkinson, *The Guns at Last Light: The War in Western Europe, 1944–1945* (New York: Henry Holt & Co., 2013), p. 112.
18. Christopher Milner, as quoted in Reynolds, *Steel Inferno*, p. 103.
19. Reynolds, *Steel Inferno*, pp. 105–6.
20. Eric Lefevre, *Panzers in Normandy Then and Now* (London: Battle of Britain Prints International Ltd, 1983), 'Schwere SS-Panzer Abteilung 101', pp. 161–81.
21. Carlo D'Este, *Decision in Normandy* (New York: E.P. Dutton, 1983), p. 196.
22. Chester Wilmot, *The Struggle for Europe* (London: Collins, 1952), p. 311.
23. Boog, Krebs and Vogel, p. 598.
24. DHH, 215C1.023, 'First Cdn Army Int Summary Number 9', 14 June 1944.
25. Boog, Krebs and Vogel, p. 598.
26. Eisenhower, *Crusade in Europe*, p. 254.
27. Churchill, *Triumph and Tragedy*, pp. 12–13.
28. Bayly and Harper, p. 388.
29. Alanbrooke, *War Diaries*, 15 June 1944.
30. TNA, PREM 4/27/9, Halifax Correspondence, Halifax to Bracken, 8 June 1944, and Bracken to Halifax, 9 June 1944.
31. TNA, INF 1/975, Bracken to Sinclair, 13 June 1944.
32. TNA, INF 1/975, Morgan, Deputy Director, BIS New York, to MOI London, 19 June 1944.

33. TNA, FO 371/38571, BIS Report No. 46, Newsreels, 12 June 1944.
34. Maddow, p. 140.
35. TNA, INF 1/975, Morgan to MOI, 19 June 1944.
36. TNA, FO 953/7, 'History of British Information', pp. 74–7.
37. See especially 'United Newsreels' for March to August 1944, International Historic Films, vols 8 and 9, 2009.
38. Survey of the *New York Times, Washington Post, Chicago Tribune, Houston Chronicle* and *Los Angeles Times* conducted for this project by Jamie Horncastle, November 2011. Horncastle identified the use of 'American and Allied' as an issue long before archival research uncovered contemporary evidence of the British complaint.
39. TNA, FO 953/7, 'History of British Information', pp. 74–7.
40. AHEC, Hansen Diary, 11 June 1944.
41. *Chicago Tribune*, 'Fighting for Two Cities', 14 June 1944.
42. Casey, *The War Beat, Europe*, p. 244.
43. Dupuy, 'Behind the Elephants', p. 137.
44. *New York Times*, 'Nazi Roads in Peril', 17 June 1944.
45. Boog, Krebs and Vogel, p. 598.
46. Roskill, vol. 3, Part II, p. 63.
47. Waddell, p. 57.
48. European Centre for Medium-Range Weather Forecasts, 'ECMWF simulates storm that destroyed Normandy invasion harbour', published online, 29 August 2017, accessed 19 December 2021.
49. AHEC, Hansen Diary, 21 June 1944.
50. Waddell, p. 61.
51. Roskill, vol. 3, Part II, p. 65.
52. Roskill, vol. 3, Part II, p. 65.
53. *Eisenhower Papers*, vol. 2, Eisenhower to Marshall, 21 June 1944; Roskill, vol. 3, Part II, p. 65.
54. Waddell, p. 80.
55. AHEC, Hansen Diary, 21 June 1944.
56. Boog, Krebs and Vogel, p. 597.
57. TNA, WO 285/9, Dempsey Diary, 19–24 June 1944.
58. Ellis, p. 274; AHEC Nevins Papers, Box 4, folder 1, SHAEF Situation Reports June–July 1944.
59. Alanbrooke, *War Diaries*, 21 June 1944; *Eisenhower Papers*, vol. 2, memo to CCS, 23 June 1944.
60. Harrison, pp. 441–2.
61. Butcher, 15 June 1944.
62. Casey, *The War Beat, Europe*, p. 245.
63. UWML, Dupuy Papers, reel 2, 'History of Public Relations Office', 12 AG, p. 8.
64. Casey, *The War Beat, Europe*, p. 252.
65. LAC, RG 24, vol. 12,369, 'Public Relations Council, SHAEF', as quoted in Annex 1 to Minutes of SHAEF PR Council Meeting, 21 June 1944.
66. TNA, WO 299/57, SHAEF 'Directive No. 1 for week ending 22/06/44', p. 330.
67. Dupuy, 'Behind the Elephants', p. 131.
68. LAC, RG 24, vol. 16,642, War Diary of No. 3 Canadian Press Reporting Group, 17 June 1944. The Canadian situation was generally satisfactory, thanks to Col. Malone's initiatives.

69. TNA, WO 229/56, Col. Joseph B Phillips, SO, Chief, Communications Branch to Acting Chief, Public Relations Division, 29 June 1944.
70. LAC, RG 24, vol. 12,369, SHAEF Public Relations Council, Minutes of meeting 23 June 1944.
71. UWML, Dupuy Papers, reel 2, figure compiled from 'Correspondents Present in European Theater, September 1945' and 'Correspondents Departed from European Theater', both of which list only American reporters with the date of their arrival and their assignment.
72. *New York Times*, 28 June 1944.
73. Raymond Daniell, *New York Times*, 25 June 1944.
74. TNA, FO 371/38673, BIS Report No. 50, week ending 24 June 1944, 'British Angst over Lack of Press Coverage'.
75. Oldfield, p. 88.
76. Casey, *The War Beat, Europe*, p. 245.
77. Bruce Muirhead, *Against the Odds: The Public Life and Times of Louis Rasminsky* (Toronto, ON: University of Toronto Press, 1999), p. 102.
78. *US News*, 23 June 1944.
79. *Chicago Tribune*, editorial, 'The Strongest Nation', 24 June 1944.
80. Butcher, pp. 593–4.
81. Russell Weigley, *Eisenhower's Lieutenants: The Campaign of France and Germany, 1944–1945* (Bloomington, IN: Indiana UP, 1981), vol. 1, Chapter 7, 'Bocage' *passim*.
82. Hinsley, *British Intelligence* (abridged edition), p. 494.
83. Reynolds, *Steel Inferno*, p. 118.
84. Pemberton, p. 222.
85. LAC, RG 24, vol. 14,465, microfilm reel T-16363, War Diary, 13th Field Regiment, RCA, 26 June 1944.
86. Reynolds, *Steel Inferno*, p. 135.
87. Hinsley, *British Intelligence* (abridged edition), p. 496.
88. Buckley, *Monty's Men*, p. 83.
89. Buckley, *Monty's Men*, pp. 84–5.
90. Michael Reynolds, *Sons of the Reich: The History of II SS Panzer Corps in Normandy, Arnhem, the Ardennes and on the Eastern Front* (Haverton, PA: Casemate, 2002), p. 30.
91. Pemberton, p. 222.
92. Reynolds, *Steel Inferno*, pp. 140–1
93. TNA, WO 285/9, Dempsey Diary, 29 June 1944.
94. Ellis, *Victory in the West*, p. 286.
95. Buckley, *Monty's Men*, p. 87.
96. TNA, WO 229/57, SHAEF Press Guidance No. 3, week of 29 June 1944.

CHAPTER 22: STALEMATE

1. AHEC, Hansen Diary, 23 July 1944.
2. See David M. Glantz, *Soviet Military Operational Art: In Pursuit of Deep Battle* (London: Frank Cass, 1991), Chapter 5.
3. *Eisenhower Papers*, vol. 3, Eisenhower to Harriman, 7 July 1944.
4. AHEC, Hansen Diary, 13 July 1944.
5. Steve Zaloga, *German Tanks in Normandy 1944* (Oxford: Osprey, 2021), p. 34.
6. *New York Times*, 'A Double Victory', 10 July 1944.

7. Beevor, p. 249.
8. Beevor, p. 249.
9. Boog, Krebs and Vogel, p. 601.
10. Sir Llewellyn Woodward, *British Foreign Policy in the Second World War*, vol. 5 (London: HMSO, 1976), see especially Chapter 62.
11. Walter Lippmann, *U.S. War Aims* (Boston, MA: Little, Brown and Co., 1944).
12. Jeffrey J. Clarke and Robert Ross Smith, *Riviera to the Rhine* (Washington, DC: CMH, 1993), p. 15.
13. Fisher, *Cassino to the Alps*, pp. 236–7.
14. Clarke and Smith, p. 4.
15. TNA, FO 371/38573, BIS Report No. 49, week ending 17 June 1944.
16. Churchill, *The World Crisis*, p. 1396.
17. Robert Dallek, *Franklin D. Roosevelt and American Foreign Policy, 1932–1945* (New York: Oxford UP, 1995), p. 455.
18. Manchester and Reid, p. 854.
19. Alanbrooke, *War Diaries*, 30 June 1944.
20. Clarke and Smith, p. 20.
21. Churchill, *The Tide of Victory*, p. 66.
22. Fisher, *Cassino to the Alps*, p. 257.
23. Smith, *Conflict Over Convoys*, p. 218.
24. Clarke and Smith, p. 16.
25. Figure 17.1 in Fennell, *Fighting the People's War*, p. 691, shows American divisions in combat surpassing those of the Commonwealth only by July 1944.
26. Boog, Krebs and Vogel, p. 597, note 35. Figures drawn from TNA, DEFE 2/431.
27. Behrens, p. 405, and see also note 2.
28. 'The Royal Canadian Navy's Part in the Invasion of Northern Europe – Operation "Overlord"', Narrative B, vol.1, draft B, RCN Naval Historical Section, *c.* 1944, p. 155.
29. *New York Times*, 'Sweepers Blazed Our "Invasion Lane"', 2 July 1944. Of the twenty-six flotillas deployed on D-Day, two were Canadian and four were American, the rest were British.
30. Roskill, vol. 3, Part II, p. 69.
31. See Milner, *The U-Boat Hunters*, pp. 137–65.
32. Roosevelt Presidential Library, Stimson Papers, Reel 9, Stimson Diary, Washington press conference, 27 July 1944.
33. *The Times*, 'Navy's Unending Duties', 14 July 1944, and *Daily Express*, 'U-Boats', 22 July 1944.
34. See the *Chicago Tribune*, 'Yanks Chuckle at Claims News Favors Them', 4 July 1944, and 'Two Great Powers', 7 July 1944.
35. Bradley, *A Soldier's Story*, p. 326.
36. *Time*, 'Battle of London: Death at Home', 24 July 1944.
37. Todman, *Britain's War: A New World*, p. 585.
38. Harry C. Thomson and Lida Mayo, *The Ordnance Department: Procurement and Supply* (Washington, DC: CMH, 1991), p. 469.
39. Bradley, *A Soldier's Story*, p. 319.
40. Ruppenthal, p. 446.
41. Martin Blumenson, *Breakout and Pursuit* (Washington, DC: Office of the Chief of Military History United States Army, 1961), p. 57.
42. Wilmot, *The Struggle for Europe*, p. 349.

43. Blumenson, *Breakout and Pursuit*, p. 56.
44. Blumenson, *Breakout and Pursuit*, pp. 59–60.
45. McManus, *The Americans at Normandy*, p. 189.
46. Blumenson, *Breakout and Pursuit*, p. 55.
47. Blumenson, *Breakout and Pursuit*, pp. 124–7.
48. Blumenson, *Breakout and Pursuit*, p. 129.
49. Weigley, vol. 1, p. 190.
50. See J.B.A. Bailey's discussion in *Fire Artillery and Firepower*, pp. 130–52. It took until 1917 for the British to perfect this kind of fire support during the Great War.
51. Blumenson, *Breakout and Pursuit*, p. 99.
52. Thompson and Mayo, p. 250.
53. Blumenson, *Breakout and Pursuit*, pp. 104–5.
54. Bradley, *A Soldier's Story*, p. 334.
55. Beevor, p. 243.
56. *Eisenhower Papers*, vol. 2, Eisenhower to Marshall, 5 July 1944.
57. Bradley, *A Soldier's Story*, p. 322.
58. AHEC, Hansen Diary, 1 July 1944; *Eisenhower Papers*, vol. 2, Eisenhower to Smith, 3 July 1944, and Eisenhower to Marshall, 5 July 1944.
59. Beevor, p. 252; McManus, *The Americans at Normandy*, p. 232.
60. Blumenson, *Breakout and Pursuit*, p. 139.
61. Weigley, vol. 1, p. 195.
62. Blumenson, *Breakout and Pursuit*, p. 205.
63. Weigley, vol. 1, p. 197.
64. Hamilton, *Master of the Battlefield*, p. 723.
65. Jonathan W. Jordan, *Brothers, Rivals, Victors: Eisenhower, Patton, Bradley and the Partnership That Drove the Allied Conquest in Europe* (New York: Calibre, 2011), p. 350.
66. Copp, *Fields of Fire*, p. 98.
67. The exact date is unclear, 26 or 27 June. See Barrett, *The History of 13 Canadian Field Regiment*, p. 44.
68. The account that follows is taken from Marc Milner, *D-Day to Carpiquet: The North Shore Regiment and the Liberation of Europe* (Fredericton, NB: Goose Lane Editions, 2006), Chapter 5.
69. Copp, *Fields of Fire*, p. 100.
70. Major A.G. Steiger, AHQ Report No. 50, Historical Section (G.S.), 'The Campaign in North-West Europe: Information from German Sources, Part II: Invasion and Battle of Normandy (6 Jun–22 Aug 44)', 14 October 1952, p. 137 (hereafter AHQ Report No. 50).
71. Copp, *Fields of Fire*, p. 101.
72. O'Brien, see pp. 330–49.
73. Alanbrooke, *War Diaries*, 5 and 6 July 1944.
74. Copp, *Fields of Fire*, p. 101.
75. Barrett, *The History of 13 Canadian Field Regiment*, p. 46.
76. Greenhous et al., p. 813.
77. TNA, WO 285/9, Dempsey Diary, 8 July 1944.
78. Beevor, p. 276.
79. Lefevre, *Panzers in Normandy*, p. 186.
80. Operation Greenline, *Encyclopédie du Débarquement et de la Bataille de Normandie*, accessed online 12 April 2022.

81. Stacey, *The Victory Campaign*, pp. 167–8.

82. Bradley, *A Soldier's Story*, p. 333.

83. Hansen Baldwin, 'Delays in Normandy', *New York Times*, 9 July 1944, p. 7; the *Globe and Mail* in Toronto carried Baldwin's story, inside, on 10 July 1944.

84. *New York Times*, 'U.S. Units Push On', 14 July 1944.

85. *Daily Express*, 'Rommel Holds on "At All Costs",' 15 July 1944.

86. Chester Wilmot, *Eclipse* (London: Hamish Hamilton, 1945), p. 122.

87. Dupuy, 'Behind the Elephants', p. 144.

88. Casey, *The War Beat, Europe*, p. 252.

89. As quoted by Larry Rue, 'British Expert Explains Lag in Normandy Drive', *Chicago Tribune*, 17 July 1944.

90. UWML, Dupuy Diary, 19 August 1944.

91. This may be the origin of that curious line in *Saving Private Ryan* that 'You gotta take Caen before you can take Saint-Lô'.

92. Wes Gallagher, 'Assert Allies [*sic*] Delay in France Helps German', *Chicago Tribune*, 16 July 1944.

93. Larry Rue, 'Allies Gain in Normandy', *Chicago Tribune*, 17 July 1944.

94. *Time*, 'Heavy Going', 17 July 1944.

95. UWML, Dupuy Diary, 16 July 1944.

96. AHQ Report No. 50, pp. 61–2.

97. Ellis, *Victory in the West*, p. 324.

98. Boog, Krebs and Vogel, pp. 599–600; Ellis, *Victory in the West*, pp. 322–3.

99. Ian Gooderson, *Air Power at the Battlefront: Allied Close Air Support in Europe, 1943–1945* (Abingdon: Frank Cass, 1998), p. 146.

100. Hamilton, *Master of the Battlefield*, p. 733.

CHAPTER 23: FANCY SKATING

1. Bradley, *A Soldier's Story*, p. 324.

2. Bradley, *A Soldier's Story*, p. 334.

3. UWML Dupuy Papers, Diary 9 July 1944.

4. Crosswell, p. 650.

5. Figures from Todman, *Britain's War: A New World*, pp. 589–90, and from Imperial War Museum, Montgomery Ancillary Collection, De Guingand Correspondence, reel II, de Guingand to Lt Col. T. Warren, 6 July 1944.

6. Crosswell, p. 654.

7. D'Este goes to considerable lengths in his well-received *Decision in Normandy* to demonstrate that Montgomery had little to do with the break-out plan. See Chapter 19, 'Planning the Breakthrough: COBRA'.

8. Bradley, *A Soldier's Story*, p. 319.

9. D'Este, *Eisenhower*, p. 558.

10. Crosswell, p. 652.

11. LHC, 15/4/85, Liddell Hart Papers, 'Operation GOODWOOD', 18 July 1944, Dempsey's expansion (18.3.52) of the notes he wrote down in brief form (on 21.2.52).

12. AHQ Report No. 50, Army Group B Weekly Report for 27 June to 2 July, dated 3 July 1944, p. 62.

13. Hesketh, p. 236.

14. Hesketh, p. 260.
15. See Hesketh, Chapter 27, 'The New Plan'.
16. AHQ Report No. 50, Army Group B Weekly Report, 27 June–2 July 1944, p. 62.
17. LHC, 15/4/87, Press Clippings, July 1944, *Manchester Guardian*, 'Berlin Speculates on New Landing', 5 July 1944. The *Manchester Guardian* provided particularly good coverage of what the German press was saying.
18. AHEC, Hansen Diary, 2 July 1944.
19. Howard Gotlieb Archival Research Center, Ingersoll Papers, unedited copy, drafts of 'Time out for a War', Box 17, file 7, Chapter 5.
20. Hesketh, p. 261.
21. Hinsley, *British Intelligence* (abridged edition), p. 500.
22. Hesketh, p. 267.
23. AHQ Report No. 50, p. 70.
24. See also Hinsley's *British Intelligence*, vol. 3, Part II, p. 216.
25. Blumenson, *Breakout and Pursuit*, p. 202.
26. Ruppenthal, vol. 1, p. 447.
27. Waddell, pp. 82–5.
28. Thompson and Mayo, p. 250; Ruppenthal, vol. 1, p. 447.
29. AHEC, Hansen Diary, 16 July 1944.
30. Alanbrooke, *War Diaries*, annotation to entry for 19 July 1944.
31. AHEC, Hansen Diary, 16 and 18 July 1944.
32. *Eisenhower Papers*, vol. 3, Eisenhower to Montgomery, no. 1840, 17 July 1944.
33. Bradley, *A Soldier's Story*, pp. 324–5.
34. Hamilton attributes this quote to Dempsey's Diary, but it is actually from Liddell Hart's notes of an interview with Dempsey in 1952. See LHC, 15/4/85, Liddell Hart Papers, 'Operation GOODWOOD', 18 July 1944.
35. Hamilton, *Master of the Battlefield*, pp. 726–7.
36. Stacey, *The Victory Campaign*, p. 169.
37. Ellis, *Victory in the West*, pp. 338–9.
38. Will Townend and Frank Baldwin, *Gunners in Normandy: The History of the Royal Artillery in North-West Europe, January 1942–August 1944* (Cheltenham: The History Press, 2020), p. 402.
39. He repeated that claim after the war, see LHC, 15/4/85, Liddell Hart Papers, 'Operation GOODWOOD', 18 July 1944.
40. Townend and Baldwin, pp. 400–1.
41. Pemberton, p. 225.
42. Buckley, *Monty's Men*, p. 101.
43. Buckley, *Monty's Men*, pp. 97, 100.
44. Townend and Baldwin, p. 404.
45. Buckley, *Monty's Men*, p. 100.
46. LHC, 15/4/85, Liddell Hart Papers, 'Operation GOODWOOD', 18 July 1944.
47. Reynolds, *Steel Inferno*, p. 177.
48. Wilmot, *The Struggle for Europe*, p. 360.
49. AHQ Report No. 50, p. 74.
50. UWML, Dupuy Papers, reel 2, pp. 2112-2129 'Talk to West Point, 24/04/69'.
51. Hamilton, *Master of the Battlefield*, p. 736.
52. AHEC, Hansen Diary, 6 August 1944.
53. Wilmot, *The Struggle for Europe*, p. 361.

54. LAC, RG 24, vol. 16,642, 3 CPRG WD, July 1944, Appendix No. 15, PR Liaison Letter No. 11, para 6.
55. De Guingand, p. 382.
56. Hamilton, *Master of the Battlefield*, p. 737.
57. AHEC, Hansen Diary, 19 July 1944.
58. Crosswell, pp. 658–9.
59. Stacey, *The Victory Campaign*, p. 174.
60. Copp, *Fields of Fire*, pp. 147–8.
61. TNA, WO 285/9, Dempsey Diary, 20 July 1944.
62. Windsor, Sarty and Milner, p. 350.
63. George G. Blackburn, *The Guns of Normandy: A Soldier's Eye View, France 1944* (Toronto, ON: McClelland & Stewart, 1995), p. 233. See p. 206 when he dates this rate.
64. For an account of Canadian gunners during this period see Blackburn, Chapter 28, 'Gun Barrels Glow Red Like Candles'.
65. Blackburn, p. 206.
66. Doug Delaney, *Corps Commanders: Five British and Canadian Generals at War, 1939–45* (Vancouver, BC: University of British Columbia Press, 2011), p. 224.
67. AHQ Report No. 50, para 180.
68. Lawrence James Zaporzan, 'Rad's War: A Biographical Study of Sydney Valpy Radley-Walters from Mobilization to the End of the Normandy Campaign 1944', unpublished MA thesis, University of New Brunswick, 2001, see pp. 203–13.
69. AHQ Report No. 50, para 179.
70. Hamilton claims, with more than a little hyperbole, that at this stage, 'the roof began to fall about Monty's ears', *Master of the Battlefield*, p. 736.
71. Crosswell, p. 659.
72. Crosswell, p. 665.
73. De Guingand, pp. 380–3.
74. D'Este, *Eisenhower*, p. 558. Quote from Allan Millett and Williamson Murray, *A War to Be Won* (Cambridge, MA: Harvard UP, 2000), p. 428.
75. Blumenson, *Breakout and Pursuit*, pp. 217–19.
76. Windsor, Sarty and Milner, p. 350.
77. AHEC, Hansen Diary, entries for 22 and 23 July 1944.
78. Weigley, vol. 1, p. 223.
79. Blumenson, *Breakout and Pursuit*, pp. 221–2.
80. Blumenson, *Breakout and Pursuit*, p. 227.
81. Hamilton, *Master of the Battlefield*, p. 752. See also his map, p. 753.
82. Barrett, *The History of 13 Canadian Field Regiment*, p. 50.
83. Townend and Baldwin, p. 434.
84. Stacey, *The Victory Campaign*, p. 185.
85. AHQ Report No. 50, para 168.
86. AHEC, Hansen Diary, 24 July 1944.
87. Calhoun, p. 321.
88. Blumenson, *Breakout and Pursuit*, p. 229.
89. Blumenson, *Breakout and Pursuit*, pp. 230–1.
90. Bradley, *A Soldier's Story*, pp. 345–6.
91. Copp, *Fields of Fire*, pp. 174–6.
92. Copp, *Fields of Fire*, p. 178.
93. Copp, *Fields of Fire*, p. 179.

94. James Jay Carafano, *After D-Day: Operation COBRA and the Normandy Breakout* (Boulder, CO: Lynne Rienner, 2000), p. 246.
95. Gregory Liedtke, 'Canadian Offensive Operations in Normandy Revisited', *Canadian Military Journal*, vol. 8, no. 2, Summer 2007, p. 62.
96. Townend and Baldwin, p. 441.
97. Delaney, *Corps Commanders*, p. 224, gives the figure of 1,149 for 20–1 July, while Copp, *Fields of Fire*, p. 179, claims 1,500-plus for Spring alone, of which 450 were dead. No casualty figures for II Canadian Corps have apparently been published for 22–4 July.
98. AHQ Report No. 50, paras 182–5.

CHAPTER 24: BREAK-OUT

1. *Chicago Tribune*, editorial, 'The Strongest Nation', 25 June 1944.
2. Drew Middleton, *Where Has Last July Gone? Memoirs* (New York: Quadrangle/ New York Times Book Co., 1973), p. 118.
3. Manchester and Reid, pp. 847–8.
4. Roosevelt Presidential Library, Stettinius Diary, 21 June 1944.
5. The *Washington Times-Herald* editorial of 22 August claims 993,000 Polish-born Americans and 5 million Polish descendants in the USA.
6. TNA, INF 371/38574, 'Review of the Foreign Language Press in the United States', Reports No. 77 and 78, June 1944.
7. Dallek, *Franklin D. Roosevelt and American Foreign Policy*, pp. 453–4.
8. TNA, INF 371/38574, 'Review of the Foreign Language Press in the United States', Reports No. 77 and 78, June 1944.
9. Roosevelt Presidential Library, Stettinius Diary, 21 June 1944.
10. Roosevelt Presidential Library, Stettinius Diary, 22 June 1944.
11. Dallek, *Franklin D. Roosevelt and American Foreign Policy*, p. 458.
12. TNA, INF 371/38574, BIS Report No. 59, week ending 29 July 1944, 'The Truth About the French'; Demaree Bess, *Saturday Evening Post*, 29 July 1944.
13. Howard Gotlieb Archival Research Center, Ingersoll Papers, BU Box 70.
14. Dallek, *Franklin D. Roosevelt and American Foreign Policy*, p. 459.
15. Eric Larrabee, *Commander in Chief*, p. 633.
16. Dallek, *Franklin D. Roosevelt and American Foreign Policy*, p. 462.
17. *Washington Times-Herald*, 'The French Empire – Ah!', 17 July 1944.
18. Reynolds, *Steel Inferno*, pp. 188–9.
19. Ian Kershaw, *The End: The Defiance and Destruction of Hitler's Germany, 1944– 1945* (New York: Penguin, 2011), *passim*, but see especially pp. 44–51.
20. Klemens von Klemperer, *German Resistance Against Hitler: The Search for Allies Abroad, 1938–1945* (Oxford: Clarendon Press, 1992), pp. 385–7.
21. Robert Skidelsky, *John Maynard Keynes*, vol. 3: *Fighting for Freedom* (New York: Viking, 2001), p. 338.
22. See the Appendix, 'Harry Dexter White: Guilty and Naïve', at the end of Skidelsky's Chapter 7; Skidelsky, *John Maynard Keynes*, vol. 3, quotes Bruce Craig, 'Treasonable Doubt: The Henry Dexter White Case', unpublished PhD thesis, American University, 1999, pp. 596–7.
23. Susan Howson and Donald Moggridge, eds, *The Wartime Diaries of Lionel Robbins and James Meade, 1943–45* (London: Macmillan, 1990), entries for 24 and 26 June 1944.

24. Robert Skidelsky, *Keynes: A Very Short Introduction* (Oxford: Oxford UP, 2010), p. 116.
25. Steil, pp. 206–7.
26. Skidelsky, *John Maynard Keynes*, vol. 3, p. 349.
27. Skidelsky, *John Maynard Keynes*, vol. 3, p. 338.
28. Steil, p. 197.
29. Skidelsky, *John Maynard Keynes*, vol. 3, p, 349.
30. Skidelsky, *John Maynard Keynes*, vol. 3, p. 349.
31. Robbins Diary, 12 July 1944.
32. Muirhead, pp. 106–7.
33. Steil, p. 215.
34. Steil, pp. 215–16.
35. Both quotes from Robbins Diary, 22 July 1944.
36. Muirhead, p. 107.
37. TNA, FO 371/38574, BIS Report No. 58, week ending 25 July 1944.
38. Skidelsky, *John Maynard Keynes*, vol. 3, p. 358.
39. Skidelsky, *John Maynard Keynes*, vol. 3, p. 358.
40. D. Clayton James, *The Years of MacArthur*, vol. 2: *1941–1945* (Boston, MA: Houghton Mifflin, 1975), p. 526.
41. William Manchester, *American Caesar: Douglas MacArthur, 1880–1964* (Boston, MA: Little, Brown and Co., 1978), p. 365.
42. James, vol. 2, p. 528.
43. James, vol. 2, p. 324.
44. Hamilton, *War and Peace*, p. 323.
45. Manchester, *American Caesar*, p. 371.
46. James, vol. 2, p. 534.
47. James, vol. 2, p. 534.
48. Hamilton, *War and Peace*, p. 325.
49. Boog, Krebs and Vogel, p. 606.
50. Blumenson, *Breakout and Pursuit*, p. 227.
51. Blumenson, *Breakout and Pursuit*, p. 236.
52. AHEC, Hansen Diary, 25 July 1944.
53. AHEC, Hansen Diary, 25 July 1944.
54. Craven and Cate, p. 235.
55. Blumenson, *Breakout and Pursuit*, p. 243.
56. Lt Col. Dawnay, as quoted in Hamilton, *Master of the Battlefield*, p. 761.
57. Waddell, p. 87.
58. This writer can find no accounts of the attacks of the V, VIII and XIX US Corps on 26 July. Even Blumenson, *Breakout and Pursuit*, fails to describe them.
59. Blumenson, *Breakout and Pursuit*, p. 250.
60. AHEC, Hansen Diary, 26 July 1944.
61. Blumenson, *Breakout and Pursuit*, p. 260.
62. Boog, Krebs and Vogel, p. 607.
63. AHQ Report No. 50, para 192.
64. AHQ Report No. 50, para 171; Buckley, *Monty's Men*, p. 156.
65. AHQ Report No. 50, paras 187–93.
66. Hamilton, *Master of the Battlefield*, p. 757.
67. Atkinson, *The Guns at Last Light*, p. 147.
68. See Hinsley, *British Intelligence*, vol. 3, Part II, pp. 231–5.

69. *Eisenhower Papers*, vol. 2, Eisenhower to Montgomery 28 July 1944,
70. Hamilton, *Master of the Battlefield*, pp. 766–7.
71. TNA, WO 285/9, Dempsey Diary, 26 July 1944.
72. TNA, WO 285/9, Dempsey Diary, 28 July 1944.
73. Hinsley, *British Intelligence*, vol. 3, Part II, p. 235.
74. Buckley, *Monty's Men*, pp. 155–6.
75. Wilmot, *The Struggle for Europe*, p. 396.
76. Pemberton, pp. 226–7.
77. Buckley, *Monty's Men*, p. 161.
78. Pemberton, pp. 226–7.
79. Stuart Hills, *By Tank into Normandy* (London: Cassell, 2002), Chapter 6.
80. Wilmot, *The Struggle for Europe*, p. 398.
81. Reynolds, *Steel Inferno*, p. 200.
82. McManus, *The Americans at Normandy*, p. 333.
83. McManus, *The Americans at Normandy*, pp. 336–9.
84. Blumenson, *Breakout and Pursuit*, p. 333.
85. Thomas Alexander Hughes, *Over Lord: General Pete Quesada and the Triumph of Tactical Airpower in World War II* (New York: The Free Press, 1995), p. 228.
86. AHEC, Nevins Papers, Box 4, folder 1, Situation Report of 31 July 1944.
87. AHEC, Hansen Diary, 27 July 1944.
88. AHEC, Hansen Diary, 5 August 1944.
89. Olivier Wieviorka, *Normandy: The Landings to the Liberation of Paris* (Cambridge, MA: The Belknap Press, 2008), p. 340.
90. As quoted in Wieviorka, p. 340, from TNA, CAB 106/989, Report No. 6, 12 August 1944, National Staff of the FFI.
91. Waddell, p. 144.
92. Wilmot, *The Struggle for Europe*, pp. 400–1.
93. AHQ Report No. 50, paras 207–9.
94. Atkinson, *The Guns at Last Light*, p. 151.
95. As quoted in John Terraine, *The Right of the Line* (Ware: Wordsworth Editions, 1985), p. 659.
96. Munro, p. 165.
97. AHQ Report No. 50, para 198.
98. Atkinson, *The Guns at Last Light*, p. 152.

CHAPTER 25: GET 'EM ALL AND HAVE DINNER IN PARIS

1. *Daily Express*, 5 August 1944.
2. Churchill College Archives, Grigg Papers, PJGG 9/8, Sir James Grigg to Montgomery, 25 July 1944 and 1 August 1944.
3. Bradley, *A Soldier's Story*, p. 324.
4. Bradley, *A Soldier's Story*, p. 325, emphasis added.
5. Hamilton, *Master of the Battlefield*, p. 736.
6. AHEC, Hansen Diary, 12 August 1944.
7. Sherwood, p. 442.
8. *New York Times*, 'Australia Praised', 21 July 1944, p. 6.
9. *Chicago Tribune*, 'The Victory is American', 2 August 1944.
10. See summaries in TNA, FO 371/38574, BIS Reports No. 57, 25 July 1944 and No. 61, 8 August 1944, 'Newsreels (As seen in New York)'. OWI newsreels

covering this period were released much later under the 'United News' label. They were generous to America's allies, especially the British and Canadians, but were not representative of what Americans saw in the summer of 1944.

11. Survey of the *New York Times, Chicago Tribune, Washington Post, Houston Chronicle* and *Los Angeles Times* compiled by Jamie Horncastle, November 2011.

12. TNA, FO 3712/38574, BIS Report No. 60, week ending 5 August 1944, '"Washington Whispers", Normandy Offensive'.

13. UWML, Dupuy Papers, reel 1, 'History of Public Relations Office', by Lt Col. John Redding, p. 13.

14. Oldfield, p. 106.

15. Dupuy, 'Behind the Elephants', p. 149.

16. *The Times*, 'Panzer Divisions Brought Over', 4 August 1944.

17. AHEC, Hansen Diary, 2 August 1944.

18. LHC, 15/4/88, Press Clippings, August 1944.

19. *Washington Times Herald*, 'Yanks Blitz on to Paris', 10 August 1944.

20. AHEC, Hansen Diary, 6 August 1944.

21. Reynolds, *Steel Inferno*, p. 215.

22. Reynolds, *Steel Inferno*, p. 211.

23. Reynolds, *Sons of the Reich*, pp. 72–80.

24. Blumenson, *Breakout and Pursuit*, p. 469.

25. Reynolds, *Steel Inferno*, p. 214.

26. Reynolds, *Steel Inferno*, p. 217; Blumenson, *Breakout and Pursuit*, p. 473.

27. Reynolds, *Steel Inferno*, p. 217.

28. McManus, *The Americans at Normandy*, pp. 381–2.

29. Brian H. Reid, *No Holding Back: Operation Totalize, Normandy, August 1944* (Toronto, ON: Robin Brass Studio, 2005), p. 109.

30. RAF Narrative, 'The Liberation of North-West Europe', vol. 4: 'The Break-Out and the Advance to the Lower Rhine 12 June to 30 September', Air Historical Branch, n.d., p. 86.

31. Mike Bechthold, 'Spitfires, Typhoons and Mustangs: RCAF Fighters in Normandy', *Royal Canadian Air Force Journal*, vol. 8, no. 2, Spring 2019, pp. 48–70. See pp. 56–62, 'Operational Research and Mortain'.

32. See 'Air Attacks on Enemy Tanks and Motor Transport in the Mortain Area, August 1944', No. 2 Operational Research Section, 21 Army Group, n.d. Reprinted in Terry Copp, ed., *Montgomery's Scientists: Operational Research in Northwest Europe* (Waterloo, ON: Laurier Centre for Military Strategic and Disarmament Studies, 2000).

33. Reynolds, *Steel Inferno*, p. 220.

34. RAF Narrative, 'The Liberation of North-West Europe', vol. 4, p. 87.

35. AHQ Report No. 50, para 216.

36. Atkinson, *The Guns at Last Light*, p. 157.

37. Reid, *No Holding Back*, p. 73.

38. See the illustrations and discussion in Reid, *No Holding Back*, Chapter 6.

39. See John Grodzinski, '*Bron Pancerna*: A Brief History of the 1st Polish Armoured Division', Appendix F in Reid, *No Holding Back*, pp. 431–45.

40. Stacey, *The Victory Campaign*, pp. 211–13.

41. Townend and Brown, pp. 499–503.

42. Reid, *No Holding Back*, p. 103.

43. Reid, *No Holding Back*, p. 103.

44. Wilmot, *The Struggle for Europe*, p. 411.
45. Pemberton, p. 228.
46. Wilmot, *The Struggle for Europe*, p. 410.
47. Middlebrook and Everitt, eds, *Bomber Command War Diaries*, 7 August 1944.
48. Reid, *No Holding Back*, p. 175.
49. Buckley, *Monty's Men*, p. 172.
50. Reid, *No Holding Back*, p. 209.
51. Stacey, *The Victory Campaign*, p. 220.
52. Delaney, *Corps Commanders*, p. 232.
53. Pemberton, p. 227.
54. Zaporzan.
55. Zaporzan, p. 249.
56. Reid's *No Holding Back* contains a lengthy appendix assessing the incident, and concludes that the SFR killed Wittmann. Zaporzan, Radley-Walters's son-in-law, came to the same conclusion, but confided that Rad really did not care who killed Wittmann. The radio logs of the SFR and the 2nd Armoured Brigade were destroyed in the short bombing incident.
57. Reid, *No Holding Back*, p. 246.
58. Reid, *No Holding Back*, p. 267.
59. Townend and Brown, p. 507.
60. Reid, *No Holding Back*, p. 290.
61. Reid, *No Holding Back*, p. 282.
62. Stacey, *The Victory Campaign*, p. 275.
63. Wilmot, *The Struggle for Europe*, p. 414.
64. See the transcript of telephone calls in AHQ Report No. 50, para 222.
65. AHEC, Hansen Diary, 8 August 1944.
66. Atkinson, *The Guns at Last Light*, p. 159; Blumenson, *Breakout and Pursuit*, p. 492.
67. Stanley P. Hirshon, *General Patton: A Soldier's Life* (New York: Harper, 2002), p. 513.
68. Hirshon, p. 512.
69. Blumenson, *Breakout and Pursuit*, pp. 501–2.
70. Copp, *Fields of Fire*, p. 218.
71. Blumenson, *Breakout and Pursuit*, p. 503.
72. Hirshon, p. 515.
73. Stacey, *The Victory Campaign*, p. 246.
74. Copp, *Fields of Fire*, p. 220.
75. Hamilton, *Master of the Battlefield*, p. 787.
76. Crosswell, p. 680; see also Hamilton, *Master of the Battlefield*, p. 785.
77. Stacey, *The Victory Campaign*, p. 246.
78. University of Toronto Archives, Stacey Papers, Box 28, 'United States Army in World War II: The European Theater of Operations: Breakout and Pursuit', by Martin Blumenson, 'Comments by Historical Section (GS) Army Headquarters, Ottawa, p. 13.
79. TNA, WO 285/9, Dempsey Diary, 13 August 1944.
80. Hamilton, *Master of the Battlefield*, p. 516.
81. Bradley, *A Soldier's Story*, p. 375.
82. Copp, *Fields of Fire*, p. 233.
83. Bradley, *A Soldier's Story*, p. 375.

84. Atkinson, *The Guns at Last Light*, p. 163.

85. Copp, *Fields of Fire*, p. 232.

86. Stacey, *The Victory Campaign*, p. 248.

87. As quoted in Copp, *Fields of Fire*, p. 229.

88. Stacey, *The Victory Campaign*, p. 251.

89. Blumenson, *Breakout and Pursuit*, p. 527.

90. Hamilton, *Master of the Battlefield*, pp. 794–6.

91. *A History of the 90th Division in World War II* (Nashville, TN: The Battery Press, 1999), p. 22.

92. AHQ Report No. 50, para 258, report from the WD of 5th Panzer Army, 16 August 1944.

93. AHQ Report No. 50, translation of Eberbach's memoir, see para 263.

94. Copp, *Fields of Fire*, p. 238.

95. Ellis, *Victory in the West*, p. 440.

96. Stacey, *The Victory Campaign*, p. 257.

97. Donald E., Graves, *South Albertas: A Canadian Regiment at War* (Toronto, ON: Robin Brass Studio, 1998), p. 146.

98. Conversation with Trooper Carson W. Daley, Saint-Lambert-sur-Dives, June 2014.

99. Brig. Gen. Denis Whitaker and Shelagh Whitaker, with Terry Copp, *Victory at Falaise: The Soldiers' Story* (Toronto, ON: HarperCollins, 2000), p. 276.

100. Copp, *Fields of Fire*, p. 242.

101. Copp, *Fields of Fire*, p. 247.

102. Townend and Brown, pp. 549–53.

CHAPTER 26: PARIS

1. Dupuy, 'Behind the Elephants', p. 160.

2. Hamilton, *Master of the Battlefield*, p. 801.

3. Stephen Ashley Hart, *Colossal Cracks: Montgomery's 21st Army Group in Northwest Europe, 1944–1945* (Mechanicsburg, PA: Stackpole Books, 2007), pp. 55–9.

4. Dupuy, 'Behind the Elephants', pp. 155–7.

5. AHEC, Hansen Diary, 14 August 1944.

6. Wilmot, *The Struggle for Europe*, p. 424.

7. Blumenson, *Breakout and Pursuit*, p. 573.

8. Copp, *Fields of Fire*, p. 247.

9. Blumenson, *Breakout and Pursuit*, p. 537.

10. Whitaker et al., *Victory at Falaise*, p. 275.

11. Stacey, *The Victory Campaign*, p. 262.

12. Reynolds, *Steel Inferno*, p. 278

13. Whitaker et al., *Victory at Falaise*, pp. 269, 278, 279.

14. Stacey, *The Victory Campaign*, p. 261.

15. Reynolds, *Steel Inferno*, p. 279; Reynolds, *Sons of the Reich*, pp. 86–7; AHQ Report No. 50, para 277, quoting from Eberbach's memoir.

16. Munro, p. 183.

17. *Into Action with the 12th Field*, pp. 78–9.

18. G.W.L. Nicholson, *The Gunners of Canada: The History of the Royal Regiment of Canadian Artillery*, vol. 2 (Toronto, ON: McClelland & Stewart, 1972), pp. 327–8.

19. Copp, *Fields of Fire*, p. 249.

20. Stacey, *The Victory Campaign*, p. 263.
21. Matthew Douglass, *The New Brunswick Rangers in the Second World War* (Fredericton, NB: Gooselane Editions/The Gregg Centre for the Study of War and Society, 2020), p. 28.
22. Whitaker et al., *Victory at Falaise*, pp. 286–7
23. Whitaker et al., *Victory at Falaise*, p. 293.
24. Munro, pp. 187–9.
25. Atkinson, *The Guns at Last Light*, p. 170.
26. AHQ Report No. 50, para 277.
27. Ellis, *Victory in the West*, p. 447.
28. Blumenson, *Breakout and Pursuit*, p. 555.
29. Copp, *Fields of Fire*, p. 247.
30. James Holland, *Normandy '44: D-Day and the Epic 77-Day Battle for France* (New York: Grove, 2019), p. 642.
31. *The Times*, 'A German Army's Death-Blow', 23 August 1944.
32. Martin Blumenson, *The Battle of the Generals: The Untold Story of the Falaise Pocket – The Campaign That Should Have Won World War II* (New York: William Morrow and Co., 1993), p. 262.
33. Hinsley, *British Intelligence,* vol. 3, Part II, p. 367.
34. AHEC, Hansen Diary, 16 August 1944.
35. Blumenson, *Breakout and Pursuit*, p. 574.
36. Blumenson, *Breakout and Pursuit*, pp. 574–7.
37. Stacey, *The Victory Campaign*, p. 267.
38. For an excellent description of the topography between Falaise and the Seine see 'Canadian Participation in the Operations in North-West Europe, 1944, Part IV, First Canadian Army in the Pursuit (23 Aug.–30 Sep.)', AHQ Report No. 183, para 13 (hereafter AHQ Report No. 183).
39. For the best account of these reinforcements see Hinsley, *British Intelligence*, vol. 3, Part II, pp. 257–65.
40. AHQ Report No. 50, para 282; see also Appendix M, Hitler's Directive of 20 August 1944.
41. Robert L. Hewitt, *The Story of 30th Infantry Division in World War II* (Washington, DC: The Infantry Journal Press, 1946), pp. 79–81.
42. TNA, WO 285/9, Dempsey Diary, 24 August 1944.
43. Ruppenthal, pp. 486–7.
44. Mark Calhoun, ' "Your Exploits Will Rank Among the Greatest of Military Achievements": Lt. Gen. William H. Simpson and the Fight for the Wesel Bridges', *Army History*, Fall 2023, p. 46.
45. Hamilton, *Master of the Battlefield*, p. 814, emphasis in the original.
46. Hamilton, *Master of the Battlefield*, p. 818.
47. Calhoun, ' "Your Exploits Will Rank Among the Greatest" ', p. 46.
48. AHEC, Hansen Diary, 25 August 1944.
49. 'The Effectiveness of Third Phase Tactical Air Operations in the European Theatre, 5 May 1944–8 May 1945', Army Air Forces Board in the European Theatre of Operations, August 1945, p. 131 and the map following.
50. Copp, *Cinderella Army*, p. 18.
51. AHQ Report No. 183, para 56.
52. AHQ Report No. 183, para 59.
53. Copp, *Cinderella Army*, p. 27.

54. LAC, RG 24 vol. 16,642 3 CPRG WD, 24 August 1944.
55. LAC, RG 24 vol. 16,642 3 CPRG WD, 22–5 August 1944.
56. 'The Liberation of North-West Europe, vol. 4: The Break-Out and the Advance to the Lower Rhine, 12 June to 30 September 1944', Air Historical Branch, Air Ministry, p. 112.
57. Maxwell Air Force Base, Air Force Historical Research Agency, microfilm reel B5602, 9th USAAF Commander's Meeting, 18 August 1944, records that airfields near Le Mans would not be ready until 23 and 25 August 1944.
58. Lt Col. Robert H. George, 'Ninth Air Force: April to November 1944', Army Air Forces Historical Studies, no. 36, 1945, pp. 205–16.
59. David N. Spires, *Air Power for Patton's Army: The XIX Tactical Air Command in the Second World War* (Washington, DC: Air Force History and Museums Program 2002), see especially p. 98.
60. 'The Campaign in Northwest Europe: Information from German Sources, Part III: German Defence Operations in the Sphere of 1st Canadian Army (23 Aug–8 Nov 44), Historical Section (G.S.), Army Headquarters, AHQ Report No. 69, 9 July 1954, para 21. (Hereafter AHQ Report No. 69.)
61. Copp, *Cinderella Army*, p. 28.
62. Copp, *Cinderella Army*, p. 30.
63. Copp, *Cinderella Army*, pp. 30–5.
64. 'The Effectiveness of Third Phase Tactical Air Operations', p. 124.
65. *The Times*, evening edition, covered the war on p. 4. During August only four sub-headlines, on the 3rd, 11th, 12th and 30th, featured British efforts.
66. TNA, FO 371/38574, BIS Report No. 64, 22 August 1944, week ending 19 August 1944.
67. TNA, FO 371/38674, BIS Report No. 65, 29 August 1944, for the week ending 26 August 1944; *United States News*, 'When Peace Is Won', and 'People of the Week', 25 August 1944.
68. LAC, RG 24, vol. 16,642 3 CPRU WD, 25 August 1944. The War Diary for 3rd Canadian Public Relations Unit for 25 August notes that American trucks were now using the Bayeux–Caen highway, travelling at night with lights and moving 20mph faster than Anglo-Canadian vehicles.
69. 'Patton Regilded', *Time*, 28 August 1944.
70. AHEC, Hansen Diary, 21 August 1944.
71. *Eisenhower Papers*, vol. 4, Eisenhower to CCS, 22 August 1944, pp. 2087–9.
72. Dupuy, 'Behind the Elephants', p. 160.
73. Dupuy, 'Behind the Elephants', p. 161.
74. LAC, RG 24 vol. 16,642 PR Liaison Letter No. 14 (21 AG), 15 August 1944, 3 CPRG WD, August 1944, Appendix 8.
75. Dupuy, 'Behind the Elephants', pp. 150–1.
76. LAC, RG 24, vol. 16,642 PR Liaison Letter No. 15 (21 AG), 23 Aug 1944, 3 CPRG WD, August 1944, Appendix 9.
77. Wieviorka, pp. 352–3.
78. Blumenson, *Breakout and Pursuit*, pp. 601–3.
79. Wieviorka, p. 351.
80. Dupuy, 'Behind the Elephants', pp. 163-172.
81. Atkinson, *The Guns at Last Light*, p. 171; see also Terry Mort, *Hemingway at War: Ernest Hemingway's Adventures as a World War II Correspondent* (New York: Pegasus, 2016), Chapter 11.

82. Mike Neiberg, *The Blood of Free Men: The Liberation of Paris, 1944* (New York: Basic Books, 2012), p. 213.
83. Blumenson, *Breakout and Pursuit*, pp. 603–15.
84. Dupuy, 'Behind the Elephants', p. 172.
85. Ralph Allen, 'Nazis Never Knew It, but Paid Canada Rent', *Globe and Mail*, 30 August 1944.
86. Dupuy, 'Behind the Elephants', p. 173.
87. TNA, WO 229/56 and 57, 'Report on Coms Dev.', by Capt. H.C. Butcher, USNR, 2 February 1945.
88. Atkinson, *The Guns at Last Light*, p. 179.
89. AHEC, Hansen Diary, 26 August 1944.
90. *Globe and Mail*, 'City Wild with Joy, Ignores Bullets' Whine', 28 August 1944.
91. AHEC, Hansen Diary, 27 August 1944.
92. The mood is well reflected in the comments by Ellis, *Victory in the West*, see p. 458.
93. Ellis, *Victory in the West*, p. 458.
94. Neiberg, p. 245.
95. *Life*, 18 September 1944, 'March Through Paris', p. 33.
96. Based on a survey of the *Sydney Morning Herald*, *Courier Mail* and *Western Mail*, by Jamie Horncastle, November 2011.
97. *Chicago Tribune*, 'American Power in Battle', 30 August 1944.
98. LAC, RG 24, vol. 10,420, AHQ file no. 205C1.013 (D1), Eisenhower's Despatches, 31 August 1944.
99. MRC, McCormick Papers, Larry Rue, I-62, 1942–1950, Box 8, folder 3, Rue to McCormick, 13 September 1944.

CHAPTER 27: AMERICAN VICTORY

1. As quoted in TNA, FO 371/38575, BIS Report No. 74, 28 September 1944, week ending 23 September.
2. Bodleian Library, Robert Brand Papers, Box 196, 'Diary Letters', Brand to Sir John Anderson, 23 August 1944.
3. Lt Robert James Brand was killed in action on 22 March 1945.
4. Woods, *A Changing of the Guard*, pp. 158–68.
5. *Chicago Tribune*, 'US Bases Sold to Canada at 13 Million Loss', front page, 28 August 1944.
6. Robert C. Hildebrand, *Dumbarton Oaks: The Origins of the United Nations and the Search for Postwar Security* (Chapel Hill, NC: University of North Carolina Press, 1990), pp. 38–40.
7. Hodson, *And Yet I Like America*.
8. Hodson, *And Yet I Like America*, p. 291.
9. Churchill College Archives, CLVL 1/6, Colville Diary, 20 September 1944.
10. As quoted in Manchester and Reid, p. 874.
11. Peter Clarke, *The Last Thousand Days of the British Empire: The Demise of a Superpower, 1944–47* (London: Penguin, 2007), p. 63.
12. Todman, *Britain's War: A New World*, p. 625.
13. Clarke, *The Last Thousand Days*, p. 66.
14. Reynolds, *Sons of the Reich*, p. 104.
15. Crosswell, p. 709.

16. Howard Gotlieb Archival Research Center, Ingersoll Papers, Box 70, Ingersoll Diary, 16 September 1944.

17. Dan Crosswell is quite clear that Eisenhower lacked a grip on the campaign and that Bradley and Patton were complicit in ignoring his directives at this stage of it. See pp. 710–17.

18. *Newsweek*, 'Spanning the Fortress Moat', 2 October 1944, emphasis added.

19. TNA, FO 371/38575, BIS Report No. 74, week ending 4 October, and BIS Report No. 77, week ending 7 October 1944, 11 October 1944.

20. Clarke, *The Last Thousand Days*, p. 81.

21. Wilmot, *The Struggle for Europe*, p. 535.

22. Crosswell, pp. 738–45.

23. Howard Gotlieb Archival Research Center, Ingersoll Papers, Box 89, Ingersoll to George C. Hotaling, 14 May 1946.

24. Crosswell, p. 706.

25. Stacey, *Arms, Men and Government*, pp. 460–84.

26. Copp, *Cinderella Army*, p. 172.

27. Information courtesy the Bevrijdingsmuseum, Zeeland.

28. TNA, FO 371/38575, BIS Report No. 71, week ending 16 September 1944, 'Fortress Pacific'; *Collier's*, 26 September 1944.

29. Clarke, *The Last Thousand Days*, pp. 108–15.

30. Clarke, *The Last Thousand Days*, p. 118.

31. Clarke, *The Last Thousand Days*, p. 103.

32. Charles P. Kindleberger, *A Financial History of Western Europe* (London: George Allen & Unwin, 1984), p. 427. The original notion was raised by Alan Milward, *War, Economy and Society* (Berkeley: University of California Press, 1977), p. 351.

33. W.K. Hancock and M.M. Gowing, *British War Economy* (London: HMSO, 1949), pp. 528–33.

34. Roosevelt Presidential Library, Hopkins Papers, Box 154, *Statistics Relating to the War Effort of the United Kingdom*, Cmd.6564, and the covering letter of 29 November 1944.

35. Clarke, *The Last Thousand Days*, pp. 101–6.

36. Hancock and Gowing, p. 532.

37. *Washington Despatches*, diary entry for 10 December 1944.

38. Ruppenthal, vol. 2, see tables and discussion on pp. 281–3.

39. TNA, WO 285/10, Dempsey Diary, 7 December 1944.

40. Clarke, *The Last Thousand Days*, pp. 152–3.

41. Isaiah Berlin, as quoted in Clark, p. 146.

42. As quoted in Clark, pp. 146–8.

43. *The Economist*, 'Noble Negatives', 30 December 1944, vol. 147, no. 5288, pp. 1–2.

44. Clarke, *The Last Thousand Days*, p. 148.

45. Churchill, *The Second World War: Triumph and Tragedy*, pp. 281–2.

46. Hamilton, *Monty: Final Years of the Field Marshal 1944–1976* (New York: McGraw Hill, 1986), p. 283.

47. Clarke, *The Last Thousand Days*, p. 220.

48. Clarke, *The Last Thousand Days*, pp. 212–13.

49. Robert Ross Smith, *Triumph in the Philippines* (Washington, DC: CMH, 1993), Appendix H, p. 692.

50. Wilmot, *The Struggle for Europe*, p. 678.

51. Clarke, *The Last Thousand Days*, p. 257.

CONCLUSIONS

1. Carew, 'Table 11.1: U.S. Long-Range Bomber Fleet in World War II', p. 239.
2. Maury Klein, *A Call to Arms: Mobilizing America for World War II* (New York: Bloomsbury Press, 2013), p. 774.
3. Calculated on the accepted wartime rate of £1= $4.03 USD. See 'Financing the British War Effort', review by J.R.T. Hughes of R.S. Sayers and Keith Hancock, *Financial Policy, 1939–1945*, in *The Journal of Economic History*, no. 2, June 1958, pp. 193–9. Figure on national wealth from Hancock, p. 551.
4. Clarke, *The Last Thousand Days*, p. 402.
5. As quoted from Sayers and Hancock by J.R.T. Hughes.
6. The text of the 'Financial Agreement' was published on 6 December 1945. See Parliamentary Archives, Beaverbrook Papers, BBK/D/478.
7. Woods, p. 375.
8. For a brief summary of this process see Charles P. Kindleberger, *A Financial History of Western Europe* (London: George Allen & Unwin, 1984), pp. 425–7.
9. Kindleberger, pp. 430–3.
10. Todman, *Britain's War: A New World*, pp. 585, 643–4.
11. MRC, McCormick Papers, I-60, GB Newspapers – Gen., 1927–1959, *Chicago Tribune*, 6 June 1945.
12. LAC, MG 31, E42, vol. 3, Swettenham Papers, interview of 13 January 1965.
13. DHH 010.013 (D5), Lt Col. H.A. Pollock, 'Invasion of Northwest Europe 1944', prepared for the Cabinet Office, n.d.
14. Ellis, *Victory in the West*, p. xviii.
15. David Edgerton, 'The Nationalism of British History: Historians, Nationalism and the Myth of 1940', *English Historical Review*, vol. 136, no. 581, August 2021.
16. C.P. Stacey, 'Harry Hopkins and General Eisenhower: Two War Books of First Rate Importance', *Canadian Army Journal*, vol. 3, May 1949, p. 32.

BIBLIOGRAPHY

PRIMARY SOURCES

UK

BBC Written Archives Centre, Caversham
Bodleian Library, Oxford
British Institute for Historical Research, York
British Library, London
British Museum, London
Churchill College Archives, Cambridge
Imperial War Museum, London
Liddell Hart Centre for Military Archives, King's College London
The National Archives, Kew
Parliamentary Archives, London

USA

Air Force Historical Research Agency, Maxwell Air Force Base, AL
Dwight D. Eisenhower Presidential Library, Online Collection
Howard Gotlieb Archival Research Center, Boston University, MA
The Library of Congress, Washington, DC
The Marshall Library, Virginia Military Institute, Lexington, VA
National Archives, College Park, MD
Colonel Robert R. McCormick Research Center, Wheaton, IL
Franklin D. Roosevelt Presidential Library, Hyde Park, NY
University of Wisconsin-Madison Library, Madison, WI
US Army History and Education Center, Carlisle, PA
US National WWII Museum Archives, New Orleans, LA

Canada

Directorate of History and Heritage, National Defence Headquarters, Ottawa, ON
Library and Archives of Canada, Ottawa, ON

Public Archives of Nova Scotia, Halifax, NS
University of Toronto Archives, Toronto, ON

Unpublished Narratives[1]

'The Campaign in North-West Europe: Information from German Sources, Part II: Invasion and Battle of Normandy (6 Jun–22 Aug 44)', Historical Section (G.S.), Army Headquarters, AHQ Report No. 50, 14 October 1952

'The Campaign in North-West Europe, Information from German Sources, Part IV, Higher Direction of Operations from Falaise Debacle to Ardennes Offensive (22 Aug.–16 Dec. 1944', Historical Section (G.S.), Army Headquarters, AHQ Report No. 77, 30 September 1957

'Canadian Participation in the Operations in North-West Europe, 1944', Historical Section, Canadian Military Headquarters, CMHQ Report No. 147, 3 December 1945

'Canadian Participation in the Operations in North-West Europe, 1944, Part II, Canadian Operations in July', Historical Section, Canadian Military Headquarters, CMHQ Report No. 162, 22 January 1948

'Canadian Participation in the Operations in North-West Europe, 1944, Part IV, First Canadian Army in the Pursuit (23 Aug.–30 Sep.)', Historical Section, Canadian Military Headquarters, CMHQ Report No. 183, 22 September 1947

'The Effectiveness of Third Phase Tactical Air Operations in the European Theatre, 5 May 1944–8 May 1945', The Army Air Forces Board in the European Theatre of Operations, August 1945

'Ninth Air Force: April to November 1944', Lt Col. Robert H. George, Army Air Forces Historical Studies, No. 36, 1945

'The Preliminary Planning for Operation "Overlord": Some Aspects of the Preparations for the Allied Re-entry to North-West Europe, 1940–1944', Historical Section (G.S.), Army Headquarters, AHQ Report No. 42, 5 March 1952

'R.A.F. Narrative, The Liberation of North-West Europe, Volume IV, The Break-Out and the Advance to the Lower Rhine, 12 June to 30 September', Air Historical Branch, n.d.

'The Strategic Role of First Canadian Army, 1942–1944', Historical Section, Canadian Military Headquarters, CMHQ Report No. 182, 23 May 1949

Note: AHQ and CMHQ reports are available online through the Canadian Directorate of History and Heritage.

SELECTED SECONDARY SOURCES

Adleman, Robert H. and Col. George Walton. *The Devil's Brigade* (New York: Chilton Books, 1966)

Alanbrooke, Field Marshal Lord. *War Diaries 1939–1945*, ed. Dan Todman and Alex Danchev (London: Weidenfeld & Nicolson, 2001)

Aldgate, Anthony and Jeffrey Richard. *Britain Can Take It: British Cinema in the Second World War* (London: I.B. Tauris, 2007)

Aly, Gotz. *Hitler's Beneficiaries: Plunder, Racial War and the Nazi Welfare State* (London: Verso, 2006)

American Battle Monuments Commission, *A Guide to the American Battle Fields in Europe* (Washington, DC: US Government Printing Office, 1927)

Atkinson, Rick. *An Army at Dawn: The War in North Africa, 1942–1943* (New York: Owl Books, 2002)

—— *The Day of Battle: The War in Sicily and Italy, 1943–1944* (New York: Henry Holt & Co., 2007)

—— *The Guns at Last Light: The War in Western Europe, 1944–1945* (New York: Henry Holt & Co., 2013)

Baer, George. *One Hundred Years of Seapower: The U.S. Navy, 1890–1990* (Stanford, CA: Stanford UP, 1993)

Balkoski, Joseph. *Beyond the Beachhead: The 29th Infantry Division in Normandy* (Mechanicsburg, PA: Stackpole Books, 2005)

Balzar, Tim. *The Information Front* (Vancouver, BC: University of British Columbia Press, 2011)

Barnett, Correlli. *The Audit of War: The Illusion and Reality of Britain as a Great Power* (London: Papermac, 1986)

—— *The Collapse of British Power* (New York: Morrow, 1972)

—— *The Desert Generals* (Bloomington, IN: Indiana UP, 1982)

Barr, Niall. *Eisenhower's Armies: The American-British Alliance During World War II* (New York: Pegasus Books, 2015)

Bayly, Christopher and Tim Harper. *Forgotten Armies: Britain's Asian Empire and the War with Japan* (London: Penguin, 2005)

Bechtholdt, Mike. *Flying to Victory: Raymond Collishaw and the Western Desert Campaign 1940–1941* (Norman, OK: University of Oklahoma Press, 2017)

Behrens, C.B.A. *Merchant Shipping and the Demands of War* (London: HMSO, 1955)

Bell, Christopher. *Churchill and Seapower* (Oxford: Oxford UP, 2013)

Bidwell, Shelford and Dominick Graham. *Fire-Power: British Army Weapons and Theories of War 1904–1945* (London: George Allen & Unwin, 1982)

—— *Tug of War: The Battle for Italy, 1943–1945* (New York: St Martin's Press, 1986)

Blackburn, George G. *The Guns of Normandy: A Soldier's Eye View, France 1944* (Toronto, ON: McClelland & Stewart, 1995)

Blom, Philip. *Fracture: Life and Culture in the West, 1918–1938* (Toronto, ON: Signal, 2015)

Blumenson, Martin. *Breakout and Pursuit* (Washington, DC: Office of the Chief of Military History United States Army, 1961)

—— *Mark Clark* (London: Jonathan Cape, 1985)

Bohlen, Charles E. *Witness to History 1929–1969* (New York: W.W. Norton & Co., 1973)

Bond, Brian. *Liddell Hart: A Study of His Military Thought* (London: Cassell, 1976)

Boog, Horst, Gerhard Krebs, and Detlef Vogel. *The Strategic Air War in Europe and the War in the West and East Asia, 1939–1944/5* (Oxford: Oxford UP, 2006)

Bourque, Stephen Alan. *Beyond the Beach: The Allied War Against France* (Annapolis, MD: USNI Press, 2018)

Boyle, Andrew. *Poor, Dear Brendan: The Quest for Brendan Bracken* (London: Hutchinson, 1974)

Bradley, Omar. *A Soldier's Story* (New York: Popular Library, 1951)

Braim, Paul F. *The Test of Battle: The American Expeditionary Forces in the Meuse-Argonne Campaign* (Newark, DE: University of Delaware Press, 1987)

Briggs, Asa. *The War of Words, 1939–1945*, vol. 3: *The History of Broadcasting in the United Kingdom* (Oxford: Oxford UP, 1970)

British Security Coordination: The Secret History of British Intelligence in the Americas, 1940–1945 (New York: Fromm International, 1999)

Bryce, Robert B. *Canada and the Cost of World War II: The International Operations of Canada's Department of Finance, 1939–1947* (Montreal: McGill–Queen's UP, 2005)

Buckingham, William F. *D-Day: The First 72 Hours* (Stroud: Tempus Publishing, 2004)

Buckley, John. *British Armour in the Normandy Campaign* (London: Frank Cass, 2004)

—— *Monty's Men: The British Army and the Liberation of Europe* (New Haven, CT and London: Yale UP, 2013)

Buckley, John, ed., *The Normandy Campaign 1944: Sixty Years On* (London: Routledge, 2006)

Budreau, Lisa M. *Bodies of War: World War I and the Politics of Commemoration in America, 1919–1933* (New York: New York UP, 2010)

Butcher, Captain Harry C. USNR. *My Three Years with Eisenhower* (New York: Simon & Schuster, 1946)

Butler, J.R.M. *Grand Strategy*, vol. 2: *September 1939–June 1941* (London: HMSO, 1957)

—— *Lord Lothian (Philip Kerr) 1882–1940* (London: Macmillan, 1960)

Calder, Angus. *The Myth of the Blitz* (London: Pimlico, 1991)

—— *The People's War* (London: Pimlico, 1969)

Calder, Robert. *Beware the British Serpent: The Role of Writer in British Propaganda in the United States, 1939–1945* (Montreal/Kingston: McGill–Queens UP, 2004)

Calhoun, Mark. *Gen. Lesley J. McNair: Unsung Architect of the US Army* (Lawrence, KS: University Press of Kansas, 2015)

Campbell, John. *Dieppe Revisited: A Documentary Investigation* (London: Frank Cass, 1993)

Carafano, James Jay. *After D-Day: Operation COBRA and the Normandy Breakout* (Boulder, CO: Lynne Rienner, 2000)

Carew, Michael G. *Becoming the Arsenal: The American Industrial Mobilization for World War II, 1938–1942* (Lanham, MD: University Press of America, 2010)

Casey, Steven. *The War Beat, Europe: The American Media at War Against Nazi Germany* (Oxford: Oxford UP, 2017)

Charmley, John. *Churchill's Grand Alliance: The Anglo-American Special Relationship 1940–1957* (New York: Harcourt Brace & Co., 1995)

Chisholm, Anne and Michael Davie. *Beaverbrook: A Life* (London: Hutchinson, 1992)

Churchill, Winston S. *The Second World War* (Boston, MA: Houghton Mifflin, 1948–53)

—— *The World Crisis 1911–1918* (New York: Charles Scribner's Sons, 1923–7)

Clark, Lloyd. *Blitzkrieg: Myth, Reality and Hitler's Lightning War – France 1940* (London: Atlantic Books, 2016)

Clarke, Jeffrey J. and Robert Ross Smith. *Riviera to the Rhine* (Washington, DC: CMH, 1993)

Clarke, Peter. *The Cripps Version: The Life of Sir Stafford Cripps, 1889–1952* (London: Allen Lane, 2002)

—— *The Last Thousand Days of the British Empire: The Demise of a Superpower, 1944–47* (London: Penguin, 2007)

Clayton, Anthony. *The British Empire as a Superpower, 1919–1939* (Athens, GA: University of Georgia Press, 1986)

Coffman, Edward M. *The Regulars: The American Army 1898–1941* (Cambridge, MA: The Belknap Press, 2004)

Cole, G.D.H. and R.S. Postgate. *War Debts and Reparations: What They Are: Why They Must Be Cancelled* (London: The New Statesman and Nation, [1932])

Colville, John. *The Fringes of Power: 10 Downing Street Diaries 1939–1955* (New York: W.W. Norton & Co., 1985)

Conn, Stetson, Rose C. Engelman and Byron Fairchild. *Guarding the United States and Its Outposts* (Washington, DC: CMH, 2000)

Cook, Tim. *Clio's Warriors: Canadian Historians and the Writing of the World Wars* (Vancouver, BC: University of British Columbia Press, 2006)

—— *Shock Troops: Canadians Fighting the Great War 1917–1918* (Toronto, ON: Viking, 2008)

Cooper, John Milton. 'The World Wars and American Memory', *Diplomatic History*, vol. 38, no. 4 (2014), pp. 727–37

Copp, Terry. *Cinderella Army: The Canadians in Northwest Europe, 1944–1945* (Toronto, ON: University of Toronto Press, 2006)

—— *Fields of Fire: The Canadians in Normandy* (Toronto, ON: University of Toronto Press, 2003)

Crane, Conrad C. *Bombs, Cities and Civilians: American Airpower Strategy in World War II* (Lawrence, KS: University Press of Kansas, 1993)

Craven, Wesley Frank and James Lea Cate. *Europe: Argument to V-E Day, January 1944 to May 1945* (Chicago, IL: University of Chicago Press, 1948)

Crosswell, D.K.R. *Beetle: The Life of General Walter Bedell Smith* (Lexington, KY: University of Kentucky Press, 2010)

Cruickshank, Charles. *The Fourth Arm: Psychological Warfare 1938–1945* (London: Davis-Poynter, 1977)

Cubbage, T.L. 'The Success of Operation Fortitude: Hesketh's History of Strategic Deception', in Michael I. Handel, ed., *Strategic and Operational Deception in the Second World War* (London: Frank Cass, 1987), pp. 327–46

Cull, Nicholas John. *Selling War: The British Propaganda Campaign Against American 'Neutrality' in World War II* (Oxford: Oxford UP, 1996)

Danchev, Alex. *Very Special Relationship: Field Marshal Sir John Dill and the Anglo-American Alliance 1941–44* (London: Brassey's, 1986)

Dallek, Robert. *Franklin D. Roosevelt: A Political Life* (New York: Viking, 2017)

—— *Franklin D. Roosevelt and American Foreign Policy, 1932–1945* (New York: Oxford UP, 1995)

Darwin, John. *The Empire Project: The Rise and Fall of the British World System, 1830–1970* (Cambridge: Cambridge UP, 2009)

Day, David. 'Anzacs on the Run: The View from Whitehall, 1941–42', *The Journal of Imperial and Commonwealth History*, vol. 14, no. 3, 1986, pp. 187–202

—— *The Great Betrayal: Britain, Australia and the Onset of the Pacific War, 1939–1942* (London: Angus & Robertson, 1988)

—— *Reluctant Nation: Australia and the Allied Defeat of Japan, 1942–1945* (Melbourne: Oxford UP), 1992

D'Este, Carlo. *Bitter Victory: The Battle for Sicily, 1943* (New York: E.P. Dutton, 1988)

—— *Decision in Normandy* (New York: E.P. Dutton, 1983)

—— *Eisenhower: A Soldier's Life* (New York: Henry Holt & Co., 2002)

—— *Patton: A Genius for War* (New York: HarperCollins, 1995)

Delaney, Douglas E. *Corps Commanders: Five British and Canadian Generals at War, 1939–45* (Vancouver, BC: University of British Columbia Press, 2011)

—— *The Imperial Army Project: Britain and the Land Forces of the Dominions and India, 1902–1945* (Oxford: Oxford UP, 2017)

Delaney, Douglas E., Robert C. Engen and Meghan Fitzpatrick, eds. *Military Education and Empire: Professional Education and the Military, Naval and Air Forces of the British Empire and Commonwealth, 1815–1949* (Vancouver, BC: University of British Columbia Press, 2018)

Derounian, Arthur (aka John Roy Carlson). *Under Cover: My Four Years in the Nazi Underworld of America* (New York: E.P. Dutton & Co., 1943)

Dickson, Paul. *A Thoroughly Canadian General: A Biography of General H.D.G. Crerar* (Toronto, ON: University of Toronto Press, 2007)

Doubler, Michael. *Closing with the Enemy: How GIs Fought the War in Europe, 1944–45* (Lawrence, KS: University Press of Kansas, 1994)

Doughty, Martin. *Merchant Shipping and War* (London: Royal Historical Society, 1982)

Doughty, Robert A. *Pyrrhic Victory: French Strategy and Operations in the Great War* (Cambridge, MA: Harvard University Press, 2005)

Douglas, W.A.B. *The Creation of a National Air Force: The Official History of the Royal Canadian Air Force*, vol. 2 (Toronto, ON: University of Toronto Press, 1986)

Douglas, W.A.B., Roger Sarty and Michael Whitby. *No Higher Purpose: The Official Operational History of the Royal Canadian Navy in the Second World War, 1939–1943*, vol. 2, Part I (St Catharines, ON: Vanwell Publishing, 2002)

Downing, John P. *At War with the British* (privately published, 1980)

Dunn, Jr., Walter Scott. *Second Front Now: 1943* (Tuscaloosa, AL: University of Alabama Press, 1980)

Edgerton, David. *Britain's War Machine: Weapons, Resources and Experts in the Second World War* (London: Allen Lane, 2011)

—— 'The Nationalization of British History: Historians, Nationalism and the Myths of 1940', *English Historical Review*, vol. 136, no. 581 (August 2021), pp. 950–85

—— 'The United Kingdom's Disappearing Wartime Imports 1939–1945: A Statistical, Ideological and Historiographical Accounting', *The Economic History Review* (2023), pp. 1–18

Ehrman, John. *Grand Strategy*, vol. 5: *August 1943–September 1944* (London: HMSO, 1956)

Eisenhower, Dwight D. *Crusade in Europe* (New York: Doubleday, 1948)

—— *The Papers of Dwight David Eisenhower: The War Years*, 5 vols (Baltimore, MD: Johns Hopkins UP, 1970)

Ellis, Jack C. *John Grierson: Life, Contribution, Influence* (Carbondale and Edwardsville, IL: South Illinois UP, 2000)

Ellis, Maj. L.F. *Victory in the West*, vol. 1: *The Battle of Normandy* (London: HMSO, 1962)

Engen, Robert. *Strangers in Arms: Combat Motivation in the Canadian Army, 1943–1945* (Montreal/Kingston: McGill–Queens UP, 2016)

Fennell, Jonathan. *Fighting the People's War: The British and Commonwealth Armies and the Second World War* (Cambridge: Cambridge UP, 2019)

Fisher, Jr., Ernest F. *Cassino to the Alps* (Washington, DC: CMH, 1993)

French, David. *Raising Churchill's Army: The British Army and the War against Germany 1919–1945* (Oxford: Oxford UP, 2000)

Fussell, Paul. *The Great War and Modern Memory* (London: Oxford UP, 1975)

Gardiner, Juliet. *Wartime: Britain 1939–1945* (London: Headline, 2004)

Garland, Lt Col. Albert N. and Howard McGraw Smyth. *Sicily and the Surrender of Italy: The Mediterranean Theatre of Operations, United States Army in World War II* (Washington, DC: CMH, 1993)

Garnett, David. *The Secret History of PWE: The Political Warfare Executive 1939–1945* (London: St Ermin's Press, 2002)

Gibbs, Norman. 'British Strategic Doctrine 1918–1939, in Michael Howard, ed., *The Theory and Practice of War* (New York: F.A. Praeger, 1965), pp. 185–212

—— *Grand Strategy*, vol. 1: *Rearmament Policy* (London: HMSO, 1976)

Gilbert, Martin. *Churchill and America.* (Toronto, ON: McClelland & Stewart, 2005)

Golway, Terry. *Together We Cannot Fail: FDR and the American Presidency in Years of Crisis* (Napierville, IL: Sourcebooks MediaFusion, 2009)

Graham, Dominick and Shelford Bidwell. *Coalitions, Politicians and Generals: Some Aspects of Command in Two World Wars* (London: Brassey's, 1993)

Granatstein, J. L. *The Greatest Victory: Canada's One Hundred Days, 1918* (Toronto, ON: Oxford UP, 2014)

Granatstein, J.L. and R.D. Cuff. 'The Hyde Park Declaration 1941: Origins and Significance', in J.L. Granatstein, *Canada at War: Conscription, Diplomacy, and Politics* (Toronto, ON: University of Toronto Press, 2020)

Grant, Mariel. 'Towards a Central Office of Information: Continuity and Change in British Government Information Policy, 1939–51', *Journal of Contemporary History*, vol. 34, no. 1, January, 1999

Grattan, C. Harley. *Why We Fought* (Indianapolis, IN: Bobbs-Merrill, 1969)

Graves, Donald E. *South Albertas: A Canadian Regiment at War* (Toronto, ON: Robin Brass Studio, 1998)

Greenfield, Kent Robert, Robert R. Palmer and Bell I Wiley. *The Organization of Ground Combat Troops* (Washington, DC: CMH, 1987)

Greenhous, Brereton, Stephen J. Harris, William C. Johnston and William G.P. Rawling. *The Crucible of War 1939–1945: The Royal Canadian Air Force Official History*, vol. 3 (Toronto, ON: University of Toronto Press, 1994)

Grey, Jeffrey. *A Military History of Australia* (Cambridge: Cambridge UP, 2008)

Grigg, P.J. *Prejudice and Judgment* (London: Cape, 1948)

Grotelueschen, Mark Ethan. *The AEF Way of War: The American Army and Combat in World War I* (New York: Cambridge UP, 2007)

Guingand, Major-General Sir Francis De, KBE, CB, DSO, *Operation Victory* (London: Hodder and Stoughton, 1947)

Gulachsen, Arthur. 'The Defeat and Attrition of the 12th SS Panzer Division "Hitlerjugend": A Case Study, June 6th–July12th, 1944', unpublished MA thesis, University of New Brunswick, 2005

Gunderson, Ian. *Air Power at the Battlefront: Allied Close Air Support in Europe, 1943–1945* (Abingdon: Routledge, 1998)

Haberman, Arthur. *1930: Europe in the Shadow of the Beast* (Waterloo, ON: Wilfrid Laurier UP, 2018)

Halberstam, David. *The Powers That Be* (New York: Alfred A. Knopf, 1979)

Hamilton, Nigel. *Commander in Chief: FDR's Battle with Churchill, 1943* (London: Biteback Publishing, 2016)

—— *Master of the Battlefield: Monty's War Years 1942–1944* (New York: McGraw-Hill, 1983)

—— *War and Peace: FDR's Final Odyssey, D-Day to Yalta, 1943–1945* (Boston, MA: Houghton Mifflin, 2019)

Hewitt, Nick. *Normandy: The Sailors' Story* (New Haven, CT and London: Yale UP, 2024)

Hochschild, Adam. *American Midnight: The Great War, A Violent Peace and Democracy's Forgotten Crisis* (New York: Mariner Books, 2023)

Harris, Arthur Travers and Sebastian Cox. *Despatch on War Operations, 23 February 1942 to 8 May 1945* (Abingdon: Routledge, 1995)

Harris, Stephen J. *Canadian Brass: The Making of a Professional Army 1860–1939* (Toronto, ON: University of Toronto Press, 1988)

Harrison, Gordon. *Cross-Channel Attack* (Washington, DC: Office of the Chief of Military History United States Army, 1951)

Hart, Justin. *Empire of Ideas: The Origins of Public Diplomacy and the Transformation of U.S. Foreign Policy* (Oxford: Oxford UP, 2013)

Hart, Stephen Ashley. *Colossal Cracks: Montgomery's 21st Army Group in Northwest Europe, 1944–1945* (Mechanicsburg, PA: Stackpole Books, 2007)

Hastings, Max. *Overlord: D-Day and the Battle for Normandy* (New York: Touchstone Books, 1984)

Hatch, F.J. *The Aerodrome of Democracy: Canada and the British Commonwealth Air Training Plan, 1939–1945* (Ottawa, ON: Directorate of History, Department of National Defence, 1983)

Hench, John B. *Books as Weapons: Propaganda, Publishing, and the Battle for Global Markets in the Era of World War II* (Ithaca, NY/London: Cornell UP, 2010)

Hesketh, Roger Fleetwood. *Fortitude: The D-Day Deception Campaign* (Woodstock, NY: Overlook Press, 2000)

Higgins, Trumbull. *Churchill and the Second Front, 1940–1943* (New York: Oxford UP, 1957)

Hildebrand, Robert C. *Dumbarton Oaks: The Origins of the United Nations and the Search for Postwar Security* (Chapel Hill, NC: University of North Carolina Press, 1990)

Hill, H. Duncan. *North American Supply* (London: HMSO and Longman, Green and Co., 1955)

Hillmer, Norman. *O.D. Skelton: A Portrait of Canadian Ambition* (Toronto, ON: University of Toronto Press, 2015)

Hinsley, F.H. *British Intelligence in the Second World War* (London: HMSO, 1979–90)

—— *British Intelligence in the Second World War* (abridged edition) (Cambridge: Cambridge UP, 1993)

Hirshon, Stanley P. *General Patton: A Soldier's Life* (New York: Harper, 2002)

History of COSSAC (Chief of Staff to Supreme Allied Commander), Historical Sub-Section, Office of Secretary, General Staff, Supreme Headquarters, Allied Expeditionary Force [May 1944] (Bennington, VT: Merriam, 2000)

Hodgson, Godfrey. *The Colonel: The Life and Wars of Henry Stimson, 1867–1950* (New York: Alfred Knopf, 1990)

Hodson, James Lansdale. *And Yet I Like America* (London: Victor Gollancz, 1945)

Hopkins, A.G. *American Empire: A Global History* (Princeton, NJ: Princeton UP, 2018)

Horten, Gerd. *Radio Goes to War: The Cultural Politics of Propaganda during World War II* (Berkeley, CA: University of California Press, 2002)

Howard, Michael. *British Intelligence in the Second World War*, vol. 5: *Strategic Deception* (New York: Cambridge UP, 1990)

Howson, Susan and Donald Moggridge, eds. *The Wartime Diaries of Lionel Robbins and James Meade, 1943–45* (London: Macmillan, 1990)

Hughes, Thomas Alexander. *Over Lord: General Pete Quesada and the Triumph of Tactical Airpower in World War II* (New York: The Free Press, 1995)

Hull, Isabelle V. *Absolute Destruction: Military Culture and the Practices of War in Imperial Germany* (Ithaca, NY: Cornell UP, 2005)

Hyde, H. Montgomery. *The Quiet Canadian: The Secret Service Story of Sir William Stephenson* (London: Hamish Hamilton, 1962)

Immerwahr, Daniel. *How to Hide an Empire: A History of the Greater United States* (New York: Farrar, Straus and Giroux, 2019)

Ingersoll, Ralph. *The Battle is the Payoff* (New York: Harcourt Brace, 1943)

—— *Top Secret* (New York: Harcourt Brace, 1946)

Isby, David, ed. *Fighting in Normandy: The German Army from D-Day to Villers-Bocage* (London: Greenhill Books, 2001)

—— *Fighting the Invasion: The German Army at D-Day* (London: Greenhill Books, 2000)

Ismay, Hastings. *The Memoirs of Lord Ismay* (New York: Viking, 1960)

Jackson, Ashley. *The British Empire and the Second World War* (London: Hambledon Continuum, 2006)

—— *Persian Gulf Command: A History of the Second World War in Iran and Iraq* (New Haven, CT and London: Yale UP, 2018)

Jackson, W.G.F. *The Battle for Italy* (New York: Harper and Row, 1967)

Jackway, Gwenyth. 'Media at War: Radio's Challenge to Newspapers, 1924–1939', unpublished dissertation, University of Pennsylvania, 1992

James, D. Clayton. *The Years of MacArthur*, vol. 2: *1941–1945* (Boston, MA: Houghton Mifflin, 1975)

Jankowski, Paul. *All Against All: The Long Winter of 1933 and the Origins of the Second World War* (New York: HarperCollins, 2020)

Jaromowycz, Roman Johan. *Tank Tactics: From Normandy to Lorraine* (Boulder, CO: Lynne Rienner Publishers, 2001)

Jordan, Jonathan W. *Brothers, Rivals, Victors: Eisenhower, Patton, Bradley and the Partnership That Drove the Allied Conquest in Europe* (New York: Calibre, 2011)

Kennedy, David M. *Freedom from Fear: The American People in Depression and War, 1929–1945* (New York: Oxford UP, 2005)

—— *Over Here: The First World War and American Society* (New York: Oxford UP, 2004)

Kennedy, General Sir John. *The Business of War* (London: Hutchinson, 1957)

Kennedy, J. De N. *History of the Department of Munitions and Supply: Canada in the Second World War* (Ottawa, ON: King's Printer, 1950)

Kershaw, Ian. *The End: The Defiance and Destruction of Hitler's Germany, 1944–1945* (New York: Penguin, 2011)

Kimball, Warren. *The Most Unsordid Act: Lend-Lease 1939–1941* (Baltimore, MD: Johns Hopkins UP, 1969)

Kimble, James J. *Mobilizing the Home Front: War Bonds and Domestic Propaganda* (College Station, TX: Texas A&M UP, 2006)

Kindleberger, Charles P. *A Financial History of Western Europe* (London: George Allen & Unwin, 1984)

Klemperer, Klemens von. *German Resistance Against Hitler: The Search for Allies Abroad, 1938–1945* (Oxford: Clarendon Press, 1992)

Kurowski, Franz. *Elite Panzer Strike Force: Germany's Panzer Lehr Division in World War II* (Mechanicsburg, PA: Stackpole Books, 2011)

Lacey, Jim. *Keep from All Thoughtful Men: How U.S. Economists Won World War II* (Annapolis, MD: USNI Press, 2011)

―― *The Washington War: FDR's Inner Circle and the Politics of Power That Won World War II* (New York: Bantam Books, 2019)

Laurie, Clayton D. *The Propaganda Warriors: America's Crusade Against Nazi Germany* (Lawrence, KS: University Press of Kansas, 1996)

Law, Clive. *Drive to Victory: Catalogue of Canadian Military Vehicles* (Ottawa, ON: Service Publications, 2016)

[Lee]. *The London Journal of General Raymond E. Lee, 1940–41* (Boston, MA: Little, Brown and Co., 1971)

Leighton, Richard M. and Robert W. Coakley. *Global Logistics and Strategy: 1940–1943* (Washington, DC: CMH, 1995)

Levine, Alan J., *The Strategic Bombing of Germany, 1940–1945* (Westport CT: Praeger, 1992)

Lewis, Adrian. *OMAHA Beach: A Flawed Victory* (Chapel Hill, NC: University of North Carolina Press, 2001)

Liddell Hart, Basil H. *The Real War 1914–1918* (London: Faber & Faber, 1930)

―― *Reputations: Ten Years After* (Boston, MA: Little, Brown and Co., 1928)

Liedtke, Gregory. 'Canadian Offensive Operations in Normandy Revisited', *Canadian Military Journal*, vol. 8, no. 2, Summer 2007

Lippmann, Walter. *Public Opinion* (New York: Macmillan, 1922)

Lloyd, David W. *Battlefield Tourism: Pilgrimage and the Commemoration of the Great War in Britain, Australia and Canada* (London: Bloomsbury, 2014)

Lloyd, Nick. *Hundred Days: The End of the Great War* (London: Viking, 2013)

Lockhart, Robert Bruce. *Comes the Reckoning* (London: Putnam, 1947)

―― *The Diaries of Robert B. Lockhart*, vol. 2: *1939–1945* (London: Macmillan, 1980)

Loewen, General Sir Charles. *Memoirs*, vol. 1 (Toronto, ON: privately published, 1985)

Lysaught, Charles Edward. *Brendan Bracken* (London: Allen Lane, 1979)

MacMillan, Margaret. *Paris 1919: Six Months That Changed the World* (New York: Random House, 2001)

McDonald, Neil with Peter Brune. *Valiant for Truth: The Life of Chester Wilmot, War Correspondent* (Sydney: NewSouth Press, 2016)

McGlade, Fred. *The History of the British Army Film and Photographic Unit in the Second World War* (Solihull: Helion, 2010)

MacKenzie, Hector. ' "Little Lend-Lease": The American Impact on Canada's Mutual Aid Program', in Paul D. Dickson, ed. *1943: The Beginning of the End* (Waterloo, ON: Canadian Committee for the History of the Second World War/Laurier Centre for Military, Strategic and Disarmament Studies, 1995), pp. 83–106

McKercher, Brian J. *Esme Howard: A Diplomatic Biography* (Cambridge: Cambridge UP, 1989)

―― *Transition of Power: Britain's Loss of Global Pre-eminence to the United States 1930–1945* (Cambridge: Cambridge UP, 1999)

McLaine, Ian. *The Ministry of Morale: Home Front Morale and the Ministry of Information in World War II* (London: George Allen & Unwin, 1979)

McManus, John C. *The Americans at Normandy: The Summer of 1944 – The American War from the Normandy Beaches to Falaise* (New York: Tom Doherty and Associates, 2004)

—— *The Americans on D-Day: The American Experience at the Normandy Invasion* (New York: Forge, 2004)

Macri, Franco David. 'C Force to Hong Kong: The Price of Collective Security in China, 1941', *Journal of Military History*, vol. 77, no. 1, Jan. 2013

Maddow, Rachel. *Prequel: An American Fight Against Fascism* (New York: Crown, 2023)

Magenheimer, Heinz. *Hitler's War: Germany's Key Strategic Decisions 1940–1945* (London: Cassell, 1999)

Manchester, William. *American Caesar: Douglas MacArthur, 1880–1964* (Boston, MA: Little, Brown and Co., 1978)

Manchester, William and Paul Reid. *The Last Lion: Winston Spencer Churchill, Defender of the Realm, 1940–1965* (Boston, MA: Little, Brown and Co., 2012)

Masterman, J.C. *The Double Cross System in the War of 1939–1945* (New Haven, CT and London: Yale UP, 1972)

Matloff, Maurice. *Strategic Planning for Coalition Warfare 1943–1944* (Washington, DC: Office of the Chief of Military History, 1959)

Matloff, Maurice and Edwin M. Snell. *Strategy for Coalition Warfare 1941–1942* (Washington, DC: Office of the Chief of Military History, 1953)

Malone, Richard. *Missing from the Record* (Toronto, ON: Collins, 1946)

Margolian, Howard. *Conduct Unbecoming: The Story of the Murder of Canadian Prisoners of War in Normandy* (Toronto, ON: University of Toronto Press, 1998)

[Marshall, George Catlett]. *The Papers of George Catlett Marshall*, vol. 3, ed. Larry I. Bland and Sharon Ritenour Stevens (Baltimore, MD: Johns Hopkins UP, 1991)

Meigs, Montgomery. *Slide Rules and Submarines* (Washington, DC: National Defense UP, 1990)

Messenger, Charles. *Bomber Harris and the Strategic Bombing Offensive, 1939–1945* (London: Arms and Armour Press, 1984)

Meyer, Hubert. *The 12th SS: The History of the Hitler Youth Panzer Division*, vol. 1 (Mechanicsburg, PA: Stackpole Books, 2005)

Middleton, Drew. *Where Has Last July Gone? Memoirs* (New York: Quadrangle/New York Times Book Co., 1973)

Millett, Allan and Williamson Murray, *A War to Be Won* (Cambridge, MA: Harvard UP, 2000)

Milner, Marc. *D-Day to Carpiquet: The North Shore Regiment and the Liberation of Europe* (Fredericton, NB: Goose Lane Editions, 2006)

—— 'The Guns of Bretteville: 13th Field Regiment, RCA, and the Defence of Bretteville-l'Orgueilleuse, 7–10 June 1944', *Canadian Military History*, vol. 16, no. 4, Autumn 2007

—— 'In Search of the American Way of War: The Need for a Wider National and International Context', *The Journal of American History*, vol. 93, no. 4, March 2007, pp. 1151–3

—— *North Atlantic Run: The Royal Canadian Navy and the Battle for the Convoys* (Toronto, ON: University of Toronto Press, 1985)

—— 'Reflections on Caen, Bocage and the Gap: A Naval Historian's Critique of the Normandy Campaign', *Canadian Military History*, vol. 7, no. 2, Spring 1998, pp. 7–17

—— *Stopping the Panzers: The Untold Story of D-Day* (Lawrence, KS: University Press of Kansas, 2014)

—— *The U-Boat Hunters: The Royal Canadian Navy and the Offensive Against Germany's Submarines* (Toronto, ON: University of Toronto Press, 1994)

Molony, Brigadier C.J. *The Mediterranean and Middle East*, vol. 6: *Victory in the Mediterranean, Part I: 1st April to 4th June 1944* (London: HMSO, 1984)

[Montgomery]. *The Memoirs of Field Marshal the Viscount Montgomery of Alamein, K.G.* (London: Collins, 1958)

Morgan, F.E. *Overture to Overlord* (London: Hodder & Stoughton, 1950)

Moser, John E. *Twisting the Lion's Tail: American Anglophobia between the World Wars* (New York: New York UP, 1999)

Morison, Samuel, E. *The Battle of the Atlantic, September 1939–May 1943* (Boston, MA: Little, Brown and Co., 1954)

—— *The Invasion of France and Germany, 1944–1945* (Boston, MA: Little, Brown and Co., 1957)

Muirhead, Bruce. *Against the Odds: The Life and Times of Louis Rasminsky* (Toronto, ON: University of Toronto Press, 1999)

Munro, Ross. *Gauntlet to Overlord: The Story of the Canadian Army* (Toronto, ON: Macmillan, 1945)

Muresianu, John M. *War of Ideas: American Intellectuals and the World Crisis, 1938–1945* (New York: Garland Publishing, 1988)

Murray, Williamson. *Strategy for Defeat: The Luftwaffe 1939–1945* (Secaucus, NJ: Chartwell Books, 1986)

Murray, Williamson and Allan R. Millett, eds. *Military Innovation in the Interwar Period* (Cambridge: Cambridge UP, 1996)

Nicholson, Col. G.W.L. *The Canadian Expeditionary Force 1914–1919* (Ottawa, ON: Queen's Printer, 1962)

—— *The Canadians in Italy 1943–1945* (Ottawa, ON: Queen's Printer, 1957)

Nicolson, Harold. *Why Britain Is at War* (London: Penguin, 1939)

Nicolson, Nigel. *Alex: The Life of Field Marshal Earl Alexander of Tunis* (London: Weidenfeld & Nicolson, 1973)

O'Brien, Phillips Payson. *How the War Was Won: Air-Sea Power and Allied Victory in World War II* (Cambridge: Cambridge UP, 2015)

Odom, William O. *After the Trenches: The Transformation of the U.S. Army, 1918–1939* (College Station, TX: Texas A&M UP, 1999)

O'Hara, Vincent P. *TORCH: North Africa and the Allied Path to Victory* (Annapolis, MD: USNI Press, 2015)

Oldfield, Col. Barney USAF (Retd). *Never a Shot in Anger* (Santa Barbara, CA: Capra, 1956)

Olson, Lynne. *Citizens of London: How Britain Was Rescued in its Darkest, Finest Hour* (Toronto: Anchor Canada, 2010)

—— *Those Angry Days: Roosevelt, Lindbergh and America's Fight Over World War II, 1939–1941* (New York: Random House paperback edition, 2014)

O'Regan, James. '"Shooters": The Canadian Army Film and Photo Unit, 1941–1946', film supported by the Department of National Defence, Ottawa, 2004

Overy, Richard. *The Air War, 1939–1945* (New York: Stein and Day, 1981)

—— *The Morbid Age: Britain Between the Wars* (London: Allen Lane, 2009)

Parsons, Edward B. 'Why the British Reduced the Flow of American Troops to Europe in August–October 1918', *Canadian Journal of History*, vol. 12, no. 2, December 1977

Pemberton, Brigadier A.L., MC, *The Development of Artillery Tactics and Equipment* (London: The War Office, 1950)

Perkins, John. '"Germany Calling": Nazi Short-Wave Broadcasting to Australia in the 1930s', *Journal of Australian Studies*, vol. 18, no. 42, 1994, pp. 43–50

Pershing, John J. *My Experiences in the World War*, vol. 2 (New York: Frederick A. Stokes, 1931)

Playfair, Maj. Gen. I.S.O. *The Mediterranean and Middle East, Volume III (September 1941–September 1942): British Fortunes Reach Their Lowest Ebb* (London: HMSO, 1960)

Pogue, Forrest. *George C. Marshall*, vol. 1: *Education of a General, 1880–1939* (New York: Viking, 1963)

—— *George C. Marshall*, vol. 2: *Ordeal and Hope, 1939–1942* (New York: Viking, 1987)

Pope, Lt Gen. Maurice A. *Soldiers and Politicians: The Memoirs of Lt.-Gen. Maurice A Pope, CB, MC* (Toronto, ON: University of Toronto Press, 1962)

Reid, Brian H. *No Holding Back: Operation Totalize, Normandy, August 1944* (Toronto, ON: Robin Brass Studio, 2005)

Rein, Christopher. 'Fredendall's Failure: A Reexamination of the II Corps at the Battle of Kasserine Pass', *Army History*, PB 20-18-3, vol. 108, Summer 2018, pp. 6–21

Reuth, Ralf Georg. *Rommel: The End of a Legend* (London: Haus Books, 2008)

Reynolds, David. *In Command of History: Churchill Fighting and Writing the Second World War* (London: Allen Lane, 2004)

—— 'Lord Lothian and Anglo-American Relations, 1939–1940', *Transactions of the American Philosophical Society*, vol. 73, part 2, 1983

Reynolds, Michael. *Sons of the Reich: The History of II SS Panzer Corps in Normandy, Arnhem, the Ardennes and on the Eastern Front* (Haverton, PA: Casemate, 2002)

—— *Steel Inferno: I SS Panzer Corps in Normandy* (New York: Sarpedon, 1997)

Rhodes, Benjamin D. 'The Image of Britain in the United States, 1919–1929', in B.J.C. McKercher, ed. *Anglo-American Relations in the 1920s* (Edmonton, AB: University of Alberta Press, 1991)

Rickard, John Nelson. *The Politics of Command: Lieutenant-General A.G.L. McNaughton and the Canadian Army 1939–1945* (Toronto, ON: University of Toronto Press, 2010)

—— 'The Test of Command: McNaughton and Exercise "Spartan", 4–12 March 1943', *Canadian Military History*, vol. 8, no. 3, Summer 1999

Ricks, Thomas E. *Churchill and Orwell: The Fight for Freedom* (New York: Penguin, 2017)

Ritchie, Charles. *The Siren Years: A Canadian Diplomat Abroad, 1937–1945* (Markham, ON: Fitzhenry & Whiteside, 1974)

Ritgen, Helmut. *The Western Front: Memoirs of a Panzer Lehr Officer* (Winnipeg, MB: J.J. Fedorowicz Publishing, 1995)

Roberts, Andrew. *'The Holy Fox': The Life of Lord Halifax* (London: Phoenix, 1997)

—— *Masters and Commanders: How Roosevelt, Churchill, Marshall and Alanbrooke Won the War in the West* (London: Allen Lane, 2008)

Roskill, Captain S.W. *The War at Sea*, vols 1–3 (London: HMSO, 1954–61)

Ruppenthal, Roland G. *Logistical Support of the Armies*, vol. 1: *May 1941–September 1944* (Washington, DC: CMH, 1995)

Schaefer, Ronald. *Wings of Judgment: American Bombing in World War II* (New York: Oxford UP, 1985)

Schreiber, Shane. *Shock Army of the British Empire: The Canadian Corps in the Last 100 Days of the Great War* (St Catharines, ON: Vanwell Publishing, 2004)

Sebald, W.G. *On the Natural History of Destruction* (New York: The Modern Library, 2004)

Self, Robert. *Britain, America and the War Debt Controversy: The Economic Diplomacy of an Unspecial Relationship, 1917–1941* (Abingdon: Routledge, 2006)

Sheffield, Gary. *Forgotten Victory: The First World War – Myths and Realities* (London: Headline, 2001)

Sherwood, Robert. *Roosevelt and Hopkins*, vol. 2: *From Pearl Harbor to Victory* (New York: Bantam, 1950)

Simonds, Frank H. *America Must Cancel: An American Reviews War-Debts* (London: Hamish Hamilton, 1933)

Skidelsky, Robert. *John Maynard Keynes*, vol. 3: *Fighting for Freedom, 1937–1946* (New York: Viking, 2001)

Smith, Kevin. *Conflict Over Convoys: Anglo-American Logistics Diplomacy in the Second World War* (Cambridge: Cambridge UP, 1996)

Smith, Richard Norton. *The Colonel: The Life and Legend of Robert R. McCormick, Indomitable Editor of the 'Chicago Tribune'* (New York: Houghton Mifflin, 1997)

Smythe, Donald. *Pershing: General of the Armies* (Bloomington, IN: Indiana UP, 1986)

Spires, David N. *Air Power for Patton's Army: The XIX Tactical Air Command in the Second World War* (Washington, DC: Air Force History and Museums Program, 2002)

Stacey, C.P. *Arms, Men and Governments: The War Policies of Canada 1939–1945* (Ottawa, ON: Ministry of National Defence, 1970)

—— *Canada and the Age of Conflict*, vol. 1: *1867–1921* (Toronto, ON: Macmillan, 1977)

—— *Canada and the Age of Conflict*, vol. 2: *1921–1948, The Mackenzie King Era* (Toronto, ON: Macmillan, 1981)

—— *Six Years of War: The Army in Canada, Britain and the Pacific* (Ottawa, ON: Queen's Printer, 1957)

—— *The Victory Campaign: The Operations in North-West Europe, 1944–1945* (Ottawa, ON: Queen's Printer, 1960)

Stargardt, Nicholas. *The German War: A Nation Under Arms, 1939–1945* (London: Vintage, 2015)

Starr, Paul. *The Creation of Media: Political Origins of Modern Communications* (New York: Basic Books, 2005)

Steil, Benn. *The Battle of Bretton Woods: John Maynard Keynes, Harry Dexter White and the Making of a New World Order* (Princeton, NJ: Princeton UP, 2013)

Steiner, Marlis G. *Hitler's War and the Germans: Public Mood and Attitude During the Second World War* (Athens, OH: Ohio UP, 1977)

Stettinius, Edward R. *The Diaries of Edward R. Stettinius, Jr., 1943–1946*, ed. Thomas M. Campbell and George Herring (New York: New Viewpoints, 1975)

—— *Lend-Lease: Weapon for Victory* (New York: Macmillan, 1943)

Stewart, Gordon T. 'An Objective of US Foreign Policy Since the Founding of the Republic', in Phillip Buckner, ed., *Canada and the End of the Empire* (Vancouver, BC: University of British Columbia Press, 2005)

Stimson, Henry L. and McGeorge Bundy, *On Active Service in Peace and War* (New York: Hutchinson & Co., n.d.)

Stoler, Mark A. *Allies and Adversaries: The Joint Chiefs of Staff, The Grand Alliance and U.S. Strategy in World War II* (Chapel Hill, NC: University of North Carolina Press, 2000)

—— *George C. Marshall: Soldier, Statesman of the American Century* (Boston, MA: Twayne Publishing, 1989)

Swettenham, John. *McNaughton*, 3 vols (Toronto, ON: Ryerson Press, 1968–9)

Taylor, A.J.P. *Beaverbrook* (London: Hamish Hamilton, 1972)

Terraine, John. *To Win a War: 1918 The Year of Victory* (London: Papermac, 1978)

Thomson, Harry C. and Lida Mayo. *The Ordnance Department: Procurement and Supply* (Washington, DC: CMH, 1991)

Todman, Daniel. *Britain's War: Into Battle, 1937–1941* (New York: Oxford UP, 2016)

—— *Britain's War: A New World, 1942–1947* (New York: Oxford UP, 2020)

Tooze, Adam. *The Deluge: The Great War, America and the Remaking of the Global Order, 1916–1931* (New York: Penguin, 2015)

—— *The Wages of Destruction: The Making and Breaking of the Nazi Economy* (London: Penguin, 2007)

Townend, Will and Frank Baldwin. *Gunners in Normandy: The History of the Royal Artillery in North-West Europe, January 1942–August 1944* (Cheltenham: The History Press, 2020)

Trask, David F. *The AEF and Coalition War Making* (Lawrence, KS: University Press of Kansas, 1993)

Travers, Tim. 'Allies in Conflict: The British and Canadian Official Historians and the Real Story of Second Ypres', *Journal of Contemporary History*, vol. 24, no. 2, 'Studies on War', April 1989, pp. 301–25

—— 'Currie and 1st Canadian Division at Second Ypres, April 1915: Controversy, Criticism and Official History', *Canadian Military History*, vol. 5, no. 2, Autumn 1996

Trotter, Reginald G., Albert B. Corey and Walter W. McLaren, eds. *Conference on Canadian-American Affairs* (New York: Ginn and Company on behalf of the Carnegie Endowment for International Peace, 1937)

Trout, Steven. *On the Battlefield of Memory: The First World War and American Remembrance, 1919–1941* (Tuscaloosa, AL: University of Alabama Press, 2010)

V Corps Operations in the ETO, 6 Jan 1942–9 May 1945 (n.p., n.d.)

Vance, Jonathan. *Death So Noble: Memory, Meaning and the First World War* (Vancouver, BC: University of British Columbia Press, 1997)

—— *Maple Leaf Empire: Canada, Britain and Two World War* (Don Mills, ON: Oxford UP, 2012)

Van Engen, Abram C. *City on a Hill: A History of American Exceptionalism* (New Haven, CT and London: Yale UP, 2020)

Villa, Brian Loring. *Unauthorized Action: Mountbatten and the Dieppe Raid* (Toronto, ON: Oxford UP, 1990)

Waddell, Steve R. *United States Army Logistics: The Normandy Campaign* (New Haven, CT: Greenwood, 1994)

Washington Despatches 1941–1945: Weekly Political Reports from the British Embassy, ed. H.G. Nicholas (Chicago, IL: University of Chicago Press, 1981)

Wedemeyer, Albert C. *Wedemeyer Reports!* (New York: Henry Holt & Co., 1958)

Weigley, Russell. *Eisenhower's Lieutenants: The Campaign of France and Germany, 1944–1945*, 2 vols (Bloomington, IN: Indiana UP, 1981)

Weinberg, Sydney. 'What to Tell America: The Writers' Quarrel in the Office of War Information', *Journal of American History*, vol. 55, no. 1, June 1968

Weintraub, Stanley. *Final Victory: FDR's Extraordinary World War II Presidential Campaign* (New York: Da Capo Press, 2012)

Wette, Wolfram. *The Wehrmacht: History, Myth, Reality* (Cambridge, MA: Harvard UP, 2006)

Whitaker, Brigadier General Denis and Shelagh Whitaker, with Terry Copp. *Victory at Falaise: The Soldiers' Story* (Toronto, ON: HarperCollins, 2000)

Wieviorka, Olivier. *Normandy: The Landings to the Liberation of Paris* (Cambridge, MA: The Belknap Press, 2008)

Williams, LCDR Ethan Rawls, USN. '50 Div in Normandy: A Critical Analysis of the British 50th (Northumbrian) Division on D-Day and in the Battle of Normandy', unpublished MA thesis, US Army Command and General Staff College, Fort Leavenworth, 2007

Wilkins, Mira. *The History of Foreign Investment in America, 1914–1945* (Cambridge, MA: Harvard University Press, 2004)

Wilmot, Chester. *Eclipse* (London: Hamish Hamilton, 1945)

—— *The Struggle for Europe* (London: Collins, 1952)

Windsor, Lee. ' "The Eyes of All Fixed on Sicily" Canada's Unexpected Victory, 1943', *Canadian Military History*, vol. 22, no. 3, Summer 2013

Windsor, Lee, Roger Sarty and Marc Milner. *Loyal Gunners: 3rd Field Regiment (The Loyal Gunners) and the History of New Brunswick's Artillery, 1893 to 2012* (Waterloo, ON: Wilfrid Laurier UP, 2016)

Winik, Jay, *1944: FDR and the Year That Changed History* (New York: Simon and Schuster, 2015)

Winkler, Allan M. *The Politics of Propaganda: The Office of War Information, 1942–1945* (New Haven, CT and London: Yale UP, 1978)

Woodward, Sir Llewellyn. *British Foreign Policy in the Second World War*, vol. 5 (London: HMSO, 1976)

Young, Kenneth. *Churchill and Beaverbrook: A Study in Friendship and Politics* (London: Eyre & Spottiswoode, 1966)

Young, Nancy Beck. *Why We Fight: Congress and the Politics of World War II* (Lawrence, KS: University Press of Kansas, 2013)

Zabecki, David and Douglas V. Mastriano, eds. *Pershing's Lieutenants: American Military Leadership in World War I* (Oxford: Osprey, 2020)

Zaloga, Steven. 'Debunking an OMAHA Beach legend: The Use of "Armored Funnies" on D-Day', *Journal of Military History*, vol. 85, no. 1, January 2021, pp. 134–62

—— *German Tanks in Normandy 1944* (Oxford: Osprey, 2021)

—— *US Anti-tank Artillery 1941–45* (Oxford: Osprey, 2005)

Zaporzan, Lawrence James. 'Rad's War: A Biographical Study of Sydney Valpy Radley-Walters from Mobilization to the End of the Normandy Campaign 1944', unpublished MA thesis, University of New Brunswick, 2001

Zimmerman, David. *Top Secret Exchange: The Tizard Mission and the Scientific War* (Montreal/Kingston: McGill–Queens UP, 1996)

Zuehlke, Mark. *Holding Juno: Canada's Heroic Defence of the D-Day Beaches, June 7–12, 1944* (Toronto, ON: Douglas and McIntyre, 2005)

—— *Tragedy at Dieppe: Operation Jubilee, August 19, 1942* (Toronto, ON: Douglas and McIntyre, 2012)

Zwonitzer, Mark. *The Statesman and the Storyteller: John Hay, Mark Twain and the Rise of American Imperialism* (Chapel Hill, NC: Algonquin Books, 2016)

INDEX

References to images are shown in bold